Social History in Museums

Social History in Museums
A Handbook for Professionals

Edited by
David Fleming
Crispin Paine and
John G. Rhodes

Published in association with
the Board of Trustees of
the National Museums
and Galleries on Merseyside
and the Museums Association

London   HMSO

ISBN 0 11 290529 3

British Library Cataloguing in Publication Data
A CIP catalogue record for this book
is available from the British Library

Design by HMSO

6003768054

🏛 HMSO

HMSO publications are available from:

HMSO Publications Centre
(Mail, fax and telephone orders only)
PO Box 276, London, SW8 5DT
Telephone orders 071-873 9090
General enquiries 071-873 0011
(queuing system in operation for both numbers)
Fax orders 071-873 8200

HMSO Bookshops
49 High Holborn, London, WC1V 6HB
(counter service only)
071-873 0011 Fax 071-873 8200
258 Broad Street, Birmingham, B1 2HE
021-643 3740 Fax 021-643 6510
Southey House, 33 Wine Street, Bristol, BS1 2BQ
0272-264306 Fax 0272-294515
9-21 Princess Street, Manchester, M60 8AS
061-834 7201 Fax 061-833 0634
16 Arthur Street, Belfast, BT1 4GD
0232-238451 Fax 0232 235401
71 Lothian Road, Edinburgh, EH3 9AZ
031-228 4181 Fax 031-229 2734

HMSO's Accredited Agents
(see Yellow Pages)

And through good booksellers

Foreword

Of the 1500 or so museums in England and Wales, the great majority are concerned with social history. Yet it is only a few years ago that social history items in museums were scorned as 'bygones', and even today the lion's share of resources goes into art museums.

Social history curators have made huge strides in recent years, in developing a greater professionalism in public services, in improving their care of the collections entrusted to them, and in the theoretical underpinning of their subject. Moreover, they have shown great determination in reaching out to ever-widening audiences, with interpretative and other techniques designed to engage as well as to inform.

Much of this progress has centred on the Social History Curators Group, which conceived this book. Social historians working in museums have been greatly influenced by developments in a wider field of history, by people's history, women's history, oral history, and the work of historians elsewhere in Europe and the Americas. Social historians in museums, however, have a very distinctive contribution to make, not simply because their audience is the general public, but because, uniquely, their work is based on the collection of historic artefacts.

This book (regrettably long in gestation) brings together forty-one chapters, by leading specialists, covering much of the field of social history in museums. Some are directly practical, others more reflective, but we hope all will be of help to social history curators, and of interest to a much wider readership.

David Fleming
John G. Rhodes
Crispin Paine

Contents

A Note on the Editors

David Fleming is Director, Tyne and Wear Museums.

Crispin Paine is a freelance museums consultant and Secretary to the Committee of Area Museum Councils.

John G. Rhodes is Head of Museums and Tourism, Reading Museum and Art Gallery.

Preface

The Trustees of the National Museums and Galleries on Merseyside are delighted to co-sponsor *Social History in Museums: A Handbook for Professionals*. In the museums of the United Kingdom, social history is a relatively young discipline, but the vigour and commitment of its curators is clearly demonstrated by the valuable collection of essays in this volume.

The sources, evidence and methodologies used by curators in this field are extremely diverse, and their work intermeshes closely with a large number of other disciplines. This volume is intended primarily to provide guidance to newly qualified curators but it should also prove useful to experienced colleagues.

It fills a pressing need for a practical reference work on the subject and is sure to remain a standard work for some years to come. I would like to thank all the contributors to the volume and to acknowledge the help of my colleague Loraine Knowles, Curator of Regional History, who represented my Trustees on the Editorial Board.

Richard Foster
Director, National Museums and Galleries on Merseyside

Part One   Theory

Introduction

The discipline of social history is, in academic terms, very young, and its introduction into museums is a recent phenomenon. Both of these factors are powerful undercurrents to all that is contained within this volume. Definitions are fluid, controversy is rife, and structures are lacking. In particular, there are unresolved problems about fusing the study of social history with material evidence and its interpretation, and an uncertainty about what both 'social history' and 'heritage' actually are. Some, for example, see social history as embracing all aspects of human activity; others believe that the essence of social history is the history of the working classes, and other exploited groups. With 'heritage' come connotations of fakery, nostalgia and history for profit. The issue of how to 'collect' and record information about contemporary society, moreover, is undecided, and is probably impossible to address in any realistic sense.

And yet, one feels that confidence is high (see Chapter 2). Social history in museums has, in less than a decade, developed rapidly, vigorously and radically. It has struck chords with different sectors of the community which have begun to broaden the base of the museum-going public and open up new eyes to the fascination and value of our past. We can, perhaps, view this as the greatest achievement so far of the social historian, museum-based or otherwise, in society. Certainly, museums today can justifiably jostle with television and the books of Catherine Cookson for a valid role in the enlightenment of people about our past.

Furthermore, social history museums, like all museums, are expensive to run, but the vicissitudes of their financing, and the threat under which many currently lie should not obscure the fact that they can become firmly embedded in communities. The key to the appeal of social history museums is that they deal with people, with their daily lives, and on a local scale. This enables curators to make museums popular and relevant.

In his introductory survey of social history in museums, Stuart Davies considers some of the influences on curators, notably that of W.G. Hoskins and the Leicester School of English Local Historians. These have contributed to a museum emphasis on social themes and storylines, at the risk of relegating the importance of objects as sources and as a means of illustrating social development. This trend is also discussed in Gaynor Kavanagh's chapter. Folk life studies, meanwhile, is an older discipline with a stronger emphasis on objects and a clearer 'academic methodology' than social history.

Davies does not see museums primarily as research institutions, and therefore social history curators are only infrequently 'at the frontiers of knowledge'. Their prime role is to disseminate historical knowledge to a lay public, through exhibitions, popular publications and other methods.

Gaynor Kavanagh charts the erratic history of social history museums. The late nineteenth century produced an incoherent pattern of provincial history museums, and an accompanying intellectual confusion among the new curatorial profession. The foundations for a history museum discipline were only laid in the 1930s by folk life specialists, especially in Scotland, Wales and the Isle of Man.

The growth in the museum movement since the 1940s has been largely in relation to industrial development, based in changes in the social and economic

1

fabric. While Kavanagh cites MERL and Beamish as important milestones, she sees the hijacking of a growing interest in the past by the 'heritage industry'.

Kavanagh perceives some lack of confidence, and a confusion in the purpose of social historians in museums, but sees a readiness to raise issues and face challenges. She would like there to be a consensus on what a history museum is.

David Fleming

1 Social History in Museums: The Academic Context

Stuart Davies

Principal Officer, Museums and Galleries, Kirklees Metropolitan Council

History is vast. In terms of immensity it is perhaps rivalled only by space. Time is the real final frontier.

As human beings struggle to come to terms with these concepts they desperately try to reduce them to manageable proportions. They set boundaries for themselves so that their enquiries can be structured, tentative conclusions reached and their perceptions of the past communicated to others. They establish methodologies, ground rules and a technical language all of their own. They become historians.

And the subject of their study, the past and its interpretation (history) becomes fragmented and splintered. Thus it is that a myriad of varieties of history develop, all offering a different viewpoint on the past and not even internally consistent as the historians themselves disagree on points of interpretation, and indeed just who they are.

I remember, several years ago, an Organisation of American Historians Annual meeting in New York City. A squat, rather dishevelled looking little man squinted at my name tag through his wire rim glasses. 'Bruce Craig, National Park Service. Hum...' After a long pause, he asked, 'Oh, the Park Service - do they have historians?' Well, needless to say, I was shocked, I was dismayed. How could any respectable academic not know that the Federal Government employed historians and the Park Service yet! Since that time, I've found that few 'Academic' historians (loosely defined as those who teach history in colleges and universities) have an understanding of what 'Public Historians' (broadly defined as those who hold history related positions outside academia) do, or where such persons are employed. Of the many kinds that exist, some public historians are historical interpreters – they bring history to the people.[1]

Any discussion about the social history context must therefore begin with some attempt to define the term 'social history'. What makes it different from 'history'? Where does 'social history' end and 'economic history' begin? How does it relate to 'local history' and 'folk life'? It would be as well to start with G.M. Trevelyan who is popularly attributed with the glib statement that social history is history with the politics left out. This, however, is unfair, for Trevelyan, in his *English Social History* (1944) had much more to say about the subject than simply that:

Social history may be defined negatively as the history of a people with the politics left out. It is perhaps difficult to leave out the politics from the history of any people, particularly the English people. But as so many history books have consisted of political annals with little reference to their social environment, a reversal of that method may have its uses to redress the balance. During my own lifetime a third very flourishing sort of history has come into existence, the economic, which greatly assists the serious study of social history. For the social scene grows out of economic conditions, to much the same extent that political events in their turn grow out of social conditions. Without social history, economic history is barren and political history is unintelligible.

But social history does not merely provide the required link between economic and political history. It has also its own positive value and peculiar concern. Its scope may be defined as the daily life of the inhabitants of the land in past ages: this includes the human as well as the economic relation of different classes to one another, the character of family and household life, the conditions of labour and of leisure, the attitude of man to nature, the culture of each age as it arose out of these general conditions of life, and took ever-changing forms in religion, literature and music, architecture, learning and thought. [2]

Trevelyan was not actually the first English historian to champion social history. Even in the nineteenth century there were those who reacted against E.A. Freeman's aphorism, 'History is past politics, and politics is present history.' John Richardson Green, in his *Short History of the English People* (1874), turned away from 'drum and trumpet history' (Green's phrase) to concentrate on social history.

Unfortunately, social history did not gain academic respectability until the 1970s when its rise was probably due in part to the growing influence of the social sciences and it being embraced by the new universities. Arthur Marwick has spoken of the disservice done to the subject by Trevelyan and his predecessors, who have been criticised for reducing it to the impressionistic 'polite chat about the past'. He and the new breed of social historians in the 1960s made far more strenuous claims.

Effectively all history (the study of man and society in the past) is really social history, so that the term is really tautological; but it has the virtue of tautology – extra emphasis. To speak of social history is a means of emphatically denying an exclusive interest in diplomatic or constitutional or, for that matter, economic or intellectual history. [3]

This broad definition has been generally accepted both in Britain and in America.

Social history is history, an approach to the entirety of the past. It is not a topic, like intellectual history, or even a set of topics ... It is panoramic, asking questions broader than most historians have previously raised and dealing with an unprecedented combination of familiar sources and materials essentially untapped before. The established topical fields of history – political, intellectual, even military ... are all part of social history.[4]

To many this has become essentially 'total history'.[5] As this broad concept of social history gained ground it was taken up with enthusiasm, not only in this country, but also in America. The growth of the subject in universities can be charted by the development of academic journals devoted either to the whole subject or recognised branches of it.

The *Journal of Social History* is published by the Carnegie Mellon University Press of Pittsburgh, and first appeared in 1967. It is international in scope and contains a great deal of material relating to British social history. It has always happily published thoughtful (if sometimes introspective) articles about social history and its relationship to the rest of historical studies. Particularly important was Volume 10 (number 2) in 1976 which devoted a whole issue to that subject and includes Harold Perkin's immensely useful bibliographical article 'Social history in Britain'.[6]

Rather more obscure, but still worth mentioning, is the journal *Comparative Studies in Society and History*, an international quarterly founded by the Society for the Comparative Study of Society and History in 1958-9. Although published by the Cambridge University Press and certainly truly international in its content, it nevertheless has a strong American bias. It publishes articles on subjects and periods from across the world, but tries to encourage comparative studies of common problems or issues. A recent article by Jack Goldstone, for example, compared seventeenth-century political 'crises' in Stuart England, Ottoman Turkey and Ming China. Museums make no impact in this sort of company but its thirty volumes to date are a fertile ground for broadening horizons and discovering the unexpected.[7]

In 1976 two important new journals appeared in Britain. The Department of Economic and Social History at the University of Hull started the journal *Social History*, under the editorship of Janet Blackman and Keith Neild. This is not exclusively British in context, but remains the principal journal expressly given over to the subject in this country.[8] At the same time a new journal emerged out of the history workshops which had been held at Ruskin College, Oxford, over the previous ten years. *History Workshop: A Journal of Socialist Historians* was not confined solely to social history but did in fact embrace the philosophy of social history as 'all history'. It has allowed unfashionable and (academically) non-established historians to explore new ground, and in so doing has encouraged those whose interests lie outside the accepted mainstream to persevere. Furthermore, it has spawned a number of influential collections of essays or monographs.[9]

Other journals also include, to a greater degree, material which may be regarded as social history. The most notable example is *Oral History*, founded in 1972 as 'Oral History: An Occasional News Sheet' by Paul Thompson of the University of Essex. Others include *Victorian Studies* (a 'quarterly journal of the Humanities, Arts and Sciences') published by Indiana University, and the more broadly based historical journals such as *History* and *Past and Present*. Specialist journals now abound, the most relevant perhaps being the *Urban History Yearbook* and the *Journal of Transport History*. Recent years have also seen the publication of regional journals, *Midland History*, *Southern History*, and *Northern History*. To these must of course be added the whole range of local and county historical and archaeological journals which can always be profitably mined for little social history gems. Finally, specialist journals such as *Regional Furniture* can help bridge the gap between connoisseur, dealer and curator.

On top of the periodical literature there is an immense number of books now published on social history in this country. It is in the nature of academic subjects that, after a few years of periodical skirmishing and increasingly specialised monographs, general textbooks eventually begin to appear. Social history is no different. As an introduction to the range and depth of the literature now available one should perhaps be content to refer to the *Pelican Social History of Britain* which is gradually providing all social historians working outside the universities with a framework upon which to base their own studies.[10]

How have the vast literature of academic social history, and the social historians themselves, viewed museums? It has to be said that, by and large, they have been ignored. One can trawl through the major (and minor) social history journals but look in vain for either any interest in material culture or indeed any suggestion that museums or curators figure at all in the world of social history. The *Journal of Social History* and *Social History* are certainly oblivious to our existence. *History Workshop Journal* has been rather more welcoming. The first three issues even had a 'Museums' section, revived intermittently in later issues as part of an 'Archives, Museums, Collections, Things' or 'Archives and Museums' column. Even this is in abeyance though potential contributors are invited to submit manuscripts about the practice of history in museums, among other things. Nevertheless, relatively few curators have taken advantage of this offer. The situation is somewhat better in *Oral History* (published by the Oral History Society, Colchester) because museums, if only as archive holders, have always held a respectable place in this subject. Museums frequently appear in its news columns and a number of articles about museum projects have been published.[11]

Not all social history, however, appears under that banner, as the definition of it that we have accepted makes clear. One important influence on the development of social history in museums since the Second World War has been the writings of W.G. Hoskins and consequently the work of the Department of Local History at Leicester University. The local history approach has encouraged much that is good about social history in museums today. Museums and their curators have concentrated their attention on studying local communities and their material culture. This is especially reflected in exhibitions on topography, vernacular architecture, craft industries, retailing and transport, all characteristic strong points of local history. The result of local history percolating through the ranks of curators in the 1960s and 1970s has been the development of numerous local museums or local history galleries along lines which can generically be traced back to W.G. Hoskins' *Local History in England* (first published in 1959).[12]

Typically they begin with an assessment of the site of the town or village and its archaeology, proceeding then through the manor and church of the Middle Ages. The sixteenth and seventeenth centuries give an opportunity to explain and illustrate local vernacular architecture. Thereafter further well-worn themes (such as Georgian growth and Regency elegance), increasingly peppered with relevant objects, leads on to the Victorian and Edwardian periods which allow major sections on industry, transport, housing, retailing, local government institutions and the like. In all probability there will be a section on the Second World War and, finally, a token gesture towards 'modern times'.

The essence of this approach is, of course, the strong storyline. For curators and museums adopting it the most important thing is to tell visitors about the history of the town, for it is an approach perhaps best suited to and most used in museums in market towns. Analysing and interpreting the story of a community has obvious attractions for members of that community. Furthermore, in the course of telling the story attention is necessarily drawn to some of the principal surviving attractions of the locality – the parish church, a castle, and other notable features. In this way the museum may also naturally act as a tourist guide to the town.

The disadvantage of this approach is, of course, the fact that objects tend to become secondary to the primary purpose of 'telling the story'. Some of the elements in the story can only be told through two-dimensional material and relevant objects are few. And there are, of course, large parts of the social history collections which are not at all important in telling the story. Perhaps less obviously the story becomes stereotyped. How far did the market towns of England really all fall into one pattern? Does following Hoskins' lead actually encourage the curtailing of individual enquiry and unique thought?

Another problem is that Hoskins was concerned with *writing* local history. His methods, approaches and presentation of results fit in with that model. He was not primarily concerned with *presenting* history in the form of an exhibition or museum display. Exhibiting history must like all other museum and gallery activities, be essentially a *visual* experience. The dangers of ending up presenting a 'book on the wall' are well known, but even the most aware of historian-curators can still be deceived into presenting history (the written interpretation of the past) rather than images of the past which will stimulate and excite, while still accurately informing.

Until the 1970s when the term 'social history' gained the ascendancy, most curators dealing with British history in museums were usually considered to be dealing with 'bygones' or 'folk life'. The study of 'folk life' in Britain has a long history but owes its modern, scientific development to the inspiration of

Scandinavian museums in the 1930s (see Chapter 2). 'Folk life' is basically the study of people and would be indistinguishable from social, economic and local history if it were not for three points. Firstly, there is an emphasis on material culture which is generally lacking in the others. Secondly, 'folk life' has come to be associated either with the history of people before industrialisation or more commonly, the survival of pre-industrial, rural or 'traditional' aspects of culture in an industrialised and urbanised society. Finally, 'folk life' studies have always been naturally linked to museums, thus allowing museums at the local level to achieve links through 'folk life' with national institutions in Wales, Scotland and Ireland.

One result, it may be argued, of this link is that a modern academic methodology has evolved for folk life studies in museums. This may best be described as a sympathetic mixing of documentary research, fieldwork and formal presentation. Critically for museums it lays particular stress on the importance of documenting objects as they are collected, whether through collecting supporting documentation as well, conducting archival research, or using oral history methods. Research, collection, interpretation and exhibition are all brought together.

Because this methodology is available, (and has been for several decades), and is actively used, there is a considerable volume of folk life literature available to the social history curator. The principal source of periodical literature is *Folk Life,* the Journal of the Society for Folk Life Studies, which was founded as *Gwerin* in 1956, and has appeared annually ever since. This publication (like the Society) is very catholic in its content. Articles are contributed from amateur enthusiasts, university professors and museum curators alike. The only test of relevance is that articles relate to the everyday life of folk: a definition which G.M. Trevelyan would have understood and approved of.

Although the periodical literature is impressive, the range of monographs and full-length studies is less developed than in social history. There are, of course, exceptions, most notably Peter Brears' contribution of works based on material evidence.[13] However, one strength of folk life studies in museums which has been largely missing among social history curators has been the production of collection catalogues, the way being shown by the publications of the Welsh Folk Museum and York Castle Museum.[14]

Another influence on the development of social history in museums has been the phenomenal interest shown in industrial archaeology and history since the late 1950s. Although not entirely neglected before then, it was only as Britain entered a period of deindustrialisation that interest in its industrial past enjoyed a sudden popularity. This has produced a great wealth of published material on almost all industries and particularly on transport. Canals and railways have been very well served by their historians, many of them genuine 'amateur' enthusiasts with very high standards of scholarship.

Of all the myriad branches of social history, industrial and transport history have had the greatest impact on museums, leading to the creation or development of a huge number of sites. Ironbridge is, of course, the industrial site museum *par excellence,* but there are many others. Interestingly enough, it is the national museums which have taken a lead in at least trying to put industry and transport in their social history context rather than treating them purely as technology museums. One thinks in particular of the National Railway Museum at York, the National Museum of Photography, Film and Television in Bradford, and the National Waterways Museum at Gloucester. Far more could be achieved at all of these but they still manage to offer a broader social history experience than many of their local authority or independent counterparts.

There have, of course, been influences on the development of social history in museums other than local history or folk life. The pure 'collectors' cannot be ignored for there are still many curators whose primary motivation is not research, interpretation or presentation but simply the act of accumulating and caring for certain types of artefact. Their interests, and indirectly the interests of many others in museums, are served by the huge army of professional and amateur collectors (and dealers) who have created or stimulated a category of literature perhaps greater in voume than social history, local history or folk life.

The guide books to various categories of 'antiques' or 'collectables' are now legion. They extend from the *Shire* series of publications through to very detailed studies of narrow specialist areas. If at one time this literature may have been viewed with caution or even distrust, the last ten or fifteen years should have dispelled this. Some of the finest artefact studies published in recent years have been carried out by collectors and dealers. Curators may be sensitive to their motives but should readily acknowledge the considerable scholarship many of them exhibit.[15]

Within the museums profession there have been three main outlets for folk life or social history studies. The *Museums Journal* has been an important publication because the articles in it reach the entire museums profession. The second source is the publications of the Social History Curators Group (formerly the Group for Regional Studies in Museums).[16] Over the last decade SHCG has developed its 'Newsletter' into a substantial journal, which is now the principal medium for the publication of articles, comment and reviews on social history theory and practice as relating to museums. Lastly, many museums have, of course, also published the results of curatorial research in various forms. Guide books vary enormously in quality but the best ones can be so much more than a 'this is roughly what we've got' job.[17] Individual exhibitions are sometimes supported by excellent publications which are able to expand greatly on the main themes presented visually to the visitor.[18] Some museums services have managed quite impressive series of publications. Oxfordshire's pioneering efforts were linked not only to museums and their exhibitions, but also to a programme of (more or less) planned fieldwork and research in the county. Equally well known is the Welsh Folk Museum series of booklets.[19] Occasionally museum services embark on project-based research and collecting, leading to an exhibition and publication which makes a significant contribution to the literature. Birmingham's 'Change in the Inner City' project and Harborough's oral history projects are perhaps the best examples to date.[20] Many more museums have managed to publish more modest information sheets which can add up to a substantial contribution to the social history of their collections and their locality.

Because social history studies which may be considered relevant to the purpose of museums (beyond providing specific information for specific exhibitions) are scattered through many publications it is all the more difficult to direct new entrants into the profession towards examples of either good practice or stimulating thought. However, the Department of Museum Studies at the University of Leicester has gone a long way towards filling that gap by the annual production of its Learning Goals and Bibliography for Museum Studies Training (History Option). This is an indispensable guide to museological literature in Britain, America and Scandinavia.

What does all this literature reveal about the principal concerns of social historians in museums over the past twenty years? The periodical literature contains much about collecting theory and methodology, with particular emphasis placed in recent years on contemporary and twentieth-century collecting.[21] Surprisingly little attention has been given to the methodology of artefact studies, and this still remains an uncomfortable weakness with many social historians.[22] On a wider front there have been attempts to formulate practical guides on how to tackle social history with limited museum resources.[23] Finally, there have been a number of general critiques about interpretive practice in museums.[24]

Apart from these museological interests, social historians in museums have also begun to make a significant contribution to the literature of social history in Britain. The 'folk life' scholars have been doing so for many years, as witnessed by the contents of *Gwerin* and *Folk Life,* as well as collected essays like Alexander Fenton's *The Shape of the Past 1: Essays in Scottish Ethnology* (1985) and monographs. The latter have been especially strong on the craft industries, domestic life, food and folk art.[25] More recently the history of children,[26] women,[27] and domestic interiors[28] have all been quite well represented in the literature. Many social historians also contribute to local history, vernacular architecture and industrial archaeology, each of which, of course, now has a vast literature of their own.

Nevertheless, it has to be remembered that museums are not primarily research institutions, and so one should perhaps not expect the social historians in them to be frequently at the frontiers of knowledge. They can contribute to the literature in a significant if limited way, but much more importantly they are prominent among those disseminating new knowledge to the lay public. And, in particular, they are doing this through exhibitions, popular publications and living history.

The new achievement of social historians in museums in the last twenty years has been the veritable explosion of local, social and industrial museums on to the 'heritage scene' in this country. The development of these museums (and relevant galleries within the larger and older institutions) reflects both the civic amenity movement and a genuine upsurge in popular interest in the local past. It is because of this that the Hoskins school of local history has had so much influence on history in museums and it will only be gradually that the broader discipline of social history will come to make its mark.

The strengths of 'academic' social history seem to lie in the very fact of its breadth and diversity. Social historians are at their most stimulating and original when exploring relationships and connections between conventional topics. It is then that our understanding of the past is enriched. Conversely, it has to be said that they are at their most tedious when either constructing 'models' for the past or getting entangled in ideological contortions.

Social historians in museums probably do not escape enough from the topic-orientated approach to studying the past. In both research and exhibition they tend to follow well worn stereotyped paths. It is, of course, difficult to do anything else given both the constraints of time and money, and again one must always remember that they are interpreting the past for a lay public, not an academic audience. However, it would be refreshing if they were able to 'break the mould', whether it be orientated to a topic or to the locality, rather more often. Both exhibitions and publications should be academically respectable while still being firmly relevant to the presentation of history to a lay public.

Some would say that the social historians working in universities and polytechnics should be doing the pioneering research, channelled through and reflected in museum displays. The reality is that the interests of academic social historians rarely mesh with those of social historians in museums. Many of them would regard our overriding interest in 'everyday life' and how to present it in museums to the general public as peripheral to the mainstream. However, it is a little more encouraging to note that some social historians do have interests which have a direct and legitimate link to museums and museum collections. The appearance of some of these as guest speakers at conferences organised by the Social History Curators Group may help to forge links, and the publication of books like Asa Briggs' *Victorian Things* might also help. He has reminded his readers that 'However many words are read, there is no substitute for seeing collections of things'. This may alert other social historians in research institutions to the potential of museum collections.[29]

The relationship between academic institutions and museums has always been erratic. The best example is at Ironbridge Gorge Museum which, through the Institute of Industrial Archaeology has established close working links with Birmingham University. The Department of Local History at Birmingham Museum collaborated with the University of Aston in the early 1980s in conducting research on its buckle and steel toy collections, and many individual curators have personal contacts within academia, but the overall picture is not a particlarly healthy one.

However, despite the general indifference of academic institutions to museums, the single most important contribution so far to the methodology and philosophy of social history in museums has come out of a university. The Department of Museum Studies at the University of Leicester appointed a lecturer specialising in history museums in 1980. Since then 'Leicester' has been increasingly influential in moulding the views and attitudes of new entrants into the field of social history in museums, and, possibly to a lesser extent, on those already established in their careers. The salient features of this influence are contained in Gaynor Kavanagh's *History Curatorship* which surveys the history, theory and practice of 'history museums'.[30]

Schlereth has recently attempted a similar assessment of the place of museum-based social historians (he calls them the material culturists) in North American social history. Although he is optimistic about the growing interest in material culture among social historians it is equally clear that our colleagues across the Atlantic face similar difficulties to ourselves.[31] The real problem has been that although much good work has been done and a valuable contribution made by museum workers (whether they see themselves as folk life, archaeology, history or social history scholars) to the study of local history, much of it is like social history itself – diffuse and obscure. If social historians in museums want to achieve an acceptable working philosophy and achieve some measure of academic credibility (and respect) then they must overcome their tribal prejudices and agree a unified methodology which truly reflects the aspirations of 'social history' as a vital and mainstream element in historical studies which should and can be represented in museums. It is to be hoped that this volume will go a long way towards finally establishing social history in museums as a recognised academic as well as museological discipline.

Notes and References

1. B. Craig, 'The public history movement and the training of historical interpreters', in J. Lunn (ed.), *Proceedings of the First World Congress on Heritage Presentation and Interpretation*, Heritage Interpretation International and Alberta Culture and Multiculturalism, Edmonton, Alberta, 1988, p. 279.

2. G. Trevelyan, *English Social History*, Longman, 1944, p. vii.

3. A. Marwick, *The Nature of History*, Macmillan, 1970, pp. 47-8, 59, 61.

4. P.N. Stearns, 'Coming of age', *Journal of Social History*, vol. 10, no. 2, 1976, p.252.

5. Ibid.

6. The managing editor, Peter N. Stearns, has published in *Journal of Social History* review essays assessing the progress of social history in the USA. See, for example, 'Some comments on social history', vol. 1, no. 1, 1967, pp. 3-6; 'Coming of age', vol. 10, no. 2, 1976, pp. 246-55; 'Modernization and social history: some suggestions and a muted cheer', vol. 14, no. 2, 1980; 'Applied history and social history', ibid., pp. 533-7; 'Social and political history', vol. 16, no 3, 1983, pp. 3-6; 'Social history and history: a progress report', vol. 19, no. 2, 1985, pp. 319-34. For Britain, however, the single most important contribution in this journal remains H. Perkin, 'Social history in Britain', vol. 10, no. 2, 1976, pp. 129-43.

7. A. A Goldstone, 'East and West in the seventeenth century: political crises in Stuart England, Ottoman Turkey and Ming China', *Comparative Studies in Society and History*, vol. 30, 1988, pp. 103-42. See also, as a sample from the journal, H. Medick,' "Missionaries in the rowboat"? Ethnological ways of knowing as a challenge to social history', vol. 29, 1987, pp. 76-98; E. Rosenhaft, 'History, anthropology, and the study of everyday life: a review article', vol. 29, 1987, pp. 99-105; F.E. Brown, 'Continuity and change in the urban house: developments in domestic space organisation in seventeenth century London', vol. 28, 1986, pp. 558-90.

8. Perhaps the most relevant article to social history in museums published to date in *Social History* is A. Macfarlane, 'History, anthropology and the study of communities', vol. 2, no. 2, 1977, pp. 631-52. But see also C.J.Calhoun, 'History, anthropology and the study of communities: some problems in Macfarlane's proposal', vol. 3, 1978, pp. 363-73.

9. Of special interest from *History Workshop Journal* may be R. Samuel, 'Art, politcs and ideology', vol. 6, 1978, pp. 101-6; T. Judt, 'A clown in regal purple: social history and the historians', vol. 7, 1979, pp. 66-94; T. Kusamitsu, 'Great exhibitions before 1851', vol. 9, 1980, pp. 70-89; T. Mason, 'The great economics history show', vol. 21, 1986, pp. 3-36; J. Beckett and D. Cherry, 'History on exhibition', vol. 26, 1988, pp. 153-7. Influential among the occasional publications have been R. Samuel (ed.), *Village Life and Labour*, Routledge, 1975, and *People's History and Socialist Theory*, Routledge, 1981.

10. J. Youings, *Sixteenth Century England*, 1983; R. Porter, *English Society in the Eighteenth Century*, 1981; J. Stevenson, *British Society 1914-45*, 1984; A. Marwick, *British Society Since 1945*, 1982 – all published by Penguin Books.

11. See especially, vol. 14, no. 2, 1986, on 'Museums and Oral History'. The most useful guide to technique remains K. Howarth, *Remember, Remember... Tape Recording Oral History*, North West Sound Archive, Clitheroe, 1984. See also S. Davies, 'Museums and oral history', *Museums Journal*, vol. 84, no.1, 1984, pp. 25-7; G. Griffiths, 'Memory Lane: museums and the practice of oral history', *Journal of the Social History Curators Group*, vol. 14, 1987, pp. 26-8.

12. See also, W. G. Hoskins, *The Making of the English Landscape*, Hodder & Stoughton, 1955; M. Beresford, *History on the Ground*, Lutterworth, 1977.

13. See, for example, *The English Country Pottery*, David & Charles, 1971; *Horse Brasses*, Country Life, 1981; *The Gentlewoman's Kitchen*, Wakefield Historical Publications, 1984; *Traditional Food in Yorkshire*, John Donald, Edinburgh, 1987; *North Country Folk Art*, John Donald, Edinburgh, 1989.

14. I. C. Peate, *Guide to the Collection of Welsh Bygones*, 1929, and *Welsh Folk Crafts and Industries*, 1945, published by the Welsh Folk Museum, Cardiff; P. C. D. Brears, *The Kitchen Catalogue*, 1979; P.C.D. Brears and S. Harrison, *The Dairy Catalogue*, 1979, published by the York Castle Museum, York.

15. Well known examples include E. H. Pinto, *Treen and other Wooden Bygones*, Allen & Unwin, 1969; R.A. Salaman, *Dictionary of Tools used in the Woodworking and Allied Trades, c. 1702-1970*, Allen & Unwin, 1975.

16. S. Davies, 'Social History Curators Group', *Museums Journal*, vol. 85, no. 3, 1985, pp. 153-5.

17. The guides produced by Sheffield City Museums are a model: J. Peatman, *Shepherd Wheel 1584-1984*, 1984, and *Abbeydale Industrial Hamlet*, 1985; D. Bostwick, *Tudor and Stuart Sheffield*, 1985; P. G.

Smithurst, *Sheffield Industrial Museum, Kelham Island*, 1985. Other good examples include the guide books produced for Beamish, Cogges Farm Museum, and the Weald and Downland Open Air Museum.

18. See, for example, E. Frostick, *Schooldays*, Hull City Museums and Art Galleries, 1988; P. Ballard (ed.), *A City at War: Birmingham 1939-45*, Birmingham City Museum and Art Gallery, 1985.

19. For an assessment of the Oxfordshire series, see D. Viner, 'Bells, blankets, baskets and boats', *Museums Journal*, vol. 85, no. 2, 1985, pp. 105-7. The Welsh Folk Museum has produced a major series which covers individual building on site, particular collections, and discrete subjects. See, for example, J. G. Jenkins, *The Rhaeadr Tannery*, 1973, and *Boat House and Net House*, 1974; J. G. Jenkins and T. A. Davies, *Crefft y Turniwr Coed/The Woodturners Craft*, 1975; C. Stevens, *Samplers from the Welsh Folk Museum Collection*, 1987; S. Minwel Tibbott, *Cooking on the Open Hearth*, 1982; J. Williams-Davies, *Cider Making in Wales*, 1984.

20. R. Wilkins, *Turrets, Towels and Taps*, Birmingham City Museum and Art Gallery, 1984; Karen Hull and P. Jenkinson, *A Taste of Change: Some Aspects of Eating in the Inner City, Birmingham 1939-85*, Birmingham City Museum and Art Gallery, 1985; M. Glasson, *City Children at Work and Play 1900-1930*, Birmingham City Museum and Art Gallery, 1985; S. Mullins and M. Glasson, *Hidden Harborough – The Making of the Townscape of Market Harborough*, Leicestershire Museums, Art Galleries and Records Service, 1985; S. Mullins and G. Griffiths, *Cap and Apron: An Oral History of Domestic Service in the Shires, 1880-1950*, Leicestershire Museums, Art Galleries and Records Service, 1986.

21. See especially the collections of articles in the *Museums Journal*, vol. 85, no. 1, 1985; *Journal of the Social History Curators Group*, vol. 13, 1986; ibid., vol. 14, 1987; V. Bott (ed.), *Labour History in Museums*, Museum Professionals Group, 1988.

22. G.Kavanagh, 'Objects as evidence, or not?', in S.M.Pearce (ed.), *Museum Studies in Material Culture*, Leicester University Press, 1989, pp. 125-37.

23. J.G.Jenkins, 'The collection of ethnological material', *Museums Journal*. vol. 74, no. 1, 1974, pp. 7-11; S. Davies, 'Change in the inner city', *Journal of the Social History Curators Group*. vol. 11, 1983, pp. 33-5; S. Mullins, 'Beyond a collecting policy: projects as policy at the Harborough Museum', ibid., vol. 14, 1987, pp. 20-22.

24. G. Kavanagh, 'History and the museum: the nostalgia business?', *Museums Journal*, vol. 83, nos 2/3, 1983; D. Fleming, 'From shepherds' smocks to EEC: interpretation in rural museums', *Museums Journal*, vol. 85, no. 4, 1985, pp. 179-86; S.Levitt, 'A Delicious Pageant of Wedding Fashion Down the Ages: clothes and museums', *Journal of the Social History Curators Group*, no. 15, 1987-8, pp. 6-10; S. Wood, 'Obfuscation, irritation or obliteration? The interpretation of military collections in British museums of the 1980s', ibid., pp. 4-6.

25. Alexander Fenton, *The Shape of the Past 1: Essays in Scottish Ethnology*, John Donald, Edinburgh, 1985. Examples from just two authors could include J.G.Jenkins, *The English Farm Wagon*, 1972, and *Nets and Coracles*, 1975, David & Charles; and P.C.D. Brears, *The Kitchen Catalogue*, op. cit., *Traditional Food in Yorkshire*, op. cit., and *North Country Folk Art*, op. cit.

26. See, for example, *Journal of the Social History Curators Group*, vol.16, 1989, pp. 3-33.

27. A pioneering publication was G.Durbin and D.Jones, *Women's Work and Leisure: A Guide to the Strangers Hall and Bridewell Museums*, 1983. See also the Social History Curators Group conference proceedings, *Women, Heritage and Museums*, 1984. Also, G.Porter, 'Putting your house in order: representations of women and domestic life', in R. Lumley (ed.), *The Museum Time Machine*, Comedia/Routledge, 1988.

28. See, for example, *Journal of the Social History Curators Group*, vol. 14, 1987, pp. 7-17; R.Allan, 'Research: social history – a case study', in J.M.A. Thompson (ed.), *Manual of Curatorship: A Guide to Museum Practice*, Butterworth, 1984; M.Suggitt, 'Heals to Habitat – museums and modern interiors', *Museums Journal*, vol. 85, no. 1, 1985.

29. Asa Briggs, *Victorian Things*, Batsford, 1989, p. 426.

30. Gaynor Kavanagh, *History Curatorship*, Leicester University Press, 1990.

31. T.J.Schlereth, 'Material culture research and North American social history', in S.M.Pearce (ed.), op. cit., pp. 11-26.

2 History in Museums in Britain: A Brief Survey of Trends and Ideas

Gaynor Kavanagh

Lecturer, Department of Museum Studies,
University of Leicester

The history of the social history museum cannot be served by a gentle genealogy. There has been no smooth incremental passage from crude beginnings to a modern form. Instead, museum provision in Britain provides evidence of spasmodic rather than coherent development, where forces and arguments outside museums are frequently more relevant and instrumental to change than those arising within curatorship.

Similarly it would be unwise to claim that 'social history' in museums has 'evolved', as this would suggest a degree of both unity and continuity. Although the term is now in common use, its configurations and discords, both now and in the past, raise many questions. If social history in museums has 'evolved', it has been the evolution of a term, and of late an identity, rather than a definable and recognisable discipline, with tried and tested theories and methods. This is not to under-estimate or under-value the work of many able curators, nor to ignore how important recent developments within the field have been. But, while a growing number are consciously testing their approaches and the assumptions that underlie them, others have not. Care therefore needs to be taken over the claims made.

In particular, we should not overstate the freedom of curatorship. Its degree of influence has always been dependent on the far greater force of the political and social moment. Moreover, it has never been and can never be neutral or innocent. As Dr Jeanne Cannizzo has pointed out,

museums are symbolic structures that make visible our public myths: the stories we tell about ourselves are institutionalised and materialised in our museums.(Cannizzo, 1987, p.22)

In recent years, the history of museums has been attracting an increasing amount of scholarly attention (Hopkin, 1987; Marsh, 1987; Van Keuren, 1984; Skinner, 1986; Wallace, 1981). These and awaited studies are laying foundations for a more critical understanding of history museums, not as institutions that are created in a moment of intellectual purity and professional worthiness, but as forms of remembrance shaped, enabled or stunted by a range of intellectual and social forces. Curatorship in this new reading is not the instigator as much as an instrument of dominant trends.

A number of texts on the history of history museums exist. Perhaps the best summary to date is provided by J.W.Y. Higgs (1963). But recent works by Marsh (1987) and Wallace (1981) have shown that new ground can be broken by bringing new questions and more thorough research techniques to bear. In different ways, they open up the history museum to detailed scrutiny and attempt to see it in its social and political contexts.

Dieter Hopkin's study of the history of railway museums has indicated how sectors of museum provision have specific histories, at variance in many respects with general trends, yet not isolated from them (Hopkin, 1987). Thus there is not one story, one history, but many. Therefore, alongside Hopkin's work, we need similarly detailed and analytical studies of museums devoted to science, technology, education, costume, city history, rural life and regiments if we are to grasp the nature and import of museum provision, past and present. Other studies are urgently required – for example on the history of collections and collecting; on how curatorial views of the past have changed; and the ways in which exhibitions have explored human history.

This very brief survey can only highlight some of the principal moments that have brought or precipitated some form of advancement or change. Attention will be directed at museums and curators that laid claim to representing or recording the history and lives of *ordinary people*.

Therefore the history of national museums, historic houses, the National Trust, art galleries, broader trends in Europe and North America, overseas museums that had little if any influence in Britain, and museums that failed altogether, will not be dealt with here.

The Nation's History 1850-1920

Regardless of earlier precedents, the public museum in Britain is essentially a nineteenth-century creation. Funded by the heaviest of the fruits from Britain's industrial growth, the provincial museum became a credential of urban sophistication, the cultural goal of a rapidly expanding industrial nation.

The national museums became symbols of Britain's self-confidence in its cultural superiority. In many ways they embodied the tension that existed between the relative dynamism of an industrial, urban and palpably unequal state, and a forceful social elitism that favoured a rising myth of a distinguished past. This myth was imaginatively extended by notions of an established order selected from the histories of ancient civilisations, and further buttressed by righteous convictions in the ennobling processes of imperialism.

The nation's history had therefore to be heroic, illustrated by stories of great men and great events. In this light, the nation's first 'history' museum, the National Portrait Gallery, was opened in 1856. It aimed to provide a national history of Britain through the collection and display of portraiture. A portrait was included in the collections if its sitter was one distinguished by intellectual or political achievement, active or heroic actions, or moral deeds, in the fields either of religion or philanthropy. Most of the portraits were of men (Hooper-Greenhill, 1980, p.39).

In the provincial museum, history was far less confidently defined. Although antiquarian interest in folklore and local sites was a distinctly local and lively preoccupation, provincial museums appeared unable to find either a clear role in recording the old ways, or a definite purpose in the collection of local material. Thus, by the First World War, provincial museum collections relating to local or regional human history were a jumble of oddments, frequently called bygones. This was confirmed in 1916 when the British Association in a survey of 134 museums found that 60 laid claim to having sections dealing with archaeology and antiquities, 22 industrial art, and 20 history. The research showed that these subject definitions were very confused. The observation was made that

far too much prominence is given to specimens that are the easiest to acquire, and that museums depend too largely on the force of circumstances. (British Association, 1916)

One of the exceptions to this pattern was the museum at Farnham, Dorset, established in 1880 by Augustus Pitt-Rivers. At the museum, collections of local material were organised and displayed along typological lines. To add to the enjoyment of the visit, bands played in the pleasure gardens near the museum.

Pitt-Rivers saw his museum as a means of edifying and instructing the masses:

If no more good come of it than to create other interests, which would draw men's minds away from politics, that greatest of all curses in a country district, good would be done. (Van Keuren, 1984, p.185)

The significance of the museum at Farnham lies in Pitt-Rivers' convictions that a properly organised museum could teach history, control a view of the past, and have measurable political and social consequences.

In general, the development of provincial museums became a problem in this period. Perhaps this is not surprising, given the general intellectual confusion and contradiction that arose within the newly created curatorial profession (the Museums Association was founded in 1889), composed of an incongruous mix of academics, pseudo-academics, committed museum enthusiasts and elevated town hall clerks.

As a result, by the early years of the twentieth century, progress was slowing down. By the 1920s museums were in a state of stagnation. In 1928, Sir Henry Miers' report on the provincial museums in Britain presented a picture of neglected museums and a conspicuous lack of ideas (Miers, 1928). This was the position until the early 1930s when museums began passing from the generations who had founded and fostered them, to much younger men, and later women, more concerned with museums as a service.

It should not be overlooked, however, that in the years up to 1920 there were a number of initiatives that provided very useful, even inspiring, direction to history museum practice and some indication of the potential of museums. Two are worth identifying here: the work of Artur Hazelius in Sweden (Alexander, 1983), and the formation of the Imperial War Museum in 1917 (Condell, 1985; Kavanagh, 1985, 1988).

Hazelius (1833-1901) has been credited with founding the first fully-fledged open-air museum, on a hill in Stockholm called Skansen (meaning the 'redoubt' after a fortification built there). This museum, opened in 1891, is seen as the beginning of the folk museum movement and the first open-air museum. In fact, the impetus Hazelius gave, even when stripped of its fervently nationalist and romantic configurations, is much more substantial and important than perhaps has been allowed. He set out to record the different ways of life of the Swedish people, at a moment of profound social change, by detailed fieldwork in which material culture and oral traditions were given equal attention.

Through his work, Hazelius demonstrated how social change and contrast were evident in a range of material, from buildings to food, from stories to stringed instruments, that had hitherto been outside the interest of museums. He demanded comprehensive studies and high levels of scholarship from those he employed, and in 1881 instigated a museum yearbook for the publication of research. In effect, Hazelius established the academic field of regional ethnology, thereby giving all museums an intellectual basis from which curatorial practice could develop. Significantly, the first Institute of Ethnology was founded in Stockholm in 1918, across the road from Nordiska Museet and with joint staff appointments.

Further, Hazelius made evident the need for a solid academic core to museum provision. Nordiska Museet, completed in 1907 and founded on the collections and records he began gathering in 1872, was planned as a centre for research and serious study. The open-air museum at Skansen was developed as the popular, expansive and educational partner of Nordiska Museet. Dioramas, room-settings, demonstrations and performance became integral parts of the museums' presentations. Such was the strength of Hazelius' vision that the museums he created did not falter after his death in 1901. By the outbreak of the First World War, they were firmly established as Sweden's national museums.

In contrast and in spite of conditions that might have suggested it was possible for a centre for the study of British ethnology or a national folk museum to be established in England, no such institution developed. Imaginative but unsuccessful proposals were made for an Imperial Bureau of Ethnology to be established at the British Museum. Similarly, an active campaign for a national folk museum, led by F.A.Bather of the Natural History Museum and Henry Balfour of the Pitt-Rivers Museum, found little support and was lost in the years of the Great War (Marsh, 1987, pp.30-48).

During the war many museums, including the nationals, were closed. In those that remained open, curators had the challenge of producing exhibitions and providing services relevant to the home front and the war effort. Some of these challenges were met with flair, many more were lost. The circumstances of the war itself led to the establishment of a National War Museum in March 1917 (called the Imperial War Museum from 1918). Born out of a propaganda initiative, but led forward by a group of people anxious for the museum to hold a full record of the experience of the war, it developed a radically different approach to collecting and recording.

The museum's committee divided the responsibility for collecting material between sub-committees, each consisting of specialists who were both well informed in their fields of interest and well placed to gather material. The sub-committees, including those for the Admiralty, the Red Cross, Women's Work, Records and Literature, Air Services, and Munitions, brought together a quality and range of material that is now fundamental to our understanding of the war. The process of delegated, contemporary collecting was quite extraordinary and in its scale and scope is unrivalled in museum projects in Britain before or since. The closest parallel to it is the contemporary documentation work of Swedish curators and their co-operative efforts, since the late 1970s, to create a record of contemporary Swedish life through the organisation SAMDOK (Rosander, 1980). But in the post-war years, all interest in and knowledge of the IWM initiative was lost. The notion that museums could be archives of contemporary or recent experience was abandoned.

Folk Life and Follies 1920-1950

In the inter-war years, there was an appreciable expansion in the number of museums devoted to folk life, especially in the 1930s. Expansion during this period can be ascribed not just to the prime years of a small number of highly motivated curators, but more powerfully to a social climate that attempted to put behind it or at least out of its mind, the war, depression, social division, industrial strife, and the apparent and threatening changes taking place in Nazi Germany. Therefore, circumstances were conducive for the establishment of museums that recorded and celebrated ways of living in what were thought to be less threatening and more secure times, before the advent of the industrial revolution. Although the time was ripe for folk museums, it was not sufficiently so that government would sponsor them. Proposals made to the Ministry of Works by a special working party looking at a possible National Folk Museum for England failed to capture the political imagination (Wheeler, 1934). Instead, individual initiatives developed: Iorwerth Peate at the National Museum of Wales (Stevens, 1986); William Cubbon and the founding of Cregneash and the Folk Life Survey on the Isle of Man (Harrison, 1986); and the gathering of collections for a Highland Folk Museum by Dr I. Grant (Cheape, 1986; Noble,

1977). Their collective work did much to lay the foundations of folk life studies and professional curatorship in Britain.

In 1927, Iorweth Peate (1901-82) joined the Department of Archaeology at the National Museum of Wales, which had a collection of 'bygones'. He worked carefully and enthusiastically on this collection examining, measuring, dating and locating each object. He wrote labels in both Welsh and English and in 1929 produced a bi-lingual guide to the collection. This was a landmark for the collections in Wales and for folk life studies in Britain, in that he not only listed the objects but outlined and discussed the historical and cultural contexts from which they came. In this way, Peate drew up an agenda for folk life study in Wales. Moreover, he lifted 'bygones' out of a rut of casual interest into an arena of genuine study.

Peate developed from this a vision of a national folk museum in Wales and a conviction of the role it should play in national life. In 1938 he wrote that the museum should be

a home for new life and not a collection of dry bones, since there will be gathered together in it every national virtue until it becomes in Welsh history ... the heart of Welsh Life ... a means of uniting every movement in our land into national identity ... so that we may, by drinking of its living well, quench our thirst, ready for our national purposes in the future. (Quoted in translation in Stevens, 1986, p.6)

Peate's nationalism was extreme and passionate in a period in Welsh history when a growing intellectual movement sought to consolidate and protect the essence of Welsh identity. His intensity of commitment led him to record and recover what he saw as the purity of Welsh life and tradition. This he wanted to be shown through the museum as unaffected by mass production, industrialisation, and outside influences.

His patriotism and nationalism were held through deep convictions, ones that did not prevent him from being a conscientious objector in the Second World War. Peate was dismissed for a time from his job because of his pacifist beliefs, but ironically found his dreams of a Welsh Folk Museum fulfilled precisely because of the war. In 1942, the Welsh Reconstruction Advisory Committee proposed that 'an open-air museum was an essential auxiliary to the National Museum of Wales'. In 1949, the Welsh Folk Museum opened in St Fagans near Cardiff, in the castle and grounds formerly owned by the Earl of Plymouth. It was Peate's interpretation of the Scandinavian model of folk museums, revised and translated for Wales.

The work of Dr I. (Elsie) Grant (1887-1983) in Scotland was even more remarkable. It sprang from her own initiative and resources and was without benefit of the security of a major national institution fostering or supporting her efforts. Dr Grant's interests in the traditions and industries of the Highlands took form in 1924 in the publication of her first book *Everyday Life on an Old Highland Farm 1769-1787* and reached a peak with her carefully gathered and organised collections being presented in the 'Highland Exhibition', held in Inverness in 1930. Through the exhibition and its catalogue, she was able to articulate her hopes for a Highland folk museum, drawing on the Scandinavian models of folk museums.

Her work to this point had parallels with that of Peate: a concern for detailed fieldwork and for competent recording; a conviction that a museum should be recovering and explaining ways of living already past or on the verge of extinction through modern influences; and a keen awareness of how much had been achieved in the Scandinavian countries. But her arguments for a Highland folk museum went largely unheeded and in 1935 she established her own

Highland Folk Museum on an inadequate site on the Isle of Iona. In 1944, she moved her collections to their present home in Kingussie. Lack of official status and recognition seriously handicapped the museum's development up to and after her retirement. That she achieved the museum at all, in the face of much indifference and at times non-co-operation, was quite remarkable.

The Isle of Man lays claim to the United Kingdom's first open-air museum, with the opening to the public of Henry Kelly's cottage in the village of Cregneash in 1938. At the opening ceremony, the director of the Manx Museum, William Cubbon, dedicated the house as a memorial to the spirit of the old crofting communities and as a reminder of the environment in which they lived and worked. The ceremony again focused Manx attention on the fragile evidence that remained of the traditions, skills and outlook of the people of these rural communities (Harrison, 1986, pp.190-205).

Significantly, at the opening was an invited delegation from Ireland, from whom Cubbon learnt of the work of the Irish Folklore Commission. Established in 1935 and taking inspiration from developments in ethnology in Sweden, the Commission was making a comprehensive record of Irish folk tradition in its many oral forms (Almqvist, 1979). The war interrupted plans, but in 1948, with the assistance of the Irish Folklore Commission, work began on the Manx Folk Life Survey. This built on earlier records, but was substantially developed through active fieldwork and recording. The Survey still continues its work today, making it one of the richest archives of popular culture and tradition in any museum.

There were other initiatives during the inter-war years and many of them hinged on private collections of bygones. The most celebrated and misunderstood of these was that of Dr John Kirk, which led ultimately to the founding of the Castle Museum, York. It was the scale and audacity of his approach that distinguished Kirk.

Throughout his career as a doctor, Kirk collected objects obsessively, using all means at his disposal. Some objects he acquired on his rounds, others he bought through the *Exchange and Mart* or through antique shops and dealers. He purchased, swapped and traded material, sometimes buying complete collections from redundant museums or from libraries unable or unwilling to care for their museum collections. As far as is understood, he made no effort to record the social detail associated with the objects or their places of origin. He was not an inheritor of the ethnology movement, but owed more to late nineteenth-century amateur antiquarianism, especially that branch which took vague though muddled note of developments in evolutionary (or colonial) anthropology. This led some curators to seek type series in recent material, as Kirk's efforts in his early galleries show.

The Castle Museum at York, with its street scene and collections arranged in loose series or attractive patterns, and the sheer size of Kirk's collections were seen in England as the way ahead for museums. But it was a false lead. The absence of research and documentation, the lack of clarity in his ideas, the blatant romanticising of the past, and the use of reconstructions as a means of organising random collections were inadequate foundations for professional curatorial practice.

The English museum world lacked an individual of the character (Thomas Sheppard of Hull notwithstanding), intellect and vision similar to those taking folk museums forward elsewhere in Britain. In the absence of any initiative from museums in England, other organisations entered into various forms of social documentation. The work which is closest to ideas of social recording in Scandinavia, and to a degree in Ireland, was the work of Mass Observation between 1937-49 (Calder and Sheridan, 1984). Although owing little if anything to museum practice abroad, it illustrated that such recording was a possibility in England.

The work of Peate, Grant and Cubbon and many who shared their views and methods gave regional ethnology and folk life museums a chance to develop into a coherent form. Albeit highly selective and at times hopelessly romantic, their style of curatorship sought to create long-term social archives and the development of museums with distinct cultural purposes. They embodied active, purposeful and directed curatorship which did not rest on convenience. The folk life specialists operated to high standards of scholarship, while at the same time working for and with, in Peate's phrase, 'the people who matter'. They laid the foundation for an academically respectable and socially relevant museum discipline.

In contrast the work of Kirk and many other public spirited collectors-cum-curators has to be seen in the first instance in the private world of collecting. Their prime aim was the creation of a secure home for their collections and, perhaps, a permanent public place for their names as collectors.

History Museums 1950-1988

There has been a terrific growth in the number of museums in Britain since the Second World War. From somewhere in the region of 700 museums, there are now over 2,000. A substantial number of these are associated with collections, sites and ideas related to Britain's industrial past (Prince and Higgins-McLoughlin, 1987). This has had many implications for professional history curatorship: it has in effect created it. The background is a significant and profound change in the social and economic fabric of Britain since the war.

Britain's fragile optimism of the 1950s gave way to gradual industrial decline in the 1960s. By the 1970s Britain's industrial base was being steadily dismantled. The chief beneficiaries of its redundant plant were scrap metal dealers and museums. By the 1980s, service industries, rather than extractive and manufacturing industries, were thought to be the way ahead. That which referred to older ways of living was marginalised, dispensed with as uneconomic or re-cycled into a new 'product'. Britain's skill-centred, community-based industrial and agricultural past, of little economic value anywhere else, swiftly became the museum's message and centre of concern.

The idea of the museum as part of social and cultural provision is still strongly held in curatorial philosophy. But this has been challenged by a more recent concept: the museum as a commercial element within the leisure and tourist industry. In a growing number of enterprises and in some museums, the past has become a package, called heritage, a commodity often neutered and sterilised of its power and meaning. The history museum has been facing huge challenges and has had to prove its worth. The contribution of the museum to the local economy is increasingly being assessed. It is within this context that historiographic and curatorial standards are being tested and judged. Yet there is much for curatorship to build on. The last forty years have been filled with energy and ideas, ever battling against disinterest, amateurism, poverty of intent, and lack of investment. Some of the more significant moments can be identified here.

The founding of the Museum of English Rural Life (MERL), at the University of Reading in 1951, marked the beginning of a new era for museums. It gave England its own national museum and brought history museums into the university sphere. But these advances were relatively short-lived and have been eclipsed. In the long term, MERL has had significant influence on professional practice in Britain through its insistence on thorough fieldwork and recording techniques, and through its development of a system for classifying museum collections, which was subsequently adopted widely. In the wake of MERL, other rural museums came into existence, profiting from the vast range of objects rendered obsolete as rural industries and agricultural practices changed dramatically or ceased altogether. Many of these, such as the Museum of Lincolnshire Life (founded 1969), host records of ways of living and working which have long since moved beyond popular memory.

In parallel was the rise of the industrial museums, borne on the back of industrial change. As heavy and skilled industries closed, museums opened. This expansion, in the late 1960s and early 1970s, was enabled not only by the fact that material and sites were becoming available in vast quantities, but also because the public's imagination and concern had been captured by the sometimes irresponsible destruction of industrial sites and urban structures. Both the political and social climate of opinion in many local and regional cases found themselves in alignment. Without this, museums like Ironbridge Gorge (1968), Abbeydale Hamlet in Sheffield (1970), Gladstone Pottery in Stoke-on-Trent (1971), could not have come into existence.

The expansion of history museums was further promoted by a revived self-consciousness in local government, which came to a head in the reorganisation of 1974. Many districts and counties took the opportunity then to establish or expand museum services, a distinct element of which was the representation of the history of the authority's area. This, coupled with sometimes deep social and economic dislocation, produced or fostered many museums, such as the North of England Open Air Museum at Beamish (1970). Known affectionately as Beamish, this museum became the proving ground for post-war ideas of open-air museums and for the amalgamation of the representation of social and industrial experiences. Thus, Beamish took over where Peate's ideas at the Welsh Folk Museum had fallen short.

History Curatorship: An Overview

With the growth in the number of museums, there has been a slow, but conspicuous development of 'history' curatorship. This has accelerated in recent years to the point where that area of museum work devoted to things, sounds and images of a recent human past is the dominant museum specialism. The name and nature of this have altered several times over the last forty years.

Until the late 1960s curators largely worked within 'folk life', in theory, with specific emphasis on the relationship of people of all classes to their natural, social and cultural environments. In practice, however, the working brief was too often restricted to pre-industrial times. The inadequacies of folk life were made clear when museums began encompassing material from industrial processes and urban environments. In line with, although maybe not conscious of, events in Sweden, where the term 'folk life' was already being abandoned in favour of 'regional ethnology' and 'cultural history', curators began to look instead to 'regional studies'.

Regional studies appeared to allow a wider, flexible and perhaps more critical brief, unhampered by confusion over who the 'folk' might be. Seen at its best in Oxfordshire museums in the 1970s under the direction of Richard Foster, regional studies brought together a number of strands from relevant disciplines and used them purposefully in research and interpretation. The first organisation for history curators was founded in 1974 and took the name Group for Regional

Studies in Museums (GRSM). At times, regional studies gave way to the more specific area of 'local history', this time taking its bearings from the English school of local history that developed from the work of W.G.Hoskins. The history of a place, as understood from landscape, buildings and documentary evidence, was the main theme.

In general terms, social history in Britain began to emerge in the late 1960s and led to an explosion of activity. It opened up the discipline to a far broader and democratic constituency than hitherto had shared the field. By the early 1980s social history had became the dominant term in history museums, but this was not without some confusion. Some curators saw social history as being only about domestic things, while others could not see it relating to industry, work, travel or transport, health, the land, the sea, war or money – the very areas where critical social history practice outside museums was making advances. A number of curators, who saw social history as the study of social conditions and change, went so far as to question the value of objects as evidence and hence the worth of gathering collections. In so doing, they inadvertently questioned the relevance of the discipline to the museum.

However, the 1980s saw the development of a very useful debate about history in museums. Largely generated by the Social History Curators Group (which had evolved from GRSM) and supported by a growing literature within this field, significant advances have been made in both theory and practice. It is evident that social history curatorship is more cohesive and united than perhaps at any point in its history. Barriers between subject areas are beginning to come down.

Because of this, further exploration of the field has been possible. In particular, there has been expansion of the debate to address 'labour history' and 'women's history', aspects of the past too often ignored by museums in the past. 'Community history' has become the most recent term used by curators to decipher their field of study. This has been particularly evident in those museums seeking to represent more fully and fairly Britain's multi-cultural society.

The compass of each of the terms used to define history practice in museums has implications for the subject matter and collections. Each of them has areas of inclusion, exclusion and emphasis. Such mobility would seem to indicate a lack of clarity and confidence in the parameters and purpose of the curator's field. (What sort of 'history' is being 'curated'?) To a degree this is true: the continual re-orientation of the curator's claimed discipline has not assisted stability, or fostered an atmosphere in which useful theoretical or methodological models can steadily develop. This is particularly evident in the ways in which the ideas about the museum, the roles of collections within it, and the value of material and oral evidence have altered within curatorial debate. Compare, for example, Higgs (1963) with Davies (1985).

On the other hand, the emergence of different approaches to the past indicates that in some quarters there is some preparedness to expand the curatorial view. This is marked by a readiness to raise issues and face challenge. Such developments have been supported and enabled by a number of factors, including the increasingly confident work of the Social History Curators Group; a growing literature, both critical and methodological (for example, Horne, 1984; Lumley, 1988; Rosander 1980; and Szabó, 1986); and greater opportunities for pre-entry and career-long specialist training. This can do no other but continue to invigorate curatorial methods. Such developments bode well for the future.

However, it has to be recognised that muddle and division about history in the museum still exists. One of the anomalies of history curatorial practice is that, regardless of the opportunity for cross-disciplinary effort and fluid movement between areas of study, there are some exclusive orientations which act as inhibitors. In spite of numerous efforts, division exists between approaches to costume, technology, folk life, transport, decorative art and social history collections. This is most evident in how the object is viewed as evidence and the questions brought to it in the process of interpretation. But this is more than just a question of naming and defining a specific field: such different orientations disclose very different ways of viewing the past.

A number of history-related specialist groups now exist (SHCG, 1988). Three of the groups have particular roles to play in strengthening curatorial practice and museum provision. The Society for Folk Life Studies has a respected journal and a reputation for stimulating conferences. Established in 1963 by Iorwerth Peate, its key role now would appear to be the maintenance and promotion of scholarship in the field of regional ethnology. This necessitates the Society enlarging its remit through reference to more recent work in allied fields.

The Social History Curators Group has a different role to play. Through conferences, seminars and publications, SHCG maintains a forum for professional concerns and provides opportunities for practising curators to continually up-date and revise their skills and ideas. Its work on the Social History and Industrial Collections Classification System, now used throughout Britain, is some indication of what can be achieved through the collective effort of curators willing to find solutions to common problems.

Women's Heritage in Museums (WHAM!), founded in 1984, alerts curators to the representation of women (or the lack of it) in museum exhibitions, in all disciplines. Its most vital contribution is to stimulate a more critical and liberated view of people through, and within, the medium of the museum.

The role of the individual in carrying forward the theories and practices of curatorship, as in the past, will continue to be vital. Since the last war the profession and hence all professionally run museums have benefited from the work and ideas of a number of people. In this regard many could be named. But it would not be unreasonable to cite the following by way of example: on the interpretation of costume, Anne Buck (1976) and Jane Tozer and Sarah Levitt (1983); on fieldwork and recording techniques, Geraint Jenkins (1969, 1972, 1974, 1987); on creative curatorship, Frank Atkinson (1984); and on critical and astute approaches to history and curatorship which illustrate the very essence of professionalism, Elizabeth Frostick (1990), Peter Jenkinson, (1989), Elspeth King (1986a, 1986b, 1988), Mark O'Neill (1987), and Gaby Porter (1988).

In spite of the obvious quality of curatorship, it would be ridiculous to claim that all is well with history museums. Uncatalogued collections, rigid and limited approaches, museums that have few ideas about subject and collection development, exhibitions that appear without any depth of research or meaning, are still evident. As this occurs at a time when the past has been treated by heritage entrepreneurs as a trade good or product like any other, it is not surprising that history museums have become easy targets for a growing number of critics (for example, Hewison, 1987; Lumley, 1988; Wright, 1985).

The future of history museums is hard to predict and will not be solely in the hands of curators. It seems certain that history curators will need to be not only highly professional, but also shrewd, brave and extremely imaginative to meet the challenges ahead. They will need to put aside those curatorial traditions and conventions which do not support the development of museum provision relevant to people's lives.

It is important that there should be a joint sense of what a history museum actually is, and hence what it is not. Here is my contribution to this debate.

A history museum exists in the first instance to develop coherently a collection of material relevant to the changing cultural contexts in the museum's area.

Therefore, the museum's primary role is to collect material and oral evidence of social experiences (ways of living, working, and believing) in all their contradictions and contrasts. This approach makes no exclusions based on work, gender, class, ethnic origin, religion or period.

A museum is committed to the safe-keeping of its collection and associated archive for more than one generation and more than one life-time.

Of equal importance, the museum exists to examine key themes and issues from the body of material amassed. It does this in partnership with its visitors and those who live within its catchment area.

In sum, a history museum is a location for social and sometimes personal remembrance, a place where change is charted, a site for communal archives. It is a means of discovering and sharing ideas about the nature of human experience.

Above all, the history museum is a forum in which to explore and talk about the relationship of the past with the present.

Whether any history museum is permitted to be like this, however, will ultimately depend not just on curatorship and the museum, but more powerfully on the social and political environment in which they are fostered.

References

Alexander, E. P. (1983), 'Arthur Hazelius', *Museum Masters*, AASLH, Nashville, pp. 241-75.

Almqvist, B. (1979), *The Irish Folklore Commission: Achievement and Legacy,* Folklore Studies Pamphlet 3, Dublin.

Atkinson, F. (1984), 'Open-air museums and the public', *Museums Association Conference Proceedings*, pp. 15-16.

Atkinson, F. (1987), 'The Beamish Open Air Museum', *Museum*, vol. 155, pp. 132-8.

British Association (1916), Haddon Papers, 3067, University of Cambridge.

Buck, A. (1976), 'Costume as social records', *Folk Life*, vol. 14, pp. 5-26.

Calder, A., and Sheridan, D. (1984), *Speak for Yourself: A Mass Observation Anthology 1937-49*, Jonathan Cape.

Cannizzo, J. (1987), 'How sweet it is: cultural politics in Barbados', *Muse*, Winter, pp. 22-7.

Cheape, H. (1986), 'Dr I. F. Grant (1887-1983): The Highland Folk Museum and a bibliography of her written works', *The Review of Scottish Culture*, vol. 2, pp. 113-25.

Condell, D. (1985), 'The Imperial War Museum 1917-1920' (unpublished M.Phil. thesis), University of London.

Davies, S. (1985), 'Collecting and recording the twentieth century', *Museums Journal*, vol. 85, no. 1, pp. 27-9.

Frostick, E. (1990), *The Story of Hull and its People*, Hull City Museums and Art Galleries.

Harrison, S. (1986), *100 Years of Heritage*, Manx Museum and National Trust, Isle of Man.

Hewison, R. (1987), *The Heritage Industry*, Methuen.

Higgs, J.W.Y. (1963), *Folk Life Collection and Classification*, Museums Association.

Hooper-Greenhill, E. (1980), 'National Portrait Gallery: a case-study in cultural reproduction' (unpublished MA dissertation), University of London.

Hopkin, D.W. (1987), 'Railway preservation: railways, museums and enthusiasts' (unpublished MA dissertation), University of Leicester.

Horne, D. (1984), *The Great Museum: The Re-Presentation of History*, Pluto Press.

Jenkins, J. G. (1969), 'Folk life museums: some aims and purposes', *Museums Journal*, vol.69, no.1, pp. 17-20.

Jenkins, J. G. (1972), 'The use of artifacts and folk art in the folk museum', in Dorson, R. M. (ed.), *Folklore and Folklife*, University of Chicago Press, pp. 497-517.

Jenkins, J. G. (1974), 'The collection of ethnological material', *Museums Journal*, vol.74, no. 1, pp. 7-11.

Jenkins, J. G. (1987), 'Interpreting the heritage of Wales', *Folklife*, vol. 25, pp. 5-17.

Jenkinson, P. (1989), 'Material culture, people's history and populism. Where do we go from here?', in Pearce, S. M. (ed.), *Museum Studies in Material Culture*, Leicester University Press, pp. 139-52.

Kavanagh, G.E. (1985), 'Museums and the Great War' (unpublished M.Phil. thesis), University of Leicester.

Kavanagh, G.E. (1988), 'Museum as memorial: the origins of the Imperial War Museum', *Journal of Contemporary History*, vol. 22, pp. 77-97.

Keuren, D. K. Van (1984), 'Museums and ideology: Augustus Pitt-Rivers, anthropological museums and social change in late Victorian Britain', *Victorian Studies*, vol. 28, pp. 171-89.

King, E. (1986a), 'The cream of the dross: collecting Glasgow's present for the future', *Journal of the Social History Curators Group*, vol. 13, pp. 4-11.

King E. (1986b), 'Case study: People's Palace Museum, Glasgow', in Ambrose, T. M. and Kavanagh, G. E. (eds), *Recording Society Today*, Scottish Museums Council, Edinburgh, pp. 20-27.

King E. (1988), *The People's Palace and Glasgow Green*, Drew Publishing, Glasgow.

Lumley, R. (ed.) (1988), *The Museum Time Machine*, Comedia/Routledge.

Marsh, G. D. (1987), 'The development of social history museums in Britain with particular reference to the London area' (unpublished MA dissertation), University of Leicester.

Miers, Sir Henry (1928), *A Report on the Public Museums of the British Isles (Other than the Nationals)*, T. & A. Constable, Edinburgh.

O'Neill, M. (1987), 'Quantity versus quality. Or what is a community history museum?', *Scottish Museums Council News*, Spring, pp. 5-7.

Noble, R. R. (1977), 'The changing role of the Highland Folk Museum', *Aberdeen University Review*, pp. 142-7.

Porter, G. (1988), 'Putting your house in order: representations of women and domestic life', in Lumley, R. (ed.), *The Museum Time Machine*, Comedia/Routledge, pp. 102-27.

Prince, D.R., and Higgins-McLoughlin, B. (1987), *Museums U.K. The Findings of the Museums Data-Base Project*, Museums Association.

Rosander, G. (1980), *Today for Tomorrow: Museum Documentation of Contemporary Society in Sweden by the Acquisition of Objects*, SAMDOK, Stockholm.

Skinner, G. M. (1986), 'Sir Henry Wellcome's Museum for the Science of History', *Medical History*, vol. 30, pp. 383-418.

Social History Curators Group (1988), *Newsletter*, no. 17.

Stevens, C. (1986), *Writers of Wales: Iorwerth C. Peate*, University of Wales Press, Cardiff.

Szabó, M. (1986), *Some Aspects of Museum Documentation: Methodological Questions No. 1*, Nordiska Museet, Stockholm.

Tozer, J., and Levitt, S. (1983), *Fabric of Society*, Laura Ashley Publications, Carno, Powys.

Wallace, M. (1981), 'Visiting the past: history museums in the United States', *Radical History Review*, vol. 25, pp. 63-96.

Wheeler, R.E.M. (1934), 'Folk museums', *Museum Journal*, vol. 34, pp. 191-6.

Wright, P. (1985), *On Living in an Old Country: The National Past in Contemporary Britain*, Verso.

Part Two   The Study of Objects

Introduction

Our subject is a relatively new player on the museum stage, at least under that name. 'Bygones' to 'folk life' to 'social history': the growth in concepts, complexity, status and social relevance within museums has been fairly rapid, though occasionally halting, and there is still some way to go. The development has taken place mostly in the last twenty years which, in a museum movement extending well over three centuries, is no time at all. It is not surprising that all stages of the long process are still with us, in the oddly assorted but compelling assemblage of the village museum as well as in the exemplary project collection, well rounded and well documented, which has been put together when museums and communities work productively together.

If social history has been one of the most vigorous, if diffuse, areas of museum study and interpretation in the recent past, it has happened without the well established academic and teaching base which characterises most other museum disciplines, whether in the natural sciences or the fields of human and cultural history. Not possessing such a base, its practitioners within museums have come from a considerable diversity of academic background, each with its own raw material, philosophies and methodologies. Inevitably, these differing approaches, along with personal and social assumptions, accompany working curators into their role as collectors and interpreters of social history; a new area of museum-based study has grown up which borrows from and constantly impinges on existing disciplines while attempting to forge its own directions, priorities and ways of working.

Part Two is concerned with some of these varied approaches to the study of material, considering first the nature of social history within the broad span of museum collections and related disciplines. Further chapters by specialists working in these other areas set out their own approaches to the study of objects, showing what characterises them and what can be of value to the student of social history. These other and mostly older areas of study are, of course, themselves not static, but developing and exploring new directions. These developments have been almost universally towards a greater interest in social context. The relationship can thus become even closer and more productive, as new and illuminating associations are made and fresh insights achieved.

No body of material is the preserve of one academic discipline, and a broad-based study such as social history includes a regard for all social documents and all aspects of the life of a society. The section concludes with chapters on particular areas of study which are central to the work of the contemporary social historian and where, in writing or re-writing history, new approaches are being developed to both material and non-material sources.

John G. Rhodes

3   The Social History Approach

Mark Suggitt

Assistant Director (Curatorial),
Yorkshire and Humberside Museums Council

Always there must be an idea, for the idea gives the form. The importance rests not in the objects shown but in the relationships established between them. (Pick, 1938)

The curator of a social history museum will encounter during a career a whole range of different objects and approaches to the study of those objects. Some of these approaches are discussed in greater detail in the following chapters. However, my purpose here is to lay down a more general critical framework for the study of objects within which other approaches can operate.

The inclusion of so many other museum disciplines in Part Two is interesting in two respects. Firstly, it exposes the way in which we continue to follow the Victorian tradition of classifying and pigeon-holing human experience, and secondly, it exposes the rather obvious fact that the term social history covers an enormous range of cultural and historical enquiry. The disciplines that we find ourselves in can be very artificial, created for administrative purposes rather than academic sense (Suggitt, 1987). Social history in museums grew not out of a method of enquiry – as did archaeology and ethnography, both of which have a life outside museums – but from a range of objects. A result of this is that some social history curators see their collections as vehicles for addressing the history of society, while others may see them as all the evidence they will ever need, capable of creating an untarnished truth through simply being. It is not unusual to find such divergent attitudes within a single museum, little empires maintaining separate ideologies about the role of objects (Kavanagh, 1989, p.24), highlighting the fact that 'history' and 'social history' in museums are curious affairs, with complex ranges of approaches and preconceptions (pp. 125-6). So indeed is the study of 'academic history' which does have a document-based framework, even if it chooses to ignore other avenues. What separates the two is that 'history' begins with enquiry and 'social history' in museums does not, leading to a poverty of theory that has led to 'not so much a charming diversity of cultural expression as a form of sanctioned professional anarchy' (Jenkinson, 1989, p.140).

We will return to this theme later on. Before doing so we must consider the nature of objects, those things produced and used by society which may end up in our collections. We must address our attitude to them and how we as curators understand them and pass that reading on to others.

Let us use clothes as an example. Like all things they have meaning, they can talk to us. Umberto Eco wrote 'I speak through my clothes' and I would suggest that few of us, even in a profession that is 'as a whole not renowned for its snappy dressing' (Levitt, 1988, p.9), could deny the truth in this statement. We select, by a combination of income and inclination, from a range of commodities, and display them on ourselves to our satisfaction. Our clothes are individual attempts to express ourselves through a visual language that can be read in semiotic terms on a number of levels. Our clothes are cultural artefacts that many would claim lack any interpretation or ideology. At first sight they may say, 'I wear clothes to keep warm', but to the wearer (and to others) the choice of clothes conveys message and meaning based upon their own experience and prejudice.

The link with museums is clear. We choose objects – by personal bias, survival rate, and income – and display these 'material traces of culture' (Beckow, 1982, p.117) as public markers of the passing of time. We also know that like clothes they do not exist in isolation and need to be understood and interpreted. Objects alone can communicate to the learned eye, which will decode the message through its own experience, but if we are trying to advance ideas and arguments through museums, reliance on objects alone is a recipe for the production of, at worst, mystification, and at best, a babble of differing voices resulting from an exhibition that never had a voice of its own.

We have now arrived back in the museum, and just as we can no longer accept 'I wear clothes to keep warm', we cannot accept 'We display things which tell us about society'. We need to be constantly aware of those outside influences, those other things, those myths, memories and images that collide with our objects. But, what of the museum itself, a place 'concerned with objects and with people' (Lewis, 1989), a rest home for burnt-out technologies and ideologies, but a special place, with a special dilemma, neatly summarised by Sir John Pope-Henessy (1987, p.11).

The whole museum situation is inherently an artificial one. The works exhibited were intended for a vast variety of purposes ... the only purpose for which we can be confident they were not designed was to be shown in a museum ... they have been wrested from their setting and alienated from whatever role they were originally intended to perform. This is the museum dilemma.

For the historian of society this dilemma is heightened by the existence of the museum in the first place. Society places things in museums, and that building then assumes ideological assumptions through its structure.

The decisions on how to display in turn decide how those displays will be received before their content has been detailed. These decisions help to set the limits not only on what is shown but how it is shown. Museums reproduce in physical terms prevailing ideological notions about what the presentation of the past is, framing our thinking of it as a place to go *into* to be *presented* with things.

How have the 'social historians' coped with this dilemma, this combination of historical and artefactual enquiry, this dialogue between people out there and things in the museum? This dilemma has faced curators for a long time and will continue to affect how we approach our work: how (if) we collect, how we display and interpret, and with whom and what we allow those collections to associate.

How we perform these fundamentals will produce an approach, an approach which may be termed 'social history'. At this point it is worth considering the work of John Higgs, one-time Keeper of the Museum of English Rural Life at Reading and author of a paper with the unassuming title of 'Folk Life Collection and Classification' (1963). Full of wisdom and plain common sense, this booklet laid down a sensible approach to the collecting of objects which looked at the experience of Sweden and Britain, producing a sound, succinct methodology for the 'home market'.

I have to say that in its day it was almost totally ignored. I feel that curators must have skipped the first part and moved on to plunder the classification system. The bulging stores of undocumented unknowns are a sad testimony to this. As an illustration of collective failure I have selected four important points from Higgs' analysis of collecting and studying what he terms 'folk culture'.

A folk museum is not dealing primarily with objects; it is dealing with people and their lives.

The museums failed; instead of engaging with the dynamism of popular history they ignored this simple piece of advice and continued to collect increasing amounts of ordinary, everyday objects through passive collecting. These mainly middle- or upper-working-class survivals now form the crate loads of christening gowns and mountains of mangles from Aberdeen to Penzance. Museums were too object centred, too keen to build up big collections as a form of museological machismo, while lacking the staff and the will to document them properly. In short, they were badly managed and lacked a disciplined approach to collecting. The objects, which should have been a means to an end, became the end in themselves. Curators took exactly the opposite view to Higgs who argued that:

The number of exhibits must not be regarded as a criterion of success.

He also stated:

It is not difficult to obtain objects for a Folk Museum. It is much more difficult to control the flow, to find enough details and to build up a collection that is representative.

The last point I wish to highlight relates to documentation.

Folk Life material usually has little intrinsic value of its own. It is thus of the utmost importance to record all possible information about its origin which enables it to assume a value in relation to the community in which it was used.

The key is to record, to document the information that makes the object of value to your museum. It has taken over twenty-five years for this statement to sink in. It is the link between Jenkins' farm wagons (1961) and Kavanagh's blankets (1989, pp.128-30); both are valueless without their context and social significance. If our collecting policy allows them to be collected then questions have to be asked of them. Why were they produced? Where? How? By whom? Who bought them? For how much? Where? How did they use them? Where? For how long? How did they perform? How were they disposed of? To whom? When? etc. In short, we have to relate this 'evidence' to the society in which it lived out its useful life. Such questions have to be asked at the time of collection, for it is then that we stand a far greater chance of recovering people's experience, especially if we are collecting mass-produced objects. It is far harder to ask these questions later when all you have is a one-line entry and a donor, who could have died or left the area.

Mass production brings us to the present, where social history museums are wrestling with the problems of collecting the output of liberal democratic consumer capitalism. Mass production and the consumer society pose real problems for the social history museum. They also pose a threat to the sacred cow of the object being at the centre of museum activity, especially when we consider the twentieth century. Stuart Davies has argued that in the twentieth century artefacts have little or no value as evidence (1985):

When writing the history of the Renaissance World and earlier, objects are a major primary source. Thereafter they become less and less important as a primary source material to the historian, who has an increasingly wide range of literary sources at his or her disposal from the sixteenth century onwards.

It is interesting to note that in the late twentieth century the curator now has far more choice than just the objects, and so does the public. One of the reasons museums were set up was to educate the public. At the time they were one of few choices. Now, the choices are no longer few (Shaw, 1985). Today the museum is one of many: film, photography, radio, TV, recorded sound, video and computers. All of these have been adopted by educational establishments and by some museums, using them as interpretive devices.

So, if we can produce a convincing argument that museums are clumsy tools and almost obsolete, why are they so popular and why do they keep springing up at an alarming rate? If we are to produce an approach that can place objects in a social context, I feel we must briefly consider why we cannot do without these objects and their remaining presences. We now have the technology to reconstruct 'reality' and present a fantasy out of the real. Museums will have to consider this when using 'the real thing' to attempt to prove what life could have been like while simultaneously communicating with future generations raised in a televisual culture. The problem is illustrated by Umberto Eco in his essay 'Travels in Hyperreality'. His tour around the theme parks and waxworks of the USA proposed that 'Disneyland tells us that technology can give us more reality than nature can' (Eco, 1986), or to put it another way, 'technology can give us more reality than objects can'.

What can save objects? We must accept that their role is changing and that they may no longer be primary evidence but we must also accept that we continue to value them for the association of the experience that we have with them. Hyperreality presents an experience too perfect to get emotional about. Social history collections present the opposite. Living in a three-dimensional world we are in a continual dialogue with the objects which inhabit our imperfect lives. We may find our emotions are directed towards objects, rather than actions (Williamson, 1986), or that objects connect with memory to produce a therapeutic power that is the key to reminiscence therapy (Wright, 1985). Museums are unconsciously building on this as they use objects to preserve evidence on which history can be based, and can present that history to the public in a lively and entertaining way. If social history is attempting to look at how people lived their lives, we cannot remove objects from that experience. It is interesting to note how they assert themselves in projects that did not even set out to collect them. The Peter Liddle Archive of World War One (now in Leeds University Library) set out as an oral history project to record the experience of 'ordinary' men and women during that war. By collecting their memories Liddle also collected a huge archive of personal papers and a substantial amount of objects, all of which were bound together by the experience of the interviewees. A second example is the establishment of the Manchester Jewish Museum, which grew out of a combination of academic history (Williams, 1976) and the Manchester Studies Oral History programme.

We have now arrived at an approach that is based on enquiry, one that has room for both ideas and objects, instead of the post-war pattern of simply collecting more and more everyday objects as a response to the increasing value attached to the 'local' and the 'everyday'. Despite the addition of oral history and sophisticated design techniques, 'objects first, thought later' remains the order of the day.

How can this enquiry-based approach be achieved? To begin with we must ask ourselves whether we are capable of writing history through our interpretation of a wide range of sources (including our collections), rather than merely providing illustrations of other people's views. It has been argued that if social history museums begin to 'develop this approach they will begin to develop a proper methodology and be treated as significant historical institutions rather than refined versions of nineteenth-century waxworks' (Marsh, 1984).

The project-based approach to both the existing collections and future collecting has been proven as a way forward. Such projects do not necessarily have to be inspired by existing collections. This approach has been taken at Birmingham with 'Change in the Inner City' (Davies, 1983), at Market Harborough with projects on housing, domestic service and shopping, at Hull with linked displays and publications on schooldays and popular entertainment. 'The People's Story' in Edinburgh has followed this approach for its new displays. These projects did not start out with their sole objective being the collection of objects, but to collect people's experience along with the other methods of evidence, including photography, oral testimony and documents. This 'people-centred' approach allows greater public involvement in the museum and the history that it is producing, although, as Jenkinson observed, the curator is still retaining the controlling hand: 'We cannot claim that we have suddenly surrendered our gate-keeping role, that we are "allowing" self-representation' (1989). Nevertheless, this active approach outside the walls of the museum allows access to what is often the best evidence, that which will not always be found in the library or the record office but in the home or the memory. The use of one form of enquiry, oral history for example, does not exalt one form of evidence over another. A lead given by oral history may need to be backed up by literary records or objects. Patents and the object itself can verify that the processes (and adaptations) described were possible. One form of enquiry should make the curator hungrier for other avenues. Once gathered all should be subject to critical examination, for as Raphael Samuel has stated, 'The living record of the past should be treated as respectfully, but as critically as the dead' (1976, p.206).

This enquiry, concept-based approach, need not be limited to the timescale of living memory. If objects become more valuable as evidence the further back we go, then it is time we began to question them more. It is also time for museums to prove to historians that they can provide evidence that is more than just illustration.

This critical, questioning approach to a project in no way alienates the object, but places it in a more social, human context. It is no longer paramount, but, equally, it is no longer fetishised. This combined approach should be equally liberating to other areas of study, like oral history and historical geography, which are in danger of being isolated and therefore incomplete, like museum objects. It should also continue to value the old curatorial concern with the materials and construction of an object, while providing a framework to lift it out of the confines of object fetishism. Such project work takes time and effort, but it provides a sensible way for a social history museum to get to grips with its responsibility as a recorder of change within the area it serves. A number of detailed and completed studies of aspects of a particular area's history will be more useful than a nebulous attempt to cover all aspects through one medium – the collection of objects. The next step is to find out what the public might want to experience through its museum.

This enquiry-based approach allows the museum to collect actively and responsibly, but what of the continuing tradition of passive collecting, the unsolicited donation? Clear aims and objectives, tied to a collecting policy, ought to politely reject those things we do not need. If we do accept something, then the wider framework of enquiry should prompt us to ask the right questions. For example, a donor may offer a 1960s twin-tub washing machine. One curator may check that the museum needs one to complete a sequence (like collecting stamps) and then collect it. But another may ask questions around it and discover that it was purchased on hire purchase from a certain shop (the bills may be remembered, tucked away in a drawer), that it replaced another one, that it was used by the mother to wash children's clothes long after they had left home to get married, and that it was then passed on to someone else. The washing machine becomes no longer one of millions but part of a record that has value to the researcher and potential to the curator in a number of ways – to investigate domestic appliances, the rise of consumerism, mass production, the family, the 1960s, and women and the home.

In conclusion, I hope that this chapter has presented a framework for the study of objects in social history museums. It is hoped that we will be able to improve our technique through a re-examination of our role in society. The social history approach must be one that not only collects information but also one that constructs and interprets it. If we are researching historical evidence then there should be no reason why the museum should not be the place to write and disseminate it in an accessible way. Social history in museums has the chance to break down the disciplines of the museum framework, as it is not just the study of things but a way of looking at them and rehabilitating them within society.

References

Beckow, Steven M. (1982), 'Culture, history and artifact', *Material Culture Studies in America*, AASLH, Nashville, p.117.

Davies, Stuart (1983), 'Change in the inner city', *Journal of the Social History Curators Group*, vol. 11, pp. 32-4.

Davies, Stuart (1985), 'Collecting and recalling the twentieth century', *Museums Journal*, vol. 85, no. 1, pp. 27-9.

Eco, Umberto (1979), quoted in Hebdige, Dick, *Subculture: The Meaning of Style*, Methuen, p. 100.

Eco, Umberto (1986), *Faith in Fakes*, Secker & Warburg, pp. 39-48.

Higgs, John (1963), 'Folk life collection and classification', in series *Handbooks for Curators*, Museums Association, London.

Jenkins, J.G. (1961), *The English Farm Wagon*, David & Charles.

Jenkinson, Peter (1989), 'Material culture, people's history, and populism: where do we go from here?', in Pearce, S.M. (ed.), *Museum Studies in Material Culture*, Leicester University Press, p. 140.

Kavanagh, Gaynor (1989), 'Objects as evidence, or not?', in Pearce, S.M. (ed.), *Museum Studies in Material Culture*, Leicester University Press, pp. 125-6.

Levitt, Sarah (1988), 'A Delicious Pageant of Wedding Fashion Down the Ages : clothes and museums', *Journal of the Social History Curators Group*, vol. 15, p. 9.

Lewis, Geoffrey (1989), Preface to Pearce, S.M. (ed.), *Museum Studies in Material Culture*, Leicester University Press.

Marsh, Geoff (1984), 'Yuccas to Yorkies – twentieth century collecting in social history', *Social History Curators Group News*, no. 7.

Pick, Frank (1938), 'The form and purpose of a local museum', *Museums Journal*, vol. 38, no. 6.

Pope-Hennessy, John (1987), quoted in Hall, Margaret, *On Display*, Lund Humphries, p. 11.

Samuel, Raphael (1976), 'Local history and oral history', *History Workshop Journal*, vol. 1, p. 206.

Shaw, John (1985), 'Museums: an obsolete medium?', *Museum Professionals Group News*, vol. 21, pp. 1-4.

Suggitt, Mark (1987), 'Social history collecting', *Museums Journal*, vol 77, no.2, pp.86-8.

Williams, Bill (1976), *The Making of Manchester Jewry, 1740-1875*, Manchester University Press.

Williamson, Judith (1986), *Consuming Passions: The Dynamics of Popular Culture*, Marion Boyars, p. 12.

Wright, Patrick (1985), *On Living in an Old Country*, Verso, p. 217.

4 The Fine Art Approach[1]

Giles Waterfield

Director, Dulwich Picture Gallery

Paintings appear in significant numbers in British houses in the sixteenth century, especially during the reign of Elizabeth I. With rare exceptions, the motive of such collectors as Bess of Hardwick at Hardwick Hall or Lord Lumley at Lumley Castle was to make a statement about the importance of their own dynasty, a major consideration at a time when many noble families were newly established. The Long Gallery at Hardwick Hall, a room largely intended for the display of paintings, contained numerous portraits of the owner's family, connections and dependants, and crowned heads of Europe, these portraits being supplemented in other rooms by topographical works. The identification of the artists is not listed in the Hardwick inventory of 1601, since the purpose of this group of pictures was documentary and their artistic quality negligible.

This tradition of portraiture, including 'portraits' of houses and estates, animals and dependants, was to provide the backbone of English patronage until this century, and many artists capable of better things suffered from the limited vision of the upper classes. Though standards of taste became more sophisticated, especially under the influence of Van Dyck in the 1630s, this prime requirement that art should provide a visual record links the art of painting, and, in the form of funerary monuments, sculpture, directly to social history.

In the seventeenth century relationships with the continent became closer after the cultural isolation of Elizabeth's reign. Charles I assembled an outstanding collection of paintings, notably of the Italian Schools (of which fragments remain in the form of the Raphael Cartoons and Mantegna's *Triumph of Caesar*), but with the dispersal of his possessions at the end of the Civil War his influence was relatively short-lived. At the end of the century, however, two developments were perceptible which were to have a powerful effect: the Grand Tour and the growth of the art trade.

The Grand Tour, by which a young man would travel for up to seven years in France and Italy, began to emerge in the 1680s and by the middle of the next century was commonplace. The purpose of the Tour was to educate the young man in the manners of foreign countries and, often, to give him an opportunity to collect antiques, paintings, drawings, books and medals. These treasures would then be sent home, and in many cases a new house was built to accommodate them. For those unable to travel, large numbers of paintings were imported into England by the increasing number of professional art dealers, and sold either at auction or through dealers' private negotiation with clients. This activity was based on a new attitude to paintings and sculpture. The productions of foreign artists were regarded as works of art rather than as documents, like English portraits, and an increasing interest was shown in acquiring works by the most famous masters. Within the town and country houses for which they were bought (until at least the 1760s the most important objects seem to have been kept in London), specially designed settings were created, with sculpture galleries containing niches for classical pieces (as at Holkham Hall, Norfolk, built for Thomas Coke from 1734 to 1765) and state rooms with symmetrical arrangements of paintings in matching frames, as seen at Kedleston Hall, Derbyshire, the house of Viscount Scarsdale. The permanent consideration was the creation of a fine decorative *ensemble* in which the works of art formed a part of the total effect. In such houses, the purpose of the works of art illustrates social development in that these historic interiors illustrate the way of life of the British ruling class in the eighteenth and early nineteenth centuries; and, as at Kedleston, the paintings are often of more interest as a collection than as individual specimens. From the 1880s in particular, such collections began to be broken up, partly as a result of the agricultural depression, and it was only in the 1930s, when the Marquess of Lothian introduced to the National Trust a scheme for saving such houses, and himself presented Blickling Hall in Norfolk to the Trust, that an understanding developed of their importance and of their uniqueness in a European context.

Around 1800 an important development took place, precipitated by the French Revolution and the consequent arrival in England of huge numbers of fine paintings sent from such collections as that of the Duc d'Orléans. It has been estimated that between 1790 and 1820 the number of Old Master pictures of high quality quadrupled in Britain, most of them entering noblemen's collections. From 1800 it became fashionable for such owners to erect picture galleries in their houses, as at Attingham Park, Shropshire; these were often top-lit and were intended purely for the display of paintings. At the same time, under the influence of the Royal Academy which from its foundation in 1768 had organised annual exhibitions of contemporary British works, an increasing number of galleries were erected in London for the display of works of art to the public. Often, like Boydell's Shakespeare Gallery of 1788, these were commercially based, but they contributed to the growing feeling that Britain needed a national gallery for the display of works of art, which could be used by young artists for their studies, a feeling that was also stimulated by the opening of the Louvre to the public by the French Revolutionary Government. In 1811 Sir Francis Bourgeois left his collection to Dulwich College and when the Dulwich College Picture Gallery opened to the public in 1817 it provided the first public art gallery in England. It was followed in 1824 by the opening of the National Gallery, in John Julius Angerstein's house in Pall Mall.

The increasing seriousness with which pictures were regarded stimulated a native literature on the arts, to supplement foreign works and such narrative accounts as Horace Walpole's *Anecdotes of Painters in England* (1761-71). A notable example is J. Smith's *Catalogue Raisonné of the Works of the Most Eminent Dutch, Flemish and French Painters* of 1829, one of the first books in England to attempt a systematic account of a foreign School. It was followed by a number of serious works on art, such as Crowe and Cavalcaselle's *History of Painting in Italy* of 1856.

Increasing knowledge of the history of paintings produced a shift in attitudes towards the arrangement and display of pictures. In place of the aristocratic Regency custom of placing pictures according to visual criteria with a feeling for a picturesque ensemble, museum directors led by Sir Charles Eastlake (1793-1865), influenced by developments on the continent and notably in Germany, arranged their collections chronologically and according to School. The quasi-scientific idea of a comprehensive collection representing all important aspects of (Western) art, dominated the formation of the collections of the National Galleries in London and Edinburgh, and influenced collectors elsewhere.

In the mid-nineteenth century John Ruskin produced a large number of books, such as *The Stones of Venice* of 1851-3, which applied literary and moral attitudes to the study of art. Art was given a new moral significance as a force capable of rescuing society from the degradation into which, in Ruskin's view, it had sunk. Ruskin's influence can be detected in the widespread belief among late-nineteenth-century philanthropists in the improving effect of art on the deprived classes. Encouraged by such major events as the Manchester Art Treasures Exhibition of 1857 and the Great Exhibition of 1861, public-spirited people founded such institutions as the Bethnal Green Museum, established in 1872 from public funds, the Whitechapel Art Gallery of 1901, and the Ancoats Museum, set up in the Manchester slums to bring a glimpse of a happier life to the deprived inhabitants. In each case, delighted surprise was expressed in the press at the appreciation shown by what were regarded as the lowest classes of society for works of art. The improvements in communications in Britain from the middle of the nineteenth century onwards strongly affected not only the popular demand for paintings and prints, but the type of work produced by British artists. The battle to establish academic art in England (that is, art as taught in the academies and based on a study of ancient and Renaissance prototypes) was abandoned in favour of a popular art depicting recognisable events in which the story was predominant, and which could be 'read' by the spectator. Outstanding among these narrative artists was W.P. Frith (1819-1909) whose paintings such as *Derby Day* were the first to require the protection of a rope at the Royal Academy Summer Exhibitions. For the social historian, the paintings of this School, widely bought by provincial museums from the 1860s into the 1920s, have an obvious documentary value. Frith remained content to depict the surface of society, but many artists of the time used the medium of narrative painting for outspoken social commentary much as writers such as Dickens employed the novel. The tradition stretches from the middle of the century, in the work of such artists as Augustus Egg (1816-63), to its conclusion: paintings such as *Newgate: Committed for Trial* of 1878 (Royal Holloway College) by Frank Holl (1845-88) with its bitter denunciation of society's neglect of urban poverty, caused a public sensation, fuelled by its reproduction through prints and in newspapers.

The growing interest in the establishment of museums through the nineteenth century was reflected in the accumulation of paintings for documentary rather than aesthetic purposes. A prime case is the National Portrait Gallery, set up in 1856 with the brief of collecting depictions, in any form, of notable Britons; the remit of acquiring great examples of the art of portraiture was added officially only in the 1960s. A similar tendency can be seen in the policy, in both national and provincial museums, of making topographical collections, as at the Victoria and Albert Museum. One of the most interesting and productive examples of this approach can be seen in the art collections of the Imperial War Museum, based largely on the commissioning of Official War Artists in the First and Second World Wars to depict the conflict both at home and abroad. A similar use of paintings as illustrations of social phenomena can be seen in the Geffrye Museum, London, where the bulk of the pictures has been accumulated in this century.

The public attention given to paintings grew steadily through the century, encouraged by, for example, the outstanding purchases of Italian Renaissance paintings for the National Gallery by Sir Charles Eastlake in the 1850s and 1860s, and the gift to the nation of the Wallace Collection in 1897.

By the end of the century paintings, and to a lesser extent sculpture, had become the first choice for acquisition of the newly rich industrial magnates. The north-west of England is studded with monuments to the beneficence of such men, generous if conservative collectors, who frequently built municipal art galleries to house the paintings that they also chose to give. Resplendent among such institutions is the Lady Lever Art Gallery at Port Sunlight of 1922, erected to house his own collection by Lord Leverhulme, and placed in the centre of the model community, Port Sunlight, that he designed to house the workers at his factories. Here, surviving almost intact, is epitomised the late Victorian belief in the healing power of art. A similar motive can be seen in the numerous major public art commissions of the period, from the murals of the House of Lords to Manchester Town Hall.

The monumental and complacent character of the late Victorian art world – it was a time when successful painters became phenomenally rich, as the artists' mansions of Holland Park Road, London, still attest – was shaken by the aesthetic movement of the 1880s and 1890s, dominated by J.M.Whistler and Oscar Wilde, as well as by the Arts and Crafts Movement. Growing dissatisfaction with the productions of the Victorian Royal Academicians was encouraged by the new approaches to painting apparent in the work of Bernard Berenson (1865-1959) and Roger Fry (1866-1934). Berenson made widely available a new style of criticism based on the comparison of works of art and on visual attributions, a study much assisted by the growth of photography. Roger Fry introduced to the deeply conservative art public of Britain, practically unaware even in the 1910s of the innovations made on the continent by the Impressionists and their successors, the work of the continental avant-garde in such exhibitions as the two *Post Impressionist Exhibitions* held at the Grafton Galleries in 1910 and 1912, and wrote a series of books in which he forcefully and influentially expressed his admiration for such artists as Cézanne. Though the Tate Gallery, established in 1897 as a National Gallery of British and Modern Art, remained unadventurous in its acquisition policy until the 1930s, the advent of John Rothenstein as Director in 1937 revolutionised – alas, rather late in the day – official policy on the acquisition of British and foreign works of art.

The twentieth century has seen a gradual maturing in art historical studies in Britain. The first university art history department was established as early as the 1870s in Edinburgh, but its next successor was not founded until Samuel Courtauld endowed the Courtauld Institute in 1932, its first Director being Johannes Wilde, one among several influential exiles from Nazi Germany. A new interest in the interdisciplinary interpretation of art, and notably in iconography, was stimulated by the transfer from Hamburg to London in 1933 of the Warburg Institute. A comparable abandonment of old-fashioned connoisseurship, in favour of attributions and dating based on archival research, can be seen in the outstanding series of National Gallery catalogues, began by Martin Davies and his fellows in the 1940s, which exerted an international influence.

Since the Second World War, history of art has been increasingly recognised as a proper subject for study, with the establishment of departments at numerous British universities, the foundation of an Association of Art Historians, the emergence of an increasingly academic art press led by the *Burlington Magazine,* and the publication of an extensive literature. A new style of art historian has emerged, often as interested in the social context of a work of art as in the object itself. In the 1980s this approach has blossomed into the 'New Art History', applying the methodology of structuralism, Marxist historical methods and feminist perspectives.

This approach has been accompanied by a growing interest in the physical history of paintings, which have come increasingly to be scientifically analysed in terms of their structure and of the insights that these can provide into the artist's working process.

A growing literature has addressed itself to the history of taste and of collecting, a subject broached by John Steegman in the 1930s and developed by Francis Haskell since the 1960s. It is an approach which exerts a particular appeal in an age obsessed by the nation's past, and which illustrates the inseparability of the history of art and the history of society.

Note

1. The term 'fine art' is generally taken to cover architecture, sculpture and painting, but this piece will not cover architecture. Broadly speaking, remarks on painting can be applied also to post-classical sculpture, which has often been treated as a subsidiary art form in this country, as it still is. Classical sculpture, like architecture, represents a field in itself.

5.1   The Decorative Art Approach: Furniture

Sarah Medlam

Deputy Curator, Furniture and Woodwork Collection,
Victoria and Albert Museum

The Development of Furniture Studies

Furniture naturally provokes speculation about the life of its original owners. Antiquarians in the eighteenth-century collected medieval and 'Old English' furniture chiefly for its romantic associations with an idealised chivalric life. Authenticity and quality were of secondary importance.

In the nineteenth-century this cult developed into a dominating aesthetic of historicism. Modern furniture was made in the style of each century in turn. Though Gothic revival dominated the mid-century, as early as the 1820s interiors were decorated in rococo-revival style, with furniture imitating pieces made only two generations earlier. This decade also saw a widespread trade in early (pre-seventeenth-century) carved oak panels, largely from the Low Countries. New furniture and room fittings were created, using early panels and imitating them. The trade of antique dealer had emerged, also encouraged by large imports of French seventeenth- and eighteenth-century furniture, following the revolutionary upheavals in France. This, the grandest furniture ever produced, encouraged a new generation of collectors. These were few in number but connoisseurship rapidly developed, and by the end of the century questions of quality, authenticity and condition were of concern, not least because of the camp-following trades of copyist and faker.

Interest in antiques soon began filtering out to a wider circle, and the first books on the subject appeared. At first these concentrated on establishing a chronology of styles in grander furniture. Because the picturesque cottage style had become fashionable following the Arts and Crafts movement, certain higher quality examples of country furniture were accepted as 'honorary antiques'. By the 1920s and 1930s several comprehensive studies of furniture had been published, including the three-volume *Dictionary of English Furniture*. The value of these works is immense though they are more descriptive than analytical. They provided the framework for all later studies, and, with the flourishing art journals of the period, encouraged the first discussions of the works of individual makers and the earliest studies relating furniture to archival records.

So far the furniture historian's eye had concentrated on single pieces of furniture, their design and craftsmanship. Two influences served to widen the vision. Developments in art historical method in Europe and America showed the value of considering furniture in relation to its original setting, using secondary source material such as inventories, bills, and contemporary letters and diaries, to discover not only the names of makers, but also such matters as original use or appearance, or relationship to other pieces now scattered from their original setting. Meanwhile, the new discipline of social history began to be interested in furniture as evidence rather than object of reverence. An approach via the craft of furniture making naturally channelled interest towards the rural and the traditional, where the furniture historians admired the grand and the innovative. As the latter had first cut their teeth on antiquarian oddities in the early nineteenth-century, so early social historians showed a preference for the quaint: baby-walkers, lambing chairs and bacon cupboards.

The Period Room was an obvious stratagem to develop from these new interests, as a device for reconstituting the environment which was increasingly seen to be important in understanding the furniture. It was certainly popular, but because of its powers of suggestion, pitfalls abounded. What it did point up was the need for rigorous research to inform the displays. A collection of furniture of vaguely the same date was not enough.

The first books treating of furniture specifically in terms of social history appeared in the 1960s. In 1964 the expansion of furniture studies was both marked and encouraged by the foundation of the Furniture History Society. The society has always been chiefly interested in fashionable furniture, and avowedly international. But it has encouraged a wide variety of approaches to a wide variety of furniture, producing studies of the organisation of the furniture trades, of furniture of all dates from medieval to contemporary, of regional furniture, of taste in collecting, or of patterns of commercial importation.[1]

This expansion of furniture studies has shown how much is still untouched. Standard works have appeared surprisingly recently. A properly researched life of Thomas Chippendale was not available until 1978, and a comprehensive *Dictionary of English Furniture Makers* was published only in 1986. The compilation of this illustrated the huge size of the field of study. Four hundred contributors combed trade directories, bills, newspaper advertisements, and more general sources such as parish registers and fire insurance records. It is recognised as a preliminary study, and the long process of identifying furniture made by even a fraction of the people listed will be a continuing task. Marking of English furniture is so rare that identification must be pursued by use of secondary sources. Diaries, letters and contemporary illustrations may also establish its original appearance, arrangement or function (all aspects of furniture history currently attracting much interest). American influences on methodology have introduced the meticulous study of woodworking techniques, decorative motifs, woods, paints and varnishes, as an aid to grouping hitherto anonymous furniture and its possible attribution to workshop or region.

Current Areas of Interest

Furniture studies become ever more catholic. After years of poring over mahogany and gilding, attention has recently turned to all aspects of upholstery (textile hangings, beds, seat-furniture, carpets) as we realise how much *more* important these were in many cases than wood. The same questions of maker, method of manufacture, stylistic development and use beckon from this new field. New fields are also opening out in exploration of what may be called minor and ephemeral furnishings (floorcloths, blinds, light-fittings) or specialist furnishings (as for schools or churches, military or trade use). Whereas interiors were at one time considered as static entities, we are now beginning to rescue the knowledge of how they were cleaned, protected, arranged and used, and to understand the conventions which separated day-to-day living from ceremonial living in all but the poorest houses. Great-grandmother's parlour is seen to have aristocratic ancestry in seventeenth-century rooms of parade. Two newer societies reflect particular interests. The Regional Furniture Society concentrates on furniture outside the fashionable and metropolitan spheres,[2] and the Design History Society studies furniture after 1850, particularly industrially produced furniture.[3]

Museums have responded by emphasising specialities within collections. A general show of seventeenth- and eighteenth-century 'brown furniture' is no longer a desideratum in decorative art museums. Specific collections are forming, as of Arts and Crafts furniture in Cheltenham or High Victorian furniture at Bedford. Astonishing increases in furniture prices have reinforced selective collecting, and funds are now concentrated on pieces with known provenance or particular art historical interest, though changes of interest may mean that these qualities are recognised not just in fashionable furniture.

Exhibitions have also become specific, and Temple Newsam House, Leeds, in particular, has shown how successfully they can be used as a spur to research, with the catalogue as a lasting record on such subjects as 'Back-stairs' (servants') furniture, or fireplaces and their impedimenta. Active information recording is also developing. The Victoria and Albert Museum was first in the field and their departmental archive on furniture is the most wide-ranging. But specialist archives are following specialist collections, and most decorative art museums maintain archives also covering local collections, local makers and local traditions.

Notes

1. The Furniture History Society – Membership secretary: Dr B. Austen, 1 Mercedes Cottage, St John's Road, Haywards Heath, Sussex RH16 4EH.

2. The Regional Furniture Society – Membership Secretary: Mrs B. D. Cotton, The Trout House, Warrens Cross, Lechlade, Glos. GL7 3DR.

3. The Design History Society – enquiries to Stuart Evans, Central School of Art & Design, Southampton Row, London, WC1B 4AP.

Bibliography

Agius, Pauline, *British Furniture 1880-1915*, The Antique Collectors Club, Woodbridge, Suffolk, 1978.

Beard, Geoffrey, *The National Trust Book of English Furniture*, Viking/National Trust, 1985.

Beard, Geoffrey, and Goodison, Judith, *English Furniture 1500-1840*, Phaidon/Christie, 1987.

Clabburn, Pauline, *The National Trust Book of Furnishing Textiles*, Viking/National Trust, 1988.

Joy, Edward, *English Furniture 1800-1851*, Sotheby's/Ward Lock, 1977.

Thornton, Peter, *Authentic Decor: the Domestic Interior 1620-1920*, Weidenfeld & Nicolson, 1984.

Beard, Geoffrey, and Gilbert, Christopher (eds), *The Dictionary of English Furniture Makers*, The Furniture History Society/W. S. Manley & Son Ltd, 1986.

5.2 The Decorative Art Approach: Costume

Naomi E.A. Tarrant

Department of History and Applied Art,
Royal Museum of Scotland

Clothing is a part of everyone's life. Perhaps because of this it has been treated in a rather offhand way in the past by curators and social historians. Occasional dressed figures have been put into a display to convey scale rather than being used to enhance the information to be conveyed.

There were several histories of fashion written in the nineteenth century by people who were genuinely intrigued by the development of fashion, or who wanted to find out about medieval dress so that they could recreate it in paintings. Fancy dress balls were immensely popular and great effort was made to get the historic costumes correct.[1] The theatre also acted as a spur to historic costume studies with some actors being especially particular about accurate details.

The serious study of the history of clothes started to gather momentum with the work of Dr C. W. Cunnington in the 1930s. Cunnington saw clothes as evidence which revealed the tastes and prejudices of past generations, and he was concerned to collect the typical items worn by ordinary people, not high fashion garments. Although his theoretical writings are today rather quaint, his monumental works on nineteenth- and twentieth-century women's dress and his series of *Handbooks* are still the standard works.[2]

Other writers this century have seen dress as a suitable subject for psychological studies, or even more esoteric work such as in semiotics. It seems to be the rapidly changing styles of western European fashion which attracts attention, in contrast to the supposed stability of clothing styles in folk dress and in non-European cultures.

Over the last forty years costume studies have proliferated. Two main lines of approach have been followed. In one the chronological development of dress and fashion in western Europe has been charted, sometimes in books which cover the total span of human history, or in works which detail some shorter time span. Whilst the general approach can do no more than touch on the context of dress within a period, it does allow an impression of the progress of styles and shows the influences that affect clothes.[3] The more particular study, if well researched and written, can show something of the place of clothing within the social, economic and artistic trends of the era.[4]

The other approach has been a detailed study of surviving garments by looking at their construction. Although some earlier works had attempted to show patterns drawn from actual specimens,[5] it has been the vogue for greater historical accuracy in dressing theatre and television plays which has led to this interest in patterns. These studies of often fragile surviving pieces have extended our knowledge of the development of dressmaking and tailoring techniques which enables us, amongst other things, to understand how the effects seen in portraits are achieved.[6]

The majority of large costume collections in Britain have been assembled in art-based museums and this has tended to lead to exhibitions which chart the fashionable image. Dress has so many interactions with other aspects of life that this narrow view has been unfortunate. At its best this approach can give a good chronological display, as at the Victoria and Albert Museum in London,[7] or show the work of a single designer in detail, such as the splendid, 'The Genius of Charles James' at the Brooklyn Museum and the Chicago Historical Society Museum in 1983.[8]

There are pitfalls to the chronological approach which can result in a misleading picture. Often the quality of material is variable because of the vagaries of survival. The twentieth-century pieces are usually high fashion obtained from the aristocratic and very wealthy, or directly from a designer, and do not necessarily show what makes a designer popular with clients. Nearly all the pre-twentieth-century pieces will have been worn and can show an individual's dress sense and flair, but because the dress of the wealthiest in society rarely remains from the past, the effect overall will be misleading.

Many of the couturiers of the present century have been involved in the major artistic trends of their day and this has been reflected in their clothes. In turn, this has led to dress being given a more prominent position in art studies than it has had before. It has, however, led to a distinction being created between the fashion or trend-setting work of the couturier and the more realistic and wearable clothing provided by the ready-to-wear firms. Whilst the former may find a place in an art show the latter is seen to belong to the social history display. Within the last decade the two costume museums in Paris, the Musée de la Mode and the Musée de la Mode et du Costume, have both had large exhibitions devoted to specific designers or periods of time.[9]

One of the most successful costume exhibitions was 'Eight Chicago Women' at the Chicago Historical Society in 1978, which related the clothes to their wearers. This show displayed the clothes of eight prominent women from the 1870s to the 1920s. An outline of their lives and quotations from their diaries and letters added life to the clothes, revealing the personality behind the clients who bought from the best Parisian houses. Their clothes fitted into the art museum but, by applying social history techniques, the display was enriched and made much more enjoyable for the visitor,

There have been disappointments in the art-based displays. Despite three major exhibitions on eighteenth-century dress in the 1980s, all in the USA, not one of them really came close to giving a true appreciation of the complexities of dress within the different cultures of Europe.[10]

An attempt to recreate the figure in an eighteenth-century portrait can also be disappointing as the conventions of portraiture do not always show the kind of clothes which survive. Plain coloured silks are easier and cheaper to paint, but in real life plain silk is easier to cut up, alter or dispose of to less fortunate relatives. Patterned silk dresses therefore survive in far greater numbers than plain silk ones.

The most extravagant displays of costume in recent years have been the series initiated in the 1970s by Diana Vreeland for the Costume Institute in the Metropolitan Museum of Art, New York. Miss Vreeland's approach was individual, preferring to give the flavour rather than the substance, precise dates being irrelevant, and incongruous juxtaposition being seen to add spice to the display. These were shows rather than exhibitions and earned for the Costume Institution a somewhat two-edged reputation.

There is a need for some new thinking about ways of using costume within art-based museums, but the recent concern of the social history museum with the working life of the lower social strata has thrown up some unjustified criticisms of the collections of costume. No museum can produce for display garments which have not survived from the past. The reason why clothes do not survive is worth considering. Apart from the obvious dangers such as insect damage, fire, and wear and tear there are other factors which determine what may remain. Until well into the eighteenth century cloth was an expensive commodity and clothes were regularly left in wills to individuals who would remake them. In wealthy households valets and maids had their 'perks', and although they might not wear the cast-off clothes of their employers they could be sold on to the thriving second-hand market. What is remarkable is that so much mid-to-late eighteenth-century clothing survives, although very little is unaltered.

Each museum has to find a way to display clothes which is most suitable for their particular collections. No two collections are comparable in their range or method of past acquisition, and differences between costume exhibitions can be seen as a reflection of the rich variety to be found in dress.

Notes and References

1. The frequent editions of *Fancy Dress Described* by Ardern Holt, published by Debenham and Freebody for the first time in 1880, are testimony to this popularity.

2. See C. W. Cunnington, *English Women's Clothing in the Nineteenth Century*, Faber, 1937; *English Women's Clothing in the Twentieth Century*, Faber, 1952; C. W. and P. Cunnington, *Handbook of English Medieval Costume,* Faber, 1973.

3. See for example, François Boucher, *A History of Costume in the West*, Thames & Hudson, 1987; Milia Davenport, *The Book of Costume*, New York, 1948; James Laver, *A Concise History of Costume*, Thames & Hudson, 1969.

4. For example, Anne Buck, *Dress in Eighteenth Century England*, Batsford, 1979.

5. For example, Talbot Hughes, *Dress Design*, John Hogg, London, 1913.

6. See Janet Arnold, *Patterns of Fashion*, Vol. 1 1660-1860, Vol. 2. 1860-1940, Vol. 3. 1560-1620, Macmillan, 1985-9.

7. See Natalie Rothstein (ed.), *Four Hundred Years of Fashion*, Victoria and Albert Museum, 1983, the catalogue for the Victoria and Albert costume gallery.

8. See E. A. Coleman, *The Genius of Charles James*, Brooklyn Museum, New York, 1982.

9. See Guillaume Garnier *et al.*, *Paris-Costume-Années Trente*, Musée de la Mode et du Costume, Paris, 1986, and Dominique Sirop, *Paquin*, Adam Biro, Paris, which were both issued in conjunction with exhibitions.

10. Linked to the exhibition at the Fashion Institute of Technology, New York, was Kyoto Costume Institute, *Revolution in Fashion: European Clothing 1715-1815*, English language edition Abbeville Press, New York, 1990. The catalogue fills in the background which the exhibition missed out.

5.3 The Decorative Art Approach: Ceramics

Pat Halfpenny

Keeper of Ceramics, City Museum and Art Gallery, Stoke-on-Trent

The full technical meaning of the word 'ceramic' embraces the products of all the silicate industries, including pottery, glass, vitreous enamel and hydraulic cement. The term 'pottery' is similar but also covers a bewildering range of materials such as earthenware, bone china, porcelain, vitreous china and sanitary fireclay. Both terms are commonly used when discussing items made from clay.

The typical decorative art collection usually includes tablewares and ornamental pottery, with occasional examples of kitchen and sanitary ware. Most of the important collections of pottery are built upon the foundations laid by large individual bequests made to local museums which then employ staff (usually trained in fine and/or decorative arts) to curate them.

The City Museum and Art Gallery, Stoke-on-Trent, has exceptionally large collections which were built up in this way. The city was formerly six individual towns and a number of these had their own museum with ceramic collections based on large donations from individuals. The six towns were amalgamated into a borough and eventually achieved city status in 1925. The collections were amalgamated after the First World War, creating one of the most important museums for the study of English pottery.

The majority of museums acquire examples of pottery because of the long traditions of collecting and the reluctance of collectors to see their life's work dispersed after their death. Amongst the earliest of recorded collections is that of Chinese porcelain made by Queen Anne. Once the royal family had started the trend for collecting, the activity became more widespread and travelled down the social scale.

Collections usually reflect the status of the collector. The wealthy shipping magnate Williamson, whose collection is now in Tullie House, Carlisle, bought over 600 pieces of expensive porcelain, particularly acquiring the showy ornate gilded figure groups of the last quarter of the eighteenth century. Porcelains such as these are much less popular with collectors today and mark Williamson as a fashionable collector of the early twentieth century. Today's wealthier collector is more likely to be interested in the early English porcelains of the mid-eighteenth century or the more easily available bone chinas of the nineteenth century. The study of twentieth century art and design is increasingly popular and has led to a proliferation of collections of 1920s-1950s pottery, which, owing to greater accessibility and lower prices, are found across a broad social band. Collectors are also interested in themes, either amassing the work of individual factories or a particular form of vessel such as the teapot.

As a consequence, very few museums have comprehensive collections of pottery and the resulting eccentric assemblages are very difficult to interpret. Often, because these objects are not collected primarily for their cultural significance, they are assigned to an 'arts' department in a museum. Many of the museums housing important collections of ceramics exhibit only from the arts, e.g. the Victoria and Albert Museum, the Fitzwilliam Museum, Cambridge, the

Cecil Higgins Art Gallery and Museum, Bedford. The pottery within these institutions is inevitably looked upon as a collection of semi-precious objects (only fine art being truly precious). In this context pottery can only be seen as an expression of fashionable taste and style. The collections tend to be formed of finely wrought pieces from the most prestigious manufacturers which can be fitted into an art or design history context, so only those pieces which exhibit features which can be readily categorised into periods or styles are usually acquired or displayed. The City Art Gallery, Manchester, has decorative art material, including pottery, displayed in the main galleries housing painting where decorative and the fine arts can be seen in context. This is a completely justifiable way of displaying certain ceramics for they were made purposely to be viewed in that way. Josiah Wedgwood's neo-classical stonewares were deliberately conceived as expressions of that art movement, just as in the nineteenth century Herbert Minton commissioned his colleague Pugin to create neo-Gothic designs suited to pottery production.

The art or design historian may also use the decoration on pottery as an interpretive feature. Sources for patterns and designs often relate from one material to another; fine art and sculpture can provide motifs and models for manufactures. The location and identification of these sources can tell us how some aspects of the pottery trade operated. Exhibitions at Temple Newsam House, Leeds, and the Fitzwilliam Museum, Cambridge, showed how mass-produced lead and plaster sculpture was available in reduced sizes and at reasonable costs from many London suppliers. Manufacturers were, therefore, able to buy examples as models and it was shown that the pottery industry did not rely solely on local pottery workers.

The identification of printed patterns and relating them to an original source confirms that pottery manufacturers were aware of the work of fashionable London print-makers and that wares were produced for specific markets e.g. scenes depicting events in North America were destined for sale across the Atlantic. The great number of surviving pieces in Canada and the USA provide some evidence of markets and trading patterns.

Many decorative arts collections, however, are not suited to the purely art historical approach. It is more usual to find that certain areas of ceramic history are more heavily represented than others or that the material is not prestigious enough to complement fine art displays. In these cases different approaches to the subject may be taken depending upon the nature of the collection. A collection of pottery cats in Norwich Museum, for example, offers problems of interpretation, as does the herd of cow cream jugs at Stoke-on-Trent. Once it is established that the cats function only in an ornamental capacity and that all the cows are an eccentric form of milk jug, it is difficult and unnecessary to find several hundred ways of saying this, one for each piece. Yet the demands from the visitor (or in some cases the legal restrictions of the gift) require that the collections are displayed.

Where collections are restricted to a certain date or period and form part of a mixed decorative art collection then the material may be interpreted by showing its use. Collections at Pickford House in Derby illustrate upstairs and downstairs life in a provincial house of the late Georgian period. The creamware collection at Lotherton Hall, Leeds, is more specific still, comprising a large quantity of late eighteenth-century tablewares of a similar type. Nowhere else could a large supper-table have been laid according to the customs of the times with the appropriate earthenware. This, combined with a study of relevant factory pattern books, offers new insights into the names of pottery shapes and the table manners of the period.

A more recent development in pottery interpretation by decorative art historians is to show pottery in terms of the development of manufacturing techniques. Understanding pottery techniques not only helps to identify and date wares but also makes us aware of the circumstances in which they were produced. Knowing the processes can lead to an understanding of the problems of production both technically and socially. In learning about the development of industrialisation we also come to terms with factory conditions; in knowing about lead glazing we learn of lead poisoning in pottery workers. The ceramic galleries at the Harris Museum, Preston, include references to the problems suffered by the workforce in pottery making. There are, however, difficulties in disseminating information about the manufacturing processes away from factory premises. The historical aspect of the ceramic industry has little illustrative or oral material, except for the most recent past, and few decorative art departments are able to maintain an active collecting policy in the area of contemporary industrial ceramics.

There is no one decorative arts approach to ceramics; different collections require different interpretations and decorative art curators have responded to these challenges in a variety of ways. In summary, any one or more of the following avenues of study may be adopted:

1. Art/design history – in which the style of an object may be studied in isolation or in context with other material and in which identification and chronology play a major role.
2. Design influences – investigating the source of patterns or models and the methods by which this information was communicated.
3. Social context – studying the users and producers of ceramics.
4. Manufacturing techniques – understanding pottery through a knowledge of methods of production and collecting evidence of working practices and developments.

All these approaches are governed by the nature of the collections involved which may be biased in many different ways. In particular, the highly selective practices of collectors and past curators may weight collections in particular areas. It should also be borne in mind that pottery, being fragile, may be easily broken and disposed of so that surviving pieces may be unrepresentative, dominated either by prestigious or ornamental pieces preserved in china cabinets or by heavy duty durable wares.

The decorative art approach to the study of ceramics is principally object-based but, in recent years, has moved away from the traditional concept of connoisseurship towards a more methodological approach supported by archaeological and historical research. Recent publications on ceramic subjects rely heavily on primary sources of information in all the areas of study outlined here, and offer tools for the study of ceramics to curators in all disciplines.

6 Science and Technology:
Un-natural Science and In-human History

Andy King

Assistant Curator of Technology,
Bristol Industrial Museum

History

When the first flood of new museums began in the early years of the nineteenth century, the learned societies which established them were interested in the exciting new fields of archaeology, zoology, geology and 'machines and models of the useful arts'. Thus in the early accession registers of the forerunner of Bristol City Museum, amongst the stuffed animals, fossils and Egyptian relics, the following entries can be found:

Feb. 1824 – Messrs Dobbins & Greasley – one of their brass sheaves for reducing friction.

Feb. 1825 – Model of air pump.

Mar. 1831 – Model of John Murray's arrow for communication with shore in shipwreck.

1838 – Model of an alarm with revolving lights for preventing collision at sea.

The acquisition of material which we would today class as 'science and technology' thus has a long history. Like 'social history' (*née* folk life), however, it took over one hundred years for the subject to achieve the separate identity long enjoyed by other museum disciplines.

Certainly in most local authority museums, the skeleton of a technology collection existed by the 1900s, often hidden under the departmental headings of 'industrial art' or 'bygones'; for many years even the Science Museum existed as a branch of the Victoria and Albert Museum, and was poorly regarded by comparison with its more effete neighbour. Primarily, the material in these neo-collections tended to be of the attractive brass variety – microscopes, telescopes, and so on – and was, for the most part, displayed as decorative items. Later, many museums began to collect vehicles of one sort or another, mainly the disappearing posh horse-drawn carriages, but, particularly in the case of Hull Museum, early motor vehicles too. By the early 1930s, several museums had bitten the bullet of larger industrial machinery, concentrating on early steam engines. Even then, the reason for collecting these things tended towards their decorative qualities or their value as 'bygones'.

After the Second World War, many museums established folklife collections with their own staff, and usually transferred the technological exhibits into the care of these. While what Harold Wilson later described as the 'white heat of the technological revolution' reached cherry red in the early 1960s, so technology departments sprang into being all over the country, concurrent with the appearance of a myriad of railway preservation societies, industrial archaeology societies, and numerous other enthusiast clubs. Many of these went on to form their own private museums; some have grown and lasted well, others have disappeared.

One result of all of this is that there are now more museum staff involved with what might be classified as science and technology material than any other discipline: probably less than half of these people would consider themselves to be specialists in this field, because the scientific or technological material in their care has been collected for its value in interpreting the social history with which it is connected. This in itself could entirely justify an object's place in a museum, but the importance of the item in terms of the history of science and technology should also be borne in mind.

Philosophy

In common with all museums, those which collect scientific and technological material do so in the belief that material evidence of human endeavour in the past is of interest and value to the present and future. Although the reasons for collecting material are influenced by the intended interpretation of the object, this basic concept is the keystone.

The Victorian view of displaying scientific and technological material in international exhibitions and in museums is summed up neatly by W.S. Jevons writing in 1883:

There seems to be a prevalent idea, that if the populace can only be got to walk through a great building filled with tall glass cases, full of beautiful objects, especially when illuminated by electric light, they will become civilised.[1]

This approach has continued to the present day, material being displayed in an isolated and idolised way in some museums, with the object of communicating its place in the taxonomy of development. Even in 1883, there were doubts about the effectiveness of this. Jevons again;

... to comprehend the purpose, construction, mode of use and history of a single object or machine would usually require, from (say) half an hour up to several hours or days of careful study.[2]

At this time, it could be safely assumed that almost everyone had practical experience of some sort of machinery or other; the mechanisms of machines in use at this time were open for all to see, and the introduction of the sewing machine even extended this to well-to-do women. The gradual introduction of guards for safety, combined with increasingly complicated apparatus and invisible modes of operation such as radios and telephones, reduced the chances of readily understanding the technology of everyday life. Science museums took up the role of trying to help their visitors to understand.

However, as Jevons pointed out, this sort of thing can be found in books, so one should be able to visit a museum 'to learn what cannot be learnt by words'.[3] This could be taken to mean setting the technology of the past and present in its context, relating it not only to the way in which a type of machine has developed, but also to the economic and social causes and effects of its introduction. This approach has been adopted more and more frequently in recent years.

Much the same criteria influence the selection of scientific and technological material as in any other discipline. The main areas of selection might be the importance of an individual machine, whether as a prototype or as an example of an important design; particular importance within a local industry; a strong association with a person of note in the area; and so on. Two extra criteria are involved, which might be summarised as size and workability.

More so than other disciplines, science and technology involves very large objects. Often the decision has to be made whether to collect the real thing, or whether to record it sufficiently to build an accurate model. This is always a difficult decision, because the sheer scale of an object is often the very thing one wishes to communicate. At the same time, this makes it prohibitively expensive to collect and maintain; aircraft and ships are the best examples of this.

'Workability' – the ability of a specimen to carry out its function – is also more important than in other disciplines. Science and technology material is generally less familiar (and often downright strange) to the visitor. Setting a machine into full, clattering motion conveys far more than several hundred words of text, provided that the machine is thoughtfully set up; too many steam engines in museums operate in isolation, apparently for the entertainment of engineers.

The science and technology discipline is perhaps fortunate in that the proportion of mass-produced material which makes up collections is higher than in any other field. This means that it is usually easy to acquire a duplicate object to allow sectioning or demonstration while still retaining a machine for posterity. This being said, justifying the storage of two identical machines of considerable size can be difficult, and the ethics of operating machinery are still heatedly discussed.

Collecting Areas

Several national museums could be seen as being primarily made up of science and technology material; apart from the Science Museum itself, much of the collection of the National Maritime Museum, the Imperial War Museum, the RAF Museum and others fall into the category of 'large machinery'.

Because of the local funding base of the majority of science and technology museums, most also have a local bias in their collecting. Several have taken a wider view of the subject, however; these include the Museums of Science and Industry in Birmingham, Manchester and Newcastle. Others have chosen to develop specialist collections of material which may or may not have local significance: motor vehicles at Hull and Coventry, textile machinery of both local and national significance at Bradford, Leeds, Huddersfield, Nottingham and Leicester, for example. Many other single-subject museums exist in the independent sector, the National Motor Museum being an obvious example, and one could perhaps include company museums in the same group.

Inevitably, a certain amount of duplication occurs between museums with similar local industries; there are no less than six museums within a radius of twenty miles of Manchester with almost identical spinning mules. Attempts have been made to reduce this duplication, which can waste scarce resources; in the East Midlands, the industrial collections at Northampton, Derby, Nottingham and Leicester were reorganised to allow each museum to concentrate on a few industries of regional importance. Other museums have looked at their own collections and compared them to the national picture, before deciding to concentrate on scantily collected areas; in Bristol, for example, it was decided to collect heavily in the tobacco and packaging industries. All these efforts have been only partially successful, and sometimes have been undone by the overnight appearance of a company museum.

Science and Technology and Social History

As science museums steer away from the purely educational approach to interpreting their material, so they veer nearer to the area of social hstory. There is much common ground; to begin with, the materials of which both disciplines' objects are made are the same. Perhaps what separates them is the point of view from which curators look at their objects: social historians tend to look from the perspective of the user, science and technology curators from that of the maker or supplier.

Nevertheless, every scientific discovery and every technological change has been initiated by a perceived requirement in society, whether it be a vaccine to cure a disease or an atomic bomb to kill the maximum number of the enemy at the least expense to the originator. One cannot easily display smallpox, but one can display the instruments that were the personal property of Jenner; one cannot 'nuke' one's visitors but one can display replicas of the bomb and an impression of the carnage it is capable of causing.

As scientific and technological change accelerates, and as each part of the discipline becomes more specialised, so the task of explaining to people how things work becomes less easy. The better science and technology museums now spend a lot more time and effort on showing the way in which this rampant 'progress' has affected and is affecting the lives of ordinary people. Society is the common factor between the two subjects, and it is perhaps the opportunity a museum offers to relate exhibits to the people who were associated with them that makes it worthwhile to its visitors.

Notes and References

1. W.S. Jevons, quoted in Eugene S. Ferguson, 'Technical museums and international exhibitions', *Technology and Culture*, vol. 6, 1965.

2. Ibid.

3. Ibid.

4. The Science and Industry Curators Group publishes an extensive bibliography of general interest at intervals; copies can be obtained from C.N. Brown (Secretary), Science Museum, South Kensington, London SW7 2DD.

7 Artefact Study in Archaeology: Typological Tradition and Socio-economic Themes

Jenny Mattingly
Freelance researcher, Leicester

Introduction

To social historians based in museums, the working methods of their archeological colleagues may, with some justification, seem alien. The high degree of specialisation brought by archaeologists to their study of artefacts is minutely detailed, without, it sometimes appears, greatly increasing our understanding of how people lived in the past, a topic which has unquestionably high importance for social history curators. This section will examine the traditional techniques of study used by archaeologists and then point out new methodologies which are emerging.

Why do archaeologists study artefacts and what do they aim to achieve by doing so? These are obvious questions whose importance is borne out by the history of the methodological development of archaeology. The main aims of the nineteenth-century pioneer archaeologists, struggling free of the earlier antiquarian tradition, could be summarised as follows:

1. to date/assign chronological sequences to artefacts;
2. to gain understanding of the geographical/cultural distribution of artefacts;
3. to develop an aesthetic appreciation of the qualities of artefacts.

These aims were applied to bodies of material for which little or no conceptual framework then existed, and in some cases relating to civilisations for which no historical data pertaining to the society existed. In so far as the evidence allowed, social questions (particularly relating to prehistoric societies) might be broached, but such analyses were bound to be seriously flawed prior to scientific excavations of the various classes of site to which the objects related. Because these three approaches have continued to dominate much subsequent archaeological research it is not surprising that less progress has been made on these social aspects than might have been hoped for. This has much to do with the methods developed for the study of archaeological data which are based principally upon classification and typology.

Methods for the Study of Archaeological Data

Classification

The organisation of archaeological evidence by classification has its roots in the work of the earliest archaeologists who gradually developed methods of systematic observation of detail and ordered the evidence yielded (see Greene, 1983, pp.12-34). For the purposes of study, archaeologists divide objects into classes and then subdivide these as far as necessary for more detailed analysis. The classes are normally defined by material – bone, metalwork, ceramics, etc. Expertise in object analysis is usually developed in one material class. This applies whether one is studying objects from a museum collection, which may have varying levels of archaeological context to amplify the information contained within the object itself, or whether objects are being analysed as part of an excavation (or post-excavation) process. Indeed, the standard structure of archaeological reports separates the excavated artefacts in this way and responsibility for publication is divided between many different specialists, each considering small, distinct groups of material. Artefacts are compared with parallels in their class for other sites and for collections, and the body of knowledge about that class of object is thus augmented. Study along these lines necessarily limits the scope of questions which may be asked about an object, but provides immense detail about material, method of manufacture, size, parallels, etc. (This becomes the basis for further, typological, study.)

As long as the process enables the dating of objects, either absolutely or relatively, and thus of the structures from which they were excavated, this limitation has not been considered a drawback. The primary concern of the archaeologists, and the main role of excavated objects, has long been to date the past. However, this reliance upon the use of objects primarily as a tool for dating has until recently rather restricted the scope of object study in archaeology.

Typology

Careful observation of the attributes of objects within their classes enables their organisation into types bearing similar characteristics. Attributes such as size, form, and special features are noted. The representative members of the system are known as the type series, similar to the practice in natural history of using type specimens. Once described, the types are organised by their similarity with each other and the closeness or distance of their time/space relationship may be analysed. Comparison of two types may illustrate the development of the object by revealing functional improvement or change in manufacturing method. Limitations of typological study lie in the frequently uncertain level of accuracy and objectivity in the original object analysis, in the validity of the sample worked, and in the underlying assumption that typological change is always progressive and not regressive.

Yet the discipline that this method imposes on recording and analysing the technology and function of objects ensures that it still has an important and valid place in the study of archaeological material. The immense detail obtained by this method in some fields of study permits analysis where few other methods (apart from historical/documentary evidence) would be useful. For example, specialists in Greek vase painting are able, often from the smallest fragments of pottery, to identify individual known workshops and painters, using the minute detail of form, style and technique observed. Conversely, this art historical approach can tell us very little about the ways in which these objects were used, their values, status in ancient society or role in the ancient economy. Typology alone is not sufficient to answer those wider questions regardless of how finely developed it has become. Lack of contextual information, encouraged by a buoyant collectors' market, has ensured that the vast majority of objects in this class are studied outside their archaeological context and thus their analysis is only relative.

Although many questions still may not be addressed by this method, typological study has generated a vast database of comparative information for archaeological study. For all manner of artefacts, reference can be made to standard works, as for instance *The Roman Imperial Coinage* volumes (RIC). With a second edition in progress, this series represents the cumulative efforts of generations of numismatists at the British Museum and is typical of the way in which typologies of all object classes are continually being revised and developed.

The sophistication of specialist study in many classes of artefact can be used at two levels: first, as the basis for expert analysis of material from a site/collection, and second, as an aid to instant identification by those responsible for wider groups of material. The information contained in these corpuses will vary, but generally will provide guidance to the provenance of an object, its attributes, and perhaps most important of all, its date.

Sequence Dating/Seriation

The use of typology in dating can be refined in several ways further. If assemblages, rather than individual artefacts, are studied (as multiple typologies) the gradual nature of typological change becomes much more apparent, and demonstrates the processes of cultural change as well as chronology.

Sequence dating, and its more modern manifestation seriation, are two such methods for studying assemblages rather than individual artefacts, establishing chronologies as the basis of the association of different objects. These methods are particularly well suited to studying artefact-rich deposits, especially cemeteries, where broad changes in the composition of assemblages can be observed, controlled by statistical analysis, and can be translated into a relative chronological sequence. At its best, this method can contrast the frequently gradual nature of typological change with more dynamic cultural events such as the rise and fall of civilisations.

Scientific Dating Techniques

Up to the 1950s typological analysis was the primary tool of archaeologists in constructing chronological frameworks. Since then the development of scientific techniques of dating, principally radiocarbon dating, has caused something of a revolution (Renfrew, 1973).

Several scientific dating techniques provide further relative dating: pollen analysis, flourine, nitrogen and uranium tests, and obsidian hydration dating add to the insights already available through typology and stratification. For absolute dating, the best known method is radiocarbon dating although there are several alternatives, including dendrochronology, varves, radioactive decay, potassium-argon dating, thermoluminescence, and archaeomagnetic dating.

But it is radiocarbon dating which has been most universally applicable on site, and which, particularly for prehistorians, has completely refocused the debates within the subject (for a concise explanation of these techniques and their application, see Greene, 1983, pp. 103-21).

Towards Wider Understanding?

The methods described briefly above have in common their primary aim of answering questions on chronology. Therefore the information sought by the researcher is shaped, and to an extent constrained by this aim. There are standard steps employed in seeking this information and the process of examining material for style, dimensions, etc. can inevitably lead to a standardised result.

Certain classes of object attract from archaeologists a more art-historical approach; in this case observation and study is primarily aesthetic in quality, and iconographic, artistic and stylistic information tends to eclipse chronology and its importance and in the priority it receives in study.

The range of information sought by archaeologists from artefacts has increased with the development of scientific techniques in addition to those employed for chronological analysis. Techniques from an ever-increasing variety of other disciplines have been employed to enable archaeologists to gather more data on their artefacts. Whether studying methods of manufacture, use, materials or composition, and whether using scientific or more traditional methods, archaeologists are largely dependent for their understanding of material culture on the information to be found within the object, and seek to refine their abilities to extract that information. Yet this contributes to an ever-increasing body of data rather than to new approaches which permit new questions and lines of thought.

At the same time, some archaeologists who recognise the value of information to be found *outside* the object are employing other evidence to complement that found within it – primarily evidence for the entire archaeological context. In addition, the methodologies of other disciplines – ethnography, anthropology, history and sociology – may be used to enhance object evidence and its interpretation.

Artefacts and New Archaeology

As we have seen, until recently object study was constrained by the overwhelming need to date the past. While classification and typology were the main tools of the object analyst, archaeologists' dependence on these methods for dating was understandable.

But some archaeologists have now begun to ask new question about artefacts, introducing new methodologies, and wishing in the main to return to basics. By looking at all the site evidence as a whole – structures, artefacts, ecofacts, etc. – and recording along with objects their spatial relationship to other objects and structures, questions about how objects were used, what for, who by, how long for, etc. may be addressed. These are aims familiar to social historians, but long denied to archaeologists studying collections built up decades, even centuries ago. Even now it is an approach which is a realistic possibility only with newly-excavated material.

Lewis Binford, one of the champions of New Archaeology, studies objects on his sites primarily as evidence for human activities. Artefacts are used to interpret processes (social, economic, etc.) in past societies. In the preface to *In Pursuit of the Past* Binford outlines his views on how the object study methods of archaeologists do not best serve the advancement of archaeological thought itself. By a concentration on specialist areas, and by applying the methodology of one field of study to archaeology, particularly in the case of scientific study, the researcher best serves that discipline: its potential application for solving archaeological problems is secondary. Binford rejects theories based heavily on inference. Earlier archaeologists, he argues, proceeded through methodologies which produced what appear to be valid observations of the record, but do not warrant the inferred interpretations of the past.

Through his recognition that different human activities produce varying patterns of archaeological evidence and that the rift between that production (dynamic) and its surviving evidence (static) is a barrier to understanding the past, Binford justified the development of new archaeological methods of study of the dynamics of hiring systems and their static consequences, that is, the processes by which particular artefacts arise in specific contexts on a site. The research on Inuit hunters is but one example of historically documented archaeology to be adopted by archaeologists.

Binford and other archaeological anthropologists are experimenting in one particular area. He is self-critical about his methodologies and their effectiveness, and indeed the theories are not universally acclaimed. But these approaches will probably hold some meaning for and generate sympathy with social historians.

Socio-Economic Themes

Ceramic study, frequently regarded as one of the most conservative and moribund areas of archaeological specialism, on closer examination can also be seen to have changed dramatically in recent decades. Traditionally dominated by the art-historical approach to a fine pottery appreciation, exemplified by Greek painted pots and red gloss wares of the Roman world, the key questions asked by researchers have been those of chronology, style and attribution.

The focus has now shifted, for some researchers at least, on to economic themes, and on to the social context of pottery production and use. A line of inquiry might be:

a. provenancing through detailed fabric analysis of particular wares, in part assisting

b. the extension of typology from fine to coarse wares (particularly bulk shipping containers (amphorae)), leading to

c. quantitative studies of pottery assemblages totalling tens of thousands of sherds from certain sites, allowing the possibility to

d. compare quantities of imported and local vessels from particular sites and to reconstruct quite detailed information on zones of economic contact. (However, it must be remembered that while pottery survives well, many other traded goods were perishable and are poorly represented in the archaeological record.) This also depends in part on

e. the uses to which the pots are put. The social context in which pots occur archaeologically (domestic, religious, funerary, etc.) may also reveal something of the significance and value placed upon them by those acquiring them. Thus the social differentiation within archaeological sites ought to become increasingly clear. To return to the point of production, much more thought needs to be given to the organisation and scale of the operation.

In his important and highly readable study of all these aspects, Peacock (1982) provides a particularly satisfying exploration of this last point combining ethnographic and archaeological data. Although it ought to be self-evident, it emerges from his study as something of a surprise that not all pottery is produced in the same socio-economic setting, and he argues that clear distinctions can be drawn from the archaeological record of kiln sites, ceramic forms and their distributions, to differentiate several levels of production ranging from the basic domestic supply to major manufactories.

This example has concentrated on ceramics, but similar developments apply in a host of other areas of archaeological object study, encouraging the further development of socio-economic research. Social historians should welcome these developments and explore and exploit these emerging areas of common interest.

References

Binford, Lewis R., (1983) *In Pursuit of the Past: Decoding the Archaeological Data*, Thames & Hudson.

Greene, Kevin (1983), *Archaeology: An Introduction*, Batsford.

Peacock, D. P. S. (1982), *Pottery in the Roman World: An Ethnoarchaeological Approach*, Longman.

Renfrew, C. (1973), *Before Civilisation: The Radiocarbon Revolution and Prehistoric Europe*, Penguin.

8 Ethnographic Approaches to the Study of Objects

Len Pole

Curator, Saffron Walden Museum

Anybody who works with objects in a museum benefits from having an approach for dealing with them, a method of handling collections in an intellectual sense which mirrors their physical ordering for purposes of storage. Much of what constitutes such an approach is common to all museum work. What, then, separates the approach of museum ethnographers from that of workers in other museum-based disciplines?

If ethnography is defined as the study and interpretation of the material evidence from human societies, without any further qualification, then it is immediately obvious that its scope is far greater than that covered by the ethnographic collections in museums in this country. It includes the products of industrialised societies, all material aspects of social history, all forms of painting and sculpture, from Chinese bronzes to the works of Frink and Bacon. Such breadth may seem unwieldy, but it is important to be clear about the unity and universality of the subject. There is no philosophical or logical distinction between the study of the significance of St Paul's cathedral to the peoples of seventeenth-century England and the study of the significance of a tambaran men's house to the peoples of the Sepik River in New Guinea.

The practice, however, is very different. 'Ethnography' in British museums refers to the study of non-European material culture, the collections mainly originating from the former British Empire. This is distinct from the use of the word in practically every other country, which encompasses the pre-industrial traditions of the home culture. 'Ethnography' has a specifically exotic meaning in Britain which it conspicuously lacks elsewhere. Ethnographic collections often include the products of the industrialised world in as much as they have become part of the material culture of the Third World, but not the industrialised procedures of those societies in which industrial economic structures predominate.

Ethnographic material in British museums comes from many cultures of vastly differing geographical origin, of a greater degree of distinctiveness than the differences (great as they are) within the array of communities and social classes in this country. But this delimitation of subject coverage is a matter of historical development leading to a pragmatic division of responsibility among the staff of museums. It should not be taken to imply any lessening of the universal scope of the subject. Some of the other topics within the present section of this book (e.g. 'women's history', 'agricultural history', 'urban history') assume a more focused and western field of view. Each viewpoint has its advantages. The academic framework for museum ethnography maintains a varied gene pool of comparative material supplying the more particular studies with a global cultural context.

What are these ethnographic objects? Broadly, they are the material evidence of other cultures – from everyday things to the most esoteric. Museum ethnographers examine and seek to understand the working social mechanisms of a community through this material evidence. The objects need to be set in relation to each other, so that we get to know what objects would have been used together (for instance, in a daily, domestic setting), and also in relation to objects which would be used in a similar setting by visitors to the museum. Thus an essential part of the museum ethnographer's work relates to communicating information as well as recording it. In order to do this well, it is obvious that museum ethnographers need a knowledge of both the exotic cultures and of the local culture in which their museums operate.

The significance of the context of colonial and trading relations between Europe and the rest of the world, which has led to the establishment and development of ethnographic collections in the countries of European influence, cannot be overestimated. Subsequent to the establishment of cabinets of curiosities some gentlemen collectors became more specifically interested, in the seventeenth and eighteenth centuries, in 'artificial curiosities'. The Tradescant collection comes immediately to mind, as does the collection of Sir Hans Sloane. These formed the nuclei of the Ashmolean Museum in Oxford and the British Museum respectively.[1] Both contained substantial numbers of objects which now come under the heading 'ethnographic'. Interest in the cultures of the Pacific increased enormously as a result of the public reaction to the voyages of Cook and others in the later eighteenth century. Much of the Cook material was incorporated into museum-like ventures such as the museum of Sir Ashton Lever in Leicester Square in 1774.[2] The high-minded concern for the moral state of the so-called 'savages' in other parts of the world engendered waves of missionary activity, which promoted interest in cities and towns up and down the country in collecting objects illustrative of the 'Arts, Manufactures and Habits of Different Nations'.[3] These were exhibited in the rooms of the nation's literary, scientific and philosophical societies, incorporating gew-gaws from sundry travellers, traders and missionaries, displayed to engender a feeling of moral superiority in the casual visitor, to raise money for further missionary activity, to justify military aggression, as well as to satisfy curiosity. Many collections have since been split up, but some remain more or less as they were, for instance the Brassey collection at Hastings Museum.

A more rigorous approach to the study of the objects was adopted by Colonel Lane Fox, later General Pitt Rivers. He was interested in tracing '... the succession of ideas by which the minds of men have progressed from the simple to the complex'.[4] He donated his collections to the University of Oxford and imprinted this approach on the museum which bears his name. In the same year (1884), Cambridge University established its own museum to house, among others, collections from Fiji which had been made as a result of a strong ethnographic interest.[5] Later, in the 1890s, the university encouraged the first ethnographic fieldwork emanating from this country, resulting in the systematic collection of material from the Torres Strait, between Australia and New Guinea. Other large-scale collections of ethnographic material were being amassed at this time, for instance by Frederick Horniman, although in this case the collections came mainly from dealers. The survey of ethnographic collections in UK museums recently undertaken by the Museum Ethnographers Group points to the great wealth of material which was amassed in the nineteenth century, much of it in the most haphazard way.[6]

Collecting in the twentieth century has been equally wide ranging, from the most inconsequential mementoes to comprehensive evidence assembled by trained anthropologists, sometimes with a specific museum-related brief. In general, as the focus of the collecting range broadens, the quality of the documentation decreases. At one end of the continuum stand the well-formed collections with copious documentation. At the other end are the many hundreds of totally unplanned small collections made up of individual objects. These items are virtually useless in isolation and without documentation in museums where there is no material of similar origin; but where such collections are gathered together, usable groups have been produced. However, the cultural context is threadbare. It therefore has to be supported by extraneous information which may or may not be correct for those particular objects. The majority of these collections come from Africa, Asia, the Americas, the Pacific, and, in some museums, Europe. But there are geographical gaps which can be related to the historical circumstances outlined above, especially in relation to parts of the world which fell under colonial control from European countries other than Britain. There is comparatively little material from former Spanish, Dutch or French territories, for instance.

The study of the more systematic of these collections resulted in theories which sought to account for the diversity and similarity of forms of objects. Some employed diffusionist hypotheses, some constructed elaborate culture complex analyses, others emphasised individual human inventiveness. The development of social anthropology in Britain in the last hundred years produced a wealth of detailed particular studies of social processes in which the material element was insignificant, although some anthropologists nevertheless made important collections. More recently, an integrative impetus linking disciplines has become apparent, based on the insights and analytical methods of anthropology applied to old and new ethnographic collections.

The distinctive approaches of these separate but linking disciplines can be highlighted by reference to an example: a weight made of copper alloy used in Asante, Ghana, for weighing gold. The weight is in the form of a snake biting a bird. The art historian approaches it as a piece of sculpture, examining the way it tackles the problems of expression of bodily forms in relation to the constraints of the technology used, in this case lost-wax casting. The ethnographer sees it as an element in an anthropological landscape, related to its place in Akan society. This is only one of a number of elements, not all of them material – for instance, the context of use in relation to fines levied in gold to deal with transgression of state laws. There is also the proverbial reference, as a result of which the Asante world view can be explored; the example suggests the proverb, 'The snake lies upon the ground, but it has caught the hornbill', which relates to the story of the bird which had borrowed money and refused to return it, being eventually caught by its creditor. The hidden meaning of this is not to take for granted a situation in which you appear to have the advantage.[7] Then there is the manufacturing background, that such items may only be made by certain skilled artisans having a specified economic relationship to the office of the chief – here the method of manufacture is again relevant, but in a different framework of study.

It may be said that many of these issues are also of concern to the art historian. But over and above this, museum ethnographers, entirely within the confines of their professional concern with the cultural context in which the object has been an element, have to consider what the gold weight has meant to others through whose hands it has passed. Many such gold weights have been illegally smuggled out of Ghana. The concern expressed in the pages of national newspapers from time to time (also in the Museum Ethnographers Group *Newsletter*, in *Museum*, in publications of the Royal Anthropological Institute, and elsewhere) about the restitution of cultural property, and about the traffic in cultural heritage, is the best publicised example of the way in which ethnographic objects continue to have significance. This significance is just as much the legitimate subject matter of the ethnographer as their meaning within the cultural milieu in which they were originally made. But it would be of no concern to the art historian or archaeologist as part of their professional study, no matter how much they may be involved as players on the stage. Archaeologists have been rightly involved in the fate of the site of the Rose Theatre, but their concern is as participants in the discussion about the significance of the site, not directly as excavators. In the case of the pottery figures from the Middle Niger delta in Mali about which the MacIntoshes wrote in *Museum*,[8] they were passionate participants in the debate, but were also elements in the description of the changed significance of the objects themselves, since they helped pin down the the the origin of the figures and so increase their value on the open market. They are part of the ethnographic documentation of these objects. From the ethnographic point of view, therefore, it would be equally legitimate to use these objects in a display highlighting the relationship between scholars, dealers on the international art and antiques exchange, and the Third World, as it would be to use them in an exhibition on cultural expression in tenth-century Mali. The latter exhibition could also be seen as an art historical or archaeological exhibition; the former could not.

The essential difference between the approach of ethnographers and that of workers within other disciplines therefore relates to their perception of the boundaries of their fields of discourse. That of ethnographers is universal, holistic, yet comparative. At their most ambitious, ethnographic exhibitions have succeeded in providing a complete picture of the material elements of a culture. The more accessible examples inevitably come from the small-scale end of the cultural spectrum, for example the Hadza hunter-gatherers, in exhibitions both at the Horniman Museum and the Museum of Mankind. On a different scale was the Asante exhibition also at the Museum of Mankind in 1981,[9] a valiant effort to present something of the 'complexity of Asante society and culture' with a significant historical dimension indicating developing artistic and governmental devices. A distinctive link between these exhibitions is the assumption that it is conceivable to present a comprehensive picture.

There are dangers and advantages in this attitude. The temptation to make generalised statements which in fact apply only within a small range of specified circumstances is difficult to resist. The requirement to present a partial picture as part of a greater whole rather than being complete in itself tends towards an excess of graphics to the detriment of the three-dimensional objects. But it usually results in an emphasis on the context of use, meaning and significance of the objects. This is a distinct advantage since it brings out the social dimension in all things. For most ethnographers, the most significant aspect of the study of objects is the extent to which they can be understood as the distillation or embodiment of social relationships.

This traditional ethnographic approach has sought in the past to show a functioning community at a particular moment in its development, at the same time giving the impression that this image is a fair and accurate representation of that community throughout its development. Until the 1950s, the ethnographers were wont to regard the historical dimension represented in their collections as irrelevant.[10] Small-scale societies were seen as living in a kind of anthropological aspic, stuck and isolated from outside influence. In more recent decades, the diachronic element has become more important in the ethnographic attitude and is now an integral part of it. One of the most encouraging developments which has taken place over the past decade or so is the increasing emphasis placed on detailed studies which include an historical element. This emphasis has sometimes carried over, not surprisingly, into exhibition work. It is is instructive to compare the approaches of the Museum of Mankind in its Asante exhibition, with its accent on the historical perspective, and the 'Arts of Ghana' exhibition mounted by the Museum of Cultural History at UCLA in 1977,[11] which, while taking the whole country as its canvas, eschews the historical dimension.

It is also necessary to be aware that the exhibitions themselves are part of the contemporary world, therefore they should be viewed against a background of political realities. The presentation of information about other societies, particularly in relation to cultural change which is always taking place, is bound to be seen as part of the debate, even if the museum authorities would prefer it to be otherwise. The 'Hidden Peoples of the Amazon' exhibition was widely criticised for giving insufficient coverage to the contemporary situation of the Amazonian peoples, being accused of presenting too Rousseauesque a vision of 'the noble savage' in contrast to the present reality of their ravaged society and forest environment.[12]

Some recent ethnograhic exhibitions refer only obliquely to the influences of other cultures. In these, the traditional world has been presented as if it were pristine, safely tucked away from outside influences. It is not so much that this picture is incomplete – there are examples in which at some period cultural isolationism existed. What requires clarification is the distinct usages of the idea of multi-culturalism. Multi-culturalism refers both to a way of expressing the fundamental inter-relatedness of cultural elements on the one hand, and on the other to a means of communicating these ideas to ethnic minority groups in a prevailing cultural milieu in which they are ignored or undervalued.

In today's ethnographic museums in the UK there is a dislocation between the collections they hold and the main task required of those museums by their multi-national audience. The collections have their roots in the colonial era and carry with them the attitudes implied in the colonial relationship. These are inappropriate in a world approaching the twenty-first century. Collecting and research undertaken now gives museums the opportunity to present a more balanced view. However, there is a danger that the older collections and their historical significance will then be ignored. Their meaning can be reinterpreted in the light of the post-colonial perspective. This is one of the most difficult tasks the museum ethnographer faces – how to use nineteenth- and early twentieth-century collections to represent the past relationship between Britain and the wider world without alienating the multi-cultural audience.

It is not a matter of not giving offence to museum visitors. Aspects of the colonialism are offensive; presenting it honestly is bound to give offence. It is necessary to encourage visitors to see the whole colonial relationship as one of inequality. Recent issues of the *Museums Journal* [13] contain an interesting juxtaposition of articles which both focus on distortions in display presentations and recent attempts to present a more balanced picture. The example from Liverpool of the policy of involving the black community in an exhibition about the city's trading past can be mirrored across the world. In the United States, New Zealand and Australia examples abound of involvement of first nation representatives in community exhibitions.[14] This emphasises the fundamental point that museums are the continually changing product of an informational process involving their communities, however they are defined. It is an embodiment of the ethnographic approach which should be universally applicable to all human history museums.

The central issue which museum ethnography is meeting today is the re-establishment of its context within museum work as a whole. All museum objects are ethnographic in the sense that they are part of the multi-cultural universe of discourse in which museum collections operate in this country. Within some disciplines some might say this is a very insignificant part. What, for instance, is the ethnographic element in the museum presentation of a particle accelerator or a Constable? Reference to the social standing of the Constable family in the Stour valley at the end of the eighteenth century adds a great deal to our understanding of the place of the figures in a Constable landscape. Reference to the capital development costs of Concorde in the light of spending on the National Health Service during the same period highlights social priorities in late twentieth-century Britain. Both of these angles are generated by viewpoints which are sociologically indistinguishable from examinations of the social significance of Ijaw masquerades or the impact of technological innovation in eighteenth-century Polynesia. This is the perspective in which the ethnographers' principal contribution to the development of museum studies is manifested.

Notes

1. For a summary of the collecting activities of the Tradescants, see G. Lewis (1984, p. 24) and V. Ebin and D. A. Swallow (1984, p. 7). For information about Sloane's collection, see G. de Beer (1970, pp. 13-14).

2. A brief account is given in G. Lewis (1984, p. 26); see also R. Altrick (1978).

3. A phrase used by the Trustees of the Saffron Walden Museum to describe their collecting policy in 1834. Quoted in L. Pole (1987, p. 3).

4. Quoted in B. Blackwood (1970, p. 8).

5. See V. Ebin and D. A. Swallow (1984, pp. 9, 10).

6. See Y. Schumann (1986).

7. See M. D. McLeod (1981, p. 129).

8. See R. and S. MacIntosh (1986).

9. See the accompanying book by M. D. McLeod on the Asante (1981).

10. See, for instance, B. A. L. Cranstone's monograph on Melanesia (1960), in which there is little evidence of the changing circumstances in Melanesia in the twentieth century.

11. See H. M. Cole and D. H. Ross (1977).

12. See, for example, D. A. Jones' review (1987).

13. See the following articles in the *Museums Journal*: Tariq Mehmood on the representation of Blacks in Liverpool Museum, Giliane Tawadros on cultural imperialism, Sally MacDonald on the Geffrye Museum, all in vol. 90, no. 9, September 1990; David Jones responding to Tariq Mehmood in vol. 91, no. 1, January 1991; Angela Fussell on anti-racist collecting policies in vol. 91, no. 2, February 1991; a review of 'Staying Power', a Liverpool exhibition of black history, by Loraine Knowles, Marij van Helmond and Lenford White; and Moira Simpson on recent exhibitions in North America in vol. 92, no. 3, March 1992.

14. To take just one example, recent exhibitions in New Zealand and Australia covering Maori history and culture have been produced with the participation of Maori people. See the introduction to the catalogue accompanying the Maori exhibition in Australia, *Taonga Maori – Treasures of the New Zealand Maori People,* The Australia Museum, 1989, and the catalogue to the exhibition, 'Garments from the Past' at the Taranaki Museum, *Nga Kakahu Tuku Tho,* Taranaki Museum, New Zealand, 1987.

References

Altrick, R. D. (1978), *The Shows of London*, Harvard University Press.

Blackwood, B. (1970), *The Classification of Artefacts in the Pitt Rivers Museum*, Occasional Papers on Technology, no. 11, Pitt Rivers Museum.

Beer, G. de (1970), 'Sir Hans Sloane and the British Museum', in Braunholtz, H. (ed.), *Sir Hans Sloane and Ethnography*, Trustees of the British Museum, 1970.

Cole, H. M., and Ross, D. H. (1977), *The Arts of Ghana*, UCLA, California.

Cranstone, B. A. L. (1960), *Melanesia: A Short Ethnography*, Trustees of the British Museum.

Ebin, V., and Swallow, D. A. (1984), *The Proper Study of Mankind...*, Cambridge University Museum of Archaeology and Anthropology.

Jones, D. A. (1987), Review of 'Hidden Peoples of the Amazon' exhibition, in *Museum Ethnographers Group Newsletter,* no. 20, February 1987.

Kaeppler, A. (1978), *Artificial Curiosities*, B. P. Bishop Museum, Honolulu, Special Publication 65.

Lewis, G. (1984), 'Collections, collectors and museums in Britain to 1920', in Thompson, J.M.A. (ed.), *Manual of Curatorship*, Butterworth, 1984.

MacIntosh, R., and MacIntosh, S. (1986), 'Dilettantism and plunder – illicit traffic in ancient Malian art', *Museum*, no. 149, pp. 49-57.

McLeod, M. D. (1981), *The Asante*, British Museum.

Pole, L. M. (1987), *Worlds of Man*, Saffron Walden Museum.

Schumann, Y. (ed.) (1986), *Museum Ethnographers Group Survey of Ethnographic Collections in the United Kingdom, Eire and the Channel Islands,* Museum Ethnographers Group Occasional Paper, no.2.

9 Artefacts as the Social Anthropologist Sees Them

Susan M. Pearce

Director, Department of Museum Studies,
University of Leicester

Anyone who uses that comforting phrase 'a nice cup of tea' invariably means Indian tea ... Tea should be made in small quantities – that is, in a teapot ... There is also the mysterious social etiquette surrounding the teapot (why is it considered vulgar to drink out of your saucer, for instance?) and much might be written about the subsidiary uses of tea leaves, such as telling fortunes, feeding rabbits, healing burns and sweeping the carpet. (Orwell, 1970)

The history of social anthropological collections in British museums remains to be written, although a number of very interesting individual studies are beginning to appear, in the pages of the Museum Ethnographers Group *Newsletter* and in papers like those edited by Stocking (1986). Considerably more effort has been put into considering ways in which this accumulated material culture may be interpreted, and it is on this that this chapter will concentrate.

The formative work was performed partly before the Second World War, by functionalists like Malinowski (1922) and Radcliffe-Brown (1952), and partly in the post-war period by structuralists like Lévi-Strauss (1972) and Leach (1976). These foundations have been built upon more recently by Hodder (1982, 1986), Shanks and Tilley (who have applied their thinking to modern beer cans, 1987), Barley (1983), and Miller (1985). I tried to explore some of these ideas in a series of three articles in the *Museums Journal* (Pearce, 1986a, 1986b, 1987), and many related themes recur in the book *Museum Studies in Material Culture* (Pearce, 1989). All these issues, difficult but fascinating, are best approached by way of an actual artefact.

Let us imagine then, a reconstructed kitchen/living room of about 1935, and of the respectable working class – the kind of display with which we are all familiar. It is the early evening of a working day. The new gas cooker with the kettle on it stands against the wall, and close by are two easy chairs, with a rug between them. A table and wooden upright chairs occupy most of the rest of the space. The table is laid for the evening meal, with plates, knives, forks and spoons. A teapot, with its own mat and knitted cover, accompanied by its teacups and saucers, stands on the corner of the table which is nearest to the cooker. The teapot is of brown glazed earthenware, with handle, spout and lid, its fat body accentuated by two narrow, yellow stripes. The problem before us is to try and express ways in which we can understand the nature of the teapot.

It is clear, first, that a range of evidence may be gathered about the raw materials and the technology which went into the making of the pot, about the way in which it was designed, and about its commercial and domestic history, from all of which it will be possible to infer a good deal about this complex society. It is important here to note two things. Firstly, what has been gathered is *data* which awaits interpretation. Secondly, this data is not natural 'raw material'; it has already been subjected to the operation of culture, which is another way of saying that the compilers of the data are working within the limits of their own personalities and period and ordering their questions and conclusions accordingly.

The interpretation of material culture starts from the premise that it is meaningfully constituted rather than random and meaningless, that is to say that all artefacts are, in some way or another, social being transformed into material form by the individuals who make up the society and make, use and relate to the material things. It follows that it may be possible to devise ways of interpreting material culture so that the nature of the social body, and of the individuals who form it, may be appreciated. The nature of this appreciation, and the part of the individual are points to which I shall return. The nature of artefacts as a transformation of social being suggests three ways in which the interpretation of material culture can be approached, although all three will be operating simultaneously through the same artefact, and all are, in any case, inter-dependent (Hodder, 1986; Shanks and Tilley, 1987). We may consider:

1. Artefacts as objects – that is, as lumps of the natural material world worked upon by technology to produce the material culture which enables each society to survive.

2. Artefacts as signs – that is, as a medium of communication which creates distinctions or social categories.

3. Artefacts as meaning – that is, with historical depth recognised by social members, so creating the manipulation and dominance which makes possible the local ideology.

Armed with these interpretative possibilities, we may return to our teapot. As a result of data gathering we know that it was used to brew hot tea, a commodity which was grown in India, transported in huge quantities to Britain and distributed through a complex system of wholesale tea merchants and local retailers. We know that the pots were similarly manufactured and distributed from Stoke-on-Trent. We know that this beverage was a staple drink of the working class, that it formed an important part of the best meal of the day, often itself called 'tea', that it was normally consumed domestically in the kitchen/living room, and that the teapot was usually handled in brewing, pouring and washing-up by the solitary wife, the senior woman of the small nuclear family.

The interpretation of artefacts as objects takes a materialist or functionalist stance, starting from the presumption that all design, technology, style and symbolism – that is all cultural meaning embodied in the artefact – has come into being in order to 'confer adaptive advantage' (Hodder, 1986, p. 20), to help the society in question to carry on being itself. Typically, such analyses start with environment and economy, continue with social institutions, and then move to ritual, predicting the functions upwards from the material base.

So, with teapot we might argue that the environment, economy and population size of Britain between the two World Wars required, on the one hand, a very extensive seaborne trade and, on the other, a large home manufacturing workforce, and that it was helpful to the maintenance of these systems that they should extend into general and intimate daily habits like tea drinking. The size of the teapot and the role of the housewife in its use helped to establish and confirm the nature of the family units in which this society worked, and the ritual of presiding over the pot gave the woman prestige which helped to maintain the social fabric, while the different qualities and designs of teapot available offered one way in which wealth and social distinction could be expressed. Much more might be said, but this gives an idea of the way in which such an analysis might run, and these are often expressed within a broad systems analysis model which might look something like that shown in Figure1.

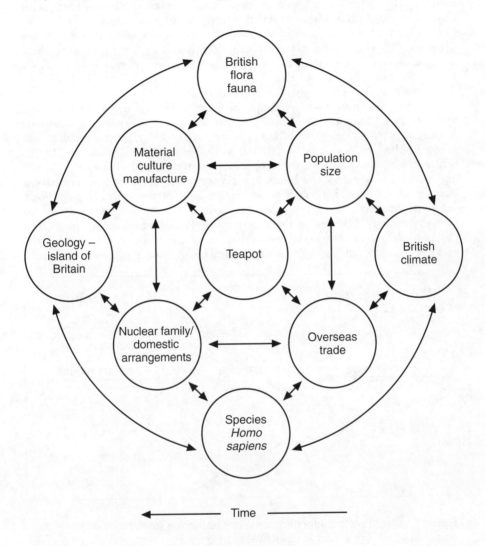

Figure 1   Functionalist model of teapot as object

This kind of approach concentrates upon the *material* functions of all cultural forms, including artefacts, and reduces all symbolic behaviour to a *utility* value. It has a number of implications, which show its limitations. In the first place, it assigns a passive place to the individual who, it assumes, simply lives out the role which society requires without any personal thoughts, feelings or actions which are not in tune with adaptive social process, and without any desire to create change; and this, we know, is simply not true. Equally, it places a low value on artefacts (and on cultural constructs of all kinds) which it regards as merely the mechanism for satisfying social needs which arise from environment and population; but this, we feel, does not account adequately for the value we sometimes attach to things. Finally, although materialists try to describe simply how social processes inter-lock, they cannot, in fact, do so without making assumptions about the ideas in the minds of the people, or in the communal 'mind' of the society, which they are describing. To take an obvious example of this, the analysis given above assumed a distinction between teapots and coffee pots, which is, indeed, a valid distinction, but only a subjective difference distinguishes them, and material functionalists can only complete their interpretation if they share in this subjective knowledge – if, that is to say, they know something of the underlying ideas current in the society which are not themselves, necessarily, simply relative to survival.

To try to penetrate to a perception of these underlying ideas, we may view artefacts as a communication medium, like language (or kinship systems, or settlement plans). This whole broad approach is usually called structuralist, and many of the key concepts originated with Ferdinand de Saussure (1983). Structuralism depends upon the proposition that apparently 'irrational' beliefs and actions (which is to say, beliefs and actions which apparently do not have a clear function of social survival) are obeying a logic of their own, that this logic can show that social beliefs and actions are reducible to sets or binary pairs which embody the 'deep structure' of the society concerned, operating below the level of the infinitely various day-to-day events but giving rise to these, and that we can come to an understanding of the deep structure by applying appropriate analysis.

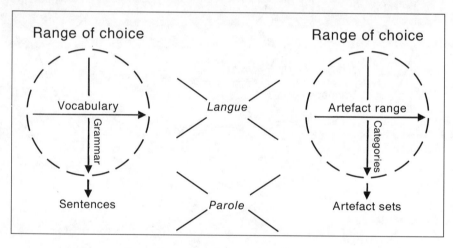

Figure 2   Saussure's distinction between the langue *(the choice of artefacts) and the* parole *(the object in daily use)*

At the heart of this lie two fundamental concepts. The first is Saussure's famous distinction between *langue* and *parole,* which also presupposes an original stage which we may call 'the range of choice' (Figure 2). Each society, theoretically, has open to it a range of possibilities from which it 'chooses' what it will be – what marriage patterns it will permit, how it will organise its domestic space, and so on. The choice is not infinite because 'practical' or 'material' considerations will be important (you cannot choose to create social distinctions by wearing different coloured loin cloths in the Arctic), but it is not wholly materialistically determined either (the Inuit can choose to suppose that venison and seal meat must not lie together on the same house floor). Equally, it is not historically determined because groups, often influenced by charismatic individuals, will choose which areas of their inherited traditions to keep and which to forget.

This body of 'choice', that is, the nature of the society, Saussure called its *langue*. Within the *langue* are all the chosen elements, the 'vocabulary', but these cannot make sense, cannot be 'used', unless they are organised according to rules, just as the vocabulary of a spoken language cannot be used unless the words are organised according to the rules of grammar. Just as some vocabulary and grammar could be deduced from a page of written text, so, the argument runs, can the elements and rules, the deep structures, governing other systems like kinship or material culture be deduced by watching kin systems or artefacts in daily use. It is this daily use that Saussure called *parole*.

The second concept has been clearly set out by Leach (1976) and involves a recognition that *parole* works by operating in sets, since one word or one object is not in itself meaningful but acquires meaning in relation to other words or objects. All the items in a set are intrinsically related and are therefore said to have a metonymic relationship to each other, while another set, which is clearly differentiated from the first but which is its equal and equivalent, is said to bear a metaphorical relationship to it.

Let us turn again to our teapot and see how all this can be worked through. Observation has shown, and all who know the society in question would agree, that teapots are not meaningful alone, but only in association with their cups, saucers, sugar bowls and milk jugs: this gives us a metonymic set. On the other hand, coffee pots also come with their own sets, and we would agree that making tea in coffee pots is 'not done', an instinctive social recognition of the metaphorical distinction between them pointing the way to the creation of categories deep in our own social *langue*. In fact, a working-class household of the kind we started with did not drink coffee at all; for it the equal but equivalent set to the tea things might be beer-drinking equipment. So the first analysis might look like Figure 3, where part of this society's *parole* is set out in an organised fashion.

coffee-pot		teapot		beer barrel
coffee-cups		teacups		pint mug
saucers	:	saucers	:	half-pint mug
milk-jug		milk-jug		
sugar-bowl		sugar-bowl		

Figure 3 The daily use of artefacts in sets constitutes Saussure's parole

It looks as if a distinction between tea gear and beer equipment is one of this society's rules, and the accumulated data shows that this distinction is not single, but, on the contrary, associated with a number of similar distinctions in related areas of life (Figure 4). Beer is clearly male, tea and teapots female, ('Shall I be mother?', 'Ask your mother if there's another cup in the pot'). Tea drinking is private, domestic and intimate, while beer and its mugs normally operate in a public house. The social space in the kitchen is organised so that the woman's area carries the cooker, with the hot water kettle, the tea things and her eating place, while the man's has his cup and eating place. Beer will not be provided at home on ordinary days, but it may be for Sunday dinner, say, and it will certainly be for a family funeral, at which the men will drink it while the women drink tea. The last line in Figure 4 gives an entry into the moral values, which in 1935 were differently articulated between the sexes. We can, then, set out a series of binary pairs, all of which are transformations of each other, and all of which may give an inkling of the deep structures by means of which this society is formed.

tea	:	beer
tea things	:	beer things
female	:	male
private	:	public
heart of kitchen/home	:	periphery of kitchen/home
ordinary	:	special
sobriety	:	licence

Figure 4   Binary set suggesting social norms associated with tea drinking and beer drinking

One of the characteristics of structuralist analysis is that, unlike functional materialism, it brings artefacts into the centre of the picture. Teapots and beer mugs are not simply a functional need taking a convenient form; they are as much an embodiment of their own society's character in the fullest sense as the manufacturing processes which created them. Equally, the central concept of category creation by an axis of similarity/distinction is applicable to *all* societies; it offers a general principle underlying perceived variety and shows how, at a fundamental level, all human beings operate in the same way. The intellectual difficulties in structuralist thinking have recently been well reviewed by Wylie (1982) who shows that the admittedly subjective choices which the analyst makes are not different in kind from those which any study requires.

It is clear, however, that, just as material functionalist explanations are brought up short by the irreducible 'irrational' social habits which they cannot explain, so structuralist analyses have ground in common with explanatory models based on systems analysis, and parts of what they show can be explained in functionalist terms: for example, teapots are parts of the women's preserve because they can easily be used at home, and women must be at home because that is where this society requires its children to be cared for. But structuralist ideas can tell us why tea is not here a public drink for men, as it is in many parts of the world, why we never keep beer in teapots, and why tea is not drunk out of the saucer, none of which have an obvious functionalist rationale.

We must now turn to the third approach, that is of the meaning, the intrinsic historical or ideological content of artefacts, which has to do with the exercise of social power and domination, and which will be elucidated by the normal methods of the historian. Such exercise of power is, of course, implicit in all artefacts and all societies, but remains passive until it is recognised by individuals, and so we are brought to the individual humans who have so far been barely visible, and to their role in creating the historical process of social and artefactual change. So far what has been said depends upon the creation of norms, the reduction of very many detailed individual lives to a small number of general observations. We must do this in order to do anything at all, but it leaves out a great deal, and it makes the process of change very difficult to explain, although we know that change is continuous and that much of it is, precisely, intended to re-shape the prevailing ideology.

To get at any understanding of change we need a very fine mesh capable of catching small individual shifts, the aggregate of which make up social change, and a theory which can make sense of these by integrating the individual and society. The mesh will give us questions like, when the teapot breaks will the woman buy another which is similar or different? Does she buy a pot which is like or unlike her mother-in-law's (a clear move in the ideological power struggle)? Does she have a second teapot which holds the milk money? And will her daughter employ one of them as a sitting room ornament? Several thinkers (especially Giddens, 1984, pp. 1-40; Bourdieu, 1984, pp. 169-76) have begun to develop what Giddens calls 'structuration', an idea which links the structure, or social norm (Figure 4), and the process of change by supposing that each individual's mind-set is like, but not exactly the same as the structure of each individual's society and so, although individual practices arise from that structure, they also transform it; people generate and negotiate their own changes in the ideological climate, and so structures are changed, sometimes very slowly and in tiny ways, sometimes rapidly and radically.

Two very important points remain to be made. Firstly, students from all disciplines do well to remember that we do not, and probably cannot *explain* why societies have particular artefacts and do particular things with them, any more than we can 'explain' a human individual. We can only, from all our different angles, try to *describe* more fully and to understand with greater perception what seems to be going on. Secondly, the note of subjectivity has been struck throughout this chapter, with its underlying anti-positivist presumption that artefacts, like any other social constructs, do not have 'a real meaning'; they have a range of possible, and perhaps equally valid, meanings, separate discourses which exist, as it were, in parallel and depend upon the eye of the beholder. The teapot is perpetually re-interpreted as functioning brewing vessel, as ornament, as part of a collection, and as part of a display, and all these discourses unite the history of the pot and its role in structure and re-construction with the observing individuals who also have their part in these processes. We are, in the last analysis, very close to writers of serious fiction who select and arrange their material in order to illuminate the relationship between individuals and their society.

What are the implications of all this for curatorship, or some of them? It places upon us, I think, an obligation to be much clearer to ourselves and to our public that interpretation is precisely that. It begins to offer a multi-faceted conceptual framework, a theory of objects within which our understanding and appreciation of artefacts can be developed, both generally and at the level of a single piece, which starts to redress the 'poverty of theory' to which Jenkinson has recently referred (1989). It should begin to give a basis from which more integrated and more broadly based and yet more specific (and more interesting) exhibitions may be articulated. At the heart of this lies loving work: objects may be like texts waiting to be read, but they yield more if, like tea, they are taken with sympathy.

References

Barley, N. (1983), *Symbolic Structures*, Cambridge University Press.

Bourdieu, P. (1984), *Distinction: A Social Critique of the Judgement of Taste*, Routledge.

Giddens, A. (1984), *The Constitution of Society: Outline of the Theory of Structuration*, Cambridge University Press.

Hodder, I. (ed.) (1982), *Symbolic and Structural Archaeology*, Cambridge University Press.

Hodder, I. (1986), *Reading the Past*, Cambridge University Press.

Jenkinson, P. (1989), 'Material culture, people's history, and populism: where do we go from here?' in Pearce, S.M. (ed.), *Museum Studies in Material Culture*, Leicester University Press.

Leach, E. (1976), *Culture and Communication*, Cambridge University Press.

Lévi-Strauss, C. (1972), *Structural Anthropology*, Allen Lane.

Malinowski, B. (1922), *Argonauts of the Western Pacific*, Routledge.

Miller, D. (1985), *Artefacts as Categories*, Cambridge University Press.

Orwell, G. (1970), 'A nice cup of tea', in Orwell, S., and Angus, I. (ed.), *The Collected Essays, Journalism and Letters of George Orwell*, vol. 3, Penguin Books, pp. 347-52.

Pearce, S.M. (1986a), 'Thinking about things: objects high and low', *Museums Journal*, vol.86, no.2, pp. 79-82.

Pearce, S.M. (1986b), 'Thinking about things: objects as signs and symbols', *Museums Journal*, vol.86, no.3, pp.131-5.

Pearce, S.M. (1987), 'Objects in structures', *Museums Journal*, vol.87, no.4, pp. 178-81.

Pearce, S.M. (ed.) (1989), *Museum Studies in Material Culture*, Leicester University Press.

Radcliffe-Brown, A. (1952), *Structure and Function in Primitive Society*, Routledge.

Saussure, F. de (1983), *Course in General Linguistics* (trans. Roy Harris), Duckworths.

Shanks M., and Tilley, C. (1987), *Re-Constructing Archaeology*, Cambridge University Press.

Stocking, G. (ed.) (1986), *Objects and Others: Essays on Museums and Material Culture*, History of Anthropology, vol. 3, Wisconsin University Press.

Wylie, M. (1982), 'Epistemological issues raised by a structuralist archaeology', in Hodder, I. (ed.), *Symbolic and Structural Archaeology*, Cambridge University Press.

10 The Labour History Approach

Myna Trustram

Keeper of Collections, National Museum of Labour History

From the outset, it is worth clearing up one common misconception about labour history, that it is concerned solely with the history of the Labour Party. Labour historians examine all manner of working-class organisations and activities, and not just those which owe their inspiration to the left. Political parties, trade unions and working-class organisations like the co-operative movement are the bread and butter of the labour historian. And class is the primary analytical tool. When tracing the historiography of their discipline, labour historians refer with respect to the pioneering work of people like J. L. and B. Hammond, Sidney and Beatrice Webb, G. D. H. and Margaret Cole.

As an area of historical enquiry, labour history is in some respects as old as the working-class movement itself: people have always used the past as an instructor in how to bring about change. Not all historians or collectors are as bold as G. D. H. Cole who, having assembled an exhibition of 'left' history in 1937, argued that such a collection 'should form part of the permanent equipment of the Left for its struggle against the power of reaction'.[1]

The founding of the Society for the Study of Labour History in 1960 by a relatively young group of scholars (including Asa Briggs, Eric Hobsbawm, J. F. C. Harrison and Royden Harrison) marked labour history's growing confidence. From this period, labour historians were instrumental in the quiet revolution which has moved through the history profession in the last 30 years. Under the umbrella of 'history from below', socialist, feminist, radical and black historians have transformed the practice of social history. Labour history retained a strong presence within this movement, but received criticism from historians who began to question the received definitions of 'labour' and 'political'. In 1974 Sheila Rowbotham wrote:

Much labour history has accepted a strictly political definition of what history is about, merely substituting working class leaders and institutions for those of the dominant class. Formal organisations leave records. This kind of source produces a particular kind of history, which excludes people who have not been prominent in formal labour organisations.[2]

This criticism is now being addressed both by historians and those museums which are tackling labour history directly. An examination of *Labour History Review* and its predecessor, the *Bulletin of the Society for the Study of Labour History*, indicates that its readers and contributors are interested in both gender and race, as well as class, as tools for historical analysis. They share areas of interest such as penology, migration, poverty and popular culture with the more general social historians. This might suggest that labour history is nothing more than a subsection of social history. But the value of the concept for social history curators does not lie so much in its delineament of subject matter, but as a reminder of class as a crucial factor in defining people's historical experience. It focuses the mind on concepts like resistance, power and struggle. As such, it shares much with women's and black history. In the move away from a focus on organised labour, it can serve as a guide as to where to draw the boundaries.

It is only recently that labour history has been embraced in a self-conscious way by a small number of museums. In the nineteenth century, museums were established in part to help provide an education in arts and sciences for working people. The recording and presentation of working-class institutions and culture was not part of this mission. The first half of this century saw a growing interest in working-class customs, especially rural life. Post-Second World War and current attempts to present the history of everyday, ordinary life have been characterised as resulting in

a 'peopling of the past' in which the cultures and values of non-elite strata are subordinated to bourgeois culture and values just as effectively as they are in the great public museums which developed in the nineteenth century.[3]

So whilst it might appear that the subject matter of labour history is discussed now in some museums, the mode of presentation tends to encourage nostalgia for an idealised past and discourages a more critical appraisal. We are only relatively recently attempting to run museums which allow working-class people to use their own voices. Hitherto museums have been for and about but not *of* the people.[4]

In the 1970s a number of museums began to examine labour history in a concerted manner. The People's Palace in Glasgow has one of the best labour history collections in Britain. The museum has pioneered a collecting policy which integrates the collection of labour history material with more general social history items. By all accounts, from its inception the People's Palace has been true to its name:

Labour history has always been considered part and parcel of local history in Glasgow. In 1900 antiquarians were depositing trade union banners of the 1830s along with stone age axe heads and pieces from the cathedral roof. There has never been any question of regarding the history of labour as something different.[5]

The National Museum of Labour History was founded in 1975 at Limehouse Town Hall in London. It developed from the collections of the Trade Union Labour Democratic History Society, a group of labour history enthusiasts whose collection of trade union and socialist memorabilia and archives had outgrown their living rooms. In contrast to the People's Palace, the museum collected narrowly from the organised labour movement. The museum has one of the largest collections of banners, some 250, along with badges, tokens, ephemera, posters, ceramics and emblems. The museum moved to Manchester in the late 1980s and re-opened on May Day 1990. It is committed now to developing displays which illustrate the last 200 years of the labour movement and the lives of working-class people, both organised and unorganised.

The Museum of Labour History in Liverpool opened in 1986 following a commitment from Merseyside County Council to establish a museum about ordinary people's lives. The People's Story in Edinburgh opened in 1989, the result of a 1984 District Council Labour election manifesto which promised a museum of labour and trade union history. It is significant that both these initiatives stemmed from elected members rather than museum professionals or indeed commercial sources.

It is also of significance that both these museums have responded to the charge that labour history tends to marginalise the unorganised. They collect and display general working-class material. What distinguishes them, however, from other municipal social history museums is the importance they attach to working-class organisation and their commitment to working alongside the people whose history they are presenting.

These museums have been singled out because they contain labour history in their brief or have demonstrated a major commitment to its interpretation. Many other museums contain labour history in their collections and displays. It is likely, though, that such collections receive less curatorial attention than those of, say, civic or military memorabilia. It is alarming that museums have not kept abreast of the radicalising of history in the last thirty years. 'History from below' is now the dominant approach within social history. Raphael Samuel has referred to a 'common sense radicalism' widespread amongst history school teachers.[6] One is hard pushed to make such an observation about curators.

Failure to embrace 'history from below' does not necessarily stem from cowardice at interpreting controversial material. Curators face a major problem in applying documentary-based research to collections of material culture. By and large labour historians have used objects only as illustrative material or have not attempted to incorporate their findings into wider-ranging debates.[7] One exception to this is the discussion of labour iconography, but it is significant that we are here straying into the discipline of art history, which unlike social or labour history is based on material as opposed to documentary evidence.[8] Moving beyond the confines of conventional labour history, there is a growing number of historians looking beyond archives for evidence. For instance, Ruth Schwartz Cowan's exploration of the history of housework, *More Work for Mother*, is a stimulating work for curators wishing to examine issues of gender and household equipment.[9]

The degree to which museums have incorporated labour history into their work depends amongst other things on curators' enthusiasms and existing collections. A seminar in 1985 on 'Labour History in Museums' offered a glimpse of the work done by a few museums in this area. At Norfolk Rural Life Museum, for example, problems whereby the museum was seen to serve the farmers and not their employees were overcome during the organisation of an exhibition about the farmworkers' union.[10] Labour history can be found in surprising palaces. The Victoria and Albert Museum, for example, collects Labour Party and Tory posters, 'as design objects in their own right; part of the history of marketing, as well as resources for the study of design'.[11] This apparent interest in design at the expense of content seems strange. But in fact, it is abandoned in the case of AIDS posters which are collected 'for their social comment as much as for their aesthetic merit'.[12] There are also, of course, museums whose subject matter is the very stuff of labour history, like the Rochdale Pioneers Museum and New Lanark.

The labour history approach to social history curatorship is about more than, say, adding a trade union banner to existing displays. Nor is it about tracing the glorious, inevitable growth of socialism. It is a much more complex business of forging alliances with others in the history business and asking who controls representations of working-class history. Britain has no significant monuments to working-class political history on the same scale as those which celebrate ruling-class culture and politics and which can be seen at their most triumphant in South Kensington. The popular struggle for democratic rights, fair wages and welfare benefits is recorded, if at all, in small pockets of collections scattered up and down the country. History museum visitors can see reconstructions of domestic interiors and village shops, but learn little of the fight to earn the money to buy the goods. Chartism, the first of Europe's working-class movements, receives no significant commemoration. Labour history curatorship searches for ways of remembering which do not merely appeal to some national past which irons out conflict or states pieties about ordinary folk.[13]

Labour history alerts us to the power relations within the museum. Museums are not neutral spaces for the recording of the past but are themselves part of that process whereby power is lodged in class, gender and racial privilege. Social history curators are charged with finding ways of displaying material which is potentially threatening to the established order within an institution which traditionally stands for permanence. For the labour historian, the museum itself is problematic because it posits a separation between history and the present, history being the instructive lifeline of the labour movement, and the present carrying the urgent imperative for change. The National Museum of Labour History recently re-erected a shelter used in the 1989-90 ambulance workers' dispute. The very incongruity of the shelter, made of polythene and pallets, standing next to the classical pillars of the gallery force questions about how to display labour history. Was the museum undermining elite notions of museum practice or merely being ridiculous?

The concerns of labour history can be promoted through alliances with people who are not hidebound by working with limited collections or resistant to using their own personal histories. For some time now, oral history has provided information which documentary and material sources fail to offer. The People's Story has made substantial use of oral testimony in the development of its displays. Labour history promotes an awareness of the role groups of people play in making their own history. This model can be used within the museum so that groups within the community are encouraged to use the resources of the museum in the recording and presentation of their history. The labour history approach questions the role of curator as guardian of history and seeks to establish a more reciprocal relationship between the museum and the communities it serves. Curators expect to enter people's lives, remove their treasured objects and write their histories. In return, we can open up our galleries and stores. Attempts to work with community groups are handicapped when curators themselves have little experience of their own community networks. The passionate identification of the People's Palace curators with Glasgow is a major factor in the museum's success. An excessive concern for standards can mean that community initiatives are thwarted, taken over, or relegated to 'community galleries' or community centres.

Labour history does not necessarily demand a search for new collections. A labour history approach to existing social history collections raises questions about the class relation within the society being documented. It looks at both the powerful and the powerless and asks how were the two positions maintained or overturned. Labour history seeks out new interpretations and endeavours to afford people a dignity often denied them. An examination of, say, early twentieth-century urban women's poverty might look at the networks of self-help and female unity which ensured that poor women were more than a silent, defeated backdrop to history. Their paid and unpaid work at home and in factories and workshops might be examined.[14] Objects, photographs, oral history, reconstructions, reproductions, film, and perhaps the work of contemporary installation artists: all these need to be mustered together when tackling this sort of subject, a subject which resists the straitjacketing of conventional interpretation and display.

Acknowledgement

I would like to thank Dorothy Fenton and Nicholas Mansfield for help in preparing this chapter.

Notes and References

1. G.D.H. Cole, 'An exhibition of "Left" history', *Left Review*, August 1937, p. 409.

2. Sheila Rowbotham, 'Search and subject, threading circumstance', in *Dreams and Dilemmas*, Virago Press, 1983, pp. 170-1. See also Sally Alexander and Anna Davin, 'Feminist history', *History Workshop Journal*, Spring 1976, pp. 4-6.

3. Tony Bennett, 'Museums and "the people"', in Robert Lumley (ed.), *The Museum Time-Machine*, Comedia/Routledge, 1988, p. 73. See also Chris Waters, 'The Americanization of the masses: cultural criticism, the national heritage and working class culture in the 1930s', *Journal of the Social History Curators Group*, vol.17, 1989-90, pp. 22-5.

4. Bennett, op. cit. I have borrowed and extended Bennett's wording here.

5. Elspeth King, 'Labour History at the People's Palace', in *Labour History in Museums: Papers from a joint seminar held at Congress House, London, 18 October 1985*, SSLH-SHLG, 1988 p. 12. See also Elspeth King, *The People's Palace and Glasgow Green*, Drew Publishing, Glasgow, 1985 .

6. Raphael Samuel, 'Educating Labour', *New Statesman and Society*, 6 April 1990, pp. 16-17.

7. See, for example, John Gorman, *Images of Labour*, Scorpion, 1985.

8. See, for example, Eric Hobsbawm, 'Man and woman in socialist iconography', *History Workshop Journal*, vol. 6, Autumn 1978, pp. 121-38. Also Sally Alexander, Anna Davin, and Eve Hostettler, 'Labouring women: A reply to Eric Hobsbawm', *History Workshop Journal*, vol.8, Autumn 1979, pp. 174-82.

9. Ruth Schwartz Cowan, *More Work for Mother: The Ironies of Household Technology from the Open Hearth to the Microwave*, Free Association Books, 1989.

10. Nick Mansfield, 'The George Edwards celebration', *Labour History in Museums*, op. cit., pp. 7-9.

11. From an exhibition label in 'Collecting for the Future: A Decade of Contemporary Acquisitions', Victoria and Albert Museum, 6 June - 12 August, 1990.

12. Ibid.

13. Donald Horne, *The Great Museum: The Re-Presentation of History*, Pluto Press, 1984. Patrick Wright, 'A blue plaque for the labour movement', in *On Living in an Old Country*, Verso, 1985, pp.135-59.

14. Carl Chinn, *They Worked all Their Lives: Women of the Urban Poor in England 1880-1939*, Manchester University Press, 1988.

11 The Women's History Approach

Gaby Porter

Curatorial Services Manager, Museum of Science and Industry, Manchester

Many women have observed that mechanical equipment is manufactured and assembled in ways that make it just too big or too heavy for the 'average' woman to use. This need not be a conspiracy, it is merely the outcome of a pre-existing pattern of power ... Many processes could be carried out with machines designed to suit smaller or less muscular operators or reorganised so as to come within reach of the 'average' woman. (Cynthia Cockburn[1])

Women's history is, by its very existence critical. It claims a special attention for women whom, it is argued, have been neglected by other historians. Women's history is also political. The women's movement has argued that we live in a society organised by sexual difference, in which men have power over women. Women have campaigned for change; they have turned to history to uncover earlier struggles, to trace 'hidden' histories of adversity and achievement. Thus Sheila Rowbotham's seminal work, *Hidden from History*, is subtitled '300 Years of Women's Oppression and the Fight Against It'.[2]

Women's history challenges the prevailing assumptions, practices and categories of history. Women often work together, in groups with lay members and professional historians. They emphasise personal experience – oral history and autobiography – as a way of linking past and present, of uncovering women's past and offering different histories from those of 'official' sources. They move beyond the restricted definition of work as waged, and often male waged, labour; they have drawn attention to changing patterns in the household. They have broken the barriers between public and private to look at the 'interpenetration of family and production'.[3] Finally, women's history itself expected to serve a function beyond the usual limits and institutions of history. Thus it is widely circulated and put to use in publications and campaigns.

Detailed studies of the workplace and the home have contributed to the history of both women and men. Many studies are incidentally linked with the material culture through their very subject – the workplace, the home, health, housing – but they have originated and been applied mainly outside the museums. The challenge for women's history in museums is to apply these perspectives in the study of objects.

The most obvious approach to objects for women's history is to look to those areas and skills which are socially distinct and most obviously 'belong' to women, usually within the domestic sphere, such as handcrafts. Here, studies may emphasise training, craft and skill, celebrating women's handwork. For middle-class women's work, studies may draw on tools and materials, samplers, magazines and pattern books, watercolours and drawings, diaries and novels. For working-class women, studies may draw on few other sources than the tools and products themselves, the chance accounts of visitors' or commentators' memory, and on present experience. Thus, for example, an exhibition on women's rugmaking at Sheffield Museums contained contemporary and historical work, and included detailed interviews with rugmakers. Such studies are likely to extend and enrich collections, collecting and interpretation. They also instate makers and objects with a new visibility and significance through study and publication or display. However, they do not address the bulk of the actual and potential collections of social history museums.

A second approach is to look at those objects and activities in which women have achieved brief and exceptional visibility. Examples of such projects in museums relate to outstanding female figures, or heroines, to women's suffrage movements (e.g. the People's Palace, Glasgow,[4] and the Museum of London), or to women workers in the two World Wars. In these events or activities, women receive attention in public and political life and thus become visible and evident to the historian/curator. The relative abundance of imagery, sources and objects makes such studies attractive, while demonstrating that 'men's' work can equally be done by women when politically or economically convenient.

Some objects may themselves speak directly of women's involvement – a banner, a bag for distributing suffrage papers (Stockport Museum), or a Land Girl's uniform. Others may be traced to women through their provenance – riveting tools, or a Home Guard helmet – or through their similarity to those used by women. In studying these objects and histories, women's history looks beyond the sensational headlines and official accounts or propaganda. It seeks women's day-to-day experience, to provide the context and associations of objects, through their accounts and testimony: reports of women factory inspectors and workers,[5] Mass Observation diarists,[6] oral history. In this process, it may discover new histories, and new relationships with other areas of the collections.[7]

A third approach moves beyond areas in which women have a distinct and apparently autonomous historical and material existence. It treats questions such as the sexual division of labour as not simply 'given', or natural, but as achieved, and therefore as objects of study in themselves. This approach might be used to study work processes in those areas where women's labour has been restricted or from which they have been excluded. In recent years, excellent studies have been carried out on the operation of gender in industries such as printing,[8] potteries,[9] and clothing.[10]

In the museum, this approach leads to a different appraisal of the objects in our collections and of future collecting and recording. It might focus on the design and operation of machinery and of the workplace, as suggested in Cockburn's quote above. It might study how tools and practices, even whole industries, have come to be viewed as 'men's work' or 'women's work', how these patterns have shifted over time and over place. For example, the Merseyside Museum of Labour History, Liverpool, mounted an exhibition on nursing as an occupation for women. The same approach might look at the whole structure of the workplace and range of work operations, rather than the central production processes, in which men are more prominent. It might extend this study to the consumption and use of products in the home, as in the Geffrye Museum's temporary exhibition on the East London furniture trades, 'Workshop of the World'(1987), which traced items from production to use, including women as furniture makers and also as purchasers and users. This approach might encompass patterns of work and the range of tasks, taking account of domestic and other responsibilities which more often fell to women.

Again, such an approach might compare women's jobs across industries, rather than working within narrow industrial sectors. For example, the exhibition 'Fit Work for Women', mounted by the North-West group of Women, Heritage and Museums, sought both to expand knowledge of women's work and to question the notion of 'fit' work across a range of regional industries. Although the exhibition was graphic, it was intended for use in conjunction with collections.

Finally, a 'gender' approach may look at a small group of objects critically, examining its development and its effect on women. For example, extreme fashions of the nineteenth and twentieth centuries sought to mould idealised forms of the female body at the cost of women's health. Thus women's 'weakness' was not innate, but constructed physically and materially by fashion. Or it may look again at those traditionally 'feminine' areas through objects and sources which reveal other histories and meanings. Much more interesting work in this area has been done by those working outside social history, particularly from art history and/or in art galleries, with works which are themselves figurative. For example, Roszika Parker's study of embroidery, and the subsequent travelling exhibition 'The Subversive Stitch', showed the shifts in the status and production of embroideries from the middle ages to the nineteenth century.[11] Rochdale Art Gallery's exhibition, 'Our Past – Our Struggle',[12] re-interpreted the carte-de-visite portraits of pit brow lasses; while their exhibition 'Painting Women'[13] examined the role of women painters and presented new readings of their paintings. Finally, the epic 'Edwardian Era' exhibition viewed the whole period from perspectives of gender, class and race.[14]

These approaches to studying objects carry new expectations of collections, classification and curatorial practices. They may move objects from one category to another, or ask questions which cut across existing boundaries. They may seek consistency in research, collecting and interpretation across the domestic and industrial, private and public spheres which at present receive different attention and treatment.[15]

Women's history may directly challenge the museum itself, and its version of history, by re-defining and re-interpreting objects already in the collections in relation to women. Such projects recognise that meaning is not singular or essential. Rather, each object, each piece of the culture, can be understood in a number of ways. In re-presenting it, a single meaning is selected and then this 'preferred' meaning is anchored by context, caption, illustration and positioning. 'Preferred' meanings are usually conventional, shared with other museums, other media, and public expectations of history. To choose different meanings may be to raise questions about the museum and its arrangement. Thus, for example, an archaeological display at Southampton Museums brought familiar material out of the collections and applied new categories to it.[16]

A women's history approach may invite interested groups to participate in making new histories with and around objects. It recognises a number of audiences and interests. It invites others to make their own sense of the past, by arranging objects, making displays and meanings, adding their own experience. Hitherto, few such projects have entrusted others with the collections; instead, as at Springburn Museum, they have used dummies, cameras, cartoons and pastiche.[17]

Acknowledgements

I wish to thank Marij van Helmond and Myna Trustram, of Women Heritage and Museums, for their advice and comments.

Notes and References

1. 'The material of male power', *Feminist Review*, no. 9, October 1981, p. 52.

2. Pluto Press, 1973.

3. For example, Leonore Davidoff and Catherine Hall, *Family Fortunes: Men and Women of the English Middle Class, 1780-1850*, Hutchinson, 1987; Judy Lown, 'Not so much a factory, more a form of patriarchy: gender and class during industrialisation', in E. Garmanikow, *et al.* (eds), *Gender, Class and Work*, Heinemann, 1983.

4. Elspeth King, *The Scottish Women's Suffrage Movement*, People's Palace Museum, Glasgow, 1978.

5. In 1918, the Women's Work Committee of the Imperial War Museum collected records and commissioned photographs of women at work. The photographers worked closely with women factory inspectors and workers. Jane Carmichael, 'Home Front 1914-18: the photographs of G. P.Lewis and Horace Nicholls', *Creative Camera*, no. 247/248, July/August 1985, pp. 58-63.

6. *Nelia Last's Diary*, Sphere Books, 1983; Naomi Mitchison, *Amongst You Taking Notes*, Oxford University Press, 1986.

7. An excellent example of the way in which oral testimony can reveal new histories is Jill Liddington and Jill Norris, *One Hand Tied Behind Us: The Rise of the Woman's Suffrage Movement*, Virago, 1978.

8. Cynthia Cockburn, *Brothers: Male Dominance and Technological Change*, Pluto Press, 1983.

9. Jaqueline Sarsby, 'Sexual segregation in the pottery industry', *Feminist Review*, no. 21, November 1985, pp. 67-93.

10. Angela Coyle, 'Sex and skill in the clothing industry', in J. West (ed.), *Work, Women and the Labour Market*, Routledge, 1982.

11. Roszika Parker, *The Subversive Stitch: Embroidery and the Making of the Feminine*, Women's Press, 1986.

12. Sarah Edge, *Our Past – Our Struggle: Images of Women in the Lancashire Coalmines 1860-1880*, Rochdale Art Gallery, 1986.

13. Deborah Cherry, *Painting Women*, Rochdale Art Gallery, 1987.

14. Jane Becket and Deborah Cherry, *The Edwardian Era*, Barbican Art Gallery, 1988.

15. Gaby Porter, 'Putting your house in order', in Robert Lumley (ed.), *The Museum Time Machine*, Comedia/Routledge, 1988.

16. See Sian Jones, 'The female perspective', *Museums Journal*, vol. 91, no. 2, 1991.

17. 'Springburn Mothers', an exhibition by Betty, Cathy, Jan and Rosemary, 1989.

12   The Agricultural History Approach

Roy Brigden

Keeper, Museum of English Rural Life, Reading University

Agricultural objects can be studied and interpreted by the curator in a number of different ways. The more these various approaches can be concentrated on a single item the more information of value it will yield. To begin with, a farm tool or piece of machinery is indicative of a specific agricultural practice in a certain place at a certain time. Background details, either acquired at first hand with the object itself or from literary sources, will help to identify an appropriate position in the agricultural context. It may, perhaps, mark an innovation in technique or at least a definable stage in an evolutionary pattern.

The principal stages of development in agricultural equipment are comparatively easy to chart, at least from the middle of the nineteenth century onwards. Extensive trials on the various categories of machinery were carried out periodically by the Royal Agricultural Society, and the results, together with details of the entries written up at length in the Society's annual *Journal*. To take dairying as one example, general trials of diary appliances took place in 1872, 1879 and 1889; of cream separators in 1881, 1888, 1891 and 1899; of butter churns in 1894; of milking machines in 1898. Further reports concentrating in particular on the appearance of new equipment are to be found, often indexed under the manufacturer's name, in the trade journal *Implement Manufacturer's Review* – later known as *The Implement and Machinery Review* – (1875-1968), *Power Farming* (1941 to date), and, to a lesser extent, in *The Engineer* (1856 onwards).

Alternatively, the absence of novelty may be a principal source of interest for museums attempting to build a collection of material typical of the farming in an area at a given time. Comprehensive information on regional agricultural practice, with details of its attendant equipment, really begins with the county surveys commissioned by the Board of Agriculture in the closing years of the eighteenth century. The *General View of the Agriculture of Lancashire* was produced in 1815 by R.W. Dickinson. Its 650 pages take in most aspects of the county's geography, land holding and agricultural characteristics, and include a whole chapter on farm implements. In the middle of the century, the Royal Agricultural Society initiated a similar national survey, through a prize essay competition, to check on development since the first series was completed. The winning report on Lancashire was printed in the 1849 *Journal* and more recent accounts of agriculture in the county are to be found in the issues for 1929 and 1952.

This kind of information, backed up by relevant illustrations, can establish the accurate agricultural framework within which it is then possible to interpret the objects more fully. It would be encouraging to believe that this was a two-way process: that detailed research upon the objects themselves threw up data which in turn helped to further our understanding of agricultural practice in the past. In fact, academic research into agricultural history in this country has, generally speaking, never been very closely object oriented. Written records and statistical data have become the primary raw material of the subject so that where farm equipment is brought in at all it is most often to analyse its social and economic effects rather than its physical properties or attributes. Consequently, for an assessment of the comparative efficacy of different types of

Victorian plough, for example, we are obliged to take contemporary accounts, however questionable, more or less at face value because there is no research tradition of field testing either original examples or accurate purpose-built replicas using the measuring techniques that modern science provides.

On the continent, the concept of the imitative experiment as an avenue for agricultural research has been taken further. The best way into this subject is through the pages of the specialist journal *Tools and Tillage* which has appeared annually since 1968 and is produced by the Denmark-based International Secretariat for Research on the History of Agricultural Implements.[1] Also, it contains some excellent articles, such as one on the introduction of the winnowing machine into Europe,[2] constructed around extensive historical analysis of particular implements. Archaeologically, the principle of subjecting agricultural material to very close scrutiny for the information it can give about ancient farming practice is well established. There is a history of field testing of reconstructions in England, as with the case of the Great Chesterford Roman scythe and the Donnerupland-ard,[3] both at MERL (the Museum of English Rural Life, Reading University) in the 1950s. Butser in Hampshire is the home of a long-term living experiment that has both answered questions and suggested many more about the nature of Iron Age agriculture.[4] For the farming of the nineteenth and early twentieth centuries, which has become the subject of so much museum activity, this type of enquiry has yet to make much of an impact. True, we have demonstrations of equipment and techniques in great number and these are important for both communicating a sense of the past as well as insuring the continuation of certain skills that might otherwise eventually be lost. It is open to question, however, whether they much increase our body of knowledge in any structured form.

Experimental investigation has enormous and mostly untapped potential for the exploration of pre-Victorian agriculture. Very little in the way of original equipment has survived from the eighteenth century, with less from the seventeenth and sixteenth, and this accounts for the almost exclusive pre-occupation of agricultural museums with the more recent story for which material abounds. There are some signs now that interest is broadening. At the Weald and Downland Open Air Museum, there is now a sixteenth-century farmstead using authentic, relocated buildings and reproduction equipment. With the latter, MERL has made an input. Research on the type and range of equipment commonly used by a Kent or Sussex farmer in the 1530s had to start from the beginning using contemporary sources, if available, and informed speculation, if not.

While authentic material from this period is, to say the least scarce, the historical sources were able to demonstrate that the Victorian equivalents of some implements were little altered from their sixteenth-century counterparts. A Kent/Sussex turnwrest plough in the MERL collection, for example, was built in Lewes in the 1860s and is typical of a very distinctive regional design that survived in use to the early years of the present century. In appearance and construction it accords very closely with the detailed description given in J. Allen Ransome's *The Implements of Agriculture* of 1843 and with the illustration of a turnwrest plough in Arthur Young's *General View of the County of Sussex* of 1808. In his *The English Improver Improved* of 1652, a most important seventeenth-century handbook of farming practice, Walter Blith says of this plough that it is so well known and has been around for so long that it hardly requires to be described. He does, in fact, write about it at some length and what he says conforms again with the 1808 illustration and the real thing of the 1860s. The true origin of this plough type goes back much further, possibly to Roman times, and on the basis of the evidence it is not unreasonable to suppose that its sixteenth-century form was not very dissimilar to the versions being used three hundred years later.

Other relevant literary sources include Thomas Tusser's *Good Points of Husbandry*, which on its appearance in 1572 was only the second agricultural text printed in English. Amongst its seasonal run-through of useful tips for the farmer are many references to implements and their use, together with a complete checklist of equipment for a well managed farm numbering well over 100 individual items. Finding reliable illustrations to back up these references so that replicas can be made is rather more problematical. The pictorial representations of medieval English farm implements are those that accompanied the text of the Luttrell Psalter which was produced in East Anglia in 1340 and now resides in the British Museum. Although these embody much useful and accurate information there is nothing comparable for another three hundred years. European works, particularly some fifteenth-century Flemish Books of Hours, come closer to the period in question and illustrate farm practice wonderfully well but the equipment is not necessarily applicable. They portray four-wheeled farm wagons very clearly, for example, but there is no firm evidence of them being used in England before the seventeenth century.

A further question on vehicles is posed by surviving sixteenth-century inventories for Sussex farms. 'Courtepottes' are frequently mentioned and it is clear from the content that these are wheeled receptacles, larger than a wheelbarrow but smaller than a cart, that were pushed by individuals or pulled by a single animal, and used for such purposes as removing manure from the courtyard. There are no originals to work from and no illustrations but the description is very similar to a device known as a putt which was used in Somerset into the present century and for which there are some surviving examples. Through this kind of detective work our understanding of sixteenth-century farming moves into new areas; more will be learnt from the actual process of manufacturing the equipment and, ultimately perhaps, still more from testing it in the field.

Farm tools and machinery are about more than agriculture alone because they are also a reflection of their social and technological context. The evolution of construction methods, together with the pattern of regional variations in design and decoration, are legitimate areas of study in themselves. Still the most obvious example is Jenkins' work on farm wagons, begun in 1956, and based primarily on records made in the field and upon returns from questionnaires covering some 600 vehicles in all. It led to the publication in 1961 of *The English Farm Wagon* in which he identified and analysed 28 different regional types. Four years later, his *Traditional Country Craftsmen* included some items from the farm, such as hay rakes and wattle hurdles, where what mattered was their process of manufacture, particularly the associated tools and techniques, rather than their agricultural end use.

This type of approach has perhaps lost some of its steam over the last decade, though, more happily, recent issues of the journal *Folk Life* have included contributions seeking to assess particular agricultural objects within their broadest context. In 'The Wooden Bottle',[5] for example, Stephen Harris has surveyed the evolution of this indispensable feature of the harvest field from the early eighteenth century through to the First World War. To do so involved a trawl through the available literary and pictorial sources supplemented by dialect evidence and information gained at first hand. Moreover, many wooden bottles preserved in museums and private collections were studied for details on type, distribution, construction, dating and decoration. From such an apparently mundane item a whole field of investigation has been drawn. The same breadth of approach is employed by P. R. Newman in 'The Flail, the Harvest and Rural Life'[6] and by David North in his study of one-way ploughs in southern England.[7]

A farm tool embodies information not only about its process of manufacture but also about its maker. Amongst the MERL collection is a small selection of edge tools, mostly billhooks, with the name 'Willis, Bramley' stamped on the blade. They are part of a larger group of tools brought together by the Rural Industries Bureau and exhibited at the Festival of Britain in 1951 before being subsequently presented to MERL. The real significance of the edge tools remained unrecognised until it was almost too late. Outwardly unremarkable in design and intended purpose, they appeared to be like any others. When attention was focused on their production, however, a different story emerged, for it was clear these were edge tools that had been hand forged using old farmers' rasps as the base material.

By good fortune, when these things were being investigated in the mid-1980s Herbert Willis was still alive and his forge in the Hampshire village of Bramley, though near derelict, was otherwise unchanged from the day when work had ceased nearly twenty years earlier. He was able to recall much about the business from the day when as a thirteen-year-old at the outbreak of the First World War he left school to work alongside his father. The hand forging of edge tools, principally bill hooks, reap hooks and fag hooks, was a trade he developed in the 1920s as a sideline to general smithing and shoeing. It never amounted to very much, for output was only in the region of 150 tools a year, but the local market of farms and woodland crafts was well served and it seems likely that Willis was the last practitioner of this skilled art in the south-eastern corner of England.

Whether hand tool or combine harvester, farm equipment is an expression of the technology of its time so the purely technical angle requires consideration. The mechanical characteristics, the specifications and performance of such things as steam engines, tractors, and, to a lesser extent, their associated equipment, are of absorbing interest today to a small army of collectors and enthusiasts around the country. Indeed, their energy has been responsible for the production of a good deal of important material that would undoubtedly have otherwise been scrapped. How much of this movement is driven by a simple love of machinery and the oily rag or by a deeper underlying interest in agricultural history is a question that need not be answered here. The point, really, is that technological change as expressed in farm equipment is a dimension for research and interpretation, particularly if any tendency for this approach to become too myopic can be resisted. Contemporary technical literature, certainly for the products of the last sixty years or so, is often available in some abundance to assist with the work. From here the story can be extended back to the manufacturing firm, with its own history and place in the technological picture on the one hand, and its economic and social role within a specific community on the other.

To return then to the main theme, the agricultural historian working within a museum context relies not upon one approach to the subject but many. The secret is to develop them together in harmony. It is about analysing and explaining change using the museum and collections as a medium, but it is also more than that. The changes are expressed through the landscape, through the buildings and other fixed equipment on the farm and through its people. All these, too, require to be recorded and interpreted. The museum is a witness to the transformations that have been taking place in the rural areas and should be a source of hard data on specifics. At no time has the future of agriculture and the future of the countryside itself been a more potent subject of general debate. Museums have a potential, if they are not reduced to simply recycling nostalgia, for influencing public opinion in an authoritative way and helping to ensure that the decisions curators make for the future are the right ones.

Notes and References

1. For example, Hans-Ole Hansen, 'Experimental ploughing with Dostrup Ard replica', *Tools and Tillage*, vol.1, no.2, 1969, pp. 67-90, See also Grith Lerche, 'Ridged fields and profiles of plough furrows: ploughing practices in medieval and post-medieval times – a study in experimental archaeology', *Tools and Tillage*, vol.5, no.3, 1986, pp.131-56.

2. Gotha Berg, 'The introduction of the winnowing machine in the eighteenth century', *Tools and Tillage*, vol. 3, no. 1, 1976, pp. 25-46 .

3. See F.A. Aberg, and H.C. Bowen, 'Ploughing experiments with a reconstructed Donnerupland-ard', *Antiquity*, vol. 34, 1960, pp. 144-7.

4. See Peter Reynolds, *Iron Age Farm: The Butser Experiment*, British Museum, 1979.

5. S.C.L. Harris, 'The wooden bottle 1700-1900', *Folk Life,* vol. 25, 1986-7.

6. P.R. Newman, 'The flail, the harvest and rural life', *Folk Life*, vol. 24, 1985-6.

7. D.J. North, 'The one-way plough in south-eastern England', *Folk Life*, vol. 23, 1984-5.

13   A Sense of Place, A Sense of People: An Urban History Approach

Suella Fogg Postles

Keeper of Social History, Brewhouse Yard Museum, Nottingham City Museums

Some Aims and Concerns of the Urban Historian

The explanation of towns in society has long been the preoccupation of historians. Britain became predominantly urban in the mid-nineteenth century when the urban population outweighed the rural. Urban historians have traditionally been concerned with explaining the growth and concentration of population since the eighteenth century, and the association in place and in time with industrialisation. They have also tried to explain the twentieth-century alterations which created the deconcentration of population/productivity from the urban core, and to consider whether these phenomena were cyclical. We must be aware of all five of the approaches used by urban historians (that of the containing context, the thematic, the grand processes, the urban biographical and the city-family), but will mostly be constrained by our jobs as single-community museum curator to use the urban biographical.[1] However, the urban biographical approach is not enough.

As curators involved in urban history, we must try continually to be aware of the most recent research and theories which relate to the material and popular culture of our own town, city or area, just as we try to keep abreast of new research in its history. Higgs himself saw clearly that we should attain the skills of ethnology, anthropology, archaeology, sociology, as well as history.[2]

When choosing an historical approach and/or any other academic approach we must never lose sight of the fact that the study of material culture *per se* is not yet central to most fields of academic study. It might be simpler to assume that the principal collections of interest to the urban historian would be the civic regalia and records, trade tokens, customs and ceremonial material used in a community. However, the objects and information which ought to interest the urban historian should be from the broadest possible spectrum to help construct the community's biography. There is often much of significance in the remaining structures and artefacts of individual towns which can either be used to illuminate or to illustrate chosen theories or themes. Material and information available to the urban historian will be from *all* the traditional museum disciplines: fine and decorative art, archaeology, ethnography, science and technology, the natural sciences, etc. Historic structures within the town may well also be the responsibility of the urban history curator.

To a large extent urban historians will look at and display material from the viewpoint of their relationship to the target community. For the urban historian the concepts of connoisseurship, artistic merit, or technological innovation are not often paramount. The following are some suggestions for possible usage by an urban historian of other disciplines' materials and records. There will, of course, be many other uses for each discipline than those listed.

Social history material and records These should be used to illuminate every aspect of the urban historian's work for which adequate collections exist, either for a specific community, or as examples of material which would have been used there.

Fine art material This may be seen as examples of local artists' work, topographical recording, household interiors, local patronage, products of local art schools, local competitions, and local collectors, as well as records of objects, events or activities of interest to the urban historian.

Decorative art objects These may be used as products of local craftsmen, showing their place in a national hierarchy, as objects sold by local shops, used to embellish local homes, collected by local people, or as showing views of local topography.

Costume and textile collections These may show products of local individuals, factories or retail outlets, work done at local schools, examples of interior decoration, souvenirs, hobbies and home crafts, union or celebration banners, as well as the clothing worn at home, work and at leisure.

Technology collections These can be looked at for examples of local production, work of local people, their housing, employment conditions, unions and social life.

Ethnography collections These may be seen as the work of local collectors, or institutions, examples of products and materials from the British Empire and elsewhere, or as part of the local and social history of peoples who have emigrated to a specific community.

Natural history collections These may show some of the flora and fauna which existed locally at various geological and historic periods, the hunting prowess of local sportsmen, or the activities of local collectors. They may also be used to illustrate how the local landscape has been manipulated.

Archaeology collections and records These may show examples of locally used and produced artefacts, living conditions, trade patterns, ceremony and many of the uses of the collections in the above disciplines.

These few examples of potential usage of objects and records of the various museum disciplines indicate the breadth of viewpoint which the urban historian must take when looking at the community and the means with which to interpret it.

More importantly, we must continually be aware of whatever specific concepts of history/philosophy/ideology/politics we personally hold when we undertake the task of curating, collecting and recording urban social history. If these are areas we have not yet fully investigated then whatever interpretation we choose may be seen to be inconsistent or seriously flawed.[3] We must be continually aware of the dangers of providing a 'nostalgic peepshow into a largely fictitious past'.[4]

Constructing an Operating Framework for the Study and Interpretation of Urban History

There is a wide range of factors which come into the scope of, and overlap with, the topics covered by other chapters in this book. For curators working as urban social historians one large and often daunting task is to be aware of the many threads, themes and factors which have relevance for their town and its people, and what, if any, records and objects should be collected to illustrate them. To remain efficient (and sane!), the following points should be carefully considered when constructing the curatorial parameters inside which you will be working.

Define your geographic area Where are the physical boundaries of the curator's collecting area? In an urban context the market hinterland generally extends well beyond the administrative boundaries. The importance of this geographical concept was recognised and reflected in the name of the parent group of the Social History Curators Group (SHCG), the Group for Regional Studies in Museums, when it was founded in 1975.

Define your time span A decision about contemporary collecting and recording must be made. An astute urban curator must be aware of what contemporary events and objects will be of use to both themselves and the future museum users.

Define your bias '... the past we see, in museums and elsewhere, is not just simply uncovered, but partly created by ourselves.'[5]. We cannot avoid being biased in our politics, our collecting or our interpreting. Different generations of curators will each have their own sets of bias, today's no less than the earlier ones. One's own are just more difficult to perceive. Lowenthal discusses bias in detail, pinpointing the concepts of 'conflict' and 'resistance' as being some of those of the late twentieth century. He suggests that the highlighting of doubts about the past actually draws the public into deeper involvement with the past, encouraging them to draw their own thoughtful conclusions.

Define your professional milieu in relation to other museum services The range and scope of other museums which geographically impinge on urban social history curators will dramatically determine their 'sphere of influence', especially in policies relating to setting boundaries for interpreting, recording and collecting. This museum network can range from the straightforward to the tortuously complicated. Due to the nature of urban social history, it is vital for each museum in a given area or region to be aware of, in agreement with, and to respect the objectives and aspirations of its fellows in any given geographical area.

Serious problems can be caused by the failure of some local authority, national or independent museums to be aware of, never mind to respect, the collection boundaries of other museums. This 'outside' collecting may take place without any discussion with, or notification of, the local curator and a recording opportunity lost.

Inter-museum co-operation can be facilitated by the professional curators employed as liaison officers by some of the Area Museum Services and/or by certain of the county museums. Another useful technique, which does not involve additional staff, is the regular meeting of representative curators, both professional and honorary, from a county or given geographical area to discuss activities and problems. This should ensure that fewer problems arise through personality clashes, lack of communication, ignorance or diffidence.

Define your professional milieu in relation to other museum professionals As the urban social historian is likely to be one of the most recent curatorial appointments within the museum service, there may be several other sections already curating, recording, and collecting material with urban social history connotations. Obvious examples could be in archaeology, numismatics, civic regalia, locally produced decorative arts and textile material. This situation can be either a potential minefield of contention or an area in which a solid partnership can develop. As other curators may not have a similar approach to collecting and recording, it is up to the urban social historians to be able and willing to explain to both colleagues and management their approach and philosophy in detail, asking for colleagues' help and co-operation. It is essential to be very clear, especially in the areas where there are likely to be omissions or overlaps, that there are not neglected areas where the chance to record and/or collect may be lost through ignorance of the specific areas, or lack of curatorial attention in recording detail. Particular areas where problems may occur are those where a viewpoint based solely on the concepts of technology, artistic merit, or the demands of connoiseurship may cause the museum service to miss the opportunity to record or collect over the broader human spectrum.

One basis for discussion between the curators dealing with human history is the use of SHIC, flawed though it may be in some areas, as a guide for determining the breadth of material to be recorded or collected for each urban area.[6] Once the range of material necessary to document the community is agreed in a large museum service, it then becomes much easier to decide, for example, which department collects the trade union banners, which deals with the factory machinery, and which the commercial and distribution material. It should not matter who collects or records the material as long as it is done consistently and there are not gaping omissions in the record for and of the community.

Some museum services have artists, writers, musicians and photographers-in-residence, who can be invited to become involved in any recording projects.

Define your allies An urban curator will have many potential allies. By the nature of the large and varied population, there will be a growing number of other institutions, groups and individuals in a town of any size who can and should be invited to become involved in the urgent task of recording and preserving both the contemporary and historic community.

Fellow institutional collectors of two-and three-dimensional historical material are the archives/record offices and the libraries, whose social history departments are also usually relatively well staffed and resourced. These departments are better placed to make their collections quickly available to the public than are many museums. However, some towns are without these specialist repositories and their museums have collected substantial amounts of archives, photographs and similar material, performing a much needed service for their community.

In urban communities virtually all institutions of higher and adult education will have departments which have done work on, or may be interested in helping with urban history projects. Help can be obtained from a wide range of educational sources: for buildings, the dating and analysis from metallurgists and dendrochronologists; the recording/surveying of buildings from architects and engineers. General recording help from departments of photography, social sciences and general studies is often freely given and joint projects devised which are of long-term value to the community.

Do not under-estimate the help available from enthusiastic teachers at whatever level. Their pupils can be front-line allies of contemporary or retrospective recording of their families or communities. Given an insight into the aims of the museum, school children can produce first-rate records. Here a good museum's education officer can be of great help in liaison, making sure a permanent record of the children's findings are kept.

Non-institutional groups should also be enlisted to help. Local history groups, civic/amenity societies and local collectors' groups are obvious allies, but there are many other groups of people who can be helpful. Groups from occupations/professions, charities, trades, religions, and groups from cultural, social, housing, community, sporting and other recreational organisations are also part of the community you want to record. We may disagree with their self-assessment, but they will have been alerted to the importance of keeping and leaving a record of what the group have tried to achieve for, or in, the community. We will also have alerted them to the museum's interest in their activities, history, records, and any three-dimensional material associated with them.

Finally, private heritage and exhibition centres which are partially funded, and therefore controllable by, the local authority or central government can be very useful sources of both material and information. It is possible for a local authority museum service to enter into a sensible arrangement with such places where material is loaned to them for exhibition under tightly defined conditions of interpretation, security and conservation. In return, the private institution undertakes to pass offers of donated material to the local authority museum service, and not to collect objects itself. The museum thus gains the chance to exhibit its material which would not otherwise be possible, as well as help with recording and collecting. The community gains further displays and interpretation of material which the local authority museum could perhaps not afford to mount.

Determine a sense of place, a sense of people When we consider urban history in a museum context we should be considering three main themes, which should be inseparable and intertwined. These are the factors which make every community unique. The first is a sense of place. This involves geographical factors: geological history, topography, shape of community, its suburbs, hinterland, and its boundary changes, scale and size of area. The second is a sense of people. This involves demographic factors: past and present population size and structure, emigration and immigration, community organisation and government, language (including dialect, accents, etc.). The third is the idea that people make the place. This involves considering the economic exploitation of geological and geographical features; defences; vernacular and polite architecture; the community's government; its language (dialect and accents); its timetables (i.e. the varied daily, weekly and seasonal schedules which relate to the work and leisure time of the inhabitants); local reactions to national, and international influences (i.e. to the civil war, to the Second World War, to radio, satellite and television).

Consider the interpretation of urban history in a museum context Factors influencing the way urban history is made available to the public depend upon the perceived audience, the range and scope of the museum service, its staffing, as well as the available finance. Of considerable importance are the number, chronological range and scale of its present and planned collections, buildings and grounds, and also any other bodies in the community or area involved in similar activities (civic societies, heritage centres, council planning departments, etc.). There may be as many museum approaches as there are factors involved.

Currently, the presentation of urban history is done by the museum history gallery (some examples are at Edinburgh, Birmingham, Market Harborough, Derby, Northampton, Oxford, Museum of London, Nottingham), by historic site museums (Castlefields at Manchester, Kelham Island at Sheffield), by open-air reconstructed communities (Beamish, Ironbridge, Black Country), by heritage centres and projects (The Oxford Story, Yorvik), and by the single theme permanent exhibition centre or show, usually commercial, which concentrates on an aspect of the community's history (Nottingham's Lace Hall, Tales of Robin Hood). Each type of presentation could be used in communicating aspects of urban history within one town. In fact, many more towns exhibit aspects of their local history in several museum venues (Glasgow, Bristol, Exeter, Leeds, etc.), some with museum trails linking the various sites, which may give the town more opportunity to display certain concepts in depth.

There has been in the last decade or so, and still are available, exceptional and exciting opportunities for museum urban historians. The huge interest (latent if not already present) in a community's own history is only a starting point. The community itself is a resource with many people interested and involved in collecting and recording. A fair proportion of research usually has been done and is also ongoing. This interest in local social history easily transcends race, gender, age, culture and religion, and could be considered an important cohesive factor in community relations.

In a community with a long-established museum service sizeable collections may already exist which have local significance, ranging from natural history through to ethnography. These can be supplemented by those housed by local industry, private collectors, groups, and individual families who may give or loan useful information and objects.

Finally, the town itself is a resource with its historic structures, sites and buildings (some in desperate need of another use). There is often no need to start from scratch for there may be the possibility of having a storyline based around a single building or several disparate sites, perhaps linked with a museum trail. There is often a surprising number of sources of funding for urban projects, governmental as well as local industry.

At one end of the museum scale a service may mount a single 'blockbuster' exhibition, covering many aspects of human and natural history as it applied to their area. At the other might be found a museum with several branches, which interprets different aspects of its area in each, with or without a core exhibition in the town which attempts to put it all in context. Either could have a resource centre where interested individuals or groups can both ask about and pass on information about those aspects of their local past and present which they feel are important. In an ideal world museums, archives, libraries, and schools resource centres might share a local history centre.

Exhibition areas specifically for the use of community groups and individuals are important to show aspects of local life perhaps not previously considered in the museum. It is important for such groups to have as free a hand as possible and to show as broad a range of opinions as possible.

Some exhibition approaches could be the chronological, the thematic, or the thematic chronology. Themes chosen would be the economic, social, governmental, spatial and perceptual. Whichever approach is chosen needs to be outlined at the beginning of the exhibition to orientate visitors. They will then have some idea what to expect. If there are other local places where visitors can see further information, displays or approaches, this too should be made clear.

The limitations of urban history galleries are legion. They primarily are caused by too little money, not enough space and the desire to communicate too much complicated information to the visitor. The latter is a serious problem and must be tightly controlled by use of a simple storyline written to a pre-set reading age, use of as many and varied display techniques as possible, and the provision of auxiliary printed material on selected topics for the keen local historian or teacher to use.

Notes and References

1. A useful outline of five current perspectives is given in S.Checkland, 'An urban history horoscope', in D.Fraser and A.Sutcliffe (eds), *The Pursuit of Urban History*, Edward Arnold, 1983.

2. J.W.Y. Higgs, *Folk Life Collection and Classification*, Museums Association, 1963, p. 6.

3. Gaynor Kavanagh, 'History and the museum: the nostalgia business', *Museums Journal*, vol. 83, no. 2, 1983, p. 140, and 'Beyond folk life', *Journal of the Social History Curators Group*, 1986, pp. 3-6.

4. Geraint Jenkins, 'The collection of material objects and their interpretation', in S.M.Pearce (ed.), *Museum Studies in Material Culture*, Leicester University Press, 1989, p. 123.

5. David Lowenthal, 'Bias: making the most of an incurable malady', Museum Professionals Group, *Transactions*, no. 22, 1987.

6. SHIC - Social, History and Industrial Classification. This classification scheme divides British life into Community Life, Domestic Life, Personal Life and Industrial Life. Whilst in need of revision, it forms a good basis for the discussion of collecting policies for different museum disciplines within a gle community.

Bibliography

Blake, Steven, '"The Castle of Indolence": urban history in Cheltenham Museum', *Journal of The Social History Curators Group*, no. 13, 1985-6, pp.34-7.

Bott, Val, 'Into darkest suburbia ...', *Museums Journal*, vol. 82, no. 3, December 1984, pp. 109-16.

Davies, Stuart, 'Birmingham's local history gallery', *Museums Journal*, vol. 81, no. 3, December 1981, pp. 159-60.

Green, J. Patrick, 'Machines, manufactures and people: social history at the Greater Manchester Museum of Science and Industry', *Journal of the Social History Curators Group*, no.13, 1985-6, pp. 43-7.

Knowles, Loraine, 'Merseyside Museum of Labour History – the People's Story', *Social History Curators Group News*, Summer 1986, p.4.

Jenkinson, Peter, '"A Taste of Change": contemporary documentation in inner city Birmingham', *Recording Society Today*, pp. 33-9, Scottish Museums Council, 1987.

King, Elspeth, 'People's Palace Glasgow', *Recording Society Today*, pp. 20-27, Scottish Museums Council, 1987.

Mastoris, Steph, and Mastoris, Lynne, 'Collecting contemporary advertising ephemera from a Nottingham suburb', *Journal of the Social History Curators Group*, no.13, 1985-6, p.15-28.

Mullins, S.P., and Glasson, M., *Hidden Harborough – The Making of the Townscape of Market Harborough*, Leicestershire Museums, Art Galleries and Records Service, 1985.

Murray, Janice, *The Miles Tae Dundee*, Dundee Art Galleries and Museums, 1990.

O'Neill, Mark, 'Recording modern Springburn', pp. 28-32, *Recording Society Today*, Scottish Museums Council, 1987, pp. 28-32.

Paine, Crispin, 'Local museums', *Museums Journal*, vol. 83, no.1, June/July 1983, p.21.

Some Useful Addresses

Department of English Local History, 3-5 Salisbury Road, Leicester. This contains the Marc Fitch Library of English Local History. The university library also has its own collection of English local history books on a national scale.

Centre for Urban History, University of Leicester, Leicester. This is a contact address for the Urban History Group and the Group for Early Modern Towns.

14   Reinterpreting Material History: Objectivity, Neutrality or Evasion?[1]

Nima Poovaya-Smith

Keeper, Ethnic Arts, Bradford Art Galleries and Museums

Britain has an estimated 1,324,000 people who are of Indian sub-continental descent. Of these, 779,000 are Indians, 433,000 are Pakistani and 112,000 are Bangladeshi. These 1986-88 projected figures do not include African-born Asians. But whatever the total number of Asians in this country, it is obvious that they are a substantial presence; and one of their main links with their material history is through the rich collection of Indian artefacts in various national and private holdings in Britain.

The 1980s signalled the start of a move to increase the accessibility of museums and galleries to a much wider public. Minorities were frequently identified as one of the groups for whom museums made scant provision. Although an area that still has not been satisfactorily addressed, networking in Leicester, Bradford, Hackney and Rochdale, for example, and an increasing number of contemporary and historical exhibitions reflecting cultural diversity, have set in motion a slow but emphatic change in the profile of the museum audience. A growing awareness, particularly among younger Asians, of the important role a museum plays in interpreting culture and history, and its power to create or destroy damaging stereotypes, has made the need for an increasingly sophisticated approach to this material history crucially important in the 1990s.

The issue of repatriation of important material is one that surfaces periodically, particularly in the Indian press. Often, however, moral considerations are subsumed under the political. One suspects, for instance, that the return of the golden throne of the Sikh king, Ranjit Singh (*d*.1839), would be a serious source of embarrassment to the government of India, since it could easily be seen as the symbol of a separate Sikh state. Since collections associated with Britain's colonial past have a capacity to arouse suspicion, even though a large number of the objects were quite legitimately obtained, the mode of acquisition and the history of their presence in this country should be explained where possible.

The notion of undisplayed 'treasures in museum basements' is firmly established in the minds of the general public. This is particularly true of material from the Indian sub-continent. But the factors that govern the choice of objects for display and their interpretation are an area arousing increasing interest. Brian Durrans and Patricia Kattenhorn point out how interpretation can 'reflect representational ideas or intentions, help generate cultural meaning, and advance or obstruct the interests of [particular] social groups'.[2] For instance, it has been commented upon that the newly furbished, palatial Nehru Gallery in the Victoria and Albert Museum seems to concentrate on opulent objects that relate to an elite, ruling class; the culture of the ordinary people only gets a cursory nod in passing. Since the South Kensington Museums, fairly or unfairly, are seen as bastions of cultural, social and racial privilege, the emphasis on the 'riches' of the sub-continent reinforces the notion. (But different groups have different expectations. For instance, older generation Asians on the whole tend to approve of the image of wealth and splendour the Nehru Gallery conveys of the sub-continent, since this is in positive contrast to the old image of a poverty-stricken Third World region. However, the recent appointment of a dynamic Education Officer of South Asian Arts in the Indian Department might help reconcile the different perceptions by widening the scope of the interpretation.)

Interpretation of objects should examine their meaning within the context of their own culture while keeping abreast of contemporary changes. Considerable new work has been done by scholars in India in the research of Indian art, but unfortunately they do not enjoy the same prestige and consequently do not get the same exposure as their European counterparts. In this country, collections have been looked at mainly from a white perspective. However sympathetic this perspective, it needs to be informed by other points of view, for it often does not take into consideration the depth of feeling certain objects can arouse or the impact of their symbolic messages.

Edward Said in *Orientalism* points out the impossibility of complete objectivity in such situations:

For [if] it is true that no production of knowledge in the human sciences can ever ignore or disclaim its author's involvement as a human subject in his own circumstances, then it must also be true that for a European or American studying the Orient there can be no disclaiming the main circumstances of *his* actuality: that he comes up against the Orient as a European or American first, as an individual second. And to be a European or American in such a situation is by no means an inert fact. It meant and means being aware, however dimly, that one belongs to a power with definite interests in the Orient, and more important, that one belongs to a part of the earth with a definite history of involvement in the Orient almost since the time of Homer.[3]

This is increasingly seen as an issue by scholars from the subcontinent. Kattenhorn and Durrans draw attention to the fact that during the organising of the Festival of India exhibition in 1982, one of the conditions of collaboration from the Indian side was that they be given main control over the interpretation of the material used in the exhibitions. But at present in Britain the total number of Asian and Afro-Caribbean curators in municipal, national and independent galleries adds up to less than 12 in the entire country; their remit covers both historical and contemporary art. Their involvement in the interpretation of their material history is minimal in relative terms.

This is not to discount the importance of the considerable intellectual contribution made by Europeans towards the study of Indian art. There have been imaginative exhibitions in the recent past where issues of interpretation have been handled with sensitivity and intelligence. 'The Raj: India and the British 1600-1947', organised by the National Portrait Gallery (1990-91) was largely conceived by Christopher Bayly. Although displaying occasional evidence of hasty research, this magnificent exhibition certainly made a strenuous effort to present the well-rounded analysis promised in the foreword to the catalogue:

British, Indian, Pakistani and Bangladeshi assessments of the merits of that empire, [the Raj] and of the consequences of its demise differ radically, and in this exhibition and catalogue we have attempted to present rather than minimise these differences of opinion.[4]

The exhibition, the catalogue and a lively lecture series, challenged assumptions and definitions of the Raj with surprising directness. The exhibition examined, for instance, one kind of distortion imposed on the people by the practice of colonial anthropology with its obsession for narrow and tidy classifications, and another kind of distortion imposed by the picturesque tradition that applied European conceits on to the landscape of the sub-continent. The portrayal of different levels of society, also meant that the subcontinent was not presented as the exotic 'other'.

Far less dramatically but perhaps more successfully, the British Library exhibition 'Calcutta: City of Palaces' (London, 1990; Bradford, 1991), curated by Jeremiah P.Losty, examines the role the British played in the growth and development of this extraordinary trading capital. What Losty portrays sympathetically but without sentimentality is a very human story of a muddy village expanding perhaps too rapidly into a city. Through an unrelenting documentation of financial transactions, we are made aware of the staggering sums of money that changed hands in Calcutta. The greed and corruption of several of the East India Company officials were often with the connivance of their Indian counterparts who were in any position of power. This was to the chagrin of the Company for although 'The profits to be made all along the line in the East India trade were immense, the Court of Directors fondly imagined that nobody but they should make them'.[4]

Quietly but authoritatively 'Calcutta' debunks or deflates various myths; the 'Black Hole of Calcutta', for instance, although a tragic event, aroused only a retrospective, propagandist outrage, aided by fatality statistics that were questionable. Robert Clive's ruthlessness and greed as Governor-General of India were well established historical facts with scholars, but he lingers in the popular British imagination as an unalloyed hero. The cool, clear analysis of his character in this show still has the capacity to shock the lay public. The unravelling truths are all the more forceful because text is allied with images, documents, maps and other archival material. It is a period so minutely analysed that a visit to the exhibition requires many hours of study.

In a wider context, the material held in this country not only embodies the craft and fine art traditions of the sub-continent, but is also frequently charged with historical and religious significances. As in the Indian mind they often coalesce, these objects, intimately connected as they are with the sub-continent's political or religious history, will always have a resonance that goes beyond their innate artistic content and worth. Take, for instance, the India Office's copy of the *Dasam Granth*, an important sacred text of the Sikhs and the work of Guru Gobind Singh (1664-1707), last and most dynamic of the Sikh Gurus. This nineteenth-century volume supposedly directly copied from the original (which is said to bear the signature of the Guru himself) is obviously of importance to the Sikhs.

This *Dasam Granth* was loaned to Bradford Art Galleries and Museums by the India Office Library for its recent touring exhibition on Sikh art, 'Warm and Rich and Fearless' (1991-92). The India Office placed no restrictions on the interpretation of the text apart from expressly stating that it should be treated with the respect due to its sacred status. Bradford prides itself on the ongoing dialogue it has with its various communities. It has a system of formal and informal consultation with members of the Asian, Afro-Caribbean and East European communities. The exhibition on Sikh art, for instance, was organised as a result of a request from members of the Sikh community. Consultation with the community covered aspects of interpretation and display. Bradford Art Galleries and Museums took what it thought were all the necessary steps to demonstrate respect for the holy text. The book was placed on a stool, with brocade cushions (also on loan from the India Office), and the installation was discussed with two representatives of the Sikh community. But this was to prove not fully adequate. Some Sikhs' feelings were deeply wounded because the text had not been placed under a canopy. Bradford was informed that such was the veneration for the text that even modern copies of the *Dasam Granth* were ceremonially carried on people's heads, when moved from one location to another. Hasty steps were taken to have a canopy installed. It was a moving sight to see several Sikhs remove their footwear and reverently prostrate themselves before the sacred text. Such a passionate engagement between object and audience demands a review of the way we display and interpret sensitive material on the whole.

An even better known object than the *Dasam Granth* both in Britain and the sub-continent is 'Tipu's Tiger' in the Victoria and Albert Museum. Obviously alive to the historical reverberations of this piece, the V & A has gone to unusual lengths with the interpretation, for in addition to a carefully neutral label, it is the only object that not only has a video of its own, but also one which allows a direct, contemporary Indian perspective. Its symbolic messages are, however, far more marginalised.

Tipu Sultan was a South Indian Muslim ruler, whose defiant resistance to British attempts to curb his ambition and weaken his power resulted in four battles, culminating in his death in the last one in 1799. In India he still exercises a powerful if rather ambivalent pull on the national imagination, where he figures both as a hero inspired by God and as a despot, albeit a brave one. One of India's earliest freedom fighters, Tipu Sultan was a man of his time in the bigotry and cruelty he occasionally displayed, and a man who transcended his time in his courage and vision. Today Mysore is a green and fertile land thanks largely to his interest in innovative horticulture and silviculture. His introduction of sericulture also helped transform the economy. He is the subject of a popular television series currently being shown in Britain and his palace in Srirangapatna is now a museum.

Tipu Sultan was obsessed with the tiger, a creature native to his kingdom of Mysore. He was enthralled by its ferocity, strength and graceful beauty. He had tiger dreams which he treated as solemn portents and his throne was a magnificent affair of gem-encrusted gold tiger head finials, with the howdah-like throne supported on the back of a large gold tiger. His armour, some of the uniforms of his soldiers, and the hangings in his palaces were decorated with the 'bubri' or tiger stripe motif.

His preoccupation with this image actually demonstrated a sound relationship between metaphor and reality. Mysore had a large tiger population at that point. (Today it is a focus of a Save the Tiger campaign.) Shia Muslim holymen during the festival of Mohharam are painted to look like tigers and dance themselves into a hypnotic trance. The tiger stripe was not only an attractive motif for textiles and craft objects, but the tiger's aura of mystery and menace was what Tipu Sultan wanted to convey. In terms of creating an identifiable mythology Tipu Sultan could not have hit upon a more appropriate symbol.

'Tipu's Tiger', which displays a sense of humour, albeit macabre, has a clockwork mechanism, which when set in motion produces menacing growls as the tiger looms over a helpless European. Clearly the marauding tiger was Tipu; the prone Englishman, the subjugated might of the British army. Yet the ironical truth lay elsewhere. Tipu was not only defeated and killed by the British, the final ignominy was that his sons as dependants of the colonisers were to all intents and purposes loyal subjects of the British crown.

The British had their own response to 'Tipu's Tiger' in a strange, obscure battle of counteracting one 'talismanic' image against another. After their victory over Tipu, they minted a commemorative silver coin upon which a lion (Britain) successfully vanquishes a tiger, obviously Tipu. This becomes even more ironic in view of the fact that the tiger was sometimes viewed in India as a symbol for the lion and Tipu's tiger-figures usually contain inscriptions that exalt 'the Victorious Lion of God'.

Objects such as 'Tipu's Tiger' (primarily in the South) and the golden throne of the Sikh king, Ranjit Singh (primarily in the North) have a prominent presence in the Indian psyche. Taken as booty or spoils of war they are already larger than life and highly emotive. To me as a South Indian, 'Tipu's Tiger' casts a shadow of history, myth and dream all the more powerful because of its dislocated status. Like all symbols so richly laden with historical associations, it has an ahistorial dimension that allows it to absorb contemporary meaning. There are parallels between Tipu Sultan's precarious position as an autonomous ruler in eighteenth-century India and the tiger's own threatened state today. But even though Tipu Sultan's kingdom has collapsed and the British no longer govern the sub-continent, the confident craft tradition that produced the boldly painted wooden figures of 'Tipu's Tiger' still survives. In Channapatna, near Mysore, about twenty miles from Srirangapatna, brightly painted wooden animals are produced to this day. The British-based Indian sculptor Dhruva Mistry's vividly painted guardian and human/animal creatures appear to be in the same tradition.

There is also an older artistic frame of reference. Indian sculpture in stone and terracotta often depicted composite creatures, shardulas and vyalas, part lion or tiger and part imaginary animal, locked in mortal combat with humans. The composite creatures allude to the teeming unconscious, the untamed appetites and desires and man's attempts to subdue them. In a mysterious transference of meaning, 'Tipu's Tiger' contains the same man/animal, conscious/unconscious dichotomy.

This is not the only Tipu relic in Britain. The tiger head from his dismembered throne is now in Windsor Castle and a number of objects are in Powis Castle, in Wales. That these are spoils of war from one particular kingdom seems to be of less consequence than their subsequent distribution and provenance. All these objects are in effect spatially and culturally displaced from their original location. Museum interpretation seldom confronts the moral issues surrounding their presence in this country, just as it shirks discussing the symbolic meaning of important pieces and seldom investigates what elitist or separatist notions a display may convey. Indeed, increasing numbers of the white British public are uncomfortable about the issues involved. Museums with such collections should initiate a critical debate about these issues, rather than maintain a defensive or neutral front. Since there will always be ambiguity in the response of any minority group when confronted with objects of great power and meaning to their culture, honesty is the only policy that can be used in such a situation. This honesty is due to all minorities, for in the end it is only their presence in this country that offers a justification for the continuing presence of these collections in Britain.

Notes

1. The views expressed in this chapter are the author's own, and do not necessarily reflect those of Bradford Art Galleries and Museums.

2. Brian Durrans and Pat Kattenhorn, 'Representing India: issues in the development of the 1982 Festival of India in Britain', paper presented at Representations Symposium, 13-15 February 1986, British Museum.

3. Edward Said, *Orientalism*, Penguin Books, 1978, p.11.

4. Christopher Bayly, *The Raj: India and the British 1600-1947*, National Portrait Gallery Publications, 1991, p. 11.

5. Jeremiah P. Losty, *Calcutta, City of Palaces*, The British Library and Arnold Publishers, 1990, p.19.

Part Three   Methods of Study

Introduction

Social history curatorship implies a concern for more than objects. Those working in museums in a field which will remain very wide and varied now enjoy a title which carries with it expectations. Their specialised contribution is to the study of material artefacts, but they are also part of a broader movement which draws on other forms of evidence for the past and present.

The area of study – the experience of people in a changing society – presents both an opportunity and a responsibility to go beyond objects to context and to make a real contribution to the ordering of information into a coherent attempt at history. Context is two-fold – spatial and temporal. If it is neglected, we do worse than miss opportunities to give our material historical value; we downgrade it to a position of mere curiosity, adrift in a vague and generalised past. Artefact studies in social history are critically important, and the experience particularly of North American museums in encouraging an understanding of form, function and meaning through interrogation of the object is illuminating and instructive. As curators we must believe that artefacts have a value in aiding an understanding of the past and are not solely three-dimensional illustrations of themes or narratives. As historians, however, it would be bizarre if we ignored surviving evidence for context, destroyed it by failing to collect it, and then relied on the object unsupported somehow to re-create it. There is a parallel here with modern excavation archaeology, where context is crucial in reconstructing a coherent site-history and usable record of the past. If it is disregarded, we are back with the early days of archaeology, cheerfully plundering a site (= a society) for prime collection or display material and destroying in the process the record of context which alone gives the material its value as evidence. Better not to collect at all.

Such context can only be found by seeing 'museum' artefacts as the small and portable sector of a larger scale of reference for the past. The scale extends, in the material world, to the whole physical environment (buildings, neighbourhoods, the rural or urban landscape) and, in the non-material, to beliefs, customary practices, attitudes, social structures and memory. These are primary evidence and they can be recorded, but there are other ways into them through written documents, printed material, maps, early photographs and film, prints, drawings and paintings. Each of these sources has become a specialised area of historical investigation, with its own practitioners; the social history curator will need to be not only familiar with them but also able in most cases to exploit them in helping to create a whole and properly documented view of the past.

Although objects may yield information through their fabric, form and construction, they are more co-operative as spring-boards for questions than as sole sources that can provide comprehensive answers. (Kavanagh, 1990)

The questions are legion, the body of available evidence vast and the workers on the ground very few. The curator has a crucial part to play in carrying out studies which supply some answers, initially at a local level but by accretion at a national level, and is in a supremely advantageous position to do so, generally highly visible and close to the communities served. This will give museums a clear contributory role in social history studies which they have so far not achieved.

For the museum-bound curator it will mean planned research and particularly research-based collecting, not just of objects but of supporting and associated information, with some constructive end in view. The benefits will be in properly documented and more genuinely representative collections, but also in the detail, precision, authenticity and local relevance of interpretation. If the task is faithfully to record and present the past, then the broader the range of sources used and the more we allow the sources to speak for themselves, the less is the risk of imposing on our material a preconceived frame for the past.

Collecting policies should expand to become programmes for action. Priorities need to be set which are based not so much on what our collections do contain but on what they ought to contain – objects and information – to reflect fully the experience and traditions of local communities. Such broad, research-based collecting may mean the acquisition of new skills and the involvement of specialists from outside the museum. The rewards are considerable in bringing the museum and its communities closer together, in allowing people a voice in the record of their own past, and in being able to identify and draw attention to survivals of the past which remain fixed in the real environment. The museum gallery should never become the only place where society can make links with its own past, or a vital continuum is broken.

The priorities for such programmes can only be determined locally. Are they to be set by the threats to evidence, again with the analogy to excavation archaeology and the rescue approach? If an important local industry died out in the 1930s and all that survives is in the memories of eighty-year-old former workers, should we as a rescue exercise not be collecting oral evidence which will have vanished within a decade? What of contemporary collecting? Are we better occupied, as social history curators, in identifying significant local strands in modern social life and collecting, sampling or recording all the available evidence (including objects) while it exists fresh and undistorted by partial memory and chance survival?

Some of the work of most lasting value in social history museums over the past decade has been in such planned and coherent exercises, whether aimed at recording the present, the recent past or more distant periods. They have often been most valuable when local people themselves have been directly involved in the process as participants rather than subjects. Mention is made in Chapter 3 particularly to work in Glasgow, at the People's Palace; in Birmingham with the 'Change in the Inner City' project; at Market Harborough; and in Hull.

One further example may be cited, of how productive the locally based cross-specialist approach may be, in the work by Oxfordshire Museum Services in the 1970s and 1980s. Here a detailed collecting and research programme was drawn up to identify shortcomings in the existing holdings of objects and information as a comprehensive reflection of the past, and to serve as a plan for future studies. A working group of curators and field archaeologists on the staff was added to from time to time by outside specialists and amateur local historians as a sequence of topics was studied in turn: workers' housing, the local clay industries of brick and potterymaking, brewing and malting. The group worked together to a timetable: identifying and recording field evidence by plans and photography or enriching existing records; recording oral testimony; searching the archives of early photographic material; combing the documentary sources of censuses, wills and inventories, estate, tithe and enclosure award maps, trade directories and newspapers; and locating, documenting and, where available, collecting artefact evidence. The projects produced a large amount of raw data, in some cases running from the middle ages to the present day. This was ordered for the permanent complete record, but was also synthesised and made quickly available through popular publications, articles in the learned journals, and in mobile exhibitions which toured the county. About two years was devoted to each project; the group approach sustained impetus and provided support when other demands threatened. A reasonably comprehensive record of each topic was achieved, and there were valuable and well documented additions to the collections.

The proactive, planned approach raises questions of time and justification for research in a busy life with other and seemingly uncontrollable demands. In reality it is perhaps the only approach which begins to discharge our responsibilities to collections which are more than random assemblages, and to take curatorship beyond a skilled store-keeping and exhibiting function to a genuine place in gathering and synthesising real evidence for the past. It is better to plan work to reflect long-term responsibilities than to be the passive recipients of unsolicited, ill-documented and repetitive material, with all the costs in time and other resources which that involves. (See Lord, Lord and Nicks, 1989, which also carries a useful listing of published project work recently carried out in museums.) These questions are addressed more fully in Part Four. The chapters in Part Three concentrate on the main primary and secondary sources and methods of study for broad project- or research-based approaches – to collecting, to the fuller documentation of collections, or to the construction of a locally based social history.

John G. Rhodes

References

Kavanagh, Gaynor (1990), *History Curatorship*, Leicester University Press.

Lord, B., Lord, G. D., and Nicks, J. (1989), *The Cost of Collecting*, HMSO.

Bibliography

Davies, Stuart, 'Collecting and recalling the twentieth century', *Museums Journal,* vol. 85, no. 1, 1985.

Davies, Stuart, 'Change in the inner city', *Social History Curators Group News,* 1984.

Jenkinson, Peter, 'Material culture, people's history and populism: where do we go from here?' in Pearce, S.M. (ed.), *Museum Studies in Material Culture,* Leicester University Press, 1989.

King, Elspeth, 'Case study: People's Palace Museum, Glasgow', *Recording Society Today,* Scottish Museums Councils, 1987.

15 Documents

David Fleming

Director, Tyne and Wear Museums

Introduction

The study of documents is the traditional method of research of the historian. In most civilisations, while the spoken word has been the routine form of communication, the written word has been used to record information. Certainly this is true of Britain since the medieval period. Some of these records were intended to have a short life, others were made for posterity.

All types of records need to be interrogated by the historian. Moreover, in compiling the history of a society, a historian must always use all available forms of evidence. In this way, as data is amassed, can history become less impressionistic, and more 'accurate'.

The museum-based social historian needs little encouragement to consult a variety of sources. Indeed, the social history curator has a particular, in many ways unique, interest in documents. Put a historian in a museum context and the emphasis of the work shifts: the curator's main professional purpose is not the writing of social history, but the interpretation of the past (and the present) by using (and building) the museum's collections. While university-based historians are interested in demographic structures, kinship, belief, conflict and control, the curator, who is interested in all of these, is looking more closely for evidence relating to museum collections, real and potential buildings, furnishings, clothing, ornaments, musical instruments, modes of transport, craft tools, kitchen implements, toys – the material survivals of different ages. Thus, sense can be made of object collections, and they can be interpreted for others. Objects only have meaning in terms of human behaviour, and only by synthesising all evidence of human behaviour can the full potential of object collections be realised. Furthermore, only by synthesising evidence can rational collecting be achieved. The same is true for archival, oral or photographic collections in museums. In short, while 'museums are about objects', social history curators, need not restrict analysis to objects alone, nor should they ever consider so doing (unlike, perhaps and perforce, the archaeologist and the ethnographer).[1] Any document is a potentially fertile source of information to the curator.

But should the curator be heavily involved in primary documentary research as a matter of course? Should it not be the case that the curator needs only to be able to identify collecting needs and collection needs, and to interpret collections, drawing upon research by others who do not bear the burden of museum collection management? Do curators, in the real world, have the time? Are there enough curators? And if we do undertake research, should we not confine ourselves to recent decades and leave the palaeographical mysteries of the distant past to our university-based cousins?

There are those who take an anti-scholastic view of curatorship, who believe that the essence of curatorship is management, of collections and premises, and that research is a luxury the museum world can barely afford. On the other hand, some believe that curators are essentially researchers, whose real job is primary research in the traditional manner of the university scholar; museum management and, indeed, collection management, are for others to worry about.

Clearly, there has to be a middle way, although most certainly the pressures on the social history curator are very great, and research will, in practice, often take a remote back seat. Nevertheless, every curator who has organised a social history exhibition knows of the widespread paucity of local research. In order to provide an even rudimentary context for social history displays a curator is frequently *obliged* to undertake original research, because the discipline of social history is still so young. Museums are, in fact, in the forefront of social history research, particularly for the twentieth century. Publications and exhibitions such as 'Turrets, Towels and Taps', 'City Children', and 'A Taste of Change' (Birmingham), 'Hidden Harborough' and 'Cap and Apron' (Market Harborough) and 'Schooldays' and 'That's Entertainment!' (Hull) are original contributions to social historical research.[2] All these projects perceive photographs and oral history as valid constituents of museum collections, and the need to synthesise sources. As for pre-twentieth century social history, this too is rare, and again, in order to provide context for collections and exhibitions, the social history curator is often obliged to undertake research. Even though few objects survive from the pre-industrial centuries, the social history exhibition still has to interpret the societies which created the objects – museums are not just about displaying objects, which in themselves do tell us so little.[3] Moreover, the value of museum research geared towards exhibition (and publication) is all the more important, because information via these media is accessible to many people in a way academic monographs can never be, and can be 'accurate' in a way television can rarely be. The case for research by social history curators is very strong.

There are thousands of species of documents which have been used by historians to gather evidence to write history, ranging from the most personal, private scripts, to the proceedings of the great governmental departments, of the Crown, and of the highest courts of law. Over the past three or four decades, more and more types of document have been enlisted, and in an increasing number of ways. Computer analysis is quite usual, and in particular our knowledge of family life has grown considerably with the application of sophisticated statistical techniques to what are ostensibly the most unlikely sources.

This chapter will concern itself, rather artificially, with manuscript (handwritten) sources, as opposed to those in print, so as to keep within some bounds. Analysis of the vast amounts of printed material, ranging from the instruction manual to the novel, is outside its scope. It may well be that printed documents are virtually as rare as manuscripts in certain areas of study, and can be classified as 'primary' in the sense that they are original evidence. One real distinction – although even this does not always apply – is that a manuscript was/is unique, while printed documents are not. Many manuscript sources are now, of course, in print in one form or another, so as to bring them to wider audiences. In any event, the important fact is that sources, whether manuscript or printed, contain invaluable information for curators.

A further restriction on the scope of this chapter is that while any historic document could be of value to the social history curator, I shall address primarily those sources which may refer directly to artefacts or buildings which might be held in museum collections. Such sources are comparatively rare.

Documents

It is salutary to preface a discussion on the use of documents with some basic remarks concerning their validity: we must always begin by asking what a document is, who wrote it and why, and what was its purpose. No document can be interpreted without such initial assessments. There may be scores of biases affecting the compilation and survival of documents – the great bulk evince both male perspective and sectionalism, and it is all too easy to accept documentary evidence at face value.

Somewhat surprisingly, written sources of direct relevance to museums begin 2,000 years ago. Suetonius recorded Stone Age axeheads; Julius Caesar and Tacitus each wrote accounts of Celtic war chariots such as we have remains of in collections today. While these artefacts have been recovered archaeologically and are unlikely to be in 'social history' collections, the principle of contemporary description of style, decoration and use helping us comprehend the surviving object (Is it typical or atypical, common or unusual, as old as we think it is? Who used it?) holds true. Moreover, the surviving artefact helps us understand the contemporary description: the process is two-way.

The medieval and early modern periods produced ever greater numbers of more and more complex documents, especially from the sixteenth century, although, as few social history museums contain many items which date from earlier than about 1600, it is only very rarely that such documents can be related directly to surviving artefacts, and references will almost always be incidental. Ecclesiastical documents which might provide references include sixteenth-century Chantry Certificates (which list ornaments, plate and other goods belonging to chantries and similar ecclesiastical foundations), Glebe Terriers (church buildings), Diocesan Visitation Books (church fabric, fittings and furniture, the glebe buildings), Churchwardens' Accounts (furnishings, tools and equipment, fittings, church fabric, vestments, plate, books, gravestones, bells), Constables' Accounts (gaol, armour and weaponry, stocks, ducking-stool), Church Inspections papers, Archdeaconry and other church court records, and the inventories of church goods of the Reformation period. Most references will be bare, though there may be further elaboration.

Pre-modern secular documents tend to derive from manor, town and county government, but also from national government. Among the latter are sixteenth-century Port Books, which recorded the import (and export) of goods, specifying origin, value and names of merchants, and they can be a guide to the arrival of foreign manufactures or raw materials which eventually find their way into museums. The Hearth Tax records of the later seventeenth century provide information, albeit limited, on buildings. Manor Court Rolls can contain information on mills and other buildings. Manorial Accounts may include inventories of tools and implements, and information on buildings and their contents. Quarter Sessions records include vast amounts of information relating to the judicial and administrative functions of Justices of the Peace, including trade and transport, alehouses and asylums, sport and servants.

Town records too can cover many subjects – trade, industry, communications, education, social activities, religion, and so on. Such records are by no means restricted to the 'incorporated' boroughs, and they survive in a number of forms: Minute Books, Accounts, Order Books, Ordinances, Leases, Surveys, Bonds, Rentals, Title Deeds, various legal papers, Craft Guild records, Freemen's and Apprenticeship records, Toll Books, Custumals and others. No two towns have identical series of surviving records. Any of these may include information on buildings or artefacts, but it may require detailed searches to unearth it. The sixteenth- and seventeenth-century Town Estate Accounts and Minute Book of the market town of Melton Mowbray refer to bridges, market crosses, arms and armour, the House of Correction, the parish church and its fittings and contents, the Grammar School and gallows, the spittal Chapel, the town's harness, the Swan Inn and other individual buildings in the town, shovels and pickaxes, musical instruments, clothing, food and drink, thatching, masonry, carpentry, glazing, highway repair, Melton Fair, transport, crop types and agricultural practices (hedging, ditching, molecatching, pigkeeping), and writing implements.[4] No commentary on Tudor and Stuart Melton would be possible without exploiting such sources, nor could real sense by made of any museum collections surviving from the period.

Family papers of various kinds can give clear insights into domestic life, although the social coverage is extremely limited, and only town and country gentry, and higher social classes, are likely to be represented on any scale in diaries, household books, memoirs, household and personal account books, letters, and business accounts. The quality of information contained within such documents is unpredictable, but at its best it is unparalleled.

Undoubtedly the most fruitful source relating to artefacts from the pre-industrial period is another class of ecclesiastic documents, probate records – wills and inventories – and although the bias towards the wealthier sections of society is profound, so, too, with museum collections from the period. Wills were proved in ecclesiastical courts until 1858, and before they were proved inventories of the deceased's goods had to be made by appraisers. Wills themselves usually refer to goods and property, but inventories are a quite extraordinary source of information on household goods, personal effects, agricultural and craft implements, shop stock, and other items.

There are innumerable ways to learn about past society, its ways of life and its working patterns and practices, from probate inventories. Unlike, for example, the trade catalogues of later centuries, inventories list what people actually owned and used, room by room, rather than what was merely available. Analysed for a particular place over a period, they can give an unrivalled picture of domestic, industrial and trading life, and changes therein. Individual inventories can be very useful documents, but it is only when examined in series that their potency as a source is truly revealed. We can establish the frequency with which goods appear, their relative values, room types, literacy, the changing amounts spent on domestic comforts, rising (or falling) standards, the arrival in a locality of joined furniture, tapestries, and other hangings, wallpaper, teapots, forks, looking glasses, wine, clocks, mahogany furniture – the list is virtually endless. How such items percolate down through the economic levels can also be traced.

Through, for example, the inventories of 15 Melton Mowbray mercers spanning the years 1599-1712, an image can be built up of the type of goods retailed to inhabitants of the Wreake Valley during the period. Fabrics available in 1599 included fustian from Milan, Genoa and Ulm, taffeta, canvas, silk, buckram, holland (and many more), some held in the shop of James Levett in huge quantities. Levett also sold haberdashery, curtain rings, gloves, bowstrings, spectacles, brown paper, iron, ratsbane, liquorice, starch, glue, books, pens, vinegar, turpentine, sweets, spices, nuts, rice, clothing, and scores more items. While such a source requires very careful interpretation, it remains a compelling insight into the material quality of life of at least some of the town's and valley's inhabitants. Levett's own goods are also laid out to view in the inventory, ranging from his shop scales, brass weights, and shop fittings, to his pots, pans, bellows, furniture, candlesticks, linen and silver, to his dairy equipment, cheeses, malt, brewing vessels, chamber pots, scythes, barrows, packsaddle, three carts and one wagon, his ladders, grindstones and livestock. Levett's spinning wheels show that his household was involved in the local textiles manufacturing, but were his wheels for flax or wool? His inventory does not tell, and only by studying other inventories from the locality can we guess that Levett's were likely to be for spinning flax.[5]

Near the other end of the Melton social scale was Chris Franke, labourer, who at his death in 1614 owned some pitchforks, rakes, a spade, a milk churn and some wheels.[6] Poorer still than Franke was William Deay (died 1631) whose cow comprised over one third of his wealth.[7] Women feature infrequently in probate records (in 48 out of 336 probate inventories surviving for Melton Mowbray inhabitants from the period 1537-1720) but inventories do prove that while women hardly ever played a formal role in local government, they did take their place in the economic hierarchy as mercers, haberdashers, innkeepers, farmers, glaziers, shoemakers, as well as appearing as the ambiguous 'widow' or 'spinster'.

Comparisons of those whose wills or inventories survive with sources which indicate wealth ranking – such as the Lay Subsidies of the 1520s and 1540s, local levies for contributions to the poor, militia assessments, levies for church repairs, Health Taxes – is a further approach to giving adequate context to the information contained within probate records.

From the eighteenth century onwards, the number of types of document multiplies and can be as diverse as Vestry Agreements, Farm Valuations, Production Records, and Motor Vehicle License Records. Meanwhile, older classes of document continue, and printed sources such as newspapers open up entirely new horizons for the historian and curator. Business records increase phenomenally in numbers, as do family papers. The social coverage of documents is extended, and education records, for example, become far more revelatory about working-class experience. Ultimately, while printed records and typescripts become more and more important as sources for the curator, the value of manuscripts remains, supplemented so powerfully nowadays both by oral reminiscence and by the relative closeness of modern curators to the material culture they are analysing.

It remains true that it is for the earlier periods that we are most reliant upon documents for information on artefacts, as we are more reliant upon artefacts as evidence of human activity. Today we have so much information – evidence – at our disposal as, essentially, students of human behaviour, that the relative value of artefacts as evidence is greatly reduced. The more recent the artefact, the less its relative evidential value. Consequently we place a decreasing reliance upon documents as sources to assist us with understanding artefacts. Documents from any period, manuscript or printed, have their limitations, and for the social history curator in particular the gross underrepresentation of the working-class, women and ethnic groups, is a fundamental difficulty. They will never, could never, tell us the whole story, but they will, collectively, tell us much more than three-dimensional evidence. While artefacts are wonderfully tangible, with potentially great emotional appeal, it is documentary evidence which allows us to increase our understanding of material culture, and to place that material culture in its context.

Notes and References

1. Anthony Burton, 'Planning new galleries at the Bethnal Green Museum of Childhood', *Journal of the Social History Curators Group*, vol.16, 1988-9. See also Anna Davin, 'Class and children's work and play in London in the 1890s and 1900s', ibid.; Michael Glasson, 'The City Children Project at Birmingham Museum and Art Gallery', ibid.; David Fleming, 'Social history in Wonderland', ibid.

2. R.Wilkins, *Turrets, Towels and Taps*, Birmingham City Museum and Art Gallery; Michael

Glasson, *City Children: Birmingham Children at Work and Play 1900-1930*, Birmingham City Museum and Art Gallery, 1985; Karen Hull and Peter Jenkinson, *A Taste of Change: Some Aspects of Eating in the Inner City, Birmingham 1939-85*, Birmingham City Museum and Art Gallery, 1985; Samuel Mullins and Michael Glasson, *Hidden Harborough – The Making of the Townscape of Market Harborough*, Leicestershire Museums, Art Galleries and Records Service, 1985; Samuel Mullins and Gareth Griffiths, *Cap and Apron: An Oral History of Domestic Service in the Shires, 1880-1950*, Leicestershire Museums, Art Galleries and Records Service, 1986; Elizabeth Frostick, *Schooldays*, Hull City Museums and Art Galleries, 1988; Penny Wilkinson, *That's Entertainment!*, Hull City Museums and Art Galleries, 1989.

3. Our experience at Hull Museums is that there is an almost total lack of accessible social history research on the city, and research into both pre- and post-industrial social history has to be undertaken by staff or commissioned for every exhibition project.

4. Leicestershire Record Office, DG. 36/284/1-34; DG. 25/1/1.

5. Ibid., PR/1/17/34.

6. Ibid., PR/1/26/105.

7. Ibid., PR/1/36/171 .

Bibliography

Part A *A small selection of recent works on social history research in museums*

Allen, Rosemary E.,'Research: social history – a case study', in Thompson, J.M.A., *Manual of Curatorship: A Guide to Museum Practice*, Butterworth, 1986, pp.179-86. Allen, Rosemary E. (ed.), 'Ravensworth Terrace: research, reconstruction and interpretation', *Journal of the Social History Curators Group*, 1986-7, vol. 14, pp. 13-14.

Blake, Steven, '"The Castle of Indolence": urban history in Cheltenham Museum', *Journal of the Social History Curators Group*, 1985-6, vol. 13, pp. 34-7.

Frostick, Elizabeth, *Schooldays*, Hull City Museums and Art Galleries, 1988.

Glaister, Jane, and Davies, Stuart, 'Oakwell: a multi-disciplinary project in Kirklees, West Yorkshire', *Journal of the Social History Curators Group*, vol. 16, 1988-9, pp. 36-40.

Glasson, Michael, *City Children: Birmingham Children at Work and Play 1900-1930*, Birmingham City Museum and Art Gallery, 1985.

Hayhurst,Yvonne, 'Recording a workshop', *Journal of the Social History Curators Group*, vol. 14, 1986-7, pp.18-19.

Hull, Karen, and Jenkinson, Peter, *A Taste of Change: Some Aspects of Eating in the Inner City, Birmingham 1939-1985*, Birmingham City Museum and Art Gallery, 1985.

Mullins, Samuel, and Griffiths, Gareth, *Cap and Apron – An Oral History of Domestic Service in the Shires, 1880-1950*, Leicestershire Museums, Art Galleries and Records Service, 1986.

Mullins, Samuel, and Glasson, Michael, *Hidden Harborough: The Making of the Townscape of Market Harborough*, Leicestershire Museums, Art Galleries and Records Service, 1985.

Wiliam, Eurwyn, 'Re-erection, restoration and interpretation: the Rhyd-Y-Car Houses at the Welsh Folk Museum', *Journal of the Social History Curators Group*, vol. 16, 1988-9, pp. 33-6.

Wilkins, R., *Turrets, Towels and Taps*, Birmingham City Museum and Art Gallery, 1986.

Wilkinson, Penny, *That's Entertainment!*, Hull City Museums and Art Galleries, 1989.

Part B *Some works on using documents as sources*

Emmison, F.G., *Archives and Local History*, Phillimore, Chichester, 1978.

Emmison, F.G., *Introduction to Archives*, Phillimore, Chichester, 1978.

Emmison, F.G., and Gray, I., *County Records*, Historical Association, 1973.

Hoskins, W.G., *Local History in England*, Longman, 1984.

Iredale, David, *Enjoying Archives*, Phillimore, Chichester, 1985.

Local History Six issues a year.

The Local Historian Four issues a year.

Macfarlane, Alan, *Reconstructing Historical Communities*, Cambridge University Press, 1977.

Munby, Lionel M., *Short Guide to Records*, Historical Association, 1972.

Richardson, John, *The Local Historian's Encyclopaedia*, Historical Publications, New Barnet,1986.

Riden, Philip, *Record Sources for Local History*, Batsford, 1987.

Stephens, W.B., *Sources for English Local History*, Cambridge University Press, 1981.

Story, Richard, and Madden Lionel, *Primary Sources for Victorian Studies*, Phillimore, Chichester, 1977.

Tate, W.E., *The Parish Chest*, Phillimore, Chichester, 1983.

West, John, *Village Records,* Phillimore, Chichester, 1982.

West, John, *Town Records*, Phillimore, Chichester, 1983.

16   Oral History

Gareth Griffiths

Director, Empire and Commonwealth Museum, Bristol

Oral history is at the same time the newest and oldest form of history and falls into two distinct categories, with differing implications for their status as historical evidence. The first and more familiar category is oral reminiscence – the first-hand recollections of people; secondly, there is oral tradition – the narratives and descriptions of people and events in the past which have been handed down by word of mouth over several generations. Oral evidence offers the opportunity to meet some of the deficiencies of the documentary record as well as redressing the balance of experience against artefacts in the exhibition area. Underlying the practice of oral history are two powerfully attractive assumptions. First, personal reminiscence is viewed as an effective instrument for recreating the past – a means of 'showing how things actually were' by entering into the experience of people in the past. Secondly, oral history may be seen as a democratic alternative, where ordinary people are not only offered a place in history but also a role in the production of historical knowledge. One of the most important roles performed by oral evidence in recent years has been to redefine what subjects may be covered under the umbrella of local history and extend the range of those involved in creating the historical record. Instead of allowing the documents to structure the work, the topic range is potentially considerably expanded by drawing upon oral testimony.

A survey of contemporary collecting and documentation in London has shown that whilst most social history museums have at some stage been involved with oral history, the range and quality of the work produced has been variable.[1] Seemingly, regretting the constraints of the artefact, museums have plunged too frequently into oral history with little regard either for the inherent limitations of the technique or the possible applications of the resulting work. Over the past decade a substantial body of literature has been produced on the technical aspects of oral recordings and the organisation of an oral history project. There has, however, been little attention given to the internal mechanics of the technique. Most oral historians have tended to be sanguine about the trustworthiness of the material they obtain. This uncritical interest is a danger to the value of the material obtained. As an adjunct of traditional historiography we have very little knowledge of the efficacy of oral history, and accordingly a strong methodology is required as well as closer collaboration with disciplines which are also involved with the autobiographical memory.

In questioning the reliability and usefulness of oral history, critics have focused upon the fallibility of human memory and so questioned both the reliability and validity of the data collected. Since Paul Thompson's pioneering studies little attention has been applied to the problems of long-term memory. Thompson argued that the credibility and usefulness of any particular source must be assessed in the light of existing professional knowledge. 'An experienced historian will already have learnt enough from contemporary sources about the time, place and social class from which an interviewee comes to know, even if a specific detail is unconfirmable, whether as a whole it rings true.'[2] Thompson's argument founders, however, when the interview is engaging wide areas for which traditional sources are lacking, an activity which is normally regarded as oral history's great strength. It is frequently argued that one of the attractions of oral history is its ability to 'articulate the experiences of people who, historically speaking, would otherwise remain inarticulate';[3] accordingly, any assessment of oral history must therefore involve a consideration of long-term memory construction.

While a large body of research exists examining the processes of short-term memory, surprisingly little work on long-term memory has taken place. Today, most psychologists accept the theory of memory put forward by Sir Frank Bartlett in the 1930s. Bartlett suggested that a person's knowledge of the world plays an intimate part in learning and remembering – that is, it is not possible to isolate the memory system from the rest of cognition. Bartlett's work provides a vital starting point for an understanding of the processes which are at work when an interview is taking place:

Remembering is not the re-excitation of innumerable fixed, lifeless and fragmentary traces. It is an imaginative reconstruction, or construction, built out of the relation of our attitudes towards a whole active mass of organised past relations or experiences, and to a little outstanding detail which commonly appears in image or language form. It is thus hardly ever really exact even in the most rudimentary of rote recapitulation.[4]

It is evident from Bartlett's research that we do not reproduce the past; we reconstruct it in accord with how we perceive ourselves in the present. Autobiographical memory reflects not only our past but also our personalities and beliefs about ourselves today. The process of recalling an event or episode from the past is therefore essentially one of reconstruction.

Indications as to the rates and forms of memory loss are provided by work recently completed by Marigold Linton.[5] Over a twelve-year period Linton studied her memory using diary cards to test her recall. Since what is remembered is affected by how memory is studied Linton applied a variety of techniques to examine the contents and organisation of her memory and how they changed over time. With the passage of time it was found that autobiographical memories became less detailed, harder to recall, less responsive to memory jogs and were less accurately recognised and dated. For events recorded two to six years previously, each year added a six per cent loss to her ability to recall events described in her diary cards. Linton found that the organisation of her autobiographical memory also changed, in part because events were later re-interpreted. That is, autobiographical memories for events in one time were altered by the perception and memory of later events. Further, it was found that with time distinct events fused and new categories evolved.

That the memory trace may suffer distortions and its recall may be influenced by subsequent changes in norms and values is acknowledged by Thompson. This retrospective bias is a difficult problem as it may occur in forms which the historian is unable to identify and so minimises. Thompson's solution is to minimise the problem: 'The intervention of retrospective assessment needs to be identified. But this is less difficult than might be imagined, since it is quite often conscious, and when it is not, may be identified through anachronisms with which it is conveyed.'[6] This is clearly an unconvincing response to what is a serious objection to oral history as a technique of recording history. Where occasions have arisen when what is remembered may be checked against a contemporary record, the impact of later social influences and experiences has been clearly revealed as distorting the remembered view of the past. Such a process was noted by Tom Harrison when he interviewed witnesses to the bombing of Coventry and who had deposited contemporary records in the Mass Observation Archive.[7] In spite of the catastrophic nature of the event, two observers could hardly recall being there and many significant details were lost, while other accounts were 'adjusted' to match a popular view of those nights of air-raids. The outraged reactions of the citizens of Coventry and Plymouth were equally interesting, when the contemporary accounts detailing the disorganisation and panic which followed the bombing of their cities were published thirty years later. All suggestions of feelings of helplessness and fear were strongly rebuffed – the later simplification and consequent distortion of war had clearly altered the memories of those days. Accepting that the contemporary diarists were also influenced by social bias at the time of writing, this does not affect the overall impression that a significant shifting in memories was revealed in this small sample. A second example is provided by a BBC radio programme 'Second Generation' which re-interviewed people about their attitudes to immigrants and immigration after a gap of twenty years.[8] Many of those who contributed to the programme were amazed by their previously held racist views and were unable to recall holding such views even when their earlier interviews were replayed to them. These two examples serve to highlight the complicated process whereby memory is produced as a result of a process which reworks its material under the impact of fresh social influences and experiences. Stephen Koss emphasised this point in his review of Thompson's *Edwardians*: his '"Edwardians"... have lived on to become "Georgians" and now "Elizabethans". Over the years, certain memories may have faded or at the very least may have been influenced by subsequent experience.'[9]

What at first glance may seem a fatal flaw in the armoury of oral history, is in reality one of the most interesting areas of opportunity. Accepting that the construction of memory is a social process, we may consider that individual memory is derived from a collective social memory – the earlier Coventry example is an excellent illustration of this process. What is fascinating is not so much that thirty years after the event memories were at odds with the contemporary record and so should be discounted, but that present memories reveal the collective social memory. The selective nature of recollections can contribute to an understanding of the past and subsequent events. Erroneous or misguided recollections may provoke, through the errors themselves, an understanding and insight into the way this collective social memory is formed. The opportunity therefore exists to examine the range of representations of the past which have, and still do, influence the processes of social remembrance. A research project following these lines of enquiry would enable some understanding of the complex cultural processes by which social groups draw upon their existing cultural materials in order to make sense of their collective experience and, in so doing, produce the individual's subjectivity and memory. Accordingly, this insight into the flawed nature of memory need not be viewed as a threat to the oral historian. From it, the oral historian can develop an understanding of how collective and individual remembrance changes and the bearing this has upon memory.

The whole array of stimuli given out by an interviewer – age, appearance, manner of speech, actions, preparations and credentials – will determine how the interviewer is perceived by the interviewee. This in turn will affect the content, style and quality of interview obtained. It is obvious that the way the interview is conducted is a vital factor in affecting its progress and the information received – each party has a direct effect upon the other. The oral history project on Domestic Service at the Harborough Museum allowed an opportunity to assess some of the effects of different interviewers and techniques.[10] The nature of the research topic resulted in the overwhelming majority of informants being women. Two of the interviewers were men and one a woman. Several of the informants were interviewed by all three and others by two of the interviewers, permitting some comparisons to be made. As may be expected, the majority of informants were noticeably more at ease with an interviewer of their own sex, producing interviews which were more conversational in style and richer in content. The informants happily discussed areas such as sex education, health matters and employer/employee relationships, etc. with the female interviewer; whereas these were to a greater degree taboo topics for both parties when a male interviewer was conducting the interview. In addition to the expected differences in the range of topics covered, the relaxed nature of the female interviewer's sessions does seem to have resulted in some subjective information being produced. An interesting point noted by a number of oral historians is that male interviewees when interviewed by women frequently go into more detail and explanation than when interviewed by another male who, they assume, has a full knowledge of technical processes and working methods. Another example of varying results generated by different interviewers was a study carried out in America using white and black interviewers who, using the same questionnaire, obtained startlingly different results.[11]

Once an oral history project is started it is important that the full costs are recognised and budgeted for. First, transcription: tapes are the primary documents of interviews. But they are not a practical medium to use either in research work or writing. It is essential to transcribe them if the material is to be fully exploited. It takes approximately six hours to type out one hour of recorded tape and this needs to be budgeted for, as does the accompanying indexing. Recently it was estimated that one hour's recording costs £120 in all.

Like other primary sources, oral recording often displays evocative, expressive qualities which are stimulating and exciting to listen to and use. However, like all historical evidence, it requires critical evaluation and must be deployed with other available sources. For example, Paul Thompson's *Edwardians* introduces oral evidence alongside his findings from more conventional sources and the majority of quotations are presented in an impressionistic manner as illustrative support for the various themes covered in the book. Other oral historians publish the results of their projects as straightforward edited documents allowing the document 'to speak for itself'. There is a drawback with this kind of approach as it does not permit accompanying comment and evaluation to be made. Many museums have carried out oral history projects; the material produced is often used either within a publication or in an exhibition in the form of quoted extracts. Playing extracts from tapes in a gallery requires careful thought; all too often poor sound quality and too lengthy extracts spoil impact. A more fruitful approach may be the provision of a 'library' area where the visitor may select extracts on various subjects and be provided with accompanying visual material as well.

An area of research which has only recently been looked at is the social history of language, speech and communication. Although social historians have only recently become aware of 'social linguistics', linguists have identified four main points about the relationships between language and the societies in which they are spoken; these are:

1. Different social groups use different varieties of language.

2. The same people employ different varieties of language in different situations.

3. Language reflects the society in which it is spoken.

4. Language shapes the society in which it is spoken.

Without this background knowledge of linguistic rules, explicit or implicit, oral historians run a risk of misinterpreting their 'documents' in the future. For example, it would be interesting in the future to examine recordings over a long period of time in the light of the feminist linguists' views that ordinary language, male dominated as it is, not only expresses the subordinate position of women but keeps women in that subordinate place.

Many museums and local libraries and record offices now hold oral history collections, and an index of most of these is held by the National Sound Archive. A resource which has been largely overlooked is the recorded material held by the National Sound Archive and the BBC's Written Archive Centre at Caversham. A wide range of material is held by these archives of great interest to the social historian. For example, the programmes 'SOS', 'Other People's Houses' and 'Time to Spare' – broadcast in 1933 and 1934 – used eye-witness accounts in investigative reporting with social documentation. These programmes for the first time spelt out the facts of living on the dole or in a slum by the simple and radical art of letting those who endured these conditions speak for themselves:

People often ask us, who are out of work, how we manage. Well, the answer is easy. We manage by doing without. You have probably heard how we have to manage to scrape together a few bones and cabbage leaves and odds and ends and so on, to make a dinner, but I wonder whether you know the effect a sordid struggle of this kind has on people's minds, apart from the effect on their bodies. It is not a question of 'the unemployed struggling to make both ends meet', but of men and women struggling to live. Please do not think of us as 'the unemployed', but as individuals like yourselves. We have the same ambition to get on in the world: we have just the same feelings as you have. Why should this sordid struggle for mere existence take place? My wife and I have often gone out on Saturday nights without a single penny in our pockets. We walk along the streets and see plenty of everything in the shop windows, so can you blame us for getting bitter? This goes on, not for a short time, but day after day, month after month, and as far as I can see it is going on for the rest of my life. I sometimes feel like throwing a brick through a window ...[12]

The conditions and feelings described in these programmes were a critical challenge to the prejudices and ignorance of the listening public and deserve closer examination and use today.

Finally, oral history has for many years been regarded as a liberating influence within the field of history – allowing people to make their own history. Such an influence has been accepted by museums as a potential means of broadening the accessibility of their collections and interpretation. Oral history promised a sense of place and community accessible to ordinary people, while at the same time illustrating the broader features of social history. However, there are difficulties with the generally held view of oral history as 'democratic' knowledge. Far from transforming the social relations of research, oral history in museums has reinforced the power relations involved within it. Throughout the process of producing a historical account the curator remains in control – the historian controls the interview, defines what counts as 'historically useful information' and makes the decisions on how and in what form the information eventually appears in the public realm. The process by which the curator transforms the recorded interview into a historical account involves significant alterations, as the memories are placed within a framework established by the curator and within which the memories acquire new meanings. Such a process moves in opposition to the original claims of oral history to give history back to the people in their own words. In the future, oral history is likely to become less important as historical *verité* and to increasingly extend its role in examining the construction of popular historical consciousness. It can be most usefully directed towards examining how a sense of the past is produced 'through public representations and private memory', examining not only the past but also the past/present relation – the voice of the past is inescapably the voice of the present too.

Notes and References

1. G. Griffiths, *Contemporary Collecting and Documentation in London,* AMSEE, 1986.

2. Paul Thompson, 'Problems of method in oral history', *Oral History,* vol.1, no. 4, 1973, pp.1-47.

3. T. Lummis, *Listening to History,* Hutchinson, 1987, pp. 19-20.

4. F.C. Bartlett, 'Remembering: a study in experimental and social psychology', *CVP,* 1932, pp.213-4.

5. M. Linton, 'I remember it well', *Psychology Today,* July 1981, pp.81-6.

6. Paul Thompson, *The Voice of the Past: Oral History,* Oxford University Press, 1978, pp. 243-52.

7. T. Harrison, *Living through the Blitz,* Collins, 1976, pp. 324-30.

8. 'Second Generation', BBC Radio 4, 9 November 1985. Copy of programme held at National Sound Archive, 29 Exhibition Road, London SW7 2AS, tel. 071 589 6603 (Keeper of Oral History: Dr Robert Perks).

9. S. Koss, 'Speaking of the past', *Times Literary Supplement,* 5 December 1975, pp.1435-6.

10. S. Mullins and G. Griffiths, *Cap and Apron: An Oral History of Domestic Service in the Shires, 1880-1950,* Leicestershire Museums, Art Galleries and Records Service, 1986.

11. Studs Terkel, *The Good War,* Penguin Books, 1986, p.120. Recent interesting examples of using oral history and autobiographical memory include Ronald Fraser's *'In Search of a Past',* Verso, 1984, and his fine book on the Spanish Civil War, *Blood of Spain,* Penguin Books, 1981. Tony Parker's book on a London housing estate is interesting: *The People of Providence,* Hutchinson, 1983, while Liz Heron's collection of essays by women who grew up in the 1950s makes fascinating reading: *Truth, Dare or Promise,* Virago, 1985. Heinrich Boll's essay on the Second World War and how it affects his behaviour today is interesting reading: *Granta,* vol.17, pp.153-77. The recently published *Them: Voices from the Immigrant Community in Contemporary Britain* (Jonathan Green, Secker & Warburg, 1991) and *So Much to be Done* (edited by Ruth Moynihan, Susan Armitage and Christiane Fisher Deschamp, University of Nebraska Press, 1991) are also well worth acquiring.

12. From 'SOS', held at the BBC Written Archive Centre, Caversham Park, Reading RG4 8TZ.

13. William Stott, *Documentary Expression and Thirties America,* University of Chicago Press, 1973, pp. 319-20.

Bibliography

Burke, P., and Porter, P. (eds), *The Social History of Language,* Cambridge University Press, 1987.

Clanchy M.T., *From Memory to Written Record,* Edward Arnold, 1979.

Davidoff, L., and Westover,B., *Our Work,Our lives, Our Words,* Macmillan, 1986.

*Kirklees Sound Archive Catalogue,*1988, is an example of an excellent published catalogue on oral history interviews.

Lummis, T., *Listening to History,* Hutchinson, 1987.

Oral History The journal of the Oral History Society. Published from Autumn 1972 onwards.

Seldon, A., and Pappworth, J., *By Word of Mouth: Elite Oral History,* Methuen, 1983.

Thompson, P., *The Edwardians: The Remaking of British Society,* Weidenfeld, 1975.

Thompson, P., *The Voice of the Past: Oral History,* Oxford University Press, 1978.

Weevasidnghe, Lali, *Directory of Recorded Sound Resources in the the United Kingdom,* British Library, 1989.

17 Folklore and Music

Bob Bushaway

Associate Member, School of History, University of Birmingham

Introduction

The study of Britain in the past must take account of a non-material record of popular culture and its relationship to the prevailing economic and social structures of society. This evidence is not readily accessible. The social historian has more to go on for élite culture, even for comparatively early periods of British social history. The cultural accretions of the middle and upper strata of British society provide a clear record in the form of art, literature, music, systems and institutions of knowledge, of government and of religion. Information on popular culture, particularly for earlier times, is more elusive. Its unofficial and informal structures none the less reveal motives and concerns, relationships and imperatives, and forms and functions which would, otherwise, be concealed from posterity.

Popular culture can be described as the mental world of ordinary people, their interior lives and beliefs, their rituals, ceremonies and leisure pursuits, and their calendar customs and work practices. The social historian relies on the work of a range of mediators, collectors, observers, and, less sympathetically, opponents, the agents of law and of official culture such as the representatives of church and state. Rarely is there any record left by those who organised, participated in, transmitted or defended popular culture. Social historians, until recently, have left the field to others and its features are sometimes collectively referred to as 'folklore' or individually as 'folk dance', 'folk song', 'folk belief', 'folk drama' and 'folk custom'.

History and Sources

There is no single vein of material which can be quarried. The historian must draw on a variety of scattered and very different sources, such as local newspaper files, local histories and regional studies; lives, diaries and memoirs; the papers of scholarly antiquaries from previous centuries; the papers of local field clubs, natural history, archaeological or antiquary journals; the collections of folklorists in the nineteenth and twentieth centuries and of popular antiquaries in earlier centuries; criminal records; pamphlets, local ephemera, records of manor courts; church accounts; medieval archives; ballads and songs; and, for the later period, oral testimony.

The recovery of information about popular custom is, therefore, disjointed, incomplete and complex. Accounts are, most often, provided by authorities who, at best, observed customs as outsiders, or, at worst, were hostile to them.

The earliest published works were either in the form of a catalogue or dictionary, or calendar. This model has a long history, beginning with the first printed collections such as John Aubrey's *Miscellanies* (1696) or Henry Bourne's *Antiquitates Vulgares* (1725). The latter work became the foundation for several later publications culminating in Sir Henry Ellis's monumental edition of John Brand's *Observations on Popular Antiquities* (1813). Brand's work was, itself, an expansion of Bourne's earlier collection.

Folklore has rarely enjoyed academic respectability as a discipline in Britain. Before the term was coined in 1846, the field of enquiry, previously known as popular antiquities, had been left to a relatively small number of scholars.

During the nineteenth century the subject fragmented into a range of areas of investigation from calendar customs to myth and legend, to popular superstition, to folk dance and song. The foundation of the Folklore Society in 1878 represented the culmination of the efforts of several key scholars, including Andrew Lang and George Lawrence Gomme. Some argued that survival theory explained the residue of popular culture to be found largely in the fastnesses of rural England. Others argued for an ethnographic approach which catalogued surviving customs in terms of their Aryan and non-Aryan origins. Still others saw in popular culture the record of the pre-history and early history of different races in Britain. It was controversy over this view which led to the discrediting of folklore by historians.

Perhaps the most famous of the folklorists was Sir James Frazer whose monumental contribution to the subject, *The Golden Bough,* was first published in 1890 and completed in a third edition in twelve volumes (1907-15). Frazer advocated comparative methodology and drew evidence for his general theory from a wide range of differing cultures and different historical periods. This methodology was open to criticism by historians who wished to see folklorists submit their evidence to the test of historical continuity.

The foundation of the English Folk Dance and Song Society in 1911 and the work of many pioneering collectors such as Cecil Sharp, Baring Gould, Vaughan Williams and others, further isolated these elements of popular culture to the closed world of the enthusiast. Their careful piano settings and presentation of lyrics cleansed of imperfections and vulgarities were designed to suit the tastes of a largely urban, middle-class audience for ruralism.

The principal model adopted after the foundation of the Folklore Society was the county study. This tended to provide an inadequate basis for analysis but did create a large body of source material available for future study.

Other analytical approaches have since been developed, such as the study of particular types of custom, or a regional approach where evidence is gathered from similar environments, such as pastoral districts or arable farming areas, or industrial environments. Recent studies by folklorists illustrate the current trend to depart from any analysis or conclusions beyond strictly factual ones. The accuracy of the information, itself very important, has become their principal aim. This is a deliberate and conscious attempt to veer away from the large-scale hypotheses of earlier folklorists.

Since the divergence with folklorists in the late nineteenth century, social historians have been wary of material on custom and folklore. In his study of leisure and popular recreation, Robert Malcolmson has shown that, by using a social anthropological approach, much can be learned about the social function of certain forms of popular cultural activity. E.P. Thompson, in his pioneering studies of 'rough music' and of wife-sale, has shown how custom and ritual figured significantly in social relationships in the local community.

Phythian-Adams has tried to reunite folklore and local history, and his work has influenced more recent folklore scholars such as Roy Judge and E.C. Cawte, who have provided thematic studies of particular forms of popular collective behaviour.

Problems and Methodologies

Whether in the medieval, early modern or modern periods, the small amount of information on popular culture is a principal difficulty. Victorian and Edwardian collectors of folk songs and customs, who have provided a large body of material, prized their finds as precious artefacts of a way of life which they perceived as long since lost. The contexts in which their finds were made were as foreign to them as the jungles of Africa and the deserts of Asia. The folklorists' insistence on survival theory meant that popular antiquities were explored not as a part of the cultural activities of contemporaries but as evidence of society in its infancy. This was further compounded by a tendency to regard rural communities as closer to the wellsprings of mankind and, therefore, as offering a purer and less contaminated source for the collector than towns, cities and factories. Urban contexts for popular custom have proved to be valuable, as recent studies have shown, such as those by Phythian-Adams and others. Issues concerning economic relationships, the structures of power, class conflict and political consciousness were associated with town and trade, whereas the collectors preferred what they regarded as the simplicity of country life.

Other sources are scarcely less problematical. Much of our evidence for popular culture, particularly for the earlier period, is derived from legal sources. These reveal glimpses of popular imperatives and motivations but from the standpoint of official culture in the form of the church or the law.

The habit of scholars of popular antiquities of overlaying and elaborating the work of others can also cause difficulties. The apparent evidence of historical continuity can, in some cases, be revealed as mere slavish copying. An example of this is the Whit custom of bread and cheese scrambling at St Briavels which was reported, throughout the nineteenth century, in a variety of publications. On closer inspection these accounts are simple verbatim repetitions with no further corroboration. Interpretation is also crucial. The fact that a source may mention a morris dance or a mummers' play does not mean that it describes the same activity as a similar reference in a later source. Similarly, even when scientific measures are employed to deduce the age of artefacts used during collective rituals, as was the case recently with radiocarbon dating to ascertain the age of the reindeer horns used by the Abbots Bromley dancers, it should not be assumed that this addresses questions of origin or of historical continuity.

Those folklorists who search for pagan origins or look for memories of the worship of the Golden Bough are oblivious to social transformations and to the importance of the study of popular culture in context.

Folk custom ranges freely through countless centuries and carries us back to our earliest recorded beginnings, and beyond. May day retains its essentially pagan character today, as in the past, in spite of the new accretions of political processions and the like which have been imposed upon it. The people who burn the clavie at Burghead on old New Year's Eve are doing what their Stone Age ancestors did, just as, farther south and in a milder season, the inhabitants of Helston continue to bring home the summer in the Furry Dance like their far-off forefathers before them. (Hole, 1978)

Whether these assertions are accurate or not, it does an injustice to the communities of Burghead and Helston to dismiss their annual ritual collective activities as 'stone age' rather than explore the functions which they serve and how these have changed through time.

Ideas and Concepts

Any student of popular culture must consider the question as to whose culture is being studied. Who are the 'folk'? The early collectors of popular antiquities in the seventeenth and eighteenth centuries had no doubt. They were the common people – 'antiquitates vulgares' – vulgar antiquities. The term 'vulgar' is not applied derogatively but in the sense of its Latin root 'vulgare' meaning 'belonging to the common people'. The common people clearly did not include the élite nor the 'middling sort' even if, on occasion, they could be both observers and participants in the collective rituals of the common people. Another term for the 'folk', usually avoided by folklorists, is the 'working class' or, prior to the Industrial Revolution, the labouring poor, that is those who subsisted, not through ownership of property, professional skills or through the labour of others, but by sale of their own labour. For folksong collectors such as Maud Karpeles and Cecil Sharp the 'folk' were the 'peasants' – the survivors of a dying rural culture.

In another sense, the 'folk' define themselves by their relationship to those in authority in the social hierarchy. George Lawrence Gomme wrote:

Folklore consists of customs, rites, and beliefs belonging to individuals among the people, to groups of people, to inhabitants of districts or places; and belonging to them apart from and often times in definite antagonism to the accepted customs, rites and beliefs of the State or the nation to which the people and the groups of people belong. These customs, rites and beliefs are mostly kept alive by tradition. They owe their preservation partly to the fact that great masses of people do not belong to the civilisation which towers over them and which is never of their own creation. (1913)

Gomme's notion that folklore belongs to the masses in opposition to the state is close to the conclusion of the Italian Marxist, Antonio Gramsci, who wrote of folklore as:

a view of the world and of life, in great measure implicit, of certain strata (determinate in space and time) of society, in opposition (here too mostly implicit, mechanical, objective) to the 'official' views of the world (or, in a wider sense, of the cultural parts of a particular society) that have occurred through history's development. (1968)

He also refers to

... a 'popular morality', understood as a certain whole ... of maxims of practical conduct and customs ... there exist imperatives which are much stronger, more tenacious and more effectual than those of official 'morality'. (1968)

Folklore, then, can relate to opposition between official and unofficial culture. Folklore is not a matter of quaint and picturesque survivals of pre-Christian religious practices but a vital aspect of contemporary culture.

Horizontal as well as vertical relationships in society are important. Within popular culture as a whole can be found elements which constitute women's culture, men's culture and youth culture.

Folk songs, for example, were not uniform carriers of popular culture but derive from particular local circumstances or contexts. Folk songs could have significance for different groups defined by age and gender. Flora Thompson, in her description of singing 'At the "Wagon and Horses"' captures the interaction between groups of male singers differentiated by age. The young married men, 'boy-chaps', sang novel songs, often taken from the music hall, whilst the 'men of middle age' favoured 'mournful songs' or songs of a high moral tone. The old favourites would counter this mood and would give way to older singers (Thompson, 1973).

Custom was a powerful source of legitimation for the activities of the poor. Custom had a legal meaning in the sixteenth and seventeenth centuries when applied to land tenure and the relationship between the lord of the manor and his tenants. It '... is where a custom, or usage, or other things have been used, so long as a man's memory cannot remember the contrary. That is, when such matter is pleaded, that no man, in life, hath not heard anything, nor any proof to the contrary' (Calthrope, 1635). From this narrow legal meaning, the labouring poor could derive a much wider defence for their customary collective actions, whether gathering dead wood unhindered, or raising a maypole, or processing round the manor or parish. Guy Fawkes activities on 5 November and Oak Apple Day celebrations on 29 May could claim authority from no less a source than the Church of England's *Book of Common Prayer* where they were enshrined as so-called state services. Until 1859, when these two celebrations were set aside at the specific desire of Queen Victoria, the labouring poor could defend their practices by reference to older state and church authority.

In the Middle Ages, legitimation could be drawn from the practices of feudalism itself and the administration of open fields and common land. A recent piece by Rosamond Faith on fourteenth-century England illustrates the way legal disputes could result in the ritual demonstration of popular right and the maintenance of grievance across decades (Faith, 1981).

Popular custom linked together components of local community cultural life and represented, on the one hand, the symbolism of social cohesion in which the labouring poor could maintain certain popular rights and, on the other, provided opportunities for socially critical and disruptive behaviour which, in some cases, could establish a popular cultural environment for more orthodox movements of social protest throughout Britain and Ireland.

It is essential to adopt a methodological approach to popular custom in any given period of British history which recognises its centrality, locates it within a holistic structure of values, beliefs and rights which informed the lives of ordinary men and women, and identifies it as part of a process of social change and not as some distant and unchanging baseline in the past which has only antique relevance to contemporary society. Custom enabled people to adopt assertive positions, to take initiatives and to confront the prevailing structures of power and authority which constituted official culture.

During the twentieth century those possibilities continued to be available. Not to recognise this is to consign the individual and collective aspirations and perceptions of past generations to the traditions of Victorian museum curatorship or to the specialist and closed worlds of the collector, the 'folk club' or the morris team.

References

Calthrope, Charles (1635), *The Relation between the Lord of a Manor and the Copyholder his Tenant,* reprinted by The Manorial Society, London, 1917, pp. 14-15.

Faith, R. (1981), 'The class struggle in fourteenth century England', in Samuel, R. (ed.), *People's History and Socialist Theory,* History Workshop Series, Routledge, pp. 50-59.

Gomme, George Lawrence (1913), 'Folklore', in Hastings, J. (ed.), *Encyclopaedia of Religion and Ethics,* T. and T. Clark, Edinburgh.

Gramsci, Antonio (1968), Observations on 'Folklore', in Davidson, Alastair, *Antonio Gramsci: The Man, His Ideas,* Australian New Left Review Publication, pp. 86 and 87.

Hole, Christina (1973), *A Dictionary of British Folk Customs,* Paladin, p. 6.

Thompson, Flora (1973), *Larkrise to Candleford,* Worlds Classics Series, Oxford University Press, pp. 63-9. First published 1945.

Journals and Organisations

From the folklore perspective, there are the following specialist journals:

English Dance and Song

Folk Music Journal

Folklife: Journal of Ethnological Studies

Folklore: The Journal of the Folklore Society

Lore and Language : The Journal of the Centre for English Cultural Tradition and Language

Talking/Reading Folklore

Traditional Dance

Transmission: A Newsletter for Researchers of Cultural Traditions

Wiltshire Folklife

From the viewpoint of social history, the following journals are of most relevance:

Annales

History Workshop Journal.

The Journal of Peasant Studies

Past and Present : A Journal of Historical Studies

Rural History

Social History

The principal organisations concerned with 'folk culture' include:

The Folklore Society

The Library of the Folklore Society and the Vaughan Williams Memorial Library produce bibliographical leaflets from which I would cite the following as a good example: Roy Judge, *May Day in England : An Introductory Bibliography,* Vaughan Williams Memorial Library, Leaflet no. 20; Folklore Society Library, Publication no.l.

The English Folk Dance and Song Society

European Centre for Folk Studies

The Morris Ring

The Morris Federation

British Folk Studies Forum

The Centre for English Cultural Tradition and Language produces an occasional *Register of Folklore Research* and publishes many other items (University of Sheffield)

The Royal Anthropological Institute

The Society for Folklore Studies

Welsh Folk Museum, St Fagans, Cardiff

Ulster Folk and Transport Museum, Holywood, Co. Down

Museum of Mankind

Selected Bibliography

For a detailed bibliography see those in Bushaway (1982) and Malcolmson (1973) cited below:

Burke, Peter, *Popular Culture in Early Modern Europe,* Temple Smith, 1978.

Bushaway, Bob, *By Rite: Custom, Ceremony and Community in England 1700-1880,* Junction Books, 1982.

Cannadine, David, 'Civic ritual and the Colchester Oyster Feast', *Past and Present,* no. 94, February 1983, pp 3-29.

Cawte, E.C., *Ritual Animal Disguise : A Historical and Geographical Study of Animal Disguise in the*

British Isles, D. S. Brewer Ltd, and Rowman and Littlefield for the Folklore Society, 1978.

Cawte, E.C., Helm, Alex, and Peacock, M. (eds), *English Ritual Drama : A Geographical Index,* Folklore Society, 1967.

Clark, David, *Between Pulpit and Pew : Folk Religion in a North Yorkshire Fishing Village,* Cambridge University Press, 1982.

Cunningham, Hugh, *Leisure in the Industrial Revolution,* Croom Helm, 1980.

Gammon, Vic, 'Folksong collecting in Sussex and Surrey 1843-1914', *History Workshop: A Journal of Socialist Historians,* issue 10, Autumn 1980, pp. 61-89.

Harker, Dave, *Folksong: The Manufacture of British 'Folksong' 1700 to the Present Day,* Open University Press, 1983.

Hobsbawm, Eric (ed.), *Culture, Ideology and Politics,* History Workshop Series, Routledge, 1983.

Judge, Roy, *The Jack in the Green: A May Day Custom,* D. S. Brewer Ltd, and Rowman and Littlefield for the Folklore Society, 1979.

Karpeles, Maud, *An Introduction to English Folk Song,* Oxford University Press, 1987 (first published 1973).

Malcolmson, Robert, *Popular Recreations in English Society 1700-1850,* Cambridge University Press, 1973.

Phythian-Adams, Charles, *Local History and Folklore: A New Framework,* published for the Standing Conference for Local History, London, 1975.

Pickering, Michael, *Village Song and Culture in Britain,* Croom Helm, 1982.

Reid, Douglas, 'The decline of Saint Monday, 1776-1876', *Past and Present,* no. 71, May 1976, pp. 76-101.

Samuel, Raphael, *People's History and Socialist Theory,* History Workshop Series, Routledge, 1981.

Storch, Robert D. (ed.), *Popular Culture and Custom in Nineteenth Century England,* Croom Helm, 1982.

Thompson, E. P., 'Rough music: le charivari anglais', *Annales,* 1972, no. 2, pp. 285-312.

Thompson, E. P., 'The grid of inheritance : a comment', in Goodey, J., Thirsk, J., and Thompson, E. P. (eds), *Family and Inheritance : Rural Society in Western Europe 1200-1800,* Cambridge University Press, 1976.

Thompson, Flora, *Lark Rise to Candleford,* Oxford University Press, 1945. First published as *Lark Rise* (1939), *Over to Candleford* (1941), and *Candleford Green* (1943).

Turner, Victor W., *The Ritual Process : Structure and Anti-Structure,* Routledge, 1969.

Watson, Ian, *Song and Democratic Culture in Britain,* Croom Helm, 1983.

18 Landscape History

James Bond

Freelance landscape historian and field archaeologist, Tickenham, Avon

Introduction

Landscape history is a comparatively new subject; thirty years ago the term itself would barely have been understood. It is a field distinguished more by a cohesiveness of theme than by any uniqueness of methodology. It draws upon the sources and techniques of many other arts and sciences, including geology and geomorphology, botany and ecology, social and economic history, historical geography, archaeology and architectural history. Consequently it fits somewhat uneasily into the framework of traditional university teaching, and has been slow to gain acceptance in the academic world. None the less, despite this, its practitioners would see its essentially multi-disciplinary character not as a weakness, but as a source of vigour and strength. It provides an arena for exchanges of ideas between specialists who might have no other avenues of contact or communication. It is a field where scholarly research has many practical applications for those concerned with the management of land and the planning and control of land use; and, because it is concerned with the living environment of every man, woman and child, it possesses a popular interest and appeal for the layman which is unmatched by virtually any other branch of history.

The Origins of Landscape History

Although the study of landscape history in any integrated form is barely three decades old, it represents the fusion of a number of older traditions and parallel approaches. Its ultimate source comes from the long tradition of antiquarian travelogues and surveys exemplified by the writings of Leland, Norden, Camden, Lhuyd, Aubrey, Stukeley, Defoe and Celia Fiennes. This headstream was reinforced by the contributions of some of the eighteenth-century historians such as Dugdale, Thoroton and Bridges, who showed a greater awareness of topography than most of their contemporaries. By the outset of the present century some of the pioneers of modern economic history, such as Seebohm, Maitland and Tawney, were beginning to concern themselves more seriously with aspects of medieval settlement and agriculture, topics which have been a major concern of modern landscape historians.

Amongst the work of geographers, the French school of regional geography, propagated before the First World War by Vidal de la Blache, was closely linked with Febvre's philosophy of possibilism, which rejected earlier doctrines of crude physical determinism. These ideas were pursued in Britain by Fleure and his disciples. The concept of a natural (physical) landscape evolving through human modification to the present cultural (human-made) lanscape, developed in Germany in the 1920s by Schluter and Penck and in America by Sauer, has also been influential. In Britain from the 1930s onwards historical geographers were experimenting with the reconstruction of past geographies by means of horizontal chronological cross-sections, best exemplified by Darby's Domesday studies; and also with the exploration of vertical themes, in which people were seen as the principal agent of specific pieces of landscape change – woodland clearance, agricultural expansion and the development of settlements and industry – in historic times.

While archaeology was still generally dominated by the excavation of individual sites and the classification of artefacts, a significant advance was made in the 1920s and 1930s through Fox's and Crawford's application of small-scale distribution maps to interpretative studies. Moreover, the tradition of field archaeology, developed in the early years of the present century by Williams-Freeman, Sumner and Allcroft, acquired new strength and direction between the wars through the work of O.G.S. Crawford, who emphasised the value of original fieldwork linked with the study of maps, topography and aerial photography. In terms of approach, this is perhaps the most important of all the precursors to modern landscape history.

One final, generally under-rated, contribution came from the mass of popular topographical books published during the 1930s by authors such as H.J. Massingham and C. Bradley Ford, and guides such as the 'King's England' series edited by Arthur Mee. Today these works tend to be disparaged. Lyrical in style and sentimental in outlook, designed to evoke the beauty of a still-untarnished rural England, their approach is out of tune with the more rigorous, objective and scientific modes of enquiry demanded today. Though descriptive rather than analytical, and weak in historical insight, they were none the less influential in nurturing the idea of the visual attraction of the countryside as something to be cherished. They did much to awaken public sympathy towards the newly emerging conservation movement and prepared the ground for the practical application of more serious landscape research.

The effective foundation of landscape history as an integrated field of study in England can be attributed to W.G. Hoskins, whose pioneer study, *The Making of the English Landscape*, was first published in 1955. This one book has inspired succeeding generations of scholars and has been directly responsible for the tremendous flowering of landscape studies over the last three decades. Although inevitably now in some respects dated, it remains essential reading; the most recent edition, while preserving intact Hoskins' original text, incorporates a brief commentary by Christopher Taylor summarising later changes in thinking

The expansion in popularity of landscape history has been encouraged through adult education classes, television programmes and the publication of numerous books and articles, and has been consolidated by the foundation in 1979 of the Society for Landscape Studies, publishing its own annual journal, *Landscape History*. Where museums are concerned, perhaps its chief potential lies in graphic displays as a basis for exhibition, providing an effective background and context for artefacts which at one time would have been shown in isolation.

Themes and Approaches in Landscape History

Although Hoskins' seminal volume in 1955 was an historical study adopting a fundamentally chronological structure, it none the less represented a significant departure from the traditional approaches and subject matter of social, political and economic history. Hoskins was concerned with 'the ways in which men have cleared the natural woodlands; reclaimed marshland, fen and moor; created fields out of a wilderness; made lanes, roads and footpaths; laid out towns, built villages, hamlets, farms and cottages; created country houses and their parks; dug mines, and made canals and railways; in short, with everything that has altered the natural landscape'. In particular, Hoskins stressed the importance of the landscape not just as a subject to be studied, but as a source in its own right. His oft-quoted declaration that 'The English landscape itself, to those who know how to read it aright, is the richest historical record we possess. There are discoveries to be made in it for which no written documents exist, or have ever existed' has remained a tenet of faith for landscape historians ever since. The importance of observation in the field, derived from the tradition of field archaeology, has been stressed in several of his other books and developed further in the writings of archaeologists such as Aston and Rowley (1974).

Hoskins recognised and stressed the great regional variety of the English landscape, and the publishers of *The Making of the English Landscape* initiated a series of county volumes, of which more than twenty have now been published. Landscape history has subsequently been a major component of regional series initiated by several other publishers.

Other important contributions have been period based, though taking a broader perspective than the horizontal section approach in order to illustrate the dynamics of change (Cantor, 1982, 1987). Some period studies have made graphic use of the evidence from aerial photographs (e.g. Beresford and St. Joseph, 1958).

Hoskins was concerned with the totality of the visible landscape rather than with the history of particular aspects; but each of the subordinate themes which he listed have themselves subsequently become the subjects of further more specialised studies. New areas of research have opened up which were hardly dreamed of in the 1950s, and much more thought has been devoted to the practical application of landscape history research. Only a very brief outline of some of the more important recent developments can be given here.

Recent Developments in Landscape History

As Hoskins himself has readily admitted since, in the 1950s he underestimated the significance of the prehistoric and Roman contribution to the landscape because, in many parts of the country, it was not immediately obvious. The intensification of archaeological survey and excavation in advance of major development schemes such as motorways and new towns during the 1960s and 1970s, aided by the realisation of the true potential of aerial photography, and the development of palaeobotanical studies, has overturned this view. Today no valid attempt to understand the landscape could be made without reference to its prehistoric beginnings.

Since the mid-1960s there has been increasing liaison with the work of natural scientists. Hoskins himself made contact with Max Hooper of the Natural Environment Research Council, who was beginning to develop the idea that hedgerows could be dated by means of their shrub species content. The recognition that the flora of ancient woodland and undisturbed pasture and meadowland could be a source of historical information as well as of botanical interest has been expressed in many subsequent publications (e.g. Rackham, 1986).

Amongst the specific themes listed by Hoskins, particularly important advances have been made in the study of woodland, which, until comparatively recently, was generally neglected by historians and human geographers. Woodlands had tended to be viewed only as negative areas still untouched by the processes of human settlement and agricultural expansion, remnants of the primeval climax vegetation which were of no interest or value until they were cleared and cultivated. Attitudes have changed since the 1950s in two principal respects. Firstly, the results of intensified archaeological field survey, aerial photography and palaeobotanical work have demolished the traditional view that the impression made upon the primeval woodland by early settlers was limited and that vast tracts survived to be cleared by the Anglo-Saxon settlers. Much of the woodland which existed in the Middle Ages is now understood to be secondary regrowth over land which had formerly been cleared, settled and cultivated. Secondly, there is now a much better understanding of the natural vegetation, structure and management and economic value of woodland since the Anglo-Saxon period, thanks largely to the work of Rackham. It is now recognised that even the most extensive medieval forests were not featureless, indeterminate wildernesses, but possessed considerable internal landscape variety, with areas of open wood-pasture or lawns used for grazing, separating coppices enclosed for wood production, and parks enclosed for deer. Woodland boundaries in many cases have remained remarkably stable from the early middle ages to the nineteenth century, when traditional woodmanship began to decline with the rise of commercial forestry (Rackham, 1986, and other publications by the same author).

Moorland and marshland have been less fully explored. Certain areas of marshland such as the Fens and the Somerset Levels have been studied in some detail, but apart from one collection of essays (Rowley, 1979), there has as yet been no synthesis or overview of marshland landscapes.

Much more attention has been paid to the evolution and regional variety of field systems, and there have been several recent summaries (e.g. Taylor, 1975). For the lowland zone of Britain a fundamental distinction has been drawn between the so-called 'Planned Countryside' of the east and south midlands and the 'Ancient Countryside' of the Welsh borders, the south-west and the south-east. In the 'Planned Countryside' there was some Tudor enclosure associated with village depopulation and conversion to pasture, and further enclosure by agreement after the sixteenth century, but extensive open fields survived up to the period of Parliamentary enclosure, when they were superseded by hawthorn-hedged rectangular closes. The origin of open field systems in this zone has come under renewed scrutiny, and it is no longer believed that they were a mass import by the first generations of Anglo-Saxon settlers; instead they seem to have evolved slowly out of earlier types of fields, perhaps not achieving their fully-developed form until after the Norman Conquest. In the 'Ancient Countryside', by contrast, the pre-Roman origin of some of the rectilinear field patterns still in use has now been convincingly demonstrated.

Considerable advances have been made in the study of both rural and urban settlements. In the 1950s, in defiance of the prevailing academic orthodoxy, M.W. Beresford was able to demonstrate through a combination of documentary research and fieldwork that deserted medieval villages were an extremely widespread phenomenon, thereby establishing a major new theme of settlement studies. Surveys of existing villages have transformed earlier notions of stability of site and plan, showing instead widespread evidence of fundamental changes, involving shrinkage, movement and replanning. While this necessitates the rejection of some of the earlier simplistic notions of village origins based upon morphological classification, morphological studies are still of value on their own terms with firmer principles established. Above all, the large nucleated village of the 'Planned Countryside' can no longer be seen as the medium by which the early English settlers colonised a sparsely populated wilderness; it now appears to be the product of late Saxon and post-Conquest reorganisations of settlement taking place within a pre-existing framework of much older estates. Dispersed forms of settlement associated with the 'Ancient Countryside' have so far received less investigation than nucleated villages. Various recent views on the evolution of rural settlement are expressed in Taylor (1983), Hooke (1988) and Aston, Austin and Dyer (1989).

A number of general surveys of urban landscapes have now been published (e.g. Aston and Bond, 1976; Lloyd, 1984), and several more specific aspects have received attention. The problems of Anglo-Saxon town origins and their precursors as central places have been a major concern (Haslam, 1984). For the post-Conquest period, Beresford's definition of the class of medieval new towns and his demonstration of the importance of medieval town planning has been of fundamental importance (Beresford, 1967). In the light of his work, the techniques of investigating urban morphology developed by Conzen have taken on a new significance (Whitehand, 1981). More recently Slater has demonstrated the potential which lies in the analysis of burgage patterns (Slater, 1981). Archaeological surveys and excavation reports necessitated by redevelopment have contributed an enormous amount of new information on urban origins, economy and topography (summarised most recently in Schofield and Leech, 1987).

Many other themes of landscape history – religious buildings, precincts and estates, communication, domestic and agricultural buildings, parks and country houses, industrial landscapes – have also been much advanced by recent work, but cannot be discussed here.

By its very nature landscape history remains a practical subject concerned with concrete reality. Pragmatic and empirical in its techniques, it has not so far generated much theoretical or methodological writing. None the less, it cannot remain untouched by progress in geography and archaeology, which have seen the old preoccupation with classification give way to model-based paradigms. There is an unfortunate tendency for the promise of such new approaches to be disguised behind almost impenetrable jargon, but some aspects have recently been explored in layman's terms by Aston (1985).

Finally, since the mid-1970s there has been a growing body of opinion that landscape history should not remain a mere academic study or popular pastime, but should be made relevant to the problems of the present, and to the needs of conservation in particular. This has been endorsed by its gradual incorporation into the planning process (Rowley and Breakell, 1975-77; Baker, 1983) and its application to land management. The Historic Landscapes Steering Group was founded in 1978 with the aims of developing and applying methods of landscape identification, recording, evaluation, interpretation and management (Brandon and Millman, 1978, 1980). An important part here can be played by the County Sites and Monuments Records. In England 20 per cent of these are museum based, the remainder mostly in planning departments. Initially conceived as dealing only with archaeological 'sites' in the narrow sense, many such databases have broadened their scope to become more comprehensive records of the historic landscape. While this is to be welcomed, the range of demands and advisory functions which can stem from the operation of such records carries many implications for the work of those museums in which they are based.

References

There is now a vast literature on landscape history, and only a few of the key works have been referred to in the chapter; many of them contain extensive bibliographies. The journal *Landscape History* is the only periodical to deal specifically with the subject, but there are also numerous relevant papers in national and local archaeological, historical and geographical journals.

Aston, Michael, (1985), *Interpreting the Landscape: Landscape Archaeology in Local Studies*, Batsford.

Aston, Michael, Austin, David, and Dyer, Christopher (eds) (1989), *The Rural Settlements of Medieval England*, Basil Blackwell.

Aston, Michael, and Bond, James (1976), *The Landscape of Towns*, J.M. Dent & Sons.

Aston, Michael, and Rowley, Trevor (1974), *Landscape Archaeology: An Introduction to Fieldwork Techniques on Post-Roman Landscapes*, David & Charles.

Baker, David (1983), *Living with the Past: The Historic Environment*, Bletsoe, privately published.

Beresford, Maurice (1967), *New Towns of the Middle Ages: Town Plantation in England, Wales and Gascony*, Lutterworth Press.

Beresford, M.W., and St. Joseph, J.K.S. (1958), *Medieval England: An Aerial Survey* Cambridge University Press, 2nd ed. 1979.

Brandon, Peter, and Millman, Roger (eds) (1978), *Historic Landscapes: Identification, Recording, Management*, Department of Geography, Polytechnic of North London.

Brandon, Peter, and Millman, Roger (eds) (1980), *Recording Historic Landscapes: Principles and Practice,* Department of Geography, Polytechnic of North London.

Cantor, Leonard (ed.) (1982), *The English Medieval Landscape*, Croom Helm,

Cantor, Leonard (1987), *The Changing English Countryside, 1400-1700,* Routledge.

Haslam, Jeremy (ed.) (1984), *Anglo-Saxon Towns in Southern England*, Phillimore, Chichester.

Hooke, Della (ed.) (1988), *Anglo-Saxon Settlements,* Basil Blackwell.

Hoskins, W.G. (1955), *The Making of the English Landscape*, Hodder & Stoughton.

Lloyd, David W. (1984), *The Making of English Towns: 2000 Years of Evolution*, Victor Gollancz Ltd & Peter Crawley.

Rackham, Oliver (1986), *The History of the Countryside,* J.M. Dent & Sons.

Rowley, Trevor (ed.) (1979), *The Evolution of Marshland Landscapes*, University of Oxford, Department for External Studies.

Rowley, Trevor, and Breakell, Mike (eds) (1975-7), *Planning and the Historic Environment*, 2 vols, University of Oxford, Department for External Studies, and Oxford Polytechnic, Department of Town Planning.

Schofield, John, and Leech, Roger (eds) (1987), *Urban Archaeology in Britain*, Research Report no. 61, Council for British Archaeology, London.

Slater, T. R. (1981), 'The analysis of burgage plots in medieval towns', *Area*, vol. xiii, pp. 211-16.

Taylor, Christopher (1975), *Fields in the English Landscape,* J.M. Dent & Sons.

Taylor, Christopher (1983), *Village and Farmstead: A History of Rural Settlement in England*, George Phillip & Sons.

Whitehand J.W.R. (ed.) (1981), *The Urban Landscape: Historical Development and Management: Papers by M.R.G. Conzen*, Academic Press/Institute of British Geographers Special Publications no.13.

19　Maps

James Bond

*Freelance landscape historian and field archaeologist,
Tickenham, Avon*

Introduction

Over the centuries many different classes of maps have been made for many
different purposes, and they can be used in a variety of ways. Their most
superficial function is merely decorative, filling blank spaces in museum displays
or adorning the covers of publications. Some maps can be used for finding one's
way around the country. As a research tool, small-scale maps can be used for
plotting distributions, while large-scale maps provide a base for locating areas of
natural history interest or archaeological sites within Environmental or Sites and
Monuments Records. Maps can also be used as a primary source of historical
evidence.

Any map potentially has value for the historian as a depiction of some part of
the landscape at some point in time. A sequence of maps of different dates
covering the same area ought to provide a record of significant changes in the
landscape. Large-scale maps may provide a record of ancient parish and
township boundaries, town, village and farm plans, ownership, tenancy, land
use, field boundaries, field size and field names, and a wide miscellany of other
topographical features. However, like any other historical source, maps cannot
always be taken at face value and must be used with caution. Early maps in
particular are affected by variable standards of accuracy, by the cartographer's
often idiosyncratic selection of the features to be depicted, and by rampant
plagiarism which resulted in the transmission of errors and the generation of
anachronisms. Some knowledge of the specific purposes for which maps were
made and some understanding of the evolution of survey techniques is essential
to their critical appreciation and use.

Medieval Maps

The first maps of Britain to provide any sort of accurate topographical detail
were those produced by Matthew Paris in the middle of the thirteenth century.
Four versions are extant, one of them annotated with a rather appealing apology
for squashing the shape of the island because of the limited length of the page.
The basis of Paris's maps is almost certainly a written itinerary, for all the details
are fitted around a vertical spine of place-names from Newcastle to Dover. Even
better known is the so-called Gough Map of *c.*1360, named after the antiquarian
who first drew attention to it. This shows a network of major roads over much
of England and Wales, 40 per cent of them of Roman origin. The position of
many towns is shown in their correct relationship, but again it is to be regarded
as a series of linked itineraries, rather like the London Transport tube map,
rather than as an attempt at a true geographical depiction.

Although medieval land surveys produced far more written descriptions and
perambulations than cartographic representations, over 30 large-scale local maps
and plans are now known for Britain, and further examples almost certainly
await discovery. Monasteries were important disseminators of cartographic
techniques. The earliest detailed English local plan known dates from *c.*1165,

depicting Prior Wibert's new water supply at Canterbury Cathedral Priory. A thirteenth-century diagram of the water pipe to Waltham Abbey showing the springs and settling tanks has the earliest known direction pointer, aimed east towards Jerusalem. Another early map illustrating a boundary dispute at Wildmore Fen in Lincolnshire in c.1224-49 was copied into a Kirkstead Abbey psalter. Increasing numbers of maps survive from the mid-fourteenth century. Many of them were drawn to support disputed property claims and cannot be regarded as wholly unbiased sources of evidence. None the less, they often show a wealth of incidental topographical detail, such as the barn, watermills and bridge on a mid-fifteenth-century plan in the Chertsey Abbey cartulary. An early example of a private estate plan, drawn up for Edmund Rede, lord of Boarstall (Buckinghamshire) in 1444, shows the complete layout of the now almost deserted village site with its surrounding fields and woods.

County Maps

For many English counties over a hundred separate maps were published between the late sixteenth and mid-nineteenth centuries. The first major series was produced by Christopher Saxton, who was granted special facilities by the Privy Council in the 1570s to survey every county for the publication of a projected atlas of England and Wales. Saxton's maps are of little use for detailed topographical reconstruction, but they do portray features such as deer parks and churches which may not survive. They continued to be published in various formats and with minor amendments into the following century. The next county atlas was John Speed's *Theatre of the Empire of Great Britain,* published in 1611; this proved far more popular than his *History* for which it was intended only as a supplement, and subsequent editions were still being issued as late as the 1770s. Speed's county maps were based largely upon Saxton, with the addition of the hundred boundaries, but his inset plans of the county towns were an original contribution. Most of the numerous county maps and atlases published during the seventeenth century were little more than plagiarised versions of Saxton or Speed, their only original content being their marginal decoration. Increasing dissatisfaction with this state of affairs produced some innovations, such as the addition of main roads from Ogilby's surveys, first incorporated on Robert Morden's playing-card maps of 1676. Larger scales appeared: Gascoyne's map of Cornwall (1700) was the first to be published at one inch to the mile. Beighton's map of Warwickshire (1725) was the first to be based upon trigonometric survey. The demand for better maps increased after the 1740s, with agricultural and industrial innovations promoting trade and improved transport facilities, which in turn allowed scholars and tourists to discover a new interest in the landscape. Local subscriptions were raised to support new surveys. Many of the new county map-makers were not trained as topographical surveyors, but came from other backgrounds – landscape gardening, the army, the enclosure commissions – which had the relevant practical skills, and they were able to take full advantage of the more advanced survey techniques and instruments now available. In 1760 the Society of Arts offered a £100 prize for an accurate survey of any county on a scale of one inch to the mile. Another significant event was the endorsement by the Ordnance Board of the National Trigonometric survey promoted by the Royal Society in 1791. The last generation of independent county cartographers was able to exploit the new data to good effect. Prominent amongst them was Christopher Greenwood, who covered most of England and Wales between 1817 and 1834; but private surveyors were now in direct competition with the government's maps, and their days were numbered.

Estate Maps

Private estate maps begin to appear in quantity from the middle of the sixteenth century, and they continue to be a useful source well into the Victorian period. The rapid upsurge in their generation is clearly related to contemporary technical advances in plane surveying, the emergence of professional surveyors like Ralph Agas and Thomas Langdon, and the rapid dissemination of the new techniques by the publication of textbooks such as Valentin Leigh's *Surveying of Landes* (1577) and John Norden's *Surveior's Dialogue* (1607). Even then the detailed large-scale plan tended still to be regarded as an illustrative supplement to, rather than a replacement for, the written description. In 1966 it was estimated that there were over 20,000 private estate maps dating from before 1850. The real total is certainly much greater, but is almost impossible to ascertain, since although many are now in public repositories, others remain in private hands where their accessibility to scholars and even their continued survival cannot be guaranteed. Estate maps vary enormously in character, some covering single small farms, others great estates extending over many parishes. They may include valuable elevation or perspective views of prominent buildings such as the church or manor house. Some late sixteenth and seventeenth-century surveys distinguished the walling and roofing materials and the number of storeys of buildings in villages. Pre-enclosure estate plans may enable entire systems of strip fields to be reconstructed and compared with surviving evidence of ridge and furrow or strip lynchets. Plans of enclosed landscapes provide a *terminus ante quem* for the field boundaries shown, and offer possibilities of checking hedge dates determined by botanical or other means. On big estates, plans for landscaping schemes will often be encountered. Field-names on estate maps provide evidence of contemporary and former land use (hopyards, vineyards, places where crops such as sainfoin have been grown) and clues to the location of archaeological sites (ancient settlement sites with names like Blacklands, Roman villa sites called Chessels, deserted medieval villages in fields called Old Town). In using estate maps as historical evidence it is particularly important to know the purpose for which they were drawn. It is all too easy to infer village shrinkage from gaps shown on estate maps, whereas some houses were simply not mapped because they were in different ownership and of no interest to whoever commissioned the survey. Similarly, the later destruction of grand landscaping schemes shown on maps can be inferred whereas they never progressed beyond the paper.

Enclosure Maps

The procedure of enclosure under a private Act of Parliament produced an award detailing the reallocation of land, and about half of the enrolled awards have accompanying maps. These vary considerably in character, depending upon the precise date and nature of the enclosure. Occasionally the pattern of new roads, close boundaries and drains was drawn over a plan of pre-enclosure arable strips and common pastures. Most county record offices have some sort of guide or index to the enclosure and tithe maps in their custody.

Tithe Maps

The widespread but cumbersome system of paying tithes in kind was replaced with a money payment under the Tithe Commutation Act of 1836. Between that date and 1851 tithe surveys were prepared for some 11,800 parishes or townships in England and Wales, over three-quarters of the total land area; the programme did not extend to Scotland, and did not include areas where the tithes had been commuted on enclosure. The survey documents comprised an apportionment schedule, detailing for each parcel of land the owner, occupier, field-name, land use, acreage and new tithe rental, accompanied by an accurate, detailed, large-scale map.

Transport Maps

The use of maps as travel guides is first manifested by the publication in 1675 of John Ogilby's *Britannia,* a diagrammatic survey of main roads which contains much incidental topographical detail, including a convention for whether the road passed through enclosed or unenclosed countryside. There is a vast range of maps connected with proposed transport improvements – turnpike roads, canals and railways – and other public utilities, which must be sought out by local enquiry.

Town Plans

Tudor bird's eye views or picture maps exist for a number of English towns, such as Faversham (*c.*1514), Dover (1543), Ashbourne (1547), Great Yarmouth (*c.*1585) and Chelmsford (1591). Some of these, such as Agas's plan of Oxford (1578) are remarkably detailed and accurate for their date. Portsmouth, because of its military importance, is especially well endowed, with no less than 22 maps from the sixteenth century alone. The first atlas of European town plans published by Braun and Hogenberg between 1572 and 1598 includes surveys of London, Canterbury, Exeter, Oxford, Cambridge, Ely, Norwich, Chester and York. John Speed included plans of 73 towns in England and Wales as insets to his county maps. The later seventeenth century saw little improvement in standards, but more accurate maps were beginning to appear after the 1730s, including John Rocque's plans of Bristol (1742), Exeter (1744), Shrewsbury (1746) and London (1746).

Ordnance Survey Maps

William Roy's map of the Scottish highlands, prepared for the military authorities to assist the process of pacification after the 1745 uprising, led him in 1763 to propose a complete government sponsored survey of the whole county. Before his death in 1790 he had constructed the line on Hounslow Heath which was to be the base for the triangulation. The Ordnance Survey was founded in 1791, and ten years later the first one inch to the mile map of Kent was published. An invaluable summary of the full range of Ordnance Survey maps published since 1791 is given by Harley and Phillips (1964).

Reference

Harley, J.B., and Phillips, C.W. (1964), *The Historian's Guide to Ordnance Survey Maps*, Standing Conference for Local History.

Bibliography

Periodicals dealing specifically with maps include *Imago Mundi*, the *Cartographic Journal* and the *Map Collector;* there are also relevant papers in the *Geographical Journal*. Many of the volumes listed below contain full bibliographies.

Harley, J.B., *Maps for the Local Historian: A Guide to the British Sources*, Standing Conference for Local History, 1972.

Harley, J.B., and Phillips, C.W., *The Historian's Guide to Ordnance Survey Maps*, Standing Conference for Local History, 1964.

Harvey, P.D.A., *The History of Topographical Maps: Symbols, Pictures ad Surveys*, Thames & Hudson, 1980.

Hindle, Paul, *Maps for Local History*, Batsford, 1987.

Skelton, R.A., and Harvey, P.D.A., *Local Maps and Plans from Medieval England*, Oxford University Press, 1980.

Smith, David, *Antique Maps of the British Isles*, 1982.

Smith, David, *Maps and Plans for the Local Historian and Collector*, Batsford, 1988.

20 Excavation Archaeology

Michael Farley

County Archaeologist, Buckinghamshire County Museum Service

It is unlikely that social history curators will themselves be undertaking archaeological excavation, although they may well have a substantial contribution to make to the archaeological process. For some, archaeology is merely a rather messy and imprecise aspect of 'history', for others both process and product have an attractiveness hard to resist. This chapter seeks to explain something of archaeological method and to show how the social history curator may, with caution, utilise its products.

Only a relatively small proportion of archaeologists are directly involved with excavation, in fact a smaller percentage than was once the case. Archaeologists are to be found working in museums, planning departments, for developers, as consultants, within English Heritage, the Welsh Office and SDD, the Royal Commissions, universities, the National Trust, and increasingly with independent units and trusts. The funding of archaeological work is correspondingly diverse; many excavation units, now almost totally dependent on 'developer funding' of their work programme, function like professional businesses.

The principal objective of all archaeologists in whatever field they operate is conservation of 'the past', however defined, which is regarded as a scarce and non-renewable resource. This objective has been enshrined in the Code of Conduct of the Institute of Field Archaeologists, a body consisting largely of professional archaeologists whose members' interests are far broader than the title would suggest. It is recognised that excavation is amongst the most destructive of archaeological investigative processes, however well carried out, and hence the majority of excavations are carried out in advance of the unavoidable destruction of a site once other options have failed. A recent trend is for small-scale 'evaluation' excavations to be executed, often at the request of planning authorities with the aim of testing the extent and survival of a site before determining planning applications which might affect it. There are proportionally a very limited number of pure 'research' excavations, and never is a site dug simply because 'it's there'. This is a constant source of puzzlement to the public at large who tend to presume that if a site is known but has not been excavated, it must in some way be unimportant.

The process of excavation is but one of a range of methods which may be used by archaeologists to elucidate the past, alongside documentary research, electronic survey, fieldwalking, aerial photography and many other techniques, a number of which are also familiar to social historians. It is now widely recognised that it is the total historic environment which must be considered, not just a below-ground remnant. The artificial division between buildings and below-ground 'sites', is seen as an irrelevant distinction. Landscape is, after all, organic. The same piece of land has been subject to constantly changing use over millennia; some of these activities may be documented, but the majority not. An archaeological investigation of whatever kind and wherever conducted is necessarily the exploration of only one small part of an interlocking complex, and although the term 'site' is common in archaeological literature its limitations are well understood topographically and also, perhaps of particular significance for social history curators, chronologically.

A few decades ago there was little recognised 'archaeology' later than the Saxon period, with the exception of the archaeological study of standing structures, especially churches. During the 1950s the relevance of archaeology to the medieval period came to be more fully appreciated, and since then the application of archaeological method, including excavation, to the post-medieval period, has also become fully accepted. Seen once as merely providing purely illustrative material, archaeological techniques can demonstrably provide data about the parts which existing documentation may not reach, to borrow a phrase.

With the professional conservation ethic firmly in mind, no archaeologist undertakes an excavation lightly since the fact that it is destructive brings heavy responsibilities. Each 'site', however common it may be as a class of monument, remains unique locally, and many sites will have regional or even national significance. Nevertheless, since the location and character of an excavation is commonly determined by its imminent destruction and funds are never boundless, difficult decisions have to be made over the extent of the area to be examined and the deployment of resources required to carry out effective recording. The overriding requirement will be to maximise information retrieval. Part, but only part, of the product will be in the form of objects. Archaeologists, like social history curators, are as much concerned with 'context' (Suggitt, 1987).

The means by which soil is moved during an excavation may differ according to the character of the deposit, its depth, whether it is rural or urban, or on land or under water. Some excavations are of necessity highly mechanised, moving hundreds of tons of soil with machinery, whereas at the other extreme, for example with cave site excavation, the removal of a few cubic centimetres a year may represent good progress. Whatever the process used, any excavation generates a substantial amount of local interest, and most archaeological organisations will be keen to exploit all the media opportunities which this presents. Local museum-based colleagues can frequently provide assistance in this respect, both with display expertise and occasionally space.

A wide range of specialists are likely to be involved both with the excavation and post-excavation process, depending on the character of the site. There are indeed few sciences or other specialisms which at some point or another have not contributed something to the products of excavation. Although the skills of surgeons and pathologists, called on in the study of the recently discovered Lindow man, may be needed rarely, soil scientists, petrologists, physicists, chemists, biologists, historians, finds specialists and conservators are frequent contributors. With the constant objective of maximising information from the available evidence, this is such a live area that it is hard to predict which disciplines may next become involved. Some specialists operate as independent archaeological consultants, others give their time out of interest, but particularly significant contributions come from national specialist laboratories such as that, for example, of English Heritage, and those of university departments. Some specialists who are in particular demand, for instance those dealing with animal bone, are employed directly by the larger archaeological units. The role of the archaeologist, in what may emerge as a complex inter-disciplinary situation, is to attempt to develop a substantive view, and to ensure publication of a coherent result.

The end product of archaeological excavation consists broadly of three classes of material. The first, and most significant, will be the final report itself. Because of the often substantial time lapse between completion of work in the field and publication of a final report, most organisations produce interim reports likely to be of some value to social history curators. However, it will be the final report, with its extensive specialist contributions, which will be of most significance in interpreting and presenting the results to the general public.

The second class of material is the finds. The character of archaeological finds is diverse and frequently presents both accessioning and storage problems for museums. Only a small percentage of the product will ever be suitable for display and the majority – in particular the bulk finds such as ceramic, bone, etc – will become principally a research archive for students and specialists. There is continuing debate within the museum world over the costs of storing bulk finds, but on academic grounds total retention has to be the norm. Accompanying the objects will normally be the third class of material, namely the excavation 'archive'. This is the comprehensive record made on site and subsequently during the post-excavation process. Archaeologists are nationally encouraged to deposit this material with the finds. The archive may consist of anything from A4 files to rolls of drawings, photographs, slides and negatives, as well as computer discs and printouts. The archive brings with it a responsibility since it has to be curated along with the finds and provides not only the key to understanding the objects in their contexts, but also to future re-interpretation of the site.

The delay between the execution of fieldwork, with its associated public interest, and the production of a usable final report, is often a source of frustration to the general public and to others. The initial delay arises from the execution of the necessary post-excavation programme on the material; inevitably the larger the project and the greater the number of specialists involved the greater the delay in the production process itself. Subsequent editing and delays in printing can all have unfortunate knock-on effects on schedules. There is little that a social history curator who is keen to utilise the information can do about this, but the majority of archaeologists are well aware of the problem and will willingly respond to interested enquirers and, as already noted, most excavators produce interim reports. It is to be hoped that the trend towards rapid interim publications is continuing – the York Archaeological Trust's booklet *Interim*, for example, is an excellent example of this approach. However, so far as the social history curator in search of information is concerned, there is no substitute for a direct approach to the excavation unit involved. Apart from providing information, it will frequently also be possible, subject to the post-excavation programme, for samples of relevant material to be made available for display.

Despite production delays the published annual output of archaeological reports is nevertheless prodigious. Often the only way to track down specific areas of interest is by direct bookshelf search, by personal contact, or through *British Archaeological Abstracts* (shortly to become the *British Archaeological Bibliography*), published twice yearly by the Council for British Archaeology. Plans are afoot for computerisation of this excellent publication which will considerably enhance its value as a research tool. A glance at *Abstracts* will show that although there are specific journals dealing with particular periods, namely the *Proceedings of the Prehistoric Society, Britannia, Medieval Archaeology,* and *Post-Medieval Archaeology,* there are also three major multi-period journals, the journals of Scotland, Ireland, and Wales, many county and regional journals, as well as research report series published by the Council for British Archaeology, the Society of Antiquaries of London and others, and this list is far from complete. A useful general view of what is going on in British archaeology, if occasionally idiosyncratic, can be gained from *Current Archaeology*, and from a more international standpoint from *Antiquity*.

The lay reader of any of these published works may be surprised to discover that excavation reports tend to be full of observed 'facts', but are often short on conclusions and interpretative comment. This can make them frustrating to use as sources for social history. Archaeology, with its strong roots in scientific methodology, is not, of course, unique in this cautious approach. To a minority of archaeologists, the presentation of 'facts' from an excavation is thought sufficient to justify the work, but the majority who do venture further are well aware that even a 'simple' archaeological interpretation may be open to challenge. For example, whilst it may be easy to demonstrate the existence of a circular building and to describe its structure, it may be less easy to demonstrate its function, unless for example it should happen to have contained a distinct group of associated artefacts. Even under these circumstances the possibility that the deposition of the objects was secondary to the working life of the building has still to be considered. There is an understandable reluctance to produce simplistic but highly questionable conclusions, but this lack of firm interpretation can be dispiriting to non-archaeologists seeking certainties. Working within documented periods, archaeological interpretation may be on stronger ground, although the match between the two classes of evidence is not always straightforward. Archaeologists, like historians, also recognise that for better or worse their interpretations are influenced by current conceptual models. For this reason amongst others, it is worth warning against the uncritical use of synthetic general works on archaeology more than a few years old.

The manner in which chronological terms are used by archaeologists in reports deserves a word of explanation since it often puzzling to non-specialists. For prehistoric periods, a date within a few centuries is often the best which can be achieved – '7th-5th century BC' would not be unusual, or 'early second millennium' – whereas for the Romano-British period a date within half a century would be more common. For the Saxon/Early Medieval period a date within half a century or closer is sometimes possible, but commonly for the earlier phase, particularly for domestic sites, 'sixth century' would be usual. Even in the full medieval period a date range of half a century is commonly used, except where the work was in connection with documented structures or events. It may be surprising that archaeologists continue to use general terms e.g. 'late eighteenth-century', when historically it is known what was happening on say, 23 June 1783! A full explanation of this would require a book on its own, but in brief such 'archaeological' dates depend on the particular dating method available for a specific site, on the margin of uncertainty inherent in that method, and, of course, on the context of the object or event being dated. Historical events which are discernible in the archaeological record, such as the Great Fire of London of September 1666, the sinking of the *Mary Rose* on 19 July 1545, or the documented demolition of a particular building, provide a welcome relief.

Even here, although such dates provide precise 'terminal' dates for a deposit, it has always to be borne in mind that they can rarely provide comparable precision for the beginning, since as we are surrounded by artefacts of varying age even a closely dated 'final' event will inevitably envelop both new and old. This familiar archaeological problem is one reason why archaeological excavation may have disappointingly little to contribute, for example, to the study of eighteenth-century diet in towns, except in exceptional circumstances. Even when animal bone accompanied by datable objects has been located in a suitable deposit, for example, within a pit in a garden belonging to a known occupier, there remains a chance that the act of digging the pit disturbed previously discarded bone from an earlier date, which would subsequently have become incorporated into the backfilling of the later pit, thus complicating an apparently neat story. Should such a deposit be discovered, say, within a short-lived fort constructed on previously open land, deductions on diet may be more reliable. Each deposit has therefore to be assessed on its merit.

Whilst on the theme of dating, it is worth noting that radiocarbon determinations are generally of little assistance in dating deposits from recent centuries since radiocarbon dates have of necessity to be expressed within a range of probability, and become of greatest value where a margin of a century or so is acceptable.

So far it has been the writer's intention to clarify the ground rules of the archaeologist's approach to fieldwork, and to define some of the limitations of its product. The final section will be more positive and illustrate a few examples from the vast range of material produced by the archaeologist and associated specialist which may be of interest to social history curators. In general where material relevant to the immediate locality is available this is often the most valuable, partly because of its particular public appeal, but also since strong regional variations are frequently apparent in the archaeological record. The diet of wealthy Londoners, for example, as reflected in bone, seed and shell deposits is likely to be more exotic than that of the villagers of Wharram Percy in East Yorkshire, and different again from that of the inhabitants of Aylesbury.

Where surviving documentation can be married with the archaeological field record then the results can be of great interest. In general terms this has been achieved in Exeter where Allen (1984) has used customs accounts, probate inventories and Port Books to map the spread of wealth across the city and to observe changing social styles, such as would have followed the arrival of ceramic drinking cups by c. 1500. Exotic imports were found to link closely with larger properties, and the arrival of glass both for windows and for drinking vessels can be seen to have a restricted distribution in the city. A small but interesting detail is that the leather shoes of adults of the fourteenth-to-sixteenth-century period were found to be discarded only when they were 'utterly beyond repair'. A generalised study of the animal bone from a number of sites in Southampton and in its Saxon predecessor Hamwih (Bourdillon, 1980), gives clear indications of the prosperity of the Saxon town, its inhabitants eating joints from cattle of good size but being relatively unadventurous for a seaside port in their choice of fish, eating mainly eel, plaice and flounder, and some oysters. Game was rarely eaten, and perhaps less available. On the other hand, fowl were common, but they were small.

The Southampton study provides a generalised conclusion about the town as a whole. In a number of instances the diet of those in specific properties can be considered, such as the occupants of the Greyfriars in the City of London. This produced a rich faunal group dumped into a well in the friars' garden, which had fallen into disuse in the late fifteenth century and been infilled shortly afterwards (Armitage and West et al., 1985). The deposit showed that beef was the principal meat eaten by the occupants – although often of second-class quality – followed by small quantities of mutton, but rarely pig. Interestingly, as well as domestic fowl, a wide range of wild birds was consumed including skylark, grey plover and robin. In York, intensive work has been carried out using a broad range of techniques to examine deposits with rich environmental data. Evidence studied from two Anglo-Scandinavian sites, for example (Hall et al., 1983), included insects, pollen, seeds and plant fragments, coprolites and parasites, and enabled a clear distinction to be drawn between the relatively clean Roman city in comparison with the tenth-to-eleventh-century city whose inhabitants were apparently surrounded with decomposing waste.

In Coventry work on a series of small sites in Much Park Street (Wright,1988), gave a good picture of the social effects of the growth of urbanism, commencing in the twelfth and thirteenth century with the taking in of new land defined by property boundaries, and the establishment of workshops concentrating on bronze casting and perhaps cutlery making. These crafts are amongst several metal-based small industries reflected in thirteenth-century deeds of the town. There followed much clearance in the fourteenth century, to be followed by a phase of town-house occupation reflected in the material culture recovered by excavation and in the buildings still upstanding in the street. Towns where the documentation of individual properties is available for study in depth, such as at Winchester, obviously provide enormous potential scope for inter-disciplinary research (e.g. Keene, 1985, pp. 756-67). Closely dated events also provide context as well as readily stirring the imagination. The discovery in Pudding Lane, London, of a brick-floored house cellar, destroyed in the fire of 1666 and which contained the remains of some twenty racked barrels probably formerly holding pitch, indicates not only the character of the building but also its overseas trading links (Milne and Milne, 1985).

Archaeological work in urban areas may be contrasted with evidence from the country, whether on specialised settlement types such as the Welsh transhumance settlement *hafod* (for example, Allen, 1979), or peasant house sites in general, of which very many have been examined archaeologically. A recent study of medieval peasant buildings (Dyer, 1986) integrates archaeological and documentary evidence to demonstrate, for example, that 'long-houses', accommodating both people and animals, were a rarity in the Midlands by 1350, that carpentered as distinct from earth-fast buildings were well established in several regions at an earlier date than this, and that peasant houses of later medieval England equate in size with working-class urban houses of the nineteenth century. Amongst outstanding studies of complete village settlements is that of Wharram Percy (Beresford and Hurst, 1990).

There are a number of excellent studies in industrial archaeology, such as that of the Wealden iron industry (Cleere and Crossley, 1985), which integrate excavation with field survey and documentation. Some industries, such as the pottery industry with its almost indestructible product, are inevitably more accessible to the fieldwork approach, in contrast, for example, to the early woollen or flax industries with an organic product and less readily traceable processing plant.

Waterlogged deposits, when they are located, can provide archaeological material of exceptional importance which survives in no other context. Amongst the prime examples is that of the warship *Mary Rose*. Although only interim accounts are available at present (Rule, 1982), these and the display at Portsmouth illustrate the wealth of material gradually becoming available from this particular social microcosm, sunk in 1545 – for example, equipment of the barber surgeon, his instruments and ointments, and the physical condition of the men on board reflected in the skeletal remains of those drowned, and of their clothing and pastimes.

This chapter has endeavoured to outline the contribution which archaeological excavations can make to the study of social history. The gap between the two disciplines lies in the technique rather than the objective. There is much to be gained by the two disciplines keeping firmly in touch.

References

Allen, David (1979), 'Excavations at Hafod y Nant Criafolen, Brenig Valley, Clwyd, 1973-4', *Post-Medieval Archaeology*, no. 13, pp. 1-59.

Allen, J.P. (1984), *Medieval and Post Medieval Finds from Exeter 1971-80*, Exeter Archaeological Report 3, Exeter City Council and the University of Exeter.

Armitage, P.L., West, B., *et al.* (1985), 'Faunal evidence from a late medieval garden well of the Greyfriars, London', *Transactions of the London and Middlesex Archaeological Society*, no. 36, pp. 107-36.

Beresford, M., and Hurst, J. (1990), *English Heritage Book of Wharram Percy Deserted Medieval Village*, Batsford/English Heritage.

Bourdillon, Jennifer (1980), 'Town life and animal husbandry in the Southampton area, as suggested by the excavated bones', *Proceedings of the Hampshire Field Club Archaeological Society, 1979* pp. 181-91.

Cleere, H., and Crossley, D. (1985), *The Iron Industry of the Weald*, Leicester University Press.

Dyer, Christopher (1986), 'English peasant buildings in the later middle ages (1200-1500)', *Medieval Archaeology*, no.30, pp. 19-45.

Hall, A.R., Kenwood, H.K., Williams, D., and Greig, J.R.A. (1983), 'Environment and living conditions at two Anglo-Scandinavian sites', *The Archaeology of York*, vol.14, fascicule 4.

Keene, Derek (1985), *Survey of Medieval Winchester*, Winchester Studies 2, Clarendon Press.

Milne, Gustav, and Milne, Crissie (1985), 'A building in Pudding Lane destroyed in the Great Fire of 1666...', *Transactions of the London and Middlesex Archaeological Society*, no. 36, pp. 169-82.

Rule, Margaret (1982), *The Mary Rose*, Conway Maritime Press.

Suggitt, Mark (1987), 'Social history collecting', *Museums Journal*, vol. 87, pp. 86-8.

Wright, Susan M. (1988), 'Much Park Street, Coventry: The development of a medieval street. Excavations 1972-7', *Transactions of the Birmingham and Warwickshire Archaeological Society*, vol. 92, pp. 1-132.

Bibliography

The following is a small selection of works containing useful discussions of method and examples of integration between archaeological and historical evidence for the medieval and later period.

Carver, Martin, *Underneath English Towns*, Batsford, 1987.

Clarke, Helen, *The Archaeology of Medieval England*, British Museum, 1984.

Crossley, David, *Post-medieval Archaeology in Britain*, Leicester University Press, 1990.

Steane, John, *The Archaeology of Medieval England and Wales*, Croom Helm Studies in Archaeology, 1985.

Schofield, J., and Leech, R., *Urban Archaeology in Britain*, CBA Research Report 61, 1987.

21 Advantages and Limitations of Buildings in Social History

Richard Harris

Research Director, Weald and Downland Open Air Museum, Singleton

Many social history museums have a direct interest in historic buildings, either because they have a building as their central exhibit, or because they inhabit a historic building. Open-air or site museums use *in situ* or transplanted buildings as exhibits in their own right, and even museums in completely modern premises often have rooms, façades or occasionally complete structures on display. Some museums include buildings as part of their research interest in a specific field of economic or social activity. In all cases the social history curator needs to know how to study buildings.

Buildings are complex objects and are consequently a rich source of historical information. The following list gives a sample of the range of questions that can be asked.

The construction How and when was it built? What craft processes were involved? Who were the craftsmen? How much did it cost? Who provided the money? What were the contractual arrangements?

The site Why is it there? What was the property boundary? What is its relationship with adjoining buildings and land? What was on the site previously?

Occupation Who was the owner? Who was the occupier? How was the building used?

Architecture How does the design of the building serve its use? What do the public parts tell the outside world about its use, status and ownership?

Some of these questions can be answered from an examination of the particular building, but others depend on a study of associated documents and landscape, or on a wider knowledge of 'normal' features against which to assess variations. The ideal combination is hard to achieve: the best documents often refer to buildings that have disappeared, and the best buildings often have no documents clearly associated with them. Similarly, excellent buildings may stand in a completely altered landscape.

Buildings have some major advantages as evidence in the study of social history. The main one is that they are generally well provenanced: they have usually remained in one place, and ownership can often be traced. In this they contrast with many other items of material culture, such as furniture, clothing or tools, which are often badly provenanced in terms of place of origin and ownership. Also, as major items of expenditure and investment, buildings tend to be well documented and culturally rich. Once their language has been learned they can be made to speak volumes – and the language is not very far removed from our continuing common experience. Another major advantage is that, in contrast with archaeological sites, they can be surveyed and understood in some depth in a completely non-destructive way.

They also have some telling disadvantages. In the absence of oral history or specific documentation, buildings only tell part of the story of their use. A farmhouse may have four rooms in plan, correctly identified as kitchen, dairy, dining room and parlour, but the house itself will not tell you how the parlour was furnished nor how it was used. Even when the main furnishings at a particular date are known from an inventory, for instance, there remains much about the social and hierarchical organisation of the house which has to be inferred from other sources, such as contemporary accounts and pictures. The other main problem is that of survival. An individual building can be read on its own terms, but to read wider patterns we need to know whether surviving examples are representative, and this is not easy. The mechanisms of survival and destruction are not yet well understood.

Practical Approaches and Methodology

The researcher first has to decide what buildings to study. The choice of building type will often be pre-determined in the context of a wider research project, but there are still some important decisions to be made. In some circumstances, for instance, an individual building will be studied. There is virtually no limit to the depth of detail that can be analysed and recorded in a single building over a period of time – although there is disagreement about the benefits that very detailed recording can bring.[1] When circumstances permit, a programme of investigation and parallel recording can be developed. Part of the programme may take advantage of a necessity to strip out or dismantle part of the building for other reasons, such as conservation, repair, or change of use. Such opportunities are of great importance and should not be wasted – but, regrettably, they all too often are. Archaeologists are geared up to do rescue digs on cleared sites whenever possible, but many building researchers seem to prefer the comforts of inhabited buildings, proud owners and cups of tea!

Another approach is to study a large number of local buildings for the purposes of establishing a local or regional context for a particular example. For instance, a museum curator concerned with a barn or granary might decide to survey all, or a sample of, the farmsteads in a surrounding area such as an estate, a parish or a county, or a region of similar soil types.

Working from the opposite direction, so to speak, a research project might be based on a particular documentary source. An early map or survey might be used as a basis for a detailed and comprehensive survey of all the buildings within its area of coverage. Alternatively, a set of architectural drawings or a contract might provide the impetus for a survey of a building.

What is a record of a building? Very often it consists of rather sketchy drawings, accurate to 10cm or so, with an assessment of the likely original plan and construction and major alterations (but usually excluding anything 'modern'). Sometimes it is even less than this – a couple of sentences in a listed building description, for instance, or a few photographs. Occasionally a comprehensive set of drawings and photographs is combined with a written report to produce a record of some depth. How should the choice be made between these alternatives?[2]

The main thing to remember is that the only complete record of a building is the building itself. All other 'records' are conditioned by hypotheses, sometimes consciously but more often unconsciously. For instance, measuring a building can be done in many different ways. Some people measure only roughly, perhaps believing that builders (at least, 'traditional' builders) worked to crude tolerances, or that measurements have nothing to tell us about buildings. Others may measure more accurately but without thinking about which planes and points are, or may be, significant. Others again may measure certain elements to a high degree of accuracy, or even take full-size casts or rubbings. Measurements may be taken in metric dimensions, to provide a 'neutral' record, or in imperial dimensions with their strong cultural and historical overtones. Some researchers will look for proportional systems, following hypotheses about practical methods of setting out. All these different approaches may have their place but unfortunately researchers are rarely explicit about the assumptions and hypotheses under which they are working.

Sometimes records produced with no clear aim in view can be used as raw data by thinkers and theorists. An example of this is the 'cruck catalogue' in which 3054 'records' of crucks have been summarised and mapped.[3] Most of the original records were not intended to contribute to the various debates and hypotheses stimulated by the catalogue, and were of varying content and quality.

It is important that records of buildings should be produced with clear and explicit hypotheses. One reason for this is that users of the records will then understand both the purpose and the limitations of the record. Another is that it would discourage the notion, which is uncomfortably prevalent, that once a building has been recorded by a particular researcher, the job is done. One job may be done, but others remain.

Despite these problems it is possible to suggest some components of a sound approach to recording a building. Every researcher develops his or her own method of working, some centred on drawings, some on photographs and some on written analysis, but the following series of steps would generally be considered good practice.

1. Make a preliminary assessment of the building, its original form and subsequent development – some parts of it may be straightforward, others complex and uncertain. Decide whether you are going to record the original structure in its original form or the present building in its developed form; often both will be needed.

2. Use the process of drawing and measurement to focus your attention on details of the building, developing and checking your interpretation of it as you proceed. Check every hypothesis and assumption by observation and measurement. When measuring, plan carefully how to obtain the most accurate and informative measurement of a feature. It is better to spend ten minutes taking a single reliable dimension than to take ten unreliable ones. If possible, draw to scale on site but also record figured dimensions. This provides an invaluable running check and is an excellent discipline – anything that can't be drawn on site you certainly won't be able to draw back at the office!

3. Write up your notes on site, or dictate them into a portable tape recorder. If you leave it till afterwards you will inevitably find some problem that necessitates a return visit. Develop a checklist to run through to ensure that all observations have been made.[4]

4. Photographs are important and worth taking trouble with. Good photographs are as difficult to produce as good drawings and can be even more time-consuming. They are invaluable for recording context, and the detail of complex features, but for interpretation they will usually take second place to drawings and notes. The specialist disciplines of photogrammetry and rectified photography, from which scale drawings are produced, are useful in some difficult situations.

5. If an element of stripping or dismantling is involved, then many more techniques become available, too many to mention here. All sorts of materials, including mortar, plaster, decorative surfaces, nails and screws can be extracted and analysed. Brick and stonework can be recorded in plan, course by course if

necessary; a brick chimney, for example, being taken down for some reason, can reveal many unexpected secrets if carefully recorded course by course, and alterations in stonework that may be completely invisible on the vertical surfaces become perfectly clear if a wall is recorded as it is dismantled.

Various specialist scientific disciplines have been developed to extend the study of buildings. The best known is probably dendrochronology, by which the tree-ring widths in a sample are compared with a master-curve to obtain a probable chronological anchor for the sample. Dendrochronology is developing rapidly and producing ever more impressive results. Analysis is now much quicker, thanks to the power of personal computers, and the master curves are becoming increasingly reliable, but the problems of short series (samples with less than 70 rings) and wide rings (from rapid growth) are still fairly intractable. The main practical problem is how to obtain samples. Timbers occasionally show exposed end grain that can be measured in situ, but otherwise samples have to be obtained by core-boring, which requires special equipment, or by sawing slices from timbers, which is rarely possible. Several samples from different timbers are needed for a reliable result.

Paint research has made great progress in the last decade, and reliable analysis of decorative finishes is now carried out routinely. In vernacular houses there are often remains of wall painting of various sorts, particularly from the late-sixteenth and seventeenth centuries. The main problem here is that it takes considerable skill and experience to detect and reveal such paintings when they are hidden under many later layers, and appropriate expertise is in short supply.

Some of the disciplines which are familiar to archaeologists can also be applied to buildings. Environmental archaeologists have found lichen, for instance, perfectly preserved on components of wattle and daub panels from the late-medieval period. Straw from original thatch, preserved over the centuries as a base coat, has been found to be 'headless', providing valuable evidence for the technique of cutting corn high and mowing the stubble for thatch. Daub often contains seeds and sometimes ears of cereal crops preserved in perfect condition. Buildings can be time-capsules for more than immediately meets the eye.

When the surveys and reports are done the time comes to deposit and/or publish the records. As well as the local purposes for which the research was originally done, it is important to know that the National Buildings Record (NBR) will receive and store records and make a contribution towards the cost of their reproduction.[5] The NBR is an excellent resource which should be used and supported by everyone interested in historic buildings. With their wide contacts in the field the staff at the NBR will also be able to give advice about other sources of help and support for your project and put you in touch with local or regional groups if necessary.

Resources

The study of buildings falls uncomfortably between the academic study of architecture on the one hand and archaeology on the other. Architectural historians tend to be good at the history of the work of architects but not very good at vernacular or traditional buildings, while archaeologists generally lack the specialist training necessary to get to grips with the complexities of buildings. As a result the field is an eclectic one, with historians, geographers and archaeologists rubbing shoulders with architects, art historians and, above all, expert and enthusiastic amateurs belonging to none of these disciplines. The staff and publications of the Royal Commissions on Historical Monuments in

England and Wales have made much of the running in vernacular architecture research over the last two decades, but otherwise the field is dominated by brilliant individuals,[6] and highly productive amateur groups.[7]

The national Vernacular Architecture Group is the recognised meeting point in its field and publishes the leading journal, *Vernacular Architecture*.[8] Its equivalent in 'polite' architecture is the Society of Architectural Historians.[9] The Historic Farm Buildings Group[10] was formed more recently but is now well established, and the British Brick Society fosters a high level of expertise in its field.[11]

Notes

1. The question of the desirability of highly detailed recording is discussed in papers by I.M. Ferris, R. Meeson and J.T. Smith in *Vernacular Architecture,* vol. 20, 1989.

2. See L. Smith, *Investigating Old Buildings,* Batsford, 1985; and Royal Commission on the Historical Monuments of England, *Recording Historic Buildings: A Descriptive Specification,* 1990 (available from Publications department, RCHME, Newlands House, 37-40 Bemers Street, London W1P 4BP).

3. N.W. Alcock, *Cruck Construction, An Introduction and Catalogue,* Research Report no. 42, Council for British Archaeology, 1981.

4. R.W. Brunskill, *An Illustrated Handbook of Vernacular Architecture,* 2nd ed., 1978; N. W. Alcock, M.W. Borley, P.W. Dixon and R.A. Meeson, *Recording Timber-Framed Buildings: An Illustrated Glossary,* Practical Handbooks in Archaeology no.5, Council for British Archaeology, 1989.

5. The National Buildings Record, Royal Commission on the Historical Monuments of England, 23 Savile Row, London W1X 2JQ.

6. There are several individuals whose work is outstanding. The remarkable series of volumes of research published by David and Barbara Martin is representative of the highest quality of this work (Rape of Hasting Architectural Survey, 16 Langham Road, Robertsbridge, East Sussex TN32 5DX).

7. The staff at the National Buildings Record will generally be able to advise on the existence of local groups in a particular area.

8. Secretary (1990): Bob Meeson, 16 Falna Crescent, Colton Green, Tamworth, Staffs, B79 8JS.

9. Secretary (1990): Ruth Harman, 55 Blakeney Road, Sheffield S10 1FD.

10. Secretary (1990): Roy Brigden, Museum of English Rural Life, University of Reading, Reading RG6 2AG.

11. Secretary (1990): M. Hammett, 9 Bailey Close, High Wycombe, Berks HP13 6QA. Further information on sources of information can be obtained from the specialist library at the Weald and Downland Open Air Museum, Singleton, Chichester, Sussex.

22 Domestic Interiors in Britain: A Review of the Existing Literature

James Ayres

Director, John Judkyn Memorial, Bath

The eight magisterial volumes which constitute *English Homes* by H.Avray Tipping (1921) weigh a prodigious $4^1/_2$ stone. It is a publication that is concerned with those large establishments which, with polished understatement, have become known as 'the English country house'. It is a genre that goes back to Colen Campbell *(Vitruvius Britannicus,* 1715) and beyond, and often includes Scottish houses in addition to those found in Ireland and Wales. Although many practical building manuals were produced, few have since followed the eighteenth-century example of Batty Langley in *The Builder's Jewel* (1754) by demonstrating a concern for the construction as well as the design of the smaller house. Furthermore, writers of Tipping's generation, like many who have followed them, were as concerned with the genealogy of the principal inhabitants of these establishments as with their ostensible theme. Whilst an aesthetic consideration is evident, construction was seldom examined and few if any of these early twentieth-century authorities, nurtured as they were on generations of connoisseurship, ventured beyond the green baize door. Only recently have the wider social and historical implications of these buildings received the attention they deserve as households which, in association with their surrounding estates and farms, supported a multiplicity of activities. The possibilities of such an approach have been pioneered by Mark Girouard in *Life in the English Country House* (1978). For a 'back stairs' examination of the subject, Merlin Waterson's *The Servants' Hall* (1980) carries the appropriate sub-title *A Domestic History of Erddig.* When the National Trust opened the house to the public via the servants' entrance in 1977, this 'back door' approach was seen as a remarkable innovation.

Buildings of this kind have long been acknowledged as 'Treasure Houses' most recently in the 1987 exhibition in Washington D.C. However, and despite the efforts of writers like Margaret Jourdain, the ability to interpret interior decoration as an entity rather than a confusion of its constituent parts (treasures as in 'Treasure Houses') requires a rare blend of experience and understanding. It is a difficulty and even a conflict that is reflected in the long-standing and ambiguous relationships between architects and interior decorators. It is a divide that has been reinforced by the customary fragmentation of museums into departments of woodwork, textiles and painting. The extent of this conundrum may be used as a measure of Peter Thornton's achievement in bringing together these various strands of thought in his books on interiors. His *Interior Decoration in England, France and Holland* (1978) demonstrates the way in which an understanding of textiles and upholstery together with furniture and woodwork may be combined to make an intelligible whole.

The state-rooms of great houses formed a logical and hierarchical progression which was based on traditions and conventions that were, at times, barely remembered by their creators. At Ham House, the Queen's Closet is the final room in a sequence. It is located beyond the State Bedchamber and only a privileged few would be admitted to this semi-private space. It is a small if opulent room which, with its coal-burning fireplace, offered in winter the comfort and luxury of warmth rare in seventeenth-century England.

Although in one sense the closet at Ham House may be 'read' as the last of the state rooms it was also one of the private ones and it was the presence of these private rooms that enabled the more formal interiors to survive virtually unchanged. Below stairs, the Servants' Hall was in effect the 'State Room' for the staff and in many respects it was the equivalent of the Great Hall that in medieval times served the entire household – those above and those below 'the Salt'. The near ceremonial role that the Servants' Hall retained in post-medieval Britain is implicit in the surviving lettered boards painted with 'Rules to be Attended to in the Hall'.

The hierarchy that existed below stairs was perhaps necessary for the efficient running of the household but the separate but parallel responsibilities of the butler and the housekeeper could result in differing traditions. Tables that were 'set' for meals under the supervision of the housekeeper were organised in a different way from those 'set' under the direction of the butler.

A fully staffed English country house was an entire community with rooms reserved for numerous specialised activities at many social levels. These were the conditions to which everything within such houses was subordinate – even such details as the quality and type of flooring to be found in a particular part of a house. It was the position that the *piano nobile* of Palladianism and the general horizontal emphasis of classicism did much to reinforce – the kitchens were in a raised basement and the servants' quarters were behind a parapet wall.

With these gradations of importance and use, of personage and person, of leisure and activity, one house and its household was a microcosm of Britain. The social distinctions between individual domestic buildings were no less evident. Writing in November 1660, Sir Roger Pratt asserted that architecture is 'an art teaching us to build as we ought, both in regard of ye person, for whome ye building is made; as alsoe for ye ende, for which it is cheifely intended'. This observation contains some suggestion, conscious or unconscious, of the residual influence of the sumptuary laws. A very similar view may be found in *The City and Country Purchaser* (1726) in which Richard Neve, the author of this builder's manual, defines 'Decor' as 'the keeping of due Respect between the Inhabitant and the Habitation'. Neither should it be supposed that this attitude of mind was confined to architecture. In *The Art of Painting* (1704), John Elsum argues that artists should 'suit their works to the quality of the place and the person'.

Quite what constitutes 'the smaller house' is very much a matter of opinion. The position is complicated by the way in which houses have tended to descend the social scale as expectations of privacy and comfort have risen (in the Welsh language there is no word for 'private'). Many so-called 'cottages' were intended for the yeoman class, just as many 'farmhouses' were built for the lesser gentry. Milton's 'cottage' in Buckinghamshire was described by his contemporary Thomas Ellwood in 1665 as a 'Pretty Box' at 'Giles Chalfont'. In contrast to this, Margaret Jourdain included Dyrham Park, to name but one, in her *English Interiors in Smaller Houses 1660-1830* (1923).

Fortunately an alternative approach to domestic architecture in Britain is provided by the burgeoning interest in vernacular building. The careful study of this dialect of construction, of floor plans and the use of materials, is giving greater emphasis to the history of the smaller house. The seminal book on the subject was S.O. Addy's *The Evolution of the English House,* first published in 1898. Since then numerous books have appeared (see Robert de Zouche Hall, *A Bibliography of Vernacular Architecture* (1972) – since when much has been published). The way in which standards of living have developed in the home from the mid-sixteenth century may be found not only in William Harrison's

Description of England (1577) but also most notably in surviving vernacular buildings – in grander establishments the pattern is much less clearly discerned. W.G. Hoskins' thesis (1964) of the 'Great Rebuilding' of the seventeenth century when timber gave way to stone and brick, was based upon the generality of buildings found in Britain. With modifications it is a theory that has been widely accepted. Even so, these improvements were by no means without exception and both Celia Fiennes (*The Journies of Celia Fiennes, c.1685-1712*) and Richard Gough (*The History of Myddle, 1700-1702*) cite well-to-do individuals living in caves in the seventeenth century.

So far as the interiors are concerned, Harrison was the first to acknowledge that nothing had greater influence than the widespread introduction of the chimney flue in the sixteenth century. Before its introduction the upper spaces of a house were unusable and most dwellings were of a single floor. With a flue houses could be constructed with more than one floor. As a result of this, staircases and ceilings as well as fireplaces and chimneys were, for prestige, given decorative importance. These features, together with a near obsession with roof construction, are the matters that concern students of vernacular architecture, although writers like M.W. Barley (1961) and R.W. Brunskill (1971) have done much to make such observations understandable in a wider historical content.

Rather less attention has been given to the more fugitive details of interior decoration in vernacular buildings and in working-class housing since the industrial revolution (or evolution). One of the difficulties that confronts the student in this field hinges on the basic problem of finding sufficient evidence to form an overall picture of the interiors of such houses. Inventories such as those published by F.W. Steer (1950) are invaluable particularly as they are frequently drawn from probate documents which also provide information on the house (which may survive), its location, and the status, occupation and financial circumstances of the individual concerned. The relationship of movable objects (furnishings and plenishings) to their original context is more difficult to establish. Although numerous domestic items from a particular period may survive, it is extraordinarily difficult to match the quality of an object to an appropriate setting. In this respect, as in all others, the recent past provides richer and more numerous clues. As Mario Praz demonstrated, contemporary illustrations are invaluable (1982). His book revealed that throughout Europe it became fashionable in the opening decades of the nineteenth-century for amateurs to make watercolour drawings recording the appearance of interiors. A good example of the genre is the series of watercolours by Mary Ellen Best which sample a remarkably wide social and geographical spectrum of interiors (Davidson, 1985). The Regional Furniture Society is also forming an archive of this type of information. Vernacular furniture is the theme of B.D. Cotton's publications on *The Regional Chair* (1990), a study which provides insights into the techniques involved with this type of research.

Interior decorators in the twentieth century give as much attention to carpets and curtains as did the 'upholders' in the eighteenth century. However, until industrialisation made textiles easily available for all, they remained luxuries that even the rich used sparingly. Mirrors and wallpaper occupied an analogous position partly for similar reasons but also because of the tax that was placed upon these luxuries. Today textiles, along with wallpaper, are seen as the principal vehicle for the provision of pattern and colour in the home. Before industrialisation, and particularly at the vernacular level, painted decoration was the chief and certainly the cheapest means by which an interior could be embellished with colour and pattern. Floors were painted rather than carpeted, walls were stencilled rather than papered, furniture was lined and grained rather than veneered.

The range of work undertaken by housepainters was formidable and has almost certainly been underestimated. Nathaniel Whittock's *The Decorative Painters' and Glaziers' Guide* (1827) describes, as one would expect, pigments and media and the methods of their application. In addition, this manual gives instructions for graining and marbling, for sign-writing and sign-painting, the creation of transparent blinds and the painting of murals.

Valuable though such publications may be, they remain a point of departure towards a fuller understanding of the domestic interior. In the past, an undue reliance on documentary sources, printed or manuscript, has had the effect of diverting thoughts away from the true primary source – the object under review, in this case surviving fragments, details or whole schemes of interior decoration. Material culture is best studied via the material itself. To gain the necessary facility in the literacy of 'reading' things, an understanding of the processes of making, of materials and tools is essential. Sacheverell Sitwell's *British Architects and Craftsmen* (1945) is a thoroughly elegant survey but it is not, as its subtitle acknowledges, about craftsmanship; it is about 'Taste, Design and Style'. Some, like C.F. Innocent in *The Development of English Building Construction* (1916) or Martin S. Briggs in *A Short History of the Building Crafts* (1925) have come close to a tactile understanding of the craftsman's role. In general this is rare. It is now time for a re-assessment – to come out of the library and into the workshop and to follow the example of George Sturt whose bench experience is what gives the *Wheelwright's Shop* (1942) its basic strength.

Light and heat, plumbing and sewerage, transport and the mass production of building components have all had their impact on the home as it moves irresistibly towards greater technological innovation. Changes in the family structure and population pressures are tending towards creating the conditions for ever smaller if more numerous 'units of accommodation'. In the light of these changes Philip Pacey's notions of 'Family Art' (1982) may need revision but ultimately the house is a home the character of which is determined as much by its occupants as by its time and place. It is the one art form in which we all participate.

References

Addy, S.0. (1898), *The Evolution of the English House,* London.

Barley, M.W. (1961), *The English Farmhouse and Cottage,* Routledge.

Briggs, M.S. (1925), *A Short History of the Building Crafts,* Oxford University Press.

Brunskill, R.W. (1971), *An Illustrated Handbook of Vernacular Architecture,* Faber.

Campbell, Colen (1715), *Vitruvius Britannicus,* London.

Cotton, B.D. (1990), *The English Regional Chair,* Antique Collectors Club, Woodbridge, Suffolk.

Davidson, Caroline (1985), *The World of Mary Ellen Best,* Chatto & Windus.

Elsum, John (1704), *The Art of Painting,* London.

Fiennes, Celia (1947), *The Journies of Celia Fiennes (c. 1685-1712),* ed. Morris, Christopher, Cresset Press.

Girouard, Mark (1978), *Life in the English Country House,* Yale University Press, New Haven, Conn.

Gough, Richard (1981), *The History of Myddle (1700-1702),* ed. Hey, David, Penguin Books. First published 1834.

Harrison, William (1877), *Description of England (1577),* ed. Furnivall, F.J., New Shakespeare

Society, vol, 1.

Hoskins, W.G. (1964), *Provincial England*, Macmillan.

Innocent, C.F. (1916), *The Development of English Building Construction*, Cambridge University Press. Reprinted 1971, David & Charles.

Jourdain, Margaret (1923), *English Interiors in Smaller Houses 1660-1830*, London.

Langley, Batty (1754), *The Builder's Jewel*, London.

Neve, Richard (1726), *The City and Country Purchaser*, London.

Pacey, Philip (1982), 'Introduction', in *Family Art: Essays and Bibliography to Accompany an Exhibition*, Bethnal Green Museum of Childhood.

Pratt, Sir Roger (1660), *Certain Short Notes Concerning Architechture*, London.

Praz, Mario (1982), *An Illustrated History of Interior Decoration*, Thames & Hudson.

Sitwell, Sacheverell (1945), *British Architects and Craftsmen: A Survey of Taste, Design and Style during Three Centuries 1600-1830*, Batsford.

Steer, F.W. (1950), *Farm and Cottage Inventories of Mid-Essex 1635-1749*, Phillimore, Chichester.

Sturt, George (1942), *The Wheelwright's Shop*, Cambridge University Press. First published 1923.

Thornton, Peter (1978), *Interior Decoration in England, France and Holland*, Yale University Press, New Haven, Conn.

Tipping, H.Avray (1921), *English Homes*, 8 vols, Country Life, London.

Waterson, Merlin (1980), *The Servants' Hall: A Domestic History of Erddig*, Routledge.

Whittock, Nathaniel (1827), *The Decorative Painters' and Glaziers' Guide*, London.

de Zouche Hall, Robert (1972), *A Bibliography of Vernacular Architecture*, David & Charles.

Bibliography

Airs, M., *The Making of the English Country House 1500-1640*, Architectural Press, 1975.

Ayres, James, *The Artist's Craft : A History of Tools, Techniques and Materials*, Phaidon, 1985.

Ayres, James, *The Shell Book of the Home in Britain: Decoration, Design and Construction of Vernacular Interiors 1500-1850*, Faber, 1981.

Charles, F.W.B., *Conservation of Timber Buildings*, Hutchinson, 1984.

Clifton-Taylor, Alec, and Ireson, A.S., *English Stone Building*, Gollancz, 1983.

Eastlake, Charles, *Hints on Household Taste*, London, 1868. Revised ed. 1872.

Emmison, F. G., *Elizabethan Life*, Essex County Council, Chelmsford, 1976.

Entwhistle, E.A., *The Book of Wallpaper*, Kingsmead Reprints, Bath, 1970. First published 1934.

Evans, Emyr Estyn, *Irish Folk Ways*, Routledge, 1957.

Fenton, Alexander, *Scottish Country Life*, John Donald, Edinburgh, 1976.

Fowler, John, and Cornforth, John, *English Decoration in the Eighteenth Century*, Barrie & Jenkins, 1978. First published 1974.

Gilbert, Christopher, *English Vernacular Furniture 1750-1900*, Yale University Press, New Haven, Conn., 1991.

Grant, I.F., *Highland Folk Ways*, Routledge, 1961.

Harris, Richard, *Discovering Timber Frame Houses*, Shire Publications, Princes Risborough, 1978.

Harvey, John, *Medieval Craftsmen*, Batsford, 1975.

Hewett, C.A., *The Development of Carpentry 1200-1700*, David & Charles, 1969.

Jekyll, Gertrude, *Old English Household Life,* Batsford, 1925. Reprinted 1975.

Jones, S.R., *The Village Homes of England,* Studio, 1912.

Lloyd, Nathaniel, *A History of the English House,* 1931. Reprinted Architectural Press, 1975.

Mercer, Eric, *English Vernacular Houses,* HMSO, 1975.

Moore, John S., *The Goods and Chattels of our Forefathers: Frampton Cotterel and District Probate Inventories 1539-1804,* Phillimore, Chichester, 1976.

Peate, Iorwerth C., *The Welsh House,* Hugh Evans & Sons, Liverpool, 1940.

Nicholson, Peter, *The New Practical Builder,* London, 1823-5.

Paine, Crispin, and Rhodes, John, *The Working Home : Small Houses in Oxfordshire Through Three Centuries,* Woodstock, Oxfordshire County Council, 1979.

Salzman, L.F., *Building in England Down to 1542,* Clarendon Press, 1952.

Vernacular Architecture, the journal of the Vernacular Architecture Group, published annually, first edition 1970.

Wood, Margaret, *The English Medieval House,* Phoenix House, 1965.

Wrightson, Priscilla, *The Small English House : A Catalogue of Books,* B. Weinreb Architectural Books Ltd, 1977.

152

23 Prints and Drawings

Ann Payne
Curator, Department of Manuscripts, British Library
James Payne
Collector of topographical drawings

It is a widely held belief that a picture can be worth a great many words in telling how things were. A picture can be more immediate and more vivid than the written word or the random historical relic. In cases where a picture outlives the subject it depicts, it can itself become an important historical source. The value of pictorial material in the interpretation of history, a notion long distrusted by historians, is beginning to receive more general recognition with scholars such as Simon Schama in his works on the Dutch and French revolutions making use of paintings, drawings, caricatures and engravings as an integral part of their theme.

Since humankind has been hard at work with paint and pencil for centuries, one might entertain a hope of finding a picture to illustrate almost any aspect of social life and history, even if the relevant features are tucked away in the corners and margins of the work. In editing the pictures over forty years ago for G.M.Trevelyan's *Illustrated Social History of England* (the selection of which was surely a model for others in this field), Ruth Wright found a wealth of drawn, printed and photographic material available to her and innumerable resources to ransack. Her principal requirements were that the illustrations should be from English sources and should be as contemporary as possible with the scenes they represented. Painters, however, have seldom set out to be of service to the social historians of later times; Mrs Wright, like many others, encountered gaps which obliged her here and there to stretch her rules.

There are bound to be areas and periods for which a choice of pictures is limited. The supply has not been regular, consistent or wholly to the point; preservation has been uncertain. If, for instance, the purpose is to illustrate with a contemporary work the interior of a pre-1620 London theatre, the choice will lie between two known sketches. Of the personal artefacts that survive from the Middle Ages the largest proportion is made up of illuminated manuscript books, many abounding in social detail and with the colours wonderfully preserved by the protection of the book. But the number of these medieval miniatures is almost eclipsed by the flood of artwork, both original and printed, that built up in the eighteenth century. Drawing became then not merely a craft of the paid artisan but an acceptable, fashionable pastime to be indulged in freely by the upper and middle classes. With the burgeoning of the 'tourist' phenomenon, many more people were taken to all manner of places to see and record things that pleased, interested or puzzled them. Public taste, thus aroused, fuelled an enormous boom in scenes and souvenirs turned out by a flourishing print trade. As a result, Hanoverian England supplies the social historian with an *embarras de richesses*.

There have been other imbalances. Throughout history the picture has had a bias towards wealth, comfort and cleanliness. Picture-making has been done mostly on commission, and those who commissioned have been the rich and the noble, seeking to record, and probably to enhance, their own status and grandeur. Portraits of themselves and their eminent and elegant connections, the magnificence of their extensive properties, the sophistication of their civilised pursuits, these have been in general the requirement – not their dowdy servants, impoverished tenantry or the squalid backstreets of their towns. The image produced was of Society in preference to the full social span; and it was a Society which paid painters might often be induced to tidy up and flatter. Cromwell could demand of Lely to be painted 'roughnesses, pimples, warts, and everything', but it was not always so with less buoyant egos. Pictures of ordinary people doing ordinary things in ordinary settings there have of course been, particularly when Romanticism became enamoured of the humble and the wretched, and when publishers and print-makers, understanding something of the social interests of their customers, became leading patrons of the art. Even so, it may be much easier to find images portraying the person and home of political figures than to illustrate the implementation and effects of their social reforms.

The balance against warts has been redressed to a degree by the work of the caricaturists, consistently popular and entertaining from the eighteenth century as illustrators and debunkers of social attitudes, modes and manners. But the oddities and exaggerations contained in their works have been, of course, as much a distortion of the actual look of things as the omission of blemishes from the face and foodstains from the frock coat. Moreover, while satirical draughtsmen from Rowlandson and Gillray to the present day have portrayed both high life and low, in general it has been the leaders of society rather than its other ranks who have been found the more diverting.

In considering pictures to enrich displays, books and other work, the kind of criteria promptly applied will be relevance of subject matter, artistic or dramatic effect, practicalities of size, shape and colour, unfamiliarity to the public and contemporaneity. It is as well to be mindful also of anachronisms, of deliberate propaganda, and of distortions arising from artistic licence and incompetence. In 1820, only a short time after the event, George Cruikshank produced a coloured etching of the bloody raid by George Ruthven's Constabulary upon the so-called Cato Street conspirators. It is captioned 'The Scene faithfully represented from the Description of Mr Ruthven. The View of the Interior correctly Sketched on the Spot'. Cruikshank has given us an artist's impression, not a 'photographic' image of the occasion; he was not a witness to the deeds, and so the placing of the figures, their caricatured appearance, their clothes, their gestures, are his invention. He has, however, gone to admirable pains to get his picture right. Jane Austen's old sea-dog, Admiral Croft, found enough faults to amuse him in a ship picture displayed in the window of a Bath print shop: 'But what a thing here is, by way of a boat ... Did you ever see the like? What queer fellows your fine painters must be, to think that anybody would venture their lives in such a shapeless old cockleshell as that ... I would not venture over a horsepond in it.' The Admiral could laugh heartily at it, but in its small way such a picture was conveying misinformation to the people of Bath about their maritime heritage. The shortcoming of Cruikshank's work, as an historical record, stems from the intrusion of the imagination; for Admiral Croft's artist it lies in carelessness or incompetence.

It is known that on occasion medieval scribes and illuminators were copying direct from continental originals; when aspects of social life figure in these works, therefore, the picture cannot strictly be of English society. Artists have regularly engaged in historical themes without being good historians: Renaissance illustrations of biblical subjects often say more about fifteenth-century Europe than first-century Palestine; nineteenth-century images of the medieval could be grievously muddled. From time to time, artistic fashion has dictated that the subjects of portraits must be decked in fancy or historical dress –

'the foolish custom of painters dressing people like scaramouches', as Gainsborough called it: as potentially misleading to the student of costume as the arbitrary tints used in the hand-colouring of prints or the conventional stylisations of medieval miniatures. Compositional theory has often led artists to rearrange and edit the reality of a scene. William Gilpin, for one, heartily recommended it whenever it might be necessary to convert dull nature into Picturesque image on the page. Gilpin even went so far as to contemplate — not entirely facetiously — physical rearrangement of the ruins of Tintern Abbey by 'a mallet judiciously used' in the interests of a good picture.

It is an advantage to know the purpose for which an illustration has been made and to recognise how far removed it is from the original scene. As a preliminary sketch moved to a tidied-up drawing, to a second copy, to an engraver's back-to-front drawing, to the finished print, the detail of the picture might be divorced more and more from the subject – disfigured by inferior craftsmanship, or 'improved' by superior. The engraver's ingenuity might also serve a more doctrinaire purpose. Alexander Buchan, one of the artists on Captain Cook's first voyage to the South Pacific in 1769, produced a plain, realistic, on-the-spot drawing of Tierra del Fuegans crouching in their hut. However, for the printed version prepared for publication in 1773 of Hawkesworth's *Voyages,* Buchan's savages and their humble home have become transformed with the accession of a leafy glade, a blazing fire, contented faces and healthy infants, to accord more readily with current concepts about the idyllic nature of the primitive life.

Fortunately there has been a long tradition of more straightforward record-making. Inspired by a wide range of motives to set down an honest account of what they have seen has been a goodly assortment of artists, both professional and amateur: antiquarians, soldiers, topographers, travellers, heralds, and many others. Where immediacy and attention to accuracy is required, without always the gloss of fine art, it is likely to be found in their work. Samuel Grimm (1733-94) is a good example. Grimm was a Swiss-born immigrant to eighteenth-century England with a respectable talent for painting. He had the good fortune to fall in with the ecclesiastical antiquarian Sir Richard Kaye who befriended him and employed him, and took him off on a series of factfinding jaunts around the English shires. Kaye's commission was simply that Grimm make pictorial records of their trips, of 'everything curious' that they encountered along the way. The results were bundles of drawings and paintings that give a sharp flavour of eighteenth-century life. As an antiquary Kaye's eye was probably directed to churches and monuments; Grimm's pencil ranged more freely and took in people, their pastimes and their practices.

The superabundance of drawn, painted and printed material that has recorded our social past in pictures resides in all the archives, libraries, galleries and collections of the country. To do justice to its variety and multiplicity would be impossible, certainly in any brief survey. To map its whereabouts would be a vast enterprise. For some areas the work has begun. Invaluable in the location of topographical material is the excellent *Guide to British Topographical Collections,* by M.W. Barley. Barley's catalogue can be used to trace pictures beyond the bounds of the strictly topographical. Included are many 'grangerised' volumes, sources that well repay study since they may include all kinds of unexpected material. The practice of extra-illustrating or 'grangerising' was established in 1769 when the print collector James Granger published a *Biographical History of England* that had blank leaves for the readers to fill with their own pictures. Collecting drawings, prints and autographs to complete a 'Granger' became a fashionable hobby in the nineteenth century. It moved on to other suitable texts, especially county histories. Many such collections remain to this day in private hands, since as A.N.L. Munby has pointed out in *The Cult of the Autograph Collector,* 'their cost and sumptuousness have made them unattractive to institutional librarians, in general an austere class'. For the social historian looking for visual material for a particular locality the reverse is true, and the discovery of an extra-illustrated set of county histories, in some cases expanded to five or six times their original size by the added pictures, can be a godsend.

Types of source material are varied indeed: printed books, magazines, sets of engravings, diaries, travel journals and sketchbooks, manuscripts and personal papers, illustrated reports from exploratory excursions and official commissions. One interesting source is the *Album Amicorum,* the ancestor of the modern autograph album. This was a book kept 'for remembrance sake' in which friends were invited to enter sentiments and signatures, often accompanied by handsome little drawings or woodcuts. The practice arose among students in sixteenth-century Germany wishing to retain a souvenir of their professors and other eminent persons met on their travels. Most of the best examples originate from Germany, but foreign universities were part of the academic tour, so it is possible to find items portraying life in Britain.

A hunt for material may lead through a patchwork of catalogues, indices and guides. The holdings of the Department of Prints and Drawings at the British Museum has no overall catalogue, although there are available various specialised catalogues and inventories, together with a very helpful *User's Guide.* For its collections of prints and drawings the Victoria and Albert maintains indexes of both artists and subject. Graphic works covering virtually any topic may be sought at the British Museum, the Victoria and Albert Museum and its many outposts, and, in more scattered fashion, on the shelves of the British Library. The last possesses not only illustrated books, newspapers (at Colindale) and other printed matter, but also innumerable drawings on all kinds of subjects: the Department of Manuscripts boasts the largest collection of topographical material in the country, while the Map Library houses the famous 'King's Topographical Collection' of prints and drawings which was formed by George III; the India Office Library (now part of the British Library) has over 15,000 drawings by British artists illustrating life under the Raj, and indeed the whole culture and history of European contact with South Asia.

The Guildhall Library has an excellent, card-indexed collection of prints and drawings that relate primarily to the metropolitan area, and most local museums and record offices have pictures that are of local interest. In many cases the characteristics of the quarry determine likely ground to be hunted: the British Architectural Library for architectural drawings, the National Portrait Gallery for portraits and silhouettes, the Imperial War Museum for war-time pictures, the Science Museum and the Wellcome Institute Library for medical and scientific subjects, the Punch Library and the Cartoon Study Centre, University of Kent, for caricature – a whole gamut of nationwide institutions from the Bewick Museum in Northumberland to the museum at Lord's cricket ground.

All the main national collections have photographic services: they will normally require detailed references to locate material, and a degree of patience may be called for before orders can be fulfilled. If their stringent security and conservation conditions for loan can be met, it may also be possible to borrow from them for temporary exhibition.

'He that likes not the discourse,' announced Izaac Walton modestly in *The Compleat Angler,* 'should like the pictures of the Trout and other fish.' There will be few occasions when an imaginative choice of illustrations does not add to the content of an historical discourse.

Select Bibliography

Arnold, Janet, *A Handbook of Costume,* Macmillan, 1973.

Barley, M.W., *A Guide to British Topographical Collections,* Council for British Archaeology, 1974.

Barr, John, *Britain Portrayed: Colour Plate Books and Topographical Illustration 1790-1840,* British Library Publications, 1989.

Basing, Patricia, *Trades and Crafts in Medieval Manuscripts,* British Library Publications, 1990.

Birch, W. De Gray, and Jenner, Henry, *Early Drawings and Illuminations...with a Dictionary of Subjects in the British Museum,* London, 1879.

Clark, Michael, *The Tempting Prospect: A Social History of Watercolour,* Colonnade Books, 1981.

Gard, Robin, *The Observant Traveller: Diaries of Travel in England, Wales and Scotland in the County Record Offices of England and Wales,* HMSO, 1989.

George, Dorothy M., *Social Change and Graphic Satire from Hogarth to Cruikshank,* London, 1967.

George, Dorothy M., and Stephens, F.G., *British Museum Catalogue of Personal and Political Satires,* 11 vols, British Museum, 1870-1954.

Glass, Elizabeth, *Subject Index for the Visual* Arts, HMSO, 2 parts, 1962.

Goldman, Paul, *Looking at Drawings: A Guide to Technical Terms,* British Museum Publications, 1979.

Goldman, Paul, *Looking at Prints: A Guide to Technical Terms,* British Museum Publications, 1981.

Griffiths, Antony, and Williams, Reginald, *The Department of Prints and Drawings in the British Museum: User's Guide,* British Museum Publications, 1987.

Griffiths, Antony, *Prints and Printmaking: An Introduction to the History and Techniques,* British Museum Publications, 1980.

Harris, J., *The Artist and the Country House,* Sotheby's. Revised ed., 1984.

Hunnisett, Basil, *Steel-engraved Book Illustration in England,* Scolar Press, 1980.

Munby, A.N.L., *The Cult of the Autograph Letter,* University of London, Athlone Press, 1962.

Nickson, M.A.E., *Early Autograph Albums in the British Museum,* British Museum Publications, 1970.

Payne, Ann, *Views of the Past; Topographical Drawings in the British Library,* British Library Publications, 1987.

Reynolds, Graham, *Handbook to Collections in the Department of Prints, Drawings and Paintings in the Victoria and Albert Museum,* 2nd revised ed., 1982.

Russell, R., *Guide to British Topographical Prints,* Newton Abbott, 1979.

Trevelyan, G.M., *Illustrated Social History of England,* Longman, Green & Co., 1949.

24   Photographs and Films

Gareth Griffiths

Director, Empire and Commonwealth Museum, Bristol

Gaby Porter

Curatorial Services Manager, Museum of Science and Industry, Manchester

Introduction

Photographs and films are among the most prolific and materially problematic collections in social history. Their acquisition and use has burgeoned recently in museums, archives and particularly in institutions with an emphasis on the community and on history 'from the bottom up'.[1] Museums often treat photographs exclusively as a source, a conveyor of meaning which can be stripped off the surface of the picture. Thus, although long established collections in museums may be difficult to use for social history (except to demonstrate the earlier interests and practices of the museum), photographic and film collections appear to merit attention. They may be re-classified and reconstituted within the new social history discipline.[2] Other collections may consist of groups of negatives without the prints made from them, and with little circumstantial and supporting evidence.[3]

Historic photographs and film always need to be used with caution. Their evidence is suspect: they edit, they omit, and their meaning depends to a large degree on how they are re-used. Deployed in the publicity and literature of heritage, for instance, historic photographs can appear to testify to the reality and truth of a history which in fact has been considerably simplified. Contemporary photographs, which are produced in response to the commercial forces of heritage or tourism, can reinforce and amplify the renovation of history by portraying it as attractive, exciting, consumable. It is against this background that curators face the challenge of interpreting and using film and photographs as historical evidence.

Photographs and film are used extensively by museums in a number of ways: as exhibition prints, celebrated for their art; combined with artefacts and/or texts in temporary exhibitions and permanent displays; as research sources for internal and, usually, for public reference; as illustration and evidence in publications. They are rarely used as propaganda or polemic, with juxtaposition on images and/or image text, although this approach has been important in other areas.[4]

Museums approach history through visible and tangible objects which appear to offer obvious and value-free evidence of the past. Objects are frequently seen as natural and direct reflections of the world, representing the past simply and unambiguously. Photographs appear particularly useful in this respect because they are always, at some level, true. They are fundamentally connected to some prior object or event, and bear the physical traces of a past reality. In their pursuit of the real, museums concentrate upon the recent past where objects are relatively abundant. Photography frequently plays a supporting role in this process by offering both the visitor and the curator instant gratification – history at a glance.

Photography and Film as Sources

Histories of photography are grounded on an art historical approach – a history of artist-photographers which is presented through the monograph and the exhibition – or on a technical history which stresses photography as a science, and celebrates its inventors and pioneers. Between the peaks of art and science lies a huge and amorphous body of work which employs photography as evidence in telling other histories – the history of a family, town or trade in social and local history, for example. Virtually every museum collects and uses photographs in this way.

Inside and outside museums, historians are extremely selective in their acquisition and use of photographs. In the nineteenth century, the vast majority of photographs produced were commercial portraits. In this century, and particularly in the second half of the century, the majority of photographs taken, and photographers, are amateur and personal; the photographs most widely circulated and viewed are commercial and advertising photographs. Yet, from these mountains of photographs, museums select a tiny proportion which match their own purposes and uses. They demur at commercial portraits, or amateur snaps and home movies, as too particular. Equally, they spurn obviously artistic or promotional works as too contrived. Instead, they choose the small number of photographs which show the street, the home, the workplace, the fields. They prefer the work of disinterested amateurs or professionals. Here, they seek historical evidence where material and written sources are lacking. This approach is grounded in a belief in photography as a transparent medium of recording, as a window on the world. 'The viewer is confronted, not by historical writing, but by the appearance of history itself.' [5]

However, the traditional patterns of (mis)representation and the organisational restraints on visual reporting are major concerns for the film and photograph record considered as a source for history. An exhibition on Isambard Kingdom Brunel used Brunel as a focus to examine the nature of the photographic record of the world of industry and its nineteenth-century workforce.[6] It showed that very few photographs of workers exist from the period; indeed, the catalogue of the British worker in nineteenth-century photography is one of exceptions. Of course, there are numerous photographs which show workers; but it is important to differentiate between photographs that happen to include workers and those which have workers as their main subject and purpose. In the early decades of photography, technical factors may explain some of the shortcomings of industrial photographs in general. Overwhelmingly, though, the absence of workers as subjects for the camera was the result not of technical restrictions on early photographers, but of social attitudes and economic forces. In the images by artists and illustrators which preceded the invention of photography, or coincide with its infancy, industrial workers either do not appear or play a subsidiary role in the picture. What the first decades of photography consistently fail to give us in direct evidence, however, they do provide in quite another way: 'in all those blurred, imperfect figures of workers ... hovering, semi-transparent, ghostly ... there is a perfect and haunting metaphor for the position of common people in mid-Victorian society – and indeed in the "making" of its history.'[7] In this indirect way photography tells us the marginal character of a section of Victorian society which remains almost invisible today.

Within the archive of 'documentary' photography and film, material from diverse sources, made for different clients and intended for different audiences, are contained and their differences are collapsed.[8] Curatorial practices lift the image out of context and invest it with a new authority, placing or inscribing it with another layer of meaning. On acquisition, the details of the date, place and people pictured may be recorded, but the history and provenance of the image as artefact are rarely documented. Once housed in the museum or archive, the conditions of photographic and film production – social, technical, aesthetic – are further neglected or obscured. The viewer/user looks at copy prints of uniform size, tone and finish. In research files, they may be organised according to their image content, in a classification which brings together images having the same subject matter.

The curator is both a collector and a creator of images on photograph, film and tape, whether these images are taken by her/himself or commissioned from others. The photographic/film record is assumed to be beneficial; its purpose(s) and usefulness are not analysed. Frequently, therefore, the curator creating the photographic record works within the same conventions and constraints as those of earlier photographers.[9] Recent research and display projects have attempted to reinstate the photograph as historical in itself, by examining the conditions in which photographs were made and viewed.[10] Who commissioned the photograph? Who was the photographer? With what instructions? With what intent? Where were the photographs placed and with what other materials? By whom were they viewed? How were they received and understood? For example, the carte-de-visite portraits of pit-brow lasses made and publicly displayed by Wigan photographers were produced as tourist souvenirs. They were bought by men visiting Wigan to view the curious sight of women in male attire working at the pit heads (the outdoor and most visible workers), or by commercial travellers to sell in Manchester and other cities.[11] The studio portraits concentrated on the women's working clothes, and used outdated tools and rustic settings as props. Some were sold in pairs, with an accompanying photograph of the same woman in her Sunday best. In museums, these photographs have come to represent evidence of another kind: examples of local occupations, evidence of occupational dress and tools, positive imagery of women's manual labour.

Museums apply particular criteria to the ways in which they select, collect, classify and interpret photographic materials. These, in turn, determine what is preserved for posterity, what is seen and how it is understood in the museum. Photography has a new role in museums: they rely upon it to provide the 'look of the past' in sites and displays which aim not only to interpret history, but to recreate it. Photography seems to tell us what 'it' was really like, offering the breadth and depth of context within which objects may be placed. In displays, photographs are employed generally to support objects and illustrate texts. They are used according to the accepted conventions of realism and objectivity: neutral grey, rectangular layout, no obvious intervention. The context in which the photographs were made and previously circulated is obscured through these uniform reproductions, with captions which briefly describe the content of the image. For example, museums may make use of commercial and advertising photographs – cropped and recopied to remove their references to promotion and selling – in a display showing how people lived. Again, photographs from a manufacturer's catalogue or report may be used to show the workplace and working conditions. Placed beside the material certainties of objects and the authoritative, generalising voice of the museum text, the photographs read as statements rather than arrangements; as fact, rather than intent – how people actually lived and worked, not how manufacturers wanted to persuade them to live or how employers sought to present their workforce.

Ever since the first cinematographers, such as William Friese-Greene, took moving pictures of short scenes of everyday people and events, historians have been interested in using film as a potential source of historical study. In 1934, the International Congress of the Historical Sciences began to examine the problems of collecting and sorting film material for historical purposes. As far as they were concerned, the term historical film could only be justifiably applied to those films which record a person or period from the time after the invention of cinematography and without dramaturgical or artistic purposes, that is those films which presented a visual record of a definite event, person or locality. At that stage, what interested these historians were the 'actuality' films or newsreels, not feature films or documentaries. Only relatively recently have feature films been considered as important evidence of the attitudes of the people making them and the period within which they were produced.

Film may therefore be analysed and used to provide information at a number of levels. Firstly, film offers a primary source of evidence because of the basic information it displays at the purely depictive levels, for example, information on the environment, life styles and patterns of behaviour. Secondly, film may be used to examine what 'messages' were being put across to the public at a particular period. Those categories of the film record, such as the newsreel and magazine film, may be viewed as a partial record of what the public saw of events and personalities of the day. The distinction between the information and the message which a film may contain is an important one, the basis of which is an acceptance that a piece of film is not some unadulterated reflection of historical truth captured by the camera. Sponsored films, such as *Housing Problems* sponsored by the Gas, Light and Coke Company, or *Drifters* by the Empire Marketing Board, provide insight into the motives of sponsoring institutions by revealing the views which they wanted the public to hold on contemporary issues. Viewed over a period, these films reflect changing styles and techniques of mass persuasion. Finally, what we do not see – censored footage etc. – provides a record of those social and political issues that were most likely to disturb significant groups at a given historical moment. Thus, studied over a period, excluded material records shifts in these concerns and values.

The pervasive power of film in the twentieth century is apparent, although its form constantly changes. In the 1930s, there were 30 visits per annum made to the cinema per head of population over sixteen in Britain; by 1990 the equivalent figure was 1.6 visits, although over 98% of households possessed a television and 40% a video recorder. When using film as historical evidence, it is necessary to examine carefully both its content and the context in which it was shown. For example, the newsreels of the 1930s and 1940s are records of events but also records of what a very large, socially important and relatively little documented section of the public saw and heard regularly. The importance of the medium must not be exaggerated; although it is difficult to measure accurately the influence of film in moulding opinion, enough information exists to caution us. In the early stages of the Second World War, Mass Observation looked at the relative importance of different propaganda channels in determining attitudes to the war and the understanding of the events leading up to it: 26% of the population stated that the press was the most important determining factor, 24% friends and acquaintances, 19% posters, 11% radio, 10% leaflets and books, 3% meetings and 1% films. The subtle indirect impact of film may not have been taken into account in such a survey. It is interesting, however, that the overwhelming majority of cinema audiences throughout the Second World War were very critical about newsreels, finding them largely trivial. For, as a news editor for Paramount remarked,

Theatre managers who have to show our newsreels do not think their function is to educate. They go to great effort in their theatres to set up the desired atmosphere of romance, happiness, music and soft lights, and along comes a newsreel with the latest race riot or something else that upsets the audience. Thus they are treated as part of the entertainment and the concentration on the ceremonial aspects of public affairs, sports, parades and mere curiosities.[12]

In addition to providing evidence on how and what the public were told about an event, the newsreel may also be used to provide primary evidence for what Asa Briggs described as 'those changes in the ways of seeing and feelings and the forms of perception and consciousness'.[13]

One of the most potent sources of information about the social history of Britain are the films of the Documentary Movement which, it has been suggested, present 'a cross-section of society, thus building an unique record of British life, its health, education and social services, its industries and communications'.[14] The main outlet for the films lay in non-theatrical distribution and they were shown mainly in schools and adult education groups. It is estimated that in 1936 the documentaries were shown to an audience of 500,000,compared with average weekly attendance at cinemas of 18.5 million. More research still needs to be done on the role of these documentaries and particularly upon the size, class structure and political attitudes of the audiences. However, the social importance of the Documentary Movement may have been exaggerated by individuals within the movement itself and by historians eager to find film material which contained a broader range of social subjects than was normally found in the mainstream of film making. The importance of the documentary film makers for the curator may lie in their aims and the techniques they employ to achieve these aims. The film makers sought not only to inform but also to enable the audience to see, know and feel the details of life: to feel oneself part of some other's experience. Two types of film and photographic records have been identified by documentary makers: one which gave factual information, and one which conveyed the feeling of lived experience. 'A good documentary should tell not only what a place or a thing or a person looks like, but it must also tell the audience what it would feel like to be an actual witness to the scene.'[15] As the documentary constantly addresses problems which can be changed by human intervention, the charge of propaganda and bias cannot be avoided, but it can be interpreted.

The past is a gold-mine for television/screen drama, with successful themes being reworked, producing 'codes of nostalgia'. These codes are a series of aural and visual markers which, when established, produce ways of reviving, or inventing, memories of a particular period. These codes are frequently reinforced by use in other areas such as advertising, photography and fashion, which further refines and reinforces their power. These codes of nostalgia are predominantly visual and are normally confined to certain aspects of the past — interior decoration, domestic equipment, advertising, dress. Film, together with photographs, are a part of the disparate range of forms which constitute a field of public representation operating as the infrastructure of popular memory. It is important to stress the complex and contradictory character of the field. It is a changing configuration of cultural forms, each with its own history; each evolving distinct, specific processes and relations of production and consumption; each producing meanings according to its own specific codes and conventions, for particular audiences. The adaptation of history to television exacerbates tendencies to accept versions of the past without reservation – frequently the historic dramas are taken for literal accounts of what actually happened, what life in the past was really like. The medium of film makes viewers feel they participated in the past. Books, artefacts, etc. that supplemented the memories of previous generations required interpretation and reconstruction. Film and photographs plunge us into the vivid past seemingly without mediation and inspire faith as records of reality which surpass the actual past, and mask the processes of selection, editing, and retouching.

As our knowledge of the past develops, together with a fuller understanding of the factors which play upon the historical evidence which filters down to us, a more rigorous approach to the interpretation and creation of this evidence is demanded of museums. In addition, museums are expected to be increasingly relevant both in terms of the record being generated and the interpretation presented.The recent debate about contemporary collecting in museums offered an opportunity to address some of these problems.[16] However, the discussions were largely confined to the cul-de-sac of object collecting and ignored the potential of a wider range of recording media. Little attempt has been made within museums to explore these alternative forms of recording media and to test their suitability for recording and interpreting differing forms of social activity. This will be one of the challenges of the future.

Notes

1. Such as at the Bradford Heritage Recording Unit or the Manchester Studies Unit, subsequently Documentary Photography Archive.

2. For example, the collection at Leeds City Museum. See David Fleming,'Photographic collections – a strategy for information retrieval (or curing the shoebox syndrome)', *MDA Information*, vol.9, no.1, April 1985, pp. 14-24.

3. For example, Lilian Ream Archive, Wisbech.

4. For example, Kathy Myers, *Understains*, Comedia/Routledge, 1986, pp. 90-97; Liz Heron, in *Photography/Politics: One*, Photography Workshop, 1979.

5. Allan Sekula, 'Photography between labour and capital', in Benjamin Buchloch and Robert Wilkie (eds), *Mining Photographers and Other Pictures: A Selection from the Negative Archives of Shedden Studio, Glace Bay, Cape Breton 1948-68*, Halifax, Press of the Nova Scotia College of Art and Design, 1983, p. 198.

6. Robert Powell, *Brunel's Kingdom*, Watershed Media Centre, Bristol.

7. Jeremy Seabrook, 'My life is in that box', *Ten:8*, no. 34, 1989, p. 35.

8. Paul Wombell makes this observation for photographs at the Imperial War Museum in 'Face to face with themselves', in Patricia Holland, Jo Spence and Simon Watney (eds), *Photography/Politics: Two*, Comedia/Photography Workshop, 1986, pp. 80-81.

9. This is seen most clearly in photographs of people at work, in which the work process is suspended, the subject stands or sits back from the work being done, and faces the camera. The subject is often portrayed full length and filling the frame.

10. For example, Sarah Edge, *Our Past – Our Struggle: Images of Women in the Lancashire Coal Mines 1860-1880*, Rochdale Art Gallery, 1986; Stephen Edwards, 'Disastrous documents', *Ten :8*, no. 15, 1984; John Tagg, 'God's sanitary law: slum clearance and photography in late nineteenth century Leeds', in *The Burden of Representation: Essays on Photographies and Histories*, Macmillan,1988.

11. See Sarah Edge, op. cit.

12. Quoted in Anthony Aldgate, *Cinema and History: British Newsreels and the Spanish Civil War*, Scolar Press, 1979, p. 33.

13. Asa Briggs, Introduction to conference papers on *The Distortion of History*, The Historical Association, University of London.

14. John Grierson, 'Documentary: the bright example', from Documentary 47, Edinburgh International Festival of Documentary Films, 1947. The word 'documentary', its generally accepted definition being 'the creative treatment of actuality', was first used in a film sense by John Grierson when writing in 1926 about Robert Flaherty's *Moana*. He described it as a visual account of the daily life of a Polynesian youth. Documentary became a movement in Britain in the 1930s, and the use of film for social comment was developed by the movement and eventually moved out of cinema and into television.

15. Roy Stryker (Director of the Farm Securities Administration Photographic Unit) quoted in William Stott, *Documentary Expression and Thirties America,* Chicago University Press, 1973.

16. See, for example, articles by David Fleming, Oliver Green, Mark Suggitt and Stuart Davies in *Museums Journal,* vol. 85, June 1985.

Bibliography

Coe, Brian, and Haworth-Booth, Mark, *A Guide to Early Photographic Processes,* Victoria and Albert Museum, 1986.

Edge, Sarah, *Our Past – Our Struggle: Images of Women in the Lancashire Coal Mines 1860-1880,* Rochdale Art Gallery, 1986.

Fleming, David, 'Photographic collections – a strategy for retrieval', *MDA Information,* vol.9, no.l, April 1985.

Ford, Colin, and Harrison, Brian, *A Hundred Years Ago,* Allen Lane The Penguin Press, 1983.

Hiley, Michael, *Seeing Through Photographs,* Gordon Fraser, 1983.

Marwick, Arthur, 'Archive film as source material', *Archive Film Compilation Booklet,* British Universities Film Council, 1973.

Morden, Terry, 'Documentary. Past. Future?' in Holland, Patricia, Spence, Jo, and Watney, Simon (eds), *Photography/Politics: Two,* Comedia/Photography Workshop, 1986.

Oliver, Elizabeth (ed.), *Researcher's Guide to British Film and Television Collections,* British Universities Film and Video Council, 1985.

Pronay, Nicholas, 'British newsreels in the 1930s. Part I: Audience and producers', *History,* vol. 56, October 1971.

Richards, Jeffrey, and Sheridan, Dorothy, *Mass Observation at the Movies,* Routledge, 1987.

Smith, Paul (ed.), *The Historian and Film,* Cambridge University Press, 1976.

Stott, William, *Documentary Expression and Thirties America,* Chicago University Press.

Tagg, John, *The Burden of Representation: Essays on Photographies and Histories,* Macmillan, 1988.

Taylor, John, *Pictorial Photography in Britain 1900-1926,* Arts Council of Great Britain, 1978.

Ten: 8, international photography magazine, 9 Keyhill Drive, Birmingham B18 5NY.

Williams, Val, *Women Photographers – The Other Observers 1900 to the Present,* Virago, 1986.

Photographic Collections

Photographs are held in almost every museum, public record office and local history library in Great Britain. Commercial picture libraries and press picture libraries provide materials, at a cost. Photographs are also held in many private collections.

Eakins, Rosemary, *Private Sources UK: A Guide to more than 1100 Public and Private Picture Collections,* Macdonald, 1985.

Evans, Hilary, and Evans, Mary, *Picture Researcher's Handbook: The International Guide to Picture Sources and How to Use Them,* Van Nostrand Reinhold (UK), 1986, 3rd ed.

Wall, J., *Directory of British Photographic Collections,* Royal Photographic Society/Heinemann, 1977.

Among museum collections, the following are outstanding in their organisation and content. All should be contacted by letter in the first instance to make a detailed request.

Department of Photographs, Imperial War Museum, Lambeth Road, London SE1 6HZ.

Modern Department, Museum of London, London Wall, London EC2Y 5HN.

National Museum of Photography, Film and Television, Prince's View, Bradford BD5 0TR.

Part Four   Practice

Introduction

Having looked at the theory of social history in museums, and having reviewed briefly the different approaches to the study of objects that characterise the different disciplines and some of their methods of study, we come in this section to the practice of social history in museums.

The section begins by looking at five *collecting methods* used in social history work in museums. Mark O'Neill addresses the need for a collecting policy that is not only realistic and intellectually coherent, but that reflects a real relationship between the museum and its community. Valerie Bott asks what that community really is, and examines ways in which the museum can in practice involve the community in its collecting. Mark Suggitt shows why the curator should respect and make use of the antique trade – too often a focus of curators' fear and distrust – while remaining wary. The social history curator, though, is above all concerned to acquire information with the objects. Stephen Price and Nicholas Molyneux give very practical advice on perhaps the most elaborate 'information context' – the recording of interiors. Roy Brigden demonstrates from the example of MERL how recording information can transform a collection. He stresses, too, the contribution the collectors' choices make to creating a distinctive collection. Oliver Green considers still photography and video as recording techniques, as collections in their own right, and as techniques for communicating with visitors.

More than any other museum discipline, social history involves a vast variety of types of object, of materials, sizes and problems. The following chapters therefore look at various categories of collection that frequently raise *special problems* in museums. Steph Mastoris argues the importance of printed ephemera in any social history collection covering the past century. Printed ephemera does present the curator with problems, but they are problems which it is important to tackle. Documents are vital to the historian, and often indivisible from objects. Elizabeth Frostick discusses when documents should be in museums rather than in archives, their care and ways of displaying and interpreting them. Gaby Porter advises on the management and care of 'probably the most chemically complex and physically fragile artefacts in historical collections': photographs and film. Clothes are equally challenging to the social history curator, but can be hugely rewarding in public response. Helen Clark looks at clothing as a social historian, and concentrates on collecting and display and interpretation. The biggest 'special problem' facing many a curator is the museum building itself. David Fleming gives advice on the curator's twofold task: to reconcile all collection management needs with the duty to 'curate' the building itself. To most non-specialists, plastics and rubber are a mystery. Gordon Watson summarises recent research on their history and gives many hints on how to recognise and identify them. Pharmaceuticals, too, are an area little understood by most social history curators, despite the many collections which contain pharmacy material. Kate Arnold-Forster gives comprehensive guidance on the display and care of such material, including the legal position regarding drugs. Nicholas Hall's subject, firearms, also has serious safety and legal aspects. He covers those as well as collecting, collection care and interpretation. To cover the huge subject of hazards in the collection comprehensively would require volumes. Karen Hull aims only to increase the alertness of curators to potential hazards, and to offer hints for an effective Safety Audit. Contemporary collecting is much discussed, but still too often shied away from. Rosie Crook shows that contemporary collecting really is worth doing, even with very limited resources, and offers suggestions on where to start. Stuart Davies makes a powerful case for taking coins and medals seriously, and suggests ways of using them in a social history context.

Documenting social history collections is a vitally important part of the museum's work. Stuart Holm identifies three areas where the standard museum documentation procedures must be tailored to suit the special nature of social history collections. These are the structure of the catalogue record, the terminology control used in this record and elsewhere, and indexing/retrieval requirements. The whole huge area of *restoration and conservation,* of care of collections generally, can only be approached in this book. The first approach is by Bob Child, who sets out the ethics that must guide the social history museum when it intervenes in its objects. The second approach is by George Monger, whose recommendations on preventative conservation seek to make intervention unnecessary. Annie Hood offers basic guidance on the design and management of museum *storage* for social history reserve and research collections.

A lively social history museum is constantly interacting with a variety of other institutions, professions and individuals. The next chapters cover the social history curator's *liaison with others.* David Fleming covers liaison with two professions often encountered and often misunderstood: architects and planners. Developing a sympathy with their priorities and an understanding of their work will bring direct benefits to the museum. Local history librarians are to the general public scarcely distinguishable from curators, yet our professional backgrounds differ widely. Valerie Bott shows how each profession's strengths and weaknesses can complement or compensate for the other's. Perhaps even closer to the social history museum is the record office. Kate Thompson, herself an archivist, describes the principles and approaches of her profession, and suggests areas for cooperation with museums. The world of field archaeology is changing rapidly as '80s principles are applied to public affairs in the '90s. Judi Caton describes how Archaeological Units grew up and how they operate today; she suggests a variety of ways in which museums and Units can help each other, and areas in which they can cooperate. Mark Taylor briefly sketches the role of government agencies – particularly English Heritage and the Royal Commission on Historical Monuments – and describes how social history curators can use the National Monuments Record and local Sites and Monuments Records. The 'vibrant parochialism' of the amateur local historian is as valuable as the professionalism of the history curator. Sam Mullins tackles the opportunities and the pitfalls when they work together in local societies. No social history museum with an interest in the English countryside can be unaware of the Museum of English Rural Life at Reading University. Roy Brigden describes the riches of its artefact, photograph and archive collections. Much more difficult is liaison where the parties have quite different aims and values; this can frequently be the case with museums and private collectors. David Viner describes why it is worth facing the difficulties, and how rewarding success can be. Formal education offers such a vast and such an important market for the museum's services that many curators with straitened resources are daunted. Catherine Hall takes a practical low-key approach to liaison with schools and colleges, and reminds curators that liaison is a two-way process. Jane Middleton notes briefly some of the implications for museums of the Education Reform Act, 1988.

Crispin Paine

25 Collecting Policies

Mark O'Neill

Keeper of Social History, Glasgow Museums and Art Galleries

The quality of a museum's collecting policy, whether written or unwritten, depends on the coherence of the idea of social history on which it is based, and on the clarity of the purpose which the museum serves. Being an all-embracing discipline, social history might seem to require that everything be collected. This is both practically impossible and intellectually absurd; it is the curator's job to select what is significant. As selection does take place, criteria of significance must exist, however inchoate. Material is not collected in a vacuum but on behalf of the public by members of a profession, so that there is a dual obligation to the community and to colleagues to make these criteria of selection explicit. These obligations are recognised by the Museums and Galleries Commission's Registration Scheme, which requires the formal adoption of a collecting policy. Thus such a policy is a prerequisite for the receipt of Area Museum Council grant aid. More generally, the museum's definition of its social purpose – the clientele it serves, be it a local community, a national specialist interest group, or tourists – and the way in which the collections are to be made relevant to them, are matters for the public domain. These are key factors in deciding social history priorities and in selecting objects for a museum collection. These priorities will change over time, if the museum is to maintain a relationship with the present. However, if the museum is in any doubt about the priorities it is working by at present, then the process of writing a collecting policy will be of great benefit to the museum's sense of direction.

Collecting Policies, Written and Unwritten

Unwritten social history collecting policies abound. They vary from 'I feel so guilty when I say No!' to 'The store is full'. The unselective curator, or the curator who simply exercises an intuition on the objects the public offers, collects only what members of the museum-going public think is worth saving from their past. Members of this group are rarely representative of the community as a whole, and their predilections are likely to reinforce those of the curator whose social background and education is likely to be closer to those of the visitors than to those of the general public. The exercise of curatorial expertise involves bringing the subject – in this case social history – into a relationship with the target client group, so that both are served as comprehensively as possible. The passive receipt or intuitive editing of donations is not, however, to be confused with the vigorous and omnivorous collecting practised, for example, during the formative period at Beamish, even though it is described as 'unselective' by the curator. While everything offered by the public was accepted, the museum also went to great lengths to inform the public about what was required; a travelling exhibition and newspaper appeals showed a very broad public what the museum wanted. Thus both curatorial expertise and community values played complementary roles in forming the collection. The demands of the subject, the needs and desires of the client community, and the practical constraints on resources are the key elements in constructing a collecting policy.

Existing Collections

The demands of the subject may be very different from the demands of the collections, and the decision to continue certain collecting lines depends on which of these is given priority. Many museum collections still reflect their origin in the nineteenth century, when the pervasive influence of natural history collections led to a taxonomic approach: the desire to collect an example of every type of every class of object that existed. Social history, like modern natural sciences, is much more concerned with context and relationships – be it an ecosystem or a family, a workplace or a community. The existing collection can usually be assessed by comparing it to the Social History and Industrial Classification system (using the museum's own system may simply reinforce existing predilections). This will reveal gaps, and the curator will have to decide whether these should be filled, or whether the existing strengths of the collection should be built on. The collecting policy will therefore include a virtual inventory of the collection, listing each major component of it and specifying whether or not similar or related objects will be collected in the future.

A crucial criterion for assessing strengths and weaknesses of existing collections is not, however, the number of objects, but the level of their documentation. A large collection of objects without proven relevant provenance is often less valuable than a small well-documented group. While object classification may alert one to the enduring physical properties of Victorian smoothing irons, it is not sufficient solely to ask if one wants a more comprehensive collection. A series of sewing machines in chronological order may reveal something about technological advances, but the decision on what else to collect in relation to them does not refer solely to sewing machines: if the museum is interested in how they were manufactured, then a whole complex of material is relevant. If domestic use is the theme, then a wholly different context is raised. The decision 'enough irons' or 'enough sewing machines' also requires other decisions relating to different types of object and to two-dimensional support material.

The most important decision to make about any object collected is how much of its context will be collected as well, and in what form. Removing an object from its habitat and conferring on it the new significance of being Chosen often undermines the reason for collecting it. A key factor in any collecting policy is the level of documentation that is required by any object for it to be relevant. While a locally made object may require only this fact to justify its place in the collection, one made elsewhere but locally used will need better credentials in the form of a detailed lifestory in the locality, or association with a particular person or place. One may have decided 'enough sewing machines', but if those in the collection are undocumented it may still be worth acquiring another if it is accompanied by photographs of it in use, objects made with it, descriptions of it being manufactured, etc. Alternatively, if an example of the type is in the collection, then the documentation alone may be deemed adequate.

It is a delicate matter how much of the rationale of selecting an individual object is written into a collecting policy, but it is worth specifying research, publication, interpretation and display. If the object cannot in the foreseeable future contribute to one of these functions, either by itself, with accompanying documentation, or in relationship to existing collections, storing it is a waste of the museum's space.

Most objects only become meaningful in terms of social history if they are adequately documented. The best time to collect such supporting material is at the same time as the object. Thus staff training in debriefing would-be donors is essential, and the collecting policy could very well include a simple questionnaire asking for details about the ownership of the object, the possible existence of related objects and documentation, and brief biographical information about the donor.

Recording the context from which objects are removed is now a standard part of most field collecting. This may be done with a variety of media, but the black and white photograph still provides the longest-lived record. Colour can be an important element in many contexts, and the low ASA colour slide is the best medium for this. With the availability of cheap automatic 35 mm cameras, a basic record can be made with a minimum of cost and expertise, although most museums will aspire to higher standards.

A Word about Contemporary Collecting

The foregoing remarks apply to collecting from the present as well as from the past. Difficulties arise, however, which are not so much due to our lack of clarity about the subject of contemporary collecting, but about the museum's relationship to its client group. Unless a museum is constantly renewing its relationship with the present, its collections will represent a fossilised view of the world.

For the present as well as the past it is the curator's job to select significant objects and record their contexts with a view to portraying social history for a specific group of people who are alive today. The multitude of objects available does create difficulties, but even if the random sieve of time is allowed to make the selection the museum should at least be creating a photographic record of the major contexts from which objects will be collected. The choice of media – video, tape recording, photography, etc. – will depend on the museum's resources and the amount of context required to collect the object's meaning as well as the thing itself.

Disposal

Collecting an object for a museum expresses an intention to preserve that object for ever. The Museums Association Codes of Conduct for Curators and Governing Bodies enjoin a strong presumption against disposal, as do the Museums and Galleries Commission guidelines on Registration. Every collecting policy should, however, include a mechanism for disposal and a clear statement on the conditions under which it can take place.

A number of the most important national museums and galleries are governed under Acts of Parliament which specifically prohibit the disposal of items in the collections and, even where this is not the case, various severe restrictions are placed on the powers to dispose of items from the museum or gallery.

So far as local authority and private trust museums and galleries are concerned, attention is drawn to the important advice on the legal position included in the 'Report of the Committee of Enquiry into the Sale of Works of Art by Public Bodies' (HMSO, 1964) as follows:

The basic principle upon which the law rests is that when private persons give property for public purposes the Crown undertakes to see that it is devoted to the purposes intended by the donor, and to no others. When a work of art is given to a museum or gallery for general exhibition, the public thereby acquires rights in the object concerned and these rights cannot be set aside. The authorities of the museum or gallery are not the owners of such an object in the ordinary sense of the word: they are merely responsible, under the authority of the Courts, for carrying out the intentions of the donor. They cannot sell the object unless authorised to do so by the Courts or by the Charity

Commissioners or the Minister of Education on behalf of the Courts, because they have themselves nothing to sell. If they attempt a sale in breach of trust it is the function of the Attorney General to enforce the trust and protect the rights of the public in the object by taking proceedings in the 'Chancery Division.'

It should also be stressed that even where general powers to disposal exist a museum or art gallery may not be completely free to dispose of items purchased. Where financial assistance has been obtained from an outside source (for example central government grant-in-aid, National Art Collections Fund, Friends of the Museum organisation, or a private benefactor) disposal would require the consent of all parties who had contributed to the purchase.

In those cases where a museum is free to dispose of an item (e.g. by virtue of a local Act of Parliament or of permission from the High Court or the Charity Commissioners), any decision to sell or dispose of material from the collections should be taken only after due consideration, and such material should be offered first, by exchange, gift or private treaty sale, to other museums before sale by public auction is considered.

In cases in which an arrangement for the exchange, gift or private treaty sale of material is not being made with an individual museum, the museum community at large must be advised of the intention to dispose of material through an announcement in the *Museums Journal*. The announcement must indicate the number of specimens involved, the prime objects concerned and the basis on which the material would be transferred to another institution. A period of at least two months must be allowed for an interest in acquiring the material to be expressed.

A decision to dispose of a specimen or work of art, whether by exchange, sale or destruction (in the case of an item too badly damaged or deteriorated to be restorable), should be the responsibility of the governing body of the museum acting on the advice of professional curatorial staff and not of the curator of the collection concerned acting alone. Full records should be kept of all such decisions and the specimens involved and proper arrangements made for the preservation and/or transfer, as appropriate, of the documentation relating to the object concerned, including photographic records where practicable.

Any monies received by a governing body from the disposal of specimens or works of art should be applied solely for the purchase of additions to the museum or art gallery collections.

A Sample Collecting Policy

1. The museum will collect only that material which has a proven relationship with the borough/district/county and which relates to the research, interpretation and display of its social history. The boundaries of the collecting area have been agreed with neighbouring museums (specify, and attach agreements as appendices to the policy).

2. The museum will collect only that material which is related to its specialism defined as follows (specify). When collecting material, the museum will not compete against local museums but consult them as to their intentions. In the event of conflicting claims, efforts will be made to refer the question to an independent arbiter.

3. The museum will collect material from 1500 to the present day. Earlier material will be passed on to an appropriate archaeological museum (specify).

4. The museum will acquire more of the following types of object from the following periods, to make its existing collections more complete (specify).

5. The museum will collect no more of the following types of object from the following periods as its existing collections are adequate (specify). It will, however, collect ancillary material which will increase the research and display value of the existing material (specify).

6. Every object collected will be sufficiently documented to ensure that it will serve a number of research and display purposes. Wherever possible a photographic record will be made of the context from which an object is removed.

7. Archival, photographic and other two-dimensional materials will be passed on to the following institutions except where they are few in number and accompany objects acquired by the museum (specify). The museum reserves the right to collect two-dimensional material of sufficient visual interest to be worthy of display (e.g. advertisements) and which is not in the collecting policies of the above institutions (e.g. family photographs).

8. The museum shall not dispose of its collections except in exceptional circumstances and then only with the agreement of the trustees/governors. Any object to be disposed of shall in the first instance be offered to other museums.

Conclusion

A collecting policy can be easily taken to be a paper exercise to comply with the conditions of Registration, or to conform to the latest management fashion. If taken seriously, however, it can be a really useful tool for managing collections, clarifying the purpose of the museum for staff, members of the governing body, other museums, and the general public. Such clarity is essential for efficient use of resources, good teamwork, and good social history research and displays.

Bibliography

Mayo, E.P., 'Contemporary collecting: collecting the twentieth century requires more work and a new philosophy', *History News*, vol. 39, 1982.

Museums and Galleries Commission, *Guidelines for a Registration Scheme for Museums in the United Kingdom*, HMSO, 1989.

Museums and Galleries Commission, *Guidance Notes for Museums in Scotland*, HMSO, 1990.

Museums Journal, vol. 85, no 1 is devoted to contemporary collecting and includes an article on collecting at Beamish.

Rosander, G., *Today for Tomorrow: Museum Documentation in Sweden by Acquisition of Objects*, SAMDOK Council, Stockholm, 1980.

Schlereth,T.J., 'Collecting ideas and artifacts: common problems of history museums and history texts', in *Artifacts and the American Past*, AASLH, Nashville, 1980.

Journal of the Social History Curators Group, vol. 13, 1986, has a number of articles on collecting.

26.1   Collecting Methods: Community Involvement

Valerie Bott

Curator, Passmore Edwards Museum Service

Social history, more than any other museum discipline, is the history of communities; the majority of Britain's social history museums draw their collections from a specific local community. The community is thus not only the subject for recording and research but also the primary source of artefacts and information. In addition it provides the main audience for the museum's interpretation of its past. The relationship between the curator and the community is a peculiarly sensitive one.

Defining 'the community' in the context of a museum requires great care. The community already defines itself in many ways. Individuals can identify clearly the communities in which they operate: these relate to work, to leisure activities and to the geographical area in which their homes are located, and all of them overlap and interlock. The museum must not risk becoming too closely identified with one specific community to the apparent exclusion of others. And it needs to be able to react quickly to changes in the community which affect both its collecting activities and its potential audience.

The context in which a museum operates – its origins, the sources of its funding and its style of management – affects its relationship with the community. A small museum, established as a result of the enthusiasms of a few individuals, may remain firmly their possession even though they claim to be acting for the community as a whole. In sensitive hands, whether those of an honorary curator or a professional, such a museum may blossom into something which truly involves and represents a wider, clearly identifiable community. An industrial site museum may emerge from the efforts of a group of industrial archaeology enthusiasts, campaigning to save the site from redevelopment. The struggle to survive as a commercially viable tourist attraction changes the nature of such a community effort, even though the community may still be represented by volunteer helpers and an annual grant from the local authority. While local people may remain proud of this important site virtually on their doorstep and may welcome the prosperity its visitors can bring, the museum's role is less likely to be focused so closely on the life of the community itself.

Local authority museums face different problems in defining their community. The local council may expect the museum to operate within the authority's boundaries, providing a service targeted specifically at those who live there and who fund it. Such an area may not form a coherent entity historically, having been created comparatively recently as a unit of local government. Even though such an area may embrace a number of very diverse communities, its history can be recorded and represented within one museum service. Though few people would claim that there are many votes in museums, the local authority provides a democratic and direct means of funding and managing a museum for its community. There have been, and still are, local authorities which undervalue and neglect their social history collections and some make no contribution to recording their communities' history at all. But the combination of an energetic and knowledgeable curator, an informed demand from within the community, and an enlightened local council can ensure that exhibitions tell the local story, show a wide range of material and provide a strong sense of place.

Collecting the history of a community, therefore, depends on a close understanding of its nature, past and present, and on curatorial sensitivity to the relationship with that community which makes collecting possible. While a certain amount of material can always be purchased in the junk shop or at auction, the principal source of provenanced social history objects remains donations from the owners, makers or users of an object, or their relatives. The stories such donors can tell about the origins of the object, the ways in which it was used or modified, how much it cost and who used it, provide a crucial context unavailable from any other source. Potential donors must feel that their contribution will be well cared for and wisely used; such gifts often come at some personal cost to the donor, whether sentimental or financial. The museum must provide an atmosphere of trust to give donors the confidence to offer unsolicited objects or information. Once this is established active collecting becomes much easier.

How, then, can we create the comfortable atmosphere which encourages visitors to become involved in the process of building a collection? Many small touches in the displays can signal the fact that the museum welcomes their involvement. The simple acknowledgement by name of donors and lenders on display labels is an inexpensive way of indicating the source of the collections and a much more 'user-friendly' method of providing an official provenance than a bald accession number which few understand. Interpretative text can make clear the fact that some information is still missing from the story being told; this may take the form of an explicit request for a specific kind of object or it may be a simple statement indicating that any further information about this local activity would be welcomed. A great deal can be gained from creating the idea of a partnership between the museum and its public in this quest for more knowledge as this is exactly the relationship the curator needs to build with the community.

Perhaps even more important is the way the museum staff handle an offer of material for the museum collection. Museum attendants and reception staff must be sufficiently knowledgeable about the work of the museum to react sympathetically to such an offer. They need to explain that the relevant curator needs to see the object – and contact that curator immediately if that is practicable. If this is not possible, taking an accurate record of what is on offer and where the donor can be contacted not only ensures that the object is not lost but also reassures the donor that his or her offer may be of value to the work of the museum. A casual attitude at this point, or a request to come back another day on the off-chance that the curator might be available could be very damaging to the welcoming image the museum needs to project to its public.

In addition the attendants need to be able to soothe the donor who is disappointed to find that a recent gift is not on show, explaining how the collection works, that some items in store are used for research or for handling sessions, that displays of recent acquisitions are organised at regular intervals to show off such gifts and underlining the museum's role as collector for the future as well as interpreter for the present day. All this may seem obvious to the curator but it should be built into the training given to all museum staff who have contact with members of the public.

Other factors contribute to the museum's image as an accessible institution for the whole of its community. Intellectual accessibility is reinforced by the use of simple language rather than jargon in exhibitions and publications, by the style of the exhibitions with lively colour and plenty to see rather than restrained decor and a few objects treated as icons on elegant plinths. Physical accessibility applies as much to the able-bodied as to the disabled. Clear signing and large display text positioned where it can easily be read, objects positioned low enough for children and those in wheel-chairs to see, flooring that is comfortable to stand on and seating available at regular intervals in public galleries – all reinforce the feeling that the museum has been planned with the visitors in mind.

So, if the philosophy of the museum is right, if it feels welcoming and comfortable to visitors, if it takes care to avoid appearing to be the possession of one limited group within the community, how does the curator ensure that the objects which are needed come pouring in? While the factors outlined above will encourage successful passive collecting, with visitors offering whatever they think may be of use, active collecting, in accordance with a clearly defined policy, requires something more. This policy must be written in language that everyone can understand and should be published, if only in a typewritten and photocopied form. The museum's attendants will feel happier about explaining that something offered may not be accepted if they can show a potential donor a copy of the policy. The governing body of the museum, whether local councillors of not, will be in a better position to become part of the museum's public relations machine if they have adopted a policy which they can support and whose implications they understand. And defining a policy, recommended by the Museums Association's *Code of Practice for Museum Authorities* and required by the Museums and Galleries Commission's Registration Scheme, is an extremely good discipline for the curator when coupled with a careful assessment of the resources needed for its implementation.

Active collecting must be just that. Defining priority subject areas and establishing a timetable for developing them should be part of the creation of the policy. Implementing the policy requires some skill in publicity and public relations to ensure that as wide a cross-section of the community as possible knows that its help is needed. And an end-product, in the form of an exhibition, a publication or an event, provides a crucial opportunity for sharing the success of the project and thanking those who were involved as well as signalling a role for those who may be able to help in future. It is unlikely to be enough merely to publicise a project of this kind to museum visitors. Indeed, it ought to provide an excellent opportunity for involving people who have never used the museum before. The local press, radio and television may provide useful publicity. However, it may be useful to enlist the help of a relevant organisation, local or national, to start the ball rolling; they will benefit from the publicity and it will make a better media story. Publicise both successes and failures as the project goes on; it can be equally useful to admit that a project is proving more difficult than expected as to trumpet astonishing finds, for both can prompt a reaction of support from the community.

Keeping the community informed about the museum's activities can become a full-time job, as indeed it is in some larger museums. But there is a direct benefit to the curator who can operate in this way, for regular contact with the community, in the museum and elsewhere, provides a barometer to its current concerns and to ways in which it may be changing. It is essential that collecting and the interpretation of collections is based upon detailed local knowledge rather than the curator's personal interests, otherwise the record left for the future will be very distorted.

Close contact with local council departments will provide key information about the community today and in the recent past and, sometimes, projections for the future. Education and Social Services Departments will have their own analyses of recent Census data prepared to help with evaluating the service they currently provide and planning changes for the future but of great value for the museum. Knowledge of current or forthcoming schools' priorities may provide unexpected links with the museum's projects. Many library services employ specialists to deal with minority languages or other minority interests, ranging from children to the housebound, from Asian to Polish communities. These specialists have a unique knowledge of the groups they serve within the wider community and may be happy to share it. Do not be surprised to find as a result of links with such groups that requests for objects to borrow or handle prompt conversation with stroke victims, assist reminiscence work with elderly people or provide a new vocabulary for those learning English as a second language. Such activities may not be central to the museum's purpose but may provide it with an unexpected point of contact with members of the community who would otherwise never have access to its rich resources.

The local museum's regular audience is likely to be drawn from among the very old and the very young. The former makes up an expanding sector of our population which has time to spare for museum visiting and for voluntary work; it is also a major source of acquisitions for the social history museum, sometimes welcoming the chance to find a permanent home for something they have treasured which they fear might otherwise be discarded after their death. Many young visitors come first on school outings. Children relish the role of the expert and will often bring parents and siblings to show off their new-found expertise after an enjoyable group visit. They are thus the key to reaching the adults of their parents' age group who may think in terms of a museum to which they can take the family for a day out and miss the museum on the doorstep.

Other groups may feel that the museum is not for them. Communities which originated with comparatively recent immigration into the district may need some convincing of a curator's interest in their lives but they should be represented in the collections and exhibitions of their local museum. Museum staff remain predominantly white, the museum as an institution may appear to have an intimidating 'official' status; for many the experience of coming to Britain was an extraordinarily painful one and one that is so recent that it is difficult to perceive as history – all these factors combine to make building the right relationship a difficult one. If employing black curators is the only way to reassure black communities of a genuine museum interest in their lives, then we must find ways of doing it. There are as many ways of making museums more friendly and less 'official' as there are of convincing people that museums are interested in the very recent as well as the distant past, however painful or controversial. In the short term we can move away from our narrowly Eurocentric interpretation of collections and widen their relevance. The use of mahogany for fine eighteenth-century furniture provides a link with the Caribbean, fabric and ceramic designs have drawn their inspiration from India and China for several centuries, while everyday food and drink – tea, coffee, spices, sugar – continue through modern trade some long-standing colonial connections.

Very little has been written about museum work with the community, yet most social history curators are doing it every day with varying degrees of success and most find it immensely valuable to exchange ideas with colleagues. An approach that proves successful with one community may alienate another; care must be taken to get the relationship right. Social history curators must repeatedly place themselves in the position of the museum's potential audience to assess the image it presents to the outside world. The curator must get to know the community or active collecting will be irrelevant and displays will target the wrong audience. Curators must base their work upon a philosophy of generosity and openness, and should be prepared to recognise the scope for the community's own contribution based on its own vision of its past. It will take time to educate the community about the principles on which a representative historical collection should be based and you may have to accept some artefacts which are not really needed in order to allow some people to get involved in person. You need your community more than it needs the museum – it is your subject matter, your source of artefacts and information, it will provide political support, and raise funds for you. Treat it with care!

Bibliography

Blackburn, Margaret, 'Polar bears in the community - a new role for a traditional museum,' *Museum Professionals Group News,* Spring 1987.

Bott, Valerie, 'Into darkest suburbia...', *Museums Journal,* vol. 84, no.3, December 1984, pp. 109-16.

Bott, Valerie, 'Beyond the museum', *Museums Journal,* vol.90, no.2, 1990.

Clark, Helen, 'A place to stay - Springburn housing 1780-1987', *Social History Curators Group News,* no.17, Spring 1988.

Greene, J. Patrick, 'Norton Priory - history for a new town', *Museums Journal,* vol.75, no.2, September 1975, pp. 75-7.

Locke, Stephen, 'Communities and professionals', *Museums Journal,* vol. 91, no. 4, 1991.

Mullins, Sam, 'Beyond a collecting policy: projects as policy at the Harborough Museum', *Journal of the Social History Curators Group,* no.14, 1986-7, pp. 20-22.

'The museum and the community', report of a session at the Museums Association Conference 1973, *Museums Journal,* vol.73, no.3, December 1973, pp. 100-106 .

Thomson, John, 'A Bradford project in community involvement', *Museums Journal,* vol.71, no.4, March 1972, pp. 161-3.

Thomson, John, 'Cities in decline: museums and the urban programme 1969-1979', *Museums Journal,* vol.79, no.4, March 1980, pp.188-90.

West, Andrew, 'Communities and professionals', *Museums Journal,* vol.91, no. 4, 1991.

26.2 Collecting Methods: The Antique Trade

Mark Suggitt

Assistant Director (Curatorial),
Yorkshire and Humberside Museums Council

The collection of objects for a social history museum in now seen as a selective process, one that should be based on clear aims and objectives. The curator should be working within the clearly defined guidelines of a collecting policy and collection management statement. Selection is now of paramount importance owing to the decreasing capacity of stores and the vast amount of material available to the social history curator. The mass production of the nineteenth and twentieth centuries, coupled with the continuing generosity of the public has allowed social history museums to build up very large collections indeed. Many such museums can boast that they have had to purchase only a tiny proportion of their collection. Unlike many art galleries, the recent reduction or obliteration of a purchase fund is not seen as the death knell for any future collecting activity.

The advantages of this tradition of donation are enormous. The curator is usually in contact with either the donor or their immediate family (the people who know something of the history of the object) and has the chance to gain valuable information about that object – when it was purchased, by whom, for whom, what it cost, its effectiveness, longevity, etc. Such information is the backbone of good interpretation in the future.

All this, not unnaturally, begs the question of whether the social history curator needs the commercial world of the antique trade. I would suggest that curators do, and for a variety of reasons which I intend to examine.

First of all we must consider what is meant by the antique trade. The word 'antique' can be used to describe almost anything that is old-fashioned, out of date, or considered a collector's item. This definition is followed by many of those involved in the antique trade and should also be followed by the curator. A seventeenth-century gate-leg table is an antique, so is a Victorian match-case, and so is a 1960s Japanese tinplate toy robot. Such a definition widens the scope of this market, from the large auction houses, through antique shops, junk shops, market stalls, charity shops and car boot sales to jumble sales. The benefits and pitfalls of these institutions will be discussed later, now we must consider what possible reasons there could be to induce the curator out of the office to hunt down objects for the collection.

The first port of call must be the collecting policy. This, and only this, can set the limits of what a museum collects. Such documents are the result of informed curatorial thought and act as help rather than hindrance. Let us take an example. A local museum has a policy that

1. restricts collecting to its local authority region,

2. collects twentieth-century material,

3. plans to re-open a historic house that has little of its original seventeenth-century furniture,

4. and has an active enquiry service.

Now, let us see how the antique trade can aid this museum in those four areas.

1. A good relationship with a local auction house can alert the museum to significant local objects such as clocks, silver, furniture, tools and machinery. If such things fit into the collecting policy, then the museum has the chance to purchase them.

2. Local junk shops, car boot and jumble sales can produce cheap items of recent manufacture and local use.

3. If the museum plans to use seventeenth-century furniture it will have to look to the auction houses or better antique shops.

4. An active enquiry service can be informed by subscriptions to Sale Catalogues. (I am assuming no values will be given by the museum.)

This example clearly illustrates the use of the trade and highlights the main reason why we enter into it – to fill gaps in the collections entrusted to our care. Such gaps can appear through taking on new responsibilities or they can result from a collections review that reveals gaps left by passive collecting or curatorial prejudice, or by unethical (and occasionally unlawful) disposals. The best reason of all should be to acquire an object that will enhance the role of the museum. That gap should be spotted in a well documented collection. Whatever the reason for the gap there are ways in which to fill it. Let us now step outside the museum and see who is out there in the market place.

Auction Houses

There are numerous auction houses throughout the country, but the ones that immediately spring to mind are Christie's, Phillips and Sotheby's. All of them act as auctioneers and valuers. They can be organised in different ways, although the large ones are companies. They all share a common function.

They act as agents for the vendor; of the large ones only Phillips operates under the rules of the Society of Fine Art Auctioneers. Their income derives from the commission charged on all sales, from valuation fees, catalogue subscriptions and occasional publishing.

The vendor has made the decision to sell and the auction house will estimate a selling price (the estimate) and possibly fix a reserve price (the reserve). This is the confidential figure below which the object will not be sold. The auction house will place the objects in sales of like with like, be it Delftware, art nouveau, tinplate toys or rock 'n' roll ephemera. The reasons for doing so are obvious; the right sale and the right catalogue will attract the right market for those goods. A recent example has been the great interest shown in Sotheby's foray into 'British Folk Art'.

Such sales attract museums, who may come across that relevant gap described or even illustrated in the catalogue. Assuming that the Director and the budget have been consulted, what procedures should the curator follow?

1. Check the description in the catalogue for remarks on date and condition. Subscribers to catalogues are sent the actual prices realised after sales, so check if a similar item has been sold recently and that the estimate appears fair.

2. If possible go and view the object on the specified viewing days. These are publicised in the catalogue. This may seem extravagant for a London sale but if your museum is prepared to spend over £500 the cost of a cheap day return is a small price to pay for peace of mind. You can handle the object and look for signs of damage or old repairs which may need further conservation.

3. Once you have seen it and decided that it is acceptable then set your budget limit. The estimate will help as a guideline. You should also decide if you are

going to go for a 'limit plus one' i.e. one bid over your limit. This can be a useful precaution against losing an object by just one bid.

Whatever you decide the golden rule is never to go above it. If your committee or trustees have set your limit then never get carried away by the theatre of the sale. At this stage it is also worth contacting the Victoria and Albert or Science Museum grant-in-aid schemes who may be able to assist with the purchase. They need time to get their forms to you and view the object themselves.

4. The sale is always by auction. You can go and bid in person. This is a useful experience for all museum staff, if only to dispel the myth that you can end up buying something by scratching your nose. Trained auctioneers always know who is in the running. I would suggest that staff should attend an auction simply as observers if they have not bid before.

If you cannot get there, a bid can be sent by post or telephone. This is the commission bid. If you telephone it is always best to follow it with a covering letter. The letter should include the lot number (written out in long hand) plus a brief description of the object. A marked photocopy from the catalogue is also useful. This is very important; no one wants to buy the wrong thing by sloppy administration!

Once the sale is over you can telephone to see if your bid has been successful.

5. Let us suppose you have been successful. First of all the auction house has to be paid. The larger houses will invoice your museum and payment will be made. You must let them know that you intend to pay in this way in advance. Most do not like delayed payment. Small country sales, especially farm sales, often expect payment and removal on the same day. All want you to remove material quickly; they need to clear stores for the next sale and certainly do not want to hang on to large objects.

Notice must be taken of the 10% buyer's premium paid on all objects. Phillips exempt recognised museums from this; Christie's and Sotheby's do not. The conditions of sale are always laid out in the catalogue and should be read carefully.

6. Once payment has been cleared the buyer has the responsibility of removal. The auction house may send the object to you via a reputable carrier at extra cost. If it is very delicate it would be better to employ specialist fine art carriers. Your Area Museum Council could advise on this.

It is also worth stating how you wish your material to be packed and what should and should not be done. I once received a 1910 tinplate toy battleship, well wrapped and insulated on the outside but the original cardboard box had been sellotaped to keep the lid on!

So, the object has arrived at the museum. As social history curators we need to know more about its provenance. Can the auction houses help? Generally they do not collect details of provenance for objects of a low financial value. They may occasionally include provenance in a catalogue if it will help to sell it, otherwise the closest you get is the coyly archaic 'The property of a gentleman/lady'. Vendors' names are not given to museums as this is confidential information between the client and their agent. However, the auction house can write to the vendor and inform them of the museum's interest. Then it is up to the vendor to contact the museum. There is no reason why this should not happen. Auction houses like to keep on good terms with museums and will help; it just takes a little time and patience. Sometimes you get nowhere; other times you succeed.

So far I have concentrated on the value of auction houses; now for a few cautionary words. First of all, they and their researchers are not infallible. Like curators they make mistakes. Their initial identifications could be wrong. A spectacular example is the rare Christopher Dresser teapot valued (and therefore unrecognised) at £30 to £100. The owners went elsewhere and it sold for £34,000! Likewise catalogue descriptions can be wrong or miss out important identifying marks.

We should also remember that although we are linked to them by common bonds of interest in the objects, we live to preserve them and they live to sell them. Conflicts can occur in which we could become involved. The débâcle over Mentmore[1] raised high emotions in both the art world and Parliament. Sotheby's recent publicity glides around the problem of house sales and exportation. 'Sotheby's sales of house contents *in situ* have often made headlines.'[2] No further mention is made of what those headlines said. Christie's have also come under fire, accused of 'vandalising' Orchardleigh House in Somerset prior to its sale.[3]

It is over financial value that we can fall out. The auction houses' Valuation Day and its media offspring, 'The Antiques Roadshow', can deter donations to museums as people see what is considered worth preserving becoming a commodity, and occasionally a valuable one at that.[4] As a result what was once offered to the museum could be taken to the sale-room. Despite this, the benefits of mutual co-operation between museums and auction houses do outweigh the disadvantages.

Antique Shops

Antique shops vary enormously; there are those owned by highly knowledgeable specialists and there are junk shops with pretensions. There are also 'new antique' shops, usually betrayed by a revealing acreage of lacquered brass and polished pine.

As the definition of 'antique' has broadened, so has the range of shops. Thirty years ago many of the specialist shops rarely stepped beyond the eighteenth century and certainly not after 1840. Now, there are quality shops specialising in areas such as art deco, art nouveau, bamboo and papier mâché furniture, and Staffordshire figures. Recently London and the larger provincial towns have witnessed an increasing interest in the 1950s and 1960s.

The antique trade offers an enormous range of material for the curator to examine and curators must be aware of problems that can arise. They should be on good terms with local antique shop owners but be aware of the ethical problems of being too friendly. Curators should never recommend one shop above others, nor receive gifts from their owners. In other words, the museum should act only in the role of a customer; it does not need special privileges. A good shop would try to locate a specific object for you anyway.

Prices in antique shops vary; sometimes they can be above auction prices and sometimes below. We have to remember that the auction price depends on who is there bidding. Antique shop prices reflect their overheads. This has to be taken into account; you are paying for their time and effort in collecting material.

When purchasing in such shops the curator must carefully examine what is on offer. Dates on tickets could be wrong, recent repairs unmentioned. Curatorial knowledge of material culture should reveal that a Staffordshire figure is a reproduction (look at the hole), that a Sheraton-style table is an Edwardian copy (look at the locks, drawers, etc.) or that the handle on a seventeenth-century spit jack is from a twentieth-century extending table.

Like auction houses, shops do not record provenance and it can be difficult to obtain. Often the owner simply does not remember where it came from.

No discussion of the antique trade would be complete without mentioning the exportation of material to Europe and America. Social history curators have particular problems because many of the things we are interested in fall way below the £16,000 limit set by the Waverley Committee. The Social History Curators Group has been lobbying for enlarging the criteria to include objects of local interest.[5] One of the great problems here is whether curators can actually find out what is getting into those bulk freight containers.

I now intend to review those areas of the antique trade where your status as a curator counts for little. (You may even get charged more if you admit who you are!) In such shops you need to go armed with a keen eye and a pocketful of petty cash. Warn your Administrative Officer that you may not get a receipt every time and it could be written on the back of a paper bag!

Junk Shops

Unfortunately the real junk shop is becoming a thing of the past. They have either died out or upgraded themselves (and their prices) into 'antique shops' or 'bargain centres'. Nevertheless, the original article can still be found and is not to be missed, especially if your interests run to 1960s and 1970s domestic furniture.

Market Stalls and Antique Fairs

Markets often contain regular stall-holders selling 'antiques' and 'bric-à-brac'. These offer a similar range to junk shops and charity shops and should not be confused with the dealers who turn up at the antique fairs and flea markets. These can be small affairs in country hotels or huge gatherings in civic halls. They are characterised by the enormous range of 'collectables' including silver, ceramics, coins, medals, stamps, postcards and military material. Prices are always higher at these events as the stall-holders anticipate a larger audience, many of whom are not regular visitors to antique shops. It's a day out; you'll pay more!

Charity Shops

Charity shops, such as Oxfam, Dr Barnardo's, Sue Ryder and the Red Cross, are common sights on most high streets. In the past they have exuded an image of an 'unloved, glorified jumble sale',[6] but this is changing. Oxfam shops are looking smarter and the Red Cross intend to improve their image.

Prices in these shops are going up, mainly because they realise people will pay more than 50p for every item. Second-hand clothes have become eagerly sought after by more than just the art school dressers. It is understood that cameras, flat irons, ceramics, etc. should be realistically priced. We should not complain; the charities need the money and prices are still low compared to antique shops. Charity shops are excellent for clothes (now is the time to collect 1970s clothes), records, accessories and books. They also have the advantage of giving till receipts!

Jumble Sales

These offer the same scope as charity shops but are cheaper. Truly dedicated followers check the local papers to plan a route for the following Saturday. Jumble sales can be very good for household appliances, clothes and toys. If you happen to know a regular organiser you may be allowed in early to have first pick. In such a way did one large museum's costume department acquire a jingoistic Falklands War T-shirt!

Car Boot Sales

The car boot sale is a more recent phenomenon, a form of self-interested jumble sale where families drive out to a field, open shop and attempt to sell their less durable consumer durables, clothes, toys and anything else that cluttered up the garage/loft/shed. If you really want to know where all those awful 1970s 'Top of the Pops' compilation L.P.s went to, go to a car boot sale!

Apart from being a sociologist's paradise, car boot sales give the social history curator the variety of the jumble sale with the advantage that you are often able to chat to the person who owned the object(s) and strike up a similar relationship to that with a donor. You only have to pay a few pence for that 1960s Barbie doll, and you can find out who played with it!

Such then, is the antique trade, a fascinating world of buy and sell. It has both glamour and grubbiness, greed and generosity. It can give us excellent additions to our collections and it can enhance our knowledge through its publications. As social history curators we need to keep a watching brief on its activities.

We can influence each other, often unknowingly. The antique trade only sells what it thinks people will buy. Often museums and private collectors are in the forefront of confronting taste. They should anticipate the trends first and help to formulate aesthetic opinion; what appears in the showcase one year could be in the shops the next and vice versa. In such ways we are bound together and we ignore each other at our peril.

Acknowledgement

I would like to thank Mr John Walsh of Phillips (Auctioneers) of Leeds for giving his time and advice in the writing of this chapter.

References

1. Wright, Patrick (1985), *On Living In An Old Country*, Verso, pp. 33-8.

2. Sotheby's (1983), *How to Buy and Sell At Sotheby's*, Sotheby's, p. 23.

3. Prestage, Michael (1988), 'Christie's '"vandalised" house', *Observer*, 10 January 1988.

4. Jenkinson, Peter (1986), Review of *Antiques Roadshow Book of Do's and Dont's* in *Journal of the Social History Curators Group*, no. 14, 1986-7, p. 33.

5. *Social History Curators Group News*, no. 12, summer 1986, p. 6.

6. Rumbold, Judy (1988), 'Sweet charity', *Guardian*, 16 May 1988.

Bibliography

Cooper, Jeremy, *Under the Hammer – The Auctions and Auctioneers of London*, Constable, 1977.

Meyer, Karl E., *The Plundered Past*, Penguin Books, 1977.

26.3 Collecting Methods: Recording Interiors

Stephen J. Price

Curator, The Priests House Museum, Wimborne Minster

Nicholas A.D. Molyneux

Inspector of Historic Buildings, English Heritage

Introduction

Field recording prior to the collection of objects for a museum might at first sight appear to be a luxury for the social history curator, upon whose time there are ever increasing demands. Yet the quality and extent of documentation relating to an object's original context will not only influence its future display potential within a museum gallery, but will also substantially determine its research value.

Since the social history museum is concerned with the material evidence set within its context (Brigden, 1984, p.170), the reconstructed room or workshop has for long been a popular and appropriate medium of presentation, enabling the visitor to appreciate something of the interrelated conditions in which a single object was used. However, the accuracy of many reconstructed interiors is questionable, since all too often they still rely on 'speculation' (Ayres,1981, p.18) or 'an educated guess' (Suggitt, 1985, p. 13), rather than thorough research and a body of reliable evidence. Whilst a considerable quantity of literature now exists to assist the curator in achieving authenticity by the careful study of documentary, printed, illustrative and oral sources (for example, Seale, 1979; Allan,1984), the accurate reconstruction must rely heavily on the quality and extent of field recording.

Unfortunately there are no consistent standards of field recording within social history museums in the United Kingdom, although individual museum services have achieved notable results. The techniques described below are those which the writers have found most useful in the task of recording interiors and the material evidence within them in the field.

Prior to recording it is useful to consider the aims and objectives of the exercise and what uses the interior fittings will have in the future. As Hayhurst has pointed out (1987, p.18), 'by defining and thinking through these objectives any omissions can become obvious. Recording can easily become little more than a salvage operation with a few photographs, some objects thrown in a box and a brief note on the outside hinting at their origins.' It is at this point that preliminary research finding parallels in the available literature will give a stimulus to the field recorder to consider how the interior under consideration differs from the published examples. Such enquiries will assist the curator in formulating questions for oral informants.

Measured Survey

The procedures for the recording of buildings by measured survey have been outlined by McDowall (1980), Smith (1985), Hutton (1986) and Cooper (1990). Whilst these works are principally aimed at the architectural historian, many of the techniques described are applicable to the needs of the social history curator and can be adapted accordingly. Architectural historians usually record the plan, one or more external elevations and a section. In addition, the curator will probably require internal elevations showing the position of fixtures and the context of movable items. These methods may be applied at varying levels of detail. Beginners can familiarise themselves with the conventions of architectural draughtsmanship by reference to the recent volumes of the Royal Commissions on Historical Monuments and to their published guidelines (Anon., 1990).

The selection of the precise areas to be measured and the method to be adopted will depend on the purpose of the record. Where the activity is of more importance to the recorder than the building itself, a diagrammatic representation may be sufficient. Examples of this approach, showing both the location of machinery and equipment as well as spatial relationships within buildings, are illustrated in Jenkins' plans of Welsh woollen mills (1969, fig. 21, pp. 304-8) and in Bagshawe's study of rake and scythe-handle making (1956, pl. I, p. 35).

Experience has shown that it is important to produce as finished a drawing as possible on site since rough sketches with measurements may appear as a mass of incomprehensible data when the time comes to draw them up. The writers advocate the use of an A3 layout pad with graph paper underlay over which the measured survey is drawn at the largest possible scale (so that the drawing fills the page). The drawing is built up by a series of measurements transferred to the paper at scale as they are made using a soft pencil and scale rule. This is most conveniently done by two people, one taking the measurements, the other drawing. In practice a 30-metre tape and a two-metre folding rule are the usual measuring tools. For most purposes measurements to the nearest centimetre or half inch are sufficient, unless it is a particularly detailed drawing. The choice between metric and imperial scales is a personal one, but should be consistent with the recording of the objects in the museum's collection. The scale should be indicated on each drawing together with an annotation of the site, the date of the recording and the names of the recorders.

For plans it is important to check that the walls are at right angles to one another. This may be done by measuring the diagonals and plotting the measurements using a pair of compasses to make intersecting arcs. Plans are normally drawn just above window sill level, and overhead features, such as ceiling beams, are shown by means of dotted lines. However, the curator may be equally concerned with recording floor surfaces, standing equipment and overhead machinery so that the plan can become very overcrowded. Therefore it is advisable to produce a master plan from which copies can be taken by tracing or photocopying to record these details separately. With elevations measurement proceeds from a horizontal datum line established with a spirit level. Alternatively, a horizontal level within the building may be used as a datum. Architectural historians usually draw sections from the ground to the ridge at a point just in front of a truss line to enable the construction of a building to be seen. Curators concerned with furnishings and fittings may find internal elevations of one or more floors more suited to their purpose. Such details as panelling, windows, fireplaces and fixed shelving, together with any movable items, can thus be seen in context against the 'backdrop' of the wall. Plans and internal elevations are especially important where the contents of a room or workshop are to be dismantled. A lettering and numbering system is established for each room and each element within it. The items to be removed can then be labelled or marked with their appropriate codes at the same time as the drawings are marked. Inventorying follows once the material has been safely removed to museum premises and the site records are then correlated with the museum register. Like an archaeological site, material may be stratified so that careful removal is essential – the position of even the most recent items on the top may be of interest and there could be useful items concealed underneath. 'There is always the danger that the currently insignificant detail may be held in greater esteem by subsequent enquirers' (Goodwin and Davies, 1980, p.14).

Details and internal fittings should be recorded at a larger scale. For example, it may be thought that if a piece of machinery is to be removed to museum premises then all that is required is a record of its position and a series of photographs, obviating the need for detailed drawings on site. However, much will depend on the complexity of the machinery and whether or not it is being acquired in its entirety. Equally importantly, the field recorder must consider the immediate environment around such equipment and how it has been affected by that machinery. Thus wear marks left on the structure by pulley belts or grease on floors or walls around a machine bed should be noted in the written description (Bodey and Hallas, 1977, p. 52). The understanding of complex machinery or internal fittings can be considerably enhanced by the use of isometric projection for which further measurements may be required. Similarly, the arrangement of a building may be unclear simply from the plans and elevations, and again an isometric drawing can enhance understanding. Isometric projection is a method of drawing which can be constructed from plan and elevations, and is preferable to perspective for our purposes because it shows true scaled measurements in the three planes of the drawing. It can be particularly useful for later use in museum displays (see Figure 4).

The figures on pages 193–5 show the use of measured surveys to record a small butchery business, including an isometric drawing.

Photography

Photography can provide a useful record of the context of objects before their removal to museum premises. It can also, when used with care, provide a valuable overall impression of the conditions within a workplace or home.

Good results are obtained by the use of a 35mm or medium format single lens reflex camera with black and white film which offers long-term archival stability as well as high quality photographs. Versatility and ingenuity by the photographer in the use of equipment are important. For indoor photographs a rigid tripod with a range of movement in the head is essential in conjunction with a wide angle lens to make the most of confined spaces. Small apertures will be necessary, in conjunction with long exposures, to provide a good depth of field. A balance needs to be struck between the better quality of slower film and the fact that although faster film gives a lower image quality it handles contrast better, since contrast is one of the main problems. The setting-up stage is important and each picture should be carefully thought out. The inexperienced photographer can take a number of shots, varying the exposures to ensure a good result. There are problems with movement, in particular where human activity in the photograph is concerned. This can be overcome by posing the operator in an action which they can freeze. Machinery will need to be stopped for long exposures to avoid a blurred result. The printing of the photographs is a crucial stage and is preferably carried out by the photographer or a skilled printer so that the best possible results can be obtained.

Artificial lighting, although often necessary, should be used with discretion. Available light is preferable since it is less intrusive and gives a more realistic impression of the environment. However, when the purpose of the photograph is to record the placing of artefacts artificial light can be a useful aid. Portable lighting is preferable to flash to enable fine adjustments to be made (but do remember that mains electricity will not always be available, as the writers have occasionally found to their cost!). Many successful examples of the use of a variety of lighting methods are shown by Buchanan (1983). Colour photographs can be taken for display purposes whilst 35mm colour transparencies will be useful for lectures and audio-visual presentations.

As a method of note-taking Polaroid photographs provide an instant *aide-mémoire*. However, in our experience neither the quality nor the long-term stability of the prints are acceptable for archival purposes and they will need to be copied in order to provide a negative.

Tape Recording

The application of the methods of oral history to the recording of interiors can be especially fruitful for the social historian. Oral evidence can breathe life into pure architectural recording by providing a 'direct and personal link with the past', which can contribute 'to a very detailed and accurate historical representation' within a museum (Frostick, 1986, p.59). When staff from the Oxfordshire Museums Service recorded working-class housing in the county they produced measured plans and photographed surviving examples. In several cases the recorders were assisted considerably by existing or former occupiers who described the contents of the houses as they were within living memory (Paine, 1979).

Whenever possible people who lived or worked at a particular site should be recorded on tape (Graham, 1980) which then becomes a part of the museum's documentation archive. Recordings should be made on open reel tape using a high quality recorder as outlined by Howarth (1984). (There is still considerable debate amongst oral historians concerning the quality of recordings made on cassette machines, but the present writers prefer to use them only for personal note-taking as part of a site survey.) When recording in a functioning workplace it should be borne in mind that the sounds of working machinery, although providing realism from noise levels, can detract from the informant's account, so that it may be necessary to record the background sounds separately if required, and to dub them on to an edited version of the tape. It is also important to remember that the listener cannot see what is being described so that a reference plan and clear indications on the tape of the specific locations are essential. It is not always practical or desirable for the interviewer to interrupt the informant's flow with such details, but they should be added to the transcript of the interview as appropriate. If an informant directly associated with the particular building cannot be found all is not lost, since it may be possible to persuade someone else with relevant knowledge, such as another worker from the same trade, to share his or her comments on the site. It will not always be practical to bring informants to a site but they may respond successfully to photographic records made as a part of the survey or to historic photographs showing the business in production.

Film and Video

The recorded moving image provides a useful method of documenting processes. Video is being used increasingly within museums and is particularly suitable as a means of presenting an edited version to a wider audience. For the curator inexperienced in the use of video equipment or unable to afford the capital investment, there is very considerable opportunity for liaison with other institutions which already have such expertise. In 1982 Stockport Museums Service, in conjunction with the Manchester Film and Video Workshop, produced a 20-minute colour documentary showing the methods of hat block making, which greatly enhanced visitors' understanding of the tools and equipment moved to the reconstructed workshop within the museum.

Sampling

As well as acquisition for the museum's collection of movable objects from a house or workplace, the curator may wish to preserve a record of an interior by removing samples of the fixtures and fittings. For example, the careful removal of areas of plaster, a complete pattern of wallpaper or woodwork retaining traces of paint will provide valuable information about the treatment of wall finishes at one or more phases of a building's history. This will be particularly appropriate where a reconstruction of the interior is envisaged in the final display or where an architectural collection of period details is being built up. However, removal by sampling should not be undertaken lightly and careful consideration should first be given to alternative methods of recording details, such as drawing or photography. Sampling may be appropriate when an interior is being gutted, but the curator should not be a party to the unnecessary removal of period details where there is any possibility of retaining them in their original position. Moreover, if the building is statutorily listed as of architectural and historical importance then it is an offence to remove the fittings without the consent of the planning authority, as they are legally regarded as a part of the listed building (even if not mentioned in the list description). The legal position regarding machinery is more complex because it is specifically excluded from the listing of the building unless it is a part of the structure, which can be a debatable matter (Suddards 1988, p. 15). If there is any doubt, the local planning authority should be consulted. It is also extremely important to ensure that authorisation for removal is obtained – the tenant will probably own the loose items, but those attached to or part of the building may belong to someone else.

Written Record

To accompany all the above methods the field recorder should also compile a written account. This can be divided usefully into three sections – historical, descriptive and interpretative. The latter is particularly important in showing the relationship between the different sources of evidence and enables the recorder to distinguish clearly between established fact and hypothesis. As much as possible should be written on site before dismantling commences, so that questions can be posed using the material evidence rather than the record. Further evidence will almost certainly come to light during removal and this should be incorporated into the final account rather than remain as a vague memory in the curator's mind.

Conclusion

The curator should not be daunted by the responsibility of acquiring and applying these diverse skills to the recording of interiors prior to the removal of objects for a museum's collection. Only by means of thoroughly documented occupational and domestic collections will it be possible for the researcher to gain an accurate insight into a region's personality. On the initial visit to inspect the contents of a house or workplace as potential acquisitions, the curator will need to assess its significance in deciding what to collect, how to document it prior to removal, and the level of resources to be expended. Whilst a sound knowledge of the museum's existing collections, coupled with its collecting policy statement, should provide guidance on what to collect, less help is available for the curator wanting to know just what to record prior to removal. The consideration will include an assessment of the skills and staff time available within the museum, the financial resources to hire or commission third parties, and what is available within the community. It may not always be possible to employ the full range of recording techniques described, as evidenced by the example below.

Example Showing the Use of Measured Survey

Harrison's butchery business, 423-5 Church Road, Yardley

Between 1976 and 1977 the Department of Local History of Birmingham Museums and Art Gallery undertook a programme of fieldwork investigating the standing buildings of Old Yardley Village, which lies ³/₄ mile north-east of the branch museum Blakesley Hall in an inter-war middle ring suburb. The village still gives the appearance of a rural community and is protected as a conservation area. Its buildings represent a visual asset, reflecting much of the history of the local community within easy walking distance of a museum outstation. A town trail linking the museum with the village was planned to follow the detailed documentary and architectural research. In addition it was intended that guidelines for collection would be established. Every building in the village was examined and the mid-nineteenth-century butcher's shop and slaughterhouse at 423-5 Church Road were found to have kept their contents largely intact since the closure of the shop in 1957. Between the death of the butcher's widow in the summer of 1977 and an autumn auction sale of the contents of the whole premises, access for recording purposes and a private treaty sale of the movable fittings of both the shop and the slaughterhouse were negotiated with the executors of the estate.

Although a number of trade manuals had been located the recorder had limited experience of the physical remains of the butchery trade. A retired butcher from north Warwickshire was invited to visit the site and explain the use of the tools and equipment. His assistance proved invaluable and prevented many mistakes being made.

Floor plans (Figure 1) and external (Figure 2) and internal elevations (Figure 3) were drawn recording the whole of the buildings. On the plans each feature, whether or not it was to be removed to the museum, was given a letter reference and was described briefly (Figure 5) and photographed.

Documentary evidence indicates the building of a cottage on this site for a wheelwright between 1708 and 1711, when it was described as 'new erected'. This early eighteenth-century cottage is represented by the first phase of the standing buildings and formed a symmetrical two-bay brick cottage with gabled dormers lighting the chambers. It had a lobby entry plan with a central axially placed stack. A pair of wings was added later in the eighteenth century when the building was subdivided and let to two tenants. In the final phase of development a butcher's shop with a bedchamber over was added to the cottage and a slaughterhouse was built on to the end of a previously detached stable block, now converted into fasting pens for the cattle prior to slaughter. These alterations correlate with the arrival of a butcher as tenant some time between the census returns of 1851 and 1861.

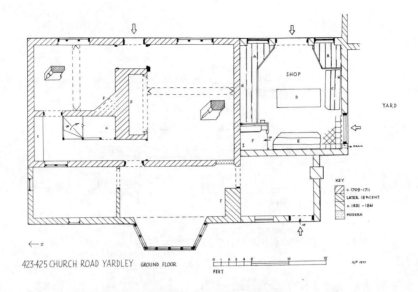

423-425 CHURCH ROAD YARDLEY   GROUND FLOOR

KEY
c.1709-1711
LATER 18 th CENT
c.1851 -1861
MODERN

Figure 1   Ground floor plan of shop and house

423-425 CHURCH ROAD YARDLEY   OUTBUILDINGS

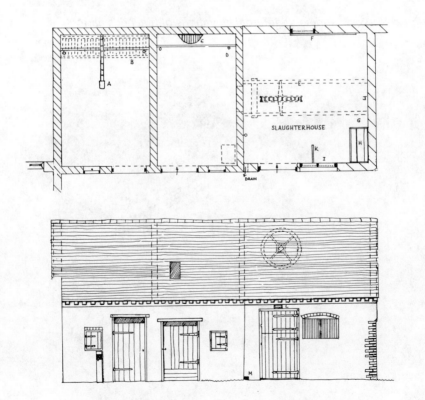

Figure 2   Ground floor plan and west elevation of buildings

193

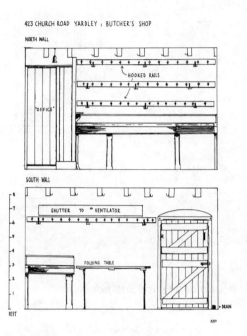

423 CHURCH ROAD YARDLEY : BUTCHER'S SHOP

NORTH WALL

HOOKED RAILS

"OFFICE"

SOUTH WALL

SHUTTER TO VENTILATOR

FOLDING TABLE

+ DRAIN

FEET

Figure 3   North and south internal elevations of butcher's shop

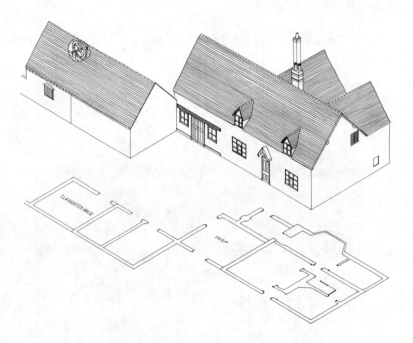

SLAUGHTER HOUSE

SHOP

Figure 4   Isometric drawing of the whole complex

194

Butcher's shop fittings: as at August 1977

Those items marked with an asterisk were acquired by the City Museums.

A*   Fixed top 3′ (0.91m) high (see separate elevation drawing).

B*   Similar.

C*   Folding table – 3 boards wide, 3′ (0.91m) high, 5′2½″ (1.59m) long. Supported at front by 2 iron legs and hung from wall by hook hanging on wall staples.

D*   Butcher's chopping block. Elm. 2′4½″ (0.72m) high comprising top 5′10½″ (1.79m) x 2′5½″ (0.75m) x 8½″ (0.22m) supported on two trestle type wooden legs fastened by iron straps.

E*   Folding table – similar to C.

F*   'Office' NW corner screened off from shop by boarded partition. Wooden floor. Cash drawer below counter. Fixed glass window 10½″ (0.27m) high and 2′10″ (0.86m) long into shop with southern 6¾″ (0.17m) open with fixed cash point below as bracketed shelf.

G*   North wall has 3 wooden rails with iron hooks for meat.

H*   South wall has 1 wooden rail with iron hooks for meat.

I*   Wooden sign painted: "FAMILY/F. HARRISON/BUTCHER". *Ex situ* from over shop door external.

J   Ceiling joists have hooks for meat on W side, except last two far W which have hooks on E.

K   Cast iron grille over windows and door of E elevation. 13′6″ (4.11m) long at 6′6″ (1.98m) height, and on S elevation for 7′6″ (2.29m) between door and outbuildings. Grille comprises panels 3′8″ (1.12m) long attached to wooden vertical posts in gap by clasps and nails. Grille is 8⅝″ (0.22m) high. Painted.
Wooden horizontal shutters behind operated from inside shop. (See drawing of grille.)

L   Shop door. Double stable type boarded door. Straight headed doorcase and windows.

M*   Hand tools hanging on hooks on N wall comprise 1 butcher's cleaver, 1 saw, and various 'S' hooks (see photograph as found) with one set of Avery scales (missing weights) on fixed top A.

N   Floor. Outer edge is 1 row of 9″ x 9″ (0.23m) red quarries and within are diagonally set 6″ x 6″ (0.15m) quarries, alternating red and blue.

O   Walls and floor joists lime washed.

P   Yard door is single stable type with segmental head.

Figure 5   List from museum files of contents of butcher's shop

Acknowledgement

The writers wish to express their thanks to Mr J. Cope, Senior Photographer at the City Museum and Art Gallery, Birmingham.

References

Allan, Rosemary E.(1984), 'Research: social history – a case study', in Thompson, J.M.A. (ed.), *Manual of Curatorship: A Guide to Museum Practice,* Butterworth, 1984, pp. 179-86.

Anon., (1990), *Recording Historic Buildings: A Descriptive Specification,* Royal Commission on the Historical Monuments of England, London.

Ayres, James (1981), *The Shell Book of the Home in Britain: Decoration, Design and Construction of Vernacular Interiors, 1500-1850,* Faber.

Bagshawe, Thomas W. (1956), 'Rake and scythe-handle making in Bedfordshire and Suffolk', *Gwerin,* vol. I, no. 1. pp. 34-46.

Bodey, Hugh, and Hallas, Michael (1977), *Elementary Surveying for Industrial Archaeologists,* Shire Publications, Princes Risborough.

Brigden, Roy D. (1984), 'Research: social history collections', in Thompson, J.M.A. (ed.), *Manual of Curatorship: A Guide to Museum Practice,* Butterworth, 1984, pp. 170-74.

Buchanan, Terry (1983), *Photographing Historic Buildings,* HMSO.

Cooper, Nicholas (1990), *Guide to Recording Historic Buildings,* Butterworth Architecture for ICOMOS.

Frostick, Elizabeth (1986), 'The use of oral evidence in the reconstruction of dental history at Beamish Museum', *Oral History,* vol. 14, no. 2, pp. 59-65.

Goodwin, Chad, and Davies, Stuart (1980), 'Recording craft workshops, Black Country Museum', *Group for Regional Studies in Museums Newsletter,* no.8, pp. 13-15.

Graham, Stanley (1980), 'The Lancashire Textile Project : a description of the work and some of the techniques involved', *Oral History,* vol. 8, no. 2, pp. 48-58.

Hayhurst, Yvonne (1987), 'Recording a workshop', *Journal of the Social History Curators Group,* vol. XIV, pp. 18-19.

Howarth, Ken (1984), *Remember, Remember ... Tape Recording Oral History,* North West Sound Archive, Clitheroe.

Hutton, Barbara (1986), *Recording Standing Buildings,* Department of Archaeology, University of Sheffield/Rescue.

Jenkins, J. Geraint (1969), *The Welsh Woollen Industry,* National Museum of Wales.

McDowall, R.W. (1980), *Recording Old Houses: A Guide,* Council for British Archaeology.

Paine, Crispin (1979), 'Working-class housing in Oxfordshire', *Oxoniensia,* vol. XLIII, pp. 188-215.

Seale, William (1979), *Recreating the Historic House Interior,* AASLH, Nashville.

Smith, Lance (1985), *Investigating Old Buildings,* Batsford.

Stockport Museums Service (1982), *Hat Block Maker* (video), Manchester Film and Video Workshop.

Suddards, Roger W. (1988), *Listed Buildings: The Law and Practice of Historic Buildings, Ancient Monuments, and Conservation Areas,* Sweet & Maxwell, 2nd ed.

Suggitt, Mark (1985), 'Heals to Habitat: museums and modern interiors', *Museums Journal,* vol.85, pp. 13-16.

26.4   Collecting Methods: Recording Information with Objects

Roy Brigden

Keeper, Museum of English Rural Life, Reading University

A few examples from the collections of the Museum of English Rural Life will attempt to show how objects can be given an additional dimension, useful for any number of subsequent interpretative and research purposes, when associated information is recorded with them. In the Museum's young days, in the early 1950s, it picked up a number of separate collections of rural material that had been accumulated by individuals during the inter-war years. These were people who, in uncertain times characterised by a sense of rural decline on the one hand and enveloping mechanisation and urbanisation on the other, turned to the traditional crafts and skills of the countryside as a source of solace and inspiration. The objects that were collected have much to reveal not only about the communities from which they originated but also the society by which they were preserved.

Lavinia Smith was a university educated lady who, in the 1930s, put together a collection of material which she referred to as 'her museum' at her home in the Berkshire village of East Hendred. All the objects, numbering 428, were collected locally, and many were farming and craft tools or household effects passed on from natives of the village who no doubt tolerated Miss Smith's acquisitiveness of such trifles with a mixture of pride and amusement. In common with other collectors of the everyday of this period, she had an artist's eye for the form and texture of objects and took a keen interest in the way things were made and the uses to which they were put. All this she recorded in notes and sketches. A lye dropper was given to her by Arthur Harrison, the village blacksmith, in whose forge it had been hanging for a reputed seventy years and a description of its use – for softening laundry water with wood ashes – was carefully noted from another inhabitant, Margaret Bradfield, who was born in 1846.

This constant tie-up to real people and places makes the component parts of the collection so interesting. The links stretch far back into the past, no more so than through the items used and given by another Hendred blacksmith, Joseph Besley, who was exactly one hundred years old at his death on 18 August 1932 and whose family had been craftsmen in the village for generations prior to that. From Henry Vaisey's in nearby Abingdon came some ropemaking equipment, a rare survival of what was once the town's staple industry. In her notes, Miss Smith recalls:

The many picturesque but unsanitary courts of Abingdon were the ropewalks. Henry Vaisey went on making halters and ploughlines for many years in the long loft in the Vineyard where his father had employed 100 men. I used to watch the making of ploughlines until 1924 when I was little in Abingdon. Hanks of hemp were put on the 4 hooks and Vaisey turned the handle which twisted and joined the strands. As the rope was formed and contracted it was straightened out by an old man with a wooden leg assisted by a rough but effective lump of wood resting on a little platform which ran on two little wooden wheels. As a last stage when the rope was completed, while it was held taut the old man filled his cupped hand with flour paste and walked along smearing it into the rope. The paste would freeze if the weather got very cold so no ropemaking could then be done in the loft.

The Lavinia Smith collection, together with notes and sketches, was acquired by the Museum of English Rural Life in 1951.

The same year brought the arrival of another collection of rural material, with 245 items in all, of perhaps even greater significance. It was put together, again in the 1930s, as a result of investigation and conversation around the southern counties by H.J. (John) Massingham, a well known writer of the day on English country tradition.[1] His offer to donate the collection to MERL came just a few months before his death. Out of context, the individual objects are interesting but not very different from the conventional stock of hand tools in any other rural museum. The difference here is that the collection provided the subject matter for Massingham's classic *Country Relics* which was published in 1939, and appropriately puts down a marker for the end of an era. In it some of the tools are illustrated by Thomas Hennell, an artist and commentator on country life who five years earlier had produced *Change in the Farm* – a finely observed account of non-mechanised farming methods prompted by a fascination with the rotting and forgotten old implements that were then to be found in almost any farmyard. It was, he said,

an attempt to collect and arrange some of this lumber, whose horny and twisted forms with their crust of fowl-dung may prevent their uses from being discerned, though upon clear scrutiny their character becomes recognisable.They are warped and rubbed down to the accustomed knots and sinews of the hands of their ancient proprietors, and so reveal themselves as emblems of family history. But what exactly were their names and uses, and what just and time-honoured methods of those who wielded them, are not in a moment to be recognised; they are to be extracted only at leisure from a welter of daily common places, the genial warmth of fire and beer bringing them ripely from the diminishing memories of the third generation back.[2]

Having perhaps captured in the idiom of his own day the spirit of social history fieldwork, Hennell himself was unable to take it into the post-war period as he was killed in Java in 1945 at the age of forty-two just as his reputation as an artist was bringing him national attention.

Massingham built a small 'museum' in his garden at Long Crendon to house his collection and called it The Hermitage because of its physical similarity to a summer house of the same name that Gilbert White had installed at Selborne in 1776. Here Massingham laid out the traditional tools of husbandry and their associated crafts, not as an epitaph to dead practices and dying skills but as a source of inspiration for the future. He was deeply suspicious of the continuing trend of ever more agricultural mechanisation, of larger farms and larger farmers employing fewer and fewer workers. It had, he said, left the land in a desperate condition and destroyed the society of the countryside. His alternative was an idealised vision of a landscape, divided up into small farming units and small communities where the industrialised practices of scientific agriculture would give way to less intensive systems more in tune with the traditional needs of the land and its people. There would then still be a future for the old knowledge and the old skills, so Massingham's purpose was to carry them through until they were needed once more.

The hand tools preserved by him would provide valuable models for a later generation to adapt and develop. Of course, it was a naive notion even in the 1930s, and the advance of technical progress in agriculture during and immediately following the Second World War would only emphasise further the nature of the absurdity. And yet now, fifty years after the publication of *Country Relics* Massingham's condemnation of the ultimate futility of continuous agricultural growth would strike a chord in some quarters. Today in the Third World, 'appropriate technology' is seen as a key factor in enhancing food-producing capacity without risking the potentially crippling side effects, both social and economical, of full mechanisation. Massingham would be pleased to know that ox yokes from the MERL collection have recently been studied as part of a project to design a more efficient yoke for use in the Indian sub-continent.

In these ways Massingham's collection is more than a random assortment of objects. It is the embodiment of one man's ideal. He documented as much assorted information as he could in order to 'wake up these "bygones" of mine in order so that they might tell their stories of the days when they were in service and before they were merely on view'.[3]

A quest for first-hand knowledge of the Gloucestershire long plough took him one day to Bangrove Farm in the Vale of Tewkesbury, home of the three old Sexty brothers whose joint lifetimes had been spent in farming and the breeding of Shire stallions. There follows a magical description of this tumbledown farm with its accretions of lumber from past generations presided over by William, George and John Sexty, all over seventy, and their equally ancient sister who kept house for them. 'House and farmyard, furniture and farm-tackle, garden and scene, all were of one piece and with their owners made one organic whole.'[4] In a granary there was indeed one dismantled long plough, which before its retirement, had been at work for thirty years, ploughing 50 acres in each. As the parts were reassembled:

The old fellows grew warm and eloquent upon the merits of the Long Plough. It was ideal for heavy land, and this was blue clay, the heaviest of all. Though it took four or five horses to draw it and even six on the headlands, it was much easier for the horses than the iron plough, and there were no wheels to lift it up and down among the clods. The ploughman gauged the right depth by his eye and he had to be careful to keep the plough behind the team. Granted that, it was a grand plough, and there were none to equal it in wet weather when the soil was like bird lime. There were no wheels to be clogged with dirt, and it was particularly comfortable for the thiller (the last) horse, because if he got 'crammed up with dirt', it 'mauled him to death'.[5]

And so on. Needless to say, the long plough found its way into the Massingham collection and even now is able to 'speak' of the Sextys and their way of life.

In these ways the Massingham objects are set into their individual context to give them identity and purpose. Collectively, they acquire an additional significance because of what we know about the intentions of the collector at the time. The same principle will apply to the present day. If, when embarking, for example, on a programme of contemporary collecting, a curator were to record in detail precisely what were the aims and objectives and why that particular type of material had been selected, there can be no doubt that a future generation would find this of great value to the interpretation and appreciation of the resulting collection.

Museum objects are by definition things that have been deliberately preserved for one reason or another. The background leading to that act of preservation may be as significant as the object itself. Perhaps a rather unlikely illustration of this point, but a personal favourite, is provided by William Smith's steam cultivating gear.

Born in 1814, William Smith of Church Farm, Little Woolston, close to the centre of what is now Milton Keynes, was a leading pioneer of the wider application of steam power to agriculture in the middle years of the nineteenth century. He devised a system of cultivation in which a heavy tined implement was drawn backwards and forwards across a field by means of pulleys and cables attached to a double winding drum powered by a portable steam engine. In the early years, a number of experimental versions were built and successfully operated on the farm, the first of them in 1855, and subsequently a modified version was offered commercially by the noted agricultural engineers Howards of Bedford. The original 1855 equipment was acquired by the Museum of English Rural Life in 1980 and is the earliest example of steam cultivating machinery to survive.

Smith was a proud and fiery character so convinced of the supremacy of his system over that of others, in spite of any evidence to the contrary, that he was prepared to do battle with the whole farming establishment. The trouble started at the Chester Show of the Royal Agricultural Society in 1858 where trials were held to find a successful method of ploughing by steam worthy of the £500 prize being offered by the Society. After operational tests on different sites, the award was made to the steam ploughing system with self-moving engine devised and exhibited by John Fowler of Leeds. From the start Smith disputed the judges' verdict and entered into a long and acrimonious debate by letter and public statement with the Royal Agricultural Society, Fowlers and anybody else who cared to be drawn in. Over thirty years after the Chester trials, Smith was still writing to the Society on the subject and by now claiming interest on the £500 which he believed was rightly his.

In 1956, it was discovered that a small brick building, devoid of doors or windows and next to the house at Church Farm, contained the original set of tackle with which Smith had begun his steam cultivating experiment in 1855. Still in remarkably good condition considering its age, the equipment arrived at the Museum of English Rural Life after a roundabout route almost a quarter of a century later. Clearly it had been deliberately entombed at some stage, probably by Smith himself, in the hope that posterity would accord his invention the justice and full recognition withheld by his contemporaries. Although the whole saga had already been extensively researched,[6] the first piece relating to the how and why of this extraordinary act of premeditated preservation remained a mystery.

The answer came when a researcher at MERL came across a brief letter from Smith that was published in *Bell's Weekly Messenger*, a well known farming paper of the day, on 25 August 1879:

... I have built a museum near to my front door in which I have placed my steam windlass and smasher, with the two anchors and three snatch blocks with which I started ploughing in December 1855. They are placed upon a board floor raised two feet above the level of the ground, to keep them dry and in good order. They are built in so that they are to remain a part and parcel of my farm. There is a small doorway to go in and out to see them, just seven yards from my front door. I occasionally have my pipe in the midst of them.

It was when Smith later retired to another family farm at Eggington that he presumably had the doorway bricked up to protect the contents from the rather incurious attentions of subsequent occupiers.

The fullness of the documentation with its unique human story transforms this piece of machinery into one of the most significant survivals of Victorian progress. Of course, it is an extreme case but one that embodies most clearly a fundamental underlying principle. The more information that is collected, by whatever means, along with an object, however humble its origins, the greater will be its significance to the curator of social history, both in the present and, perhaps more particularly, in the future.

Notes

1. See W.J. Keith, *The Rural Tradition,* Harvester Press, 1975. Chapter 12 is on H.J. Massingham.

2. From the Preface to Thomas Hennell, *Change in the Farm,* Cambridge University Press, 1934.

3. H.J. Massingham, *Country Relics,* Cambridge University Press, 1939, p. 230.

4. Ibid., p. 93.

5. Ibid., p. 99.

6. See Colin Tyler, 'William Smith of Woolston', published in 3 parts in *The Road Locomotive Society Journal,* February, August and November 1974.

26.5   Collecting Methods: Photography, Film and Video

Oliver Green

Curator and Head of Museum Services, Colchester Borough Council

There can be few social history museums which do not make extensive use of photography, but in all too many institutions this essential medium for recording, interpretation and display is treated as a subject of secondary importance to a museum's 'proper' collections of three-dimensional artefacts. Curators have been slow to appreciate the importance of photography, often preferring to leave the administration of photographic collections to librarians and archivists whilst limiting their museum's use of photographs to atmospheric backdrops and window dressing for objects on display. Certainly few social history curators seem to be engaged in active photo recording projects above and beyond the minimum required just before an artefact is removed from its context and taken into the museum's collection. Film has received even more cursory treatment in museums, although until the recent advent of accessible video formats, most curators have quite reasonably been able to justify banishing film to the depths of their stores because of the cost and complications of screening it in a museum. Photography has become an indispensable aid to museum interpretation, and it is essential that curators recognise the need to take full account of photographic archives as an integral part of any collections management policy. The following notes should be considered as suggestions rather than guidelines, and are intended above all to encourage social history curators to adopt a more organised and active approach to photography.

Acquiring Existing Photographs

Every social history curator has experienced the most basic level of collections development when offered a group of old photographs by an individual or institution. Passive collecting of this kind is the standard means by which most museum photographic archives have been created (just like most museum object collections!). But it has the serious disadvantages of being both random and unstructured. No museum archive that is built up in this way will ever achieve a balanced or comprehensive coverage of its subject.

Whether or not you accept photographs that are offered to your museum out of the blue will of course be determined by their relevance to your collecting policy. Should your existing collecting policy specifically exclude photographs it is almost certainly time you re-wrote it! The degree of documentation about the photographs will probably be limited to whatever information the donor has available. Not surprisingly, few individuals or organisations maintain comprehensively documented photographic records which can be passed on intact to a museum with the images. Nevertheless, make sure you acquire as much information about the pictures as possible at the time of acquisition.

Occasionally a museum is fortunate enough to be offered a complete archive collection built up over the years by a commercial company such as a local photographer's or newspaper. The business concerned may still be in operation but have no everyday use for its historic material. In such a case what may begin as a passive acquisition in response to an offer can sometimes be turned into an active collecting arrangement for the future by agreeing a procedure for the rolling deposition of material with the museum year by year.

It is quite likely that the owner(s) of historic photographs will not agree to donate their original prints to the museum, but will allow them to be borrowed, copied and returned. Provided that good quality copy negatives are made, this can be as useful as acquisition of the original items. It is, incidentally, a procedure that should be gone through with all the museum's own original prints anyway if no negatives exist. Copy negatives are an essential precaution against damage, loss or deterioration of the originals and are of course necessary for production of copy prints for any purpose. Above all, never use unique archival prints in a display or allow them out of the museum for reproduction by a printer, without first having them copied.

Whether you acquire original negatives and prints for the museum's collection or take copies, it is important to reach a clear understanding with the owner/donor about the copyright position at the time of transfer. This will depend on the age of the image. If a photograph was taken before 1 June 1957, the duration of copyright is fifty years from the end of the calendar year in which it was taken. After that date it may be published freely by anyone. The duration of copyright in any photograph taken after 1 June 1957 is perpetual until it is first published; the copyright period then lasts for fifty years from the end of the year of publication.

Remember that a person or company donating a photograph to your museum may own that print but not be the copyright holder. The whole business of copyright is a minefield in which you are advised to tread very carefully.[1]

Picture Research

Very few social history museums have comprehensive photo archives of their own, and sooner or later you will find it necessary to do picture research outside your own institution when searching for the right images for an exhibition or publication. Copy material acquired from outside sources is not your copyright of course, and duplicate prints obtained for display or publication should not be accessioned or mixed up with your museum's own photographic archives.[2]

Archive Photo Recording

The inevitable gaps and weaknesses in any historic photo archive can usually only be filled by lucky finds or offers. However, if a museum develops an active policy of photo recording to build up a contemporary archive, future generations of curators and historians will be less dependent on serendipity. Paradoxically, although more people own cameras and take pictures today than ever before, photography of everyday life has tended to diminish as its novelty wears off.

Every social history curator should find the time to spend at least one day a month out with a camera creating new photo records, or ensure that someone is doing this on the museum's behalf. A logical starting point in the implementation of your photo recording policy might be to update your existing archives by concentrating on modern shots of buildings or activities of which you already have historic photographs. Quite apart from the intrinsic value of the new photographic record which would be built up, the 'then and now' contrast offers obvious potential spin-offs in both exhibitions and publications.

If your museum is genuinely unable to devote sufficient resources to such a project, look at ways of getting other people to do the work on your behalf. Sources of assistance, such as local photographic societies and colleges with photography courses, should be contacted to investigate potential co-operative projects.

When planning a photo recording project with anyone outside the museum, make sure you look beyond the immediate results, such as an exhibition, to the long-term requirements of your institution. Ideally, you should ensure that the museum physically acquires all negatives and/or transparencies as well as prints, and full copyright to the images. To save argument later, a clear contract signed by all relevant parties should be agreed before any of the photography takes place.[3]

The quality and value of your photo project as a record will not only depend upon the skill (and creativity) of your photographer, but also on the materials used. If you are not confident about choosing the equipment yourself, take advice from the professional photographers employed by some of the larger museums.

A few suggestions about materials and method are worth making here. First, use a larger film format than 35mm (such as 2¼ square) if you can. It is more expensive, but will give you a better quality, more flexible record. Second, use black and white film for your basic record, but use colour as an extra if funds permit. A fundamental problem with colour archival photography is that most colour film is not sufficiently stable to guarantee colour permanence. On the other hand, to restrict record photography to monochrome is to cut out an essential part of that record. Archival storage at very low temperatures in a freezer will help retard colour deterioration. Finally, make sure that the photographer (or someone else) keeps a careful record of what is taken at the time. If you leave this until you get the finished prints or slides back there will always be something or somebody you cannot identify.

Film

Movie film can bring the history of the twentieth century to life in a unique and exciting way, as the recent crop of television documentaries on aspects of modern social history have demonstrated. But using film as a medium of interpretation is a different matter from preserving it. Museums are, on the whole, ill-equipped to act as archival repositories of original film material, and very few attempt to do so. At present the only film collections in the UK to be recognised by FIAF (the International Federation of Film Archives) as meeting their standards for film preservation are the National Film Archive and the Imperial War Museum. Of the many other British film collections which exist, only a handful are based in museums and none of these has anything approaching the quantity of material in the IWM, which holds enough archival film for more than ten years' continuous viewing.

Social history curators are therefore unlikely to be faced with the task of running a full-scale film archive. Nevertheless, it is possible that your museum will hold or acquire limited quantities of film material and you should have a clear policy for dealing with it.[4] Unlike still photographs, original movie film in a museum collection is effectively inaccessible and unusable until it is copied. In order to guard against damage the master copy should not be handled or projected unnecessarily. However, having it copied is expensive, and for most museums getting the original film transferred by telecine on to videotape is the most practical and affordable option.[5]

If there is any possibility that your collection contains nitrate film stock, inspection and copying should be arranged without delay. A cellulose nitrate (celluloid) base was used for most 35mm film stock up to the early 1950s. It deteriorates continuously, and is highly inflammable, making it dangerous to store anywhere other than in special fire-proof vaults. Make sure that you are not inadvertently housing a potential timebomb in your museum. Having nitrate on the premises may invalidate insurance, and be against local fire regulations.

In the case of a nitrate film, it may be necessary to destroy the original after copying. But even if the original film is on safety stock, you may decide that your own storage conditions are inadequate and that it is better housed by a properly constituted archive such as the British Film Institute, Imperial War Museum or your nearest regional film archive. If the archive concerned accepts the film as an appropriate addition to its collection, make sure that clear conditions of deposit are agreed by both parties. Copyright conditions should also be clarified at the time of transfer, as well as arrangements for use of the film for any purpose.

Using Video

Video is perhaps best considered as a usable rather than an archival medium. It is far less likely than black and white film to survive for long periods without deterioration, and cannot (yet) offer the image quality of film. On the other hand it is cheap, flexible and easy to use. Before the advent of affordable video, few museums had the facilities to show film to their visitors and it was therefore almost impossible to use the moving image as an integral part of an exhibition or display. This opportunity now exists, although it must be said that few museums have yet developed the possible applications of video in a creative and effective manner.

Basic competence with a camera can reasonably be considered an essential skill that no social history curator should lack. This ability rarely extends to movie photography, which is a far more complex business. You may be tempted by the (comparative) cheapness and simplicity of modern equipment to make your own video programmes for the museum, but the practical side of film-making is usually best left to the professionals. If museums are to make the most of this medium for communication with their visitors, the results must not look amateurish.[6]

The most basic use of video in museum displays is to show existing film material which has been transferred on to video by telecine. Production of the video master and subsequent viewing copies can be carried out by various London labs (see note 5). This procedure should be fairly straightforward, but if the original film is not in your possession, finding appropriate material for your subject and getting copyright clearance to use it may be a lengthy task.[7]

Any public exhibition of video material is now covered by the Cinemas Act, 1985, which requires the establishment concerned to hold an appropriate film licence. This applies even when such exhibitions are incidental or subsidiary to the main activity on the premises. In other words, your museum will be treated as if it were a cinema and your premises will be inspected by the local authority for maintenance of escape exitways, fire doors, fire extinguishers, safety lighting etc. Rules may be waived or modified by the local authority but must comply with the relevant current regulations made by the Secretary of State. These are the Cinematography (Safety) Regulations, 1955 S.l. 1955 No. 1129 and the Cinematography (Safety) (Amendment) Regulations, 1982 S.l. 1982 No. 1856.

If you are considering commissioning a video, visit other museums which have made or commissioned videos for their displays and watch these existing programmes critically in context, observing the reactions of visitors. Are the videos too long or too complicated? Do visitors get bored and not watch for the whole programme? Is the script, editing and camerawork good? You may not consider yourself a very good judge of these matters, but unless you develop a sharp critical awareness of other people's videos, you may have difficulty making the right decisions about your own. It is not appropriate to dictate to the professional videomaker exactly how the work should be done, but it helps if you have a clear idea of the sort of thing you want. This in turn should be reflected in the brief which you prepare when you are commissioning the work. Find out who made the videos that have impressed you, talk to the museum staff who commissioned them, and approach more than one production company to arrange for presentations of their work before you engage the one that suits you.

When planning a video production there are a number of key areas to be considered.[8]

1. Aims and Objectives   Think carefully about your reasons for using video and what you hope to achieve with the programme. It should not be simply bolted on to an exhibition as the latest display gimmick.

2. Subject   You should make a concise summary of the subject and content you want. This will form the basis of the brief, and can be developed into a 'storyboard' by or with the videomaker.

3. Audience   Who is your video for? Is it aimed at children, specialists, tourists, or the broadest possible range of museum visitors? Your choice will partly determine the character of the production.

4. Budget   What can you afford to spend? Bear in mind that location shooting by a professional film or video crew can be very expensive. It is nearly always cheaper to use existing archival footage where it is available, particularly if you are able to get copyright fees waived. You will need to take into account the cost of playing equipment and maintenance.

5. Timescale   When do you need to have the programme ready? Is there a deadline such as an exhibition or gallery opening, and if so is your timescale adequate?

6. Length   For use as part of a museum display, a video programme should be short and simple. If visitors are expected to watch the programme standing up, it should not last more than 5-6 minutes. Even if seating is provided, beware of trying to cover too many subjects or too much detail in one production.

7. Equipment   Video comes in a number of different formats which are incompatible, but can be copied from one to another. VHS (Video Home System), which has become the most popular amateur/domestic system, uses half-inch tape. This is adequate for the home, but is less suitable for heavy or continuous play in an exhibition. The recommended industrial standard video format for museum displays is Low Band U-matic, which is on three-quarter-inch tape. Picture quality is better than VHS and the players are more robust. However, it is also worth considering the Super-VHS system, which gives a sharper and better quality picture on the compact half-inch tape size than standard VHS.

The player(s) used in a museum display must have an auto-rewind facility and, preferably, a visitor-operated start button so that there is no unnecessary wear and tear from wasted play when nobody is watching it. Videos do not normally require a great deal of attention, but you should take out a service contract on the equipment.

206

8. Location Give careful thought to the siting of your video(s) in the museum. Is there space to provide seating? How many visitors do you expect to be watching the programme at any one time? A small screen monitor may be adequate for a 'talking label' video display built into a showcase, but it can only be seen by 4 – 5 visitors at once. Even a 26" monitor is only suitable for a maximum audience of about 30. For a larger audience you will need either more than one monitor, or one of the new giant screen monitors. Alternatively you could use a projection video system, which gives a bigger picture but comparatively poor image quality.

Consider, too, the problem of sound leakage into adjacent areas of your exhibition. Careful siting and the use of directional speakers can help contain it. A good quality audio system is important; you cannot always rely on the small and usually inferior built-in speakers of a television set.

9. Resources Available Can you provide all the necessary research material for the programme – information, objects and illustrations for filming, sources of additional material? Some video production companies can offer you an additional research service, but it will, of course, add to the cost and you are going to be much better acquainted with the available material than they are. However, if you decide to write your own script, be prepared to let the videomaker edit or even rewrite your no doubt scholarly but possibly leaden prose into something more punchy and appealing!

10. The Long Term You must make provision for the archival storage of the master tapes and agree procedures for getting the playing copies you will need in the future. This could be written into your agreement with the production company.

The State of the Art

New developments in optical storage technology have widened the scope for using photographs, film and video in museum displays. Twelve-inch laserdiscs will hold 36 minutes of moving image, or approximately 55,000 still frames per side. Three-and-a-half-inch CD-ROM discs (Compact Disc Read Only Memory) can store over 270,000 text pages. This dense storage capacity, combined with high speed retrieval, offers new opportunities for documenting, managing and interpreting a museum's visual archives. Inevitably, only a few of the larger institutions in this country have been able to afford laserdiscs as yet.[9]

Soon after the opening of the Museum of the Moving Image in 1988, the new museum was described in the *Guardian* as 'one of a growing number of international showplaces where inter-active audio-visual displays and micro control systems replace dusty exhibits in glass cases'. One hopes that this is not a general trend. As more museums follow the pioneers, this new technology should be seen as the means to expand and improve the interpretation of existing collections. It is no substitute for the real thing, but it can work wonders by helping to explain to visitors why that object is important and the reasons for preserving it in your museum. Consider it an opportunity, not a threat.

Notes

1. For a useful and concise summary of the legal position, see Charles H. Gibbs-Smith, *Copyright Law Concerning Works of Art, Photographs and the Written and Spoken Word,* Information Sheet No. 7, Museums Association, 1974. A more detailed account is given in Michael F. Flint, *A User's Guide to Copyright,* Butterworth, 1990, which incorporates the major changes brought about by the

Copyright, Design and Patents Act, 1988.

2. For an introduction to picture research, though one that is geared more to the needs of professional researchers working for publishers and television companies, see Hilary Evans, *The Art of Picture Research: A Guide to Current Practice, Procedure, Techniques and Resources,* David & Charles, 1979. The most useful guide to British photo archives is Rosemary Eakins (ed.), *Picture Sources UK,* Macdonald, 1985.

3. This is all the more important in the light of the 1988 Copyright Act, which strengthens the rights of the artist/designer in an agreement. Check the new legal position on copyright carefully and contact the Arts Council's Photography Officer or your local Regional Arts Association who can advise on appropriate procedure and contracts for commissioning photographers.

4. For a brief introduction to the subject, see David Cleveland, 'Movie film', *Museums Journal,* vol. 88, no. 2, September 1988. More detailed practical guidance can be found in the Technical Notes prepared by the same author for the East Anglian Film Archive, of which he is curator. These are available from the EAFA at the University of East Anglia, Norwich, Norfolk.

5. The names and addresses of film laboratories which can provide such a service (nearly all of them in London) are given in the EAFA *Technical Notes*. Check with the EAFA on the current situation as the labs do close or change their practices. It is also worth taking advice from museums with experience in dealing with archive film, such as the Imperial War Museum and London Transport Museum, and your nearest regional film archive. For a list of collections and archives see Elizabeth Oliver (ed.), *Researcher's Guide to British Film and Television Collections,* British Universities Film and Video Council, 1985.

6. If you are starting from a position of complete ignorance, look first at some of the introductory guidebooks now on the market, such as Brian Winston and Julia Keydel, *Working with Video,* Pelham Books, 1987, and David Cheshire, *The Complete Book of Video,* Dorling Kindersley, 1990.

7. The BUFVC *Researcher's Guide* is an invaluable starting point which, as well as listing film collections, contains helpful essays on research practice and film copyright. Copyright in films is considerably more complicated than in still photographs as it involves making a distinction between fiction and non-fiction material, and, in some cases, separate rights for the music and script. There is no easy way round this, and certainly no guarantee that a request to the copyright holder(s) to waive or reduce the usual copyright fees for museum use will be successful. You may be persuasive or just lucky.

8. For some professional tips on how to set about it, see Kit Campbell, 'Thinking of an audio-visual?' in *Leisure Management,* vol. 8, no.7, 1988.

9. For an account of the Science Museum's experience with laserdiscs see Jane Insley, 'Push button to continue', *Museums Journal,* vol.8, no. 2, September 1988. See also Michael Prochak, 'Multimedia is the message', *Museums Journal,* vol.90, no. 8, August 1990.

27.1 Special Problems: Printed Ephemera and Packaging

Steph Mastoris

Keeper of the Harborough Museum, Leicestershire Museums, Arts and Records Service

Introduction

Virtually every social history museum possesses examples of printed ephemera and items of packaging, often in surprisingly large numbers. However, apart from items of known rarity or importance, much of this material constitutes rather ad hoc collections which are often poorly documented and accessioned, and little used except as 'set dressings' for displays.

The reasons for this are not hard to find. Older items are comparatively rare, while there is a superabundance of contemporary examples. Much of the material has been mass produced and has only attained rarity or uniqueness through the destruction in time of most other copies. Aesthetically, most items are nondescript, being the product of many different processes where design is greatly tempered by function. They are 'everyday' items in the truest sense, and this mundane quality has meant that more recent examples acquire 'historical' status very slowly. Many items are very difficult to date, provenance and interpret because a wide range of circumstantial, local or technological knowledge is required. Their documentation is hampered by the lack of published reference material and precise terminology. Finally, ephemera and packaging pose a considerable challenge to the curator who wishes to collect contemporary items. This material is so readily available in great quantities that it is difficult to know what and how to collect. A more general curatorial problem with printed ephemera lies in the fact that, in addition to museums, both libraries and archive repositories have traditions of collecting this material.

This chapter aims to examine these problems further and suggest ways in which they can be (even partially) overcome. Although the age of the items discussed can extend back into the seventeenth century and before, it is assumed that most collections of immediate interest to readers will date from the middle of the nineteenth century up to the present day.

The term *printed ephemera* used throughout can be defined as follows:

Transient documents, produced by printing or illustrative processes, usually not in a standard book format, which are created for a specific purpose and not intended to survive the topicality of their message.[1]

Packaging can be defined as follows:

A covering or container for goods, often made from a variety of materials which uses one or more methods of closure and can consist of a number of layers.[2]

The Value of Collection

Before examining the difficulties of curating collections of printed ephemera and packaging, it is important to look briefly at the value of these items to the social history museum.

Firstly, they constitute an important aspect of the material culture of the past two centuries. As with any other product of industrialisation, they were produced deliberately for widespread dissemination and use. They are, therefore, essential to any social history curator who attempts to understand everyday life in the past. However, the original abundance of this material should not blind the curator into a false sense of security. Being intimately associated with rapid, mass consumption, printed ephemera and packaging have always been considered expendable by their users. In this way many items have soon become unique examples.

Secondly, both printed ephemera and packaging can constitute important historical evidence. Printed ephemera especially can provide primary source material for many aspects of a community's social, political, religious and cultural life. Packaging can often fulfil this role in a more symbolic way. Their decoration often provides potent images which can explain contemporary attitudes far better than other written or oral sources.[3] Also, both types of artefact can provide a consumer's-eye view of material culture by showing the innovation of new artefacts or processes and the changes in graphic and industrial design.[4]

Thirdly, printed ephemera and packaging can be of great value in museum displays. Besides their role as subjects for display in their own right, they can act as silent interpreters of other objects. They are especially useful in cases where related artefacts cannot be displayed because they have been destroyed or are too big. Also, because the design of these items reflects current styles and fashions, they are very useful for providing the atmosphere of the period to displays.

Opportunities for Collection

Various methods can be used to collect printed ephemera and packaging. Acquisition through random donation is the most common, because of the shortage of staff, time and storage found in most museums. The one advantage of this method is the insight it provides into how the items were considered and used by members of the community. However, the attitudes and social class of the owners/donors will restrict radically the range of items donated. The collections acquired in this way are often heterogeneous and provide little interpretative information beyond what is inscribed upon them. It is therefore crucial that as full a provenance as possible is sought from the donor.

Another method of collection is through donation by a manufacturer or retailer of a former working archive. Such collections are usually well documented, having been created by a design, advertising or manufacturing department. The strength of such collections lies in the range of artefacts provided from one source during a given period. Often, a type series can be compiled for dating and provenancing similar items from less well documented sources.[5] The sudden influx of a large quantity of artefacts has to be taken into consideration, and before collection begins, the storage, conservation and documentation routines must be worked out.

Active collection of contemporary items is the third method of acquisition. Potentially, this can provide the curator with the greatest range of information. Because the very nature of the material to be collected is ephemeral, acquisition can take place very easily and at virtually no cost to the museum. The greatest difficulty lies in setting the parameters for the collection programme, which must be viewed essentially as a sampling exercise from which statistically viable data can be extracted. The fullest details of the method and circumstances of collection must be recorded, along with a detailed itemisation of the artefacts.[6] Again, extensive preparations are necessary to ensure adequate storage and reduce conservation problems.

Analysis

Virtually all packaging and much printed ephemera have been generated from some form of manufacturing or commercial activity. For this reason the provision of detailed contexts for this material is, in theory, possible. However, in reality such information is not only unavailable at the time of collection, but also difficult to research when full analysis of the artefacts is undertaken by the curator. Most reference literature relating to printed ephemera and packaging has only developed in the last twenty years, and much of what there is lacks academic thoroughness. Also, because this subject straddles the history of technology and design as well as commercial and public use, together with social attitudes, wide reading is required in areas often foreign to the social history curator. Nevertheless, such analysis as can take place is most usefully carried out by considering the following three areas of human activity.

The first area of activity is *manufacture*. Here the analysis includes consideration of an artefact's commissioner and creator and the materials from which it is made; the processes used to create each item; and its overall place in the history of technology. Local and national commercial directories provide the basic information on the producers of both packaging and ephemera which is signed in some way and those which cannot be thus attributed can normally be provenanced by an analysis of design and content. Far greater problems are posed to the social history curator by the analysis of an artefact's technological history. The history of technological advances in printing and paper technology are fairly well documented but special difficulties arise when dealing with packaging or ephemera which was originally used in conjunction with some (now lost) artefact. For items of packaging, difficulties include recognising the materials used (especially plastics and the more recent metal alloys); the shortage of accessible information on the development of manufacturing techniques; and ascertaining the great time lag which can exist between the invention of an item or a technique and its widespread dissemination or adoption by the public.

The second area of activity to be analysed is *design*. Here the style of the artefact is the focus of attention. As with the analysis of manufacture, the difficulties are far greater for items of packaging. The overriding problem is that the literature describing the details of packaging design is confined to a number of well known national brand names. Typographic style of labels and inscriptions on packaging can help to provide a rough guide to date, as can a registered design, trade mark or patent number. But it is important to remember that classic designs can remain in use for decades and rob the curator of one very useful method of dating, although it should be noted that even the most seemingly unchanging design has usually been subtly altered many times in its life. For packaging produced by smaller concerns, the curator has to rely on contemporary trade literature which can be very difficult to trace.[7] Another difficulty lies in assessing the relative responsibilities for a design between the manufacturer of the package and the manufacturer or marketer of the material contained within. This is especially true in the case of producers of stock packaging where one package design can be used for a number of products and retailers.[8]

Thirdly, the artefacts can be analysed by *use* and/or *content*. Here analysis can begin with the creator's idea of the function of the item, progress through its actual function immediately after production, and finally examine any subsequent uses of the item after it has served its primary purpose. For much printed ephemera (especially items dealing with local religion or politics), content is the most difficult area of analysis, the topicality and lack of background detail in an item frequently being the difficulty. Often there are no other sources of information to provide any context for such locally produced, non-commercial ephemera. With packaging this problem does not really arise, since the function is usually described in some way on each item. However, this artwork often includes allusions to contemporary events or attitudes which can be difficult to interpret.[9]

With much printed ephemera any secondary use is usually alleviated by destruction, but with packaging there is frequently a long history of subsequent use. This is especially true of boxes and tins which are sturdy enough to survive over long periods and, by the convenience of their design, able to fulfil a number of other uses. Interpreting such survivals requires a synthesis of the analyses of manufacture, design and use, and this, in turn can help develop a critique of success (or failure) for these artefacts.

Many of the problems discussed in this section do not apply so readily to artefacts acquired as part of an active programme of contemporary collection. In these cases, subsequent in-depth analyses can be undertaken by the curator into an artefact's manufacture, design and use. The main disadvantage of collecting material almost 'at source' is that there is no opportunity for studying any secondary uses of the item or the process by which some material survives and some does not through the course of time. However, as contemporary material seems to have a very low survival rate, if the items are not collected at their immediate point of use most will not be available a week later, let alone after a decade or two.

Curation

Conservation

The prime consideration in the conservation of printed ephemera is good storage practice. This includes avoiding creasing, folding or tearing each item and providing a safe atmospheric environment. Humidity should be kept moderate and constant (55-60% RH); temperature low, at around 13-18°C; and display light intensity low (a maximum of 5O lux). An additional consideration with more modern items printed on glazed art paper is the tendency of such items to adhere together when stored under pressure in humid conditions. Often, printed ephemera has been stored in very poor conditions prior to its collection by the museum. In cases of infestation or excessive fragility a specialist paper conservator must be consulted before attempting to move the material. Frequently, however, a little basic cleaning and preventative conservation is all that is necessary. All dust and grit should be gently brushed away before sorting, numbering and boxing the items. All metal pins, spikes or staples should be carefully removed. Any associated items which may have to be separated for specialist cleaning and conservation should be carefully noted to facilitate their documentation as a group.

The primary conservation problem with packaging occurs at its entry into the museum environment. By their very nature, packaging items have been used to contain something, very often some organic substance. It is therefore most important that before entering the museum store each item is either emptied of its contents and cleansed very thoroughly or it is ensured that the contents are well sealed into the package and will not leak out. Routine cleaning can be undertaken (where appropriate) by either a gentle washing with water and a few drops of non-ionic detergent, or by delicate brushing or use of a low suction vacuum cleaner. Professional advice should be sought attempting to empty or seal up packages containing medicines and chemicals (see Chapter 27.7). The environmental conditions for storage of items of packaging will alter according to the materials from which they are made. The conditions outlined for printed ephemera are satisfactory if there is a predominance of card and paper packaging. If most items are of glass and metal then a drier (44-50% RH), warmer (18-25°C) store is advisable. A problem arises out of recent trends in the materials used in packaging. Over the last twenty years there has been a steady decrease in the use of glass and metal in favour of easily perishable materials, such as paper and card, chemically unstable plastics and even plastics with built-in degrading agents.[10] This is bound to result in far fewer items being available for collection by future curators. Long-term conservation problems can arise through the degradation of some plastics. Again, this problem is likely to increase as a greater proportion of museum collections will contain items made from these materials. There is also a potential problem with the degradation of the adhesives used to attach labels to packages. In both cases storage at a low, constant temperature and humidity (around 18°C and 50%RH) is essential, together with the isolation of each item in acid-free tissue. A frequent check should be made to ensure no sudden advances in decay have taken place.[11]

Documentation

A range of writing equipment is required when marking accession numbers on ephemera and packaging. Paper and card items should be marked in soft pencil (4B), while Indian ink with a covering lacquer should be used, where possible, for all other items. In cases where this is impossible, some types of overhead projection felt-tip pen can be used. However, the traces of even the most 'permanent' of such markers fade to a considerable degree if placed in natural light.

Difficulty of terminology is often encountered when accessioning this material. It is often very difficult to establish rigid definitions for items of printed ephemera (when does a 'playbill' become a 'poster'?; what is the difference between a 'leaflet' and a 'hand bill'?). In the absence of any readily accessible glossary of terms, house rules for a curator's own institution are necessary if any large amount of material is to be accessioned (especially by mechanical means).[12] In the same way, difficulties can arise in the use of terminology when documenting items of packaging. However, in this case the British Standard Glossary of Packaging Terms will provide most answers. A very much simplified glossary has been produced for the packages most commonly found in museum collections.[13]

Every attempt must be made to ascertain a detailed provenance for this material. When compiling the documentary record for each item of packaging, care should be taken to include the subsequent non-standard uses of a package which often occur after its contents have been exhausted. If ephemera or packaging are being collected as part of a programme of active contemporary collection, as full a record as possible should be made of the time, place, cost and reason for purchase by those undertaking the initial acquisition. This is best done by means of proformas which are filled in partly by those collecting and partly by the curator.[14]

Although the format of museum catalogues of ephemera and packaging will depend on the institution's house style, details of these items should be arranged in at least three ways. Included should be data on the producer of each item, its commissioner and/or retailer, and its use or purpose. The item should also be classified according to its most obvious sphere of human activity (e.g. personal, domestic, community or working life).[15]

Storage

Most ephemera is best stored separately from other objects in rigid boxes made from low-acid card. Ideally two or three sizes of box should be used in order to avoid large items having to be folded or small items being buckled by larger material. Care should be taken that boxes are not over-filled (a common cause of creasing for items at the bottom) and that they are stored flat. If certain items are frequently consulted or are in a very delicate condition, they should be placed in acid-free polyester sleeves, supported further where required by a sheet of acid-free mounting board. Large items, such as posters or playbills, should be rolled around some low acid support and placed inside a storage tube. Such items in frequent use are better hung in a vertical plan chest (although the mounting strips should be applied with great care and consideration both to the information on the item and the force which will be exerted on one edge when stored in this way).

The main problem in the storage of items of packaging arises from the wide variety of materials used. One package can often be made from glass or ceramic, metal, paper and a plastic. Furthermore, packages for the same goods can often contain a wide variety of materials. Packaging is therefore best stored according to fragility of material. All items made in the main from glass or ceramic should be well padded before boxing, or stored in sub-divided boxes or crates. Metal containers, especially cans, should be checked for sharp edges left after opening before being stored together, again with each item well buffered from its neighbour. Special care is necessary with items made up of several layers of packaging (such as a glass and metal vessel in a card box) in case their weight will crush similar items which lack their inner part. Paper bags and emptied food wrappers should, like printed ephemera, be stored flat with as little creasing as possible.

Use in Display

Printed ephemera and packaging items are used in museums most widely as 'set dressing' for permanent or temporary displays, especially in recreated 'period' interiors. In this they perform a very useful function. These items often include details of prices, descriptions or illustrations of processes or events. Their design can easily impart a sense of time and place. In this way they combine a role as displayable artefact with that of interpreter of other items. However, if they are to be fully interpreted in their own right then a considerable amount of background information is required. As ephemeral items their topicality is paramount in their interpretation. Some items of printed ephemera are virtually unintelligible without some explanation of the topical allusions made in their texts or graphics. The production methods and historical importance of many types of packaging are very difficult to extrapolate from the artefacts themselves. It is very hard to impart this information either succinctly or easily, especially in the confines of a period reconstruction which aims to reduce written interpretation to a minimum.

Two further problems arise in the use of packaging items in period reconstructions. Firstly, many of the items available are well used and often very worn or damaged. Displaying items in this condition is acceptable in a traditional cased display, but ruins the sense of period reality which underlies the reconstructed setting. Secondly, museums usually only possess one or two copies of any item. It is therefore impossible to recreate a shop display which includes mass produced goods such as these. The only solution to these problems is to create facsimiles which can be replicated in quantities sufficient to provide the desired effect. An added advantage is that low security displays can be mounted containing replicas of rare museum items.

A more abstract use arises from the very ordinariness of printed ephemera and packaging. Although many items may be unique copies, they are often perceived by visitors as 'rubbish', out of place amongst the rare and beautiful objects they consider the stuff of museums. If interpreted fully, such displays can help to 'de-mythologise' the museum in the eyes of its public and bring about a greater awareness of its true role as collector and interpreter of material culture, great and small.

Use in Research

As discussed above, both printed ephemera and packaging items present a 'consumer's-eye view' of everyday life. Their transitory nature has often allowed them to become vehicles for significant observations on important historical events. They often possess circumstantial information frequently useful as a source of research which is often unrelated to the history of the artefact itself. Also, given that many of the older items of printed ephemera are unique, they are often consulted as primary historical records akin to manuscripts and are frequently used as sources for research. This can often cause problems of public access, where items are not available elsewhere and are required for frequent consultation by the public. The lack of public reference areas and adequate supervisory staff in most small and medium-sized museums can turn this public interest into a considerable problem. In such cases this material should be reproduced in microform and copies deposited in other relevant repositories. If material of this nature is of little relevance to the rest of the museum collections, then its transfer to a more suitable repository should be considered.

Printed ephemera and packaging items can also be used in more rigorous and empirical historical research programmes. Where a collection comes from a well documented source and where the criteria for its selection are recorded, its use can go beyond representations of cultural activity. By combining the circumstantial information relating to the artefact's provenance with statistical or contextural analyses of the artefacts themselves, a collection can generate new historical insights into the culture to which they belong. Generally such work arises from a programme of active contemporary collecting. With such a programme, the great problem is getting an adequate range of collection points and dealing with the large quantity of artefacts which can be assembled very rapidly.

Conclusion

This chapter has not only examined the problems of curating printed ephemera and packaging but also tried to demonstrate that they are worth tackling. Perhaps the greatest curatorial problem lies in the attitudes of the curators themselves. Like many members of the public, museum workers often consider this material interesting but too ephemeral for much time (and money) to be expended on its curation. Such an attitude not only negates the all-embracing collecting brief which most museums purport to maintain, but denies the fact that for at least the last hundred years the material culture of Britain has become increasingly diversified, mass-produced and ephemeral. For this reason alone, printed ephemera and packaging can be seen as important in any serious examination of this culture. If the consumer society continues to develop at such a rapid rate during the next century, the artefacts discussed here will develop an even more central role in its interpretation. In the 'throwaway society' the social history curator cannot wait for the archaeologist.

Notes and References

1. Adapted from C. Makepeace, *Ephemera:...Its Collection, Conservation and Use,* Gower, 1985, p. 10.

2. Adapted from British Standards Institute, *Glossary of Packaging Terms,* B.S. 3130.

3. Good examples of this can be found in J.M.MacKenzie, *Propaganda and Empire,* Manchester University Press, 1984.

4. J. Lewis, in his *Printed Ephemera,* Cowell, 1962, used examples of typography from ephemera to chart the development of type design and graphics throughout the nineteenth and twentieth centuries.

5. The collection of John Player & Son (now on long-term loan to Nottingham City Museums) is a good example of a very comprehensive archive of two- and three-dimensional advertising and packaging material which can be used to date examples found in other museums. See A. Clinton, *Printed Ephemera: Collection, Organisation and Access,* Bingley, 1981, for an account of the Robert Wood Collection at Hartlepool Museum. This collection is made up of 50,000 items from the files of a local printing firm.

6. S. and L. Mastoris, 'Collecting contemporary advertising ephemera from a Nottingham suburb', *Journal of the Social History Curators Group,* no. 13, 1985-6, pp. 15-28; S. Mastoris, 'Pre-empting the dustbin: collecting contemporary domestic packaging', ibid., no. 14, 1986-7, pp. 23-6; S. Mastoris, 'Sneinton revisited: further collections of contemporary advertising ephemera from Nottingham suburbs', ibid., no. 18, 1990-91.

7. A start can be made with British Library, Newspaper Library, *Catalogue of the Newspaper Library Colindale,* 1975; British Library, Document Supply Centre, *Current British Journals,* 1986.

8. P. Brears, *The Lightowler Collection,* Leeds City Museum, 1988; R. Opie, *The Art of the Label,* Simon & Schuster, 1987.

9. J.M. MacKenzie, op. cit.

10. S. Mastoris, 1986-7, p. 25.

11. S. Mossman, 'Plastics in museums', *Journal of the Social History Curators Group,* no. 15, 1987-8, p.32.

12. There is a useful glossary in L. Shepard, *The History of Street Literature,* David & Charles, 1973, pp. 224-5; and a checklist of items constituting ephemera in C. Makepeace, op. cit., pp.220-23.

13. This was supplied as a supplement to S. Mastoris, 1986-7.

14. Examples of these are reproduced in S. and L. Mastoris, op. cit., and S. Mastoris, 1986-7.

15. See SHIC Working Party, Social History and Industrial Classification, Centre for English Cultural Tradition and Language, University of Sheffield, 1983. The ephemera collection at the Museum of London, which contains approximately 300,000 items, is indexed by four categories: date, name of producer, trade and/or subject, and area of London to which it refers.

Bibliography

Allen, A., and Hoverstadt, J., *The History of Printed Scraps,* New Cavendish, 1983.

Bottomley, P.M., 'Conservation and storage: archival paper', in Thompson, J.M.A.(ed.), *Manual of Curatorship,* Butterworth, 1984.

Baglee, C., and Morley, A., *Street Jewellery,* New Cavendish, 1988, 2nd ed.

British Standards Institution, *Glossary of Packaging Terms,* BS.3130, 1986.

Buday, G., *The History of the Christmas Card,* Spring Books, 1954.

Clinton, A., *Printed Ephemera: Collection, Organisation and Access,* Clive Bingley, 1981.

Davis, A., *Package and Print: The Development of Container and Label Design,* Faber, 1967.

HMSO, *A Century of Trademarks,* 1976.

Hamish Fraser, W., *The Coming of the Mass Market, 1850-1914,* Macmillan, 1981.

Insley, J., *British Patent Numbers,* Group for Scientific, Technological and Medical Collections, Information Sheet No.2

Institute of Packaging, *Packaging Today Directory – Institute of Packaging Yearbook,* annual.

Jaspert, W. P., Berry, W. T., and Johnson, A. F., *The Encyclopedia of Typefaces,* Blandford, 1970, 4th ed.

King, A., *Registered Design Numbers,* Group for Scientific, Technological and Medical Collections, Information Sheet No. 4.

Lee, R., *A History of Valentines,* Batsford, 1953.

Lewis, J., *Printed Ephemera,* W. S. Cowell Ltd, 1962 (reprinted by Antique Collectors Club, Woodbridge, Suffolk, 1990). Abridged edition, Faber, 1969.

Makepeace, C. E., *Ephemera – A Book on its Collection, Conservation and Use,* Gower, 1985.

Mastoris, S., and Mastoris, L., 'Collecting contemporary advertising ephemera from a Nottingham suburb', *Journal of the Social History Curators Group,* no.13, 1985-6, pp.15-28.

Mastoris, S., 'Pre-empting the dustbin: collecting contemporary domestic packaging', *Journal of the Social History Curators Group,* no.14, 1986-7, pp. 23-6.

Mastoris, S., 'Glad tidings...: collecting contemporary Christmas cards at the Harborough Museum', *Journal of the Social History Curators Group,* no.17, 1989-90, pp.18-21.

Mastoris, S., 'Sneinton revisited: further collections of contemporary advertising ephemera from Nottingham suburbs', *Journal of the Social History Curators Group,* no.18, 1990-91, pp.30-37.

Minchington, W. E. J., *The British Tin-plate Industry,* Oxford University Press, 1957.

Mossman, S., 'Plastics in Museums', *Journal of the Social History Curators Group,* no.17, 1987-8, pp. 30-33.

Mullen, C., *Cigarette Pack Art,* Hamlyn, 1979.

Murray, J., 'A short history of glass packaging', *Journal of the Social History Curators Group,* no.15, 1987-8, pp. 34-5.

Opie, R., *The Art of the Label,* Simon & Schuster, 1987.

Opie, R., *Sweet Memories,* Pavilion, 1988.

Opie, R., *Packaging Source Book,* Macdonald Orbis, 1989.

Rickards, M., *Collecting Printed Ephemera,* Phaidon/Christie's, 1988.

Shepard, L., *The History of Street Literature,* David & Charles, 1973.

Singer, C., *et al., History of Technology,* 5 vols, Clarendon Press, 1954-8.

Sonsino, Steven, *Packaging Design – Graphics, Materials, Technology,* Thames & Hudson, 1990.

Tilley, R., *A History of Playing Cards,* Studio Vista, 1973.

Winstanley, M. J., *The Shopkeeper's World, 1830-1914,* Manchester University Press, 1983.

27.2 Special Problems: Documents

Elizabeth Frostick

Keeper of Social History, Birmingham Museums and Art Gallery

It is very difficult to define the word 'documents' precisely; according to one definition a document can be a 'thing, writing or inscription that furnishes evidence'.[1] The problem, of course, is that many objects in our collections are both objects and documents in that they furnish us with historical evidence, often in written as well as material form. An eighteenth-century gravestone is both an object and a document. Generally speaking, it is fair to say that documents are 'works on paper'. As distinct from printed ephemera, documents are often handwritten or drawn and have a greater claim to rarity or uniqueness than ephemera. There is, however, some overlap and some early printed material, for example Civil War tracts, may be legitimately classed as documents.

Within social history collections there are invariably large numbers of documents, items which fall outside accepted object or ephemera classifications. These include letters, school reports, punishment records and school registers, passports and identity cards, certificates, diaries, notebooks, drawings and sketches, accounts and inventories. Documents may also include maps, membership cards, invitations, stock and share certificates and banknotes. Other important documents in Hull Museums include the punishment record books and estate inventories from eighteenth and nineteenth-century slavery plantations in the West Indies.

No social history curator would question the value of documents within the process of historical research and understanding. Traditionally documents have been by far the major source for historical research. The curator draws upon a wide selection of sources, from objects to landscapes and oral testimony, from photographs to documents.

But should these documents form part of our permanent museum social history collections? After all, record offices and local history libraries exist to deal almost exclusively with documents.[2] Museums collect 'objects'! How then should the social history curator approach 'documents' with regard to collection management? Should the social history curator collect documents? Why? When and with what justification? What implications does collecting documents have on more practical questions of storage, documentation, accessibility, and for display?

Collecting Documents: What Justification?

The Concept of Context

One of the positive steps forward within social history thinking in museums has been the growing recognition of the importance of historical context in interpreting social history artefacts. Only with knowledge of the context in which artefacts were produced and utilized can a full understanding of them be reached. Sets of objects in themselves may tell us little or nothing about the ways of life associated with or implied by their existence. In essence, social history is about the people who made and used those objects, not simply about the objects themselves.

Should, then, the collection of a small tailoring business, of local historical importance, involve only the collection of objects? What does the curator do when faced with the postcards on the noticeboard, the shop accounts and order books, paper patterns and handwritten instructions that so characterize the particular workshop? Like the instructions book that tells us how a machine actually works, the paper 'documents' can tell us how this particular workshop 'worked' as a social and economic unit. Should the documents, however, duly acknowledged, be separated from the objects and sent to a different collecting institution? Some would argue that the trade catalogues should be placed with other trade catalogues rather than remain within the work context in which they were used. There is a case, surely, for respecting the integrity of the collection as a whole. There is a strong argument in favour of keeping material that has formed a homogeneous collection together, irrespective of the type of material involved. There is no social historical justification for separating certain items in a collection simply because they are made of paper.

The Personality Museum

There is a large number of museums, both at home and abroad, that fall broadly into the category of 'personality museum'. Wilberforce House Museum, in Hull, for example, is both the birthplace of, and now a public tribute to, the life and work of William Wilberforce, slave emancipator. The Brontë Parsonage in Haworth and the Freud Museum in London are variations on the theme. Many towns and cities have produced at least one famous person, now safely enshrined. These museums are very often run through social history departments of local authorities, although a number are independent.

In a personality museum, everything from buildings, furniture, paintings, ceramics, diaries, letters, notebooks, etc., to clothes and kitchen utensils, is of equal importance. The historical significance of these 'objects' and 'documents' lies predominantly in their association with that person. Letters and personal documents, in particular, are significant for the insights into the personality that they can provide. Personality museums become repositories for information about the life and works of an historical figure, interpreting the person within the context of their birthplace, home or studio.

Whether or not the aims of personality museums are legitimate – much of the context is, of course, completely recreated – they can become recognized centres of specialist knowledge and information. A further strength is that they can enable nationally important material to remain in the local museum. Documents, therefore, form a justifiable part of the personality museum's collections.

The 'Displayability Criterion'[3]

Some collecting of documents and two-dimensional material seems to be dictated by whether the item in question could be useful for display. While there can be no philosophical justification for collecting social history material because 'it would look good on display', the practical problems of limited storage and display areas may inevitably influence decisions. Reconstructions and a contemporary obsession with 'the real thing' may tempt the curator to collect more material than is necessary. Given that theoretically all information relating to a particular historical situation is relevant, it can become very difficult to collect 'selectively'.

Rescue Social History

The social history curator is justified in collecting important documents if the material would otherwise not survive. Even if other collecting institutions are consulted, there will always remain material that falls outside official collecting policies. Available information suggests that even taking the collecting policies and strategies of parallel institutions into account, there are grey areas which would leave some material uncollected.[4] The standard of care that the documents will receive is also of concern to the curator, who should collect material that is otherwise known to be placed at risk. Clearly there is much need for judgement and discretion on the part of the curator who should be able to make decisions with confidence.

Historical Accident

Whatever justification the curator may assume for collecting documents in the present and future, many social history collections will already include large numbers of documents. While certain material may be transferred to other institutions if appropriate, this will almost certainly not involve all material. The documents will be there in the museum, for reasons we may not understand, because they have been collected in the past.

A Sense of Social History?

One of the perennial problems facing the social history curator is that many of the objects in our stores are not representative of past society. The middle-class bias inherent in many museum displays is something the social history curator must continuously strive to augment. Whilst formal written manuscripts and literary sources often contain the same problems, a personal document, for example a Micky Mouse Cinema Club membership card, Hull, c.1930, may be all we have. Similarly, a set of approximately 500 original sketches by F.S. Smith, showing detailed street views of Hull in the 1880s and 1890s are some of the most important social history documents in the collection. The appearance of shops and businesses, the details of street patterns, transport, costume, long-gone buildings and street furniture on drawings with no claims to artistic merit are quite happily cared for by the social history department. The drawings are similar to photographs, furnishing information that exists nowhere else; each drawing is a unique historical document.

Given that many social history curators will find themselves responsible for collections of documents, how should they be managed; how should documents be organised, stored, conserved, interpreted and displayed?

The Care of Documents: Storage and Conservation

Documents usually require to be stored in an area separate from the three-dimensional objects. The advantage of documents, however, is that they are usually regular in shape, fairly flat and may take up relatively little space in the store. They also fit neatly into storage boxes! Detailed information on the conservation of works on paper will not be given here, although the following practical guidelines should prove useful. Good housekeeping can prevent expensive repair and conservation work, which should be left to qualified conservators.

Because paper, an organic material, absorbs moisture, the temperature and relative humidity (RH), should be kept constant. It is recommended that paper documents be kept at a RH of 50-65%, and parchment or vellum at 55-65%. Paper is generally conserved by keeping it cold but a compromise with staff-inhabited buildings is usually required. A steady 13-18°C is considered acceptable, the more constant the better.[5] Mould is likely to grow if the temperature goes much above this. Light should be excluded or kept to a minimum level, ultra violet film can be put around fluorescent tubes and over windows. Documents should be boxed to keep them as clean as possible from dirt and atmospheric pollution. It is important to ensure good air circulation. Acid and lignin-free archival storage boxes are recommended. Much nineteenth- and twentieth-century cheap paper poses particular problems for the curator because the lignin contained within it becomes acid when it absorbs sulphur dioxide and the paper disintegrates. Acid-free tissue, which is relatively cheap, should be wrapped around individual documents. Melinex-type polythene sleeves/pockets create an acid-free environment and are particularly useful as they are transparent.

Stored documents should be examined at regular intervals to check for discoloration, mould, etc.

Avoid contact with paper clips, staples and pins as these can rust leaving stains and damaging paper. Paper clips should be removed but it is important to maintain the original ordering of papers.

Handling documents should be avoided unless it is absolutely necessary and cotton gloves do protect paper from the grease and grime of human skin! All documents should be handled with great care. Do not pick up documents with the finger and thumb at a corner; support them with an archival board and view them on a clean flat surface. With regard to display and conservation, documents can be mounted against acid-free mountboard and fronted with melinex sheet. The melinex sheet can then be attached to the display board with brass pins. Melinex strips can be used to hold particular-pages open by attaching the strip to the display board crossing a page at a diagonal or the full length of the document. No attachment is ever made to the original document. Pins and Blu-tak and other adhesive agents are not acceptable.

The Use of Documents: Public Access

It is easy enough to collect documents, and looking after them is in many ways more straightforward than dealing with multi-media three-dimensional objects. But what do you do with documents once they are safely in store? There are two aspects to this question, the first, public access, and the second, display and interpretation. One of the problems caused by collecting documents of important local interest is that the public will wish to consult them. How does the curator deal with making the information contained in these documents available while ensuring the safety and preservation of the material? Museums are not simply public archives, and few museum services have the luxury of staff appointed to deal solely with the supervision of public access to records. By collecting documents and by making them available – either to the academic researcher or local school pupil – a curator is creating work. Dealing with an individual enquiry may take up to three hours or more. Where specific collections of documents are well known, the demand upon them will be even more considerable. The public, increasingly familiar with record offices and local history libraries, expect the museum to operate in the same user-friendly manner and may be discouraged by the attitude of some museums. The curator should aim to make material available if at all possible whilst taking all considerations of conservation into account. It is best to operate an appointments system of access. This ensures that the curator is available to supervise the researcher, and is a more efficient system to operate. Encourage the researcher to be as specific as possible before the visit so that you can prepare the most suitable material; this will avoid unnecessary handling of sensitive material, etc. Good indexes, storage and filing systems can help to save time.

The Wilberforce Slavery collection of documents and ephemera is constantly sought by researchers and school pupils busily engaged upon GCSE 'slavery' courses. The better the collection, the greater the demand. Unfortunately the fragile nature of documents means that if they are to be preserved for the future it is essential to make copies available, leaving the original safe in store. The publication of facsimiles, catalogues, information packs and booklets will certainly help reduce demands on the most sought-after material and save curatorial time in the long term. The creation of a photographic negative removes the need for frequent copying of original and fragile material.

The Use of Documents: Display and Interpretation

Although documents do not have an immediately obvious display value they can be used to good effect in social history displays. It should be recognized that documents are generally more effective for the information that they exhibit than for their visual appeal. Used in conjunction with other material, however, documents can add both a sense of reality and a sense of the personal, the individual in history. For example, a child's hand-written account, written at school in 1939, of the start of the Second World War, framed within an exhibition about the War, is a reminder that individual ordinary men and women lived through the War. There is a tendency in history to accentuate the strangeness of the past, as if things in the past could not happen 'to people like us'. The child's personal document brings the abstract facts, figures and atrocities back to a more manageable level. A similar effect is created by using school reports, artefacts and school exercise books within an exhibition about the social history of education. To read names, especially those written upon a very familiar document, adds immediacy. Yes, they were real people.

Documents are sometimes all we have; they can also make something incredible seem less so. Where difficult subjects are being tackled by social history staff, documents may have to be used in the absence of any other material. For example, Wilberforce House Museum attempts to explain the history of slavery and its abolition. When you see, for example, the slave-trader's accounts, the receipts for slaves bought and sold, the punishments issued written down in a book by some past person's hand, the effects can be very powerful.

The strength of documents is that, unlike many objects, they can be relatively simple, and are often immediately intelligible. To represent the past accurately, the social history curator needs as much evidence as possible; documents are too important a resource to be excluded.

The ideal social historian is an explorer who does not stay in his [or her] study: he will use his eyes and his feet as much as his brain. We learn through things as well as ideas, and through reminiscence as well as through documents – or statistics.[6]

Notes and References

1. *The Concise Oxford Dictionary,* Book Club Associates, 1979, 6th ed.

2. See Chapter 31.3.

3. Term discussed by Mr Richard van Reil at Yorkshire and Humberside Federation of Museums and Art Galleries seminar, 'Paper, Paper Everywhere! Archives in Museums', held at the Yorkshire Museum, York, 20 June 1988.

4. 'Paper, Paper Everywhere! Archives in Museums'. See note 3.

5. P. Michael Bottomley, 'Conservation and storage: archival paper', in J.M.A. Thompson (ed.), *Manual of Curatorship: A Guide to Museum Practice,* Butterworth, 1984.

6. A. Briggs, *A Social History of England,* Book Club Associates, 1983.

Bibliography

Bazelon, Bruce S., 'Curatorial and archival methods yield divergent views', *History News,* vol. 43, no. 2, March/April 1988. pp. 12-13.

Bottomley, P. Michael, 'Conservation and storage: archival paper', in Thompson, J.M.A. (ed.), *Manual of Curatorship: A Guide to Museum Practice,* Butterworth, 1984.

Briggs, A., *A Social History of England,* Book Club Associates, 1983.

Cruttenden, Philip C., 'Local history resource centres', *Library Association Record,* no. 77, vol. 8, August 1975.

Dructor, Robert, M., 'It's a record: archivist. It's an artefact: curator', *History News,* vol. 43, no. 2, March/April 1988, pp. 14-15.

McAusland, Jane, 'Conservation and storage: prints, drawings and watercolours', in Thompson, J.M.A. (ed.), *Manual of Curatorship: A Guide to Museum Practice,* Butterworth, 1984.

Sandwith, H., and Stainton, S., *The National Trust Manual of Housekeeping,* Penguin Books and National Trust, 1985.

Useful Addresses and Contacts

Atlantis Paper Company, Gullivers Wharf, 105 Wapping Lane, London El 9RW   Paper enclosures; Polyester sleeves, sheets; Mountboard; Silversafe paper; Photostore paper.

Conservation Resources Limited, Unit 1, Littleworth Industrial Estate, Wheatley, Oxon   Paper enclosures; Polyester sleeves; Mountboard; Storage boxes; Silversafe paper.

G. Ryder & Company Limited, Denbigh Road, Bletchley, Milton Keynes, MKl lDG   Paper enclosures; Solander boxes; Storage boxes.

Secol Limited, Kelvin Place, Thetford, Norfolk IP24 3RR   Polyester sleeves, sheets.

27.3 Special Problems: Photographs and Film

Gaby Porter

Curatorial Services Manager, Museum of Science and Industry, Manchester

Photographs are both artefacts and reference materials. They are probably the most chemically complex and physically fragile artefacts in historical collections, sensitive to handling, light and variations in environmental conditions. They have strong inherent qualities as artefacts, each with its own detailed history of process, production, presentation and circulation. However, they are often seen as illustrations, of little intrinsic value or importance, treated with less care and used more extensively than other parts of collections. This chapter gives broad guidelines as to the care of photographs and film, and a Bibliography for more detailed advice.

Access

Many people using photographic collections are concerned with the subject and content of images (e.g. buildings, locomotives) rather than with the history of the photograph itself. A system of copy slides or prints, which gives the content of the image, with access to information about the original, is therefore sufficient for many enquirers.

Such a system is costly to establish, but produces its own savings. These are:

protection of the photographs: handling is the main cause of damage, often irreversible, to photographs;

better physical security for the collection;

reduction in staff time supervising access;

less wear and tear on storage materials for the collection: these are expensive to purchase because they are highly specialised.

Access to photographic collections is usually through subject classification groupings, with limited or no cross referencing. A database with access through various indexing terms to the collection (for example, place, sitter, photographic process) and with copy photographs stored in numerical sequence by accession number offers a more flexible system.

In many museums, copy photographs are mounted on index and/or catalogue cards (e.g. Beamish). The Museum of London has back projection units on which users may scan carousels of slides. The slides are made *in situ* by curatorial staff, using a small copy stand, as photographs are catalogued and stored, so avoiding delays for photographic work (Seaborne and Neufeld, 1982).

Environment

Photographic collections should be stored in a cool, dry and stable environment. The general storage environment is the most important consideration and the most cost-effective investment in any photographic collection. The existing environment should be assessed with monitoring instruments to provide a profile of diurnal and seasonal fluctuations (if this has not already been done).[1] Such fluctuations may be reduced by basic housekeeping measures, or by installing plant. If stores are in damp cellars, or in attics which heat up and cool rapidly, a new and more stable location should be considered. The optimum arrangement is conditioned storage with carbon air filtration, and with temperature and relative humidity at 16-18°C, 40-45%.

Research/work areas should be separated from storage areas; lights in stores should be used only for removing/returning items. All natural light should be excluded; background lighting should have individual switches at the work surface. If fluorescent lighting is used, tubes with a low UV output should be chosen. Any other tubes should be sleeved with UV filters; these should be checked every month with a UV meter and replaced regularly.

Floors should be hard surfaces (vinyl or equivalent), which are easy to clean and free of dust, which is highly abrasive and encourages mould formation on photographic emulsions at higher humidity levels.

A cleaning roster for curatorial and cleaning staff is essential. Work surfaces should be cleared and wiped clean before and after every use. Detergents and ammonia cleaners should be avoided. Floors should be cleaned weekly, at least; cupboard doors, tops and backs, overhead pipes and light fittings should be cleaned monthly. During intensive periods of work on the collections, you may need to clean more frequently.

Storage

Curators may use a variety of storage materials, but none is universally satisfactory in very damp or very dry conditions.

Storage materials should be chemically neutral. Fittings and storage materials may introduce pollutants into the general atmosphere of the store, and into local containers. For example, compound boards contain high proportions of formaldehyde; wood and wool contain sulphur. These will tarnish silver photographic images. Many products offered as archival quality are unsuitable for long-term use: for example, buffered wood-pulp papers and boards. Be sceptical; take advice from established museum users and rely on specialised vendors and certified products.

The general considerations are as follows:

1. *Shelves and cabinets* should be made of stainless steel or baked enamelled metal, should be robust and well able to bear the heavy loads of photographic materials. You should consider the distribution of materials on shelves according to weight: the heaviest items should be stored at waist level.

2. *All storage and mounting materials* should be made of 100% polyester (tradenames Mylar, Secol, Melanex) or of 100% rag, unbuffered, lignin- and sulphur-free paper and board. Beware of commercial plastic 'photopreservers': if a plastic smells, it is probably no good.

3. *Any glues and adhesives* on storage enclosures or mounts should be starch or cellulose water-based adhesives, which are easily reversible. The emulsion surface of the photographic image should not be placed in contact with any seam or extra thickness in the storage enclosure.[2] Direct application of any adhesives to the photographs themselves should be avoided. No self-adhesive tape or labels, double-sided tape, or dry-mounting should be used.

4. *Neutral foam* (Plastazote brand) may be used as a lining for drawers and boxes.

5. *Working surfaces* should be made of neutral materials, with surfaces and edges

which do not splinter or crack. Compound boards contain high proportions of sulphur and formaldehyde: if used, they must be fully sealed. For example, thick laminates may be bonded to *both* sides of chipboard, with an edging strip of sealed hardwood. Thin laminates, and boards which are sealed on one side only, are unsuitable.

6. *Cotton gloves* must be used at all times when handling photographic materials. These are available from protective clothing suppliers. It is important to replace gloves regularly. They should be washed with a mild soap or neutral washing agent.

7. *Working surfaces* should be clean and dry: they may be cleaned with a disposable towel dampened with water. They should be covered with sheets of unbleached calico or acid-free tissue to soften the surface and cushion the material. Again, sheets should be replaced and washed as above (6.).

8. *Photographs should be well supported* in transit and while working. To move material between stores and work areas, use trolleys with a rebate and cover them with paper or cloth. Support the photographs well while handling them: hold firmly with both hands by the edges. Do not touch the emulsion.

9. *2B pencils* should be used for any writing. The photograph should be laid emulsion side down on a hard board before writing on the back, to minimise pressure on the emulsion. Waxed negatives should not be marked.

Storage varies according to the photographic process; curators and archivists should consult the standard works for detailed storage guidelines, particularly for nineteenth-century material. Recommended storage for the most common types of photographic materials is as follows:

Nitrate film   Segregate. Identify unstable material (Fleming, 1984), copy on to safety stock and refrigerate originals in sealed foil bags or store off-site. Place stable material in buffered enclosures and in well-ventilated cabinet; check regularly.

Safety film
  Strip   Captive-flap polyester sleeve, or pocketed polyester sleeve, or paper envelope or enclosure. Store on edge in box.
  Roll   Original aluminium containers, or cut and store as above.
  Sheet   Polyester sleeve, or cruciform paper enclosure, or negative envelope, stored on edge in box.

Colour transparencies
  Unmounted   Individual polyester sleeve, stored as above.
  Mounted   Pocketed polyester sheet, or box.

Glass negatives   Cruciform paper enclosure, on edge in box. Do not stack.

Broken negatives   Do not pour out of original envelope or box: place on a flat surface and slit two edges.

Lantern slides   Check binding papers and cover glasses; wrap in cruciform paper enclosure if damaged. Store on edge in slotted or partitioned box.

Prints   Polyester sleeve, cruciform paper enclosure, folder or envelope, store flat in box.

Curled prints   Do not attempt to flatten, this may fracture the emulsion. Store loose in box.

Cleaning

Photographic emulsion and suspensions are part of the history of the object.

Photographs often carry surface treatments, such as retouching and toning; they are highly sensitive to abrasion and pollution. Do not attempt to clean these surfaces. A 'bloom' or mould growth on the emulsion may signify high humidity; at lower humidity it will not spread. Silvering of the emulsion may signify acid storage materials; again, if the photograph is stored in neutral materials, it should not spread. Non-emulsion surfaces may be cleaned sparingly with soft brushes or puffers.

Display

For many display purposes, high quality copy prints may be acceptable, or even preferable, because flexible. To display original photographs, the general considerations are the same as those for storage.

Frames should have backing boards of corrugated plastic or neutral foam core board. Clean glass and acrylic with a soft lint-free cloth; avoid proprietary cleaners. Mounts should be made from rag board, with an overmatte so that the photographic image does not touch the glass or acrylic cover. Paper or polyester photo corners should be attached to the mount to hold the photograph in place.

Early prints – salt prints and albumen – are fragile and highly sensitive to water: they should not be mounted with corners or hinges. They may be mounted thus: place in position on the backboard of a window mount; place a sheet of polyester on top. Attach the polyester sheet with double-sided tape at its corners, well away from the print, to the backboard. Put the overmatte in place. Frame the print and mount: tension will hold the print in place.

Prints on heavy papers or mounts may be mounted in cases by strapping them to an archival support board with strips of polyester. The backing board may then be laid flat or firmly fixed to a display board or panel.

Disaster Plan

Any collections management policy should acknowledge the possibility of fire and flood damage and prepare a detailed disaster plan. Guidelines are laid out in Anderson and McIntyre (1985).

Notes

1. You may be able to borrow or hire measuring instruments from your local Area Museums Service.

2. The cruciform or 4-flap design provides an excellent enclosure without adhesives or seams.

References

Anderson, H., and McIntyre, J. (1985), *Planning Manual for Disaster Control in Scottish Libraries and Record Offices,* National Library of Scotland, Edinburgh.

Seaborne, M., and Neufeld, S. (1982), 'Historic photograph collection management at the Museum of London', *Museums Journal,* vol.82, no.2.

Select Bibliography

Photographic history

Gernsheim, H., and Gernsheim, A., *The History of Photography,* McGraw Hill, New York, Thames & Hudson, 1969.

Newhall, B., and Newhall, N., *The History of Photography*, Secker & Warburg, 1985.

Rosenblum, N., *A World History of Photography*, Abbeville, New York, 1984.

Processes

Coe, B., and Haworth-Booth, M., *A Guide to Early Photographic Processes*, Victoria and Albert Museum, 1983.

Crawford, W., *The Keepers of Light: A History and Working Guide to Early Photographic Processes*, Morgan & Morgan Inc., New York, 1979.

Gill, A. T., *Photographic Processes*, Information Sheet 21, Museums Association, 1978.

Reilly, J.M., *Care and Identification of Nineteenth Century Photographs*, Eastman Kodak, Rochester, New York.

Collections management and conservation

Anderson, H., and McIntyre, J., *Planning Manual for Disaster Control in Scottish Libraries and Record Offices*, National Library of Scotland, Edinburgh, 1985.

Fleming, A.E., 'Conservation and storage: photographic materials', in Thompson, J.M.A. (ed.), *Manual of Curatorship*, Butterworth, 1984.

Fleming, D., 'Photographic collections – a strategy for information retrieval', *MDA Information*, vol. 9, no. 1, pp. 14-24.

Hendricks, K., *The Preservation and Restoration of Photographic Materials in Archives and Libraries: A RAMP Study with Guidelines*, UNESCO, Paris, 1984.

Keefe, L., and Inch, D., *The Life of a Photograph*, Focal Press, 1984.

Reilly, J.M., *Care and Identification of Nineteenth Century Photographs*, Eastman Kodak, Rochester, New York, 1986.

Rempel, S., *The Care of Photographs*, Nick Lyons Books, 1987.

Ritzenhaler, Minoff and Long, *Administration of Photographic Collections*, Society of American Archivists, Chicago. Available from SAA, 600 S Federal Street, Chicago, Illinois, USA.

Seaborne, M., and Neufeld, S., 'Historic photograph collection management at the Museum of London', *Museums Journal*, vol. 82, no. 2, 1982.

Swan, A., *The Care and Conservation of Photographic Material*, Crafts Council (out of print), 1981.

Weinstein, R., and Booth, L., *Collection, Use and Care of Historical Photographs*, American Association for State and Local History, Nashville, Tennessee, 1977.

British and International Standards

BS 1153: 1975 *Recommendations for Processing and Storage of Silver Gelatin Microfilm.*

BS 5454: 1977 *The Storage and Exhibition of Archival Documents*, section 12, pp. 6-7.

BS 5687: 1979 *Recommendations for the Storage Conditions for Silver Image Photographic Plates for Record Purposes* (revised 1985).

ISO 5466: 1980 *Photography: Practice for the Storage of Processed Safety Photographic Film* (revised 1985).

ISO 6051: 1980 *Photography: Silver Image Photographic Paper Prints for Record Purposes – Storage Conditions* (revised 1985).

Suppliers of Storage and Display Materials

These materials may not have been tested independently, therefore their suitability is not guaranteed.

Atlantis Paper Company Ltd – Paper enclosures, envelopes; Polyester sleeves, sheets; Mountboard; Storage boxes; Silversafe photostore paper. 2 St Andrews Way, Bow, London E3 3PA Tel: 081 537 2727 (wholesale and archival) 081 537 2525 (retail)

Conservation Resources Ltd – Paper enclosures, envelopes; Polyester sleeves, sheets; Mountboard; Silversafe; Alpha-Cellulose papers; Storage boxes. Unit 1, Pony Road, Horspath Industrial Estate, Cowley, Oxon OX4 2RD Tel: 0865 747755

G. Ryder & Co. Ltd – Paper enclosures, envelopes; Solander boxes; Storage boxes. Denbigh Road, Bletchley, Milton Keynes MK1 1DG Tel: 0908 75524

Secol Ltd – Polyester sleeves, sheets, captive flap enclosures. Howlett Way, Fison Industrial Estate, Thetford, Norfolk IP24 3RR Tel: 0842 752341

BP Chemicals – Plastazote foam. Foams Business, 675 Mitcham Road, Croydon, Surrey CR9 3AL Tel. 081 684 3622

27.4 Special Problems: Clothing

Helen Clark

Keeper of Social History, Huntly House Museum, Edinburgh

Clothes are among the most difficult of all museum objects to care for, and, judging by numerous uninspired displays around the country, it would appear that they are extremely difficult to interpret effectively.[1] They are in a constant and inevitable process of deterioration and make huge demands in terms of adequate conditions for storage and display. For the general social history curator clothing is often regarded as a problem area and many feel a need for specialist training in order to look after the collections properly. This chapter will describe some of the problems and possible solutions in the management and interpretation of clothing

Management and Organisation

Who Looks after the Collection?

Clothing usually comes within the remit of decorative art or social history departments; sometimes it becomes a separate department of its own. Over the past twenty years, increasing numbers of decorative art and costume curators have begun to regard their collections of clothing from a social history perspective, although this is not always apparent from their displays. In some museums the collection has even been transferred from the decorative art to the social history department. However, in other museums services, such as in Nottingham, clothing is passed on to the Costume Museum by the social history department. In Glasgow, the People's Palace collects clothing as another category of object, for example, painter's overalls as industrial, a 'Support the Miners' T-shirt as trade union, an ARP uniform as Second World War civilian life, and a punk rocker's clothes as sculpture. In Bristol both the social history and the applied arts departments hold collections of clothing and textiles.

Collecting

Many museums do not have a specific policy for collecting clothing and as a result of passive collecting their stores often contain a hotch potch of unrelated, badly documented items, the bulk of it being women's Sunday best, and clothes kept for sentimental reasons and for special occasions. If museums rely on passive collecting they get what the public think they want and they are far more likely to offer the museum Mother's going away dress than Father's working overalls. The public usually offer more of what they have seen on display unless special appeals are made.

A common criterion for collecting clothing will be 'any items made or worn locally or within a certain geographical area'. If a museum were actually to implement this, thousands of items would have to be collected – more than the general social history curator has the resources to care for adequately. There are national collections which aim to be comprehensive; the small social history museums must therefore be selective. There is certainly a case for regional co-operation in the collection of clothing, with different museums concentrating on different periods and types of clothes, and attempting to fill the gaps which exist in museum collections. For example, many museums are making a special point of collecting clothing relating to the ethnic communities in their area.

The major gaps in collections are working and occupational clothing, items of local manufacture, contemporary clothing and menswear. For example, the Grange Museum, Brent, said recently, 'Despite it being the fiftieth anniversary of Y-fronts there is not one pair in the collection.' A vast array of working clothing has been lost forever, and it is not likely to turn up in Grandmother's old trunk in the attic where her best clothes were put away. At least we can save our successors in the museum this heartache by collecting contemporary working clothing. By active collecting – approaching firms and companies for examples of working and protective clothes – these collections can be built up.

Most museums are keen to build up their collections of late twentieth-century clothing. At Blaise Castle, Bristol, an outfit from a polytechnic fashion student is added to the collections each year. Some museums collect clothing catalogues which do not take up much storage space and portray a far greater range of clothes than a museum could hope to collect. Pat Clegg of Harrogate Museums estimated that 350 items would have to be collected for each year to reflect the changing 'look'.[2] She has suggested that by collecting the clothing of one adult or family it would be possible to resolve the problems encountered with twentieth-century collecting. Different museums could concentrate on a particular source across the social spectrum. Leeds Museums have collected clothing worn by a local girl. A selection of her cast-offs has come to the museum each year since her birth twenty years ago. The advantage of this approach is that the collections can be placed in a social context as a profile of the individual or family is built up.

Documentation

Many museums have poorly documented clothing collections. Often items are offered to the museum without any background information. Without documentation an article of clothing loses its associations and its social context. Ideally it should be accompanied by photographs of the item being worn, bills and receipts, and information on where it was made, where it was bought, how much it cost, where and when it was worn and so on. This could be collected as an oral history interview.

Many museums use the SHIC classification which is based on the ICOM classification and appears to be satisfactory. The MDA publish a costume card. There are some useful guidelines for describing an item of clothing in Collecting Costume by Naomi Tarrant.[3]

The Care and Storage of Clothing

Clothing can be damaged by exposure to light, dust, dirt, grease, water, dryness, insects and handling. It makes great demands in terms of resources for storage and conservation. Preventative conservation is the most cost effective way of caring for textiles. The number of professional conservators in the country is low and the cost of conservation is high. Area Museums Services will give advice and possibly a grant towards conservation. The Scottish Museums Council, with a grant from the Getty Foundation, has undertaken a survey of seven museum textile collections. Advice was given on storage, environmental control and conservation priorities. There is an increasing awareness of the fragility of clothing among social history curators and it is the policy of most not to allow original clothing to be worn.

It is not within the scope of this chapter to outline the requirements for the storage and display of clothing. These have been well covered elsewhere.[4]

Displaying Clothing

There is a general consensus of opinion that clothing should be integrated with general social history displays and related to its social and economic context. Clothes can be used to discover more about the society in which they were worn and obtained. To interpret clothing we should look at the influences of status, wealth, sex, morality, occupation, conformity, tradition, social allegiance and the social pressures to which an individual may be subject.

In many museums, costumed figures are displayed in a setting along with related social history material. At 'The People's Story' in Edinburgh, Gems models have been dressed, given names and biographical details and placed in a set. There is a domestic servant, a hotel receptionist and porter, a bookbinder, cooper, fishwife, dressmaker, a woman and her daughter in a council house, a woman in a washhouse, two women in a tea room next to two men in a pub and three teenagers in a cinema queue. Replica clothing is used to dress characters in an eighteenth-century close, a prison cell and a nineteenth-century slum, and there is a First World War clippie, and a late nineteenth-century joiner. Each set is used to make a range of points in the story of the life and work of Edinburgh's people.

Increasingly, replica clothes are being used in museums. They may be based on originals or reconstructed from visual images. Replica clothing can be used to make points where the original clothing does not exist or it cannot be displayed. Other examples of its use are a bondager's clothing at Kelso Museum, workhouse clothing at Gressenhall, Norfolk, and Levellers' clothing at Weybridge Museum.

It is important that dressed figures should not be used merely as props and set dressing. Care should be taken to interpret clothing along with other items.

Possible Themes for Displays on Clothing

There is a case for temporary displays of clothing on specific themes which can be backed up by other material.

Female Dresses

The most common display is one of female dresses and these could be brought alive by additional documentation. There could be photographs of a dress being worn, and information on where it was made or bought, how it was obtained, and how much it cost and where it was worn. Oral history quotations could be added about how the person felt wearing it – did they feel good, confident, sexy, overdressed, underdressed, uncomfortable? Why did they choose to wear it? Was it to please someone, to conform to social expectations, or to draw attention to themselves? Clothes are very personal so why not build on this aspect? Advertisements showing the cost of the item or a comparative item could also be used.

The Agony of Fashion Approach

'Fashioning the Image', an exhibition at Coventry in 1986, looked at the way the body has been restricted, altered, moulded, padded and slimmed to conform to the ideal fashionable image and at the side effects and possible reasons for this. It put clothing into a context as the outward expression of a social attitude or a response to social pressure. An exhibition at Hull Museums looked at change in fashion and the way it related to women's role in society and changing attitudes to women. Strathkelvin Museum's exhibition – 'From Corsets to Comfort' –

looked at the changes in the restrictiveness of clothing, and 'The Agony of Fashion' by Tyne and Wear Museum Service traced the changing feminine ideal through clothing.

Clothes Worn for Different or Special Occasions

This is a common theme for display and the most popular subjects seem to be sports clothes, such as those worn when bathing, cycling, walking and riding, and ritual clothes for birth, marriage and death.

Wedding dresses survive in great numbers. A display could look at the types of wedding dress worn by women from different social groups. A contrast could be made between an elaborate dress that would never be worn again and a best dress that could be worn on other occasions. A display could be backed up not only by wedding customs but displays putting the whole subject of marriage in a wider social and economic context. A wedding dress from a member of the ethnic community could add another dimension to the display.

Working and Occupational Clothing

There have been comparatively few displays of working clothing. The most frequent have been those showing rural and farmworkers' clothes, especially 'the Countryman's Smock'. Some museums display a figure at work wearing the appropriate clothes, but few have looked at the variation in working clothes and aspects such as protection and status. In 1982 the Science Museum produced an exhibition and booklet on 'Covering Up' which looked at the history and development of protective and specialised clothing. In any display it is vitally important to display working clothes in context, showing the conditions in which they were worn, the protection they offered, where and how they were acquired, and the messages they conveyed to others.

The Clothing Industry

Displays showing clothing produced by local craft and industry frequently appear in museums and attract a great deal of local interest. There have been displays showing the local dressmaking trade in Liverpool and Hull. Armley Mills Museum in Leeds shows the manufacture of cloth and the tailoring trade. Paisley Museum has a permanent gallery on the manufacture of shawls. Around the country there are displays of local lacemakers, boot and shoe manufacture and hat making. In 'The People's Story' in Edinburgh there is a display showing a dressmaker and customer, the emphasis here being on the working conditions of the dressmaker.

Gunnersbury Park Museum undertook a contemporary photographic survey of the manufacture, retailing, cleaning, care and use of clothing in the London boroughs of Hounslow and Ealing. This resulted in an exhibition 'A Stitch in Time 1880s-1980s', and an excellent booklet which is available from the museum.[5]

Some displays have shown the effects of the demands of the fashion industry. Wildlife conservation has been touched on by 'Borrowed Plumage' displays at Platt Hall, Manchester, and the Castle Museum. Displays could also look at the manufacture and supply of cheap materials from abroad. In any display on the manufacture of clothing, working conditions should not be overlooked.

How People Get their Clothes

There are re-constructions of drapers' shops at Beamish, Leicester and the Grange Museum, London. At Beamish the shop is part of a co-operative store and is used to show the importance of the store in the community, the conditions in which co-operative clothes were made and sold, as well as how people bought their clothes.

Displays can also show the movement of clothes from one person to another, for example from a mistress to her servant, and the way that they have been altered or re-made to adapt to changing fashion or function.

Displays looking at the numerous ways people obtain their clothes are rare. Gunnersbury Park looked at a range including bespoke tailoring, off-the-peg clothes, second-hand clothing, and mail order catalogues.

Display Models

If an aim of the display is to show clothing in a social context and to convey the idea that clothes were worn by people, realistic models can look very effective. Possibly the most realistic are those made by Gems of London which are articulated and can be moved into a variety of positions. These are, however, very expensive. Museum Casts make cheaper figures with a more stylised head. Old shop dummies are often used but they can be unsatisfactory as they portray the ideal shape of a period with exaggerated features and attitudes.

If realistic figures are not needed there is a variety of supports to choose from.[6]

Seigal and Stockman supply dressmakers' dummies in a variety of different shapes and sizes.

The Use of Clothing in Education and Outreach

Replica and duplicate clothing is used by many museums as part of their education activities. The most frequent situation appears to be the Victorian/Edwardian classroom with teachers and pupils dressed up in replica clothing.

Replica clothing is worn by demonstrators on site at Beamish and Ironbridge as part of the interpretation programme. In both museums a scheme was established to make the clothes which were based on original items, pattern books and visual images.

Duplicate clothing often forms part of a loans service to schools. It can also be useful in a handling collection as trigger material for the elderly. In Edinburgh a handling box entitled 'Going Out' includes clothes which have been given to the museum for that purpose.

Further Advice

The Group for Costume and Textile Staff in Museums was formed in 1975 to promote and disseminate knowledge and expertise in all the techniques and materials related to the care of costume and textile collection in the British Isles. The Group holds study days and an annual conference, it produces a bi-annual newsletter and a variety of publications, including a guide to the costume and textile publications from museum collections.[7]

The Costume Society of Great Britain publishes an annual journal which contains some papers of interest for the social history curator. There are Costume Societies in Scotland, the North of England and the West Midlands.[8]

Acknowledgements

I wish to thank all those who completed and returned the questionnaire that was sent to 70 museums in order that this chapter would accurately reflect current thought and practice in social history museums. My apologies to those who would have liked one, but I had to limit the numbers sent out.

Notes and References

1. Sarah Levitt, ' "A delicious pageant of wedding fashion down the ages": clothes and museums', *Journal of the Social History Curators Group*, no.15, 1987-8, pp. 6-10.

2. Pat Clegg, *Observations on Costume and Textile Collecting in the Twentieth Century*, Harrogate Museums and Art Gallery, 1986.

3. Naomi Tarrant, *Collecting Costume: The Care and Display of Clothes and Accessories*, Allen & Unwin, 1983, pp. 68-76.

4. See particularly Karen Finch and Greta Putnam, *The Care and Preservation of Textiles,* Batsford, 1985 (revised version of *Caring for Textiles*); J.M. Glover, *Textiles: Their Care and Protection in Museums*, Museums Association, Information Sheet no. 18, 1973; J.M. Glover, 'Conservation and storage: textiles' in J.M. Thompson (ed.), *Manual of Curatorship*, Butterworth, 1984, pp. 333-55; Garry Thomson, *The Museum Environment,* Butterworth, 1978; Tarrant, op cit., pp. 45-68.

5. Gareth Griffiths and Phil Philo, *A Stitch in Time: Clothing in West London, 1880s-1980s*, Gunnersbury Park Museum, 1987, price £3.00 including postage and packing.

6. Some of these are outlined in Janet Arnold, *A Handbook of Costume*, Macmillan, 1973; Anne Buck, *Handbook for Museum Curators – Costume*, Museums Association, 1958; K.J. Harris, *Costume Display Techniques,* American Association for State and Local History, Nashville, Tennessee, 1977; and Naomi Tarrant, op. cit. pp. 138-43.

7. Group for Costume and Textile Staff in Museums, Secretary: Joanna Marschner, State Apartments and Court Dress Collection, Kensington Palace, London W8 4PX. Tel. 071 937 9561.

8. Naomi Tarrant, op. cit., pp. 138-43.

Some Suppliers of Models

Gems Wax Models Ltd
23-5 Kensington Park Road
London, W11 2GU
Tel. 071 229 0196

Museum Casts International
4 Church Street
Cottingham
Market Harborough
Leicestershire LE16 8XG.
Tel. 0536 771127

Seigal and Stockman
2-4 Old Street
London EC13 9AA
Tel. O71 251 6943

27.5   Special Problems: Museums in Historic Buildings

David Fleming

Director, Tyne and Wear Museums

The task of the social history curator with responsibility for a 'historic' building is basically twofold: firstly, to reconcile all collection management needs with the requirement to protect the fabric of the building itself; and, secondly, to 'curate' the building itself every bit as carefully as if it were a prized item in the collections. Some buildings in use as museums are undeniably more important as 'material culture' than anything they may contain, and achieving the balance between using the building and presenting its integrity is challenging. Curators of museums housed in historic buildings must have a good knowledge of the relevant legislation.

'Historic buildings' may have the protection of the law and be listed, or designated as Ancient Monuments. Buildings are listed by the Secretary of State for the Environment. The following is an extract from DOE Circular No. 8/87, Appendix 1, 'Listing of Buildings of Special Architectural or Historic Interest – Principles of Selection':

How the Buildings are Chosen
The principles of selection for the lists were drawn up by the Historic Buildings Council (the functions of the former Historic Buildings Council for England are now carried out by the Historic Buildings and Monuments Commission (HBMC)) and approved by the Secretary of State. They cover four groups :

All buildings built before 1700 which survive in anything like their original condition are listed.

Most buildings of 1700-1840 are listed, though selection is necessary.

Between 1840 and 1914 only buildings of a definite quality and character are listed, and the selection is designed to include the principal works of the principal architects.

Between 1914 and 1939, selected buildings of high quality are listed ...

After 1939 a few outstanding buildings are listed.

In choosing buildings special attention is paid to:

Special value within certain types, either for architectural or planning reasons or as illustrating social and economic history (for instance, industrial buildings, railway stations, schools, hospitals, theatres, town halls, markets, exchanges, almshouses, prisons, lock-ups, mills).

Technological innovation or virtuosity (for instance cast iron, prefabrication, or the early use of concrete).

Association with well known characters or events.

Group value, especially as examples of town planning (for instance, squares, terraces or model villages).

Grading
The buildings are classified in grades to show their relative importance as follows:-

Grade I These are buildings of exceptional interest (only about 2 per cent of listed buildings are so far in this grade).

Grade II* These are particularly important buildings of more than special interest (some 4 per cent of listed buildings).

Grade II These are buildings of special interest, which warrant every effort being made to preserve them.[1]

Objects and structures fixed to a listed building, or within its curtilage even if not fixed to the building, providing they form part of the land and have been there since before 1 July 1948, must be treated as part of the building.

The protection afforded to listed buildings is in theory quite considerable. Causing damage is itself an offence, as are demolition, alteration or extension which affects the building's character (open to interpretation) without 'listed building consent' from the local planning authority or the Secretary of State. Alterations to interiors are controlled just as much as those to exteriors. Planning permission from the local authority may also be necessary. Local planning officers should be consulted over any alterations deemed either by curator or architect to be necessary, because the legislation is far from precise. In a recent case (1986) in the Yorkshire and Humberside region, the complete removal of several seventeenth-century chimney stacks from a Grade 1 listed museum building was sanctioned by legal advisors whose view was that this did not amount to 'demolition', as claimed by the curators involved. The building's character was not affected, according to the legal opinion, because the replacement chimney stacks (made from modern bricks) would 'look the same to the man in the street'.[2]

Listed buildings may also be scheduled as ancient monuments by the Secretary of State. Scheduling is a recognition of national importance, and any alteration to an ancient monument without 'scheduled monument consent' by the Secretary of State is an offence. Because specific consent for work to scheduled monuments is required from the Secretary of State, acting on the recommendation of the Historic Buildings and Monuments Commission, monuments which are also listed are not in fact subject to listed building procedure. Examples of museums housed in Grade I listed buildings which are also scheduled ancient monuments are Oakwell Hall (Kirklees Libraries, Museums and Arts) and the Old Grammar School, Hull (Hull City Museums and Art Galleries).

Of course, historically important buildings are not solely those with a status defined by historic buildings legislation. The social historian is as interested in mundane buildings – terraced houses, the semi-detached, prefabs, tenements, highrise blocks – as in those with outstanding architectural merit. Such mass-produced buildings are certainly more indicative of the ordinary ways of life which characterise social history. Whether or not a building has legal status, the need remains the same: to recognise the conservation of the structure and the fittings and fixtures which are part of its story, with the necessity to operate a functioning museum within it.

Nor is the custody of a historic building by any means the exclusive province of a social history curator. Nevertheless, the curator is a likely denizen of such a museum, and in any case knowledge about historic building types and styles tends to be (and ought to be) the remit of the historians on a museum's staff. Many factors affect the fabric of a museum in a historic building. These can perhaps be dealt with under three main headings : use by people; use to house and display museum collections; and inherent deterioration.

Use by People

This is the factor which brings about most physical trauma for a historic building, beyond its own inexorable decay. There has been an increasing emphasis on health and safety standards in all types of building in recent years, and tragedies such as those at Bradford City football ground, King's Cross and Hillsborough all heighten awareness and inevitably lead to ever tighter regulations. People – visitors and staff – now have every right to expect that all reasonable steps have been taken by the owner of a building to ensure the health and safety of its occupants.

The main legislation which determines health and safety standards in buildings is the Building Act, 1984, under which the current building regulations were made. These came into effect in November 1985, and they apply to repairs if extensive, and to repairs or other building works where there is a material change of use. Thus, building regulations are a governing factor where a historic building is converted to use as a museum, or where significant alteration is to take place in an existing museum.

The following list of requirements under building regulations which may affect historic buildings is adapted from Elder's *Guide to the Building Regulations 1985:*

Fire compartmentation or means of escape enclosure.

Structural strengthening or repair.

Increase fire resistance of doors, floors, etc.

Damp proofing.

Increase floor to ceiling heights.

Make construction non-combustible.

Accommodate new escape routes.

Provide sprinkler system.

Safety guards to mechanisms.

Reduce gaps between balusters.

Increase window area.

Add hand rails.

Make stairways conform to regulations.

Increase doorway heights or widths.

Hang doors to open outwards.

Provide non-combustible finishes.

Add equipment and fittings e.g. alarm bells, fire hoses. [3]

There is, moreover, other legislation which affects buildings, such as the Factories Act, 1961; Offices, Shops and Railways Premises Act, 1963; Town and Country Planning Acts, 1962 and 1971; Fire Precautions Act, 1971; Health and Safety at Work Act, 1974; and others.

Obvious conflicts arise under the legislation with the preservation of a historic building's character, particularly with the introduction of new elements and the removal or obscuring of old ones, aside from difficulties in achieving desirable circulation routes, cost implications for the museum, and the onerous maintenance of fire detection systems.

In practical terms, the curator will liaise over these matters with planners, architects, fire officers, structural engineers and safety officers, possibly also with landscape architects and archaeologists. Knowing the appropriate legislation is not easy, because it is complex and wide-ranging. Problems arise in not knowing which provisions apply to a particular aspect of work, who enforces it, and what the scope is. Parnell says of this:

Unfortunately, architects find the legislation equally confusing and they do not all have the sort of detailed understanding of it that is often needed if its effect on an historic building is to be minimised ... To gain a full grasp of most of the legislation one needs to work with it fairly constantly.[4]

Confronted with this uncertainty – which may well be shared by planners, especially in an authority which has no tradition of protecting historic buildings – the curator must develop expertise. This is one of *the* major responsibilities of a curator who works in a historic building. Thus, the curator can make full use of the fact that there is a great deal of flexibility in the regulations: buildings are very often dealt with on their own merits, and relaxations of ostensibly daunting and destructive regulations can be obtained, especially if they are argued for from a position of (reasonably) expert knowledge.

Use to House Museum Collections

The control of the environment in order satisfactorily to store or display collections is another area where compromise may be necessary. Problems can occur when the environment needed to safeguard collections is not identical to that necessary to maintain plasterwork, panelling, floorboards and other constituent parts of the building. The most critical time is usually when there is any alteration to heating systems, which can destroy an equilibrium arrived at after perhaps hundreds of years. Such alterations must be designed and monitored with infinite care. Needless to say, the appearance of new heating systems (or air conditioning, security, lighting and other electrical systems) needs sympathetic attention to match the minimising of physical disruption. In this, as in other aspects of running a museum in a historic building, a close relationship with the responsible architect is critically important. Display installation itself is a further threat to the building, and precise briefing and policing of designers is essential.

Loading bays and goods and disabled lifts are among the desirable elements in any museum, the need for which conflicts with the preservation of the building's integrity. It may well be that even the orthodox means of access to a historic building are inadequate – there is a quite real restriction on the size of items which can be fitted through the Tudor and Victorian doorways of Hull's Old Grammar School. Such constraints simply have to be lived with.

Security is a further problem. Museums are vulnerable to attack out of opening hours as well as during the day. The range of physical deterrents to attack, however, may be severely limited, in that shutters, bars and steel doors (and their mountings) can ruin both the appearance and the integrity of a building. Once again, compromises have to be found which neither devastate the structure nor give free reign to the burglar. Remember that insurance companies will not be impressed by aesthetic arguments.

Inherent Deterioration

Probably the greatest risk of all to the integrity of a historic building housing a museum is the attention to minor repairs and alterations, undertaken without the benefit of a maintenance strategy which takes account of the building's importance. Older buildings are in need of constant maintenance, and plumbers, telephone engineers, stonemasons, electricians, service engineers, roofers and tilers, glaziers, locksmiths, joiners, painters, decorators, and others, may all appear on the scene to do their bit. Perhaps none of them has any experience of working on a historic structure, or sympathy with the need to conserve as much as possible. All work should, naturally, be under the supervision of an architect who does have experience and sympathy. In turn the architect must work closely with the curator, and both should be as knowledgeable as possible about the building's history. A recognition that most damage to historic buildings is caused by human hands is a good place to begin dialogue, as is an acceptance that the terms 'repair and maintenance' are synonymous with 'conservation'. Good communication is vital. It is worth quoting from Feilden on the ethics of building conservation, which apply just as much to maintenance as to 'restoration':

The following standards of ethics must be rigorously observed in conservation work:

1) The condition of the building before any intervention and all methods and materials used during treatment must be fully documented.

2) Historic evidence must not be destroyed, falsified or removed.

3) Any intervention must be the minimum necessary.

4) Any intervention must be governed by unswerving respect for the aesthetic, historical and physical integrity of cultural property.

Any proposed interventions should (a) be reversible, if technically possible, or (b) at least not prejudice a future intervention whenever this may become necessary; (c) not hinder the possibility of later access to all evidence incorporated in the object: (d) allow the maximum amount of existing material to be retained; (e) be harmonious in colour, tone, texture, form and scale, if additions are necessary, but should be less noticeable than original material, while at the same time being identifiable; (f) not be undertaken by conservator/restorers who are insufficiently trained or experienced, unless they obtain competent advice. [5]

It follows that prevention is better than cure, and routine inspections of the fabric by an experienced architect are essential.

A historic building is likely to contain features other than structural elements which are in need of careful custody – wallpaper and other wall coverings, panelling, decorative plasterwork, floorboards, fireplaces, etc. Here, too, there is a need for close liaison between curator and architect to ensure that the value of such features is not underestimated.

Over and above the many difficulties in running a museum in a historic building are the opportunities to utilise its character and atmosphere – some consolation for having to bear a heavy burden! The building itself can stand as the prize exhibit, in which can be re-created period interiors, themselves the ideal setting for living history. A country house, a windmill, a council house, a miner's cottage, can all accommodate such interpretation. Nevertheless, the needs to match up to safety requirements, and to heat and secure the museum, will all conspire against the purity of authentic reconstruction.

With planning, care and sympathy, turning a historic building into a museum and running it effectively are achievable, but it is a task not to be underestimated. The curator so charged must know that building intimately, and must persuade others that the challenges it throws up can be met, and must not be dodged. It takes a team to cope, and the curator may need to be the central character.

Notes and References

1. Printed in The Local Government Library, *Encyclopedia of Planning : Law and Practice*, vol. 4, Sweet & Maxwell, pp. 40991-1937.

2. See Chapter 31.1, 'Liaison with Others: Planners and Architects'.

3. A.J. Elder, *Guide to the Building Regulations, 1985 : for England and Wales*, Architectural Press, 1986, p.113.

4. Alan C. Parnell, *Building Legislation and Historic Buildings*, Architectural Press for the Historic Buildings and Monuments Commission, 1987, p.60.

5. Bernard M. Feilden, *Conservation of Historic Buildings*, Butterworth, 1982, p. 6.

Bibliography

Ayres, James, *The Shell Book of the Home in Britain : Decoration, Design and Construction of Vernacular Interiors, 1500-1850*, Faber, 1981.

Baker, David, *Living With the Past; The Historic Environment*, David Baker, Bedford, 1983.

Feilden, Bernard M., *Conservation of Historic Buildings*, Butterworth, 1982.

Heap, Desmond, *An Outline of Planning Law*, Sweet & Maxwell, 1987, 9th ed.

The Local Government Library, 'Planning Listed Buildings and Conservation Areas) Act 1990, *Encyclopedia of Planning: Law and Practice*, vol. 2, Sweet & Maxwell, pp. 25001-287.

The Local Government Library, Circular No. 8/87, 'Historic buildings and conservation areas – policy and procedures', *Encyclopedia of Planning : Law and Practice*, vol. 4, Sweet & Maxwell, pp. 40991-1937.

The National Trust, *The National Trust Manual of Housekeeping*, Penguin Books/The National Trust, 1985.

Alan C., Parnell, *Building Legislation and Historic Buildings*, Architectural Press for the Historic Buildings and Monuments Commission, 1987.

Royal Borough of Kensington and Chelsea, *Urban Conservation and Historic Buildings : A Guide to the Legislation*, Architectural Press, 1984.

Suddards, Roger W., *Listed Buildings: The Law and Practice*, Sweet & Maxwell, 1988, 2nd ed.

27.6   Special Problems: Plastics and Rubber

Gordon Watson

Principal Leisure Development Officer, Wakefield Museums, Galleries and Castles

Plastics and rubber are still thought of as new materials even though they were first used to mould household items well over 100 years ago. From the 1900s they have been produced in a growing variety of forms and ever brighter colours. The designs are often exciting and sometimes quite absurd. The social history curator will find, for example, that in the 1930s and 1940s plastic was used to produce such diverse objects as art deco radio cabinets, rabbit-shaped egg cups and napkin rings, lime green pearlware dressing-table sets and even an electric bed warmer shaped to resemble a hot water bottle.

The number of plastic objects in museum collections is growing rapidly as more and more items are being made of plastic or include plastic components. As the history of plastics is gradually better understood, more early examples are being collected and more items are being identified as made of plastic rather than one of the natural products, such as ivory and tortoiseshell, that plastic often aims to imitate.

At the same time curators have come to realise that items made of plastic and modified rubber are not easy objects to look after as they are often unstable combinations of chemicals capable of ageing quickly and unpredictably. What follows aims to help the curator to identify the main types of plastic and rubber objects that may be in a general museum collection. Identification is an essential first step in the dating, cataloguing and care of plastics, but it is also useful to understand something of the different methods of manufacture.[1]

Manufacture of Plastics

The variety of types of plastic is almost matched by the number of methods of manufacture. Many of the books in the Bibliography describe these in detail; here we need only look at the main processes.

The manufacturers talk of three main types of plastic: thermoplastics, thermosetting plastics and elastomers. The first plastic, celluloid, and most modern plastics are thermoplastics, which means that they soften when heated and can be re-softened and re-moulded. In contrast, when thermosetting plastics are heated and moulded they become more rigid and cannot be altered again with further heating. Vulcanized rubber was the first thermoset. Bakelite was used for electrical components as it is a thermosetting plastic with good heat resistance and insulating properties. Elastomers, as the name implies, are synthetic materials which remain rubbery – a plastic sponge is an example.

The main manufacturing processes used today were developed in the 1920s and 1930s, but they had existed in some form much earlier than this. Most celluloid items were made from sheets which were cut off in various thicknesses from a large block. Other objects were made from extruded rods or tubes of plastic which were cut to size and then used to make the finished product. An example is the manufacture of casein buttons or fountain pens. Thermosetting plastics such as Bakelite and urea were produced by compression moulding. In this process the powdered plastic is compressed or squeezed into shape in a heated mould. The most common process used today, with thermoplastics, is injection moulding. Heated plastic is forced through a small hole into a mould where it cools in the correct shape. Objects produced by this method can usually be identified by the small sprue left where the plastic enters the mould. Laminated plastics are produced by a calendering process in which the plastic is forced between heated rollers (in a sort of giant mangle) to impregnate a base fabric or paper and thus produce both flexible and rigid sheet material. Nowadays this will probably be PVC but in the 1930s it was commonly Bakelite, urea or melamine. Other variations on these processes include blow moulding, for example, for bottles, rotational moulding for large tanks and drums, foaming and casting.

Any curator with a collection of plastics will soon realise that they are made not only in a variety of forms and all colours, but also with a wide range of patterning and texture. Early plastics are certainly not all brown. They can have marbled, mottled or speckled patterning, imitate natural materials such as ivory, tortoiseshell, amber, glass and wood, and can be inlaid, coated and polished. To produce these effects manufacturers obviously use colouring, but they also add different fillers such as wood pulp, in combination with the plastic resin or granules. Patterning is produced by combining fillers that have been processed in different ways so that they do not blend or mix together completely in the mould.

A Guide to the Identification of Plastics

The identification of different plastics is certainly not easy. The curator can only hope to know the main plastics and even then there can be many forms of any one plastic. Modern plastics are becoming increasingly complex as new combinations are investigated.

The survey below looks at the principal plastics and describes in most detail the materials used up to the early 1950s. The books listed in the Bibliography take this subject much further and illustrate a wide range of items. Some of them list the large number of trade names that have been used.[2] It is possible to obtain samples of the more modern plastics, and details of experiments that can be carried out to aid identification. As the latter often involve the destruction of part of the object they are not usually suitable for museum specimens. Probably the only sure method of identification is to consult those in the plastics industry or compare items with similar objects in well catalogued collections

Natural Plastics

Amber, tortoiseshell and horn   These plastics have a long history. The process of moulding horn is shown in Diderot's *Encyclopedia* of the mid-eighteenth century.[3] During the nineteenth century demand increased and it was the shortage of these natural raw materials which encouraged investigations into synthetic alternatives. Typical products in social history collections are amber jewellery, tortoiseshell combs and boxes, and horn cups, spoons, buttons and lamp 'glass'.

Shellac   This material is produced from the secretions of a tropical beetle *coccus lacca*. In the 1870s it was used to make union cases to contain photographs. Gramophone records were made of shellac until Bakelite replaced it in the 1930s. Other items moulded in shellac include jewellery, hair brushes, mirror backs and book covers.

Shellac is usually black or dark brown, but it was moulded with fillers which

243

could produce as well a deep reddy-brown colour. Mouldings are brittle and often quite thick but they can have very fine detail.

Rubber   There were three key breakthroughs in the use of rubber to make household goods. In 1820 Thomas Hancock showed that rubber could be turned into a useful latex or dough if it was cut up in a masticating machine, heated and kneaded. An early use of this material was the production of rain-proof cloth by Charles Macintosh. The second advance was the discovery that rubber could be turned into a hard material if it was vulcanized with sulphur. This work was carried out separately in the 1830s-50s by Charles Goodyear in the United States and Thomas Hancock in Britain. The third step forward came in 1928 when Dunlop produced the first foam rubber.

Soft rubber products include, of course, wellington boots, gloves, balloons etc., and are quite easily identified, as is foam rubber. Hard rubber, often called vulcanite or ebonite, is more similar to other plastic materials. One common product in museums is imitation jet jewellery. Others are fountain pens, vesta matchboxes, 'candlestick' telephones and medical items such as enema nozzles.

Ebonite and vulcanite generally look black, but they often have a definite brown tinge or bloom. They can have a smooth finish and sometimes designs are cut into this. They are quite brittle.

Guttapercha   This is a related, but much rarer material. It was made from a gum extracted from palaquium trees and moulded into items such as vases, trays, tubing and golf ball covers.

Semi-synthetic Plastics

Celluloid   The first plastic, discovered by Alexander Parker in 1862, was closely related to celluloid (the name now given to all cellulose nitrate plastics) which, until the 1940s, was a major plastic material. Parkesine and early celluloid items are rare, but examples are held by the Science Museum in London. During the 1890s celluloid became far more common. In this country it acquired the trade name Xylonite. Celluloid was successful even though it is inflammable, although objects made from celluloid are more stable than celluloid film.[4] Most celluloid items were formed from sheets of the plastic, but it was also produced in rods and tubes for things such as knife handles and bicycle pumps.

Celluloid was very successful as a plastic used to imitate more expensive natural materials, particularly ivory and tortoiseshell. In the 1920s it was used a little more imaginatively in mouldings with pearl patterns or plain colours such as green, blue and pink. Probably the first really successful celluloid products were collars and cuffs. Typical celluloid objects are boxes, brush and mirror backs, small trays, combs and dolls.

There are many celluloid items in museum collections. Imitation tortoiseshell is usually given away by the slightly 'better than the real thing' feel of the object. The sheet material often has parallel lines running through it. This is particularly noticeable in 'ivory'. Sometimes celluloid items smell a little of camphor.

Cellulose acetate   This was developed as a safe, non-flammable alternative to celluloid. As a clear sheet material it had a major advantage as it did not yellow with age. By the 1930s it was available as a plastic for moulding objects. One key feature is that it can be injection moulded and it was a popular plastic in Britain in the early 1950s. Objects that are likely to be made of cellulose acetate are spectacle frames, 'parchment' lampshades, toys and pale coloured telephones of the 1950s.

Casein   This is derived from the protein in skimmed milk. Casein production started just before the First World War, but it has never been a major plastic even though it can be very attractive. It was used to make buttons, buckles and fountain pens, often with brightly coloured marble patterning. Casein could be made to imitate tortoiseshell for objects that could not be made from sheet celluloid. Erinoid was the main trade name.

The multi-coloured marble patterns are quite distinctive, sometimes showing that they were made from an amalgam of pieces, or nibs, of different coloured plastic. Casein products are often machined and highly polished.

Synthetic Plastics

Phenol formaldehyde Although Bakelite was developed in the 1900s, objects made from it are unlikely to date from before the First World War. It soon became a very common plastic, in particular for electrical items and objects where heat resistance was important. Bakelite is a trade name, but somehow it has come to be applied to all early plastics. It was often used to imitate wood, but can be found in dark colours such as green and red and, of course, black. Phenol formaldehyde objects were compression moulded and it is worth looking closely at them to discover the main features of this method of production. You will find that the mouldings often have smooth lines and rounded edges and always avoid any overlap or rim as this would prevent the removal of the object from the mould. On the inside of the moulding there may be marks left by the ejector pins within the mould. Bakelite was also used as a laminate, although again mainly in dark colours.

A wide range of items was moulded in phenol formaldehyde. Those most likely to appear in museum collections are radio cabinets and other electrical items, objects relating to smoking, and imitation wood boxes, bowls and trays.

Bakelite has a distinctive, quite unpleasant carbolic smell. Mouldings are usually fairly thick, frequently brown and nearly always dark in colour.

Cast phenolic Cast phenolic products were made from phenolic resin without any fillers. As a result a wider range of colours was available, but the process was expensive and usually confined to quite small objects such as jewellery, 'amber' cigarette holders, napkin rings and writing equipment (Carvacraft, made by Dickinson & Co., designed in the art deco style in the 1940s, is a good example). Often the objects were machined from rods and tubes. Cast phenolic is sought after by collectors.

Urea formaldehyde This plastic appeared in the mid 1920s and immediately made a major impact as it could be moulded in lighter and brighter colours than phenol formaldehyde. In particular, marble patterns have become associated with the early days of urea formaldehyde (strictly speaking thiourea/urea mixes were used at the start). Certainly the shapes, the colours and the trade names of this plastic have helped to make it attractive to collectors. Indeed, who can resist cups, bowls, trays and picnic sets with the trade names Bandalasta, Linga Longa and Beatl?

In the 1930s and 1940s it was moulded in plain colours. Cream and pale green, pink and blue were popular, and it sometimes appeared in dark colours including black. Kitchen equipment such as biscuit boxes, sugar shakers, cruet sets and cream makers were made of urea formaldehyde as it did not taste or smell as bakelite did, but was similarly undamaged by heat as it is a thermosetting plastic. Urea was used to make laminates, but later it was replaced by melamine as this produced a higher quality product.

Light coloured and marbled objects of the 1920s and 1930s are more than likely to be made of urea formaldehyde and will, like Bakelite, be compression

245

mouldings. The earlier products are quite thick and, when looked at closely, have a mottled finish which is more apparent on plain colours. Usually the finish is a little dull. Later mouldings became much thinner.

Modern Plastics

The main plastics used today derive from research started during the 1930s. Most of them were improved rapidly during the Second World War and first used for mass produced items in the late 1940s and early 1950s. The raw materials are nowadays taken from oil although originally they were extracted from coal. I have listed below the principal plastics used for household items with brief comments. More detail about these and other plastics is given in some of the books in the Bibliography, particularly in Sylvia Katz's *Plastics: Designs and Materials*.

Acrylic Polymethyl methacrylate, better known as acrylic plastic or by the trade name Perspex, was first used in clear sheet form and for mouldings in the late 1930s. During the Second World War it was adopted as a strong, light-weight material for such things as aircraft wind shields and gun turrets. It only became available as a coloured plastic after the War. Common acrylic household objects dating from the 1940s and 1950s are boxes, dishes, toastracks and light fittings.

Polystyrene This was a popular plastic used for mouldings in the 1950s and it is still produced in large quantities. It can be made in a wide range of colours, has good electrical insulation properties and, like acrylic, transmits light very well. Unfortunately it is brittle and many of the early mouldings broke too easily in use. Throwaway packaging such as yoghurt pots is frequently made of polystyrene. These products have a characteristic tinny sound to them. Nowadays polystyrene is often combined with other materials to improve its qualities. Possibly the most significant of these is ABS (Acrylonitrile-Butadiene-styrene) which has good impact resistance and is moulded into items such as safety helmets and cases for electrical equipment. Polystyrene foam is used for packaging and for buoyancy aids.

PVC Polyvinyl chloride, a major modern plastic, was first produced in Britain in 1942 and is best known as a flexible product frequently used for sheeting, bottles, leathercloth, flooring and synthetic rubber. Unplasticised or rigid PVC (UPVC) has good weather and chemical resistance and is used for pipes, gutters and windows. From the 1950s gramophone records have been made of vinyl.

Polythene There are two types of polyethylene – low density and high density. The former was first produced by ICI in Britain in 1930. High density polythene was developed in the 1950s and is a much more rigid product.

Polythene is now the most commonly used plastic and there is a long list of products made from it, headed, perhaps, by plastic carrier bags. Tupperwear and other rival food containers are made of low density polythene. High density is used for lightweight furniture and large containers.

Polypropylene Polypropylene, which was developed in Italy in the mid 1950s, has similar properties to high density polythene, but it is a superior product. It has a higher melting point, good impact resistance and it does not scratch as easily. It is flexible and can be used for integral hinges on such things as brief cases and boxes. It is now moulded into a growing number of items including chairs, sterilizable bottles, rope, beer crates and battery boxes.

Nylon Nylon, or more correctly the group of plastics known as polyamides, is usually associated with artificial fibres in textiles and carpets and, of course, stockings. It was discovered by Wallace Carothers in the United States in the

1930s and production began in 1938. It soon came to be used for bristles in tooth brushes and hair brushes, and for fishing line and rope, in addition to hosiery. The first nylon mouldings were made in 1941 and now it is used for zips, gears and bearings. It is a strong, flexible plastic which resists abrasion.

Polyester and glass-reinforced plastic   The social history curator will most frequently come across polyester resin in combination with glass fibre, known as 'fibreglass' or glass-reinforced plastic (GRP). Mouldings were first made during the Second World War in the form of boats and portable shelters. It is still used for such things as well as car bodies and furniture, and smaller items such as trays and signs.

Specialised modern plastics   There are many plastics with specialised applications. Examples are polyurethane which is used widely for foams and sponges, polycarbonate, which is a very strong sheet material, and epoxy resin glues. Most of these appeared in the 1950s and 1960s and are of growing importance.

Care of Plastics

The plastics industry has often suggested that its products are somehow superior to natural materials and indestructable. The former may often be true, but the latter is frequently not. The conservation of plastics is a growing problem that affects the curator in more disciplines than social history. Some plastics, such as celluloid, can degrade very quickly and with little warning. At its worst this may take the form of sweating followed by cracking, warping and self-destruction.

Susan Mossman has suggested basic guidelines for the curator caring for plastics. She points out that 'plastics are susceptible to a number of degradation factors, the most important of which are: light, heat and oxidation'.[5] To this could be added mishandling, as some plastics become increasingly brittle and easily damaged as they age. In general terms most of the usual good housekeeping rules apply. Plastics fade in strong light so light levels need to be kept to below 50 lux. They can produce destructive gases so ventilation can be important and it may be necessary to separate different types of plastic. They need to be inspected regularly and sometimes the acid-free tissue used for wrapping may start to discolour and thus indicate signs of degradation. Humidity in stores should be kept as level as possible as rapid changes can be destructive. Casein products, for example, will shrink or craze if they get too dry. Some plastics are easily marked by finger prints.

In the last ten years, early plastics have changed from throwaway junk to collectors' items. Some mass produced plastics are quite highly priced by dealers, particularly if they are designed in the art deco style. As a result more research is being carried out on the history of plastics and there is now a Plastics Historical Society with around 300 members.[6] This society and others are looking closely at the conservation of plastics. In 1992 the Conservation Unit of the Museums and Galleries Commission and the Plastics Historical Society have published *Conservation of Plastics*, as listed in the Bibliography. The study of plastics is clearly a growth area and more information is likely to appear in the next few years.

Notes and References

1. For information on the history of plastics the best source is M. Kaufman, *The First Century of Plastics,* Plastics and Rubber Institute, 1963.

2. Contemporary catalogues and advertisements usually use trade names. I have found general catalogues issued by the following to be useful: Army and Navy Stores, Gamages, Great Universal Stores, Harrods, Hobday Bros, S.Lessor and Sons, and Littlewoods as well as more specialized catalogues issued by Brown Bros, Andersons' Rubber Co. and the many electrical goods manufacturers such as GEC and Edison Swan. Catalogues produced by the plastics manufacturers are, of course, much rarer.

3. D. Diderot, *A Diderot Pictorial Encyclopedia of Trades and Industry,* 2vols, Dover Publications, New York, 1959.

4. M. Kaufman, *The First Century of Plastics,* pp. 51-3. His discussion of the flammability of celluloid includes a note about an American farmer's celluloid leg which exploded in the heat of the sun around 1913.

5. Susan Mossman, 'Plastics in museums', *Journal of the Social History Curators Group,* vol. 15, 1987-8.

6. The Society's journal, *Plastiquarian,* is published three times a year. It began publication Winter 1988.

Select Bibliography

Braun, Dietrich, *Simple Methods for Identification of Plastics,* G. Hanser, West Germany, 1982.

British Industrial Plastics Ltd, *Plastic Antiques,* BIP Ltd, London, 1977.

British Plastics Federation, *The World of Plastics,* BPF, London, 1986.

Cook, J. Gordon, *Your Guide to Plastics,* Merrow,Watford, 1964.

Couzins, E. G., and Yarsley, V. E., *Plastics,* Penguin Books, 1941.

Couzins, E. G., and Yarsley, V. E., *Plastics in the Service of Man,* Penguin Books, 1956.

Dingley, Cyril S., *The Story of BIP,* BIP Ltd, Birmingham, 1962.

Fielding, T. J., *History of Bakelite Ltd,* Bakelite Ltd, London, 1950.

Hall, Mike, *Design and Plastics,* Hodder & Stoughton, 1988.

ICI *Identification of Plastics by Simple Tests,* ICI Plastics Division, Welwyn Garden City, 1962.

Katz, Sylvia, *Plastics: Designs and Materials,* Studio Vista, 1978.

Katz, Sylvia, *Classic Plastics,*Thames & Hudson, 1984.

Katz, Sylvia, *Early Plastics,* Shire Publications, Aylesbury, 1986.

Kaufman, M., *The First Century of Plastics,* Plastics and Rubber Institute, London, 1963.

Kaufman, M., *The History of PVC,* Maclaren and Sons Ltd, London, 1969.

Merriam, J., *Pioneering in Plastics: The Story of Xylonite,* East Anglian Magazine Ltd, Ipswich, 1976.

Morgan, John, *Conservation of Plastics,* Museums and Galleries Commossion, 1992.

Mossman, Susan, 'Plastics in museums', *Journal of the Social History Curators Group,* vol. 15, 1987-8.

Sparke, Penny (ed.),*The Plastics Age from Modernity to Post Modernity,* Victoria and Albert Museum, 1990.

Watson, Gordon, 'Celluloid to polythene', *Journal of the Social History Curators Group,* vol. 12, 1984.

Useful Addresses

The Plastics and Rubber Institute and Plastics Historical Society
11 Hobart Place, London SW1W OHL
Tel. 071 245 9555

The British Plastics Federation
5 Belgrave Square, London SW1X 8PD
Tel. 071 235 9888

The Rubber and Plastics Research Association of Great Britain
Shawbury, Shrewsbury, Salop SY4 4NR
Tel. 0939 250383

ESPI (Education Service of the Plastics Institute)
University of Loughborough, Leicestershire LE11 3TU
Tel. 0509 232065

The Science Museum
Exhibition Road, South Kensington, London SW7 2DD
Tel. 071 598 3456

27.7   Special Problems: Pharmacy History Material

Kate Arnold-Forster

Museum Curator, Museum of the Royal Pharmaceutical Society

Introduction

The history of pharmacy covers the discovery, development and application of drugs and medicines as a treatment to control or relieve the effects of disease.[1] In the broadest sense, items that illustrate aspects of its history can be found in almost any category of museum. Pharmaceutical material may belong to specialist museums, collections of science and technology, natural history and fine and decorative arts. But by far the largest proportion of pharmacy material held by museums is found among social history collections. Few museum collections of local history are without some items relating to an aspect of retail pharmacy, while several open-air museums incorporating historic reconstructed premises include complete period pharmacies.

The objects such pharmacies include will incorporate material from a wide range of museum disciplines: dispensing apparatus and laboratory equipment, glassware and ceramic storage and packaging; materia medica; measuring and weighing instruments; shop furnishings, fixtures, and fittings; pharmaceutical products; ephemera; pictorial representation; photography, infant and invalid care; medical requisites, etc.

The Use of Pharmacy History Material in the Museum

Reconstructed Pharmacies

Over fifty museums in the UK hold collections that contain complete or representative items from retail or community pharmacies.[2] Probably the most popular type of display based on this type of collection is the reconstructed pharmacy shop. There are some pharmacy displays of this kind that are now several decades old,[3] but they can still create colourful and effective exhibits, and as a piece of social history in the museum provide a valuable representation of a rapidly disappearing feature of the retail community of the High Street. Reconstructions can offer a setting for a composite collection of pharmaceutical material drawn from a wide range of sources,[4] but the majority attempt to reproduce the appearance of a particular shop using the contents of a single pharmacy.

As with all forms of museum reconstruction there are potential difficulties in re-creating an accurate impression of the original. The contents of a pharmacy acquired by a museum are likely to include the accumulated effects of a long-established business, sometimes covering a period of fifty years or more. Authenticity will not necessarily depend on limiting objects to a narrow date bracket as some of the most attractive traditional pharmacies may retain period features even though they sell and dispense products of a century or more later. However, common failings of pharmacy reconstructions are to exhibit items which would not originally have formed part of the typical composition of the 'counter' display; or items inappropriate in terms of date in the context of a particular reconstruction. Establishing information concerning the type and date of pharmaceutical artefacts and pharmaceutical products in a collection can require careful research and identification.

For a curator about to acquire the contents of a pharmacy, it is important to make as detailed a record as possible of the pharmacy *in situ*. Useful records will include a stock inventory, business accounts and records, photographs (contemporary and historical of both the outside and inside of the shop), oral or written accounts from previous owners, employees and customers, preferably including a description of the daily routine of the pharmacy, dispensing practice, specialities of the business (non-pharmaceutical products supplied, popular remedies sold, typical advice given and sought, etc.).

Certain biographical details of pharmacists and information relating to business premises can be sought from the official registers of the Royal Pharmaceutical Society of Great Britain,[5] and from local trade directories. The pharmaceutical trade and professional literature can provide background information to many areas of pharmacy practice,[6] as do pharmaceutical textbooks and reference works.[7]

Thematic Displays

A large proportion of the material found in the museum can be assigned to particular aspects of pharmacy practice, such as the variety of skills involved in different areas of dispensing, including pill rolling, powder folding and suppository making. Exhibits based on themes of this kind can be devised to demonstrate their historical development within the context of the pharmacy. Pharmaceutical material may also lend itself to displays that compare similar objects from other areas of retailing, manufacturing or general use, such as weights and measures, packaging or advertising. Alternatively, pharmaceutical items may find a place in thematic displays on general social history topics such as childhood, infant and invalid care, photography, etc.

Exploring the Social History of Pharmacy Collections

The role of the pharmacy within the community has been transformed in the past fifty years, reflecting developments in pharmaceutical science and technology as well as the structure of public health services. For the museum, pharmacy collections may provide a context through which many of these issues can be explored.

The reconstructed pharmacy can serve as a background for investigating the professional role of the pharmacist in providing expert advice and in the practice of dispensing and retail trade. Through their professional training, they are equipped with a wide range of technical, scientific, medical as well as pharmaceutical knowledge. In terms of dispensing practice, however, the majority of the skills of the traditional pharmacist have largely been replaced by the industry-based production of pharmaceuticals. Nevertheless, many of these original techniques are represented among some of the more common items of pharmacy collections, such as the suppository and pill-making equipment. Although no longer regularly practised, older pharmacists may still be familiar with these skills and detailed instructions can be found in the literature on dispensing practice of the period.[8]

The pharmacy should also be seen as an important focal point in the community, the setting in which the pharmacist acts as an adviser to the public on medicines, minor ailments and a host of practical problems ranging from rodent eradication to home brewing. This is a comparatively neglected area of the social history of pharmacy in the museum. As a basis for oral history and displays on medicine, pharmacy material can provide an introduction to the study of patient experiences and social attitudes to health care. Recollections of medical treatment and advice, memories of nursing and illness, as well as patient perceptions of the pharmacist and allied medical professionals, may all be explored with the aid of illustrations from pharmacy collections.

Identifications

Pharmaceutical Artefacts

Pharmaceutical artefacts cover all items relating to the pharmacy, excluding pharmaceutical products. Pharmacy collections can include items that would be common to general social history collections and also a range of specialised pharmaceutical equipment, apparatus, fixtures and fittings, storage containers and iconography.

There is no single exhaustive publication on pharmaceutical artefacts, but a variety of specialised reference works can be useful. The majority of manufactured items can be identified with the assistance of illustrated trade literature, technical information and catalogues produced for the pharmacist,[9] as well as more general reference works, including published museum catalogues on specialised types of objects to be found among pharmacy collections.[10] Trade marks and patent numbers are another source for identifications and provide additional information on use, dating, the operation and manufacturers of specific items.[11] Of the vast range of trade and professional journals and periodicals available, the most valuable are generally the *Pharmaceutical Journal* and the *Chemist and Druggist*.[12]

Pharmaceutical Products

This term covers all medicinal products sold or supplied through the pharmacy. The full identification and documentation of medicinal products can be important for both security and legal reasons (see p.253). For many products this will require access to technical sources. Information for dating a product, information about its ingredients, indications and legal category may only be available through a specialist pharmaceutical or medical library.

For current medicinal products available in the UK there are a variety of standard reference sources providing different types of classified information.[13] *The Medicines and Poisons Guide*, with cumulative amendments published in the *Pharmaceutical Journal,* provides the main listing of legal categories of pharmaceuticals. Among the technical information sources, *Martindale: The Extra Pharmacopoeia*, which has been published on a regular basis since 1883, provides the most comprehensive and unbiased source of drug information, but a range of publications offers useful information on particular aspects of their actions, use and control.

There is no single source for dating pharmaceutical products and it can be extremely difficult to place accurately a particular product, especially as many of the more successful proprietary medicines may have been in production over a long period.[14] Style of packaging, whether the composition is disclosed on the product packaging, whether it is marked with a Medicines Stamp Duty stamp, and what design of stamp has been used, can all provide some guidance on dating.[15] Although none are specifically intended for dating and identifying products, there is also a selection of publications that can assist.[16]

The Care of Pharmacy Collections

For the curator there are various special considerations that affect the possession of pharmaceutical products. These relate not only to the legal position of certain medicines (see below) but also to the conservation, security, and health and safety aspects of their care. Many pharmaceutical products, from all categories of medicines and related products, are potentially dangerous if consumed in sufficient quantities and so the curator has a responsibility to take due care, particularly in relation to health and safety legislation. Some products (e.g. volatile materials) will also require careful handling. Reasonable precautions must be made to ensure that pharmaceutical products are stored or displayed under secure conditions; a lockable cabinet or store with control of key holder access is the minimum necessary. Accurate documentation of the name, type and quantities of medicines held is also essential. Advice on the disposal of medicines should be sought initially from a registered pharmacist or a Drugs Inspector from the Home Office or from the Law Department of the Royal Pharmaceutical Society of Great Britain (see below).

Like many types of museum object, the packaging and contents of most medicinal products include a variety of materials, each with particular conservation requirements. Most modern medicines and, in effect, older products, are manufactured with a limited shelf or stock life. Thus it is unlikely that a museum will be able to preserve the contents of a product in its original condition. However, to prevent rapid deterioration of packaging and wrappings, pharmaceutical products should be kept under cool, dry and dark conditions (40-50%RH, and not above 18°C) and remain unopened.

Legal Considerations for Pharmacy Collections in the Museum

The main legislation controlling the retail and wholesale dealings with medicinal products relevant to the museum is contained in the Medicines Act, 1968, the Poisons Act, 1972, and the Misuse of Drugs Act, 1971.

For the curator it can be valuable to be aware of the basic legal categories of medicinal products. These include all products sold or supplied for administration to humans or animals for a medicinal purpose, or as an ingredient for use in a preparation in a pharmacy or hospital or by a practitioner or in the course of a retail herbal remedy business.[17] Medicinal products are classified in three categories under the Medicines Act, 1968:

1. *General Sale List Medicines (GSL)* With the exception of products that have been designated foods or cosmetics, these are licensed medicines which may be sold from general retail outlets as well as the pharmacy (e.g. aspirins in quantities of less than 25, extra-energy tablets, etc.).

2. *Pharmacy Medicines (P)* A medicine which can only be supplied through a registered pharmacy premises under the supervision of a qualified person, a pharmacist (e.g. cold remedies, some forms of analgesics, etc.).

3. *Prescription Only Medicines (POM)* Prescription only medicines must be sold or supplied against a practitioner's prescription and have particular labelling requirements. These include drugs controlled under the Misuse of Drugs Act, 1971, for which possession may be subject to certain additional legal restrictions.

The Use of Pharmacy Titles and the Sale of Goods

As defined by the Medicines Act, 1968, the legal position on the use, in a museum, of restricted pharmacy title is as follows: the terms 'Pharmaceutical Chemist', 'Pharmacy', 'Dispensing Chemist' cannot be used in connection with retail sales unless the premises concerned are a registered pharmacy.

The retailing of any goods from premises which use any pharmacy titles is unlawful. Thus a museum which sells postcards, souvenirs, etc. should do so from a remote sales point and not from the counter of a reconstructed pharmacy. Museums should also avoid the sale of any pharmaceutical product (as defined above).

The terms 'Pharmaceutical Chemist' and 'Chemist' are strictly professional designations, whereas the titles 'Pharmacy' and 'Dispensing Chemist' are usually associated with a business name.

Possession of Medicines and Related Proprietary Products

It is not unlawful for a museum to possess General Sale List Medicines (GSL), Pharmacy Medicines (P) and Prescription Only Medicines (POM), apart from those controlled under the Misuse of Drugs Act, 1971 (except under exceptional circumstances, see below). However, there are certain legal restrictions that relate to the acquisition of POMs which should only be supplied by a prescription issued by a registered practitioner. Exemption may be made for medicines supplied for scientific or educational purposes, a category into which museums should fall. Further advice on this matter can be sought from the Law Department of the Royal Pharmaceutical Society.

Possession of Controlled Drugs

The category of drugs controlled by the Misuse of Drugs Act, 1971, is a comparatively small group of substances, predominantly forms of narcotics. To possess drugs of this category it is necessary to be issued with the appropriate Home Office licence, but for the majority of social history collections it is unlikely that they will require or wish to hold such material. One way in which a museum may unwittingly come into possession of quantities of controlled drugs is among the contents of old medicine chests. If a museum is in any doubt about its pharmaceutical holdings, advice is available from the Law Department of the Royal Pharmaceutical Society which can, in relevant cases, provide advice through its locally based inspectorate.[18]

Notes and References

1. For general historical background to the history of pharmacy see Bibliography (Section A) and for a specific introduction to the pharmaceutical historiography of Great Britain see David Cowen, 'The history of pharmacy in Great Britain' in Alex Berman, *Pharmaceutical Historiography*, pp. 47-52, American Institute of the History of Pharmacy, Madison, 1967. For a more recent discussion of the scope of pharmacy history see J.K. Crellin, 'History of pharmacy: what is it?', *Pharmacy in History*, 1987, vol. IV, pp. 212-19, and Kate Arnold-Forster, 'Pharmacy history and the role of the curator' in K. Arnold-Forster (ed.), *The Care of Pharmacy History Collections*, Pharmaceutical Society of Great Britain (PSGB), London, 1987, pp. 3-7.

2. See Leslie G. Matthews, *Regional Guide to Pharmacy's Past*, Merrell Dow Pharmaceuticals, Hounslow, 1985.

3. The first reconstructed pharmacy exterior to be exhibited in a public museum in Great Britain is in

the Castle Museum, York, but the earliest pharmacy interior to be displayed is at Kirkstall Abbey House Museum, Leeds. See Anon., 'The apothecary's shop at Kirkstall Museum', *Chemist and Druggist*, vol. CLXV, 1956, p.580. For a study of the history of pharmacy museums see George Griffenhagen, *Pharmacy Museums*, American Institute of the History of Pharmacy, Madison, 1956, dealing mainly with the development of pharmacy collections in the United States up until the mid 1950s; an up-dated edition of George Griffenhagen and Ernst Steib, *Pharmacy Museums and Historical Collections in the United States and Canada*, American Institute of the History of Pharmacy, Madison, 1988, has recently been produced. For a discussion of theoretical and practical issues involved in museum reconstructions in presenting medical history see James Edmondson, 'The medical period room', *Caduceus: A Museum Quarterly for the Health Sciences*, vol. III, 1987, pp. 27-43, and J.F.H Connor, 'An alternative perspective: the medical period room', *Caduceus: A Museum Quarterly for the Health Sciences*, vol. 1987, pp. 44-8.

4. An example is the pharmacy collection of the Norfolk Museums Service discussed by David Jones, 'The Newstead Pharmacy Collection at the Bridewell Museum, Norwich' in K. Arnold-Forster (ed.), *The Care of Pharmacy History Collections*, PSGB, London, 1987. See also Matthews, note 2.

5. See Bibliography (section E). Although membership registers date from the formation of the Royal Pharmaceutical Society of Great Britain in 1841 (formerly the Pharmaceutical Society of Great Britain), it was only in 1868, as a result of the Pharmacy Act of that year, that legal provision was made for the registration of all practising pharmacists. Since 1936, under the Pharmacy and Poisons Act, 1933, a separate annual register of pharmacy premises has also been published by the Royal Pharmaceutical Society of Great Britain.

6. See Bibliography (section. E).

7. See Bibliography (section E) and also Leslie G. Matthews, *The History of Pharmacy in Britain*, E. & S. Livingstone, 1962, pp. 61-111, for an introduction to the pharmaceutical literature. For a detailed discussion and guide to United States publications (including US editions of works of British origin) see Nydia M. King, *A Selection of Primary Sources for the History of Pharmacy in the United States*, American Institute of the History of Pharmacy, Madison, 1987.

8. See Bibliography (section E).

9. See Bibliography (section C).This section does not list individual manufacturer's publications as these are now summarised in three comprehensive listings of trade literature and catalogues. See Audrey B. Davies and Mark S. Dreyfuss, *The Finest Instruments Ever Made*, Medical History Publishing Associates, Arlington, 1986; Michael Jones and Jean Taylor, *A Handlist of Trade Catalogues and Associated Literature in the Wellcome Museum of the History of Medicine*, Science Museum, 1984; J.T.H. Connor, *The Artifacts and Technology of the Health Sciences: A Bibliographic Guide to Historical Sources*, University Hospital, London, Canada, 1987. A valuable introduction to the use and interpretation of medical trade literature appears in Audrey B. Davies and Mark S. Dreyfuss, op. cit. Pharmaceutical artefacts were often appended to or included within general medical instrument manufacturers or suppliers catalogues. Among the principal British firms to supply the retail pharmacist in the nineteenth and first half of the twentieth century were Allen & Hanburys Ltd, London; Arnold & Sons, London; Down Bros, London; S. Maw & Son (and from *c.* 1870-90 known as S. Maw Son & Thompson, and from *c*.1900 onwards as S. Maw Son & Sons) London; and James Woolley, Sons & Co. Ltd, Manchester.

10. See Bibliography (section B).

11. *The Trade Marks Journal*, published since 1876, is the authoritative guide to registered trade marks. R. Price and F. Swift, *A Catalogue of Nineteenth Century Medical Trademarks 1800-1880*, Science Museum, 1988, lists all registered trade marks relevant to the history of medical artefacts for this period.

12. *Ulrich's International Periodicals Directory*, The Bowker International Serials Database, New York, R.R. Bowker Company Reed Publishing, 2 vols, issued annually, lists world-wide current pharmacy periodicals, including discontinued publications; see Theodora Andrews, 'World list of pharmacy periodicals', *American Journal of Hospital Pharmacy*, vol. 20. no.3, 1963, pp. 3-43, and for revised and enlarged list see Theodora Andrews, and J. Oslet, 'World list of pharmacy periodicals', ibid., vol. 32, no. 1, 1975, pp. 85-122.

Although not a cumulative index, *Current Work in the History of Medicine: An International Bibliography of References*, published quarterly by the Wellcome Institute for the History of Medicine, London, surveys a wide range of the historical and specialist literature available.

13. See Bibliography (section D).

14. The Pharmacy and Medicines Act, 1941, introduced legislation to make compulsory the disclosure of the active ingredients of any medicine recommended for the cure or relief of a disease, whether proprietary or otherwise. Matthews, op. cit., pp. 352-88, see note 7, describes the history of legal control of the supply of medicines.

15. The majority of British proprietary medicines were subject to a stamp tax duty from 1783-1941. Although originally introduced as a source of government income to help meet the interest cost of the American War, these stamps were often misconstrued as a form of official recognition for the product they taxed. Variation in the style and design of these stamps on products can be a valuable guide to dating. For a descriptive catalogue of the Medicine Tax Stamps of Great Britain see George Griffenhagen, *Medicine Tax Stamps Worldwide*, American Topical Association Inc., Wisconsin, in co-operation with American Institute of the History of Pharmacy, 1971. See also Bibliography (section E).

16. *The EBL Guide: Directory of Pharmaceutical and Related Material Available in the UK*, Edwin Burgess Ltd, provides information on all current pharmaceuticals. For earlier products, *The Chemist and Druggist Directory*, Benn (formerly *The Chemist and Druggist Diary*), first published in 1886 and published annually, lists proprietary products by name and manufacturer, and can be a valuable aid to dating. Otherwise, for sources to be consulted see Bibliography (section D).

17. For a more detailed discussion of legal and ethical issues of pharmaceuticals and museums see Gordon Applebe, 'The legal implications of pharmacy material in the museum', in Kate Arnold-Forster (ed.), *The Care of Pharmacy History Collections*, PSGB, London, 1987, pp. 10-14.

18. For a full explanation of these categories see Maureen Pearce, *Medicines and Poisons Guide*, Pharmaceutical Press, 1984.

Bibliography

This Bibliography is designed to provide an introduction to some of the principal sources relevant to the identification and interpretation of pharmacy history in the museum. It is deliberately selective, concentrating almost exclusively on publications in book form, and is not intended to offer an exhaustive survey of specialist or periodical publications.

It has been organised in sections which broadly relate to the subjects covered in the main text and referred to in the notes. The sections deal with general historical reference works; artefacts; museum, exhibition and trade catalogues; pharmacopoeias; pharmacy textbooks and guides to pharmacy practice; drug information sources; registers, etc. The majority of the technical information publications are primarily intended for use by pharmacists and allied professions but may be valuable to the curator in the identification, interpretation and dating of particular pharmaceutical products.

A   General historical reference works

Bell, Jacob, and Redwood, Theophilus, *Historical Sketch of the Progress of Pharmacy*, PSGB, London, 1880.

Berman, Alex, *Pharmaceutical Historiography*, AIHP, Madison, 1967.

Bousel, Patrice, Bonnemain, Henri, and Bove, Frank, *The History of Pharmacy and the Pharmaceutical Industry*, Askelepios Press, Paris, 1983.

Cowen, David, and Helfand, Williams, *Pharmacy: An Illustrated History*, Harry N. Abrams Inc., New York, 1990.

Kremer, E., and Urdang, G., *The History of Pharmacy*, Philadelphia, J.B. Lippincott Co., 1976, 4th ed. revised by G. Sonnendecker.

Mann, Ronald D., *Modern Drug Use: An Enquiry on Historical Principles*, MTP Press Ltd, Lancaster, 1984.

Matthews, Leslie G., *The History of Pharmacy in Britain*, E. & S. Livingstone Ltd, 1962.

Matthews, Leslie G., *Milestones in Pharmacy*, Richardson Merrell Ltd, 1980.

Matthews, Leslie G., *Regional Guide to Pharmacy's Past,* Merrell Dow Pharmaceuticals, Hounslow, 1985.

Poynter, F.N.L., *The Evolution of Pharmacy in Britain,* Pitman Medical Pub. Co., 1965.

Smith, R. B., *The Development of a Medicine,* Macmillan, 1985.

Thompson, C.J.S., *The Mystery and Art of the Apothecary,* Bodley Head, 1929.

Trease, G.E., *Pharmacy in History*, Bailliere, Tindall & Cox, 1964.

Wootton, A.C., *The Chronicles of Pharmacy*, Macmillan, 1910, 2 vols.

B   Artefacts: General reference works

This section includes a selection of general reference works relating to types of artefacts covered in pharmacy history collections. Apart from these, there is also a vast, largely ephemeral, literature of publications intended to aid the collectors of some of the smaller, often more common, ceramic, glassware and advertising items from the pharmacy. Although not represented in this Bibliography, these booklets, society newsletters, magazines, price guides, etc., can be of considerable assistance to the curator.

Bennion, Elisabeth, *Antique Medical Instruments*, Philip Wilson, 1979.

Bennion, Elisabeth, *Antique Dental Instruments*, Philip Wilson, 1986.

Connor, J.T.H., *The Artifacts and Technology of the Health Sciences: A Bibliographic Guide to Historical Sources*, University Hospital, London, Canada, 1987.

Connor, R.D., *The Weights and Measures of England*, HMSO, 1987.

Davis, Aubrey B., *Medicine and Its Technology*, Greenwood Press, Connecticut, 1981.

Drey, Rudolf E.A., *Apothecary Jars: Pharmaceutical Pottery and Porcelain in Europe*, Faber, 1978.

Fildes, Valerie A., *Breasts, Bottles and Babies: A History of Infant Feeding*, Edinburgh University Press, 1986.

Haskell, Arnold, and Lewis, Min, *Infantalia: The Archaeology of the Nursery*, Denis Dobson, 1971.

Jackson, W.A., *The Victorian Chemist and Druggist*, Shire Publications, Aylesbury, 1981.

Matthews, Leslie G., *The Antiques of the Pharmacy*, Bell & Sons, 1971. Re-published by Merrell Dow Pharmaceuticals in 3 vols, 1982-4.

Pinto, Edward H., *Treen and Other Wooden Bygones*, Bell & Sons, 1969.

Turner, Gerard L'E., *Antique Scientific Instruments*, Blandford Press, Poole, 1980.

Turner, Gerard L'E., *Nineteenth Century Scientific Instruments*, Philip Wilson, 1983.

Wilbur, Keith C., *Antique Medical Instruments*, Schifer Publishing, Pennsylvania, 1987.

There are a number of other publications not listed here in the Shire Series that covers subjects relevant to pharmacy collections. For a full list of titles contact Shire Publications Ltd, Aylesbury, Bucks HP17 9AJ.

C   Trade and museum catalogues

This section covers a selection of published catalogues of material from museum and private collections relevant to pharmacy collections, and also reproduction trade catalogues and bibliographical guides to manufacturers' literature.

Arnold-Forster, Kate, and Tallis, Nigel, *The Bruising Apothecary: Prints and Drawings in the Collection of the Royal Pharmaceutical Society*, Pharmaceutical Press, 1989.

W.T. Avery Ltd, *Avery Balances, Standard Weights and Measures Catalogue No. 100* (facsimile of 1897 catalogue), ISASC, Chicago, 1983.

Crellin, John K., *Medical Ceramics in the Wellcome Institute for the History of Medicine*, Wellcome Institute for the History of Medicine, 1969.

Crellin, John K., *Glass and British Pharmacy 1600-1900: A Survey and Guide to the Wellcome Collection of British Glass*, Wellcome Institute for the History of Medicine, 1972.

Crellin, J. K., and Hutton, D.A., 'Pharmaceutical history and its sources in the Wellcome collection No. 5: Comminution & English bell-metal mortars *c*.1300-1850', *Medical History*. vol. XVII, 1973, pp. 266-87.

Davis, Audrey B., and Dreyfuss, Mark, *The Finest Instruments Ever Made*, Medical History Publishing Associates, Arlington, 1986.

Davies, Audrey, and Appel, Toby, *Bloodletting Instruments in the National Museum of the History of Technology*, The Printer's Devil, Arlington, 1983.

Hill, C.R., and Drey, R.E.A., *Oxford University: Museum of the History of Science Catalogue No. 3: Drug Jars*, Oxford University Museum of the History of Science, 1980.

Jones, Michael, and Taylor, J., *A Handlist of Trade Catalogues and Associated Trade Literature in the Wellcome Museum of the History of Medicine*, Science Museum, 1984.

Legge, Margaret, *The Apothecary's Shelf: Drug Jars and Mortars Fifteenth to Eighteenth Century*, National Gallery of Victoria, Melbourne, 1986.

Lipski, Louis, and Archer, Michael, *Dated English Delftware: Tin-glazed Earthenware 1600-1800*, Philip Wilson, 1984.

D   *Pharmacopoeias, formularies and drug information sources*

British Medical Association (BMA) and Royal Pharmaceutical Society of Great Britain, *British National Formulary*, BMA & RPSGB.

Edwin Burgess Ltd, *The EBL Guide: Directory of Pharmaceutical and Related Material Available in the UK*, Edwin Burgess Ltd, London. 1987.

Great Britain Medicines Commission, *The British Pharmacopoeia*, HMSO, from 1883.

Royal College of Physicians of Dublin, *The Dublin Pharmacopoeia*, Royal College of Physicians of Dublin, 1818-41.

Royal College of Physicians of Edinburgh, *The Edinburgh Pharmacopoeia*, Royal College of Physicians of Edinburgh, 1699-1841.

Royal College of Physicians of London, *The London Pharmacopoeia*, Royal College of Physicians of London, 1618-1815.

Royal Pharmaceutical Society of Great Britain, *British Pharmaceutical Codex*, Pharmaceutical Press, from 1907.

Royal Pharmaceutical Society of Great Britain, *Martindale: The Extra Pharmacopoeia*, Pharmaceutical Press, from 1883.

E   *Pharmacy textbooks, guides to dispensing practice, receipt books, etc.*

There is a vast literature in this area and so this is only a representative selection of the general reference works for the pharmacist. They cover many aspects of pharmacy practice, including dispensing, retail trade and the law.

Alpe, E.N., *Hand Book of Medicine Stamp Duty*, Chemist and Druggist, 1888.

Beasley, H. *The Druggist General Receipt Book*, Churchill, from 1852.

British Medical Association, *Secret Remedies:What they Cost and What They Are* and *More Secret Remedies*, BMA, 1909, 1912.

Chemist and Druggist, *The Art of Dispensing*, Chemist and Druggist, 1888.

Chemist and Druggist, *Chemists Windows: The Art of Displaying Pharmaceutical Goods with Chapters on Ticket Writing*, Chemist and Druggist, 1915.

Chemist and Druggist, *The Chemist and Druggist Directory* (formerly *The Chemist and Druggist Diary Yearbook and Buyers Guide*), Benn, 1886.

Cooper, John W., and Gunn, Colin, *Dispensing for Pharmaceutical Students*, Pitman, from 1928.

Dale, J. R., and Applebe, G.E., *Pharmacy Law and Ethics,* Pharmaceutical Press, 4th ed. 1989.

Harman, Robin, *Patient Care in the Community*, Pharmaceutical Press, 1989.

Moss, H.G., *The Retail Pharmacists Handbook*, George Newnes, 2nd ed. 1962.

Pearce, Maureen, *Medicines and Poisons Guide*, Pharmaceutical Press, 1984.

Royal Pharmaceutical Society of Great Britain, *Annual Register of Pharmaceutical Chemists and Premises*, RPSGB.

Royal Pharmaceutical Society of Great Britain, *The Pharmaceutical Handbook formerly The Pharmaceutical Pocket Book*, Pharmaceutical Press, from 1907.

Thompson, C.J.S., *The Chemist's Compendium*, Whittaker, 2nd ed. 1898.

Useful Addresses

Royal Pharmaceutical Society of Great Britain,
1 Lambeth High Street
London SE1 7JN

British Society for the History of Pharmacy
c/o Scottish Department of the Royal Pharmaceutical Society for the History of Pharmacy
36 York Place
Edinburgh EH1 3HU

27.8　Special Problems: Firearms

Nicholas Hall

Curator of Artillery, Royal Armouries, Fort Nelson

The diversity of museums in Britain has been rightly applauded. While only one public museum in Britain – the Royal Armouries at the Tower of London and Fort Nelson – has arms and armour as its main subject, the variety of the holdings of non-national museums is such that collections of great interest exist in cities and towns of Wales, Scotland and England. There can be few local museums which do not have some weapons; even if their number is small there will often be pieces of high quality or technical interest. A problem for students of arms and armour is that no one knows what actually exists in all these museums. The problem for curators of social history, primarily concerned with the way people lived, and covering a wide range of physical evidence is that arms and armour may appear to constitute a highly technical specialism and one which inspires distaste in some people.

While the thinking behind these attitudes can be understood, it should be borne in mind that this is not the only technical subject that social history encompasses and that difficult subjects abound if one is really trying to get to grips with life in the past rather than plundering it for the bits that no one could object to, or that are marketable.

The problems presented by arms and armour for the non-specialist may be placed under the familiar headings of collection management, and in this manner made perhaps less daunting, though still real enough.

Collecting Policy

Under this heading I would consider not simply the question of what acquisitions might be collected by whatever means, but the desirability of holding a collection at all. If the collection does not fit in with the objectives of the museum in any real way, it might be better to transfer it to another museum.

However, a traditional view would be that a local museum could reasonably interest itself, for example, in weapons signed by local makers, even if made elsewhere, and arms and armour generally of a type that would have been used locally. Outright ownership, although administratively easier, may not be essential – where a particular story is being told, loans of suitable material may be available from other museums, although this should never be seen as a cheap alternative.

Identification

There is a vast and growing literature on arms and armour. A few well chosen reference works will assist in the identification of the majority of pieces the curator is likely to come across, or at the very least narrow down the possibilities.

Nevertheless, things are likely to crop up, such as a firearm of a particularly rare kind, or which has been modified in some way, where expert advice is required. Several approaches are possible. There may be local amateurs who have great expertise, but be mindful of the needs of security. It may be worth asking if they belong to a well established group such as the Arms and Armour

Society, the Historical Breech-Loading Small-Arms Association, or the Ordnance Society. Do not automatically assume that an expert on, say, modern firearms (e.g. a gunsmith) will be able to help on much earlier weapons. There may be a museum in the same Area Museum Service with the appropriate expertise.

In the event of difficulty the societies named above or the national museums should be able to help. (They will do so more willingly if they are not asked to identify standard patterns or types of arms and armour that are easily found in reference books.)

Cataloguing

Assuming that the collection is not fully catalogued already, documentation will follow from identification or acquisition. Clearly the system (eg. SHIC or Chenhall[1]) will be compatible with the museum's practice, and this is not the place to discuss the advantages of any particular computerised or manual system. It is important to decide on satisfactory classifications if the collection is of any size, for example, by ignition systems for firearms. It may be more satisfactory in other circumstances for the weapons to be classified together with other kinds of object under function – a cavalry sword with 'armed services', a target bow under recreation or sport, a silver-hilted small sword under decorative arts or even costume, while a coaching blunderbuss might be related to transport. Although a specialist would prefer them considered together as 'weapons', a functional classification may in fact help to suggest how weapons relate to other areas of the museum's collection. Despite their limitations, both SHIC and Chenhall give a lead.

Conservation

I take this to include storage. Iron and steel forming the major part of most armour and weapons, damp is their great enemy. As leather, wood, textiles, bone and ivory, for example, may also be present, storage and display conditions should be suitable for such mixed materials.

Granted that conditions are reasonably good, there is a great deal to be said for doing nothing in the way of conservation to arms and armour unless really expert staff are available, except for the careful cleaning and micro-crystalline waxing of some specimens. Even so, there are pitfalls, for example wire inlay on gunstocks, which can easily be pulled out by over-enthusiastic cleaning.

The first thing to do when handling any firearm for the first time is to ensure that it is not loaded. This should be straightforward if it is a breech-loader – open the breech and find out. If it is loaded and the cartridge extracts or ejects properly you will then have a possibly live round to deal with; live ammunition is not necessarily unstable, but expert advice will be needed. If a cartridge appears to be jammed, do not shut the breech again, in case you inadvertently fire it; instead, seek expert assistance. If you cannot see how to open the breech or if it is seized, use the standard technique for checking muzzle-loaders. Take a dowel longer than the barrel, lay it alongside the barrel with one end where the breech face, ie. the closed end of the tube, ought to be and mark the dowel level with the muzzle. Then gently push the dowel down the barrel. If it enters to the mark, good; if there is an appreciable difference – enough for a cartridge, or powder and shot or bullet – the firearm may be loaded. In this case you will need expert assistance, as you will also with any apparently live ammunition you may come across. Although ammunition is of course explosive, it can form part of a collection, and can be rendered inert for display. Ammunition might be assumed to be inert if it has been around for a long time, but this can be a very dangerous assumption. Take advice if in doubt.

Particularly dangerous are the rounds for the German First World War spigot mortar – the Grenatenwerfer 16. Numbers of these were brought back and can be found in museums. The 'grenade' itself can be highly unstable – if any are found they should not be handled. Call in bomb disposal experts. Firearms should be stored and displayed with the lock in the fired position to avoid strain on their springs. They should not be 'dry fired' although there are occasions when the lock may be cocked and carefully let down to avoid shock as the trigger is pulled. No gun should ever be pointed at anyone.

Security and the Law

Much arms and armour is very valuable and thus potentially tempting to thieves, perhaps working to order, but in this respect is no different from some other kinds of museum object. However, in the case of firearms there is the problem that some held in museums could actually be fired. This does not mean that current firearms legislation is applied to earlier types of firearm. For these – which, broadly defined, include all muzzle-loaders and the earlier breech-loaders, including obsolete cartridge breech-loaders such as pin-fire weapons – normal museum good practice should be sufficient. For firearms and shotguns that do come within the province of the current legislation, specific security requirements are laid down. If in doubt, consult the firearms officer of your local police force. If you become responsible for a collection which you think has not been held on the correct certificates, discuss this with the firearms officer at the earliest opportunity.

Certain weapons are prohibited, so cannot be held on a firearms certificate. If such weapons are not to form part of the collection, and the collection is small and not likely to be added to very often, easily coming entirely under the control of one curator, normal firearm and shotgun certificates as appropriate may be convenient. If prohibited weapons or large numbers of firearms are held or are likely to be held, it is worth considering seriously the advantages of the new Museum Firearms Licence. Issued direct by the Home Office in the form of a letter, this can offer the following advantages:

It covers all staff, not just the holder as with the ordinary kind of licence.

Prohibited weapons may be held.

Acquisitions are less complicated.

Specific security arrangements can be worked out with the local police; they have to be satisfied with the arrangements.

Other conditions may be included, but not that the firearms have to be de-activated. Under the Firearms (Amendment) Act, 1988, there is a provision for de-activated firearms to be held without a certificate. This might appear to be an attractive solution for museums; unfortunately this is not the case. If firearms are worth preserving for museum purposes they are worth preserving intact; de-activation entails such drastic alteration that the firearm would have no value for museum purposes after de-activation. It should be noted that de-activation under the Act is a closely defined procedure – removing the firing pin, or similar arrangements intended to render a firearm unusable do not constitute legal de-activation. The correct procedure is to keep firearms intact, held under an appropriate licence and proper security.

The Criminal Justice Act lays the duty of proving innocence on a person possessing a bladed weapon – for example a sword being moved from one museum to another – in a public place. If staff are to be involved in moving such weapons outside the museum it would be advisable for them to carry a covering letter. When moving firearms a copy of the licence might also avoid lengthy questioning if stopped.

Interpretation

Weapons can form an important part in displays on a wide variety of themes. Military firearms and bayonets show the tools the ordinary soldier lived and died with far more strikingly than any reading. The Victorian volunteers formed an interesting link between the regulars and commercial or professional civilian life from which most of the volunteers were drawn. A volunteer rifle – more beautifully finished than an ordinary issue version – would have been kept at home. After drills and manoeuvres, it was carefully cleaned – in the kitchen watched by all the family, if contemporary *Punch* cartoons are anything to go by.

Firearms always featured at all levels of rural life, with, for example, once elegant shotguns finding their way when obsolete into the hands of agricultural labourers. Wildfowling became a gentleman's sport, but it also remained a means of subsistence for poor families during the winter in some coastal districts. Wildfowling can be linked to nutrition, selling of surplus fowl for cash and local natural history.

Firearms tend to be displayed with little of the paraphernalia surrounding their use. Powder flasks are sometimes shown separately, but if the weapon is put into some context of its original use accessories such as shot belt, powder flask and cap box should be shown with a muzzle-loading sporting gun. Old photographs in the collection or available locally may support such displays. Occasionally old moving film may be available to illustrate weapons in use. For military aspects the Imperial War Museum has a vast film archive. Video material is increasingly available, partly as a result of the popularity of historical re-enactment in its various manifestations. If re-enactment or 'living history' is to be used to help interpret weapons in the museum, very careful thought needs to be given as to the purpose of such an event and whether the people – staff, volunteers or an existing society – are capable of achieving a good and sufficiently accurate result

Specially commissioned video work has a role in helping to interpret arms and armour collections. The Royal Armouries have produced several films, for example on how armour was put on and worn, and more recently, on the techniques of historical fencing and on fortification and artillery, including firing demonstrations.

Depending on type, firearms may relate to one of a broad range of themes in the field of the social historian. As there is undoubtedly a large number of firearms (and other arms and armour) in museum stores, it would be good to see the practice of using weapons in multi-disciplinary displays and temporary exhibitions further developed.

Note

1. See Robert G. Chenhall, *Nomenclature for Museum Cataloguing: A System Classifying Man-Made Objects*, Association for State and Local History, Nashville, 1978. Chenhall presents 'a structured system for the naming of man-made objects' but in addition to being a lexicon 'it can be

expanded by the user in a controlled manner' and is 'adaptable to British usage' according to the author. Chenhall's system for firearms is straightforward and logical, as part of 'Armament' as a whole. He gives a list of types of firearm to provide the name of the object, qualified by ignition system. Ignition systems are also listed. Other information such as country, date and calibre would follow. Chenhall could help the non-specialist curator produce his or her own scheme for cataloguing arms and armour as it is the user's choice of how detailed the classifications should be.

Bibliography

Blackmore, D., *Arms and Armour of the English Civil Wars*, Royal Armouries, 1990.

Blackmore, H.L., *English Pistols (in the Royal Armouries)*, Royal Armouries, 1985.

Blackmore, H.L., *British Military Firearms*, Herbert, Jenkins, 1961.

Blackmore, H.L., *Guns and Rifles of the World*, Batsford, 1981.

Blair, C., *European and American Arms*, 1100-1850, Batsford, 1963.

Blair, C., *Pistols of the World*, Batsford, 1968.

Blair, C., *European Armour*, c.1066-c.1700, Batsford, 1979.

Blair, C. (ed.), *Pollard's History of Firearms*, Country Life, 1983.

Elgood, R. (ed.), *Islamic Arms and Armour,* Arms and Armour Press, 1979.

HMSO, *The Armouries of the Tower of London: 1. The Ordnance,* HMSO, 1976.

HMSO, *Crossbows,* HMSO, 1976.

HMSO, *The Armours of Henry VIII,* HMSO, 1977.

HMSO, *Treasures from the Tower of London* (exhibition catalogue), HMSO, 1982.

HMSO, *Arms and Armour in Britain,* HMSO, 1986.

HMSO, *The Royal Armouries at the Tower of London: Official Guide,* HMSO, 1986.

Norman, A.V.B., *The Rapier and the Small Sword*, Arms and Armour Press, 1981.

Robinson, H.R., *Oriental Armour*, Arms and Armour Press, 1967.

Robson, B., *Swords of the British Army,* Arms and Armour Press, 1975.

27.9   Special Problems: Hazards in the Collection

Karen Hull

Collections Manager, Oxfordshire Museums

This chapter is intended to increase the awareness of curators to potential hazards; it is not intended to give technical detail. In a general sense it aims to identify areas where staff or public may be in danger, from either the physical or the chemical nature of artefacts.

It is important to note that the encouragement of a museum culture of safety awareness comes within the remit of the curator. The appointment of a safety representative is a vital step in maintaining health and safety in museums.

The Safety Representative

The safety representative's job involves regular inspection of every part of the museum to try to identify potential safety risks and health problems (the 'Safety Audit'), investigating any accident and as for as possible removing its cause, providing information and training opportunities for all staff on safety issues, and liaising with official bodies concerned with safety.

Relevant Legal Requirements

Under Section 2 of the Health and Safety at Work Act, 1974, the employer has a general duty to ensure so far as is reasonably practicable the health, safety and welfare at work of all employees. This duty extends to the safe use, handling, storage and transport of articles and substances, as well as to the provision of such information, instruction, training and supervision of employees as to ensure their safety at work. A further duty imposed under Section 3 of the Act is to ensure so far as is reasonably practicable that people who are not employed by the museum but who may be affected by its activities – i.e. members of the public and contractors working on the premises – are also not exposed to risks to their health and safety. The Control of Substances Hazardous to Health Regulations, 1988, made under the Health and Safety at Work Act place a duty on employers to prevent or control exposure of employees to any substances hazardous to health.

Hazards to Staff

All staff come into contact with the museum's collection at some time or another and it is important to create an awareness of the nature of the objects being cared for in all aspects of the museum's daily routine. For example, badly stacked storage areas or apparently harmless toxic minerals can provide unexpected hazards to the unsuspecting volunteer, curator, museum assistant, cleaner or director.

Hazards to the Public

Although the areas open to public access are restricted in most museums, collections on display can still be dangerous. Insecure heavy objects, furniture that looks sound but should not be used, or moving machinery within reach of straying hands all provide potential risk. Working farm museums pose particular problems with live animals to control, and open display areas should be looked at with a cautious eye. Simple explanatory labels can often serve a double purpose in warning the public and also increasing understanding of a museum's work and the inherent dilemmas in combining care and display. Every situation, of course, will demand different solutions and compromises.

Because they are small in size but large in curiosity, children should be given special consideration when you are looking for potential dangers in a public area. They can squeeze round and underneath rails which are quite adequate for protecting their elders. It is worth getting down on hands and knees to look for gaps, sharp corners or loose wires which might otherwise get overlooked. Sharp-edged or lead-painted objects should be especially protected.

A very common cause of accident both for children and adults is falls from heights. In old buildings visited by a public who may be unaware of the safety features built into the design of modern buildings and are therefore perhaps incautious of their own safety, special attention should be paid to the movement of the public on stairways and rooftops.

Obviously a curator cannot overcome every possible eventuality but the unexpected should be considered and there is no excuse for missing the obvious.

Types of Hazards

Hazards within a social history collection can be divided into two different types: there are the dangers which come from the physical nature of the object, and those which are caused by its chemical components.

Dangers from the Physical Nature of Objects

Moving parts   Moving machinery in some collections can present a danger, and it is sometimes the case that guarding is not wanted in the form that would be necessary in a modern factory because people will wish to see how the machine works, or because it might detract from the authentic working environment the museum is trying to create. In this case either transparent guarding or suitable barriers to keep the public safe would be needed.

Weight   Heavy objects need careful moving and lifting techniques both for limiting stress to the object and to the handler. Never drag heavy items and never rely on handles or apparently firm rims or lips. Always check that the area you lift by is sound. Take particular care of glass; it can be deceptively heavy as well as fragile and, in the case of mirrors, sometimes contained in something not designed to take extra stress.

Construction   Objects that look apparently whole often aren't. First they may be constructed in separate parts; lids, drawers, bases to sculptures can all move unexpectedly. Always separate 'pieces' before handling. Objects which have been repaired can also give a false sense of security. Look carefully for signs of conservation which may have weakened the structure.

Size   The dangers of size are much the same as weight; any large unwieldly object may be dangerous to move if the correct techniques of lifting are not applied. If in doubt ask for advice from a professional remover who is trained in the task.

Material   From chandeliers to pharmacy bottles the most difficult material to move safely is glass. It is not only at times very heavy, but also causes more danger in its broken state. Any objects that can shatter must be displayed and stored correctly. Often, due attention is taken in handling the item but little thought given to poor fixing while on display. Vibration from road, rail and air traffic as well as the 'give' in some flooring can bring glass off its shelf or display stand on to the hapless passer-by. The character of the material makes secure fixing, both on display and in the stores, essential.

The nature of previous use The way in which an object was used in its original context can be overlooked once that object has been taken into a museum's care. Sharp weapons, cutting tools, swords, knives and scalpels were all designed to pierce surfaces and skin. Care should therefore be taken both in handling and storing, and in placing on open display. Snares, mantraps and all types of weapons must also be handled with thought.

Dangers from the Chemical Nature of Objects or Treatments

In looking at the possible hazards that could occur from the chemical nature of an object, this section must be read as a general guide. It is meant to alert the reader to areas of possible danger; detailed information and analyses on types of chemicals, and their relationships and reactions one to another, must be sought from experts.

Hazardous materials These can be grouped into three main categories: toxic (e.g. lead objects, lead paint, some mineral samples, such as lead or mercury ores), inflammable (e.g. cellulose nitrate film), and explosive (e.g. ammunition). Each of these categories must be treated with extreme caution and advice taken from experts in each particular field.

Unknown chemicals Many social history collections contain artefacts that have been part of a medical, dental or pharmacy practice. Such material should always be treated with caution as the items may have been contaminated with bacteria or chemicals invisible to the naked eye. Always wear gloves when handling and lean on the advice of a conservator. Other objects may have been used in processes which involve known chemicals. Churns, for instance, may have been used to store seed dressing. Poisoned arrows may still retain the poison they were tipped with. Again, never handle without protecting the skin and wash immediately if skin contact occurs. Some modern plastics are as yet an unknown quantity in terms of how and when they will degrade; research into this question has been undertaken at the Science Museum. Cellulose nitrate plastic used in early snooker balls will deteriorate and become inflammable. If you are uncertain of the identity of a plastic, consult a conservator.

Conserved objects Any object that has undergone conservation treatment might prove hazardous especially in terms of contact with the skin. Conservation records should be consulted when they are available. Objects that have been treated with a fungicide or insecticide can show a crystalline deposit on the surface, but other treatments are not so easily recognised.

It is sensible to take the precaution of wearing gloves and washing hands after contact with all types of collections that may have been treated (e.g. collections of animal skins, or taxidermy), or collections that might in themselves be harmful (e.g. spirit collections).

Because any object in a collection may have been conserved, teaching material must be rigorously checked for previous conservation work. If there is no clear evidence that an object has never been treated it should not be used within a teaching collection.

Finally, storage areas that have been treated for insect or pest control should be well ventilated before reuse.

These guidelines may seem very obvious statements but simple principles are very often overlooked. One piece of advice remains paramount throughout – seek informed advice where any doubt over a safety issue arises.

27.10   Special Problems:
Contemporary Collecting

Rosie Crook

*Museums Officer, Sandwell Borough Council, Wednesbury
Art Gallery and Museum*

On one side plastic, formica, gadgets, nothingness; on the other beauty and culture
mummified in a museum. (Marray, 1979)

The author of this remark is not alone in regarding museums and modern objects
as incompatible: these sentiments are still heard on the lips of many a councillor,
trustee, visitor, director and even social history curator. Believing that resistance
to modern objects from the latter often stems from a belief that contemporary
collecting is a problem, I have attempted to outline firstly, some of the arguments
for the vital importance of such collecting and, secondly, some ideas and case
studies of how to go about it. Finally, I briefly consider some of the collections
management implications.

   This chapter is not intended to be paradigmatic: it is, rather, a survey of
published approaches to the issue and an individual's view of the state of the art.
Above all, as a curator commanding not unlimited resources who has tackled
contemporary collecting as an issue and found it less intimidating than expected,
I intend to encourage my colleagues who have yet to do so, and to acknowledge
our debt to the pioneers whose example has been so inspirational. It is an issue
that none of us can afford to ignore any longer.

In Praise of Formica: the Arguments for Contemporary Collecting

There is nothing new in the practice of museums collecting the material culture
of their own times: this was the original *raison d'être* of both the Victoria and
Albert and Imperial War Museums, albeit for widely different reasons (Green,
1985). What is unusual in recent years and is exemplified by social history
museums such as the People's Palace in Glasgow, is a concern for the ordinary,
the typical, the unremarkable. It is an approach which takes the usual regard of
the social historian for the context and importance of an object and extends it
from the nineteenth and earlier centuries forward into the late-twentieth. The
difference is that whereas we must struggle to recreate that context for most of
the objects in our collections, contemporary collecting allows us to collect the
full range of material – aural, visual and photographic as well as documentary –
which makes sense of that object at the time of its collection.

   The debate that was opened up in 1984 by the first SHCG seminar in York
on twentieth-century collecting focused particularly on why curators should
address the issue at all. Contemporary material is often seen as too
controversial, too complex to collect or just too banal (King, 1985-6). Like
Marray, some of us view the inclusion of the formica-topped reality within our
palaces of beauty and culture as anathema. We are too close to the material to
be able to view it objectively and this awareness of our own subjectivity is
disabling (Bott, 1985-6).

Yet many museums collect and already hold a plethora of objects from 1900-1945 and do not feel prevented from doing so by the recentness of the material. As historians we must be aware of the subjectivity we inevitably bring to our work from our own background, culture and social conditioning, and strive for the maximum objectivity we can achieve. How is it possible to show change through time if we do not collect, and above all, display, contemporary artefacts? By rejecting the contemporary because it is too close or controversial we are assuming that the museums of the future will be less interested in the social life of the twentieth century than we are ourselves in that of the nineteenth and previous centuries. All too often we are dependent upon unrepresentative survivals and painstaking research to represent the past. A recent SHCG conference on childhood in museums lamented the absence of working-class children's toys from museum collections; their very cheapness renders them ephemeral (Glasson, 1988-9). We now have the chance, if that is our aim, of collecting the 1980s versions of those toys with the context that surrounds them. We can collect the objects and the information about how they are regarded, how acquired and how used by the children who own them. Who is to say that such information would not prove as valuable in the 2090s as the few 'tip-cats' and clay marbles we now have to represent late nineteenth-century childhood?

There is, of course, an element of speculation in our assumptions about the role of museums in the future. Noting the rise of film, video and oral recording, Stuart Davies wonders whether these will supplant artefacts as the media by which museums will interpret history and culture (Davies, 1985). He concludes that even if artefacts become less important in the new museums, they will still have a relevance as supportive evidence. Artefacts can illustrate and clarify, but above all they can delight and inspire.

It is the power of the object to evoke such responses which is the strongest argument for the actual accumulation of twentieth-century artefacts; that which is banal or insignificant to us will inevitably be exciting to our grandchildren.

Several commentators on this issue have considered ways of countering the shock of the familiar which is the source of hostility from visitors to contemporary material. Val Bott (1985-6) and Mark Suggitt (1985) both emphasise the need for display, for presentation. The sense of recognition kindled in the visitor can be developed into an understanding of the place of that ordinary object in history and perhaps provide an insight into the social life of our own times. Investing a contemporary object with the significance of an 'historic' artefact starts to put the society that produced it into context and this activity has value now, irrespective of the importance of that object in the future.

A particularly good example of this kind of display is the 1981 kitchen reconstruction at the York Castle Museum, which gains immeasurably by its juxtaposition with period rooms of the nineteenth century, 1940s and 1950s. However, it is also possible to create the same effect on a smaller scale: a display of the official and 'bootleg' souvenirs of Coventry City FC's FA Cup victory in 1987, held at the Herbert Art Gallery and Museum attracted public support for the social history section's contemporary collecting policy. By choosing to highlight an area of modern life in the city that most residents felt was important, it was hoped to present the museum as an institution in touch with the everyday life of Coventry. A photographic record of the marvellous blue and white window decorations put up by shops, offices and private houses throughout the city was made as a context for the objects. Such activities are already within the remit of many museums; some examples will be considered later in this chapter. The key point about both of these displays is their potential for changing public attitudes.

The Curator with the Clipboard: Contemporary Recording

It is important to recognise a distinction between contemporary collecting and recording. The former has been discussed in the previous section and is defined in terms of the acquisition of objects, especially those dating from 1960, although it is noted that objects dating from 1900-1960 can also be under-represented in collections. Contemporary recording, of which Sweden's SAMDOK project is the earliest and best known (Rosander, 1980), is most akin to social anthropology in its approach and is often the cause of the greatest degree of curatorial alarm. It is the process of acquiring information about society today by means of statistical sampling, video or film-making, photographic recording or oral recording. It can range in scope from a small photographic survey of trends in shop window display, for example, to a full-scale survey following the model laid down by the Mass Observation Archive, recording domestic interiors and attitudes to household artefacts. (This project, entitled 'Household Choices' has been undertaken jointly by the Victoria and Albert and Middlesex Polytechnic; see Putnam, 1988.)

The value of such projects as sources of information about the context in which objects are used is immeasurable and the techniques used are only the logical extension of those curators are already using. We have worked for a long time with historic photographs, documents and oral history as research tools and we are beginning to add video to these. In borrowing a structure for our research from the social anthropologist or sociologist we are simply restating the eclectic nature of our discipline.

Scale, of course, is all. But limited resources should not prevent very useful work being done provided that the project is properly structured – an issue which I shall consider in detail.

Contemporary Collecting in Practice

Objectives and Collecting Policies

Given the plethora of contemporary objects which could be collected, most commentators are agreed upon the absolute necessity of a collecting policy. Such a policy should be drawn up as a result of a series of actions:

Definition of clear aims and objectives for the museum;

Thorough survey of existing collections;

Consideration of methods of acquisition.

Collecting areas may be defined by locality, by subject or theme, or by the museum's perceived function within the community. York Castle Museum's re-assertion of itself as a museum of regional social history was a key factor in determining what not to collect and thence to a collecting policy (Nicholson, 1985). At Gunnersbury Park Museum, a detailed collections survey revealed the quality of contextual and provenance information about each object and led to the adoption of project-based contemporary recording and artefact collection as a way of building up these collections (Griffiths, 1986-7). Looking at collections in this way identifies areas where no further expansion is wanted, but also where active collecting methods are needed.

Methods of Acquisition: Objects

Updating existing collections Perhaps the simplest method of starting to collect contemporary material is to collect direct parallels or modern versions of items already well represented in the museum, for example, 1980s and 1990s greetings cards (York Castle Museum – see Suggitt, 1988; Brewhouse Yard Museum – see Postles, 1985) to supplement nineteenth-century examples. This principle can be carried throughout the collections in those areas identified as priorities and enables museums with few resources to build up their holdings. Defined limits, or sampling, will limit growth of collections to manageable size. Some museums, anxious to avoid the isolation of multi-cultural collections from the rest of the museum, have adopted this approach to the material. In all but a very few cases, artefacts with a multi-cultural background collected in context today (as opposed to ethnographic items collected by white travellers) will mostly be new. Hence multi-cultural and contemporary collecting are often synonymous.

Projects Some museums approach active collecting by means of a short, directed project. This has several advantages:

It enables a representative selection of material to be accumulated over a fixed period, avoiding the inevitable duplication otherwise involved in collecting the products of a mass-industrialised culture;

It enables resources to be channelled effectively;

It provides an objective for collecting, other than that of straightforward preservation, by linking collecting with research, publication and exhibition.

A notable example of this approach is that employed by Harborough Museum which uses projects as a way of building the museum's collections and its support within its community (Mullins, 1986-7). An annual theme, determined by the museum's resources and objectives, is made the focus of object collection, oral history recording, photographic research and surveying and information collection. The results form a publication and an exhibition.

Other museums opt for shorter-term projects such as collecting domestic food packaging and free ephemera (Nottingham – Mastoris, 1986-7; Mastoris and Mastoris, 1985-6); responding to a national and local event like the 1984-5 miners' strike (Salford and Glasgow, amongst others – see Preece, 1985; King, 1985-6); recording in detail an aspect of popular culture such as teenage fashions (Glasgow again – see King, 1985-6).

Small-scale projects, especially if they make use of volunteers, local interest groups or school pupils, can be an ideal way of both collecting contemporary material and strengthening the museum's links with its community. This is particularly so for small museums, under-resourced ones, and those quixotic curators who desperately wish to manage their collection properly and be involved in outreach work.

Methods of Acquisition: Information

This area covers both the contemporary recording described earlier and some examples of recent or current initiatives.

Social studies For want of a better phrase, this term describes the research undertaken by museums into all aspects of life in the late twentieth century. Perhaps because so many museums already contain such extensive domestic collections for earlier periods with great gaps for later material, this is an area that many museums have chosen to concentrate upon.

Gunnersbury Park's 'In the Kitchen' survey, Middlesex Polytechnic's 'Household Choices', and Bristol Museum's 'Recording Contemporary Culture' are all projects which use a mixture of questionnaires, photography, interviewing and object collection to find out about domestic interiors and household purchases (Griffiths, 1986-7; Putnam, 1988; Dawson, 1985).

Other museums apply the same research methods to community or political life: Guildford Museum recorded changes in retailing in the town by compiling a card index of shop premises, using trade directories and maps for the earlier period and personal observation for the later (Alexander, 1985); Birmingham's 'Change in the Inner City' project traced the history of childhood, food and drink, and public baths (Mullins, 1986-7). A few museums tackle controversial yet crucial issues. The People's Palace records political and religious activity on both sides of Glasgow's Protestant/Catholic divide, collecting ephemera and banners, and photographing demonstrations. This is an essential future record – even if the material is too sensitive for display now. Coventry Museum collects the personal items relating to female hygiene and contraception, the lack of which for earlier dates is so frequently deplored by historians of the family (Mattingly, 1985). Of equal importance are the essential collections of multi-cultural material being built up by many museums – most notably Haringey, Leicestershire and Brent.

Documentary information   Contemporary ephemera has already been mentioned for its importance as a background to object collection. Of equal importance can be some or all of the following collected within defined limits. They provide information about changes in society as well as recording change within themselves (Suggitt, 1988):

Catalogues: both mail order (household goods, clothing, etc.) and free handouts from local stores and industries;

Magazines: especially those which include advice and features on DIY and interiors, but also special supplements from local newspapers;

Promotional Material: estate agents' house particulars which show interiors can be most revealing; also advertising material, political posters and leaflets, cinema or theatre leaflets.

Collections Management Implications

Conservation

A well known problem of collecting contemporary material is that we are dealing with materials the behaviour of which over time is not yet known. One museum, York Castle, has felt it inappropriate to collect some types of plastics because they are, at the moment, not conservable (Nicholson, 1985). Brewhouse Yard Museum's contemporary food packaging was cleaned very thoroughly by vacuuming and washing in non-ionic detergent solution – before being stored in low-acid containers (Mastoris, 1986-7).

It may be some time until conservators have the knowledge they require about these objects. Until then, all curators can do is to apply the same principles of care in terms of environmental control, storage and handling as we already use for objects whose needs we know more about. The newness and apparent robustness of an object should be no reason for treating it less carefully than its older counterparts.

Storage and Documentation

It is all too easy to become overwhelmed by the sheer volume of material when collecting representative samples. It is therefore crucial that the museum's resources in terms of storage and documentation are considered *before* collecting priorities are established and that, if necessary, other institutions, such as archives or libraries which might be more appropriate repositories are involved.

Since provenance is so important, it is essential to concentrate on provenanced material. This can be time consuming to document fully: once again the need for *focused* collecting is stressed. Collecting can be defined by time or locality – for example, six months' worth of manufacturer's samples from one doctor's surgery (Brewhouse Yard – see Postles, 1985) Groups of volunteers or students can be trained to undertake the follow-up documentation and thus benefit from involvement in a project from start to finish.

Oliver Green wrote despairingly in 1985 that

unless there are some dramatic changes soon in outlook and practice, our museums will enter the twenty-first century quite unable to present a full retrospective picture of British life in the late twentieth century. (Green, 1985)

It is up to the current generation of curators to prove him wrong.

References

Alexander, Mary (1985), 'Guildford Museum – the shop index', *Museums Journal,* vol. 85, no. 1, June.

Bott, Val (1985-6), 'Collecting the twentieth century', *Journal of the Social History Curators Group,* no. 13, p. 12.

Davies, Stuart (1985), 'Collecting and recalling the twentieth century', *Museums Journal,* vol. 85, no. 1, June, p. 28.

Dawson, David (1985), 'Archaeology, "Recording Contemporary Culture" and the meaning of goods', *Museums Journal*, vol. 85, no. 1, June, p. 17.

Glasson, Michael (1988-9), 'The City Children Project at Birmingham Museum and Art Gallery', *Journal of the Social History Curators Group*, no. 16, p. 18.

Green, Oliver (1985), 'Our recent past: the Black Hole in museum collections', *Museums Journal,* vol. 85, no. 1, June, p 5.

Griffiths, Gareth (1986-7), 'In the Kitchen: a contemporary documentary project', *Journal of the Social History Curators Group*, no.14, p. 15.

King, Elspeth (1985-6), 'The cream of the dross: collecting Glasgow's present for the future', *Journal of the Social History Curators Group,* no.13, p.4.

Marray, Bernard (1985), *Les Grands Magasins des origines à 1939,* Paris, 1979, quoted in Lowenthal, David, *The Past is a Foreign Country,* Cambridge University Press, 1985, p. 356.

Mastoris, Steph (1986-7), 'Pre-empting the dustbin: collecting contemporary domestic packaging', *Journal of the Social History Curators Group,* no. 14, pp. 23-6.

Mastoris, S., and Mastoris, L. (1985-6), 'Collecting contemporary advertising ephemera from a Nottingham suburb', *Journal of the Social History Curators Group,* no. 13, pp. 15-28.

Mattingly, Jenny (1985), 'Coventry Museum – twentieth-century collecting and history', *Museums Journal*, vol. 25, no.1, June, p.18.

Mullins, Sam (1986-7), 'Review of City Children and A Taste of Change', *Journal of the Social History Curators Group*, no. 14, p. 34.

Mullins, Sam (1986-7), 'Beyond a collecting policy: projects as policy at the Harborough Museum', *Journal of the Social History Curators Group*, no. 14 pp. 20-23.

Nicholson, Graham (1985), 'York 1 – collecting for York Castle Museum', *Museums Journal,* vol. 85, no. 1, June, p. 26.

Postles, Suella (1985), 'Nottingham – contemporary collecting at Brewhouse Yard', *Museums*

Journal, vol. 85, no. 1, June, p. 26.

Preece, Geoff (1985), 'Salford 2 – the Museum of Mining', *Museums Journal*, vol. 85, June, pp. 23-4

Putnam, Tim (1988), *Household Choices,* information leaflet, Middlesex Polytechnic.

Rosander, G. (1980), *Today for Tomorrow – Museum Documentation of Contemporary Society in Sweden by Acquisition of Objects,* SAMDOK Council, Stockholm.

Suggitt, Mark (1985), 'Heals to Habitat: museums and modern interiors', *Museums Journal*, vol. 85, no.1, June, p.13.

Suggitt, Mark (1988), 'Primary evidence? What future for objects', notes for the seminar 'The Twentieth Century Folk Museum', at the Ironbridge Institute, Wednesday 20 April 1988.

27.11 Special Problems: Numismatics

Stuart Davies

Principal Officer, Museums and Galleries, Kirklees Metropolitan Council

Introduction[1]

Throughout history the exchange of goods has invariably had a prominent role and therefore so too has currency. Money reveals much about social and economic history and it endures longer than most artefacts. The desire of it is the root of all evil and the care of it is the unhappy lot of many a museum curator.

The status of numismatics in museums has fallen in recent years, though the number of staff curating coin collections may have risen.[2] Generally speaking this has caused little interest or reaction among social historians. Before the rise of social and local history as museum disciplines to be reckoned with, coins and medals were usually cared for by archaeologists. Even now most social historians remain ignorant of the importance of modern numismatic items for their own interests.

Numismatics has traditionally been displayed in coin galleries as a separate discipline with the emphasis on medieval and earlier coinage. This has been unfortunate in two respects; firstly, the greater part of general numismatic collections is usually post-medieval; and secondly, when this later material is displayed in a coin gallery it is divorced from its historical context.

Both of these problems can be avoided even within the traditional framework of a coin gallery. Post-medieval items, especially medals, can make attractive and interesting displays. This may be because of a local association or simply because they are of many styles, sizes and metals. The appeal of all coin displays can be considerably increased by interpreting them in the context of wider social, economic and political history. Nor does it do any harm to introduce some explanation of the technology behind coin production.

A more radical and satisfactory solution may well be to include coins and medals among other displays and not have a separate 'coin gallery' at all. This approach should particularly appeal to historians who ought to view a museum's collection *in toto* as a resource to be used to illustrate the history of their selected subject. Coins and medals can, in this context, become flexible and interesting pieces of historical evidence rather than inhibitive and boring objects. A number of possible themes into which they can be incorporated will be suggested in this chapter. Trade, industry, politics, architecture and art may all be viewed through numismatics, particularly if they are related to local history. Coins and medals can especially take their place among other artefacts illustrating local people and events.

However, not all aspects of numismatics can be easily included in local or social history galleries. Indeed, it must be said that the now increasing popular 'local history gallery' is in some ways as restrictive as a traditional coin gallery. There still seems to be a long way to go in achieving the balance between the gallery that is an antiquarian's delight and one which has little or no local relevance at all. But it will be in galleries which present local history as a microcosm of national history that modern numismatics will best flourish.

It is obviously necessary to appreciate some of the fundamental principles of numismatics, not least because numismatic identifications make up such a large proportion of enquiries in most urban museums.[3] The rest of this chapter will therefore be given over to identifying the main numismatic types and their relevance to the social historian. Although often simply referred to as 'coins and medals' (and not infrequently simply identified as one or the other) there are in fact far more types than these two. The most common are coins, tokens, checks/tickets and medals.

Coins

Coins are essentially legal tender produced by a state. They normally have the head of the monarch (or an equivalent in the case of republics) on one side (the obverse). They also usually have a date and denomination. Two developments in the history of coinage are of particular interest to social historians. The first is that of technological change in the production of coins and the second is of economic change and its effect on the metal content of coins.

These developments should be of greater interest to social historians than some of the finer numismatic points or the art historical approach which lays great emphasis on the 'style 'of coinage. There is relatively little scope for the 'local relevance' approach but this should not preclude interpretation in an interesting and informative way.[4]

How one tackles the display of coinage in a museum obviously depends to a certain extent on the collections. But there are a number of approaches which most history curators could attempt. Coins may simply be used to illustrate the succession of monarchs, the changes in denominations current at different periods or the changes within the same denomination, as for example, the development of the penny.

But coins might also be used to introduce wider issues. It is important to remember that coins (albeit of differing denominations) are one of the few artefacts that are universal to all classes of people and to all places throughout the country. If linked to such topics as prices and wages they can become the starting point for perceptive and quite sophisticated comment on English social history in the eighteenth and nineteenth centuries.

The study of coinage can also include examining the materials from which coins are made and where they come from. It also covers the forms which coins take, including weight, design and technique of manufacture. Beyond the coins themselves, the organisation and control of their production and circulation may be considered. Their actual use in the community is also part of the general science of numismatics.[5]

The most appropriate way of dealing with non-British coinage may well be to link it to Britain wherever possible or to use it to demonstrate general numismatic themes. At Birmingham the Birmingham Mint collection of post-1850 world coinage is displayed by continent. As well as explaining the history of the mint, within these geographical areas a number of topics are covered, such as the relationship between private mints and the Royal Mint mintmarks, the decline of silver in coins and the break-up of the British Empire.

Although coins 'should be seen, not only read about',[6] they are not always self-explanatory and can rarely be adequately interpreted without recourse to supporting documentary evidence. This might include mint records, business archives or miscellaneous printed primary sources ranging from government reports to newspapers.

Tokens

Trade tokens exist for the periods 1649-1672, 1787-1797 and 1811-1815. They came into existence on each occasion because of the inability or unwillingness of the government to produce adequate quantities of small change. And on each occasion legislation was required to end their rivalry to the official regal coinage. Tokens were essentially local in character and use, and the enormous number of tokens issued and their nationwide incidence make them an obvious choice for inclusion in local history displays.[7] If a good collection exists they can also illustrate various themes of the industrial revolution: the textile industries, transport, mines and copper companies, iron and lead works, and a miscellany of other trades such as 'success to the Cider Trade' on a Hereford token. The Parys Mines Company, with its druid's head obverse, produced the greatest range of varieties, but there were other very common ones such as John Wilkinson, the Black Country ironmaster.

But in addition to these there were retailers' tokens, architectural tokens (such as the collectors' series produced by Peter Kempson) and those depicting politics and war. All in all tokens provide the local, social and economic historian with a great opportunity to interpret history through the very medium of trade during the industrial revolution.[8]

Checks/Tickets

The nineteenth century saw the appearance of a number of odd pieces which were neither coins nor tokens. They include Victorian card counters inscribed 'To Hanover' and those which imitate George III 'Spade' guineas. But the most significant group are the 'checks' or 'tickets'.

During the nineteenth and early-twentieth centuries an enormous number of metal checks and tickets were produced, most of them in Birmingham. They were made for a large range of purposes: gambling checks in public houses or concert halls, entrance tickets, and market checks were among the more common. But all of them acted as advertisement pieces for the establishments by which they were issued or in which they were used. Although there are many types, the most common is probably the public house check.[9] Each check named the issuing establishment and/or its proprietor, and most showed a monetary value. Their generic term is 'checks' rather than 'tokens' because they could be spent only at the premises of issue. There they were redeemed for beer, either at the bar or counter or, as some particular checks indicate, at the attached concert hall to which those served as admission passes. How they were issued to customers is conjectural: perhaps variously as games prizes, bonuses to regular patrons or in change. They also publicized the premises or the proprietor's arrival there.

Public house, market and tradesmen's checks have been described as among the 'byways' of numismatics. They are certainly not particularly exciting in themselves but they are useful to the social historian. Many relate to buildings, places, businesses or even people still in existence. They may therefore provide the stimulus to local enquiry or the means of introduction to facilitate a wider study. Pub checks have their place in the relationship between the public house and the community, albeit a small part of a major topic.[10] Market and retailers' checks are the pseudo-currency of a closed economic world which has largely disappeared.

Medals

The potential use of medals in local and social history displays seems to have been largely overlooked. Many medals commemorate historical events in themselves or mark important occasions which have taken on historical significance. Others relate to institutions, public or private, which have played an important role in the development of the local community. They may also depict local personalities of note or may themselves be the product of a local medallist. Indeed, of all the numismatic types medals are the most difficult to generalise about because they are so diverse. It must simply be enough to say that they ought to be consulted by every local or social historian as source material for exhibitions. Medals are also items which are still struck to commemorate local events and so should form part of a museum's modern material collecting policy.

Medals are distinct from the previous three categories in that they are not currency in any way at all. Nevertheless, the general type 'medal' does contain a number of subdivisions, including the following.

Commemorative

Some see the medal as essentially a 'monument', largely intended to inspire politically or artistically.[11] Little has been done, however, to investigate the motives behind the issue of the thousands of local commemorative medals during the nineteenth century alone. Commercial and simple commemoration motives may well be equally important.

Whatever their origin, commemoratives are the most common variety of medal and of particular relevance to historians, depicting local events, buildings and people, as well as national occasions. From a purely practical point of view they are usually large enough to be easily displayed and readily appreciated by visitors.

Award

These include prize medals (e.g. agricultural shows and exhibitions) and proficiency awards of various sorts (e.g. long service and good attendance at school). They are to be found wherever such events or institutions existed.

Advertisement

There are two basic sorts of advertisement medal. The first includes those struck specifically to publicize the subject or the maker of the medal. The second includes those which were produced as samples of a manufacturer's work but also advertised it as well. These medals are particularly useful to social historians working in those cities which hosted medallists.

'Useful'

Particularly popular in the eighteenth and early nineteenth centuries, some of these medals depicted geographical or scientific information. But the most common was the pocket calendar medal. On one side the dates of each Sunday were shown, together with the dates of more important religious festivals and, on the other side, the dates of new and full moons, details of royal birthdays, or the law terms.

Military

Military medals are rarely given much attention by social historians because it is assumed that their usefulness outside regimental displays is limited. However, service medals awarded to individuals may provide a springboard to investigating their biographical details and from there a broader understanding of the role of the military within a local community. Even if this neglected area of study is not explored, all social historians should acquire a basic knowledge of the more common service medals, if only to deal with public enquiries.[12]

Numismatics and the Curator

The actual curation of coins and medals is in many respects no different from many other museum collections. However, particular care must be exercised with regard to security and documentation. Coins are most at risk when being examined by visitors when they are in store. Good 'housekeeping' is essential. No more coins than is absolutely necessary should be taken from the trays at any one time, and their movement carefully controlled. Anyone wishing to consult the collection ought to have their credentials checked beforehand and must be thoroughly supervised.

For the purposes of documentation it is important to keep white paper discs with information about each coin (including the accession number) with the coin in its place in the tray. It is vital to make sure that these discs are not separated from the coins because accession numbers are not inked on to coins and it is often difficult to distinguish between many items at a glance.

When considering the needs of an opinion service for coins and medals curators need a fairly broad but not necessarily especially deep knowledge of numismatics. They must be able to distinguish between types (i.e. between a coin and a medal), but once that is achieved the relevant reference books may be consulted with reasonable hope of arriving at an identification.

The degree of identification will depend on the needs of the enquirer and it is therefore useful to establish those from the outset. Large numbers of coins or difficult identifications may need to be tackled at length so a proper system of receipts is required to give the curator the option of safely 'taking-in' an opinion. For dealing with the more common enquiry it is useful to have a set of simple information sheets, including a list of local dealers. Most enquirers are interested in the value of their coins but curators should not give valuations. It is useful, however, to have some idea of how valuations are arrived at so that you do not unwittingly deceive someone by your own apparent disinterest in the value of a coin. The value will depend on the metal it is struck in, the condition it is in and its rarity. By explaining this to enquirers you can often lead them to realising the potential worth of their possession themselves. Curators can also refer them to Seaby's *Coins of England* [13] but it must be stressed that this can only act as a very rough guide to market values of those coins in better condition than most.

Many hard-pressed social history curators may well feel that they have not the time to spend getting acquainted with what is to them an alien discipline. This would only be to condone and entrench the narrowest of attitudes to historical studies in museums. A refusal to try to understand the basic elements of a wide range of subjects presented in museums hinders historians from fulfiling their true role in the profession. The skill of historians must lie in familiarising themselves with museum collections of all sorts and then interpreting them in the knowledge of the historical development of a certain community or of a particular theme.

Notes and References

1. I am grateful to the late Anthony Gunstone, both for commenting on a draft of this chapter and for his guidance and support during my time as curator of Birmingham's modern numismatics collection. This contribution is a revised version of a paper entitled 'Numismatics and the historian in museums', published in the *Journal of the Social History Curators Group*, vol. 11, 1983, which gives a fuller and illustrated account of this subject.

2. Stuart Davies and D. Symons, 'Birmingham's coin gallery', *Museums Journal*, March 1983, p. 233.

3. At Birmingham Museum approximately 80% of all casual enquiries made of the Department of Archaeology and of Local History are numismatic. A wide range of simple, free information sheets is produced by both departments to try to respond quickly to the most common enquiries. Copies of these are available to anyone interested in issuing similar information.

4. To compare and contrast different approaches to displaying coins, visits to the British Museum, Lincoln, Birmingham and Glasgow (the Hunterian Museum) are recommended.

5. P. Grierson, *Numismatics and History,* Historical Association, 1951, pp. 13-15.

6. G.R. Elton, *England 1200-1640*, Macmillan, 1969, p. 230.

7. The standard reference works on tokens are G.C. Williamson, *Trade Tokens Issued in the Seventeenth Century*, Seaby, reprinted 1967; M. Dickinson, *Seventeenth Century Tokens of the British Isles and their Values*, Seaby, 1986; R. Dalton and S.H. Hamer, *The Provincial Token-Coinage of the Eighteenth Century*, The Stationers Company, reprinted 1910 ; W.J. Davis, *The Nineteenth Century Token Coinage*, Spink, 1904, reprinted 1969.

8. Particularly useful in this respect are P.Mathias, *English Trade Tokens: The Industrial Revolution Illustrated*, Abelard-Schuman, 1962; J.R.S.Whiting, *Trade Tokens: A Social and Economic History*, David & Charles, 1971.

9. R.N.P. Hawkins, *Public House Checks of Birmingham and Smethwick*, Birmingham City Museum, 1980; A. Gunstone, *Catalogue of the Collection of Tickets, Checks and Passes in Birmingham Museum*, Birmingham City Museum, 1982; A.J. Wager, 'How were nineteenth century "pub checks" used?', *Seaby's Coin Medal Bulletin*, November 1981, pp. 317-20; R.H. Thompson and A.J. Wager, 'The purpose and use of public house checks', *British Numismatic Journal*, 1982. pp. 215-33.

10. V. Hartwich, 'The public house and the community', *Journal of the Group for Regional Studies in Museums*, vol. 10, 1982, pp. 24-5.

11. E.A. Shils, *English Tradition*, Routledge, 1981, pp. 73-4. I would like to thank Jane Legget for this reference.

12. See, for example, J.H.Rumsby, 'Crimea and Indian Mutiny veterans in Huddersfield', *The Journal of the Orders and Medals Research Society*, vol. 23, no.2, Summer 1984, p. 183; S. Wood, 'Obfuscation, irritation or obliteration? The interpretation of military collections in British museums of the 1980s', *Journal of the Social History Curators Group*, vol. 15, 1987-88, pp. 4-6.

13. P. Seaby and P.F. Purvey, *Standard of British Coins : volume 1 : Coins of England and the United Kingdom,* Seaby, annual edition.

28   Documenting Social History Collections

Stuart A. Holm

Freelance museum documentation consultant, Reepham, Norfolk

In most respects the documentation of social history collections is no different from that of material relating to any other discipline. The same basic procedures of entry, accessioning, cataloguing, retrieval, control, audit, etc. apply whatever the subject matter. These procedures have been adequately described elsewhere (Holm, 1991; MDA, 1980a) and cannot be re-stated here. Some suggestions for background reading will be found in the Bibliography if needed.

This chapter will concentrate on those parts of the system where these standard procedures must be tailored to suit the special nature of social history collections. Three particular areas have been identified:

1. The structure of the catalogue record;
2. The terminology control used in this record and elsewhere;
3. Indexing/retrieval requirements.

Catalogue Record Structure

The catalogue record lies at the heart of most documentation systems. It holds all of the information known about a particular item, either directly or via pointers to other types of record. In most systems the catalogue record is structured by breaking its component data down into discrete categories. This organisation aids systematic recording and greatly facilitates indexing and retrieval. The data categories into which various types of information can be 'pigeonholed' are known as fields.

In simple systems these fields may be arranged in a logical sequence but no particular relationships between fields can be indicated, other than that they all belong together in one 'parent' record. Advanced systems allow more complex relationships to be expressed, by grouping related fields together to form a hierarchical structure, for example.

Sometimes the catalogue card or computer database record represents all the available fields. In some sophisticated systems, however, the full structure only exists as a theoretical concept. The actual catalogue cards or computer records are assembled by selection from an extensive list of pre-defined fields known as the 'data dictionary'. This data dictionary and the rules and conventions which control its use are known as a 'data standard'. Record structures can be 'tailored' to suit specific needs, whilst remaining compatible with the underlying standard and hence with one another. The only data standard widely adopted by UK museums is that developed by the Information Retrieval Group of the Museums Association (IRGMA) and currently supported by IRGMA's successor, the Museum Documentation Association (MDA) (MDA, 1991a).

The creation of social history catalogue records will present differing problems according to the type of system adopted. The main options are presented in Table 1. The implications of each of these will be considered in turn. It should be remembered that in addition to the factors mentioned here, the choice of structure may also be influenced by current and future indexing needs which will be mentioned later.

Manual System based on MDA Standard using MDA Cards

If a manual MDA-based system is chosen and it is decided to buy in standard 'off-the-shelf' MDA cards then the following problems must be resolved:

Which of the available card designs to use;

Which fields on the chosen card to complete;

Whether to add any other fields from the MDA Data Standard.

Choice of Card

Over twenty different designs of MDA card are available, all of which are based on the same data standard. Some are designed for a very specific type of collection as indicated by their title (e.g. Costume or Numismatics) and are unlikely to be relevant beyond their stated purpose. Several are intended for generic use (e.g. Museum Object), whilst others, although developed for use with particular collections (e.g. Decorative Arts or Technology), are actually quite generalised and can be successfully utilised for more diverse collections than their

```
Manual system
    Based on MDA standards
        Using MDA cards
        Using cards of own design
        Using plain cards
    Based on alternative standards
        Using cards of own design
        Using plain cards

Computerised system
    Based on MDA standards
        Using MDA MODES or compatable program
        Using other program packages
    Based on alternative standards
        Using museum packages incompatable with MDA
        Using other program packages
```

Table 1   Cataloguing options

```
Generic designs – Object
    Decorative art
    Ethnography/folk life
    History artefact
    Military artefact
    Museum object
    Technology

Generic designs – Non-object
    Pictorial representation
    Locality

Specialist designs
    Costume
    Numismatics
    Photography
    Scientific instruments [no longer available]
```

Table 2   MDA cards suitable for social history material

titles suggest. Perhaps eleven cards from the range could be appropriate to social history material; they are listed in Table 2.

Using many different designs of cards within one catalogue file is not recommended as switching between the various layouts can be confusing. It is suggested that a single generic card design is selected and used throughout, unless particularly strong and important specialist collections justify the use of additional specific designs.

The various generic designs of MDA card differ only slightly in the range of fields they offer. Some include more duplicated fields or groups of fields which may reduce the need for cumbersome continuation cards. The final choice will depend on collection needs and personal preferences. To help curators to make the most appropriate choice, MDA have produced a factsheet giving field by field comparisons between these cards (MDA, 1985). If in doubt the Museum Object card should serve as a reasonable choice for the typical social history collection. A new MDA basic object card designed specifically for small and volunteer-run museums is due for release in 1992.

Choice of Fields

There is no need to use all of the fields offered on the chosen design of card. Depending on the resources available and indexing requirements, field usage can range from a basic inventory record with perhaps five or six fields completed, to a full catalogue record with most boxes on the card filled. Only rarely will every available field be utilised.

The following fields should generally be considered mandatory and data always recorded provided it is available:

Identity number (or Record number)

Simple name

Brief description

Acquisition method

Acquisition person

Storage location

Although it is quite legitimate and often desirable to create very basic records, any existing non-intrinsic information concerning the history of the item must always be preserved. It will sometimes be best to record this data in unstructured form in the 'Notes' box until such time as it can be fully analysed and entered under the appropriate formal headings. Even if a more comprehensive record is warranted from the outset, some descriptive data is best left in free-text note form. As a general rule it is best to concentrate on analysing those data categories which will be used in indexing the catalogue.

Additional Fields

The fields considered most likely to be useful when cataloguing social history objects are listed in Table 3. Several of these do not actually appear on most MDA cards. When the cards were designed by panels of curators over a decade ago, the importance of certain concepts, such as entry records, was not widely recognised. There was also a tendency to over-estimate the importance of analysing physical descriptions and the 'Part:aspect:description' box has been the bane of curators' lives ever since. In the writer's experience few social history curators have ever used this field for retrieval yet many hours of documentation time have been spent over it and many people have been put off using the MDA system as a result. It offers a very powerful retrieval tool when properly used but, initially at least, it is often best ignored. The 'Part:summary' field can be substituted in its place. This is a note field which can be completed in free-text form. The object can be described part by part, each part name preceding its description and separated from it by a colon. A simple object can be described as a whole, the description just preceded by a colon, the part name 'whole' being implicit.

The 'Deposit reference number' field is essential for cross referral to entry records but is missing from all the cards. Entry numbers can, however, be added at the bottom of the 'Notes' box if desired. Another useful field for social historians which does not appear on all the cards is 'Event'. This is particularly likely to be needed in the 'Association' group, although it can occur elsewhere. Again it is easily added once one is aware of its existence. Anyone needing to add other additional data categories to MDA cards to make them better fit their collections is referred to the *MDA Data Standard* (MDA, 1991a). MDA staff can give further help if required.

Record number (Identity number)	Association
	Nature
Number of items	Person/corporate body
	Date/period
Identification	Event
Simple name	Place
Full name	
Classified name	Deposit
System	Reference no.
Other name	
Type	Acquisition
Title	Method
	Person/corporate body
Description	Date
Part: summary	Price
Material	
Condition	Valuation: date
Completeness	
Part: aspect: description	Conservation
Length	Method
Height	Date
Width	Reference no.
Part: dimen: reading	
Inscription	Photography
Method	Method
Position	Person
Transcription	Date
	Result
Production	
Person/corporate body	Documentation
Date/period	
Place	Temporary location
Technical data	
	Permanent location
	Recorder: date
	Notes

Table 3   basic field checklist for social history records (for a more comprehensive list see MODES *Manual, Section 3.4.9)*

Other Records

In addition to recording details about objects, the social history curator will often need to document images in the form of photographs, topographical prints, film, etc. These are catered for by the Pictorial Representation cards. Note that the Photograph card is specifically designed for documenting photographs as objects with a significant place in the history of photography, rather than for recording the images they bear.

Documents can be recorded on object cards with extensive use of association fields although this is not totally satisfactory if a very full record is required. Production of a specific archives card has been delayed pending discussions with the Society of Archivists.

Records about places (including sites and monuments) can be assembled using the locality cards. Oral history archives are not really catered for in the MDA manual system at present but can, at a pinch, be squeezed on to the Pictorial Representation card since they are, in effect, 'sound pictures'.

Biography or events are not covered at all by the current range of MDA cards. As social history curators try to interpret their local community as well as its artefacts this information will increasingly need to be documented. The MDA data standard makes provision for this and new cards may be produced if there is sufficient demand.

Manual System based on MDA Standard using Cards of Own Design

If a manual MDA-based system is chosen and it is decided to design the catalogue cards in-house, then one is faced with deciding which fields to select from the data standard and how best to lay them out on the chosen card format.

Choice of Fields

Table 3 lists the fields most likely to be relevant. It is obviously desirable to keep the cards as simple as possible, but fields which might be needed in future should not be omitted without careful consideration. Oversimplification will not be appreciated when future curators have to transfer all the records on to new cards as the existing ones are outgrown. However, if it is anticipated that the records will be transferred to a computer file before being expanded, then there is no problem and a very basic card will suffice.

As well as selecting appropriate fields from the MDA data standard, a decision will be needed over which fields or groups of fields should be repeated. For collections strong in mass produced items it may be desirable to repeat the 'Production' group at least once. Many social history objects are likely to have multiple associations and so the 'Association' group is always a prime candidate for repetition.

Layout

Once the fields have been selected and the need for repetition resolved, it only remains to lay out the headings on the card, apportioning the available space as seems most appropriate to the data to be held. Try not to separate fields which belong to the same group.

Cards designed in-house can use a comparable layout to those published by the MDA with the same conventions for continuation, etc., or, if the needs of the museum are basic, they can be much simpler such as the example shown in Figure 1. Further advice on card design is available from the MDA.

Manual System based on MDA Standard using Plain Cards

As an alternative to using a pre-printed card it is possible to use a plain card or

IDENTITY NUMBER Institution Number		Number of Items	RECORDER Name Date	
MDA : 17304		1	Holm, S.A. : 19.12.1988	

IDENTIFICATION Simple name	Full name
typewriter	electric typewriter & Olympia model ES 100

Classified name	Other name / Title
1.612.24	

DESCRIPTION Part : Summary
: light grey plastic casing, black base and keys. Daisywheel printhead with carbon ribbon cartridge. Erase facility.

Materials	Condition : Completeness
steel & plastic (various)	fair (working order) : complete

Dimensions
length 51.5 cm depth 43.0 cm height 15.5 cm

Inscription (method : position : transcription/description)
screen printed : front (above keyboard) : OLYMPIA /ES 100

PRODUCTION Person/Corporate body : Date/Period : Place : Notes
Olympia Werke A.G. : 1970 = 1976 : Wilhelmshaven & West Germany

ASSOCIATION Nature : Person/Corporate body : Place : Event : Date/Period
owned : Museum Documentation Association : Cambridge :: 1976 = 1989

used : Hopkins, Llywela, Mrs : Cambridge :: 1976 = 1989

FRONT

ACQUISITION Method	Person/Corporate body
purchase	Galloway and Porter Ltd (30 Sidney Street, Cambridge)

Date	Price	DEPOSIT Entry number
1976	£220	MDA : E704 1

CONSERVATION Method : Person : Date : Ref No
cleaned : Roberts, D.A.R. : 10.4.1981 : C362

overhauled : Galloway and Porter : 12.3.1986 : C779

REPRODUCTION Method : Date : Ref No
photographed : Light, R.B. : 12.4.1981 : 35/172 B4-6

PERMANENT LOCATION Location : Date	TEMPORARY LOCATION Location : Date	VALUATION Value : Date
gen. office D2 : 7.11.1979	Galloway and Porter : 12.3.1986	£175 : 7.11.1979
gen. office D3 : 16.3.1986		£80 : 16.3.1986

NOTES	sketch/photo
Exhibited in 'Treasures of the MDA' exhibition, Jan-Mar 1985	

Figure 1   Example of a simple MDA compatible catalogue card

sheet and enter data in a pre-determined order or prefixed with the appropriate field names. This is a highly flexible approach but can make it harder for inexperienced staff to create good records and is not generally recommended. The principles of determining the structure are exactly the same as for the previous option.

Manual System based on Alternative Standards

There is no widely accepted alternative to the MDA data standard and, as far as the writer is aware, no other off-the-shelf social history catalogue cards are available on general sale.

Most supposedly non-MDA cards designed in-house by UK museums, are actually fully compatible with the data standard, or very nearly so. This suggests that the MDA approach can meet the needs of most museums, which is hardly surprising since it was based on existing practice. In view of this, it would be perverse to create new non-MDA record structures without very good reason. The most likely alternative would seem to be a hierarchy where people, places, dates, etc. were the primary groupings, but this is beyond the scope of this chapter.

```
RECORD_NUMBER
    IDENTIFICATION
        SIMPLE_NAME
        FULL_NAME
        CLASSIFIED_NAME
    DESCRIPTION
        PART:SUMMARY
        MATERIAL
        CONDITION
        COMPLETENESS
        LENGTH
        HEIGHT
        WIDTH
        INSCRIPTION
    PRODUCTION
        PERSON
        PLACE
        DATE
    ASSOCIATION
        NATURE
        PERSON
        PLACE
        DATE
    DEPOSIT
        REFERENCE_NO
    ACQUISITION
        METHOD
        PERSON                    from:
        DATE
    VALUATION
        VALUE
        DATE
    PERMANENT_LOCATION
    RECORDER
    NOTES
```

Figure 2   A typical MODES template for social history material

Computerised System using MDA MODES Program

The most flexible way of producing true MDA records on a computer is to employ the MDA MODES software package. This program ensures conformity with the MDA data standard but imposes no other restraints on record size or structure. It incorporates powerful data validation features which can check the vocabulary and syntax to ensure consistency and hence give better recall. It allows the production of every conceivable type of printed catalogue, index, inventory, etc. MODES offers little in the way of direct on-line searching facilities but at the time of writing an enhanced version, to be known as MODES Plus, is under development. This will support on-line retrieval. In addition MODES data can be readily transferred to other packages which, whilst having less powerful data capture and reporting facilities, can offer full on-line searching.

Entry Templates

If the MODES package is used to create catalogue records, then one or more entry templates can be set up to suit the social history material being catalogued. A set of standard templates based on the MDA card range is provided with the program but it is very easy to set up special templates tailored to the precise needs of specific collections. The design principles are exactly the same as those outlined when discussing in-house card design, although the ease with which additional fields can be added when using MODES makes it unnecessary to include fields only needed occasionally. A simple MODES template suitable for basic recording of social history objects is illustrated in Figure 2. For further information on MODES templates refer to the MODES manual (MDA, 1987).

When creating a template on a system where disk storage space is at a premium, remember that linked fields (see *MODES Manual*, Section 3.5.6) use less space than separate subfields, although they may be less convenient to use.

Photographs, topographical prints, paintings, etc. can be accommodated using the supplied pictorial representation template, varied to suit the exact nature of the collection. Oral history, building, locality, biography and event records require a different selection of fields from those provided in the Museum Object format. MDA hopes to produce formats for these in the future, probably starting with locality recording. Members of the Society of Archivists have produced a MODES archives format which may be of value to museums with large archive collections.

MDA-compatible Computerised System using Other Program Packages

At the time of writing there are one or two other museum specific programs available which are broadly compatible with the MDA data standard. These range from the Museum Inventory System (MIS) developed by the National Museums of Scotland and available free of charge, to packages such as Collection and Minisis which cost thousands of pounds. MIS supports the efficient creation of very simple collection inventories but is not suitable for handling full catalogue records. The top-of-the-range systems are very powerful but beyond the reach of all but the largest museums.

If these museum specific programs do not offer the required facilities or are too expensive, then it is possible to tailor a generic database system to suit museum needs. Unless the necessary expertise is on hand to set up one of the really powerful true relational systems such as Advanced Revelation, it is best to accept a lower level of sophistication and choose one of the many low-cost (£50-£500), flat file, fixed field systems currently available. Users of such programs must create their own record structure as part of the set-up procedure, unlike users of museum specific systems which incorporate ready-made structures.

A record structure devised by the author for a social history collection database of this type appears in Figure 3. This has been used with dBase II and III and was developed from a similar structure used with Delta. It could be applied to many other similar packages and could of course be extended or modified to suit particular collection needs. It will be seen that, in order to keep the fixed length records to a manageable size, only those data categories regularly searched are included. The exception is a summary description field which, by giving a quick indication of the exact type of item selected, can minimise fruitless cross-referral to full catalogue records during on-line searches. A significant constraint is the inability to cope with more than one production or association group. This is a typical limitation of this type of low-cost solution. Inserting a set of repeated fields doesn't help much since it still doesn't cater for larger numbers of associations (e.g. a photograph of a cricket team where all players are named) and it increases the size of all records. In theory, the command language within programs such as dBase could be used to overcome some of these constraints but the programming effort would be considerable.

Despite these shortcomings, a simple database can still give useful results provided its limitations are understood and accepted. Whilst it can be more efficient to generate the database from MODES records, this is not essential. The key data can be input direct using the on-line program's own data entry facilities. The full catalogue records, including any detail which cannot be accommodated in the on-line database, can be held on MDA cards or in any other appropriate form.

Field	Field name	Type	Width	MDA equivalent
1	ID	Character	12	Record number
2	SNAME	Character	20	Identification. Simple name
3	CNAME	Character	10	Identification. Classified name
4	SUMDESC	Character	58	Identification. Brief description
5	PROLE	Character	12	Production. Person. Role
6	PNAME	Character	30	Production. Person. Person name
7	PPLACE	Character	20	Production. Place
8	PDATE	Character	9	Production. Date
9	AKEY	Character	12	Association. Nature
10	ANAME	Character	30	Association. Person
11	APLACE	Character	20	Association. Place
12	ADATE	Character	9	Association. Date
13	AQMETH	Character	8	Acquisition. Method
14	AQNAME	Character	20	Acquisition. Person. Person name
15	STORE	Character	12	Permanent location
Total			282	

Figure 3   A simple social history object record structure for use with a flat file database (dBase III+)

Computerised Systems Incompatible with MDA Standards

At present there are hardly any non-MDA-compatible museum packages on the market which are of relevance to social history material. Anyone contemplating employing such a program in the future should carefully weigh any claimed advantages against the disadvantage of deviating from the widely accepted MDA standard. The same considerations apply when thinking of tailoring a generic database package to create a non-MDA-compatible system.

Terminology Control

Once a record structure has been devised, various rules must be established to control the way in which data is recorded within that structure. These rules may cover

separators (i.e. specialised 'punctuation');

syntax (i.e. documentation 'grammar');

vocabulary (i.e. choice of words);

and are collectively known as terminology control, although purists might argue that strictly this only refers to vocabulary control.

Separator conventions, if used, are normally the same for all disciplines and need not be pursued here. (For further information see MDA, 1980a, 1980b and 1987). Syntax control generally applies to concepts common to all disciplines such as personal names, place names, dates, etc. (see MDA, 1980a, 1980b, 1987 and 1991b; Norgate, 1992). Discipline specific syntax control is usually intimately bound up with vocabulary control (e.g. inversion of simple name elements).

Vocabulary control can range from basic regulation of terms by means of a simple word list, through to sophisticated management of cataloguing language by means of a thesaurus which indicates not only the right word to use but also its relationship to other associated terms.

This area of terminology control is much more intimately bound up with subject disciplines but social historians still have much to achieve in developing and agreeing standard systems. MDA publications have stressed the need for sound terminology control and have offered suggestions for the type of control that is needed, but have seldom provided comprehensive and consistent examples which can form a model for further development. MDA is now trying to offer more positive support to encourage curators to develop standard terminology control systems co-operatively.

By far the most comprehensive published set of conventions currently available to the social history curator are those originally developed for use in Wiltshire and subsequently extended and published as *OBJECT Format Rules* (Norgate, 1992). Apart from these, published sources tend to concentrate on simple name and classified name concepts.

The most widely used source for simple names in the UK is the *Hertfordshire Simple Name List* (Hertfordshire Curators' Group, 1984). Unfortunately it is sometimes inconsistent in its handling of inversions, etc. but it offers a useful starting point for further work. As might be expected in view of its origins, the selection of terms offered reflects the interests of Hertfordshire museums. As a result it is weak in many areas (coal mining for example!). Specialist word lists which can augment the basic Hertfordshire list are beginning to appear (e.g. Cheeseman, 1988). Simple name lists are also being developed in connection with co-operative collections research initiatives (e.g. Crompton, 1988). The MDA hopes to co-ordinate these developments to ensure that a single standard emerges. A set of guidelines for constructing object name termlists and thesauri is due for release by MDA during 1992. Work is also underway on a pilot object name thesaurus and simple name wordlist.

The only other published system which appears to have had any significant influence is the American *Nomenclature* (Chenhall, 1978). This is a combination of hierarchical classification system and simple name word list. The recently published *Art and Architecture Thesaurus* (Getty AHIP, 1990), also from the United States, seems likely to have considerable influence in the future. Although developed primarily to serve art historians, this multi-faceted system has much to offer the social historian. Unfortunately, both these systems present language difficulties for the UK curator. Few British social historians would accept streetcar as the preferred term for tramcar, or faucet for tap!

Several curators of specialist collections have very sensibly turned to appropriate standard textbooks or manuals covering their subject. Several fire service museums, for example, use the Home Office Manual of Firemanship when naming equipment.

Trade catalogues can be another invaluable source for determining correct object names. Many industries have precise and consistent terminology for describing their products and where possible this should be used in preference to inventing new nomenclature.

The data category which has received the most attention from social history curators so far is that of classified name, for which a number of published classification systems are available. These group together in the same classified category items sharing particular characteristics. Different, but related, groups are brought together under a common heading higher up the classified hierarchy and so on. There are dangers inherent in using such pre-coordinate systems since they impose a particular point of view on collection research and may be a disincentive to original interpretation. Nevertheless, used wisely hierarchical classification schemes provide a useful way of organising social history collections and are popular with curators. Eventually sophisticated computerised retrieval techniques incorporating comprehensive thesaurus linkages may render hierarchical classification schemes redundant but for the time being they have a worthwhile role to play in both manual and computer systems.

The common ancestor of most published UK social history classifications is the *Classification of Objects in the Welsh Folk Museum Collections* (Welsh Folk Museum, 1982) which can trace its roots back to 1912 and has had a profound influence on other systems. Its offspring include *Museum Procedure: Classification* (Institute of Agricultural History and Museum of English Rural Life, 1978) which was formerly widely used by museums in rural areas (which often countered its agricultural bias by in-house expansion and modification), and SHIC – *Social History and Industrial Classification* (SHIC Working Party, 1983) which was developed by a consortium of museums dissatisfied with the limitations of existing systems and anxious to create a new standard system rather than perpetuate the piecemeal and unco-ordinated tinkering with MERL. *The Classification of Artefacts in the Pitt Rivers Museum Oxford* (Blackwood, 1970), *Outline of Cultural Materials* (Murdock, 1987) and *Location Code for Reserve Collections: Anthropology* (Horniman Museum, 1974), although orientated towards an ethnographic approach, have occasionally been used to organise social history collections.

Many of these systems fail to recognise that collections can be classified according to a number of different criteria and they tend to mix several approaches indiscriminately. For example, one classification scheme may group craft tools according to the trade in which they were used (classification by context), but will then group all costume or musical instruments together regardless of their contextual associations (classification by function or typology). Thus mousetraps are classified as pest extermination equipment but the Pied Piper's clothes and pipe are separated under costume and musical instrument headings. In the past this inconsistent approach actually fitted the average curator's retrieval needs tolerably well and allowed a single classification to perform several functions at once. Eventually, however, this pragmatic approach breaks down.

This was recognised by the SHIC Working Party, who after much discussion settled firmly on context as the basis for classification. Thus the pipe and piebald costume are retrieved along with mousetraps and Warfarin tins when using SHIC. As SHIC has an extended hierarchical structure, decimal notation is used to represent the 'path name' of each grouping within the scheme. If all the group titles were strung together without this abbreviation, the system would be very cumbersome to use. SHIC is rather more than just a classification system as it incorporates extensive cross-referencing between headings, giving it some of the characteristics of a thesaurus.

Whilst SHIC is far from perfect and needs developing further, it has largely displaced the St Fagans and MERL systems and is now believed to be used by over 100 UK museums. It was always intended that the system would be actively maintained and extended, although there has been little progress recently. However, the SHIC Working Party has recently reconvened and more active development may result.

Despite having the complexity to cope with large and diverse collections with sophisticated retrieval needs, SHIC can also be applied more superficially by ignoring the lower levels of hierarchy. Curators of small social history collections may, however, prefer to use a very simple, non-hierarchical list of a few dozen classification terms. Even so, it might be wise to ensure that the categories chosen relate to SHIC groupings in order to simplify future upgrading.

For many social history curators there is an obvious need for a parallel classification or thesaurus based on form and function rather than context. At present no widely adopted system has emerged. STOT (The Scientific and Technical Object Thesaurus), being developed jointly by the Science Museum and the Science and Industry Curators Group, seems the most likely candidate for widespread acceptance. Based on the very powerful *BSI Root Thesaurus* (BSI, 1985), it could probably be extended to cover non-technical objects in the future. Unfortunately it is likely to be many years before even the first edition of STOT appears.

Apart from simple and classified name concepts, work on other aspects of social history collections terminology is very fragmentary.

Indexes

Catalogue records are of limited value on their own, whichever standard they follow. The catalogue must be supported by indexes or other retrieval aids which offer a range of access routes to allow users to find records relevant to their enquiry. Users will be frustrated if they cannot find a way in to the data which matches their viewpoint, so it is important to consider who will use the system and assess what questions they are likely to ask of it.

Users of manual retrieval systems need to give indexing priorities particularly careful consideration, since each additional manual index represents a substantial investment of time and effort. Computer users may be under less pressure, since they can generally retrieve on additional fields with little extra effort. Even so, there may be substantial overheads in disk storage space and processor time if large numbers of fields are indexed. Also the cheaper database packages may impose limits on the number of indexes which can be maintained concurrently. The option of performing an unindexed 'sequential search' remains, but even on the faster computers this can be tedious if the database is of any size. As suggested earlier, the very structure of a simple computerised database may be determined by retrieval needs. Consequently almost everyone, be they manual or computer system user, will have to devote some thought to retrieval priorities.

Obviously retrieval needs will vary from collection to collection, but the checklist of indexes offered in Table 4 is based on experience with several fairly typical social history collections. Although it is difficult to generalise, those at the top of the list will probably be top priority for the majority of collections.

In addition to sorting by primary key field, it will normally be sensible to subdivide groups of similar objects by using secondary index keys to form a multi-level index. Secondary key requirements may vary greatly; those suggested in Table 4 will not suit all social history collections.

Common name	Key field	Suggested secondary keys
Classified index [1]	Classified name	(Simple/full names)
Donor index	Acquisition. Person	(Address/simple name)
Inventory	Permanent & temporary location [2]	(Simple name/ID no.)
Object name index	Simple name [3]	(Full/classified names)
Maker's name index	Production. Person	(Prodn.place/ simple name)
Associated person index [4]	Association. Person	(Nature/simple name)
Associated place index [5]	Association. Place	(Nature/simple name)
Event index	Association. Event	(Assocn.place/assocn.date)
Date index	Production. Date	(Classified/simple names)

Notes
(1)   May need more than one (e.g. by context and by typology)
(2)   Permanent location used unless there is a current temporary location
(3)   May also include other name as a primary key
(4)   Can usefully be combined with Production.Person
(5)   Can usefully include Production.Place

Table 4   Index checklist for social history collections

Skilful selection of multi-level index keys can help minimise the number of separate indexes which are needed. If an off-line computerised system is used to generate printed indexes, judicious selection of indexing keys combined with tabular output can sometimes result in indexes which can be scanned by eye more efficiently than by on-line searching.

References

Blackwood, Beatrice (1970), *The Classification of Artefacts in the Pitt Rivers Museum Oxford*, Oxford University Press.

British Standards Institution (1985), *BSI Root Thesaurus*, BSI.

Cheeseman, Robin (1988), *Simple Name List for Stone Quarrying, Masons and Mining Tools and Equipment,* unpublished.

Chenhall, Robert G.(1978), *Nomenclature for Museum Cataloging,* American Association for State and Local History, Nashville.

Crompton, John (1988), *WMSIHCRU Simple Name Terms,* West Midlands Social and Industrial History Collections Research Unit, Dudley.

Getty Art History Information Program (1990), *Art and Architecture Thesaurus,* Oxford University Press New York.

Hertfordshire Curators' Group (1984), *Hertfordshire Simple Name List,* Standing Committee for Museums in Hertfordshire, Hertford.

Holm, Stuart A. (1991), *Facts and Artefacts,* MDA, Cambridge.

Horniman Museum (1974), *Location Code for Reserve Collections: Anthropology,* Horniman Museum.

Institute of Agricultural History and Museum of English Rural Life (1978), *Museum Procedure: Classification,* University of Reading.

MDA (1980a), *Practical Museum Documentation,* MDA, Cambridge.

MDA (1980b), *Museum Object Card Instructions,* MDA, Cambridge.

MDA (1985), *Variations between MDA Decorative Arts, Ethnology/Folk Life, History Artefact, Museum Object and Technology Catalogue Cards,* MDA, Cambridge.

MDA (1987), *Modes Manual,* MDA, Cambridge.

MDA (1988a), *MDA Booksales Catalogue,* MDA, Cambridge.

MDA (1988b), *MDA Systems Catalogue,* MDA, Cambridge.

MDA (1991a), *The MDA Data Standard,* MDA, Cambridge.

MDA (1991b), *Place Names Recording Guidelines,* MDA, Cambridge.

Murdock, G.P. *et. al.* (1987), *Outline of Cultural Materials,* Human Relations Area Files, New Haven.

Norgate, M. (1992), *OBJECT Format Rules,* Norgate, Steeple Ashton.

Orna, Elizabeth, and Pettitt, Charles W. (1980), *Information Handling in Museums,* Clive Bingley.

Roberts, D.A.R. (1985), *Planning the Documentation of Museum Collections,* MDA, Cambridge.

SHIC Working Party (1983), *Social History and Industrial Classification (SHIC),* University of Sheffield.

Stone, Sheila M. (1984), 'Documenting collections', in Thompson, J.M.A. (ed.), *Manual of Curatorship,* Butterworth.

Welsh Folk Museum (1982), *Classification of Objects in the Welsh Folk Museum Collections,* Welsh Folk Museum.

Bibliography

Any curator unsure of the fundamentals of museum documentation and seeking to place the above notes into context is referred to *Facts and Artefacts* (Holm, l991) or to the relevant chapter within the *Manual of Curatorship* (Stone, 1984) for a concise explanation of the function and principles of documentation and a brief outline of how these principles can be put into practice. A more thorough practical guide to the various procedures involved will be found in *Practical Museum Documentation* (MDA, 1980a). This is based on the widely adopted MDA approach but will be of relevance to users of all but the most arcane systems. Other MDA publications offer detailed guidance in the use of specific MDA systems. *Information Handling in Museums* (Orna and Pettitt, 1980) presents a clear insight into the thinking behind good information management, independent of particular techniques or equipment. *Planning the Documentation of Museum Collections* (Roberts, 1985) provides detailed guidance for anyone contemplating creating a new documentation system or upgrading existing procedures. A select list of recommended documentation publications is provided by the *MDA Booksales Catalogue* and *MDA Systems Catalogue*, both available free from the MDA.

29.1 Restoration and Conservation: Ethics

R. E. Child
Head of Conservation, National Museum of Wales

Introduction

Ethics is the science of morals, the distinction between right and wrong; and in the ethics of conservation as with human morality, that distinction is not a fixed, immutable thing that exists through time but is in a state of constant flux, shifting, adapting and changing with changing circumstances and attitudes. The use of the ducking stool for nagging women is now considered as offensive to the humanitarian as the riveting of broken pottery is to the conservator.

The ethics of conservation cannot satisfactorily be thought of as carved on tablets of stone, but must represent the consensus view of all those who have an appreciation of art and antiquities, and therefore must alter as that consensus alters. Similarly, it would be absurd to expect the same ethical values to be applied to all classes of objects, however even-handedly people try to apply them. Depending on fashions and personal preferences different objects will always evince a different reaction and thus their conservation will be, to a degree, subjective. At present, it is thought desirable to polish silver and brass, but the National Trust are allowing their brass furniture fittings to mellow and patinate with the wood, judging this the ethical thing to do. This attitude follows the present trend in conservation ethics which is more towards preservation of the inherent nature of an object rather than its restoration to a subjective former state.

There are now a number of published statements on conservation ethics both from institutional bodies such as the International Committee of Museums (ICOM) (Allen, 1984; AIC, 1979; IIC-CG and CAPC, 1986; UKIC, 1983) and from concerned specialist conservators and companies (Frost, 1980; Harding, 1976; Wallis, 1988).

They show an unremarkable agreement on what is important, and as such can be considered to be the consensus viewpoint of the conservation world. Apart from ICOM, mentioned above, few curatorial publications discuss conservation ethics and therefore the prevailing view of museum curators is difficult to evaluate but must be broadly similar to those of the conservators with whom the ethical responsibility is shared.

Before embarking on a discussion of the ethics of conservation as applied to social history collections, it is perhaps necessary to define and explain the following terms as they are generally understood. *Conservation* is the preservation of an object by retarding or halting the processes of deterioration, without unduly altering the object. *Restoration* is the alteration of an object beyond that necessary for its preservation, in order to improve some factor of the object. It is additional to preservation and should only be undertaken for compelling objective reasons.

A broken pottery vase needs only correct storage of the fragments for the preservation of the material, but restoration through glueing the pieces back into a unified whole and applying correct storage/display conditions obviously increases its value for research, interpretation, visual impact, etc.

However, further restoration work to fill in the cracks and spray paint on the joins to make them invisible, is usually unnecessary deception, as it does not aid the object's interpretation, but denies the observer information concerning it. The repaired vase is now a fake.

Conservation Ethics

The ICOM Committee for Conservation presents the activity of conservation as that of examination, preservation and restoration.

Examination is defined in the UKIC *Guidance of Conservation Practice* as 'an adequate examination of the object and all available documentation in order to record its condition and history, and to establish the causes of its deterioration'. The examination of documentation and discussions with outside experts in order to have the fullest understanding of an object is an obvious necessary precursor to deciding on ethical treatments. The examination of the object, however, has some ethical problems; for instance, it is often the case that the necessary information on the object's condition can only be obtained through intrusive examination, say, by chemical tests or by dismantling, which may of necessity damage, remove or destroy original material. There is a great desire for work to begin on the conservation of objects without the necessary preliminary examination and recording being done. Time, space, resources, and over-enthusiasm of the staff to get started all put pressure on the examination process. The following is a basic list of the information needed for the record:

1. *Background information* – history of the use of the object to determine its 'curriculum vitae' of storage condition, details of use, maintenance details, etc.

2. *Research data* – operating manuals, manufacturers' catalogues, contemporary oral data and information on similar objects from other museums, specialists, societies, etc.

3. *Condition record* – from details of materials, fabrication methods, manufacturing details, both from the research data and visual examination, the deterioration of the object both active and historic should be recorded in detail.

At this point an evaluation should be made on the next two steps: firstly, the proposed conservation treatment; secondly, the additional examination needed to aid the conservation treatment.

If considered dispassionately, any further intrusive examination may not be relevant or necessary. If the object is not unique, such information that might be gleaned will perhaps be gained some other time on another identical article. Naturally in many cases the examination and initial recording process will be left to the conservator and will often be brief. The curator/conservator dialogue is, however, vital at the end of this procedure to decide on the conservation treatment and the proposed result of it.

Passive Conservation

The conservation treatment is essentially one of preservation, and in all cases involves what is commonly known as 'passive' conservation. This is the provision of an environment that provides it with the best possible chance of survival. The great ethical advantage of passive conservation is that it is incontrovertibly good for the objects. There is no attempt to alter the object itself, only to provide conditions for its best survival. The controversy arises when there is a conflict of interest between the needs of the objects and those of the viewer who wishes to see, handle and use them. A common complaint of the visitor to museums is the low light levels in costume and picture galleries and the intrusion of glass showcases and glazing over pictures. It is often not well explained or conveniently forgotten that the low light levels and the glass are a compromise between the object and its future, and the needs of the viewer. In many cases the objections arise through poor design and display techniques making these compromise safety measures obvious and intrusive. With the options available to conservators, curators and designers to use, for instance, higher light levels for shorter periods of time, more frequent rotation of exhibits, filtered air-conditioning, etc., most ethical conservation restrictions should be surmountable.

Active Conservation

The principle of active conservation is that it is a treatment affecting the object concerned. It can be as simple a process as dusting or as complex as the removal of fresco wall-paintings from a church. In all cases the treatment poses a potential risk to the object which has to be outweighed by the benefit to the object and to the viewer. In a great number of cases the application of a protective layer – varnish, consolidant, paint etc. – is a cheap and expedient alternative to the provision of correct environmental conditions, and when used as such it is a process to be deplored. It is a short cut to determining and providing the correct conditions and, as will be explained further, is a non-reversible treatment.

Both Pye and Cronyn (1987) and Horie (1987) note that a fundamental statement of ethical conservation is the use of reversible treatments – it should be possible to undo everything that is done to the object. They go on to demonstrate that though this is a desirable and laudable aim in theory, in practice it is not wholly possible. The treatment of corrosion removal, such as derusting, is one obviously irreversible process; however, less obvious is the irreversibility of consolidation, a process whereby a material is strengthened by impregnation with a hardening agent. Though in theory one can dissolve out such an agent with the same solvent used to thin it for impregnation, in practice it is found not to be possible – a residue always remains. In the removal of yellowed varnish from paintings or the re-glueing of old glued joints, the original varnish and glue is never completely removed. Even the lacquers put on seemingly impermeable metals need drastic solvent treatments to remove them – and some will remain. Furthermore, with the degradation of the glues, consolidants, varnishes etc. themselves, with time they tend to become increasingly insoluble and irreversible.

An even greater problem of ethics arises with the use of so-called permanent solutions to preservation problems. A backlash to the irreversibility of some processes previously considered reversible, is the hard-held opinion of some, 'that there are processes that will outlive the life of the object' and whose use is thus ethical. Unfortunately, for many of the materials and processes, time has proved them to be less permanent than their proposers had hoped, and the subsequent removal of the degraded substance has proved difficult and sometimes impossible. Conservators faced with the task of removing epoxy resin glues and polyurethane varnishes note this to their cost.

There is a grey area between what can be defined as conservation and restoration, and this again highlights the conflict between preservation and interpretation. It was common conservation practice until recently to clean costume by various methods in order to remove dirt, sweat and worse that may chemically degrade the fabric or prove an attractant to insect pests or fungi.

However, Cooke shows what evidence can be obtained from crease patterns in costume and how this information may be lost through washing (1988).

Similarly, the removal of rusted layers of iron corrosion will permanently destroy the entrapped original surface with its inherent information, irretrievably. With increased understanding of the degradative processes and the ways to overcome them, there are fewer purely preservational reasons for such irreversible processes, and if they are carried out it is for reasons of restoration.

Restoration

Restoration, by definition, changes an object from the condition in which it was accepted into the museum. Axiomatically, any change, whether through deterioration or restoration, diminishes its individual integrity, so it has to be a matter of singular importance for any object to be restored, and the objectiveness of such a restoration needs to be clearly understood by both curator and conservator. The routine refurbishment of artefacts, and the long accepted customs and practices of restoration (such as the desire that clocks should work, cars should 'go' and corrosion should be stripped off) need to be constantly evaluated especially today when original untouched examples of many museum objects are becoming increasingly rare.

The reason for restoration is usually aesthetic, regardless of the truisms that 'the significance of a broken object ... may lie in the damage it has suffered' (Organ, 1976) and 'for obvious cultural reasons, it is far more desirable to retain genuine old fabric and workmanship than to replace it with even the highest-quality modern reproduction fabric' (Waite, 1976). The tradition of the restorer has evolved from the desire of collectors to possess works of art in an immaculate state. When the demand exceeded the supply the restorer was able to refurbish damaged and deteriorated material for presentation as 'in perfect condition'. That tradition lives on in collectors of all types today who turn to museums to evaluate just how genuine their objects are when compared with the museum's authentic material. Sadly, today even museums have fallen under the spell of what is disparagingly known as the 'bright and shiny brigade'.

One of the moral dilemmas facing collectors of usable items such as machinery, clocks, scientific instruments, cars, steam engines, etc. is the 'to run or not to run' problem. All too often, however, the problem is different from that perceived by the restorer in that the use of replicas is not considered. The restorer may reject this alternative, wanting to restore the clock/piano/car in order to get an authentic appreciation of its workings. However, that very restoration process by its nature will adapt, repair, modify and change the original until there is no guarantee of authentic workings beyond general principles. However, with an accurate facsimile a greater chance of reproducing original working processes is possible as new, fresh, unworn material is being used, and in the final analysis there is always the original to compare it with.

Many institutions are overcoming the restoration problem by making a register of original items in collections and keeping them unchanged, while restoring, if appropriate, duplicates. Such an arrangement could be made on a national level to preserve a core of type specimens, as zoologists and geologists do.

Where restoration is deemed desirable, a highly detailed documentation programme of the work needs to be carried out. This is especially important where outside restorers are being used in order that there is no misunderstanding in the treatments planned and carried out, and that the degree of restoration desired is fully understood by both sides. Such a document will exist as a permanent justification of the project and a complete description of the examination, preservation and restoration work carried out.

In the case of machinery restored to working condition, there must be a schedule of operation that least jeopardizes the preservation of the object. This may include running under low loading, reduced weights in gravity-driven clocks, slow warm-up times, etc. A complete understanding of the machine and its operative capacities is necessary.

There are many manuals, guidelines and so on, on the details of restoration ethics such as the use of compatible materials or paint finishes superior to the original, the cross-over from restoration to reconstruction etc., and it is easy to get entangled in such minutiae. The general tenets of conservation satisfactorily cover all such points by appealing to the common sense attitudes of conservators and curators alike in abiding by the three main ethical considerations:

1. Preservation should ideally be the limit of conservation.

2. Conservation processes should cause the minimum of change, and where feasible be fully reversible.

3. All relevant information should be fully documented.

It is difficult, if not impossible, to give precise criteria for deciding on ethical conservation treatments; as the Standing Commission on Museums and Galleries Working Party on Conservation aptly put it

The aims of conservation and restoration ... are easily intelligible and justifiable on rational grounds ... Neither of these aims is usually capable of realisation because of the limits of technical and historical knowledge and resources.

References

AIC Committee on Ethics and Standards (1979), *Code of Ethics and Standards of Practice*, American Institute for Conservation of Historic and Artistic Works.

Allen, Nick (ed.) (1984), *Scottish Conservation Directory*, Glasgow Conservation Bureau, Scottish Development Agency.

Cooke, William (1988), 'Creasing in ancient textiles', *Conservation News*, no.35, pp. 27-30.

Frost, Murray (1980), 'Care and conservation of machinery', *Saskatchewan Museum Quarterly*, vol. 7, no.8, pp. 11-18.

Harding, Keith, (1976), *A Code of Ethics for Restorers in Antiquarian Horology*, Keith Harding, London.

Horie, Velson (1987), *Materials for Conservation*, Butterworth.

ICOM (1984), *The Conservator-Restorer; A Definition of the Profession*, ICOM, Paris.

IIC-CG and CAPC (1986), *Code of Ethics and Guidance for Practice*, Ottawa International Institute for Conservation/Canadian Group and Canadian Association of Professional Conservators.

Organ, Robert M. (1976), *Discussion, Preservation and Conservation : Principles and Practices*, Washington, The Preservation Press.

Pye, E., and Cronyn J. (1987), *The Archaeological Conservator Re-examined*, Institute of Archaeology Jubilee Conference Proceedings, London.

Standing Commission on Museums and Galleries (1980), *Conservation: Report by a Working Party 1980*, HMSO.

UKIC (1983), *Guidance for Conservation Practice*, United Kingdom Institute for Conservation, London.

Waite, John G. (1976), *Architectural Metals : Their Deterioration and Stabilisation, Preservation and Conservation : Principles and Practices*, Washington, The Preservation Press.

Wallis, G. (1988), *Dorothea Restorations Ltd, Conservation Policy Statement*, Dorothea Restorations Ltd, Bristol.

29.2   Restoration and Conservation: Preventative Conservation

George Monger

Conservator, Museum of East Anglian Life, Stowmarket, Suffolk

At the simplest and most basic level preventative conservation is a matter of ensuring good storage and display conditions. However, this is easier said than done; a social history collection includes objects composed of a number of different materials which ideally require different environmental conditions. A number of compromises therefore have to be made.

Most of the materials in social history objects would naturally be degraded by fungi, bacteria, insects and other animals, and often they do not occur naturally in the form in which they are utilised in objects. Conservation of museum objects is therefore an exercise in combating nature.

Before venturing further into this subject it is worthwhile reminding ourselves what we mean by conservation. The members' handbook published by the United Kingdom Institute for Conservation (UKIC) defines conservation as

the means by which the true nature of an object is preserved. The true nature of an object includes evidence of its origins, its original construction, the materials of which it is composed and information as to the technology used in its manufacture. Subsequent modifications may be of such a significant nature that they should be preserved. (UKIC, 1987)

Strictly speaking, therefore, all pure conservation treatments are preventative in nature; some treatments also include work of a partly cosmetic nature, such as filling a gap in a clay pot or wooden statue. Removing dirt from an object is a preventative measure as it removes a potential agent of degradation (however, old oil and grease on machinery sometimes maintain areas of original paint).

This chapter will outline some of the actions that can be taken to prevent deterioration within the museum – in stores and display – after (or even before) treatment by a conservator. Degradation can still occur after conservation treatment if the object is neglected or put into conditions which caused the degradation in the first place.

It is worth remembering that many historical objects have survived by accident – especially the everyday objects – and that they can be in greater danger of destruction in a modern building or museum than in the environment where they survived (Ward, 1982).

Because of the wide range of materials and objects found within a social history collection only a broad outline of the types of problems which can occur, and possible solutions, can be given. More detailed accounts can be found in the publications listed in the References and Bibliography.

Metals

Few metals are found in nature in a pure state; they are usually in the form of an 'ore'. For use, the metal has to be extracted from the ore and refined. The process which we recognise as corrosion is the metal reverting to a natural state.

The main agents of corrosion are water, oxygen and various reactive chemical species known as 'ions', specifically chlorides, carbonates, sulphides, sulphates and phosphates.

The actual process of corrosion, such as the rusting of iron, is a complicated set of electrochemical reactions which need not concern us here (Stambolov, 1979). Many corrosion products are hygroscopic, that is, they absorb moisture, and thus help to perpetuate the corrosion process.

Some corrosion products form a barrier over the metal surface which prevents further corrosion; a good example is copper oxide on copper and brass and the patina usually found on bronzes. Obviously such a barrier should not be removed unless absolutely necessary.

Although metal corrosion is usually associated with high relative humidities there are exceptions. Lead oxide corrosion is promoted by very dry, low relative humidity conditions.

Obviously the main causes of degradation of metals are environmental – oxygen, water vapour and other gases such as sulphur dioxide (SO_2 forms sulphuric acid on the surface of a metal). If the environment is kept free of all or some of these agents of corrosion, or a barrier formed between the metal and the corrosive agent, then degradation will be prevented.

Organic Materials

Organic materials include wood, leather, paper, textiles, waxes, rubbers and plastics. Many of the preventable causes of damage are common to all these materials so they can all be considered together.

The agents of damage with this class of material are heat, light, fluctuating (or too high or too low) relative humidity (RH), and insects, fungi and rodents. Fuller discussions of the mechanisms of damage from these sources can be found elsewhere (e.g. Hickin, 1974, 1981; Lafontaine, 1977; Padfield, 1966; Thomson, 1965, 1967, 1978, and also Bibliography). All these agents are important in the natural cycle where one type of material provides food for another.

In some cases damage is caused by accident. *Anobium punctatum* (common furniture beetle or 'woodworm') is known to have damaged books and textiles in contact with wood when biting an exit or flight hole. (Contrary to popular belief the holes characteristically produced by 'woodworm' are caused by the adult beetle emerging from the wood, *not* by the beetle entering the wood (Hickin, 1974; 1981).)

As well as the actual materials themselves, we must also consider the conservation of surface coatings, dyes and other colourants associated with any particular object.

Lastly, before considering what can be done in the way of preventative conservation we must remember that many social history items are composites of two or more different materials, for example, steel tools with wooden handles; metal, rubber and textile in gas masks; and leather and brass in harnesses. Additionally, we must remember that original historic photographs, glass negatives, cine film and audio tape are also composite materials which need specific conditions for their conservation.[1]

Prevention Better than Recurrence

The term 'preventative conservation' can be seen as tautological. A better term would be 'passive conservation' as we are considering the measures which can be taken to prevent deterioration within storage and display areas rather than actively treating the objects themselves.

The Buildings

Passive conservation begins with the buildings in which the objects are displayed or stored.

Buildings should be subjected to regular surveys and maintenance. It is no use trying to regulate the internal environment using expensive equipment (in both capital and revenue terms) if the roof leaks or the walls are damp.

Gutters and downpipes should be checked to ensure that they are working and not just channelling rainwater down the brickwork.

Is damp rising up at the bottom of the building? Where are the objects stored? If in the basement is it 'naturally' damp? If the storage area is an upper storey are the walls damp outside, or inside? What is above the ceiling? What is the floor loading?

For any museum fortunate enough to have new purpose-built object stores and/or galleries there are other considerations.

Whilst concrete in a new building is curing (i.e. setting) and drying the atmosphere will be alkaline and humid. Depending on the finishes and sealants used it can take up to two years for the alkalinity to drop to safe levels (Hilberry and Weinberg, 1981).

Materials used for the finishing of buildings – fireproofing material, plastics and types of wood – also need careful consideration (this, of course, also applies to buildings being adapted)(Hilberry and Weinberg, 1981). Such considerations are also important in display case construction and lining (Blackshaw and Daniels, 1979; Macqueen, 1979; Oddy, 1973).

The Environment

The problems and damaging effects of the environment have been well documented; it is therefore not necessary to go into great detail here (Hilberry and Weinberg, 1981; Lafontaine, 1977; Padfield, 1966; Stambolov, 1979; Thomson, 1965,1967,1968; Ward, 1982; and also Bibliography).

Briefly we are considering the damage caused by dust, uncontrolled relative humidity, light and insects. A fifth damaging factor, air-borne gases (sulphur dioxide, ozone, hydrogen sulphide, nitrogen oxides), will not be considered here. The control of these pollutants would need air filtration equipment which is too expensive for most museums. However, curators need to be aware of the problems of these gases which are fully considered in Thomson (1978).

Dust Dust is particulate matter suspended in air which may settle in still air. It can be sooty or tarry, produced by the burning of fuels, can contain sulphur dioxide and sometimes traces of metals such as iron (Thomson, 1978). Alternatively, it can originate from textile and animal sources. In this last case the dust will provide food for fungi and mites which in turn are a food source for larger insects.

The ideal is to have an air-conditioning system which filters the particulate and gaseous matter from the air. However, because of the expense involved this is not feasible for most museums; for some social history museums, which include displays in reconstructed buildings or historic 'working sites', this is totally impractical.

As with most aspects of passive conservation, good housekeeping is the key. Storage areas and galleries should be kept free of accumulations of dust and dirt. Stored objects should, if possible, be boxed, with a long lip on the box lids to prevent the ingress of dust, or else wrapped in acid-free tissue paper or loosely wrapped in polythene.

Relative humidity (RH)   Relative humidity is an important factor in preventative conservation. Good storage is a matter of several compromises; generally metalwork should be stored at a low %RH, but this would be damaging to such organics as wood, leather, paper, textile and ivory which are sometimes found in association with metals. Consequently, conditions must be chosen which are least damaging to the most vulnerable materials.

A zoned storage facility where the RH can be adjusted for the objects being stored in each area would be ideal, but this, for many museums, would be impractical.

For a mixed collection, a steady RH of 50%-55% at a temperature of 10°C-12°C is recommended. Exposed metals can be treated with a moisture barrier to decrease the possibility of corrosion. However, it is difficult to treat metals which penetrate other materials, e.g. the tang of a tool embedded in a wooden handle. If the metal begins to corrode the non-metallic element may be damaged. It is therefore necessary to regularly inspect the collection.

Although the low temperature may be uncomfortable for the staff who have to enter the store from time to time it will decrease the rate of decomposition reactions within objects.

Such a temperature would be impractical to maintain in galleries as it would be uncomfortable for the visitors and staff. It must be remembered that %RH is temperature-dependent, and that people in a room will drastically affect the RH in a gallery. It is therefore necessary to have equipment to monitor the environment as well as the equipment and expertise to control the %RH (Thomson and Staniforth, 1985).

High temperatures together with high %RH levels not only promote corrosion in metals but also provide ideal conditions for fungal growth on organic materials. High %RH also encourages insect activity and acts as a mild solvent for animal glues.

There is, however, a problem with wooden wheeled vehicles and coopered containers (wooden buckets, casks and butter churns). In use they were either damp or stored in uncontrolled environments. These objects are likely to shrink in the ideal controlled museum environment resulting in tyres becoming loose on wheels and even casks and buckets falling apart.

Light   The damaging effects of light are well known. Light can be envisaged as waves of energy packets which can activate chemical reactions within objects which we see as the fading of dyes, for example, the degradation of rubbers and plastics (Crighton, 1988), and the yellowing of newspapers (Mills and White, 1987).

Recommended *maximum* light levels are as follows:

200 lux for oil and tempera paintings, undyed leather, lacquer, wood, horn, bone and ivory (where surface colour is important);[2]

50 lux for costume, watercolours, tapestries, furniture, textiles, prints and drawings, manuscripts, wallpapers, miniatures, dyed leather and natural history objects (Thomson and Staniforth, 1985).

The effects of light are cumulative, which means that the same amount of damage is caused by illumination at, say, 50 lux for 10 hours for one day, as 50 lux for one hour per day for ten days.

Visible light is just as damaging as ultra violet (UV) light; however, by filtering out UV, using window and fluorescent light tube filters, the light damage will be diminished.

To reduce the damage caused by light three rules should be observed:

1.   Eliminate UV radiation using filters.

2. Reduce the illumination time of sensitive objects.

3. Reduce the illuminance to that necessary for comfortable viewing (Thomson and Staniforth, 1985). For a fuller account of this complex subject see Thomson (1978) and Thomson and Staniforth (1985).

Insects There are about a dozen different woodboring insects, a dozen different moth species, plus other beetles which infest textiles and leather (Hickin, 1974, 1981), so it is not possible to discuss all of these here. Most organic materials can be subject to insect attack, so all artefacts should be checked and/or treated for insect infestation before being put into store or on display.

The signs to look for are fresh frass around an object, frass coming out of holes, unusual beetles or unusual numbers of beetles in an area, moths, larvae on textiles, and cocoon cases.

Objects suspected of being infested should be isolated for treatment. However, bad infestation may require a major treatment programme throughout the store.

It is tempting to suggest that all objects should be fumigated before entering the store: however, there are many problems with fumigation both for objects and people (Dawson, 1981, 1983; Getty Conservation Institute, 1988; Rossol, 1987; Story, 1985).

Good housekeeping and vigilance are the keys to the prevention and/or containment of insect attack. It is easier to see the unusual, such as fresh frass or beetles, if the stores and display areas are kept clean. Nests and dead rodents provide breeding areas for moths, carpet beetle and hide beetle (Hickin, 1974), so it is necessary to ensure as far as possible that roof spaces and eaves are also kept clean.

Handling

The staff are one of the biggest dangers to the collection. Handling, transporting and mounting displays are all hazardous operations to objects. Rules for handling and transporting objects should be drawn up and followed. The guidelines entitled *Handling Museum Objects and Paintings*, drawn up by the Department of Conservation at Birmingham City Museum and Art Gallery, are a very good model.

Some simple rules can be outlined here:

1. Wear cotton gloves when handling objects, especially metals.

2. Plan the route before moving an object and ensure that there are no obstructions.

3. Before picking up an object, look for fragile areas and loose parts (e.g. lids).

4. Ensure that an object is adequately supported when being handled.

5. Use trolleys and/or padded carrying baskets where feasible.

6. Do not try to carry too many objects at one time.

Use of Objects

The use of objects in demonstrations is diametrically opposed to the concept of preventative/passive conservation. A certain amount of wear and tear is inevitable to any object being used, however strong and resilient it may appear to be.

Conclusion

Preventative or passive conservation is an exercise in controlling the various external factors which cause or promote degradation in objects – heat, light and the general environment. Many of the measures taken are a matter of compromise, and it is worthwhile obtaining, and using, some of the specialised information sheets available, such as the Fact Sheets from the Scottish Museums Council and the Notes published by the Canadian Conservation Institute (see Bibliography).

Regular inspection of collections, cleanliness of areas where objects are kept, and good maintenance, both internal and external, are essential.

Care must be taken in choosing materials for storage, display cases and case linings; ensure that any materials used are not liable to degrade and that any objects liable to degradation (e.g. certain plastics and rubbers) do not contaminate other objects and promote degradation in them. Last, but not least, care must be taken in handling and transporting objects.

Notes

1. At the time of writing doubts have been expressed regarding the longevity of compact discs (CDs). The printer's ink used to print the information on the disc is thought likely to degrade the lacquer layer on the aluminium disc and cause corrosion of the aluminium. This would result in a loss of sound reproduction quality. The sound quality and the indestructibility of CDs has been one of their selling points (see *Guardian*, 29-30 June 1988).

2. Lux is the unit of measurement of the strength of light (Thomson, 1967, 1978; Lafontaine, 1977; Thomson and Staniforth, 1985). See also *Scottish Museums Council Factsheets* in Bibliography. A simple, but not very accurate, method of measuring lux levels is given in the Canadian Conservation Institute Notes, sheet no. 2/5 (see Bibliography).

References

Blackshaw, Susan M., and Daniels, Vincent, D. (1979), 'The testing of materials for use in storage and display in museums', *The Conservator*, vol. III, pp. 16-19.

Crighton, J.S. (1988), 'Degradation of polymeric materials', in *Preprints of Modern Organic Materials Meeting*, Edinburgh, 14-15 April, Scottish Society for Conservation and Restoration.

Dawson, J.E. (1981), 'Ethylene oxide fumigation', *IIC-CG Newsletter,* vol. VIII. no. 2, pp. 8-11.

Dawson, J.E. (1983), 'Ethylene oxide fumigation: a new warning', *Supplement to CMA Museogramme*, March, pp. 1-6.

Getty Conservation Institute (1988), 'Vikane holds potential as a museum fumigant', *Newsletter,* vol. III, no. 1, p. 6.

Hickin, Norman E. (1974), *Household Insect Pests*, London Associated Business Programmes Ltd, 2nd ed.

Hickin, Norman E. (1981), *The Woodworm Problem*, East Grinstead, Rentokil Ltd, 3rd ed.

Hilberry, John D., and Weinberg, Susan Kalb (1981), 'Museum collection storage: Part I', *Museum News*, vol. LIX, no. 5, pp. 7-21, Washington. (See also 'Part II', *Museum News*, 1981, vol. LIX, no. 6, pp. 5-23; and 'Part III', *Museum News*, 1981, vol. LIX, no. 7, pp. 49-60.)

Lafontaine, Raymond H. (1977), 'Museum lighting' and 'Relative humidity', *Museum Round-up*, no. 68, Fall, pp. 20-35.

Macqueen, Mary (1979), 'Display and storage of metal objects after conservation', in *The Conservation and Restoration of Metals: Proceedings of the Symposium*, Edinburgh, 30-31 March,

Scottish Society for Conservation and Restoration, pp. 70-74.

Mills, John S., and White, Raymond (1987), *The Organic Chemistry of Museum Objects*, Butterworth.

Oddy, W.A. (1973), 'An unsuspected danger in display', *Museums Journal*, vol. 73, no. 1, pp 27-8.

Padfield, Tim (1966), 'The control of relative humidity and air pollution in show cases and picture frames', *Studies in Conservation*, vol. XI, no. 1, pp. 8-29.

Rossol, Monona (1987), 'Care and preservation of museum personnel', in Howie, F. (ed.), *Safety in Museums and Galleries*, Butterworth.

Stambolov, T. (1979), 'Introduction to the conservation of ferrous and non-ferrous metals', *The Conservation and Restoring of Metals: Proceedings of the Symposium*, Edinburgh, 30-31 March, Scottish Society for Conservation and Restoration.

Story, Keith, O. (1985), *Approaches to Pest Management in Museums*, Smithsonian Institute, Washington.

Thomson, Garry (1965), 'Air pollution – a review for conservation chemists', *Studies in Conservation*, vol. X, pp. 147-67.

Thomson, Garry (1967), 'Annual exposure to light within museums', *Studies In Conservation*, vol. XII, no. 12, pp. 26-35.

Thomson, Garry (1978), *The Museum Environment*, Butterworth/IIC.

Thomson, Garry, and Staniforth, Sarah (1985), 'Simple control and measurement of relative humidity in museums', *Museums Information Sheet*, no. 24, 2nd ed., and 'Conservation and museum lighting', *Museums Information Sheet*, no. 6, 4th ed., Museums Association/Area Museum Councils.

UKIC (United Kingdom Institute for Conservation) (1987), *Members' Handbook*.

Ward, Philip R. (1982), 'Conservation: keeping the past alive', *Museum*, vol. XXXIV, no. 1, pp. 6-10, UNESCO, Paris.

Bibliography

Canadian Conservation Institute, *Notes*. These cover a wide range of subjects which relate to preventative conservation. Available from CCI, 1030 Innes Road, Ottawa, Canada, KIA OM8.

Graham-Bell, Maggie, *Preventative Conservation: A Manual*, British Columbia Museums Association, 1986, 2nd ed.

Plenderleith, H.J., and Werner, A.E.A., *The Conservation of Antiquities and Works of Art*, Oxford University Press, 1971, 2nd ed.

Scottish Museums Council Factsheets, 23 titles available. These include:

1. Temperature and Humidity

2. Light

3. Air Pollution

4. Materials used in Conservation and Display

5. Care of Metallic Objects

10. The Care of Textiles in Storage

11. Preserving Photographs

15. Storage of Industrial Material.

Complete list and prices available from Scottish Museums Council, 20-22 Torphichen Street, Edinburgh, EH3 8JB.

Shelley, Marjorie, *The Care and Handling of Art Objects : Practices in the Metropolitan Museum of*

Art, New York, 1987.

Thompson, John M.A. (ed.), *Manual of Curatorship*, Butterworth, 1984.

Turner, Sylvia, and Yates, Bridget, (ed.), *Taken into Care : The Conservation of Social and Industrial History Items,* Proceedings of a joint UKIC/AMSSEE meeting, London, 1984.

30 Storage

Annie Hood

Museum Development Officer with AMSSEE

The wide range of artefacts that can be included in social history collections means that their storage represents a microcosm of museum storage as a whole. Artefacts within such collections are not only made up of a great variety of materials, often combined in one object, but also range in size, from small personal belongings to industrial plant. In this chapter various aspects of storage are discussed:

The building

Environment control

Housekeeping

Methods of storing

Requirements for different materials.

There is an overriding need in the development of an efficient storage system for advance planning and a good working relationship between curator and conservator, whether this be a member of staff or an outside adviser. If no conservator is available, advice can first be sought through the Area Museum Councils and the Conservation Unit of the Museums and Galleries Commission.

The Building

Position

The site of a store will depend on a great variety of factors, but if possible it should not be placed in the bits of space left over when everything else has been accommodated. Particularly to be avoided are attics and basements as both provide environmental problems. Access is a key factor, especially if large items are to be housed and machinery used to move it. Advice should always be taken at the planning stage for problems such as floor loading.

Security

The museum store must be as secure as possible, having both physical security and an alarm system. Entry points and windows can be reduced to a minimum, being blocked in if necessary, as this will also help to reduce light levels. Remaining doors and windows should have high standard locks and present the maximum protection against entry. Fire exits will need to be included for people working in the stores, and professional advice on both fire regulations and security should be sought.

Access

Access to the store should be closely controlled and limited to museum staff, visitors being accompanied at all times. A log book listing keys issued, and a record of people working in the stores, can be useful.

Layout

A system should be devised for entry of artefacts to the store and this should be reflected in the layout. Items should first be fully documented and labelled, and then undergo any necessary emergency conservation treatment, for example de-infestation, before being moved to the storage areas.

Environmental Control

Relative Humidity

Moisture is the most important agent of deterioration, and its action is closely linked to temperature. Relative humidity is the ratio of water vapour in the air compared to the amount it could hold if fully saturated, expressed as a percentage. High RH causes corrosion in metal, and above 65% RH can render organic materials liable to attack from mould and fungi. Too dry an atmosphere can also damage organic material by causing it to contract through water loss.

Changes in RH

The most significant damage to collections is caused through fluctuations in RH, as continued expansion and contraction, especially of organic material, can cause irreparable harm.

Ideal Conditions

The first essential is for the RH to be as consistent as possible, both daily and seasonally. As most social history collections contain a great variety of materials a compromise figure of between 50-55% RH should be aimed at. If, however, there is a tendency towards condensation, for example, because of cool conditions in winter, this should be lowered to 45-50%. If there is a substantial amount of metal in the collection, and this can be separated from other materials, a separate area with a lower RH of 40-45% can be set up for this.

Temperature

The main consequence of temperature is seen through its effect on the RH. High temperatures will increase deterioration by speeding the rate of chemical reactions, and so fairly low temperatures are expedient. In areas with public access a fairly low temperature of 18°C can be aimed at, and in other areas this can be reduced to 15°C. At the lower temperature RH needs careful control.

Monitoring Conditions

RH and temperature should be recorded on a permanent basis to gain a picture of conditions, and assess any necessary remedial work. The most useful instrument for this is a recording thermohygrograph which can monitor on a weekly or a monthly sheet. It must be regularly calibrated, using a whirling hygrometer, for example, to ensure accuracy. Temperature and humidity can also be recorded separately using thermometers and hygrometers. Separate readings should be taken in all areas of the museum, and it is advisable in large stores to check conditions in different areas, and at different heights.

Controlling Conditions

The ideal is to install permanent air conditioning equipment which will stabilise conditions by humidifying or dehumidifying when necessary, this being controlled by a humidistat. This has the added advantage of being able to control air pollutants at the same time. The next best alternative is to combine a regulated heating system, with free-standing humidifiers or dehumidifiers as required.

Remedial Measures

In the absence of plant to stabilise conditions, some emergency measures can be taken, for example by keeping artefacts away from floors and outside walls, by making sure there is adequate air circulation, and by isolating small storage areas for high risk items in which silica gel can be used as a buffering agent.

Air Pollution

Urban and industrial areas are particularly prone to pollution, which arises mainly from the burning of fuels. Dirt, soot and tar can be carried in the air, as can harmful gases such as sulphur dioxide, and traces of metals. An added danger in coastal areas is the high level of salts. If high levels of pollution are suspected, tests should be taken. Remedial measures that should be put into practice anyway include ensuring that artefacts are not left in open storage but are boxed, cased, or covered with suitable materials. If the problem is especially severe, air filtering or air conditioning should be considered, or as a compromise air filtration can be fitted to certain cases, or areas.

Light

Light, and particularly ultra violet (UV) radiation, can cause deterioration and fading in many materials with some areas such as surface pigments being most at risk. It is the total exposure to light that is important as the effect on objects is cumulative. The ideal is therefore to keep light levels as low as possible, and the length of illumination to a minimum. UV filters should be fitted to any lights, and other sources of light eliminated where possible. If there are windows in the store these should also be fitted with UV screening, or preferably fitted with blinds. Filtering material, whether it is sheeting, varnish or polyester film, should aim to reduce the UV light level entering through the window to below 75 microwatts per lumen.

Monitoring Light

Light intensity can be measured with a light meter, and UV radiation with a UV monitor. Readings should be taken regularly, and care taken that seasonal variation is checked. A low light level should be aimed at, certainly not above 200 lux, and where sensitive objects are stored, not above 50 lux.

Housekeeping

Cleanliness

Steps should be taken to make stores as dust free as possible, using sealing strips on any doors and windows, and making sure access is strictly limited. Stores should be kept as clean and tidy as possible, with dusting being done as far as possible using vacuum cleaners, as physical methods circulate particles in the air.

Storage system

It is useful for the stores to be arranged following the classification system used in its documentation, for example by SHIC code numbers. A clear guide to the store should be kept and regularly updated, and any boxes used for packing should be clearly labelled on the outside with contents, to avoid the need for continued repacking.

Moving Objects

Cotton or surgical gloves should be worn at all times when moving museum objects, to minimise the damage that can be caused by acids on the hand. This is particularly important for metal artefacts. Care should be taken that adequate support is given while moving objects, that items are moved singly, and that for delicate items suitable boxes or containers with padding are used. Bubble wrap forms an excellent packing material for transit, but should not be used for long-term storage.

Large Objects

If large industrial or agricultural artefacts are being stored, distinct gangways should be defined between major blocks of machinery and marked with paint or tape. Where the storage space permits, objects should be put on to pallets and moved using forklifts, or similar machinery. It is particularly important with this type of collection that the Health and Safety at Work regulations are carefully studied, and that all people working with them have been acquainted with their responsibilities.

Methods of Storing

Packing

A balance must be reached between packing to protect artefacts and the need for adequate air circulation, especially if there is any problem with high levels of RH. Packing, or arrangement on open shelves, should be loose to allow air flow, and if metal objects are bagged, airholes should be made to avoid condensation. Fragile items should be boxed, or ordered, so that retrieval does not put them at risk.

Materials to be Avoided

Wood Care should be taken over the choice of shelving and casing. Woods, for example, produce harmful vapours, and particularly bad in this respect are oak, sweet chestnut and the composite boards such as chipboard, plywood and hardboard, the latter also producing vapours from the adhesives binding them together. Sealing of wood can overcome the problem, by painting or varnishing, or more effectively by using aluminium foil. The adhesives used in marine plywood and exterior plywood are less harmful than in other forms.

Fabric If fabrics are used in storage these should be non-animal in origin, such as cotton, linen, or hessian, as wool and felt contain sulphur compounds. Treatment and dyes used need to be tested even on these fabrics. Testing of materials can be carried out by a conservation laboratory.

Requirements for Different Materials

Some of the major considerations for different types of material found in social history collections are listed below. Often, however, artefacts in this discipline are characterised by being composite, and compromise is often necessary in finding optimum storage conditions.

Metals

Any active corrosion present should be removed before items are placed in store. This treatment should usually be followed by coating the object with products such as Jenowax, to act as a protection while still allowing the object itself to be seen clearly. Following this the main requirement is for a low relative humidity to be maintained to prevent any further corrosion. If it is impossible to maintain a low RH throughout the store, separate storage units with containers for the desiccant silica gel can achieve localised control. Two metals which can be particularly vulnerable are lead, which corrodes easily in the presence of organic acids, and tin, which should be kept in temperatures above 10°C. Regular checks should be made to make sure that there is no new corrosion on metal objects.

Organic Materials

The main requirements are a steady RH, preferably between 50-60%, and good ventilation. Above 60% RH organic materials will be prone to attack from moulds and fungi, and this will be more severe where there is little air circulation. Organic materials are also subject to insect infestation, and should be treated before going into storage, and regularly checked for any further attack. This is especially relevant for wood, in which boring beetles can often at first go undetected. Paper should be stored flat in suitable acid-free boxes, and interleaved with acid-free tissue. Basketry is very susceptible to drying out, which causes it to become brittle, while leather can be affected by sulphur compounds.

Ceramics and Glass

The main consideration in the storage of these materials is to avoid physical damage. Packing in acid-free boxes with acid-free tissue can offer the best answer. Padded shelving can be an alternative, and care should always be taken that ceramics and glass are not left on glass or metal shelving without a lip, as they can be moved inadvertently through vibrations. Cups and bowls should never be stacked, and even if plates are stored in this way they should be of the same size and be interleaved with tissue or foam. Great care must be taken over moving such items and handles should not be used for lifting.

Plastics

Modern materials can cause their own problems, and of particular note are recent advances in plastics which have a built in obsolescence. Advice on the longevity and storage of such materials can be sought from the Science Museum, where tests are currently being undertaken on new products.

Textiles

These represent one of the most vulnerable parts of the collection and special care should be taken over their storage. As far as possible different materials should be segregated before being stored, and where possible textiles should be stored flat in acid-free cardboard boxes, packed with plenty of acid-free tissue. Large items can be rolled around plastic tubing, this being done along the warp of the material with the right side outermost, and they should be interleaved with acid-free tissue. If costumes are to be hung rather than stored flat, then padded hangers should be used, and covers made for each item from calico, or other closely woven cotton materials.

Photographs

A large number of social history collections include photographic and film material, and this is another vulnerable area. The main considerations are to maintain a RH of between 40-50% with temperatures between 16-17°C, and for inert materials to be used for storage. The ideal are specially produced polyester storage sleeves, which are then kept in steel filing cabinets. Some types of film are liable to deterioration and conservation advice should be sought for any materials that seem to be at risk.

Bibliography

This chapter has offered a brief overview of storage for social history collections. Further information can be found in the following works:

Information sheets issued by the Museums Association, and the Area Councils on various aspects of conservation and storage, including

Simple Control and Measurement of Relative Humidity in Museums, Museums Association Leaflet no. 24, 1980.

Scottish Museums Council's Factsheets, 1989.

Hoare, Nell, *Security for Museums*, Committee of Area Museum Councils in association with the Museums Association, 1990.

Edwards, S.R., *Pest Control in Museums*, Association of Systematic's collections, 1980.

Finch, Karen, and Putnam, Greta, *Caring for Textiles*, Barrie & Jenkins, 1977.

Leene, J.E., *Textile Conservation*, Butterworth, 1972.

Swann, A., *The Care and Conservation of Photographic Material*, Crafts Council, 1981.

Thomson, Garry, *The Museum Environment*, Butterworth, 1978.

UKIC/AMSSEE Seminar, *Taken into Care: The Conservation of Social and Industrial History Items*, AMSSEE, 1984.

Lists of suppliers for storage equipment and supplies need constant updating. Up-to-date lists can be obtained through the Area Museum Councils; Conservation Departments, especially in large museum services; and from the Conservation Unit of the Museum and Galleries Commission.

31.1   Liaison with Others: Planners and Architects

David Fleming
Director, Tyne and Wear Museums

Hamlets which fail to pass the planners' test
Will be demolished. We'll rebuild the rest
to look like Welwyn mixed with Middle West.

John Betjeman, *The Town Clerk's View*

Two of the professions encountered and misunderstood most frequently by social history curators are those of planning officer and architect. Both can be of great assistance to the curator in a number of ways. Equally, there is potential for disagreement and conflict which has to be recognised and anticipated in order to achieve fruitful working relationships. We can do this by comprehending the nature of their work and their aims.

Planners – What are They?

Nobody likes planners. They appear always to be responsible for permitting ugly development, allowing historic features to be demolished, or otherwise hindering people wanting to put up shop signs or to build garages, or to turn their houses into old people's homes. Planners are frequently attacked for lacking imagination and sensitivity, and for interfering where they have no business. They please neither developers nor conservationists.

These negative views of planners arise out of the main ideologies of town planning, which are to reconcile competing claims for land use, and to provide a good physical environment. The scope of planning has expanded as more and more central government legislation has tackled the growing problems of the urban environment, and the ideologies of the planner pervade many walks of life. 'Planning is by definition interested in the production of a deliberate future.[1] The chilling prospect of an institutionalised 'deliberate' future needs to be weighed against the fact that planners also look to the past in their role of policing historic buildings. Planners could be forgiven for succumbing to rampant schizophrenia in attempting to reconcile the preservation of valuable remnants of the past with their own schemes for total environments – in balancing the individuality of former ages with the uniformity and conformity of the present and future.

It is precisely because planners try to balance preservation with change that they cross paths so often with curators, who of course are doing exactly the same thing, only without the benefit of legislation and case law to assist in their deliberations. It is in the sphere of buildings and architectural detail that there is an identity (or conflict) of interest between planners and curators, though our definition of 'building' needs to encompass archaeological remains, docks, walls, embankments, street furniture and other features of the landscape.

Beyond the identity of interest in historic buildings of planners and curators there is an overlap of function in interpreting the environment in a wider sense. Within the ambit of the social history curator is the interpretation of the modern and historic environment, but who placed the following job advertisement in a

317

national newspaper in November 1987?

Heritage Information Officer

The main role will be to promote —shire's heritage of historic buildings and conservation areas, encouraging greater awareness of the built environment .... Responsibilities will include the preparation and design of advisory leaflets and publicity material, the development of interpretive and educational programmes, the organisation of seminars ...[2]

The advertisement was placed by the county's Planning and Estates Department. There are curators all over the country who feel that planners are crossing a professional divide and straying deep into museum territory. However, planners can and do claim that they have a perfectly legitimate interest in interpreting all aspects of the environment and they are not, in the immediate future, about to go away. In many ways everything a planner does is of interest to the social history curator, because the latter has such a wide brief.

The Planning Framework

The Secretary of State for the Environment is the government minister who is ultimately responsible to Parliament for all matters of planning and development control in England and Wales. Responsible to the minister are local planning authorities (47 County Councils, 333 Shire District Councils, 36 Metropolitan District Councils, 32 London Boroughs, the Corporation of the City of London and, where they are set up, Urban Development Corporations). These authorities have structure plans, local plans and unitary development plans which set out their development policies. They also have the power to grant or refuse planning permission: anyone wishing to develop land has to obtain permission from the local authority, this applying to all land, including conservation areas, and all buildings, including listed buildings and ancient monuments. Quite what constitutes 'development' is outlined in the legislation, although it is fair to say that this is a complex issue.[3]

Planning Legislation

Some familiarity with the terms of planning legislation is essential for the social history curator, although a recent book on planning law referred to 'the seething cauldron of planning Acts, Rules, Regulations, Orders and Circulars' during the 1980s.[4] The pivotal planning legislation in England and Wales is the Town and Country Planning Act, 1971. This has been amended by subsequent legislation such as the Town and Country Amenities Act, 1974; the Ancient Monuments and Archaeological Areas Act, 1979; the National Heritage Act, 1983 (which established the Historic Buildings and Monuments Commission for England); and the Housing and Planning Act, 1986. While all planning legislation is of significance to the curator, the most relevant is that affecting historic buildings, because curators very often have direct responsibility for the care of such buildings. Furthermore, curators are expected within a community to have knowledge of and expertise in historic buildings, as well as to exert influence over their fate. Buildings are artefacts which are in the public domain, just as are museum collections, and curators must be alert when dealing with them, and be in a position to argue, advise, inform, defend and encourage when necessary. Much of this communication will be with the planning officers who are directly advising planning authorities, and it must be based on a good knowledge of the relevant legislation on the part of the curator.

The most useful résumé of the historic buildings legislation at the time of writing is the Department of the Environment Circular No. 8/87 'Historic Buildings and Conservation Areas – Policy and Procedures'. DOE Circulars are sent to all local authorities to clarify government policies and provide guidance on their implementation, and they are the easiest way into the labyrinth of planning legislation. Circular No. 8/87 summarises all changes in the law and consolidates all current advice as at 25 March 1987. The Circular recognises that 'public opinion is now overwhelmingly in favour of conserving and enhancing the familiar and cherished local scene' and stresses the vital importance of historic buildings and conservation areas to the environment. The Circular explains the listing of buildings and their classification, as well as procedures for listed building control, and building preservation notices and conservation areas.[5]

Working with Planners

There are various direct benefits to be derived from good working relationships between planners and curators, whether these are conducted in an informal way, or through bodies such as Conservation Area Advisory Committees. Planners can be invaluable sources of information on changes in the townscape. Liaison between the curator and the planning department can result in the museum being able to record buildings and features before they disappear forever, and to rescue items such as shop signs, interior fittings, and even whole façades or structures (housing and environmental health officials can be helpful in similar respects).

Close relationships with planners maximises the potential for 'planning gain', wherein the local authority seeks from a developer some benefit in return for granting planning permission. This may come about through so-called Section 52 agreements. Planning gains are by no means the exclusive preserve of museums, less still of social history curators, but the bargaining system can result in the rescue of structures, or even the improvement, extension or building of new museums. A current example of a major planning gain is the £1.7 million extension to the Ferens Art Gallery in Hull, but only a close involvement by museum staff in the local planning process could normally lead to such a gain being considered, let alone carried through.

Schemes run by planners to improve the environment, such as pedestrianisation, can bring resources to museums or museum-related projects. The interpretation of Hull's Old Town is (largely) under the control of the city's Social History Department, though money for schemes such as the display of the historic Beverley Gate, of industrial items like steam winding engines, of cannon and anchors, and even of outdoor sculpture, has come not from museum budgets, but from those of the planners. In this very real sense the overlap of interests by planners and curators in the environment can be of great value to museum services.

On the other side of the coin are the disadvantages brought about by not maintaining close relations with local planners. In a recent (1986) case in the Yorkshire and Humberside region, for example, curators and planners squared up to each other in a disagreement over alterations to a Grade 1 listed building run as a museum by a social history department. The argument was settled by the local authority legal section in favour of the planners when several seventeenth-century chimney stacks were demolished to make way for modern replicas. With a closer relationship between planners and curators, a mutually heightened sense of respect for each other's expertise and sensitivity, and a longer history of determination on the part of the museum profession to fight corners, this issue would probably never have become a problem, and the original chimney stacks would still be in place, in a state of good repair. Moreover, while in this case the curators felt they were sufficiently well-informed about historic buildings to force a debate, it remains true that many curators will need to rely quite heavily on planners' expertise and advice in interpreting planning legislation – the more reason for curators to familiarise themselves with that legislation.

Finally, it is worth bearing in mind that planners report to planning committees: they have no power of their own beyond their advisory role. In common with other local authority officers it is influence which they wield, an influence which curators should match, especially where there is no historic buildings officer with special expertise in the local planning department.

Working with Architects

Reviled by many even more than planners, architects have an equally profound effect on the environment, and like planners, therefore, they operate in the same sphere as the social history curator. Architects have no statutory role like that of planners, although their work is governed by legislation, notably planning legislation and building legislation. An architect is not only a designer of grandiose new buildings, but the designer of heating and electricity systems, damp-proof courses, and disabled access arrangements.

Curators will encounter architects in a number of ways throughout their careers. Most immediately, because architects are responsible for building maintenance and repair, rare is the curator with responsibility for a museum premises who has not disagreed with or queried an architect's solution to a problem, or even a routine requirement. This kind of situation is most likely to occur in a historic building, but then so many museums do occupy such buildings.[6] In the case of the Grade 1 listed building chimney stacks cited above, the architect was fully instrumental in bringing about their demise because of lack of sensitivity and experience in dealing with such a structure (so the curators would claim). Once again, closer co-operation, mutual respect, and full discussion at an early stage, might all have led to a more satisfactory conclusion. In truth, it is the architect's job to identify building problems and find solutions, not the curator's, but foolish is the curator who leaves everything to the architect, because architects with good knowledge of historic building requirements are not common. Those with good knowledge of museum requirements in terms, for example, of environmental control, are more uncommon still.

Beyond repairs and maintenance, architects may well be involved in the construction of new displays, particularly those involving refurbishment works. As is the case with a museum designer, an architect must be fully briefed, and liaison between curator and architect must thereafter be continuous, so ideas can develop which draw upon the expertise of both. In terms of redesigning buildings, or even designing and constructing new ones, the need for good briefing and close consultation is just as great. In the end, we have to be knowledgeable and determined.

Notes and References

1. Alan Dobby, *Conservation and Planning*, Hutchinson, 1978.

2. *Guardian*, Wednesday, 4 November 1987.

3. Desmond Heap, *An Outline of Planning Law*, Sweet & Maxwell, 1987, p. vii., 9th ed.

4. A valuable summary of what constitutes development can be found in Heap (see note 3).

5. Printed in The Local Government Library, *Encyclopedia of Planning : Law and Practice*, vol.4, Sweet & Maxwell, pp. 40991-937.

6. See Chapter 27.5, 'Special Prolems: Museums in Historic Buildings'.

Bibliography

Davies, Keith (ed.), *Butterworths Planning Law Handbook*, Butterworth, 1987.

Dobby, Allan, *Conservation and Planning*, Hutchinson, 1978.

Heap, Desmond, *An Outline of Planning Law*, Sweet & Maxwell, 1987, 9th ed.

The Local Government Library, *Encyclopedia of Planning : Law and Practice*, 4 vols, Sweet & Maxwell.

McAuslan, Patrick, *Land, Law and Planning: Cases, Materials and Text*, Weidenfeld & Nicholson, 1975.

Matthews, Geoff, *Museums and Art Galleries: Design and Development Guide*, Butterworth Architecture, 1991.

Parnell, Alan C., *Building Legislation and Historic Buildings*, Architectural Press for the Historic Buildings and Monuments Commission, 1987.

Royal Borough of Kensington and Chelsea, *Urban Conservation and Historic Buildings: A Guide to the Legislation*, Architectural Press, 1984.

Suddards, Roger W., *Listed Buildings: The Law and Practice*, Sweet & Maxwell, 1982.

31.2   Liaison with Others: Local History Libraries

Valerie Bott

Curator, Passmore Edwards Museum Service

Many local historians, both amateur and professional, see 'local history' as something related purely to documentary collections and not to objects at all. Most researchers wishing to discover the history of a place and its people are likely to start at the local history library or archive office rather than the museum. Certain classes of material, however, are likely to be found in museums as well as libraries: ephemera, maps and topographical works of art, photographs and film, oral history tapes and transcripts, and some classes of archives. A knowledgeable librarian or archivist will want to be able to refer researchers to the other relevant collections, including those in museums.

Both the quality of the record our collections provide and our ability to offer a reasonable service to users depend upon some degree of professional co-operation. After all, it makes very good sense to preserve the archives of a local manufacturer, the company's collections of packaging and advertising material, and photos of people at work as well as obsolete tools, samples of raw materials and past products. Indeed, the archival material is sometimes more difficult to interpret without access to the objects in question. But the preservation of such items is irrelevant if we cannot find a way of providing access to both kinds of material – preferably together – because of an accident of history which created separate collections or because of the failure of different professions to work closely together. Most local history library collections are to be found within the public library system, though some are held by old-established antiquarian societies and some form part of university or other specialised libraries. A recent survey of local history collections in university libraries shows that their content and use vary considerably;[1] many are primarily used for studies associated with specific courses in local or regional history. Some have been established within the last thirty years while others are much older; the one at Durham, for example, dates back to the tenth century. Some concentrate only on their immediate locality; others have a wider coverage. For example, at London University's Institute of Historical Research and at Leicester University the collections are drawn from the whole of England, while the Welsh collection at Bangor is especially strong on Anglesey and Caernarfon and also includes material on Welsh communities outside Wales such as that in Patagonia.

Many public library local collections are as old as the institutions of which they form a part, a tribute to the commitment of the early public librarians.[2] These Victorian and Edwardian librarians were conscious that their new services represented burgeoning civic pride and provided the mass of ordinary people with their first access to a rich cultural resource. In this context, providing an understanding of the identity and history of the local community was an essential element. This was achieved by collecting local books (including those by local authors), pamphlets, newspapers, maps and topographical illustrations, often associated with a county collection to put it into a wider context. In many places the core of the local collections consisted of a local antiquarian's collection purchased or bequeathed for the public benefit.

Warrington, Canterbury and Salford had established public libraries under the provisions of the Museums Act of 1845 and local collections began to be made early on. At Warrington, for example, this began in 1848 with the gift of a collection of books from the mayor. Following the Report of the Select Committee on Public Libraries in 1849 and the Public Libraries Act of 1850, a number of large towns and cities established public libraries. Manchester and Liverpool opened theirs in 1852, Cambridge in 1855 and Bristol in 1856; all included special local collections which included contemporary as well as historical items.

Many of these collections were personally supervised by chief librarians and some were even kept within the librarian's office! A few public libraries, like those at Glasgow and Plymouth, had provided separate accommodation for their local collections before the First World War but it was not until the large-scale rebuilding of libraries after the Second World War and the restructuring of library services after local government reorganisation in the 1970s that separate accommodation was provided for many other collections. Even today some local collections are managed as just another part of the reference library.

As early as the 1860s Birmingham's local history library had its own member of staff but this was exceptional. Over the last thirty years or so, interest in local history has blossomed and local history library collections have begun to be treated with more care and respect. Public demand and the reorganisation of local government have resulted in the appointment of specialist staff to manage local history collections. It is still common, however, to find only one properly qualified and experienced local history librarian in quite large library services, while few employ paper conservators or provide environmentally controlled accommodation for their collections. In addition, the status of this specialism within the library profession remains low, with some librarians seeing it as isolated from the mainstream and a barrier to future career development.

Museum curators and archivists have learnt a great deal in the last thirty years about the problem of balancing the need to use special collections of this kind against the need to preserve them. The librarians' approach remains one which is dominated by their perception of collections as a source of information. So in some libraries old photographs, prints and drawings are still being pasted on to cheap acidic paper or slotted into overfull folders, original bindings are replaced with cheap modern ones, sellotape and other self-adhesive films are still used for paper repairs and light levels are not considered important when material is displayed. (Indeed, the recent *Manual of Local Studies Librarianship* only considers conservation and environmental control in detail in the context of archival collections in libraries and suggests that the mounting of illustrations is one of the simple duties which can be undertaken by non-professional – i.e. unqualified – library staff.)

While even non-specialist librarians should be able to retrieve information from local history collections, this should not be at the cost of their long-term preservation. Poor security, non-existent environmental controls, and a casual attitude towards conservation and the handling of collections in libraries are also the cause in some local authorities of curators' unease about sharing the management of collections with librarians. There are still some social history museums which could care for their collections better and we should not damn all local history librarians for the failings of a few, but these differences in the treatment of historic collections serve to emphasise the benefits to be gained from joint working relationships, where knowledge and skills can be shared for mutual benefit.

The technique of interpreting three-dimensional material as historical evidence is little known outside museums except in the context of archaeology (where virtually no original documentary evidence is available) and art history (where the study of the actual works has long been recognised as academically valid). In the library world careful cataloguing and the organisation of collections are generally seen as having a higher priority than interpretation.

While many specialist librarians in this field are immensely knowledgeable about their collections, the district whose history they record and the information which can be drawn from specific kinds of material, they are less likely than curators to see the material in their care with an interpreter's eye. A librarian may, for example, discard multiple copies of an ephemeral handbill which the curator would preserve because of the potential the group might offer in a future display; and in the library ephemera is often pasted into scrap books for convenience of filing and retrieval but thus becomes virtually undisplayable as anything other than a collector's specimen. Again, it is important that fellow professionals compare notes about their preferred practices because valuable opportunities may be lost through a simple lack of understanding.

Many of the local museums and galleries which were established as part of the same burst of civic pride which produced libraries were administered by and housed with library services. Neglected and ill-cared-for collections of objects can still be found in store in some libraries, their documentation lost or non-existent, their contents depleted. My own research into lost local history collections in Greater London[3] revealed considerable contempt for such collections on the part of some of the Borough Librarians I interviewed in the late 1970s. Pressure from local societies and constructive advice from area museum councils has eventually embarrassed local politicians into creating new local museums.

Surprisingly few local authorities manage their historical collections within one service, yet where both are funded and managed by the same local authority there is a strong case for the establishment of a formal relationship which recognises their common purpose. Leicestershire's County Museum Service embraces the county record office though not the local history library collections. Wiltshire's Library and Museum Service has a local studies officer in charge of local history library collections who is responsible to the museums officer rather than directly to a chief librarian.

The idea of a 'local history centre', housing related two- and three-dimensional collections, attracted interest in the early 1970s and an article on this subject written by a curator appeared in a library periodical in 1975.[4] Oldham's local history library and museum collections had been successfully combined in 1972 into a 'local interest centre' which provided information about the town, past and present. And in the same year, the London Borough of Bexley, created in 1965, brought together the museum collections from two of its constituent authorities, with local history library collections from two former boroughs and one and a half urban district councils, at Hall Place, Bexley.

This pattern of combined collections is probably more common in the London boroughs than anywhere else. Some have been managed in this way for decades while in other boroughs the amalgamation of collections is a comparatively recent practice. Vestry House Museum in Walthamstow, established in 1930, is a good example of an old-established combined collection. It received early recognition as an official archive repository as well as a museum, though the first full-time staff were not appointed until the 1950s.

At the amalgamation of Walthamstow with Chingford and Leyton in 1965, creating the new borough of Waltham Forest, no provision was made for expanding the service to cover these areas. However, changes in staffing in the mid-1970s and a restructuring of the Libraries and Arts Department resulted in the creation of a local history service which embraces library, museum and archive collections. The former Leyton library collections and those of the Chingford Historical Society now form part of the same service.

Similar collections had been combined for many years in the London Boroughs of Haringey, Enfield and Barking, though the object collections were in the care of librarians and were not actively developed until the appointment of professional curatorial staff in comparatively recent years.

The creation of a new museum for the London Borough of Brent in 1975 provided another opportunity for linking existing collections. In this case existing archive and local history library collections were removed from the reference library and housed in the same building as an antiquarian collection assembled by George Titus Barham and a new collection of local objects to form the Grange Museum of Local History. For the first time the posts of Local History Librarian and Museum Keeper came into being and within a few years the presence of a very accessible local history collection, available to virtually every museum visitor, created a public demand which could barely be met. Donations of objects and documentary material poured in and the eighteenth century building has twice been extended.

Informal links and joint projects can reduce the problems of separate ownership and administration but they are no substitute for the kind of structural link which ensures that related collections are managed and used as a coherent entity. Many social history curators work very closely with specialist librarians and archivists although they are employed by separate departments within one local authority or by completely separate governing bodies. This may take the form of teams from different institutions working on specific projects such as an exhibition, or a longer-term working party managing a joint publications programme.[5]

All three professions recognise the need for co-operation where their collecting practices overlap geographically or in subject matter. In some cases detailed agreements have been drawn up to clarify responsibility for various kinds of collections. Co-operation in defining collecting policies where two institutions are working in the same geographical or subject area is crucial if museum and library are to have a reasonable working relationship. A joint working party of the Museums Association, the Society of Archivists and the Library Association published a Statement of Policy relating to archives in 1981 which outlines the potential areas of overlap and conflict, and suggests local agreements which are relevant to library as well as archive collections.[6]

In a few cases, however, personality clashes and professional jealousy are still doing unnecessary damage to the comprehensive recording of the history of a locality. Here, it seems, there is no alternative to laying down a formal relationship which can reduce the damage so easily done in such circumstances. Sometimes such problems can be explained by past history and sometimes they arise from the very circumstances of having to depend on the goodwill of a specific member of staff without any political or other support, but these factors are irrelevant to frustrated potential users of collections which are inaccessible or incomplete as a result.

It is relatively simple to describe the benefits to be had from a close relationship between museum and local history library staff, both for the related collections and for their users. It is more difficult to quantify any financial or other benefits to be gained by the governing bodies of such collections. It is possible that there are minor economies of scale to be had where collections are combined though it would be dangerous to think that linked collections need fewer resources for their care and exploitation than they would if kept separate.

The combination of collections in this way may have an unexpected benefit; a small team of staff working on local collections will provide higher status for the team leaders and have a clearer identity than single, isolated staff working in large separate departments. This can serve to raise the profile of the collections within the local authority hierarchy and may lead to increased funding and influence in the longer term.

Notes and References

1. Michael Dewe (ed.), *A Manual of Local Studies Librarianship,* Gower, Aldershot, vol. I, 1987, vol. II, 1991. Chapter 4 gives the text of the survey questionnaire and an analysis of the returns.

2. *A Manual of Local Studies Librarianship* (see note 1) contains useful background information on the history and origins of local history collections. See T. Kelly, *A History of Public Libraries in Great Britain 1845-1975,* Library Association, 1977, for a more general history of the library service.

3. Valerie Bott, *Local Collections in Greater London,* unpublished dissertation, 1980, for the MA in Museum Studies, University of Leicester.

4. Philip C. Cruttenden, 'Local history resources centres', *Library Association Record,* vol. 77, no. 8, August 1975, p. 179.

5. Stuart Davies,'Change in the inner city', *Journal of the Social History Curators Group,* vol. 11, 1983.

6. 'Statement of Policy Relating to Archives', Museums Association/Society of Archivists/Library Association, *Museums Journal,* vol. 81, no. 3, December 1981, p. 165-6. See also *Code of Practice on Archives for Museums in the United Kingdom,* Museums and Galleries Commission, 1990.

31.3   Liaison with Others: Record Offices

Kate Thompson

County Archivist, Hertfordshire County Council

The Structure, Organisation and Work of Local Record Offices

There are over 1,000 record offices listed in the second edition of *British Archives*.[1] These include many repositories established solely to serve their parent organisation and which do not offer a public service in the usual sense of the term. Liaison with museums will normally be confined to publicly funded record offices, although examples of other joint ventures may exist. The structure of publicly funded record offices is a complicated one and includes the major national repositories, local authority record offices, and university archives/manuscripts departments. Details on all publicly funded record offices can be found in 'the red book' – *Record Repositories in Great Britain,* published by the Royal Commission on Historical Manuscripts.[2]

The size and resources of County Record Offices (CROs) is very variable and this situation is even more marked in other repositories. For example, at the end of March 1990 Suffolk Record Office had 40 members of staff in its three branches, compared with one in Powys. There are historical and other reasons for this enormous range but little logic in the situation. Like museums, a record office is often a 'Cinderella' service and the amount of money spent on it can be a reflection of the importance it is seen as having to the County Council.[3]

Traditionally record offices were part of the administrative service of the local authority and many CROs still come under the County Secretary/Solicitor. However, in recent years some have been transferred to a 'leisure' department, with Leicestershire being the only CRO in a museums department. Most archivists still see the service they provide to the local authority as being extremely important.

The most recent area of debate for many record offices has been security. While the problem of thefts has always been uppermost in museum curators' minds, it has been comparatively minor in record offices until recently. However, a series of thefts over the last few years has meant that archivists have carefully examined their security procedures and in many cases tightened them. Several record offices now require reader's tickets and about 20 CROs are part of the County Archive Research Network by which one ticket is valid for all participating offices.

The work of a local record office can be divided into a number of tasks: preservation, conservation and 'exploitation'. The first duty of a record office is the preservation of archive material relating to its sphere of collection (normally its local authority area): this involves collecting the records, cleaning and fumigating them if necessary, and listing them.

Not every record office has a conservation section but most CROs do. Others, however, may have a joint arrangement with a neighbouring office or contract out the work. Archive conservation has many similarities to fine art conservation although there are certain specialised skills which can only be learnt by practice. Increasingly, archive conservation is becoming more scientific and the old 'craftsman' skills are not so important as they were.

There is clearly little point in keeping archives if they are never likely to be consulted, and one of the most difficult decisions to make is whether or not to destroy material. Research requirements change over the years and yesterday's non-subject can become today's popular topic. A more frequent problem is that many owners of archives do not appreciate their value and destroy them, either deliberately or through neglect. In addition, some types of document are becoming collectable, and record offices with a small or non-existent purse may have to compete with wealthy individuals or overseas institutions when material comes on the market. Export restrictions still do not prevent archives from leaving the country. All these problems are familiar to museum curators, especially in the arts field.

The most important element of 'exploitation' is the public searchroom. Particularly since the onset of the family history boom, public use of record offices has grown enormously but the space available is frequently inadequate. Though an average 10,000 readers a year in a medium-sized CRO may seem very small, these visitors are not 'static': documents have to be produced for them and returned afterwards, and their myriad questions need to be answered. Each reader may take an average 15-20 minutes of staff time. For this reason, as well as for the better preservation of the archives, record offices are increasingly turning to the use of microforms, often on a self-service basis. This also provides an opportunity to make copies available outside the record office.

Archivists are becoming increasingly aware of the need to become more publicity conscious and many are taking active steps to promote the service they offer. Requests for talks and exhibitions are increasing[4] and most CROs see them as a good opportunity for 'spreading the message' even though they are often time-consuming. If the office is able to provide an educational service, opportunities exist to create an awareness of and interest in the value of archives to a younger 'clientele', and the introduction of the National Curriculum has increased the emphasis on the use of original archive material, primarily in the study of history, but for other subjects too.

Each record office is different from the rest in its resources and the use of those resources; similarly, the way in which archives are accessioned and listed varies to quite a large extent. To some this lack of uniformity is frustrating but others see it as part of the charm of using record offices!

Record Offices and Social History Museums

To an outsider the contents of a record office and of a social history museum are very much the same, and researchers may be confused by what material is stored where. Theoretically there should be no overlap between the two but in practice this is rarely the case; even when the record office is part of the museum service it does not apply! The most important distinction lies in the way the material is accessioned, listed and stored: museum artefacts are usually dealt with thematically but the archivist is much more aware of the need to preserve the archive group or 'fond'. Each item in an archive has a relationship with the others and it is essential that the integrity of the whole is not broken, thereby destroying important incidental information. Any thematic listing should be done by indexes or selective lists; this does mean, however, that record office lists can seem daunting and difficult to use. The kind of list usually produced is a 'schedule' which should provide sufficient information to enable searchers to know whether or not they need to look at the document.

Archivists (the author included!) are very bad at using the correct terms – archives and records are different but are generally used interchangeably. The definition of these terms has been discussed at length; in 1919 Charles Johnson wrote: 'Archives consist of one or more groups of documents no longer in current use, each group of which has accrued in the custody of an individual or a department in the ordinary course of business, and forms an organic whole, reflecting the organisation and history of the office which produced it.'[5] Since then other authors have attempted more precise definitions[6] but the basic philosophy is unaltered. The salient point is that archives are formed naturally and not artificially, and this distinguishes a record office from a library or museum.

It is therefore quite easy to identify archives *per se:* the difficulty lies in the 'grey areas' which are not strictly speaking archives but which archivists are anxious to have in their offices because they may be the sole surviving example and merit archival 'treatment'. They include a wide range of printed material such as posters, broadsheets, photographs, and ephemera. It may be possible to draw up guidelines laying down precisely who collects what but this does depend on mutual trust and goodwill, and the situation may change with the personnel. The only clear rule is that where this material forms part of an archive it should remain with it, although there is no reason why copies cannot be provided for another institution. Similarly it is an archive principle that 'out-county' material is rarely divorced from an archive and transferred but that its existence is notified to any offices which may be interested. In the end the important consideration is that material falling into this area is stored and listed correctly and its existence notified to any interested body – its precise location is a matter for mutual agreement. There is a growing trend for information about archives and documents to be more widely disseminated; the National Inventory of Documentary Sources (NIDS), for example, is an attempt by a commercial microfilming publisher to film record office schedules and produce sets of microfiche for general sale, and this initiative has already proved useful.

Record Offices and the Museum Curator

There have been moves to bring together the 'information professions' and local examples of joint projects are increasing. The most obvious ways in which this can be achieved are exhibitions and publications. Some of the best exhibitions are those which combine the aesthetic and evidential qualities of the museum object with the background information available from the archives. Although archives have been exhibited[7] they are not generally very suitable. Few documents have a great deal of visual appeal and, more importantly, they will deteriorate if exposed to ultra-violet light for any length of time; for this reason therefore UV filters are essential. Also, unless the item is a single sheet, there is the question of only being able to display a minute proportion of the total piece. Good quality reproductions are just as acceptable to all but the purist and can be used in many more ways than the original for maximum effect. Exhibitions of this sort can harness the skills of both archivist and social history curator.

Joint publications are another way in which the two professions can usefully collaborate. A book on domestic utensils could include extracts from a diary describing the first vacuum cleaner to be introduced to a house, an account book listing the purchase of such items or a probate inventory detailing the contents of a house. The use of oral evidence is yet another dimension which can add to the overall presentation of information. There may be other ways in which archivist and museum curator can usefully collaborate and in most cases the record office will benefit from the higher public perception enjoyed by most museums.

There are two caveats: it takes time to become familiar with record office routines, finding aids and so on, and research always takes longer than one imagines. In addition, few archivists have the time to do more than indicate the sort of material that may be useful. Both archivists and museum curators are used to the request for 'everything you've got on ...', but in the case of record offices it may literally be thousands of items. The best advice is to get to know the archivist in charge and discuss how the two institutions can help one another. In the thorny field of collecting policies most archivists will react violently to any attempt to 'poach' archive material but will be happy to come to an arrangement over the 'grey areas'. The old 'ivory tower' image of record offices is now luckily a thing of the past, nevertheless there are certain archive principles that are still sacrosanct. If you learn the rules and ask first you should have no problems!

Notes

1. Janet Foster and Julia Sheppard, *British Archives*, Macmillan, 1989.

2. *Record Repositories in Great Britain*, HMSO, 1991, 9th ed.

3. The annual *Archive Services Statistics* published by CIPFA (the Chartered Institute of Public Finance and Accountancy) provides some interesting statistics on the resourcing and use made of the archive services.

4. *Archive Services Statistics*, CIPFA.

5. Charles Johnson, *The Care of Documents and Management of Archives*, SPCK, 1919, pp. 8-9.

6. See, for example, Michael Cook, *The Management of Information from Archives*, Gower, 1986, pp. 4-8, 17-18, 20.

7. For example, 'The Common Chronicle' held at the Victoria and Albert Museum in 1983 and at Leicester in 1987.

31.4   Liaison with Others: Archaeological Units

Judi Caton

Assistant Keeper of Antiquities, Oxfordshire Museums

The Origins and Diversity of Archaeological Units

Archaeological units were set up in a rush all over England in the mid-1970s. The great increase in urban and rural development at that time threatened more sites of archaeological importance than the old-style archaeological committees, university groups and local societies could easily deal with. The increased demands of rescue required a formal body to co-ordinate the archaeological process, from the monitoring of planning applications, through excavation to publication. It was in response to this new situation that archaeological units were born, and in Britain there are now some 63 such bodies in operation.[1]

The term 'unit' was first coined by Martin Biddle for his excavation team at Winchester in the 1960s, and the Winchester Excavation Unit became a prototype for units all over England. But units were by no means established in a uniform manner. Some 20 of the 63 currently operating are in museums, 11 in universities, 18 in local authority departments, mainly county planning departments, and the rest are independent trusts. The diversity of units' governing bodies forms a picture all too familiar to social history museum curators.

This diversity extends into their fields of operation. The Trust for Wessex Archaeology, for example, covers Berkshire, Dorset, Hampshire, Wiltshire and the Isle of Wight. The Kent Archaeological Rescue Service operates in one county while the Chelmsford Archaeological Trust works in one town. Yet other units, such as the Trent and Peak Archaeological Trust, are not confined to areas related to local government divisions, while English Heritage's Central Unit may undertake survey or excavation anywhere in England. The archaeological coverage of Britain is therefore haphazard and uneven.

A clear illustration of this unevenness can be seen in the contrast between two counties, Hampshire and Cambridgeshire. Hampshire falls within the sphere of the Trust for Wessex Archaeology, but there are other units working in the area, in the Test Valley, Southampton, Winchester and in Portsmouth. At the opposite end of the scale, Cambridgeshire has no true field archaeology units at all. Curators will once again be struck by the similarity of field archaeology and museum provision in these contrasting counties. Archaeological units are no more capable than museums of forming a state service with national coverage.

To make matters even more difficult, this already complicated situation is today very much in the melting pot. Archaeological units are evaluating their position and reconsidering their aims, strategies, and function. This new situation has resulted from changes in funding over the last few years. There are now new government strategies in funding archaeology, for the emphasis has shifted from excavation to preservation as a method of rescuing archaeological sites, and English Heritage's Historic Buildings and Monuments Commission (HBMC) has largely withdrawn funds for new excavation projects. Consequently, all new excavation work must be developer and/or local authority funded. Given the financial situation of local authorities, units must now attract money from the private sector or face winding up their activities in rescue archaeology. Today the old fields of operation, the county or the town, while they may still be respected, are no longer seen as essential. Units now see themselves as entitled to tender for work, which increasingly means consultancy work as well as excavation. Contract archaeology is now firmly part of a unit's world, and some have already been involved in competitive tendering with other units. I shall return to these issues later, and discuss how social history curators might be involved with the unit of the future. I shall now turn to units' aims, what they currently do, and how these relate to the work of social history curators.

The Aims and Functions of Archaeological Units

A synthesis of Units' perceived aims and roles might appear as follows.[2]

Aims

To co-ordinate and normally execute archaeological activity in a given area

To promote public awareness of archaeology

To prepare and carry out research plans

To create archaeological archives for the future of archaeological research and for the public benefit

Roles

Planning and liaison with Sites and Monuments Records

Surveys of archaeologically sensitive areas

Assessing threats to archaeological sites

Defining priorities

Excavation (from major set-piece to salvage)

Creating an archive of site data

Performing consultancy work

Publishing reports

Raising funds

The unit field officer, then, is simply engaged in a different part of the same business as the curator of a social history collection: that of interrogating, preserving and interpreting the past for the benefit of research and of the public. The field officer collects objects in a different way, but like the social history curator, seeks to conserve heritage as a resource for study, enjoyment and dissemination.

Liaison Between Curators and Units

Curators, of course, often care for archaeological as well as social history collections. In this case they need close links with units, and all other relevant archaeological bodies, if they are distinct and separate. County archaeologists, museums, Sites and Monuments Records, HBMC, universities and local societies, all play their part in the archaeological process from the formation of the research plan to the use of the excavation archive in the museum. As the Dimbleby Report stated, 'It must be recognised that the creation, housing and use of an archive is a single continuous process.'[3] But the particular needs of these curators will not be considered here. I shall concentrate rather on the benefit of liaison with units for social history curators who neither receive excavation archives, nor curate archaeological material.

There are four major areas of benefit which can result from liaison between curators and units: an exchange of knowledge about the history of the area; an exchange of knowledge about collections; the pooling of expertise and resources in shared activities; and the formation of a lobby of people with common aims.

Unit staff come to know a great deal about the history of the geographic area in which they work. The preparation of each excavation report requires patient searches of local histories and documents to build a detailed history of the site concerned, enabling archaeologists to place their structures and finds in context. Staff mobility, or rather the lack of it, also plays a part in this process. After the initial flurry of jobs in the setting up of units, promotion and the creation of new jobs has been slow or non-existent. One consequence has been that individuals have built up a very detailed historic picture of their areas. Today, unit staff not only have great expertise in the consultation of local resource material but also produce reports and excavation archives which themselves form a body of resource material for local history studies.

Since there is often a considerable delay between excavation and publication and the preparation of usable archives, close liaison with units allows curators to keep well up to date with new developments in local history. Since, too, curators are experts in the matter of local studies, their knowledge and advice is often of great value to unit field officers in the preparation of reports and consideration of evidence. Both social history curators and unit field officers generate historical research and data and it is to their mutual benefit to communicate.

In exactly the same way curators and archaeologists can inform each other about collections. The curator will often find it extremely helpful to be able to consult the unit about objects brought to the museum for identification. These may be objects that fall outside the sphere of social history collections, perhaps shards of Beaker pottery or a fragment of a Neolithic polished stone axe. Equally they may be objects which fall within the normal sphere of social history but which overlap with post-medieval archaeology. Most archaeological units have developed type series of local artefacts such as pottery and clay pipes. These reference collections, and the specialist staff who have developed them, are often vital in making proper identifications, whether the objects concerned have been excavated or not. The curator in turn can enhance the reference collection by regularly adding information about new examples which are brought to the museum.

In the interpretation and explanation of artefacts, too, curators and unit staff have much to offer each other. The field officer or finds specialist is more likely to consider objects contextually, chronologically, and typologically. In the field of pottery studies, for example, archaeological techniques may include fabric analyses, the study of stratigraphic relationships and geographic distributions. The curator, from a slightly different standpoint, is more likely to consider the objects in their social historical context. Probably the curator will regard pottery in terms of its function, the social classes who made, bought, sold and used it, and its value as a domestic or art object.

This difference in approach should not be overemphasised. Many archaeological pottery specialists employ the considerations of social history at least in their synthetic works. The point is that there is a difference in emphasis, and the curator and unit can benefit from discussion.

The interpretation of the historic environment forms the third area where both parties should benefit from working closely together. Unit staff, like curators, give lectures to WEA and extra-mural groups, put up exhibitions, hold open days, conduct guided walks, publish leaflets and perform many other activities to bring archaeology to the public. The promotion of public awareness of the past is an important part of the work of both groups, and each can support the other.

If the units' recent work is displayed in the form of regular temporary exhibitions at the local museum, then they will benefit from the provision of the venue, equipment and display expertise provided by the curator. The curator in turn benefits from the origination and research for the exhibition carried out by the unit. Most of all the public can enjoy the results.

This sort of collaboration can be carried through to the setting up of lecture series or the running of historical or archaeological clubs. Pooling the resources and skills of a number of people in the time-consuming business of promoting the past has its obvious rewards. Perhaps even more important than sharing these activities, however, is the forming of a lobby for the past. A social history curator may be quite an isolated person at work. The post often involves running a museum in a town or rural area where there are no curatorial colleagues. One of the links which goes a long way towards avoiding a feeling of isolation is that with the archaeological unit which covers the area. Unit staff often have designated posts, not just for a particular period, but also for a particular area, and are pleased to collaborate with curators of local museums, which either stand alone as in the previous example, or perhaps where a county museums service has branch museums.

Isolation is an important consideration for many curators, but such collaboration can be actively effective. Unit staff and social history curators can form joint policies for tackling both problem areas and research projects. A jointly conceived policy for metal detecting will be far more effective than going it alone, as indeed will joint representations about planning matters, and jointly produced research strategies. When a curator and unit understand each other they can put their heads together to form strategies for the promotion of the past. Finding opportunities for being in each other's establishments is a preliminary way of generating the sort of exchanges under discussion.

New Developments

Today these exchanges are not only advantageous as we have seen, but in many places are common practice. Contract archaeology and the consequent widening of units' boundaries do threaten to change all this for the units and curators of the future. Units will have to build relationships with more curators, and curators will be faced with having to make links with more units, and with the new archaeological consultancy firms. The Institute of Field Archaeologists (IFA) conference at Birmingham University (1988) investigated these new developments.[4] Several points of interest to curators arose from the papers and discussion. Firstly, there are new terms used to name those involved in the archaeological process. The 'client' is the developer who pays for the archaeology, the 'contractor' carries it out and the 'curator' is the county archaeologist or Inspector of Ancient Monuments or unit who exercises general supervision over the care of the past. Many units are in fact both 'curators' and 'contractors'.

Secondly, the meeting distinguished between contract archaeology, which was found to be acceptable, and competitive tendering which was not. The meeting came to the conclusion that the IFA should set up a committee to monitor the contractors who carry out archaeological work.

The findings of this conference are given here both as the most up-to-date information (at the time of writing) about the work of units, and to alert social history curators to the potential problem of fly-by-night consultancies. The first step in the formation of links with the archaeological unit of the future may be to contact the IFA for its credentials. For the moment, though, there has never been a more important time for curators to liaise with units. The liaison process could create a crucially needed forum for discussing how the units themselves might best develop to face their uncertain future and maintain their high standard of archaeological work.

Notes and References

1. The Association of County Archaeological Officers (ACAO) produces a mailing list of members. Contact Ken Smith, County Planning Department, County Offices, Matlock, Derbyshire. The Standing Committee of Archaeological Unit Managers (SCAUM) also produces a mailing list of members. Contact Ms J. Wills, County Planning Department, Gloucestershire County Council, Shire Hall, Gloucester, GLl 2TN. The Historic Buildings and Monuments Commission produces a list of County Sites and Monuments Records and a mailing list for rescue archaeology: Fortress House, 23 Savile Row, London WlX 2HF.

2. T.G. Hassall, 'Museums and field archaeology: the view of an "independent" unit director', *Museum Archaeologist,* no. 2, January 1979; and J. Hinchcliffe, *Preservation by Record: The Work of the Central Excavation Unit 1975-85,* English Heritage, 1985.

3. R. Dimbleby, *The Scientific Treatment of Material from Rescue Excavations,* Department of the Environment, 1978.

4. 'Professional and Public Archaeology – Contract Archaeology Session', *Archaeology in Britain 88,* the Second Annual Conference of the Institute of Field Archaeologists, University of Birmingham, 18-20 April 1988.

Bibliography

Contract Archaeology Study Group and British Archaeologists and Developers Liaison Group, 'Code of Practice', *The Field Archaeologist,* no.8, February 1988.

Davies, D. Gareth, 'Museums and archaeology – a lost cause?', *Museums Journal,* vol. 78, no. 3, 1978.

English Heritage, *The Work of the Central Excavation Unit 1986-7,* English Heritage, 1987.

The Institute of Field Archaeologists (By-laws), *Code of Conduct,* adopted June 1985.

The Institute of Field Archaeologists (By-laws), *Disciplinary Regulations,* adopted July 1986.

The Institute of Field Archaeologists (By-laws), *Area and Special Interest Groups,* adopted July 1986.

Selkirk, A., 'Competitive tendering', *Current Archaeology,* vol. 110, July 1988.

Society of Museum Archaeologists, 'Dust to dust', *Field Archaeology and Museums Conference Proceedings,* vol. 11, 1986.

Useful Addresses

Standing Committee of Archaeological Unit Managers (SCAUM)

Ms J. Wills
County Planning Department
Gloucestershire County Council
Shire Hall
Gloucester GL1 2TN
Tel. 0452 425683

Association of County Archaeological Officers (ACAO)

Ken Smith
County Planning Department
County Offices
Matlock
Derbyshire
Tel. 0629 814321

Institute of Field Archaeologists (IFA)

The Assistant Secretary
Minerals Engineering Building
University of Birmingham
PO Box 363
Birmingham B15 2TT
Tel. 021 471 2788

IFA also have 7 area groups either in existence or in the process of being set up. Contact Birmingham for details.

Historic Buildings and Monuments Commission

Fortress House
23 Savile Row
London W1X 2HE
Tel. 071 734 6010

Society of Museum Archaeologists

The Secretary
Dr S. Greep
Verulamium Museum
St Michael's
St Albans
Herts AL3 45W
Tel. 0727 54659

31.5 Liaison with Others: Government Agencies and Sites and Monuments Records

Mark Taylor

County Archaeologist for West Sussex County Council

The Background to English Heritage and the Royal Commission

At a national level, there are principally two bodies responsible for the historic environment, English Heritage and the Royal Commission on Historical Monuments (RCHM). English Heritage, the shorter title for the Historic Buildings and Monuments Commission, was set up in 1984 under the National Heritage Act as a quango to advise the government on all heritage issues. Formerly a directorate in the Department of the Environment, it can trace its ancestry back to the Ministry of Works and the Commissioners of HM Works set up under the first Ancient Monuments Protection Act of 1882. The three Royal Commissions on Ancient and Historical Monuments were initiated in 1908, with the appointment of Commissioners for Scotland by Letters Patent followed not long after with Commissions for England and Wales. The Scottish Commissioners were appointed to 'make an Inventory of the Ancient and Historical Monuments and Constructions connected with or illustrative of the contemporary culture, civilisation and conditions of life of the people in Scotland from the earliest times to 1707, and to specify those which seem most worthy of preservation'. These terms of reference were adopted for England and Wales, but again with a cut-off point at the beginning of the eighteenth century which would be unthinkable today. The production of detailed lists of archaeological sites and historic buildings through survey and recording, a key role of the three Commissions, now includes many important twentieth-century buildings.

The importance of indexing and compiling inventories was highlighted in 1905 by Professor G. Baldwin Brown in *The Care of Ancient Monuments*. By drawing attention to the advances being made in Europe at that time compared with the rather tentative moves in Britain, and stressing that 'inventorization' as practised abroad was a necessary preliminary to any scheme of preservation and care, Baldwin Brown influenced the form which the Royal Commissions later took.

After the First World War, another major step forward was taken when O.G.S. Crawford was appointed as the Ordnance Survey Archaeological Officer. Crawford, in conjunction later with C.W. Phillips, gathered information to identify archaeological sites on Ordnance Survey maps and continued and extended the process of establishing proper records. Archaeological correspondents, often ministers and schoolmasters, were recruited in each county, and were invited to add information on archaeological sites which the Ordnance Survey might be unaware of. From these beginnings, the Ordnance Survey's records were to form the foundation for the National Monuments Record and County Sites and Monuments Records.

In some cases, the Ordnance Survey correspondents were museum staff who recognised the virtue of keeping their own local register of archaeological sites as well as finds brought in for identification. At the City and County Museum in

Lincoln, for example, Arthur Smith and F.T. Baker instituted a card index before the Second World War which anticipated the concept of a locally based Sites and Monuments Record (SMR). As yet, the process of 'inventorization' had simply resulted in an ever-growing mass of information, but the distinguishing characteristic of SMRs is their capacity to analyse and retrieve archaeological information, not merely to acquire it (Burrow, 1985, p. 10). A landmark in the development of SMRs arrived when Don Benson, the first keeper of the field section of the Oxfordshire City and County Museum at Woodstock, established a formula for recording archaeological information which gave each site, structure, find or historic building a unique reference number. The 'Primary Record Number' system looked forward to the technological benefits of computerisation and set a standard which was widely copied by SMRs elsewhere in creating machine retrievable databases of archaeological information. The development of locally based SMRs in the 1970s and 1980s has resulted in a resource which can offer information in greater depth than that available to the National Monuments Record, but depending upon the parent organisation which houses the SMR, and the level of staffing, provision for public access may be less well catered for.

Organisation of the National Monuments Record

The National Monuments Record is organised into three sections: the National Buildings Record (NBR), the National Archaeological Record (NAR), and the National Library of Air Photographs (NLAP). The NAR and NBR can be consulted at Fortress House, Savile Row, without prior appointment during weekday office hours after 10 a.m. The Southampton section of the NAR and the NLAP based in Swindon can be consulted during weekday office hours by prior appointment. Details of opening hours and facilities may be obtained from RCHM(E), Fortress House, 23 Savile Row, London W1X 2JQ. Collectively, the range of material held by the RCHM covers records of archaeological sites; photographs of archaeological interest from the 1860s onwards; the National Excavations Index and archives; the archives of the former Ordnance Survey Archaeology Division; and reports, drawings and photographs compiled by the Royal Commission and other field workers. The National Library of Air Photographs contains over 600,000 oblique photos from the early twentieth century to the present, and three and a half million vertical air photos dating from the beginning of the Second World War to recent years. Another national archive with extensive air photographic material is the Cambridge University Collection based at the University of Cambridge Department of Aerial Photography, The Mond Building, Free School Lane, Cambridge, CB2 3RF.

English Heritage: The Organisation

English Heritage was set up under the National Heritage Act with responsibility for safeguarding and conserving the historic environment, but it is also responsible for looking after and presenting many of the monuments in care. The two main operational groups consist of the Conservation group and the Properties in Care group. The former deals with protection of the historic environment; advice and assistance, including grant aid to owners; advice to government; research programmes; and publication and maintenance of records. The latter maintains monuments open to the public which are in English Heritage's direct care. Presentation and education are an important element of this work reflecting a growing concern in recent years for high quality interpretation. The English

Heritage Education Service offers a range of facilities which reflect the recommendations of the National Curriculum History Working Group in providing for field visits, a 'hands-on' approach to objects and artefacts, and opportunities for role-play to bring social history to life. The English Heritage Education Service offers free publications: *Information for Teachers* – a booklet listing all the English Heritage sites, and *Remnants* – the journal of the education service which offers practical help for teachers in applying archive resources and site visits directly to the requirements of the National Curriculum. The education service also offers a list of publications aimed specifically at teachers, teaching packs and handbooks for sites together with videos and computer software. Further details are available from English Heritage Education Service, Keysign House, 429 Oxford Street, London WlR 2HD.

County Sites and Monuments Records – Functions and Facilities

At the local level, Sites and Monuments Records can offer an impressive range of resources and may provide more detail on local sites than the index of information held by the NAR. However, public access will in all cases need to be arranged by prior appointment within weekday office hours and the availability of such facilities as a search room will depend largely on which department of the local authority houses the SMR. For example, the majority of SMRs are located in County Planning Departments, with Leisure Services which have incorporated museum service departments the second most common location. A few others are found in other local authority departments, education departments and universities. This reflects the fact that the function of a SMR can be defined under three main headings (Fraser, 1984; Hedges, 1975; ACAO, 1990):

1. *Planning and development control.* The SMR provides the database against which planning applications and land management enquiries can be assessed for archaeological constraints. This accounts for about 70% of demands made upon the SMR.

2. *Internal archaeological research.* The SMR can be the starting point for determining priorities for future fieldwork and site visits by local authority archaeological officers, for publishing the results of previous fieldwork, producing exhibition material (especially for museum-based SMRs), or on-site interpretation.

3. *External archaeological research* – by members of the public, academic and non-academic, covering a wide range of educational and leisure interests.

The Range of Resources Available to Local SMRs

At its best a local authority SMR and the parent organisation which houses it can offer a range of data comprising a computerised database with full description of site backed up by detailed record files, record maps, air photographs and a range of plans and drawings amongst other facilities. Some authorities even offer computerised mapping which could produce a made-to-measure distribution map of specific types of site. However, where the SMR is still in the process of computerisation, the paper record and card index may still be needed for retrieval on a county-wide basis. SMRs will normally have a range of air photographic material to hand; in a planning department this may be a resource shared by other sections, but it may be easier for members of the public to obtain copies of photographs where the department holds copyright (as with the national air photo collections). Other facilities normally available include large-scale maps, geological maps, and access to the Department of the Environment Listed Building records, although computerised Historic Buildings lists are the exception rather than the rule at the moment.

Content of SMRs and Continuing Development

The breadth, depth and content of the SMR may vary from one institution to another. Broadly speaking, a recent paper on Sites and Monuments Records (ACAO, 1990) indicates that 'standing structures' make up the largest single record type (half of which are listed buildings), while findspots of artefacts etc. form the second largest category. However, the survey also suggested that in some cases, categories of information such as urban sub-surface deposits and industrial archaeological sites were significantly under represented or, in isolated cases, deliberately excluded. It must be stressed that SMRs (including the national record collections) are only a reflection of the present state of knowledge and past research preferences. As more material is gathered and further research undertaken, the pattern may change, and on occasion previous views about the nature of an archaeological site may be overturned. Therefore, although every effort is made to ensure that data entered on to an SMR is accurate and verified, it is not necessarily definitive and new information may turn up at any time in the course of development or archaeological fieldwork. In terms of the history of archaeological activity in this country as a whole, SMRs and computerised databases are still in their infancy relatively speaking, and content and sophistication will undoubtedly develop into the next century.

The Future Role of the RCHM Regarding SMRs

In the 1980s, SMRs were largely indebted to English Heritage for financial and technical support in transferring data on to computer. Latterly, in 1989, when Mrs Virginia Bottomley was then Under Secretary of State for the Environment, the decision was taken that the RCHM should take on a 'lead role' for SMRs whereby County Sites and Monuments Records would interface with the National Monuments Record as the 'National Archaeological and Architectural database for England' (DoE, 1990). It was confirmed that the Royal Commission should continue in existence as the independent body of survey and record while taking on a co-ordinating role in managing archaeological information. The Royal Commission intends that the NAR should serve as an index to information held at county level and should not duplicate the entire contents of local SMRs. In several instances data exchange has already taken place in which the NAR now hold an index of sites or updated information previously unavailable to the national record.

This approach may influence the extent to which social history curators and teachers directly approach their local SMR. As noted above, the majority of SMRs are housed within planning departments, often in offices which have no specific provision for search room facilities and where staff whose primary duties relate to planning and development control have to divert from these tasks to answer enquiries from members of the public. SMRs housed in other locations such as Leisure Services departments or universities will, by their nature, be better equipped to deal with enquiries and may have search room facilities on hand. Moreover, the task of answering enquiries may be accorded a much higher priority and greater staff time allocated.

How to use the SMR or the NAR

In all cases, it will help the SMR or the NAR staff if social history curators or teachers can be as specific as possible about the purpose of their enquiry and provide useful information such as six figure National Grid references (where appropriate); details of sites or the subject/s of interest and local topographical information such as the civil parish; and finally an address (or county if consulting the NAR). In most cases, information will be supplied free of charge to bona fide users for the purposes of research and teaching, but there is an increasing trend for county councils to operate a charging policy for information held on computer database, especially where substantial amounts of information are requested by independent consultants to incorporate in reports for clients. Some SMRs have produced or have in preparation printed catalogues with basic edited data covering, for example, topics such as Romano-British or medieval sites to save duplicating effort over the most frequent enquiries.

Bearing these points in mind it will normally be more convenient to make an appointment to visit the SMR in person rather than write a letter with a daunting list of requests which may end up very low on the SMR officer's list of priorities. To get the best from these records, at local or national level, the guidelines in publications such as *Remnants* or *Information for Teachers* will be invaluable, but the county archaeological officer or staff of the national record collections will also be pleased to help with a project design.

Some of the foregoing comments may be inclined to dissuade rather than encourage users, particularly of locally based SMRs, but it is only through increased public demand for facilities that local authorities will take action to improve the arrangements. Besides, the flow of information may not be all one-way; researchers who have taken advantage of the SMR as a starting point may end up in a position to offer something in return as a result of their own observations.

References

ACAO (Association of County Archaeological Officers) (ed.) (1990), *Sites and Monuments Records – Some Current Issues.* (Contributions by N. Lang, N. Chibb, and Dr R. Leech.)

Baldwin Brown, G. (1905), *The Care of Ancient Monuments,*London.

Burrow, I. (ed.) (1985), *County Archaeological Records: Progress and Potential*, Association of County Archaeological Officers, printed by Somerset County Council.

Department of the Environment *et al.* (1990), *This Common Inheritance – Britain's Environmental Strategy*, HMSO, p. 132.

Fraser, D. (1984), *England's Archaeological Resource: A Rapid Quantification of the National Archaeological Resource and a Comparison with the Schedule of Ancient Monuments*, Department of the Environment.

Hedges, J. D. (1975), 'Archaeology within a county planning department – Essex', in Rowley, Trevor, and Breakell, Mike (eds), *Planning and the Historic Environment*, Oxford University Press.

31.6 Liaison with Others: Local Societies and the History Curator

Sam Mullins
Director, St Albans Museums

To be truly effective in their work, history curators need to establish a wide variety of links with their local community. A museum isolated or divorced from its surroundings stands in danger of becoming merely antiquarian. In every city, town and village there exists a network of interest in the past and present life of a place: amenity societies, local history groups, friends of the museum, evening classes, reminiscence groups, history workshops, etc. The history curator needs access to this penumbra of interest as a source of local information, voluntary help, political support, fund-raising and other specialist expertise. Such groups are also the most likely source of regular visitors and sustained interest in the local museum.

Local history, perhaps above all other museum-based subjects, offers the part-time enthusiast, the amateur, the opportunity to participate. While local history is increasingly being written by professional historians, the primary sources for local history are sufficiently available through libraries and record offices to allow almost anyone to explore the history of their house, family, parish or suburb.

A broadly based boom of interest in the local community's past has been sustained since the 1960s. The establishment of the Department of English Local History and the pioneering work of Finberg, Hoskins, Everitt and others at the University of Leicester since 1955 transformed a previously antiquarian pursuit into a major source of information on the social and economic history of England. The acquisition of academic credentials by the professional local historian has been paralleled by a sustained groundswell of interest at the grass roots level. Extra-mural classes have spawned local history societies, research groups, village exhibitions, genealogical societies, family historians and a host of books and pamphlets for local consumption. The attendances of evening classes and the growth of such groups and societies has in many places appeared to be a response to rapid change in the local environment caused by redevelopment, new housing, new roads and accelerating social changes.

The rise of the local history society occurred as many of the traditional county-based archaeological and historical societies have either declined or been found inappropriate for more parochial enthusiasm. As archaeology has become more rigorous and scientific, it has tended (with such notable exceptions as Leicestershire's community archaeology groups) to turn its back on the amateur and to disparage their contribution. The reverse is true of local history. While not always at the cutting edge of the subject, the part-time local historian has played a valuable role, both in the collection and preservation of source material and in its interpretation. The local history curator has an important role to play in both encouraging and focusing local interest and relating it to the wider regional or national picture.

It is almost impossible to generalise about local societies, as they come in so many shapes and sizes. (The same, of course, remains true of history curators.) Some follow the more traditional pattern of providing lecture meetings for members when the fruits of local labours, both amateur and professional, are presented. Others, often descended from extra-mural classes, are working groups, meeting to work co-operatively on projects such as census analysis or probate inventory transcription. Many local societies are founded with historical artefacts as their priority and a local museum or at least regular exhibitions as their goal. Indeed, the local history exhibition has become almost as fixed a feature of the village fête as the white elephant stall. In the industrial and restoration field societies tend to be looser groupings of collectors and enthusiasts, dedicated to restoring steam engines or buses, following the steam fair or working the demonstrations circuit. Whatever their motives of association, all such groups have some degree of interest in the local past in common and the history curator should seek regular contact with them all.

The Curator as Facilitator

The vulnerability of local societies' research, collection and exhibition is its impermanence. The history curator should be in a position to offer the museum (or the archive) as a permanent repository for the results of their labours by copying the photographs they collect, preserving unpublished manuscripts or reminiscence archives, by recording the weekend exhibitions or by enabling the publication of the results of research, whether short notes or extended articles and manuscripts.

While the growth of public interest in local history owes much to a need to know about the place in which you live, this vibrant parochialism is also a major drawback. As W.G. Hoskins noted in his inaugural lecture as Professor of Local History at Leicester in 1965, 'it has been well said that antiquarians collect facts; historians discuss problems. Too many local historians are still stuck at the antiquarian stage, and even those who are trying to move beyond it may not always be sure what are the fundamental problems they should be tackling' (1967).

Indeed, he went on to suggest that while the amateur's achievement can equal that of the professional historian, the average standard of the professional is likely to be considerably higher. While the pages of the *Local Historian* in recent years stand as ample testimony to the high standards attained by the cream of part-time historians, it remains difficult to persuade even the best of extra-mural classes to look beyond the confines of their own patch and, by so doing, slough off the tag of antiquarianism.

Here again, the history curator is uniquely well placed to bring the breadth of vision, the comparative approach, to the material enthusiastically gathered and researched by members of the local society. The history curator can encourage a wider study of the *pays* perhaps by co-ordinating the work of several village or community groups. An annual one-day conference can perform this role usefully, while local history newsletters, informal training in techniques such as oral history interviewing, recording buildings or palaeography encourage and enable the part-time contribution to be more effective. The local museum can offer a meeting place, a library, a store or a publisher, be a clearing house for projects and lecturers, encourage better practice in storing local society collections or archives, and link them to the advice and initiatives of other museums or the area services. Over time this involvement ought to raise the standards and aspirations of the society members and may serve to broaden at least a few members' horizons.

The role of the history curator as a co-ordinating influence is of particular importance in the larger conurbations. Here the curator will be dealing with a large number of societies, rendering his role of necessity fairly distant. None the less, great potential exists for the bringing together of disparate groups and societies. In Birmingham, for example, the pioneering local history department founded in 1987 the Birmingham and District Association of Local History Societies which publishes a substantial newsletter, the *Birmingham Historian,* twice a year from subscription. Such an organisation keeps the museum in touch with local initiatives and achievements. In rural South Leicestershire, an annual conference is held for the half dozen or so societies in the villages around Market Harborough, and the Harborough Museum assists the local Market Harborough & District History Society to publish a modest annual journal – the *Harborough Historian.* If parochialism is evident in local history, such initiatives encourage at least a few heads above the parapet of particularism and serve as publications of record.

The curator will find particular problems in museums either brought into being by local societies or administered by them. As already noted, the motivation of curator and society member tends in practice to be at variance. Introducing more rigorous standards, such as a collecting policy, documentation and printwork, can run contrary to the society's established practices and attitudes. Bringing a society museum into a local authority service can be a traumatic experience for both parties, leading to a radical change of respective roles. The authority will not, for example, view the society member's personal satisfactions as the only token of success and will demand professional standards which are not easily reconciled with part-time or occasional member involvement or group work.

Other curators will find similar problems in the 'pastoral care' role with society museums on the professional museums patch. Societies are commonly run by a small committee consisting of active members, and contact with and guidance of this group is crucial. Hence the curator's link with the advice and possible grant aid of the Area Museum Council may be a useful catalyst for good practice – access to bulk purchase of storage materials, agency conservation work or photographic copying, for example. The society museums have grown apace in recent years, especially those arising out of the local history exhibition. Whether long-established or recent, their collections and connections are generally too good to be ignored, and even in the best-serviced areas, they do a job to which history curators are able to devote no more than a small fraction of their time.

The Curator's Role in the Local Society

A significant area of difficulty for the history curator is deciding how much to be involved in the workings of the society. It is a question all history curators should face as participation in the local society ought to be regarded as part of the job. Most societies are determinedly independent and can resent interference in their affairs, and yet the curator is often asked, even expected, to participate by serving on the committee of the society. Once installed, it can be very difficult for the professional curator not to tread on toes by bringing knowledge and higher standards to bear on the running of the society. While high standards of presentation, for example, are of great importance within the museum, they may not always be appropriate to the local society. An attempt, for example, to raise standards of presentation of labels in the village exhibition, the annual programme or quarterly newsletter of the society, or their posters on the parish notice board, may be a laudable but ultimately short-term gain. This can mean that these aspects of the society's work are 'professionalised', robbing the members of involvement and replacing them with the typesetter, photographer or printer. If involvement is the main reason for the society's existence, it must be damaging to 'improve' it in this way, unless such skills can be attracted to join the society itself. This is a relationship which the curator should handle with great care, avoiding any suggestion of takeover. All local societies depend for their health above all on the enthusiasm, initiative and involvement of their members. Nearly all fully-fledged societies rely for their running on a small minority of active members. It really does not matter if some appear to come merely for the chat or seem instinctively drawn to making the tea. The society has broad social as well as intellectual objectives. Local history societies should not be expected to be research pioneers. Indeed, the sociability of the society and the passive consumption of a lecture programme is the primary motivation for the large majority of society members. Any gains in the research or publication line should be regarded as a bonus. No museum can afford to ignore the heterogeneous motivations of the local society member and should indeed seek to emulate it in its own programme of events and activities.

It is common for professional curators to become officers of local societies. It is all too easy for a society to become over-dependent on the curator as chair or secretary and lose in the process the vitality from which the society was formed. It is mutually beneficial for curators to be co-opted on to society committees, but curators are best suited to posts demanding specific contributions such as editor or meetings secretary. The editorship of a county journal or record, the transactions of the local society or even a modest broadsheet style of publication are the single permanent record the group leaves behind for posterity of its earnest endeavours. The highest standards are required in the editorship of this record, ensuring that it is above all factually correct, scholarly in its quoting of sources and references, and deposited with local libraries, archives and museums. History curators' skills are widely employed in this role and through it exert a significant influence over many local societies.

Similarly a year or two as meetings secretary can bring the curator's network of contacts to bear on the arrangement of a varied and lively programme for the society, mixing fellow professionals with the local talent, perhaps prompting new initiatives and directions, breaking out of a rut of worthy but dull speakers, showing examples of good practice from nearby or far away. The meetings secretary, who is usually left to this thankless task with some alacrity, can have a considerable influence on the health and direction of the society. Wherever possible, local societies should be encouraged to meet on museum premises. This brings society members closer to the day-to-day workings of the museum and to some understanding of the curator's preoccupations. It breaks down barriers and ensures that a small part of the local community sees, and we hope, tells the rest about new developments, changed exhibitions and new acquisitions in the museum. The museum on our doorstep is all too easily neglected or taken for granted. If the museum has a lecture room or meetings room, a wide variety of local societies might be encouraged to meet there and make the museum their headquarters.

Local societies form a pool of potential help for the history curator, whether directly as volunteers engaged in simple housekeeping of the collection or indirectly spreading the word beyond the museum's four walls. The small museum invariably needs the help in kind to be found in the local photographic society or cine club, or the skills and contacts possessed by society members who in their 'other' lives are research chemists, railwaymen or the local Hoover agent. The local society can raise funds by becoming the publishing arm of the small museum, lead appeals for modest object purchases, or organise social and open evenings in the museum. The curator should be prepared to be opportunist, carrying at all times a mental list of tasks and objectives against which offers of help or members' skills can be matched.

The curator should proceed with care in relations with amenity societies. Civic societies arose in the 1960s and 1970s and remain influential today. Many such societies are formally consulted in the planning process while others lobby through the columns of the local newspaper, freesheet or community press. They regularly cross swords with the local authority over planning issues. The local authority curator needs to take particular care in this area if conflicts of interest are to be avoided. Many history or archaeological curators have formal access to the planning process and can influence this where historic buildings, shopfronts or archaeological remains are concerned.

The history curator may find it useful to create a local society or formal research group. This accords well with the view of the curator as a facilitator, offering the meeting space, objectives, methods and materials for a project needing more than one pair of hands. Oral history recording, the transcription of probate inventories and census analysis all require resources of time unavailable to the curator but readily volunteered by a group of enthusiasts. Such groups can be the extension of an extra-mural class, giving members an opportunity to get stuck into some real history. Great benefits can accrue from the application of local knowledge to problems of topography and dialect, and the group can carry the middle-class curator into areas normally closed or difficult of access.

Adult Education

The important role of extra-mural classes in the establishment of local history groups and societies has already been alluded to. History curators have often served as tutors for such groups and fostered their achievement of publications, exhibitions and artefact collections. At the time of writing things are changing fast in the world of adult education as the funding of extra-mural departments of local authorities and universities and the Workers' Educational Association have come under pressure. Indeed, it is now not possible to speak of an extra-mural system, as provision and content of classes varies from area to area depending on the approach of the relevant university. Suffice it to say that adult education is moving increasingly away from the non-vocational class, for example the village history group, towards vocational courses, certificates in local history, part-time degrees and MAs.

Courses such as Leicester University Adult Education Department's Certificate in Local History, are producing skilled local historians with the ability and innovation to return to their locality and research it. The opportunities for the support of local history courses in the villages and suburbs are reduced by this trend away from non-vocational courses, although the demand remains. The long-term effects of this trend are difficult to assess. Suffice it to say that history curators should keep in touch with their extra-mural departments both with a view to acting as tutors or occasional lecturers and to recruiting the skills or local knowledge of certificate or part-time degree students for museum-based research.

The History Curator and the Community

A final warning is for the curator not to become exclusively dependent on local societies for direct contact with the community. The museum's programme of events should not be orientated only towards membership but include plenty of opportunity for other circles of interest in the surrounding community to have access to the museum. All local societies' vitality ebbs and flows and the museum needs to avoid becoming overly associated with any one group. Societies can become clique-ridden, introspective and as a consequence offputting to the newcomer or potential new member. Their members can become fossilised and moribund, dissuading the young newcomer from joining the group.

It needs noting that interest in the local past is commonly the pursuit of middle-class newcomers, often the instrument or at least the symptom of those very changes which they decry. Such incomers are almost invariably the leading lights of the local society. They have chosen to live there, and seek the mythical rural past which motivated that choice through the pages of the Victorian census or the reminiscences of elderly villagers. Their interest might also be seen as a barely conscious attempt to establish roots by tapping into the local past. This role should not be disparaged; indeed, perhaps, it is a phenomenon to be documented.

By no means all part-time local historians are members of local societies. Many prefer to join the working groups rather than the lecture societies. The very best local historians almost invariably do not feel the need to join a society. After all, their motivation is personal; they are creators rather than consumers, and quite prepared to plough a more solitary furrow in the pursuit of history. Ultimately historical research and writing, whether for publication, exhibition or lecture, is inevitably a solitary activity. Many people can contribute to the gathering and ordering of information or artefacts, but only one person sits facing a blank sheet of paper to give shape to the story suggested by that evidence. It is as the facilitator of both collection and dissemination that the history curator plays a vital role.

While it is easier to preach to the converted, the curator must always seek to extend awareness of the museum's work. Hard-pressed meetings secretaries of all manner of groups and societies welcome the history curator as an occasional speaker. It is often a salutary experience, revealing how little known the museum is in the wider community, but invariably good publicity and essential public relations. Well established groups such as Women's Institutes, parents/teachers associations, the local art club, Sunshine Club or Scouts and Brownies will also be interested in holding the one-off or occasional meeting in the museum itself. National Trust, Historical Association and NADFAS groups can also be valuable sources of volunteer help. A public open evening to launch an exhibition appeal or research project invariably brings in people who otherwise might not have considered the museum as a place for them.

If the museum wishes to have a genuine role as a centre or focal point for the community, it should be a meeting place for almost any voluntary society. Its facilities are more attractive and welcoming than most village halls and there is often a shortage of this type of meetings space in larger cities. As a community centre the museum might even find a source of revenue or at least donations for the box or turnover for the shop. Less tangible benefits are spreading the word, breaking down set views of the museum and simply persuading people to cross the threshold. Museums and their grounds are good locations not only for evening meetings but for a wide range of activities and events – fêtes, performance art, concerts, film settings, treasure hunts, craft shows, etc. All help to bring a lively feel to the place, bring people who might not otherwise consider a museum visit and generally propel the museum closer to a varied but central cultural role in the communities which surround it.

While curators have always blithely, if correctly, assumed that the community needs a museum, it is clearer today than ever before that museums need the community. If the future funding or the role in formal education of the local museum is in doubt, then the curator must place the museum closer to the focal points in the cultural and social life of the community, whether large or small, metropolis or market town. The local society represents the hard core of potential community support for the history curator's aspirations, a valuable link with the wider community and source of help. In building on this support the aspirations and motivation of those local societies should ever be borne in mind. History curators must draw a fine line between facilitating their activities, and forcing a pace that stifles enthusiasm and involvement. As museums become more conscious of their unique role and immense potential in rapidly changing communities, so their response to the demands for involvement and participation becomes ever more crucial.

Acknowledgement

The author acknowledges the assistance of many colleagues, but particularly Stuart Davies, in the writing of this chapter.

Reference

Hoskins, W.G. (1967), *English Local History: The Past and the Future*, Leicester University Press, p.10.

31.7   Liaison with Others: The Museum of English Rural Life, Reading University

Roy Brigden

Keeper, Museum of English Rural Life, Reading University

This chapter is about the museum as a specialist resource and information centre. The two-dimensional collections at Reading, covering the broad span of rural life but concentrating particularly upon agriculture, are in great demand by other museums, enthusiasts, researchers and commercial organisations both home and abroad. Consequently, one arm of the organisation is devoted to handling this business and in the process has accumulated a considerable measure of expertise. It is a time-consuming activity, which is not fully self-supporting financially, but one that carries the institution's name to some of the remoter corners of the world.

The biggest single element within the information archive is the trade record collection. Its contents date from the early nineteenth century through to the 1980s and chiefly comprise the business records of agricultural machinery manufacturers, dealers and contractors, together with material from other agricultural servicing concerns such as seedsmen, agro-chemical companies and animal feedstuff producers. The depositors have been the manufacturers themselves – partly as the result of substantial rationalisation in the industry over the last twenty years – government departments, agricultural journals, machinery dealers and private collectors. Today the importance, not to mention the financial value, of these records is taken for granted though in the 1960s and 1970s some of the most important items had to be rescued from the bonfire or from the rubbish tip following the demise of some distantly established, but no longer viable family firms. In all, the collection contains a combination of business records, advertising and technical literature issued by some 3,000 British and foreign firms.

For other museums, all of this represents information that may shed light on farm equipment and ancillary material in their collections. Access is best gained via the name of manufacturer and from there it is a straightforward process to produce a catalogue, if one exists, for a particular product. This will in many cases provide some idea of a date, give an illustration, a certain amount of technical detail and perhaps a price. It may also suggest, perhaps by referring to appearances or awards at trade exhibitions and trials, starting points for further researches in the contemporary agricultural literature.

Where the firm's archive is more extensive, this may be only the beginning. The production records that survive from Marshalls of Gainsborough, to take an example, will reveal precisely to the day when the steam engine, threshing machinery or whatever was built, give a full run-down of its specifications, and name the original buyer or dealer to whom it was supplied. Amongst the collection deposited by Ransomes, Sims and Jefferies of Ipswich is a complete photographic record of products back to the late 1850s which was originally compiled to assist with the making of catalogue engravings. There is also a large selection of advertising literature, including a range of very colourful and amusing posters from the 1890s on. Original engineering drawings of products, vital for restoration work, can be supplied from a number of firms, most notably John Fowler, the Leeds-based steam engine builders.

More often than not, the interest of the enquiring museum is in gathering together information and illustrations that will assist in the wider interpretation of agricultural material to an audience having little or no prior knowledge. Dealing with the enthusiast and private collector fraternity, on the other hand, implies a much more single-minded and narrow approach to the minutiae of technical detail. Here a working knowledge of the more obscure trade names and model numbers, together with an ability to pull out spare parts lists and instruction manuals on demand, are essential. Contacts overseas are strong in this respect for two reasons. Firstly, considerable quantities of British agricultural machinery were exported in the Victorian and Edwardian periods to the colonies, to the European mainland, South America and so on. After languishing for years in a forgotten part of the outback or hidden corner of a sugar plantation, bits and pieces are now being rescued and, if some British enthusiast hasn't got there first and repatriated them, they are being preserved and restored in their adopted country. Consequently, a request for technical information on the equipment concerned very often follows.

The second reason is that for many years now there has been a thriving export trade of second-hand and reconditioned farm material, often tractors and their associated implements, to the Third World. There they may remain in use, perhaps passing through a number of different hands, long after the original manufacturer has ceased to stock the relevant servicing and technical literature. As I write, a request has come in from a Tanzanian farmer who has recently acquired two egg incubators, of pre-war vintage and originating from Gloucester, which he has been unable to operate effectively. A photocopy of the instruction manual is now on its way to him.

Recent legislation in this country requires anyone selling farm machinery to provide the purchaser with an instruction book. Some of the bigger manufacturers such as Massey Ferguson and Case, who now control what used to be International Harvester, keep very little of their own non-current product information. Instead, it has been passed on to Reading so that dealers and farmers are coming to us for material on tractors that are no more than ten or so years old. It is also now the case that an enthusiast who has restored an old tractor or traction engine can purchase an appropriate period licence number from the DVLC at Swansea as long as proof of the vehicle's age can be demonstrated. This means matching up serial numbers against manufacturer's records, where they exist, or supplying other information specific to the date of introduction of the particular model.

The photographic collection is the other element in the archives that accounts for most interchange with outside organisations. Photographs have been accumulating since the early days of the museum, though initially the emphasis was on recording the object collection and upon fieldwork. An historical collection was being established as well, but the total number in the mid-1960s was still under 10,000 images. Since then the rate of acquisition has accelerated sharply so that today the collection is approaching one million prints and negatives and has become a first-rate historical resource for the subjects of rural and agricultural history. In the late 1960s, the *British Farmer and Stockbreeder* and the *Farmers Weekly* photograph libraries were added, both of which give extensive coverage of farming practice and innovation over a fifty-year span, from the inter-war period. To this have been added the work of commercial agencies and professional photographers, of amateur researchers like Dorothy Hartley, with her interest in rural occupations and pastimes, and C.F. Snow, who produced some marvellous photographs of woodland crafts in the 1940s, and of organisations like the Council for the Protection of Rural England, illustrating the evolutionary process of planning and development in the countryside from the 1920s onwards. Overall, the earliest images date back to the 1850s, the bulk cover the period 1920-1960, and current acquisitions are dealing principally with photographs taken over the last two decades. The far-reaching changes now enveloping both the countryside and the agricultural industry are rendering even the more recent components of the collection of great value as an information resource, and this trend can only continue.

There is much more besides. The library contains 30,000 books on rural and agricultural history, together with complete runs of most of the major relevant journals, and is supplemented by the extensive records of national institutions like the Royal Agricultural Society, the National Union of Agricultural and Allied Workers, the National Farmers Union, and the Country Landowners Association. There are herdbooks and flockbooks from breed societies, individual records from around 1,400 farms, statistical records compiled over many years by the Ministry of Agriculture and sound records that include twenty-five years of the BBC's programme, 'On your Farm'. Then there is, of course, the object collection, which particularly in the areas of rural crafts and agricultural hand tools, provides a further store of reference and research material.

The aggregate value of all of this is easily demonstrated by the diversity of its users. Whether they are scholars working for a higher degree, pupils doing a GCSE project, publishers compiling another glossy slice of rural nostalgia, advertising agencies using the past to market the present, or television companies producing a historical drama, there is something to interest them all. For the other rural and agricultural museums dotted around the country, the benefits, too, are clear. They very often take a local or regional perspective of the subject for which there are materials and sources both in their own collections and close by. These can then be supplemented when appropriate by reference to the archives at Reading which, in the main, are made up of components that are multi-regional or national in their scope. The result is a partnership that has proved its worth over the years because it works.

31.8   Liaison with Others: Private Collectors

David Viner

Curator of Museums for Cotswold District Council

The Growth in Collecting

Private collecting is a widespread phenomenon. An obvious indication is the great increase in the promotional activity of London-based auction houses, and in particular their spread of interest into the provincial auction market. The columns of both the daily and Sunday national press contain regular reports of saleroom activity, usually spiced with the flavour of extravagant hammer prices or the wranglings of interested parties which have led inexorably to a final showdown in the saleroom of the auctioneers. Such press interest remains strong for both metropolitan and provincial 'stories'. At a more mundane level, the junk end of the spectrum has gone steadily up-market – in promotional terms, at least – to find itself hyped into antique markets or that irresistible attraction, the 'flea market'. A more recent variation is the car boot sale.

The stimulus for so much fervent activity in the market place and saleroom is derived from two phenomena of recent years : firstly, a noticeable growth in collecting activity by an increasing number of people, coupled with a broader range of areas of collectable interest. The second factor underpins the first : an increased awareness over a broader spectrum of the community that collectables offer more than just the thrill of the chase and the pleasure of acquisition, but an investment opportunity as well.

No social history curator observing the activities of the local saleroom or flea market can avoid the conclusion that her or his particular discipline has been affected by this increase in both promotion and activity. Curators of fine and applied art have long been required to rationalise some form of working relationship – or alternatively determine none at all – with the network of local and national auction houses.

Not so the curator of local or social history, for whom the relationship, if it existed at all, has probably been rather more occasional in nature. This has changed. Or, indeed, it should have changed, as the acquisitive habits of the nation's private collectors have extended into virtually all the fields of social history with few exceptions. I have no doubt that from their various contacts amongst local private collectors, the membership of the Social History Curators Group could produce a collector for virtually every type of social history object or item of ephemera, however obscure!

Attitudes and Approach

Private collecting is essentially about acquisition. This may seem a superficial assessment, but it represents a significant difference in emphasis to which the social history curator has to relate. At whatever level of collecting the relationship between a curator and a private collector may be established, it will have this different assessment of objective as a primary factor in that relationship. Fletcher (1980) illustrates this point effectively in an all-too-brief survey. For reference, 'private' should here be defined as belonging to an individual – or sometimes groups of individuals – as opposed to an element of corporate if not public ownership which shapes the philosophies and determines the activities of the majority of social history curators.

Relationships

Contacts between curators and private collectors take many forms. It is extremely unlikely that social history curators seeking to develop to the full the potential of their collections can do so without some contact – and in some detail – with other collectors in the private field. Much of the museum's existing collections may well have sprung from collections previously built up by individuals, and the curator will frequently need to maintain at least a rapport with those whose efforts have endowed the collections at some time in the past. Such relationships need not be oppressive, but can for various reasons sometimes become unbalanced.

Let us assume, for example, that a museum's collections have been enriched by a particular collection of, say, period toys. It is limited in scope, reflecting perhaps little more than the financial resources and developing expertise of the collector through the period of acquisition, prior to the sale or gift to the museum. The weaknesses in the collection have quickly become obvious to the curator, who nevertheless feels justified in acquiring the collection because it substantially advances the museum's own (we must assume, approved) collecting remit in this particular subject area.

The museum must formulate its early response to the incomplete nature of the collection. Should it in itself proceed to collect directly (using its own financial and staffing resources) via the saleroom or the antique market generally? What is the position of the collector involved? Is the collector's interest in period toys now exhausted, leaving the field clear for the museum's own collecting in the same field? If so, then the obvious potential for conflict is reduced.

However, should the collector continue an interest in period toys, then such potential conflict remains, and this can show itself most spectacularly in that great test of nerve and organisation, the process of bidding at auction. In the negotiations which have accompanied the acquisition of the original collection, the curator should be anticipating this problem and seeking to establish in discussion what the future activities of the collector might be and how the potential for conflict might be reduced or removed. It may be that the museum's financial resources and the collector's knowledge of the subject (and perhaps more especially the many contacts established by the collector) could be linked to advantage.

Such relationships are fraught with ethical problems. How can museum curators legitimately use to the proper advantage of their institutions the known interest and knowledge of private individuals within their respective fields of interest and expertise? Much potential for community involvement and support is lost if an appropriate balance cannot be struck here. The curator must ensure that the clear objectives of the collecting policy of the museum are understood – and agreed – to be the basis of any relationship with others. Indeed, it might be argued that all interested parties in such a relationship will be looking for clear objectives of this kind. The onus is firmly with the curator to ensure not only that these objectives exist, but that they are actively promoted.

It should not be assumed that private collectors are necessarily sympathetic to the attitudes of a public museum, any more than vice versa. It is not uncommon to find private individual collectors feeling resentment against the 'authority' which they perceive museums to represent, an attitude often linked with a similar perception on the availability of financial resources. A weak financial base can often be the cause of closure of a private collection operating as a museum, thus posing a real challenge in diplomacy if the local museum curator does in fact also represent the local authority in any discussions on dispersal or transfer of the collections.

Co-operation

These comments are not to suggest that private individuals with particular areas of interest and expertise cannot make significant contributions to the social history collections of most museums. Indeed, the opposite is the case. Community involvement in museum activity frequently takes just this form: the sharing of expertise, usually voluntarily given, and linked with the collections within the museum's care, to generate a broader appreciation not only of the particular subject under scrutiny but the value of the collections generally. Frequently, the greatest stimulus comes from those with their own collections of objects, the process of sharing knowledge in the form of workshops, demonstrations and loan exhibitions being an obvious vehicle of linkage between the public and the private interest.

Herein lies probably the most frequently occurring opportunity for the curator to cultivate the private/public relationship. Most museum special or temporary exhibition programmes incorporate private collections in one form or another; many rely upon this as a major source of supply. Tangible benefits result : a temporary exhibition is an obvious, and usually well promoted, form of co-operation. Sometimes closer links are formed, which may lead to a future commitment which would transfer the collection permanently into public care at some future date. It is worth studying temporary exhibition programmes for both large and small institutions to detect these trends at work. Some assessments have been published; Viner (1982) detected something of this phenomenon and also indicated the potential for exhibiting material from subject areas which did not, do not and will not form part of the museum's policies for its permanent collections.

Collectors frequently exhibit a depth of interest in particular subjects which others do not share; the minority element of this phenomenon can again be a useful research aid for the curator to develop. For example, a museum's collections of local historical photographs might contain a given number of views of inns and public houses, probably recorded more for their contribution to the street scene than as individual buildings. A local historian with a specialist collector's interest in postcard views of public houses, on the other hand, would be able to contribute to the museum record a body of knowledge not only of local public house history but also the potential for a small exhibition of both photographs and postcards and a leaflet/booklet/article on the subject. Such a specialism might also arouse a wider media interest with obvious spin-off benefits for the museum involved.

It is not infrequently the case that such opportunities are the catalyst around which the rather disparate research of the private collector can be pulled together and take on a more structured form. Such a statement might seem condescending, but experience suggests its validity. Where a museum takes a deliberate policy to mount a special exhibition programme of well researched topics both from within and without its own collections, it can considerably advance both the quality and the quantity of local historical research around the chosen subject areas. The consistent and excellent series of smaller exhibitions mounted over a number of years at the Gloucester Folk Museum is well worth reference here.

Coincidentally in the same county, the fruits of a very personal and specialist collecting interest forms the theme – as well as the total content – of a privately owned museum of the history of packaging. The Robert Opie Collection housed in a warehouse in Gloucester Docks comprises nearly 300,000 packaging and promotional items from the nineteenth and twentieth centuries, the fruits of its owner's personal crusade of specialist collecting. Associated publications (see Opie, 1985 and 1987) develop and deepen appreciation of this subject area.

Loans

Aside from co-operation on acquisition and on special exhibitions, a further area requires mention: the arrangement of permanent or long-term loans into the museum collections from a private source. The arguments against loans in principle need not be rehearsed here, but they raise an additional concern where gaps in the museum's holdings are thus filled by individual objects or groups of objects. It is tempting to regard such 'infilling' as an adequate method of shaping collections, but the prospect of future problems if loans are subsequently returned should be a real concern, not least as the cost of acquisition of adequate replacement objects will inevitably have grown and availability diminished. Even the museum's possession of loan objects might tell against it in the future, as the mere reference to museum possession of objects can sometimes increase their saleroom value. In general terms, loans for other than specific, short-term objectives such as exhibition needs, ought to be avoided on the assumption that all loans must be assumed to be returnable and therefore 'temporary' in the life span of the museum's collections.

Ethics

Duggan (1984) has dealt with the ethical considerations in the general approach of curators to their collections, reflecting the Code of Conduct which the Museums Association (1983) now has as a central document of policy. Here the difficult question is discussed of the individual curator building up a private collection. The issues need not be repeated, but it follows that some curators will inevitably bring with them to a particular curatorial appointment the legacy of their own previous collecting habits. These may stretch back into childhood, the collection(s) of Meccano and Dinky toys being every bit as relevant to the argument as later, perhaps more mature, acquisitions of a more esoteric nature.

It is important that such private collections of whatever vintage should be 'declared' from the outset, and clarity can only be retained if such collections do not grow further during a curator's period of office in a particular institution. A ban on curatorial private collections is neither enforceable nor desirable, but in the context of this chapter it is essential that personal curatorial collecting instincts must not compromise any relationship which may be developed on the museum's behalf with a private collector operating in the same subject area as the museum itself. Shared enthusiasms might well pose temptation.

The Collectors' Legacy

Such issues extend beyond the process of acquisition into the care of collections already within the museum's control. Problems of documentation, conservation and ultimate presentation are all implicit in the relationship between the individual approach and that of the museum. It is a commonplace to find reference within museum circles to the inadequacy of documentation associated with many private collections. Linda Fletcher (1980) cites what might be regarded as a case study, the collection of over 6,000 treen and other wooden objects accumulated by the Pinto family and subsequently acquired (part gift, part purchase) by Birmingham City Museum and Art Gallery in 1965. Her brief analysis is worth studying for its relevance to this point.

The Pintos, says Fletcher, were keen collectors without financial restrictions whose motivation was the gathering together of as many examples as possible of the uses to which wood could be put. She points out the general lack of documentation on usage and provenance, arising not least from the method of acquisition of much if not most of the collection through antique dealers and auctioneers. Use of middlemen leads to loss of information and lack of personal involvement with any 'original' owner of a given object. A further complication is the unreliability of information which is added (in contrast to being removed) in this process of acquisition, and especially comments by dealers upon the rarity value of a particular object. The inevitable consequence of scarcity is an enhanced financial valuation, which process must be treated with considerable caution.

A further telling point is the lack of any framework for an appropriate provenance for items in the collection. Purchases were made from all over the United Kingdom at least – a factor which must of course always be a major constraint against the acquisition of such collections into museums with local, well defined collecting areas. Some recompense which might be expected from the collector's publication of the fruits of his long-term interest (Pinto, 1969) is offset by the realisation that the deficiencies in the collection are perpetuated in the publication, which has nevertheless become 'used by many museums as a bible on the subject of wooden bygones' (Fletcher, 1980, p.3). Even a systematic re-inventory of the Pinto Collection by City Museum and Art Gallery staff cannot eradicate this particular problem.

Other problems come to the fore with different types of collections. Even the briefest of analyses of the many technology or agricultural history collections now incorporated into public museums will reveal a wide disparity of approaches to conservation/restoration. For the social history curator with however modest a, say, agricultural history collecting brief, this is a very real problem. Private collections of farm implements are notoriously prone to partial – and often ill-considered – restoration which ignores (or at least postpones) the real issues of conservation need. The trained curatorial eye will immediately recognise this problem when approaching a private collection on display; further analysis will reveal something of the stages as well as sources of acquisition by which the collection has grown, and the issue of presentation is frequently the most convenient way of breaking down any particular collection into its 'original' component parts.

More testing is the curatorial response to differing approaches within a collection once inherited by or acquired into the public domain. Here clear guidance is required but experience varies considerably. A complete change of approach often offends those whose generosity may have brought about the transfer of material. Perhaps a group of volunteers has been involved, whose talents and enthusiasm the curator is particularly unwilling to lose. As with the process of acquisition itself, so too the accompanying policies of documentation and conservation need to be addressed at an early date in any debate over transfer. Such early confrontation of these issues may overcome many later difficulties. Hallam (1984) tackles some of the issues in relation to technology collections.

These are some of the major negative issues, and there will be countless less obvious examples of whole or part collections now residing in public care which have presented more than their share of difficult curatorship. It remains to pursue a more positive note, by examining how significant many erstwhile private collections have been in the development of social history museums generally.

In terms of individuals, the name of Dr John Kirk is certainly significant. The story of the tortuous and difficult path he followed in order to establish his collection of North Yorkshire Moors 'bygones' in a suitable public home is well summarised by Peter Brears (1980). That this superb collection so impressed other curators at the time is worthy of note, and so too is its central function as the key collection around which the Castle Museum in York has been developed since 1938. Kirk's story is as much about the strengths of private collecting as it is about some of the weaknesses upon which it is so easy to dwell. Without his single-minded determination (and in poor health too), the transfer of his collections into public care might have faltered yet again at York's door as it had done previously elsewhere in the county. Dispersal of the Kirk collection by auction would have been a major loss, rendered even more obvious by hindsight.

Half a century later, such a process of transfer continues with attendant difficulties which Kirk would have recognised. The parallels are striking between the housing of the Kirk collection in a former prison building and a similar solution which retained together the Lloyd-Baker collection of Gloucestershire agricultural history in the former House of Correction at Northleach, to form the basis of the Cotswold Countryside Collection. The story of this particular saga from 1975 to 1981 has yet to be written, but it exhibits all the factors of strength and weakness in private collecting with which this chapter has been concerned : documentation of variable quality, a mixed legacy of conservation problems, part of a difficult and continuing struggle with an inheritance which could not be checked with its compiler and primary source of inspiration. Miss Olive Lloyd-Baker died in 1975 before the future of her collection of agricultural history had been determined. The fact remains that without John Kirk and Olive Lloyd-Baker and thousands like them with less obvious profiles, the collections which they amassed – and often also dispersed to other collectors in their lifetime – would not be available for public enjoyment at all. It is in the field of social history that the debt owed to such individuals is particularly clear. Leaving aside the difficulties with professional matters of curatorial management, such collections large and small continue to form a major endowment to public museums, a legacy of substantial public appreciation and enjoyment.

References

Brears, P.C.D. (1980), 'Kirk of the Castle', *Museums Journal,* vol. 80, no. 2, September, pp. 90-92.

Duggan, A.J. (1984), 'Ethics and the curator', in Thompson, J.M.A. (ed.), *Manual of Curatorship: A Guide to Museum Practice,* Butterworth, 1984.

Fletcher, Linda (1980), 'A collector's collection', *Group for Regional Studies in Museums Newsletter,* no. 3, October, pp. 3-5.

Hallam, John (1984), 'Conservation and storage: technology', in Thompson, J.M.A. (ed.), *Manual of Curatorship: A Guide to Museum Practice,* Butterworth, 1984.

Museums Association (1983), Code of Conduct for Museum Curators, in Thompson, J.M.A. (ed.), *Manual of Curatorship: A Guide to Museum Practice,* Butterworth, 1984.

Opie, Robert (1985), *Rule Britannia: Trading on the British Image,* Penguin Books.

Opie, Robert (1987), *The Art of the Label,* Quarto.

Pinto, E.H. (1969), *Treen and other Wooden Bygones,* Bell & Sons.

Viner, David (1982), 'Ringing the changes – a review of the special exhibitions programme at the Corinium Museum, Cirencester', *Museums Journal,* vol. 82, no. 3, December, pp. 139-41.

31.9   Liaison with Others: Schools and Colleges

Catherine Hall

Senior Curator (Historic Houses), Kirklees Cultural Services

For the busy social history curator wrestling with an exhibition brief or battling with a stores reorganisation, requests from schools can seem to be little more than an annoying distraction. We are all familiar with the very time-consuming nature of work with schools or colleges, especially if the museum has no education officer on the staff. However, there are effective ways of both responding to school requests and initiating projects with them which could, in some cases, benefit the museum as well as the school.

In any relationship with schools and colleges it is important to acknowledge the likely expectations on both sides, since friction between curatorial and teaching staff often derives from misunderstandings of each other's position. From the curator's point of view, security and time are an issue; locating objects, researching supporting material, devising appropriate programmes of work for a particular age range are time-consuming activities. Some teachers have a limited knowledge and appreciation of how museums operate. As an education officer I received requests ranging from 'I would like a large painting to decorate the Head's office,' to 'Could you bring the museum collection of Greek pots to school; we are doing a project on the Olympics.' Part of the problem of lack of understanding relates to the fact that few teacher training courses have traditionally included training on the use of museum resources.

Another potential source of misunderstanding can lie in the teacher's expectations of the type of material housed in museums. Requests are often for documentary or map material which many museums do not hold. This artificial division between repositories for artefacts (museums), photographs (museums or libraries) and documents (usually record offices but sometimes libraries and museums) can pose problems, although an education project drawing on the skills of curators, archivists and librarians can be a useful way to bring all three together.[1]

Looked at from the teacher's point of view, museums offer the chance for a wide variety of experiences for pupils. Many schools relate museum work to projects at school. Sometimes these can be anticipated; in 1988 the Olympics and Australia were high on the list of most requested topics. When schools television series are broadcast on the Victorians or the Vikings, museums with relevant (or not so relevant) collections are inundated with requests. With the introduction of the National Curriculum in history this problem is likely to become more acute.

Expectations of the type of work that can be carried out in a museum are likely to be influenced by the policies of leading sites in the heritage field. Requests to 'dress up' in period costume or to use original artefacts, which are politely refused on security or conservation grounds may be followed by 'Oh, when we went to X we were allowed to do that.' You will find it necessary to explain your museum's philosophy and perhaps encourage alternative teaching approaches accordingly. While museums offer the chance to try out innovative projects in a new environment, teachers are also under pressure to maximise the opportunities of a visit, either by bringing more than one class of pupils or visiting several galleries on a single visit. In these cases teachers need adequate briefing about supervision and gallery capacity.

Teachers also approach museums to undertake work which cannot always be related to the artefactual collections of museums. Requests for material on the Tudors or the Vikings, both popular school topics, are not well represented in the collections of most local museums, however it may be possible to use a single relevant item such as a suitably protected coin with a class group as part of a time-line exercise putting the object in its chronological context.

Changes in the education system, such as the Local Management of Schools, and the National Curriculum, have left the education system in a state of flux and confusion. The National Curriculum is in many ways prescriptive in terms of the range of courses offered at a particular age range but it does offer opportunities for museums to market their potential to schools.

The National Curriculum in English includes assessed elements in each stage of the child's career to evaluate speaking and listening skills. Museum visits of all kinds offer tremendous opportunities to develop verbal and aural comprehension. All museums would be advised to acquire copies of the new curriculum documents. Some museums have decided to offer very specific visit plans closely related to the requirements of the curriculum attainment targets while others prefer to offer general guidelines for the type of visit plans that teachers may wish to adopt.

As the National Curriculum comes into use across the age range, many museum staff will be concerned either that they will be overrun by group visits if the museum theme fits neatly into a prescribed history study unit, or alternatively that there appears to be no link between the museum and the curriculum at all. For museums which feel they fit into the latter category there is always scope to work with teachers on school-designed themes and on an introduction to historical sources including artefacts, oral history and visual sources. Museums which fear that they will be inundated by requests will need to look carefully at their teacher briefing sessions and visit scheduling to retain a degree of quality in their programme.[2]

It would be unfortunate if social history curators identified the history curriculum alone as relevant to their museums. Cross-curricular themes including environmental education are fundamental to the new curriculum and geography and art will offer further scope for visit programmes.

For museums without their own education staff, one of the most effective ways of meeting educational needs is through training teachers to use the museums independently. Indeed some museums refuse admission to schools where the teacher has failed to attend a training course. Organising courses during the school day is best achieved via the appropriate education adviser in the LEA. The adviser may be prepared to support the course and provide the funds to cover for staff absence from the classroom for the day. Advisers in appropriate disciplines are very useful potential ambassadors for the museum service. After-school 'twilight' courses are an alternative, but attendance could be poor. Organise these with light refreshments, on a late night shopping day if you are based in a town centre; giving teachers the chance to shop after the course can be an incentive to attend. The introduction of training days – the so-called 'Baker Days' – provides the chance to introduce the whole staff of a primary school to what you have on offer.

Useful contacts can be made with colleges offering B.Ed or PGCE courses; they might be willing to pilot resource material for you. It is also worth tapping into courses already offered by local polytechnics or colleges for teachers of local history. Another useful ally could be your local school inspector (HMI). There are many reports from the school inspectorate outlining good practice in museum education.[3] Teachers' Centres and other curriculum centres are useful venues to display information, talk to teachers and co-ordinate courses. Education offices in each district will be able to supply contact lists and can usually arrange free mailing of course information with school bulletins. Independent schools cannot be reached through that route and you may want to consider some type of mailing subscription for them.

Nationwide initiatives can offer useful opportunities to reach teachers; the inauguration of the Young Historian's scheme in 1988, for example, was used by many museums to liaise with teachers from the secondary sector, which is not well represented among museum users. The annual history days organised by the scheme provide the opportunity for high profile activities bringing children into contact with a wide variety of sources. At the Harris Museum and Art Gallery, Preston, the first history day brought together archive film, oral history tapes, artefacts and role play. The aim of the day was to introduce children to the problems involved in the interpretation of a variety of types of source material. A historical open day of this type requires a great deal of organisation but is attractive to teachers and is likely to attract repeat visits or follow-up studies. [4]

One of the dilemmas facing curators in their dealings with schools is just how much support and advice can, or indeed should, curators provide for teachers. There is a danger in any relationship with schools that the curator provides inappropriate material.

An over-zealous adherence to worksheets is one area of possible conflict. Many teachers expect worksheets to be provided; others will make a visit bringing reams of closely worded worksheets of their own. The problem can be that the wording of worksheets may be too difficult for the reading age of the children, or, equally worrying, the questions might be inappropriate for the museum context, directing children to labels rather than encouraging them to explore and interpret objects on display.

Another pitfall with worksheets is the tendency to offer a game of hide-and-seek, searching for objects in a gallery without providing an educational experience. The alternative to worksheets is to offer teachers a series of guidance notes with suggested teaching approaches which are impossible for teachers to photocopy as worksheets.

For many children making a first or second visit to a museum, a worksheet is probably not required. The real value of museums as learning environments lies in the variety of approaches to learning that are possible. Children with limited reading skills can use their visual perception and verbal skills to interpret what they see; such an opportunity could be ruined by the use of a worksheet which both confuses and creates anxiety for the child in an unfamiliar setting.

A discussion session with children about the form and function of objects is a very valuable approach to take, particularly with very young children. If worksheets are being used try to retain some of the interest in the objects and comparative questions brought out by discussion. There is a world of difference between closed questions which assess factual knowledge and could be better answered from a book at school and open, comparative questions which bring together unknown artefacts and familiar, everyday objects and encourage discussion of their likely use and ownership.

Handling sessions with artefacts are a vital component of museum education visits. Go into any cased gallery after a school visit and notice the finger and nose prints on the glass. There is a need to get close to objects, if possible to lift them, view them from all sides, even use them if possible. Clearly as professional curators our primary concern is for the objects and their long-term survival, so the risks of allowing handling must be assessed. A separate, non-accessioned handling collection is an option but for some social history collections the use of robust duplicates is a possibility.

Handling sessions require careful supervision, with adults and children, so brief the teacher well and look out for objects which can be pocketed. Even where the objects themselves are strong and secure, look out for possible problems; while leading a time-line session I once caught a child wielding a stone-age axe head on a tin of dried egg! If you are working with a selection of small objects it is useful to cover the table with paper and circle around each item to keep track of it. At the end of each session the children find it intriguing to return each object to its allotted place while you can see instantly if an item is missing. Even with a separate education room it is often preferable to conduct handling sessions with children seated on the galley floor. Half a dozen well chosen objects relating to others on display may be enough for a satisfactory session.[5]

One of the recurring requests curators receive from schools is for loans, either for school displays, assemblies or teaching sessions. Unless the museum has a loan service it is best politely to decline such requests and encourage groups to visit the museum instead. The administration of loans is very time consuming, and poses serious problems of security and insurance. An alternative strategy could be to put together a single loan box of newly arrived unaccessioned items or even low value purchases: flat irons, christening gowns, glove stretchers are exactly the type of objects requested by schools and are available quite cheaply. Alternatively, a practical session with teachers introducing them to the techniques of handling and discussing artefacts could encourage them to establish their own school boxes of recent material.

Even if your museum cannot provide an artefact loan service to schools it may be possible to provide copy photographs of local interest. These can be loaned or sold to schools, indeed the new curriculum offers many museums the chance to market resource materials to schools. The interpretation of visual evidence is one of the requirements of the History National Curriculum. Photographs should not be used merely as visual aids to storytelling; they should be argued over and analysed. Even the youngest child is capable of this. When showing slides or photographs to pupils make sure that they do more of the talking than you do; encourage observation and comparison with familiar scenes to stimulate discussion.

Another possible resource for schools is oral history; again this is featured in the new curriculum. Training sessions for teachers in interviewing and recording techniques can be worthwhile. Oral history tapes can be used with children; good examples of high quality tapes include those produced by the Imperial War Museum. Excerpts from tapes need to be short, and primary children can find strong dialect impossible to comprehend on tape, so it is vital that pupils work on their own projects with parents or grandparents as willing 'victims' and only at that stage introduce them to pre-recorded tapes which can take memories back to the earliest years of the century. As someone whose grandfathers fought in the First World War, I find it necessary to remind myself that the average primary child's grandparents may not remember the Second World War. A decreasing number of the staple school loan items, such as writing slates or clogs, now evoke memories.

While the relationship between schools and museums is seen as largely one-sided with museums providing help for schools, there are opportunities for working with schools for the benefit of the museum. A moribund toy collection could be revitalised and interpreted by a group of children who could also suggest ways to add contemporary items to the collection. A class could document their own experience at school to accompany an exhibition of material on education in the last century, children's perceptions of their own town could contrast with the oral testimony of older residents: the opportunities are endless.

Requests for work experience placements for school pupils or college students are becoming more frequent as schools encourage children to experience the world of work. Requests will need to be considered on their merits. It is useful to interview students before making a decision; you may find that the student has been pressurised by an over-zealous teacher. A realistic view of the career options for budding curators is essential.

College students may be interested to review your latest exhibition or devise and implement a visitor survey. Polytechnic students undertaking historical methods courses may be able to research and interview for oral history and exhibition projects.[6] Others could offer support for projects with schools such as graphics and editing input to children's guides or teachers' packs.

Many opportunities for collaboration with schools and colleges exist; find teachers with enthusiasm and stamina equal to yours and the potential benefits for both sides are enormous.

Notes and References

1. One example of a collaborative project to generate teaching materials is the Cheshire Museums and Archives Education Project.

2. Useful National Curriculum documents include Department of Education and Science, *National Curriculum History Working Group Final Report*, April 1990; Department of Education and Science, *History for Ages 5 to 16*, July 1990.

3. HMI reports on museum school services are numerous and free. One of the more thorough recent examples is Department of Education and Science, *A Survey of the Use Some Schools in Six Local Education Authorities Make of a Museum Service*, DES 53/87.

4. For further details of the Young Historian's Scheme and local co-ordinators contact John Standen, Young Historian's Scheme Co-ordinator, The Historical Association, 59a Kennington Park Road, London SE11 4JH.

5. For excellent practical guides to using artefacts and images see G. Durbin, S. Morris and S. Wilkinson, *Learning from Objects*, English Heritage, 1990; S. Morris, *Using Portraits*, English Heritage, 1989.

6. An example of such work is the oral history and photographic research undertaken by Lancashire Polytechnic students at the Harris Museum and Art Gallery. I am grateful to Sally Coleman, Keeper of Social History, for information about the project.

31.9. i   Liaison with Others:
Schools and Colleges:
A Note on the Education Reform Act, 1988

Jane Middleton

Education Officer, The Historic Dockyard, Chatham

Museum learning is entering a new and exciting period of development. Many institutions have entered a period of re-appraisal of their educational responsibilities, unleashed by a number of factors including changing patterns of employment; the growth of the heritage industry and consequent acceptance of the notion of market forces; increased accountability; and a downturn in the economy. Changes in the formal education sector have undoubtedly had a part to play in the increased emphasis which many museums now place on their services to the general public and to schools and colleges.

In the past, changes in the formal education sector have had only marginal effects on visits made to museums by students. It has always been relatively easy for teachers, publishers and museums to adjust to the changes. Even GCSE, introduced in 1985, was assimilated by schools and galleries/ sites/ museums relatively rapidly. Moreover, it was impossible to have any real notion of exactly what aspects of history, for example, were being studied by 5 to 14-year-olds. Consequently, exhibitions could be planned in the certain knowledge that some groups would take up the theme, although cunning curators consulted the educational broadcasting schedules to ensure a minimum take-up. However, that is no longer the case. The developments which have shaken the formal education sector since the mid-1980s have been so profound and are so all embracing, that museums ignore them at their peril.

The changes instituted by the Education Reform Act of 1988 are the most radical and comprehensive this century. This makes any introduction to them and their effect on the educational market an enormous task. Moreover, the phased introduction of the reforms, the National Curriculum in particular, makes it extremely difficult to produce a summary which will remain accurate for the shelf life of this publication. The National Curriculum Council and other bodies, such as the Curriculum Council for Wales, School Examination and Assessment Council, the Department of Education and Science, and the National Council for Vocational Qualifications, have produced huge quantities of documents as part of the process of change. From 1990, consultative papers have been issued for all subjects considered to be essential within a broad and balanced curriculum. These have been followed by NCC reports and recommendations and, ultimately, by statutory orders and non-statutory guidance notes. The Group for Education in Museums has attempted to represent the museums profession throughout this period and has submitted comments wherever possible, but developments have been rapid and it remains difficult to present an overview.

A useful attempt to provide this has, however, been made by *The National Curriculum: A Guide for Museums, Galleries, Historic Houses and Sites*. Published by the NCC, the folder will develop into a brief guide to the key changes which are being phased into schools over the next five years. It contains case studies and extracts from programmes of study in subjects which have passed the final stages of debate and become law. As expected, history has proved to be one of the most contentious areas of the curriculum and, in consequence, the programmes of study have been modified to be less detailed and retain a relatively large number of options at all key stages.

The programmes of study for History, Art, and for cross-curricular themes may well be daunting, but they offer those responsible for social history collections an unparalleled opportunity. For the first time it is possible to produce educational material based on the collections, which will have a mass educational market. Indeed, visitor trends are already beginning to indicate that the pattern of school visits is changing. Teachers can no longer justify visits with vague or philosophical objectives: they need to demonstrate links to the new curriculum. Moreover they are working under other very real constraints – the timetable, reduced budgets and unfamiliar themes. Those museums which can demonstrate an understanding of the demands of the National Curriculum, produce material which can be used in classroom teaching to back up a given programme of study, and which can offer a relevant museum experience will reap rewards.

Part Five   Interpretation

Introduction

Just what is it that social history curators 'interpret'? Many might claim, first and foremost, that our task is to analyse and interpret material evidence i.e. objects. Explanations about the past should derive from the study of objects, with other sources playing a subsidiary role. Real objects are what make museums distinctive, and they are our basic currency.

A rounder view, perhaps, is that social history curators, like all social historians, should integrate the study and interpretation of material evidence with other sources – documentary, pictorial, oral, the landscape. Ultimately, it is the most successful integrations that produce the most effective explanations, providing that the nature and needs of our audiences are given their due primacy: interpretation is only worthwhile if the messages are received. The museum curator as interpreter must always ask the question – for whom?

There are many tales to tell for the social history curator, and no two tales will be the same. No two historians using the same evidence will manage to draw identical conclusions. Unlike the university-based historian, however, or even the television historian, social history curators have a variety of means at their disposal for communicating with audiences. It is the purpose of this section to consider some of these. None is exclusive of any other, and any comprehensive museum programme of bringing people into contact with their own history, or that of others, will assuredly use a range of methods and media. Nor by any means is the process of communication restricted by the walls of a museum, nor is it necessarily a one-way process, nor should we be paranoid about subjectivity.

It may be that the issue of veracity should be touched upon here, in the sense that the social history curator by definition trades in many of the more disturbing and unpleasant aspects of human life, such as poverty, oppression, abuse and exploitation. In themselves few objects surviving from the past readily illustrate these themes, and yet we have somehow to strive to ensure they do so. We must not be tempted from these aspects of life by restricting ourselves to presenting and 'interpreting' objects which can readily be made to illustrate other themes, such as prosperity, administration, technological development. Nostalgia is a powerful emotion, but historians should make use of it, not allow themselves to be seduced by it.

David Fleming

32   Conventional Displays

Loraine Knowles

*Head of Regional History Department, National Museums
and Galleries on Merseyside*

What is meant by 'conventional' social history displays? Definitions of such a
term will probably vary with the definer and the time of definition. Here I take
the definition as meaning displays relating to the history of a locality which
communicate primarily by means of objects. This may seem an obvious
statement but the trend in local history displays in recent years has been away
from objects towards the use of more graphics and other media in the interests of
improved interpretation.

Many social history curators today consider it their role to tell the story of
their locality, and displays may therefore be 'storyline-led' rather than 'object-
led', with two-dimensional material and text filling in the gaps where objects do
not exist or are, for example, too large to be accommodated. Whether objects
predominate or not, conventional social history displays tend to be arranged on a
chronological basis rather than thematically. They tend also to represent
spectacular or extraordinary events rather than commonplace history, and from
the point of view of the ruling classes rather than from that of the ruled – with
scant consideration of race and gender.[1] They may also use taxonomic methods
of display which concentrate on the technological evolution of the object rather
than on its function and social significance.

The reasons for this are various: the chronological approach to display
reflects the way in which history is taught in our schools and universities. It may
be considered as enabling visitors to locate themselves, relatively speaking, in
time, but historical evidence in the form of artefacts rarely survives, or has been
collected, evenly across the centuries so that chronological displays are inevitably
unbalanced in their coverage. The tendency towards displaying objects
associated with extraordinary or spectacular events or personalities must owe
something to the 'cabinet of curiosities' tradition within museums as well as to
the relatively recent appearance of social history as a museum discipline.[2]

Curators are bound by their Code of Conduct to present museum objects on
display in 'a clear, accurate and balanced exposition and must never deliberately
mislead'.[3] However, a critical examination of some social history displays would
lead to the logical conclusion that in many periods of British history the role of
women, of black people and of the working classes was insignificant or non-
existent.

Women are absent from virtually every trade and craft workshop in small museums and
barely visible in the larger industrial museums. Except as domestic servants, shop
assistants, and occasionally munitions workers, the museum visitor might be forgiven for
thinking that women in the past did not work outside the home at all and spent most of
their time sitting at home sewing.[4]

Class is invariably denoted by an 'upstairs, downstairs' or 'rich and poor'
approach, leaving visitors to draw their conclusions about the political context
which gave rise to these divisions in society.[5] It is impossible, however, to
separate museum collecting policies of the past from the prevailing political
ideologies of the time. The absence of race as an issue from museum displays is a
case in point. Black history, for example, is to be found in our museums but it is

more likely to be within an ethnographical or anthropological context reflecting British colonial life than within a social history context.

This neglect of the contribution which other ethnic groups have made to British society has resulted in the formation of special interest groups within communities themselves. In some cases links have been forged with the local museums; in other cases there has been resistance to the idea of ethnic history 'leaving' the community.[6]

There is plentiful evidence, if we wish to look for it, that Black people (and Asians, and Jews, and Irish men and women, Flemings, Dutch, Hugenots and many others), lived here and played a part in shaping British history. Such people were a part of the ordinary life of the country, and it is their exclusion from the historic record which should arouse comment, not their inclusion.[7]

Thus, although there may be far more concern these days to present displays which are balanced in their treatment of history, the modern-day curator is faced with the problem of reconciling increasing public expectation of a 'different' kind of history with lack of the appropriate collections to fulfil this demand. Many items of material culture which are now considered of interest by the social history curator no longer survive. They were either of poor quality to start with or they were not considered worthy of collecting at the time they were available, or in some cases they have passed into private collections.[8] A positive collecting plan may do much to remedy this situation, especially with regard to the modern period; otherwise the curator has to draw on media other than the object.

The way in which museums present or should present history and the effects on the museum world of the so-called heritage industry have been the subject of much debate in recent years.[9] The museum's advantage over the heritage centre lies in the fact that museums are the custodians of real objects. The potency of this tangible link with the past should never be underestimated. Yet, as has been illustrated above, it has its shortcomings. No systematic study has been made of the reaction of museum visitors to conventional as opposed to contextual displays in the field of social history alone.[10] But the inherited wisdom, which applies to many other museum disciplines, is that there is still a category of visitor who prefers the 'Aladdin's cave' type of museum to that with a more didactic approach. Indeed, there is a school of thought within the museum world, most obviously represented in the fine art tradition, that the object should be allowed to speak for itself. This assumption must be open to question, however. Although conventional displays may allow the opportunity to display more of a museum's collections and, it might be argued, they are easier and cheaper to produce, to change and update, consideration is needed as to whether this should be at the expense of interpretation. A taxonomic approach might more appropriately be adapted in a study/storage display rather than in a primary gallery situation. [11]

The undoubted popular success and proliferation of the open-air or site museum over the last ten to fifteen years, such as Beamish, Ironbridge and Wigan Pier, is due in no small part to the opportunities available outside the confines of a conventional museum gallery for presenting a seemingly more complete and evocative representation of the past than is achievable in the traditional museum showcase.[12] Who can blame the general visitor who is drawn to the museum which displays a wooden butter pat in a reconstructed dairy setting rather than in a showcase alongside a dozen others, even though they may all be carved with different patterns?

The physical nature of the museum building may have caused some curators to dismiss all thought of contextual displays, but physical space need not necessarily be a constraint.[13] If the purpose of social history displays is to convey more than how objects evolved technically and stylistically, the question of who used them, why and to what end, which is rarely answered in conventional social history displays, must be addressed. As Susan Pearce has demonstrated, the potential 'questioning' of many museum specimens − a Victorian dress in the case of social history, for example − is extensive, and results in a wider appreciation of the culture in which that dress was made and worn.[14]

The question for curators must be this: can conventional social history displays adequately convey a sense of the past and all its complexities rather than merely providing 'a nostalgic peepshow into a largely fictitious past?'[15] Some would argue that museums cannot attempt to do so if they confine their role primarily to the collection of objects.[16] Whilst the collection and care of objects distinguishes the museum curator from other workers in the field of history, the value of those objects depends on a corpus of associated information, be it documentary, photographic or oral, to give the object context. The reproduction of that context is what many conventional social history displays fail to achieve for some of the reasons outlined above. Whilst any picture of the past will be selective and incomplete, that which divorces objects from their social context is artificially so. In planning conventional social history displays curators should, therefore, always be clear as to objectives and make those objectives clear to the public.

Notes and References

1. Valerie Bott, 'The spectacular vs. the commonplace', Museum Professionals Group, *Transactions,* vol.20, 1985.

2. Major cities such as Manchester and Liverpool, where municipal museums and galleries were founded in the nineteenth century, have only recently begun to extend their work into the field of social history, reflecting the trend away from world history on which their founding collections were based. The establishment of the People's Palace in Glasgow in 1898 with the aim that 'the permanent collections to be formed should relate to the history and industries of the city' was exceptional. In Birmingham's case the desire to see Birmingham history illustrated in the Municipal Museum and Art Gallery was expressed as early as 1895 but only achieved in 1981 when the Local History Gallery was opened.

3. Rule 5.5 of the Museums Association's *Code of Conduct for Museum Curators: Rules and Guidelines* .

4. Gaby Porter, 'Putting your house in order: representations of women and domestic life', in Robert Lumley (ed), *The Museum Time Machine,* Routledge/Comedia, 1988, pp. 102-27.

5. The recent touring exhibition 'How we used to live, 1900-1926' produced by the Museum and Art Gallery Service for Yorkshire and Humberside, in connection with the Yorkshire TV series of the same name, took this approach.

6. Leicester and Kirklees Museums Services have made positive steps to involve local ethnic groups in the representation of their history. See, for example, Julia Nicholson, 'Tinsel, terracotta or tantric: representing Indian reality in museums', Museum Professionals Group, *Transactions,* 1987, vol. 22, pp. 26-31.

7. Rachel Hasted, 'Whose history? Racism and censorship', *Journal of the Social History Curators Group,* 1987-8 vol. 15, pp. 19-22.

8. See, for example, John Gorman, 'What to collect', in Valerie Bott (ed.), *Labour History in Museums: Papers from a Joint Seminar held at Congress House,* 1985, Society for the Study of Labour History and Social History Curators Group, Methyr Tydfil, 1988, pp. 3-7.

9. This debate was started in Patrick Wright, *On Living in an Old Country*, Verso, 1985 and developed most recently by Robert Hewison, *The Heritage Industry: Britain in a Climate of Decline*, Methuen, 1987.

10. Most museums conduct visitor surveys to assess visitor reaction to displays and to establish the geographical origin and social class of their visitors, but few publish the results.

11. A good model here is the new ceramics study centre at the Liverpool Museum, opened in 1987, which is adjacent to the primary gallery where showcase displays are arranged chronologically but with a strong sense of 'period'.

12. For a critique of Ironbridge see Bob West, 'The making of the English working past: a critical view of the Ironbridge Gorge Museum', in Robert Lumley, op. cit., pp.36-62 (see note 4).

13. Displays in some of the branch museums of the Oxfordshire County Museum Service such as the Museum of Oxford, and Wantage Museum, and the recently opened County and Regimental Museum, Preston, have good examples of effective contextual displays in relatively small spaces.

14. Susan M. Pearce, 'Interpreting objects – an outline of theory', Museum Professionals Group, *Transactions*, vol. 24, pp. 5-10.

15. J. Geraint Jenkins, 'The collection of material objects and their interpretation', in Susan M. Pearce (ed.), *Museum Studies and Material Culture*, Leicester University Press, 1989, pp. 119-24.

16. Peter Jenkinson, 'Material culture, people's history and populism', in Susan M. Pearce, ibid., pp. 139-52.

33　Re-erected Buildings

Eurwyn Wiliam

Curator, Welsh Folk Museum, National Museum of Wales

There are three main ways in which buildings can be preserved and presented, namely by conservation or restoration *in situ,* by reconstruction or copying, and by re-erection.

Restoration *in situ* is the ideal approach for any individual building for it preserves the relationship that has developed between the structure and its immediate environment, physical, ecological or historical. Groups of buildings so preserved and presented in a museum context are frequent on the European mainland, but an example such as Kumrovec Memorial Park in Yugoslavia shows both the strengths and weaknesses of this approach. Josip Broz Tito was born here in 1892, and today a dozen cottages in the centre of the village have been restored to their appearance when Tito lived there. The buildings are in their original location and preserve their original relationship to each other and to the immediate surroundings, and the village is alive with modern peasants going about their day-to-day business, some living in similar houses, others in modern bungalows. But the village was almost entirely a peasant village and Kumrovec today enables no questions to be answered about the living standards of other classes and occupations in this part of Yugoslavia : the presentation thus has both great strengths and great weaknesses. The classic example of this approach in Britain is Cregneash (1938) while Auchindrain and Glencolumbkille in Co. Donegal are similar in nature; and of course there are hundreds of buildings individually presented *in situ* in all parts of Britain.

Reconstructions, namely the copying of buildings which exist, existed, or whose existence may be inferred from archaeological or documentary evidence, can be carried out either *in situ* or elsewhere. The 'street scenes' of museums such as York Castle and Salford belong to this genre, as do striking examples in theme parks such as Flambards, debatably of more interpretative interest than most museum presentations. Several British open-air museums include reconstructions of buildings amongst their exhibits, such as the Hangleton medieval cottage at the Weald and Downland Open Air Museum, a thirteenth-century croft at the Ryedale Folk Museum, and iron-age round-houses at several locations. This approach is entirely to be applauded when honestly done and is extremely useful as experimental archaeology. Its great virtue is that it enables museums to fill the gaps in the surviving record where, for example, medieval peasant buildings or poor eighteenth-century cottages no longer survive, and without examples of which a museum would be presenting an unbalanced picture of the past, wittingly or unwittingly. Reconstruction may also be necessary in special cases where a building does survive: the Ulster Folk and Transport Museum's only reconstructed building is an exact copy of an earth-walled cottage which it was not technically possible to dismantle and re-erect.

For a number of reasons, restoration *in situ* will not always be possible or desirable. Finance and access problems resulting in dubious viability, impending and unavoidable demolition, or the pedagogical desire to exhibit buildings in groups, may all contribute to a decision to exhibit and interpret a building elsewhere than on its original site. Several British open-air museums, notably the Weald and Downland Open Air Museum, the Avoncroft Museum of Buildings and the Ryedale Folk Museum, have developed from local initiatives to save particular buildings from destruction, while others, such as the Ulster Folk and Transport Museum, the Welsh Folk Museum and Beamish have all developed from conscious policy decisions to create collections of buildings as an aspect of interpreting social history.

Such conscious decisions lay behind the formation of the first open-air or folk museums in Scandinavia at the end of the nineteenth century, amongst them Skansen in Stockholm, Kulturen in Lund (both 1892), the Norsk Folkemuseum at Bygdøy (1894) and Frilandsmuseet, Copenhagen (1897). These museums were both educational and nationalistic in purpose, social history (properly managed) being a useful tool to any emergent state or movement. The ethics of re-erection were then little considered, though today some would argue that a building is better destroyed than removed: 'ethos' and 'spirit of place' are quoted in defence of such a position. However, it has always been usual to move timber buildings, and frequently the building is the only thing of its age to survive in a neighbourhood: its immediate environment has often been changed out of all recognition, particularly in the countryside. A collection of re-erected buildings exhibited together in one spot may well do more for the cause of education and conservation than very many individual structures restored *in situ,* though that in itself should never be taken as an excuse to demolish a building.

The concept of the open-air folk museum spread across northern and eastern Europe, and by today there are least 250 such sites masquerading under such titles as 'Folk Museums', 'Folk Parks', 'Open-air Museums', 'Museums of Buildings', 'Ethnomuseums' and 'Skansens', these latter terms common to eastern Europe. Their nature varies considerably. Some are purely collections of buildings (as both Avoncroft and the Weald and Downland were originally, though both institutions are now beginning to furnish their buildings, sometimes with reproductions and sometimes with original material); others comprise buildings and their contents, such as the Ryedale Folk Museum; others again have buildings, contents and major collections such as Beamish; while yet others have all this and are major research and publication centres, notably the Ulster Folk and Transport Museum and the Welsh Folk Museum, both closely based on the old Scandinavian folk museums and the only state-funded open-air museums in Britain, with all the implications that has (or had) for staffing levels. Some of these museums are national or supra-regional, others regional (the Chilterns Open Air Museum, for example), others more local still (the Black Country Museum). The most ethical museums will accept only threatened buildings. In a museum of buildings these will be chosen to show past building craftsmanship, but the national museums will only accept a building if it fits into a carefully considered strategy of what is typical and representative in order to interpret past life, rather than architecturally unique examples (though what is now architecturally unique may of course have once been commonplace). The basis of collection needs to be carefully defined, though it can change with time: the addition of the Rhyd-y-car miners' cottages to the Welsh Folk Museum marks a departure from a previously entirely rural collection of buildings.

The formation of any collection will throw a number of fundamental problems into sharp relief. The value of bringing buildings from different sources (and therefore differing building traditions) together in a comparative collection is counter-weighed by the problems of understanding that this brings about. Only a very large site will adequately solve this problem, as in the European museums where farmsteads from different areas are clustered together in regional groups, in a three-dimensional map of the country, as it were (e.g. Ballenberg, Switzerland; Bucharest, Romania; Kommern, Detmold etc., W. Germany). The smallish regions largely represented in the British museums normally enable this problem to be avoided, while in others 'village' or 'urban' aspects are catered for by grouping relevant examples together apart from the other buildings. Eastern Wales has timber-framed buildings unknown in the stone regions of the west, and in theory this could pose problems for the proposed village centre at the Welsh Folk Museum. In practice, however, villages were remarkably few in this land of scattered settlement before the middle of the nineteenth century, when railway-borne materials became common over the whole country. The age of the buildings re-erected may differ considerably and be a further potential source of confusion, with new techniques, materials and plans being introduced. Only a minute proportion of visitors will be aware of such pitfalls and it is the curator's task to convey such facts to visitors. Likewise, because only the homes of the richest normally survive from any period of history (for it was they alone who could afford the best building materials) it may not be possible to display the full social range of buildings : it is difficult in many German museums, for example, to believe that the owners of the massive, ornate farmhouses re-erected there were really 'peasants' in the narrowest definition of that world. The Welsh Folk Museum is amongst the luckiest British open-air museums in this respect, in that its *in situ* sixteenth-century mansion house, St Fagans Castle, is open to the public.

The time-frame or frames chosen for presentation can also lead to problems. 'Freezing' the time-frame is done at several of the most successful British open-air museums, such as Beamish, the Black Country Museum, and the Ulster Folk Museum, where buildings from the seventeenth century onwards are presented as they would have been in 1900. There are many interpretative advantages to such a policy: costumed attendants or interpreters can be used, and at Ironbridge's Blists Hill visitors can change their modern money to buy services and souvenirs with old money. (Classically, this is the approach at Colonial Williamsburg and Plimoth Plantation.) However, a static picture of the past results from such a presentation, with no link to the present and certainly no pointers to the future. The chosen period is idealised and may be seen as a panacea to today's ills. The converse approach taken at Avoncroft, the Weald and Downland and the Welsh Folk Museum, namely to present and interpret each individual building according to a different period, leads to its own problems, such as practical difficulties in introducing costumed interpreters. At St Fagans, a step forward has been taken by presenting six houses in a terrace at differing periods of their history (1805, 1855, 1895, 1925, 1955 and 1985), thus introducing the concept of historical change in both fabric and fittings to the public at the same time as providing them with their own links to the past. Older members of family groups have been seen taking on the role of interpreter and, by linking them to their own background, explaining objects entirely strange to a modern child in terms they can relate to and understand. In such a case, history can be seen as literally starting on one's own doorstep.

The need for accuracy in such a context is paramount: curators will inevitably shape the past they choose to convey to their public but they should be careful how they tamper with the evidence itself. Most buildings offered to museums will have been altered in numerous ways: a sixteenth-century farmhouse might have had wings added in both the seventeenth and eighteenth centuries, it might have been re-fenestrated in the Victorian period when new fireplaces were also inserted, and it may have had both gas and electricity added. To what period of its history should it be re-erected? Each building can only be considered on its individual merits, for there is no hard-and-fast rule that can be applied. Such a decision will probably have been made before the building was accepted by the museum. Accuracy of re-erection varies greatly between British museums and even within museums: a three-storey weather-boarded water mill at Stowmarket has every piece of new timber branded, for example, yet the same museum had a fourteenth-century aisled hall with sheet-glass panels blocking its smoke louvres. At the Black Country Museum doors and windows in one shop were 'moved' from one wall and 'replaced' in another, the better to suit the topography of the new site; the Ryedale Folk Museum has had to introduce metal fire-escapes into a medieval longhouse; while at Beamish a row of cottages has had new connecting doors inserted for the public's benefit. Those museums with the luxury of their own building staff, however meagre in numbers, pride themselves on the craft accuracy of their re-erections, often rediscovering lost building techniques in their quest for perfection.

Finally, furnishing such re-erected structures offers pitfalls in interpretation. The one great difference between furnished re-erected houses and period room settings is that the former provide the proper context for both buildings and contexts: one, after all, was designed for the other. Both structure and furniture were often made by the same craftsmen in earlier times, though museums of buildings *per se* need not always attempt to show this. Even those centres with the wider brief of folk museums sometimes face problems: because buildings normally last longer than their contents, a fifteenth-century house may of necessity have to be interpreted as it might have looked in the late eighteenth century, for example. The Weald and Downland Open Air Museum has partly overcome this problem by furnishing some of its houses with period reproduction material, an approach still largely anathema to the more traditional folk museums with their often extensive reserve collections.

34   Period Rooms: The House of Fiction has Many Windows

Susan Underwood

Director, North of England Museums Service

Wherever you may be while reading this chapter, at home or in the office, it is unlikely you would describe it as a period room. What would be the effect if it were transported into a museum? What would it convey to the visitor about how you and the majority of people live today? Would you want the room to be reconstructed exactly as it is now? Would you feel that it represents how you really are, your role in society, how your relationships work? Would you want to change it so that it represented you at your best, and not after the bad week you have just had, even if only to the extent of tidying it up a little? Why would anyone want to preserve or recreate a room like this in the first place? What would future, or even present, audiences need to be told to know how this room represents your role in society, and how should this best be done? The technical difficulties in reconstructing a room so that it looks authentic vary from period to period, but the issues of how typical the room is, the acceptable degree of compromise in using replica sets and partial reconstructions, the constraints of display in a public building, and the challenge of using the room as a medium of communication are common to all. It is only by carefully working through all of these problems that period rooms can achieve their full potential in social history museums.

The attempt to place objects in the physical context in which they were used solves many curatorial problems. It enables the curator to place varied, numerous and often mundane objects into a context to which the visitor can relate more easily than to the glass display case selected according to academic or abstract criteria. This can often be an easy option, designed simply to get a lot of material from the store on to display, but it also has great potential as an interpretative device and is now a standard part of the repertoire of social history museums.

There are many types of period room, and many reconstructed environments which are not rooms, but which raise similar issues. The room can be a recreation or preservation of a specific place with a great number of the original fittings and furnishings intact, such as at the Freud Museum in London, or a more generalised typical setting. Settings can illustrate interiors at a particular time, ranging from the Roman (Cirencester) to the medieval (Merchants House, Southampton), right up to the recent past (e.g. the 1980s kitchen in York Castle or the 1990s lounge in the Old Grammar School, Hull. Other settings may be a combination of indoor and outdoor, with no real, but lots of replica objects e.g. Jorvik (Viking) and 'A Celtic World' at the Hull and East Riding Museum (Iron Age). Non-domestic settings are also often reconstructed, with chemists' shops, school rooms and wheelwrights' workshops being keen favourites. The Wellcome Museum of Medicine has some of the most specialised and most elaborately realistic room settings, including a full modern operating theatre. Another type of period display is the sequence of period rooms at York Castle or the row of cottages at St Fagan's, Cardiff. Street scenes, with shop windows, are used to create a context for displays of sales goods, vehicles and street furniture. York Castle has the most widely imitated example of this genre, with offspring in the Glasgow and Hull museums of transport. A more recent variation of the period room is the railway platform at the National Railway Museum, York, and the booking office at Monkwearmouth Station Museum, Sunderland. Another variant is the preserved building, whether on its original site like Oakwell Hall, Batley, or moved to an open-air museum such as Beamish, Ironbridge, or the Weald and Downland, Singleton. These museums were based on the Scandinavian models, which also influenced Dr J.L. Kirk when he was setting up the York Castle museum displays. The Swedish models were developed as a response to the destruction of the traditional rural way of life by industrialisation. They were influenced by folklife studies rather than by museum taxonomies, so that the period room was seen as a far better medium for displaying a way of life than, say, the classification system used to arrange the Pitt-Rivers collection at Oxford.

Period rooms will always be used where there is a need to convey a rounded picture of daily life in the past. The main problems are the degree of physical accuracy which it is possible to achieve, and the interpretation of a way of life through a setting. The attempt to recreate the context in which objects were used involves compromises. The first compromise is the very fact of preservation or reconstruction. A medieval period room is not a medieval room lived in by medieval people, with objects subject to normal wear and tear, but an arrangement of medieval objects in a museum. Even if the room had been transported by a time machine from the past, and was perfect in every detail, placing it in a museum and the effort to halt the normal forces of change and decay render it artificial, and less than authentic.

The amount of information available for the recreation of a period room varies greatly due to the haphazard survival of records. Even the most faithful reconstruction is, however, an interpretation. Like all history, reconstruction reflects the spirit and state of knowledge of its time. This is obvious in an archaeological period, where new interpretations may drastically alter our ideas of how people lived. Even if we did have our time machine, the very act of choosing the date at which we would freeze the room is an interpretative act with a strong subjective element. The very sense of reality which is the purpose of the recreation can often lead to complacency about the curatorial role, especially when the period being recreated is relatively recent. Thus Kirk's view of the Victorian street now seems very dated, conveying a romantic and carefully sanitised view of that period. Recent developments in the social history of sanitation, public health and crime are nowhere reflected in the displays, which now seem more like sets from the Hollywood version of *David Copperfield* than real streets. Many recent reconstructions will appear dated very quickly, not just because the time they refer to will recede further into the past, but because they will reflect the concerns and interests of the 1970s, 1980s and 1990s.

Choosing something which is typical can also be problematic, as the typical is often less interesting visually than the extreme. The chemist's shop at Blists Hill is a splendid example of a museum pharmacy, but it is too big and luxurious for the kind of village being recreated. The typical also gives rise to problems in that it often creates an artificial uniformity. Does everything in the room you are in date from the same period? Does everything you own come from Habitat, or have you, like most people, accumulated a range of possessions of different age? Even if you have redecorated the entire room and bought all the furnishings and fittings at exactly the same time, within a short time anomalies will be introduced; Charles Rennie McIntosh may have bought cats to match his sitting room decor, but few people go to these lengths. Thus the typical 1930s or 1950s interior recreated in the museum, is often quite atypical, and in fact represents historical mismatch, or rather overmatch. The period rooms created by curators with a decorative arts bias (even if they are masquerading as social history curators) are most often guilty of this viewing of the past through a filter of 'good taste'.

One way around these problems is not to reconstruct typical rooms but instead create very specific rooms for which accurate records exist. These can be typical, but have enough individuality for them to look like they might have been lived in by real people. The level of research required for such interiors is much greater. Two fine examples can be seen in the Museum of Oxford. The rooms of named families of different social classes, from different parts of Oxford, are juxtaposed to make a specific point about the range of living conditions in the nineteenth century. Even if such records do not exist, it is possible to create an individual but typical room by constructing a storyline about the kind of family which would have lived there. From census returns, health and sanitation inquiries and other sources it is possible to find out for most of the nineteenth century for any particular area what a typical family would have been like – where the mother and father would have come from, what possessions each would have brought to the marriage, whether one of them would have owned or rented the house before the marriage, how many children they would have had, and the number of possessions they would have been able to afford. Many period rooms are untypical simply because they have far too many objects, no matter that all of them are individually 'correct'. Another approach, used most extensively by the Museum of London, is not to pretend to recreate period rooms, but to use a number of key objects in a partial reconstruction. This can be atmospheric and suggestive, but does not claim to be a perfect representation of a total reality. It indicates that curators have made a choice in order to make a particular point about what they think is important.

The acknowledgement of the element of subjectivity and choice in even the 'most perfect' reconstruction is the crucial first step in successfully creating a period room. It is then possible to make explicit decisions about what the room is for, and what level of 'authenticity' is aimed at. The purpose of the room must be more specific than to show what a 1950s kitchen looked like – there must be an intention to answer particular historical questions about the period, through using these objects in this particular way. The same room can be used to answer questions about interior design, domestic technology, family structures, economic and social status, health and hygiene. Once these questions have been formulated, the nature and extent of the research required can be determined, and a solid basis built for ethical decisions about the amount of authenticity which is being aimed at.

A brief discussion like this is not the place to list the whole range of sources which may help in the creation of period rooms. But having specific objectives does make it clear exactly what kind of information is required. This is often a stimulus to the ingenuity needed for recreating interiors. For earlier periods, archaeological excavations, plans, inventories, wills, household and commercial accounts, engravings, paintings and literature may all give clues. The more recent the period, the more abundant the sources. Photographs and film, sales catalogues, newspaper and magazine advertising and features, along with oral history are among many which may yield results. Having an aim beyond getting some of the collection on show will determine which and how many of these will be used.

Determining the level of authenticity, or rather the acceptable level of inauthenticity, is crucial. As compromises are inevitable – if only due to the restrictions of the museum building, the requirements of health and safety and fire regulations, and the need to conserve and provide security for the objects – serious ethical decisions are only possible if the reconstruction has a clearly defined purpose. Thus the much maligned Jorvik has far greater integrity than, say, the reconstructed street in the Glasgow Museum of Transport. The former has a clear purpose – to interpret a specific archaeological site. The latter involves almost the same degree of fabrication as Jorvik (the shop fronts are not real) and conveys very little information about the period which it represents. Indeed, it probably conveys much 'misinformation'.

Part of the purpose, therefore, must include a plan to communicate the historical point for which the period room was created. The messages that period rooms convey are never simple and cannot be taken for granted. Just as individual objects do not speak for themselves, groups of objects in period settings *need* interpretation. The context can make interpretation much easier, by providing an atmosphere sympathetic to the objects which is human in scale and stimulates the imagination and the interest of the visitor. But the interest and empathy must be given more than visual information about how the past looked. Whether you are trying to capture changes that took place over time, or convey what daily life was like for people in the past, uninterpreted period rooms are not enough in themselves. Interpretation can take many forms, the choice being determined by the objectives of the room. Labels can be placed within the room, deliberately pointing out its artificiality, or on lecterns where the invisible fourth 'wall' is. Portable labels are unsatisfactory. They require a lot of maintenance, are difficult to provide in sufficient numbers for busy periods, and often go missing. If resources permit, the simple device of a dispenser outside the room with free photocopied text is very effective. Modern technology provides a wide range of options. Recorded commentaries can be delivered through fixed amplifiers, through portable cassette players (of which the Jorvik-type ride is a variant), or through infra-red broadcast systems, such as that used by the Rock Circus in Piccadilly. Period music and songs can be used to add atmosphere.

Mannequins are often used to humanise the displays, and the quality of those available has improved a lot recently. There is nothing more distracting in a museum display than those bizarre parodies of human beings with ill-fitting clothes and extraordinary wigs which used to be all too common. The customisation of these figures so that their posture and expressions help communicate the message of the room is a vast improvement on the period costume on tailors' dummies.

The use of 'demonstrators' or actors in period costume is a refinement in the creation of atmosphere and the conveying of the meanings of the recreations. They are most often seen at open-air museums, but are used to good effect in period houses or even individual period rooms. Their most extensive use indoors is in the Museum of the Moving Image, where the use of actors is particularly appropriate to the subject of the museum. Like period rooms, period people involve compromises with authenticity (Ironbridge permits glasses, but not watches) and a clear interpretation policy is essential. Whether the actors/demonstrators are to pretend to be living in the period (first-person interpretation) or simply to be guides whose costume helps create a more integrated atmosphere (third-person interpretation), will depend on the purpose of the reconstruction.

Period rooms are very popular with both the public and curators. They are a natural part of the language of museums, using objects which are closely related to each other, and being themselves three-dimensional. To be an effective part of a social history display, they must provide answers to historians' questions. These questions will give clear objectives to the display, determine the research carried out, guide ethical decisions about the level of authenticity which is required, and provide the basis for selecting an effective method of interpretation. An effective recent use of period rooms which meets all these criteria is in the People's Story in Edinburgh. Period settings – often partial rather than full reconstructions – are here peopled with mannequins, most of which are based on real, named individuals, with taped sound based on oral history or scripts written in consultation with local people. These are integrated into an overall historical narrative, which allows for the evocation of nostalgic and other emotions, and uses this to draw the visitors into a sense of the causes and consequences of change in a city's life over two hundred years. The difference between this use of period rooms and, say, the York Castle displays, is the difference between social history and antiquarianism. The former uses period rooms to communicate the results of research into life in the past. The latter confuses the recreation of the surface appearance of the past with interpretation.

35 Audio-Visual Presentation

Penny Wilkinson

Museums and Cultural Services Officer, Wansbeck District Council

This chapter looks at the role and value of audio-visual presentations in social history museums. It covers the use of sound, slide-tape, video and film, and also hyper media, that is the inter-use of computers and audio-visual systems.

Audio-visual displays can be a useful addition to all museum exhibitions. They provide a change of pace by bringing movement into a gallery, and they bring noise into a gallery which helps to dispel the silent scholarly atmosphere of the museum. Many visitors will find it easier to absorb information from an audio-visual than from conventional text because they are more used to this format through television than to the increasingly alien mode of the written word. Video in particular is very familiar to most visitors and its use in the museum helps to make the museum a more familiar and less intimidating environment. Those visitors who do not read easily will also find it easier to access information from an audio-visual display.

Audio-visual material is particularly useful for the social historian. Social history curators try to present historical themes and ideas and these are often the starting point for exhibitions, rather than objects. This may mean that the range of objects relevant for an exhibition is very limited or even non-existent. In this situation audio-visual techniques are invaluable in providing an alternative way of dealing with a topic without having to resort to extensive use of text and graphics. At Merseyside Maritime Museum the exhibition 'Emigrants to a New World' faced exactly this problem. The subject of emigration was poorly represented in the museum's collection but despite this the exhibition was developed using audio-visual amongst other techniques to put information across. Two sections of the exhibition contain no objects, and here taped extracts from diaries and letters are played and archival film is shown which relate and illustrate the emigrants' experience. In this way 'the true historical experience of the very human story of emigration has been recognised despite the paucity of objects'. [1]

The use of archival film in this exhibition also demonstrates how audio-visual material allows the presentation of other primary sources for the social historian apart from objects. Archival film and sound, oral history, and film and television footage are all important sources of information and evidence and can be effectively presented in their original format in an audio-visual display. At the Museum of the Moving Image in London extensive use has been made of original footage to present the history of film and television. Archival film has also been integrated into many displays in Hull Museums. At the Old Grammar School successive temporary exhibitions have used compilations of film and television footage to present the treatment of school life by the cinema and the media, and the development of British film. Period music and the use of oral history were also a feature of these exhibitions.[2] In the permanent social history galleries – The Story of Hull and its People – archival film of dockers is shown in the section looking at work and a compilation of children's television programmes is included in the section on childhood. Archival material has also been edited together with other visual material to produce a video on housing in Hull. This would have been very lengthy and wordy presented as conventional graphics and shows how large amounts of two-dimensional information can be presented more effectively as an audio-visual display.

Sound and vision can also be used as effects to create atmosphere and provide context. At Woodhorn Colliery Museum in Northumberland sound effects are used throughout the galleries: the sound of showers running plays where the displays look at pithead baths and the noises of a pub are heard next to a seated figure drinking beer and playing dominoes. In the reconstructed colliery kitchen two women have a conversation. Here the use of sound not only brings life into the display, it also provides information about the objects on display because they are discussed in the conversation. The conversation itself is in local dialect and conveys the companionship between women in pit communities that would otherwise have to be discussed in a label. Sound can therefore be used to develop interpretation as well as to provide effects.

Audio-visual techniques can also be used simply to provide additional information about an exhibit. A display of tools can be supported by audio-visual material showing the tools in use, for example, and is much more effective than a series of photographs of the process.

Audio-visual material can also be produced for sale in the same way as publications and catalogues are produced, so extending the ways in which the museum can disseminate information.

What to Use and How To Do It

Technology changes rapidly and it is therefore impractical to recommend particular systems or to quote costs. It is, however, possible to consider the advantages and disadvantages of available systems and to compare their usefulness in different circumstances. This section will look at slide and slide-tape, video disc, film, cassette tape, compact disc and digital sound.

Slide and slide-tape presentations using 35mm slides continue to be useful methods of presenting visual information. Slides can be cheaply and easily produced, in-house if necessary, as can a soundtrack on tape cassette. The use of more than one projector and phased projection can result in a highly sophisticated presentation, as in the programme on the Border Reivers at Tullie House in Carlisle which uses nine projectors. The advent of new technology has not relegated slides to the scrap heap and in many museums they can be an appropriate choice. Their main disadvantage is that projectors can jam.

Video is another way of presenting a sequence of images and stills with the added advantage of being able to show moving images. Video images can be stored on either tape or disc. Videotapes are less easy to produce in-house without specialist equipment, unlike slides, although the development of the camcorder does make it easier to record your own material. The cost of producing a video commercially will obviously depend on many factors, such as length and complexity, although it may be possible to avoid these costs by involving local television companies or colleagues in the project, as has been done in Hull Museums. The main disadvantage of videotapes is that the quality of the image deteriorates as it is copied and the quality of the final copy will deteriorate through use and will need to be replaced.

Video disc, however, is much more hard-wearing and presents a better quality image than tape. Here the sound and images are stored on a 12" disc similar in looks to a compact disc, rather than on tape. It is not possible, however, to produce your own disc and the costs at present are significantly higher to produce a disc than to produce a tape; the cost of a video disc player is also higher than that of a videotape player. Because video disc lasts longer than tape it may, however, be cost-effective for an audio-visual display in a permanent exhibition.

Video disc also has the advantage of random access as well as sequential play. This allows visitors to select the information they want to see or hear. Video disc can also be linked to a computer to produce interactive displays which give visitors an even greater degree of choice in the information they can view.[3] These recent developments clearly have implications for exhibition interpretation as the amount of information that the visitor potentially has access to is far greater than could previously be presented.

Sound presentations can be recorded on to loop cassette tapes available from any good hi-fi dealer or on to ordinary tapes which can then be pre-set to re-wind at the end of a sequence. These can be played through a domestic hi-fi system. Alternatively, there are specially produced message repeater systems which also use tape. The chief problem with sound on tape is that eventually the tapes either snap or unravel and have to be replaced. Cassette tape is increasingly being replaced by compact disc as a storage and playback method for sound. Compact disc players are now relatively cheaply available. The chief disadvantage of compact disc compared to cassette tape is that the production of the compact disc master and copies can only be done by a commercial company, whereas it is possible to produce audio tapes on cassette yourself. For high quality tapes it is necessary to use professional recording equipment, but where cost is an issue it is possible to produce an acceptable standard on domestic equipment.

Sound can also be digitised and stored on silicon chip. This is said to be everlasting but is expensive to produce and has to be done professionally. A disadvantage of this method is that the length of presentation that can be stored is relatively short at present.

Practical Hints

1. How Long Should an Audio-Visual Display Be?

This will depend on the purpose of the audio-visual display and how many visitors you want to see it. For example, if it is an introduction to the museum that all visitors should see, then it should not be too long. At the Ulster American Folk Park staff found that visitors who came into the museum when the twenty-minute introduction had begun would not wait for the next showing. It is impossible to state exactly how long such a presentation should be, but under ten minutes would be reasonable. If the audio-visual material is a supplement rather than a core element, then it could be longer; fewer visitors will choose to see it and those who do will be prepared to wait if necessary and will also remain interested through a longer presentation. A label stating the length of the presentation is useful for the visitor.

2. Where Should You Put the Audio-Visual Display?

The audio-visual display can be located in a separate lecture theatre, in an enclosed part of the gallery, on a screen placed openly in the gallery, or as an integral part of the display itself. At MOMI imaginative design has been used to integrate the audio-visual presentations into the displays in many cases; for example, a video of a 1920s Russian propaganda film is shown inside a reconstructed propaganda train. This not only places the video in its correct context but lends depth and authenticity to the period reconstruction.

3. Sound Overflow and Distraction

Where an audio-visual display is located within a gallery the sound may overflow into other parts of the gallery, and if more than one display is in use the sounds will compete. This may not be a problem if you are happy with a noisy gallery, but it can be distracting for visitors. This can be countered by directing sound, reducing sound levels, by placing the display in a covered area, and by sound-proofing. There is a danger that the audio-visual installations may be used as a game rather than for their intended purpose. This can be the case where computers or interactive video, for example, are in use, and could have a bearing on whether you choose this type of installation.

4. Using Archival Film

Cinema film, newsreel, and television can all be used in audio-visual presentations. Much cinema and newsreel footage is held by commercial film libraries or companies: the British Film Institute will usually be able to tell you who owns or holds a particular film. Television companies can be contacted with a view to using their footage, but the fees charged may run into thousands of pounds per minute of film used, although companies may consider reducing or waiving their fees for museums. If film is held only on reel then it will need to be transferred on to another storage medium. This can be expensive if commercial rates are charged. Locating material, negotiating for its use and preparing the final programme can be a lengthy and time-consuming process.

5. Licences

The public performance of music is regulated and if you are using commercially available music you may need a licence from one or more of the following bodies: Performing Rights Society; Phonographic Performance Ltd; Mechanical Copyright Protection Society. The museum may also need to be licensed for the public performance of music.

Notes and References

1. Michael Hall, 'Emigration – a human approach to its interpretation', *Journal of the Social History Curators Group*, vol. 15, 1987-8, p 23.

2. For reviews of these exhibitions see *Social History Curators Group News*, nos 18 and 22, Summer 1988 and Winter 1990.

3. See *Museums Journal*, vol. 90, no. 8, August 1990, which includes a feature on multi-media displays.

Bibliography

AIM, *An Introduction to Slides/Tape Audio Visuals*, Guidelines No. 10.

Peirson-Jones, Jane, 'Interactive video and the Gallery 33 Project', *Museum Development*, June 1990, pp. 10-16.

36   Site Interpretation and Trails

Jon Price

Organiser of Time Travellers *(Live Interpretation Consultancy and Provision)*

In Britain and Ireland the environment or landscape is the largest artefact that social historians must interpret. By its nature it presents particular problems; it cannot be arranged or re-arranged with ease, it is not always easy to visit, and it suffers from weather. This applies whether the landscape is rural or urban. Some landscape elements, or even whole landscapes, have been incorporated into museums, for instance at Acton Scott where a farm has become a museum, at Beamish where existing farms have been incorporated into a larger open-air museum of reconstructed buildings, or at Ironbridge where an attempt has been made to include the whole landscape of the gorge into a museum environment. To a lesser extent the provision of carefully built viewing windows into conventional museums, such as at the Museum of London or Tullie House in Carlisle, allows landscape elements to be included within displays. More often interpreting the landscape allows social historians to leave the artificial environment of the museum and to emerge into the real world outside. Once out there they have generally opted for one or more of the following interpretative mechanisms: trails, outdoor panels, interpretation centres, live demonstration or working environments.

Trails

Linear trails are probably the commonest form of landscape or site interpretation since at their simplest – duplicated trail leaflet – they are within the means of even the poorest resourced service. Unfortunately, as a result of this ease of production, many organisations or even individuals can and do produce trails whose value is strictly limited.

A trail is created by selecting and highlighting a feature through space or time, such as a waterfront or town wall, or by drawing together similar thematic elements, such as public houses, and marrying them to a route which can be easily followed. Even where the route is circular the visitors' experience of a trail always has a beginning, a linear progression, and an end. Where the visitor is self-guided by leaflet, or led by information panels, information must be produced in self-contained episodes, since visitors will tend to join the trail at different points along its length, and will travel in their own chosen direction. Panels must therefore contain some form of map or instruction on how to reach either of the neighbouring panels. Just as in exhibitions, attempts to force the visitor to take a prescribed direction are doomed to failure.

The use of guides presents its own problems. The cost of providing full-time staff is usually prohibitive, and curatorial staff cannot be counted upon to turn out more than a couple of times a year. The usual solution is to use either volunteer or self-employed guides with tour-leading skills, as well as a fair degree of local knowledge; others will require a training programme. A sheaf of hastily scribbled notes is not an adequate training programme and will lead to poor interpretation.

Outdoor or Interpretative Panels

Distributed single panels allow the interpretation to escape from the confines of a simple linear progression but unless they are specifically aimed at the casual visitor they demand much more visitor commitment. At the simplest level they convey a single 'fact' about a structure or place. The most common use of this approach is the 'blue plaque' system adopted in a number of towns after the London model, and which note the presence of a 'famous person' in the past. Other uses are the panels at some battlefields, of which the Flodden interpretative panel in Northumberland is a good example. More sophisticated versions are linked together thematically, and one of the best early examples of this was the system of panels at Lissoy in County Westmeath around the site of an abandoned settlement which was thought to be a model for Oliver Goldsmith's poem 'Deserted Village'. Here the relevant verses could be read at the sites of the buildings to which they were presumed to refer.

The same requirements for legibility of text apply to outdoor panels as to indoor exhibitions. In addition, whilst siting may be governed by planning or safety regulations, the siting will also govern the potential complexity of the content: a long text might be suitable at a rural viewpoint whereas a more succinct text will be required on a busy main street. The 'listening post' is a specialised form of panel and often includes some form of illustration. The chief problem with this kind of equipment is one of maintenance, although another problem is the volume level – too loud and it will disturb people and animals – too quiet and no one will hear it in heavy traffic or high winds.

Interpretation Centres

The concentration of information at a node point or interpretation centre is a common practice. In country parks information is usually concentrated at an access point such as a car park to maximise visitor use. At its simplest this form of interpretation is represented by the single panel – in its most developed form it becomes an entire museum in itself with its own display of relevant objects. This type of museum has a number of advantages over the large central museum: it is generally less exhausting for the visitor; it is likely to present a concise and limited range of concepts instead of an eclectic group of subjects; and it is physically smaller. The benefit of displaying objects in close proximity to their point of use or production should be clear to any social historian.

Live Demonstration

The distribution of interpretative activity at a series of node points throughout a site allows a variety of activities to be presented in their correct context. The type of activity will depend on the constraints of the site and on the range of themes to be interpreted. This method of interpretation can be linked to a linear trail and in practice the requirements of visitor flow will inevitably require a degree of linearity to be built into the interpretation.

Live demonstration at a series of node points is increasingly used where there are intact buildings to interpret, although good examples on open-air sites exist. The cost of employing staff is the most obvious limiting factor which tends to mean that either a peak period employment pattern is used, or the live demonstration occurs at special events where a high density of live demonstration can be achieved for a limited time. In this case it is usual to hire or subcontract a group or agency.

Working Environments

All the forms of interpretation so far described are to a greater or lesser extent separate from the environment which they are intended to interpret. It is, however, possible to make the interpretation an integral part of its environment by distributing an actual process, which is itself an interpretation, throughout the site or building. Single theme examples would include a working industrial or agricultural process such as is found in a cotton mill or in a managed woodland. More complex examples can range from a working farm where the focus is on the production processes of farming, to character interpretation where the process being interpreted is the everyday social interaction of a group of historical characters.

Who Interprets Sites?

All these interpretative processes can be carried out by museum services or related bodies in the existing environment, although often versions are produced by other local authority services such as planning simply because they have a greater resource base of staff, equipment and funding than most museum services. It is, however, important for museums to be actively involved in these projects, even if they are not able to run them alone. Interpretation is a primary museum function and the sensitive nature of the interpretation of social history means that it should not be left to someone without proper training or guidance. There are too many examples of museum authorities originating these interpretative processes to provide a comprehensive list; however, here are a few examples.

In Hull a set of scripts for thematic town trails was produced in-house. These scripts are intended for use by self-employed guides who are paid on a commission basis. The trails explore the old medieval core of the city. In Southampton a design company was brought in to produce trail panels, outdoor displays and pavement furniture for a trail around the town walls.

A good example of a site interpretative centre is the Culloden Visitor Centre which deals with the 1745 battle in its social and political as well as its military context. In general, however, the use of interpretative centres is more common in a natural history context.

Live demonstrations are not widely used in existing environments except on an occasional or seasonal basis and this reflects the resources available to pay staff. At the Merseyside Maritime Museum demonstrations are regularly carried out in the pier master's house and the coopering shed, and at a number of industrial museums single point demonstrations of industrial processes can be seen on a more or less regular basis. An example of a process continuously carried on throughout an environment is the working of the fields by horse at Acton Scott.

Reconstructed Environments

An alternative to interpreting the existing environment is to create a purpose-built environment. Within such an environment the same interpretation processes can be carried out. At rural life museums such as St Fagans or Singleton the collecting together of disparate elements means that interpretation must be distributed at node points throughout the site. At the Black Country Museum or at Beamish the assembly of structures of a similar period in a simulated environment allows the potential for continuous process interpretation. At the Black Country Museum this occurs on 'Live Ins' when the Friends of the museum live in selected buildings for a weekend. At Beamish the concept of first-person interpretation has been used to attempt to present the social structure of the colliery village.

For the most part museums move existing indigenous structures to a single site and arrange them in 'typical' environments. Other approaches are possible. The Ulster American Folk Park has brought North American buildings to Ulster to complement its local examples and show both ends of the social history of emigration. At Gosport in Hampshire a completely simulated squatters' hamlet was built by a re-enactment society and subsequently taken over by the local authority.

The benefit of reconstructing an environment is that in theory precisely those elements best suited for interpretation of particular processes or social activity can be selected and condensed into a limited space. The major disadvantage is the enormous cost of dismantling, transporting, and re-erecting a building. This will affect the interpretation, as inevitably sponsorship is easier to obtain for a 'nice' structure like a chapel than for a slum courtyard or a workhouse. The philosophical question of what relationship a reconstructed building, more often than not adjusted to fit site and safety requirements, bears to the original artefact is beyond the scope of this chapter. By far the greater part of outdoor interpretation is derived from natural history or archaeology. Where a historical angle is used the interest is often in the history of architecture. There are some social history driven schemes such as the Weavers Triangle in Burnley, or the New Lanark scheme, but at the time of writing they are chiefly notable by their rarity. To fully interpret the human environment social historians need to go beyond the walls of their museums.

Select Bibliography

Any list of sources will inevitably rapidly go out of date. A good starting point would be to look at David Uzzell's two volumes of papers from the Second World Heritage Interpretation Conference at Warwick. In addition, the regular journals produced by the Centre for Environmental Interpretation (CEI) and the Society for the Interpretation of Britain's Heritage (SIBH) carry details of current good (and bad!) practices in this area.

Anon. 'Have open air museums got a future?', *Museum News*, vol.41. May 1988, pp. 1-2.

Atkinson, Frank, 'Beamish Open Air Museum', *Museum,* no. 155, 1987, pp.132-8.

CEI, *Environmental Interpretation,* Summer 1985, issue on outdoor panels. Summer 1986, issue on interpretation panels.Winter 1986, issue on trails.

Friedman, Renee, 'Of trees and teacups:the landscape as artifact', *History News*, vol. 43, no. 4, July/August 1988, pp. 34-6.

Hudson, Kenneth, 'Making sense where it matters – some thoughts on site museums', in Southworth, Edmund (ed.), *The Interpretation of Archaeological Sites and Monuments*, SMA, 1988.

Kerr-Wilson, I.A., 'Approaches to the interpretation of unrestored heritage sites', *Museum Quarterly*, vol. 17, no. 1, February 1989, pp.33-5

Korn, Randi, 'Self-guiding brochures: an evaluation', *Curator*, vol. 31, no.1, March 1988, pp. 9-19.

Lawson, Myra, and Duncan, Fenella, 'The problems of open air interpretation', *Heritage Scotland*, vol. 4, no. 1, Spring 1987.

Stevens, Terry, 'Open air museums: taking the lid off interpretation', *Leisure Management*, vol.8, no. 6, 1988, pp. 38-41.

Stevens, Terry, 'War and peace: battlefields interpretation', *Leisure Management*, vol.9, no.1, 1989, pp. 60-64.

Tanner, Kathy, *Museum Projects: A Handbook for Volunteers, Work Experience and Temporary Staff*, AMCSW.

Wood, Chris, 'Interpretive policies and practices in the national parks of England and Wales', *Heritage Interpretation*, vol. 40, Winter 1988, pp. 6-8.

Uzzell, David (ed.), *Heritage Interpretation* (2 Vols), Bellhaven, 1989.

37 Living History

Penny Wilkinson

Museums and Cultural Services Officer, Wansbeck District Council

'Living history' is a broad term used to describe a wide range of activities – from actors pretending to be emigrants to America, to schoolchildren dressing up as Victorian servants, from buxom wenches serving mugs of foaming ale, to re-enactors living in a reconstructed seventeenth-century hamlet. The common factor between these methods of interpretation is the presence of people. Living history uses people to simulate life in the past. There are two basic approaches to living history – re-enactment and drama.

Re-enactment

The aim of re-enactment is to portray accurately and authentically aspects of history. This may be done by people pretending to be from the past – first-person interpretation, or by people describing the activities of people from the past – third-person interpretation.

The most well known aspect of re-enactment in this country is battle re-enactment. There are a large number of battle re-enactment societies covering almost every period of history from the Dark Ages to the Vietnam War. These societies attempt to re-create historic warfare through the use of reproduction weaponry, armour, costume and military tactics. Whilst some societies attain a high standard of display, many battles tend towards pageant and entertainment rather than careful interpretation. This is due partly to the amateur status of these organisations and partly because the battles are scaled down simulations rather than full-scale re-enactments. Because of this, battle re-enactment has limited value as a method of interpretation for museums. Many of the groups do, however, give displays of drill and use of weapons which avoid the disadvantages of battles.

Some battle re-enactors carry out small-scale first or third-person interpretation re-enactments of civilian or military life. In general they refer to these as 'living histories'. In contrast to battle re-enactment, these events re-create all aspects of life in a particular period which is acted out as realistically as possible, and the participants take on roles appropriate for the setting and period. Events of this kind have taken place regularly at Gainsborough Old Hall, Blakesley Hall in Birmingham, and at Avon Croft Museum of Buildings. This will usually involve careful reconstruction of setting and environment, including food and living arrangements (even down to sanitary provision at some events!) as well as costume. There are now also groups set up specifically to provide living history events and who disassociate themselves from battle re-enactment groups.

This type of re-enactment is relatively new in Britain, although it has been incorporated into museums in America for some years. The most well established re-enactment site in America is Colonial Williamsburg, which has its origins in 1926. Here the eighteenth-century capital of Virginia has been rebuilt and populated with 450 interpreters using a range of interpretative methods including first and third-person re-enactment.

There are no sites of this nature in Britain. Most re-enactment events take place as one-offs when re-enactment groups are hired for a single event, usually for a weekend or a week. Many open-air museums in Britain, such as the Black Country Museum at Dudley and Blists Hill at Ironbridge, do use real people in their displays. At these sites guides and demonstrators may dress in authentic reproduction costume but rarely take on a period role. They explain and discuss the history of the buildings and the work they are involved in or representing, but they are not expected to pretend to be the actual inhabitants. For the most part the use of interpreters is at a basic level and does not extend beyond straightforward activity or craft demonstration.

Re-enactment may require role play (adoption of an historic persona) by the participants but not the public. Some museum education departments have adapted re-enactment to involve children in the role play too, so that they can begin to understand the attitudes and feelings of people other than themselves in situations very different from their own. Clarke Hall is run as a living history venue by the Yorkshire Consortium for Education Joint Services. Schoolchildren, mostly between the ages of 5 and 12, visit the hall where staff take on the roles of the Clarke family and servants in 1680, and develop themes and ideas during the role play which have been prepared with the teachers. The children usually dress in costume, take on roles and carry out a range of tasks and activities. This type of event has much in common with drama and is usually referred to as theatre in education (TIE). English Heritage runs similar events, and some museum education departments, such as at Bolton, incorporate role play into their general programme.

Drama

There is no firm division between re-enactment and drama, and living history events will probably contain elements of both. Drama, however, does not attempt to provide a full historical picture like re-enactment. Instead, historical events are used as a basis for dramatic presentations which develop and explain historical themes. Drama has been used at Merseyside Maritime Museum to interpret the experiences of emigrants sailing to America. The voyage was condensed into a sequence of events which lasted for approximately twenty minutes. The play did not recreate the voyage but it created an understanding of the experience of being on board. The use of actors need not imply any reduction in the accuracy of information presented. At Wigan Pier Heritage Centre all scenarios are carefully researched and where possible are based on real people and events in Wigan.

Living history has been taken up enthusiastically by museum educationalists because they have identified its potential for allowing people to empathise with the people of the past to gain understanding of them, their ways of life, their attitudes and beliefs (Beamont and Stevens, 1987). This potential can equally be exploited by the social history curator. Living history can take the presentation of material culture beyond object and function towards an interpretation of the whole human situation. It puts objects into their human context by injecting ideas and emotions into an otherwise mechanical demonstration of craft processes.

This is popularly referred to as 'bringing the past to life'. This claim for living history has attracted criticism from people who argue that it is impossible to understand and so recreate past attitudes and ways of life (Ronsheim, 1974). It is certainly impossible truthfully to recreate the past, but it is quite possible to present an interpretation based on current research. Like any other museum display, living history presents a view (in a very realistic way) of the past and, as such, it can be as accurate, and as useful, as anything else we do in the museum.

Some living histories have had a tendency to present an attractive, simplistic and nostalgic view of the past, which concentrates on the wealthier or more exciting members of society. Social history curators are all too well aware of the paucity of information concerning the poorer sections of society, but where information is available it can and should be incorporated into presentations. The presence of vagrants and vagabonds at a seventeenth-century living history event at Bramall Hall, Stockport, in 1988, was based on evidence from the manorial court records. At Colonial Williamsburg it was recognised that the presentation was one-sided and the lunatic asylum was added to the site, as were slaves, to indicate that life in eighteenth-century America had its unpleasant aspects (Olmert, 1985).

Living history can be a very useful technique for interpreting social history and all historical periods up to the early twentieth century can be presented. It is theoretically possible for living history also to be used as an interpretative method for the recent past, and drama may well be appropriate to deal with events such as the Second World War. Re-enactment, however, will encounter problems if the visitors have direct experience of the scenario being presented because they will have more knowledge of the events than the participants. The role of re-enactment in helping visitors understand the past is largely redundant when the past is still within living memory, or recorded on film, and so living history of the recent past is unlikely to prove useful.

Putting on an Event : Problems and Practical Hints

This section refers to temporary re-enactment and drama events.

Aims and objectives The first stage in preparing an event is to decide what is the aim. As with any display, the curator must have clear aims and objectives, and must determine the parameters, content and emphasis of the display. The participants will be able to make suggestions about how the event might develop, but the curator should retain overall control.

Research The content of the event must be researched carefully. Living history is frequently criticised for being clichéd and stereotyped. To avoid this all aspects of the event should be researched, including costume and settings, as well as the historical background and content.

Choosing a living history group Living history is becoming popular in this country and there are a large number of re-enactment societies in existence. The quality of presentation and interpretation varies and some groups do not reach the standard necessary for a museum display. You need to vet groups thoroughly by seeing them in action, if possible, by discussing with the group who they recruit, how they organise and operate, and what training, if any, they have. It is also worthwhile contacting any museum or venue where the group claims to have worked before.

Venue An obvious venue for living history is an historic house which immediately provides a suitable period environment. It is, however, quite possible to create a setting. Military living history can be suitably staged in a tented encampment. Alternatively, it is feasible to erect buildings. At Gosport in Hampshire, a set of dwellings was built using authentic building methods by the Historic Builders Group of the English Civil War Society in 1984 at a cost of £5,000. The site was purchased by the local council and was regularly used by them for living history. Living history can also be successful within a modern museum. At Wigan Pier actors present a range of scenarios, using both specially created areas of the museum like the schoolroom, or open space in the main display hall. The National Army Museum has used an empty gallery to recreate the interior of a seventeenth-century inn on a small stage approximately 10 feet square. Lack of an authentic period setting does not, therefore, make living history impossible.

Use of collections and reproductions One of the advantages of living history is that it shows objects in use. The use of collections is an ethical problem which has to be decided by the curator before the event. Most re-enactment groups can provide a range of smaller items themselves, such as pottery, cutlery, etc., but this could be a problem if the quality and accuracy of items is not high. Larger items such as furniture are not usually provided, and the use of furniture in historic houses can cause problems. Living history is messy, and collections may not stand up to spilt beer or gutting fish, for example. Period furniture may also not stand up to the wear and tear of daily use. The curator must consider all this, discuss with the event organisers what their needs are, and then either use objects or provide replacements. This may mean the use of reproductions. Kirklees Museum Service has re-opened Oakwell Hall, a seventeenth-century house, and uses it for a variety of living history events. Some rooms, such as the kitchen, have been refurnished with reproduction items which can be used. Other rooms have original furniture on display and are exhibition rooms only.

There are a large number of manufacturers of reproduction objects for all periods, who are too numerous to list here. Re-enactment groups can provide information about the suppliers they use.

Use of buildings Most buildings today contain smoke detectors. Find out whether the group expects to be using candles, smoking tobacco, or creating smoke in any other way. If smoke detectors cannot be switched off then this must be made clear to the group.

Visitors Like any special event, living history will probably attract a higher number of visitors than usual. This has implications for staffing levels, and facilities like shops, toilets, car parking and first aid. How visitors are to use and view the event also needs consideration. If visitors are allowed to wander freely, it may result in certain locations becoming clogged up. It can be preferable for visitors to be organised into guided groups to ensure a regular flow through the display. Another point to consider is whether visitors will walk through the display or remain behind the barriers. Will visitors be able to touch items as they see the participants do, or will a 'hands off' approach be maintained? Will visitors be encouraged to ask questions, or just watch?

Insurance Make sure that the living history group has the standard liability insurance cover for £1 million. This will cover any accident or damage during the event which may be caused by the group.

Use of firearms If an event involves the use of blackpowder and/or firearms the group needs clearance from the police, fire brigade, your Health and Safety Officer, and must have the relevant Home Office licences.

Contract Any event needs a contract which clearly states what is to be provided by both parties.

How to find a re-enactment group Local libraries often have details of local societies which may include re-enactment groups. A list of re-enactment and living history organisers, nationally, covering all periods, entitled the Living History Register, has been compiled and is available from Roger Emerson, 21 Oak Road, Woolston, Southampton S02 9BQ. There are now also a handful of suppliers of living history events operating commercially or semi-commercially.

References

Beamont, M., and Stevens, A. (1987), 'Change: a constant theme', *Journal of Education in Museums*, no.8, pp. 15-17.

Olmert, Michael (1985), 'The new no-frills Williamsburg', *Historic Preservation*, October, pp.27-31.

Ronsheim, Robert D. (1974), 'Is the past dead?', *Museum News,* vol.53, no.3, Washington, pp. 17-19, 62-63.

Bibliography

Anderson, Jay, *Time Machines : The World of Living History,* American Association for State and Local History, Nashville, 1985.

Beamont, M., and Stevens, A., 'Change: a constant theme', *Journal of Education in Museums*, no.8, 1987, pp. 15-17.

Burcaw, G. Ellis, 'Can history be too lively?', *Museums Journal,* vol.80, no. 1, 1980, pp. 5-7

Centre for Environmental Interpretation, *Environmental Interpretation*, complete issue on living history, Manchester, March 1987.

Fairclough, John, and Redsell, Patrick, *Living History, Reconstructing the Past with Children,* HBMC, Colchester, 1985.

Olmert, Michael, 'The new no-frills Williamsburg', *Historic Preservation*, October 1985, pp. 27-31.

Ronsheim, Robert D., 'Is the past dead?', *Museum News*, vol. 53, no. 3, Washington, 1974.

Schlereth, Thomas J., 'It wasn't that simple', *Museum News*, vol. 62, no. 3, Washington, 1984, pp. 60-65,

The *Journal of Education in Museums*, which is the newsletter of the Group for Education in Museums, contains a number of useful articles on living history.

38   Demonstrations – Ethics and Techniques

Lesley Colsell

Curator and Assistant Director, Museum of East Anglian Life, Stowmarket, Suffolk

Two important functions of a museum are to educate and to entertain. There are many methods of achieving this, from conventional displays to interactive computers and video equipment, or by the use of museum objects through demonstration. Working exhibits and demonstrations are often the more effective because they clearly show museum objects as they would have been used, thereby enabling the visitor to achieve a greater understanding of them.

Using museum exhibits in this way has been a matter of conscience for curators and conservators. It is inevitable that accidents will occur from time to time which will damage an artefact, sometimes irretrievably. Even if no such accidents occur, wear and tear has to be taken into account. There do not appear to be any written rules for curators to be guided by. This chapter shows how some museums have addressed the problem of using their collections and some of the issues involved. It also puts forward some suggestions.

Craft Demonstrations

Among the numerous craft demonstrations the Museum of East Anglian Life puts on for its visitors, approximately eight days per year are organised for intensive school use, over and above the regular school visits. Over 300 children a day are shown specially organised craft demonstrations, from blacksmithing to the laundry, to help them to discover something of life around the turn of the century. They are encouraged to participate wherever possible. For butter-making a small glass churn is used so that the process can be observed easily. It is possible to buy new glass churns so that if the churn is broken, approximately £30 will replace it. The replaceable churn means that all the children can take a turn at butter-making. At present, butterhands and markers from the collection are used. Probably replicas of these should be made for use in the butter-making, leaving the originals for the display.

One way of minimising the use of the collection is to bring in demonstrators with their own equipment. At the Museum of East Anglian Life, spinners and weavers, for example, have been used in this way.

Very often craft demonstrations in museums are intended to show the technique rather than the artefact itself; the demonstration then leads to a greater understanding of the artefact. Some museums employ full-time actors or demonstrators to bring their displays to life – cooking on the Victorian range is very popular.

Somerset Rural Life Museum has used drama and live music in the attempt to attract visitors. Good use can be made of the County Drama Advisers who can take children around the museum and act out the part of a Victorian teacher, or whatever part is appropriate. One headmistress wrote after a visit to the Somerset Museum, 'They (the actors) are certainly to be congratulated on giving the children a truly educational experience which impressed them so much that I am sure they will remember it all their lives'. (Brown, 1982)

Working Machinery

Quarry Bank Mill at Styal uses demonstrators to work the textile machinery and explain the various processes involved in this industry. Indeed, without that human element it would be an extremely difficult process to interpret and make interesting. However, 'Not everybody, it may be granted, wishes to employ talking labels dressed in historic costume and present the museum as a theatrical experience' (Brigden, 1982).

Other alternatives have been explored, such as the use of video and other audio-visual aids, with some success, but they cannot replace the importance of seeing a process in action. It means that the machinery at Quarry Bank Mill, and other museums like it, is in constant use and will need much maintenance. The alternative of leaving it static renders many of the machines nearly impossible to understand, and much less attractive to the visiting public. However, should museum curators contribute in no small way to the wearing out of museum exhibits?

When considering an item for use it is essential to determine how much of it is original and ensure that evidence is fully recorded. If it is in original condition then I feel it is not ethical to replace any worn parts in an attempt to return it to working order. Every care should be taken to preserve the integrity of the exhibit and conserve it.

An account of one museum's experience of acquiring a unique pair of steam ploughing engines may prove useful here. These were purchased about five years ago by the Museum of East Anglian Life. The engines were made by Charles Burrell & Sons of Thetford who contributed no small amount to the development of steam power in agriculture and for road haulage, so to acquire this pair of engines was of extreme importance. As soon as they arrived at the museum, it was under pressure from the public and from the steam fraternity to bring them to full working order.

Staff at the museum traced the history of the engines back to their original specification, and found an individual who had worked with them in the 1920s. After they had lain derelict for years, they were bought by a private steam museum and 'restored'. When the Museum of East Anglian Life acquired them, the decision was taken to bring the engines to working order as very little remained of the original engines. They had been given new fireboxes and boilers which were welded rather than riveted – the museum hopes to rectify this in the future.

The engines are 'worked' very gently about three times a year and steamed several times more. Some of the original parts are wearing; for example, it is feared that the teeth on one of the big gear wheels will break. If this happens three options will then remain – to retain the engines as a static exhibit, to have a completely new gear wheel cast, which will be very expensive, keeping the original part for research purposes, or to build up and repair the original. The second option seems preferable to keeping them as a static exhibit, particularly in view of their unsympathetic 'restoration'. A cold engine does not convey as much as a steaming, working one. Also, by steaming them much has been learned about the lives of the people who used them and about the technology itself.

The smell of steam and hot oil, the thump and vibration of the piston and boiler, the movement of the flywheel and governor – the least technical person must be impressed with a working steam engine in a way that the static object can never achieve. From this the visitor can begin to gain an understanding of techniques, of technical innovation, of manufacture and applications. (Greene, 1983)

The third option – building up the teeth on the gears with weld – would cover up the original and is therefore untenable.

Many open-air or site museums have other types of working machinery. Watermills, for example, are difficult to understand if they are not operating. The Eling Tide Mill was restored to full working order and an eighteenth-century replica flour dresser was built to work.

When operating this type of exhibit, alterations have to be made to the building as unobtrusively as possible to take into account required safety measures. Fire escapes and fire detection equipment, and barriers and guards for working machinery (usually at the request of the Health and Safety Executive) have to be installed. Such compromises with authenticity are necessary.

Agricultural Museums

The agricultural museum encounters even greater difficulties. In order to farm it is preferable to have duplicates for the working machinery in order to prevent damage to the originals. In most cases an agricultural museum keeps livestock; however, 'On real farms animals have always been kept for profit and not as pets or demonstrators, so there can be a basic lack of authenticity about the farm museum's approach' (Thomas, 1984). Similarly, 'Another drawback to interpretation which applies to most aspects of farming is that things happen slowly ... even buttermaking has stages which are not evident on "churning day" ' (Thomas, 1984).

Replicas

It is often wise to have replicas for use in demonstrations, while keeping the originals on display. Certainly costume should never be worn – 'Replica costume could be the answer for those who believe wearing is important for an understanding of costume. If historic specimens are used, the experience of a very restricted number of wearers is being put above the appreciation of many potential viewers, both present and future' (Sykas, 1987). With larger machinery it is generally too costly to build a replica; however, the National Railway Museum at York has a replica of Stephenson's 'Rocket', which is steamed. The Lincolnshire Museum Service has considered commissioning a new farm wagon. This would not be considered a replica in the strict sense of the word because it would be made by a wheelwright working in the traditional way. This would be a new wagon which could be used and would become an exhibit in its own right.

I believe that we should make use of our collections, albeit in a restricted way, for these reasons:

1. It keeps skills alive and aids our understanding of them, whether it be making butter, a craft, driving a steam engine or ploughing by horse power.

2. The use of the museum's collection allows the visitor a 'living' experience of days gone by, and a chance to see something they have only had explained or read about.

3. The public has come to demand it, and the museum needs it through the additional revenue earned by putting on special events and demonstrations.

We need to work towards an agreed set of guidelines for the use of artefacts in museum collections since there is increasing pressure from our governing bodies and from the public for more working demonstrations.

References

Brigden, Roy (1982), 'Where will it all end?', *Museums Journal*, vol.82, no.4, pp. 199-203.

Brown, Martyn (1982), 'One museum's drama experience', *Museums Journal*, vol. 81, no.4, pp. 208-9.

Greene, Patrick J. (1983), 'Independent and working museums in Britain', *Museums Journal*, vol.83, no.1, pp.25-8.

Thomas, T. (1984), 'Old Macdonald's ark: livestock in museums', *Museums Journal*, vol.84, no.4, pp.135-6.

Sykas, Philip (1987), 'Caring or wearing', *Museums Journal* vol.87, no.3, pp.155-7.

39　Temporary Exhibitions

Loraine Knowles

Head of Regional History Department, National Museums and Galleries on Merseyside

Temporary exhibitions are an important aspect of a museum's programme for a number of reasons: they attract new audiences and encourage repeat visits; they provide a means of focusing on aspects of the collections which, for reasons of space, may not be dealt with in much detail in the primary displays; they provide a stimulus for researching and collecting in new areas; and they may even be used as a means of building up a completely new museum collection.[1]

There are a number of options available when it comes to organising a temporary exhibitions programme: curators can choose to generate all the exhibitions from their own resources; to hire in exhibitions from outside sources; or to construct a programme around a mixture of the two. The latter is probably the most practicable. Organising a temporary exhibitions programme, of whatever kind, is expensive in both staff time and resources so the availability of resources is likely to dictate how many exhibitions a year are mounted and whether they are generated in-house or hired from outside.

Sources of exhibitions for hire, especially in the field of social history, are increasingly hard to find: Area Museum Councils, the Crafts Council and even, occasionally, the Arts Council of Great Britain are the obvious sources. Exhibitions from the latter are likely to be photographic. Some photographic galleries originate and circulate their own exhibitions direct rather than through an agency such as the Arts Council.[2] Occasionally, museums generate their own exhibitions for touring but this is exceptional principally because the administrative arrangements required to organise a tour are considerable and if an exhibition is to travel it must be designed to do so in the first place.[3] There is also the consideration that many social history exhibitions are distinctly local or regional in emphasis and so unless they are conceived with a wider audience in mind their appeal may be limited.

Temporary exhibition galleries vary considerably in size from museum to museum and whereas it may be possible to edit an exhibition down a bit, it is not so easy the other way round, although a curator can successfully augment a touring exhibition with local material and even add showcases and graphics. It is, however, worth consulting colleagues either through the forum of an Area Council Newsletter or County Curators Group to establish right at the outset whether your planned exhibition may be of interest to others. In the author's experience a temporary exhibition in the region of 1000 sq. ft. is the optimum for a local museum. Anything smaller than this means that the choice of touring exhibitions will be extremely restricted and it will be difficult to create an impact with the museum's own exhibitions. The location of the exhibition gallery within the museum is also extremely important: a ground floor location is best (unless you have a goods lift and loading bay) in that it will be easier to move specimens, crates, and display systems in and out of the building; it is also desirable from the visitors' point of view in that the temporary exhibition will be easily accessible, not tucked away. At the same time it is important, for reasons of security and public appearances, that the gallery is located so that it can be closed off when exhibitions are being changed over. There is nothing worse than seeing an empty gallery on entering a museum.

The gallery should be designed or adapted so that it is possible to control light levels and temperature and humidity levels otherwise the curator's choice of exhibitions will again be restricted. The installation of a flexible, modular display system which can be adapted for each new exhibition, although involving a substantial capital outlay, will save design and installation time and be more cost effective in the long run. It needn't mean that every exhibition will look the same.[4] A regular temporary exhibition programme will also necessitate a store for spare showcases, packing materials, etc.

Hire exhibitions are normally only available for periods of 4 – 6 weeks so the curators will invariably be forced to devise their own programmes in addition to hiring in. A rapid changeover of exhibitions is very demanding on the curator and good advance publicity is required, otherwise a month's showing may be almost over before the publicity has had any impact. A minimum of two to three months is recommended. The policy of Market Harborough and Hull Museums in recent years has been to mount temporary exhibitions for a year at a time but to do a very thorough job by producing accompanying tape-slide shows and/or videos and publications. The programme as a whole should be planned twelve to eighteen months in advance and, depending on the size of the exhibition gallery, a period of at least six to twelve months is required to undertake the necessary research to produce the finished design brief.

Producing a temporary exhibition is no less demanding than producing long-term displays and, because an exhibition may be temporary, it is perhaps even more important that a permanent record of it, in the form of a publication, should be left behind. Timetables and budgets have to allow for this extra dimension, however.

Ideas for temporary exhibitions need not come only from the curator. If curators are in touch with their community suggestions are likely to be forthcoming from individuals and groups within that community and this may result in local people becoming actively involved in the presentation of their own history, provided curators are willing to step back and act as facilitators rather than as experts.[5] Certain events or anniversaries within the community, such as the centenary of a firm or of the birth of a leading figure within the community, are obvious subjects for exhibitions. Collaborative research projects between the museum and a university or polytechnic department can also be made available to a wider public through an exhibition and are a tangible end-product for members of the public who may have contributed to the research process through oral history, for example.[6]

As has already been mentioned the production of a temporary exhibition is as demanding as that of a longer-term exhibition. The same planning process is required for both. If designers are to be involved in the production of the exhibition a briefing document will be required. Even if no design services are available the use of a briefing system forces curators to organise their thoughts and objectives and provides a good record of the contents of the exhibition. This document or 'brief' should contain a statement of the exhibition's aims and objectives, and its target audience; a summary of the sections into which the exhibition is divided and detailed information on each object included in the exhibition, whether loans or accessioned items; copies of all photographic images and diagrams to be used, their source and negative numbers etc.; as well as all headings, main text, captions and object labels which should be typed ready to be sent straight to the typesetters. (Word processors now allow for such 'copy' to be sent to the typesetters on disk but hard copy will still be required for reference.) Sample briefing forms are reproduced in Figures 1 – 6.[7]

Design Office
Briefing Form DO/B1

LIST NO.

Exhibition Title

Brief Summary of Aim of Exhibition

Section No.	Title	Number of Items

Figure 1

Design Office
Briefing Form DO/B2

LIST NO.

Exhibition Title

Section Title

List No.	Category (tick)							Brief Description
	Exhibit	Photo	Graphic	Caption	Label	Text	Other	

Figure 2

Design Office
Briefing Form DO/B3

LIST NO.

Exhibition Title

Section Title

Object   Accession No.

Storage Location/Source

Dimensions: Length   mm   Breadth   mm   Height   mm

Display Dimensions
(if different from above)

Weight

Viewing Details

Conservation Before Display

Conservation Requirements When On Display

Is a Mount Required   YES / NO (delete)   Is a Case Required   YES /NO (delete)

Special Security Requirements

Illustration (photo, contact, or good xerox)

Designer   Curator   Date Required

Figure 3

405

Design Office
Briefing Form DO/B4

LIST NO.

Exhibition Title

Type of Graphic: Photo ☐ Diagram ☐ Map ☐ Illustration ☐ Other (tick one)

Source / Location of Original Reference

Negative No.

Illustration (photograph or good xerox of complete image area)

Notes

Designer   Curator   Date Required

Figure 4

406

Design Office

Briefing Form DO/B5

LIST NO.

Exhibition Title

Section Title

Caption / Label / Text (delete) | To Accompany

Notes

Copy (Show headings and titles as required. All should be typed upper and lower case, double spaced, marking any italics or bolds required. No indentations, extra line space between paragraphs. All punctuation and spelling to be correct.)

Design Details

Edited by:

Date:

Approved for Production by:

Date:

Figure 5

Design Office
Briefing Form DO/B6

LIST NO.

Exhibition Title

Section Title

A/V Title

Text/Dialogue	Details of Image	Source of Image

Edited by:	Approved for Production by:
Date:	Date:

Figure 6

If an audio-visual programme is being produced as part of the exhibition a separate brief will be required for this. A sample briefing sheet is reproduced in Figure 6. Any publication would also require a separate brief although there is likely to be overlap from a design and artwork point of view.

Once the design brief has been handed over to whoever is producing the exhibition and the production schedule has been agreed, the curator can concentrate on promotional arrangements which should have been put in train at the outset of the planning process. If the exhibition is to have an official opening and a special opener then a date must be agreed well in advance. The time of year, the day of the week and the time of day are all important factors to bear in mind when choosing an opening date and the criteria will vary according to the locality. An official opening or private view is a good means of thanking all those members of the public who have contributed to the exhibition as well as an opportunity to introduce a new audience to the museum and to invite the local press to see for themselves what the press release you will have sent them is all about. Depending on the likely interest in the exhibition you may wish to organise a separate press call rather than combine it with the opening or private view.

If your exhibition is of particular relevance to schools you may wish to organise teachers' courses which will provide an opportunity for teachers to have their own private view of the exhibition and to hear all about it from you, the expert, and then discuss how they might make the best use of it. You may wish to organise a programme of linked events such as gallery talks, demonstrations, film shows, readings etc. throughout the period of the exhibition's showing as an extra means of promotion. The nature of the programme would vary according to the nature of the exhibition.

Once the exhibition is up and running you may wish just to breathe a sigh of relief and forget all about it. It is important to remember, however, that from the public's point of view this is just the beginning. Evaluation of the exhibition should now begin. This may take two forms: an internal assessment of the exhibition's production process exploring whether the end product met with the curator's expectations, and if not, why not; and formal evaluation by means of questionnaires, interviews with visitors, and tracking of their movements through the exhibition.[8] If resources do not exist to carry out such a formal evaluation, a staightforward visitors' book in which comments can be made can be very revealing.

Producing a summary report of the exhibition is good practice and useful for those who come afterwards. This, together with the exhibition brief, administration file, press cuttings, photos of the exhibition and of its opening, sample posters, leaflets, publications, visitors' book etc. should form the exhibition archive which can be stored for future reference.

Acknowledgement

I would like to thank Jon Hall of HRA Design and Communication for reading and commenting on this chapter.

References

1. The Harborough Museum at Market Harborough, established in 1982, has built up its collections through a series of (until recently) annual temporary exhibitions making extensive use of oral history and the collecting/recording opportunities presented in the course of research for the exhibitions. It

has often produced an accompanying publication for each exhibition. See, for example, Samuel Mullins and Gareth Griffiths, *Cap and Apron: An Oral History of Domestic Service in the Shires 1880-1950*, Leicestershire Museums, Art Galleries and Records Service, 1986.

2. The Impressions Gallery of Photography, York, the Photographers Gallery Ltd, London, and the Stills Gallery, Edinburgh, are examples of galleries which generate and tour photographic exhibitions which from time to time may be of interest to social historians. See the *Arts Review Yearbook* for addresses.

3. The 'Brass Roots: 150 years of Brass Bands' exhibition organised by Bradford Art Galleries and Museums and partly funded by the Museums and Galleries Commission's Travelling Exhibitions Unit; and 'Fit Work for Women' produced by WHAM! (Women, Heritage and Museums') are two recent examples of such touring exhibitions.

4. Hull Museum had such a system designed by HRA Design and Communication for the temporary exhibitions gallery on the ground floor of the Old Grammar School.

5. Mark O'Neill's work at Springburn used the facilitator approach for some exhibitions. See Mark O'Neill, 'Springburn: a community and its museum', in F.Baker (ed.). *Writing the Past in the Present,* 1990; 'Springburn – a community museum', British Association of Friends Yearbook, 1989.

6. The Docklands History Project, an initiative of the University of Liverpool, worked in close collaboration with National Museums and Galleries on Merseyside. The project's aim was to involve the community in the recovery and presentation of its own history which was then made available in exhibition and publication format. Photographs, objects and an extensive oral history archive were then deposited with the Merseyside Maritime Museum. See, for example, Kevin Moore, *The Mersey Ship Repairers: Life and Work in a Port Industry,* Docklands History Project, 1988. The recent 'Household Choices' exhibition at the Victoria and Albert was organised in conjunction with Middlesex Polytechnic. See Tim Putnam and Charles Newton, *Household Choices,* Future Publications Ltd, 1990.

7. The DO/B1 form is used for summarising the contents and aims of the exhibition; DO/B2 for listing the contents of each section – text, graphics, photographs, captions, objects and labels – and giving each element a unique identity number; DO/B3 is for objects; DO/B4 for graphics; DO/B5 for all copy whether text, captions or labels; and DO/B6 is for A/V presentations. For other systems and a description of the process from brief to production see Giles Velarde, *Designing Exhibitions,* Design Council, 1988; and *Museums Journal,* April, June and August 1990.

8. Recent evaluation of National Museums and Galleries on Merseyside's galleries was conducted through the University of Liverpool's Department of Education. The Department's Centre for Research in Primary Science and Technology (CRIPSAT) and Liverpool Evaluation and Assessment Unit (LEAU) have both been involved. See, for example, T.J. Russell, 'Formative evaluation of interactive science and technology centres: some lessons learned', in D. Uzzell (ed.), *Heritage Interpretation Volume 2: The Visitor Experience,* Bellhaven, 1989. A range of other evaluation reports published by CRIPSAT and LEAU are available from CRIPSAT, LEAU or the Department of Education and Public Programmes at the National Museums and Galleries on Merseyside.

40   Outreach

Derek Janes

Assistant City Curator, Huntly House Museum, Edinburgh

Introduction

When talking of 'outreach', the first problem is to arrive at a satisfactory definition. It is like a word in a foreign language the meaning of which we know, but find difficult to express. Outreach, of course, is itself a word from a foreign language – the language of social work. It is not a well-liked word, although the activities it is thought to embrace are generally popular. Perhaps the very fact of its being drawn from social work is indicative of its meaning in museum terms. It is to do with the community and with people.

In its broadest sense outreach in a museum could encompass exhibitions, displays, publications, lectures, guided tours, loan kits, education, etc. It is prudent, however, to try to arrive at a fairly clear and concise area of work to be covered by the term.

The basic principle of 'outreach' is to involve the local community in the work of the museum. It is an area of activity – like work with the elderly – where the main beneficiary is not the museum itself, but the community. It involves working with groups and individuals and helping them to look at their own history, the history of their area or workplace. It involves the curator in an enabling role, not a directing one. It is not necessarily the quickest, most efficient means of achieving narrow museum objectives but is a crucial means of gaining the support of the community and enhancing the museum's credibility as a part of that community. It requires particular attitudes on behalf of the museum staff involved – modesty, tact, confidence, for example.

The Objectives of an Outreach Programme

Before embarking on an outreach programme it is important to have a clear idea of why it is being undertaken. It is important that there is a genuine commitment to outreach as an activity which benefits the community, not as a technique, for example, to develop the museum's collections. It is also important that staff at all levels believe in what they are doing, because it is also possible to see the setting up of an outreach programme as a means of winning the favour of local councillors or the Directorate of the Recreation Department. If a 'conservative' museum management attempts this the result is likely to be disappointing all round. If there is no belief in the importance of providing a service to the community, then an outreach programme is unlikely to succeed.

Having ensured that the motivation is correct, then attention should turn to the purpose of an outreach programme. It is essential that, as good social historians, curators have a clear understanding of the community served by their museum. An outreach programme based on firm foundations can then be developed. It is a fact of life that very few curators are natives of the area they serve. It is part of their professional expertise to overcome this handicap.

A community history-based outreach project might have as its prime objective the development of understanding of the growth of a particular community, or the fostering of a feeling of community in an area. It might be simply to enable a group of people to look at and get to know their own history or the history of their workplace. One attitude that all these schemes would have in common is that they could be accused of being 'political'. It is likely that some of them might have political consequences. Working with a group of interested, articulate people on, say, a run-down council housing scheme, may well have consequences. A project on just such a scheme in Coventry revealed that there was a scandal, leading to a public enquiry about jerry building in 1915. It also showed a history of rent strikes and political activity in the 1920s. In this case the history helped to explain why the area was so badly thought of, and also indicated how problems had been dealt with in the past.

The results of an outreach project could, then, be politically sensitive. If, however, the objectives are clearly thought out and the museum staff's role is that of expert/adviser/facilitator, then the museum is clearly performing a legitimate activity, not setting out to cause trouble. The problem with recent history is that it is recent and so almost bound to provoke disagreements.

Another accusation which can be made against outreach is that of social engineering. Again, if objectives are clearly defined and the curator's role is that of a modest adviser, this accusation would not stand up. Museums should help to create a sense of community. If, by bringing people together and helping them to appreciate more clearly a common interest, an outreach project changes the perspective of a local community, then that, surely, is a good thing.

Setting up an Outreach Programme,

Having decided on the objectives of a project, the next step is to get it on the road. In the past it was very useful to be able to make use of the Community Programmes (CP) on an experimental basis. With the demise of CP it is now important that such programmes are very carefully planned as they have to be part of the museum's mainstream activities.

The keys to a successful outreach programme are knowledge of the community and sensitivity. It is usually possible to gain access to a group of people via an existing organisation, be it the WEA, tenants' associations, or community groups. It might be that there is already an interest in community history, a desire to put on an exhibition, or an existing reminiscence/reunion group. It is, for example, often possible to set up a group from a dispersed 'slum clearance' area for reminiscence/oral history work for a short-term purpose and leave behind a permanent, free-standing group. This is usually very rewarding – especially as curators may bring together people who have not met for many years – and is a prime example of an outcome that is of little direct benefit to the museum but which actually improves the quality of people's lives. An example of this was a group at Red Lane, Coventry. Drawn together from all over the city by stories in the press, initially for work on a book, they continued to meet as an 'Old Residents' Group' with the community history element fading into the background once the book was published.

When a museum seeks to involve itself with an existing group it is important not to seem to be moving in, taking over the work of the group. The purpose is to help and encourage people to research their own history. This can be – usually is, in fact – much more difficult and time consuming but is much more rewarding for the people involved. The role of the specialist in this case is to give advice about sources and techniques and be prepared to act as a dogsbody – where, for example, the group cannot easily get to record offices or local history libraries. The museum can also provide facilities for tape recording, photocopying, copying photographs, holding meetings, etc. All of this develops the role of the museum in the community and strengthens its support.

Sometimes an outreach project may fail – it might not be possible to put together a group, for example. This is almost inevitable in this field. Remember that such projects depend on people having the interest and the time. If no one has, then that's nobody's fault. It's a fact of life of genuine community-based schemes.

Some Examples of Schemes

These examples are mostly drawn from my own experience, so that I can comment on their success or otherwise.

Community History Workers, Coventry

This was a CP scheme intended to encourage people to work on their own history, very much on the enabling system. It was a partial success. One area of 'failure' was on a peripheral housing estate, where we tried and failed to set up a community history group. On the other hand, one of the workers became involved almost full time with a very successful group based on an inner city community centre, and acted as their dedicated worker. He became heavily involved in the group and the museum benefited in the indirect way of becoming well thought of. For example, the Social History Section got invited to the community centre Christmas party!

We also failed to develop any contact with the Asian community. Part of the problem here was that the workers were all white males. One of them, however, was heavily involved with the Afro-Caribbean community in developing the historical content of a major exhibition at the Art Gallery.

Not strictly outreach, but the team helped co-ordinate the Coventry Local History Centre, which brought together local societies, amateur historians, the university, polytechnic, museum and archives into a loose body to try to co-ordinate activity in the city.

Dance Band Daze, Coventry, 1984

It's hard to know whether to define this as 'outreach' or not. Technically it was an exhibition organised jointly with a local enthusiast for dance bands. What made it different was the busy programme of dances held in the exhibition during its run, culminating in a grand finale attended by some 400 people, featuring two dance bands and a bar. The programme for this is now itself a collector's piece. The success of the event was that it brought into the museum a 'community' – followers of dance bands and dancing – which had largely never heard of the Art Gallery, let alone set foot in it. It also changed people's lives, in that people met again after perhaps years, and one person in particular started playing his saxophone once again after forty years and re-lived his local stardom of the 1930s. Another feature of successful outreach was that it led to a long-term result – tea dances continued at different venues round the city, making use of the stage set created for the exhibition.

Renfrew District Council

Margaret Blackburn's work in Renfrew is well known.[1] She has enabled the former Paisley Museum Service to expand its coverage to the new Renfrew District by means of lively exhibitions and activities in libraries and community centres and with the creation of a genuine community museum at Lochwinnoch, a small community on the edge of the District. The important lesson from

413

Lochwinnoch is the need to have a member of staff on the spot to enable the museum to develop proper roots in the community.

Edinburgh District Council

The Social History Section in Edinburgh was created in 1985, by which time there was a great deal of community history activity in the city. The need, therefore, was for tact and sensitivity. Helen Clark helped set up a federal structure for these groups and took on the editing of a regular newsletter. This way the museum was seen as participating in the work of the groups without taking over.

The People's Story museum has been developed with substantial input from reminiscence groups, in collaboration with the WEA. Possibly this would not be seen strictly as outreach, but it again relies on staff having those particular qualities to enable the museum to learn from ordinary people. Growing out of this work was the development of handling kits aimed primarily at groups of elderly people.[2]

Many local museums do outreach work instinctively as part of their normal work without labelling it as such. Two other examples from Scotland are Springburn in Glasgow and Alloa, Clackmannan. These are both new museums in industrially depressed areas which have worked hard with local community groups, including teenagers, a group museums often shy away from.

The Open Museum, Glasgow

As part of the re-organisation of Glasgow Museums, responsibility for outreach has been vested in the Social History Section. One of their first projects, in early 1991, has been the 'Open Museum'. Glasgow, like Scotland's other cities, has a belt of peripheral housing schemes. A group of women from one of them acted as the pioneers of this project, selecting items from the museum collections and mounting an exhibition themselves in their local community, with the help and support of museum staff, but with minimal intervention. As with most outreach projects one of the objectives was to 'empower' people, to give them ownership of the product. Doubtless as the project develops it will change and adapt but the simple ideas involved – with their quite complex consequences – should be enough to spark ideas.

Southampton – Female Footsteps

This was a project put together by Sian Jones and Jean H. Cook of Southampton City Museums to mark Women's International Week. As with all good ideas it used a simple, even old-fashioned concept – the guided walk – and used it for a new purpose – to demonstrate how women have been 'hidden from history' in the clearest way. Jean H. Cook has described the excitement involved in researching and developing the project and then the pleasure of actually putting it into effect.[3] The project has outlived Women's International Week, 1990, and has run again in 1991, as a bus tour, using local women to speak for themselves. The aim of the project is to 'encourage individuals, groups and societies to explore their streets, villages and towns, and to discover for themselves their own local heroines'. There really is no better summary of the aims of outreach work itself!

414

How Does Outreach Relate to Museum work?

I have heard criticism of workers in small museums who do nothing but outreach work. The criticism suggests they barely count as museum professionals. The work of social historians in museums is to tell the story of their local community with particular reference to what is known as material culture. Museums certainly need to continue to develop, research and interpret collections. In addition, however, they also should work with the people who live in their area to develop further understanding of, and interest in, the community's history. Objects have a vital role to play – for example as 'trigger material' for reminiscence groups – but they should not dominate social history work to the exclusion of other activities. New museums in urban areas will not find it easy to develop collections. Poor people have few possessions. Poor people who have been re-housed will have nothing to give to museums but they do have a history, and a right to have that history reflected in the activity of museums.

Conclusion

Outreach is the key to involving museums in their communities. It needs to form a recognised part of a museum's mainstream activities, not to be tacked on as camouflage. In a small museum in a small town it can become the dominant activity, as it should. In such a setting a museum can firmly establish itself as a vital part of the community.

In a big city outreach can be a means of contacting groups otherwise alienated from the museum – people on peripheral estates, teenagers, elderly people, immigrant communities, etc. The contacts made through outreach programmes will enable museums to reflect more completely the lives of everyone who lives in their catchment area and will also widen the support in that area for the museum. In times like these museums must be seen to be playing an important role in their community or they will be increasingly marginalised into catering for the local elite and tourists.

Notes

1. Margaret Blackburn, 'Polar bears in the community – a new role for a traditional museum', *Museums Professionals Group News*, no. 25, pp. 1-3.

2. This project has been described in Liz Beevers, Helen Clark, Sally Griffiths and Susan Moffatt, *Memories and Things – Linking Museums and Libraries with Older People,* WEA, Edinburgh, 1988.

3. See Jean H. Cook in *WHAM! Newsletter*, no. 16, April 1991.

41 Education

Elizabeth Frostick

Keeper of Social History, Birmingham Museums and Art Gallery

Introduction

'The Educational uses of Museums' was debated by the British Association as early as 1853, and is a subject that has been with museum professionals ever since.[1] The many education officers and departments, school loan collections, visiting school groups, GCSE projects and work for the National Curriculum bear testimony to the continuing educational value of our museums. Much has been written and published about specific educational practice, including changes to the National Curriculum, information which requires constant updating. The intention of this chapter is rather to explore some of the philosophical assumptions underlying 'educational' activity in social history museums.

What do we mean when we talk about education in social history museums; isn't education just something that teachers and education officers do? Apart from selecting objects for a school visit and worrying about the likely damage, is education important to the hard-working social history curator? Not to accept some responsibility for education, however, is to put the integrity and potential of social history in museums at risk. To develop as a 'serious' museum discipline, social history needs to remain clearly distinguishable from nostalgia, fantasy, the 'heritage industry' and pure entertainment. The use of material evidence in historical research needs developing fully if we are ever to understand the 'man-made' world in which we live. To achieve this, social history curators need clear definitions of education and history and should strive actively to promote their resources.

The role of education within a social history museum will be determined in part by the interpretation of the words 'history' and 'education'. Is 'education' different from museum 'interpretation'? Does it make sense to look at education as a separate activity; is not all interpretation educational? If all interpretation is not educational then we need to know why. How do we know? Is a living history activity of greater educational value than a conventional 'display'? Different lessons may be learned from different activities; the point is that education is not so much a 'thing' or an 'event', rather it is an activity and a process. Education is not simply something visitors take home with them, purchased at the museum shop. Like any commodity, however, there is good and bad: the content and quality, accuracy, integrity and effectiveness are all very important.

Aims of Education

The philosophy of education is an enormous subject, so little more than some basic principles will be provided here. In its most basic form, education is the passing of skills and ideas from one generation to the next; we go on learning all our lives. Organised schooling or formal classroom education has been available to most people in Britain since the late nineteenth century. Schooling has become a major part of most people's lives and involves the preparation of individuals for life. Moving away from the acquisition of knowledge, recent emphasis in state education has concentrated upon the acquisition of skills. The Education Reform Act, 1988, has brought the greatest changes to education in Britain since 1944. It introduced a national curriculum; it also clearly illustrates the transience of educational aims. Exactly what and why people should learn are inextricably linked to the ideas, needs and politics of the day.[2]

There are three broad categories of educational aims which may all apply to a greater or lesser extent at any time. Firstly, that education has intrinsic aims; knowledge and skills learned are valuable for their own sake. Secondly, that education promotes the development and well-being of the individual, and thirdly, that education promotes and develops a better society, whether this is moral or economic. The social history curator should strive to embrace all three aims. Social history museums can be used to impart knowledge, i.e. to explain and stimulate interest in the collections and in social history. They should also encourage children and adults to learn for themselves, to acquire skills which promote personal development. Learning about the past can help people to develop their own sense of history and with it a sense of psychological well-being. Social history museums, in particular, can be used as a means of educating contemporary society about the past. It has been argued that there is a social need for social history, both by individuals and by societies.[3] Museums as conveyors of history must also aim to challenge ignorance and myths about the past and put into perspective the 'achievements' of the present. Too often we are presented with nostalgia, blatant political bias or, more usually, the absence of any critical view. As such, many social history museums are not educational at all.

The Role of Education

'A museum is an institution which collects, documents, preserves, exhibits and interprets material evidence and associated information for the public benefit,' where 'interprets' includes display, education, research and publication.[4] It is clear from this definition of a museum that education is one of several primary functions of a museum. The opportunity for social history curators in education lies in the nature of history itself. Unlike art or geology, (social) history is, by definition, 'educational'. For centuries history has been studied for the past it reveals, for the instruction it might provide for the present, and for the skills it employs. An historian, in this case the social history curator, is a writer and educator. Social history curators cannot afford to let others define the messages of history. The separation of education and history in museums is a very artificial one. If visitors to museums are to be educated about history and not something else, then curators must involve themselves in this process. Just as the curator and not a designer determines the content and historical integrity of an exhibition or publication, so the curator and not the education officer should be involved in determining the historical content of educational work. Of chief concern to the social history curator should be whether visitors are learning history; as such, the role of education is one of the most important in the museum.

Education or Interpretation?

Education and interpretation are used increasingly as interchangeable terms, but what difference, if any, is there between them? In some cases, the looser term 'interpretation' has been used to justify a less critical approach to the messages that emerge from our history museums. There are strict limits to objectivity in history, but the response must not be to adopt a less rigorous approach, or to succumb simply to political or expedient options. Admission charges in particular have led to some museums telling the story that visitors want to see because they have come to the museums to 'have a nice day'. The full historical picture may prevent a return visit. Much so-called interpretation in contemporary museums contradicts the educational aims to inform, to instruct, and to dispel historical myths, while still claiming the rewards for offering valuable educational 'experience'. Some interpretation has become entertainment: quite legitimate, if that is what it claims to be. One of the most disturbing imports from America is an increased blurring of fact and fiction, and of fantasy and reality. In this country, the association of museums with tourism and leisure has led to a diffusion of educational aims: curators are under increased pressure to raise money or to provide a 'Mutiny on the Bounty' experience.

Interpretation includes museum display, research, publication and education. It might be better to include interpretation, i.e. *the methods of communication* within the aims of education. If in explaining the past the interpretative method misinforms, then it cannot be justified. Education should be the overall aim of all aspects of interpretation, drawing on the great variety of ideas on offer in our museums. Some museums have already begun to draw up interpretative strategies along these lines. The problem for the social history curator is that the interpretation of social history is so open to abuse; the historical messages as well as the interpretative methods are crucial.

History, Museums and Education

History is both the actuality of events and it is our sense and knowledge of them. Written or published history (such as a social history exhibition) is an analysis of the past and interpretation for those living in the present. History is that which we come to know as a result of enquiry: Why? What? When? How? To what end? By careful examination and validating of evidence, written, oral, or material, conclusions can be drawn. 'History is essentially an imaginative study, a reconstruction of a past which is gone and cannot be directly inspected or perceived' does not mean that museums can start making up history.[5] So what can our visitors hope to learn from studying history, particularly history in a museum?

The educational benefits of learning history include the acquisition of a sense of values about different aspects of life in a community. History is an exercise of judgement, determining the relative priorities of a former age. History provides the chance to synthesise areas of life that are not directly experienced. This horizontal perspective, or study in depth, offers particular opportunities for social history museum involvement. The vertical perspective, looking at developments through time, enables us to determine what was of ephemeral importance and what ideas, seemingly unimportant at the time, affected many generations. Understanding the past helps us to ask more penetrating questions in the present (and vice versa).

The wealth of historical material in social history museums makes them an ideal focus for historical study for the professional and, increasingly, for the school pupil, adult or family group. Bruner and others have suggested that 'any object could be taught to any child in some form without losing its integrity'.[6] The point of the 'spiral curriculum' is that children develop conceptual and abstract thinking only gradually; they move from concrete known facts to more abstract ones.[7] At certain ages one can expect children to have reached certain levels of understanding. This movement from known to unknown, however, is not peculiar to children; all good teaching aims to start where the pupil is and to encourage them to develop. History is a difficult subject to learn, difficult because it uses so many abstractions and concepts. 'Poverty', 'Revolutions' or 'Trade Unions' may mean very little to a fifteen-year-old. Social history museums, with their vast collections of buildings, domestic interiors, domestic appliances, industrial relics, photographs, and ephemera, can directly illustrate some of these concepts and help develop conceptual thinking. Social history collections, with their generally ordinary things, can also more often start from where the learner is. All children should go to school: to organise a lesson about past schooldays will mean that they have a place to start. Old desks, ink-wells and attendance medals, common to most social history collections, make it much easier to explain the problems of attendance in nineteenth-century schools. Social history as a subject does not alienate groups of people because it is a synthesis of past ordinary life. Written history has been slower to reflect minority groups and such imbalances can be rectified by using different kinds of evidence. The mangles, hoovers and dolly tubs say as much about women's history as any academic volume.

Education in Practice: Is it History?

Site Interpretation

Social history museums, which include collections of buildings over large sites, have developed various forms of 'interpretative education' to unify the sites and to make the collections intelligible. These may include labelling, demonstrations, character actors, re-creation of historical events, written guides, etc. Colonial Williamsburg, USA, a site museum set in the 1780s, is an example of a museum with an overall 'education policy'. The Department of Interpretative Education has produced not only an impressive handbook for interpreters on the site, but also a booklet entitled 'Teaching History at Colonial Williamsburg'. This overall thematic interpretation was used in the mid-1980s as a basis for all their educational 'programs'. '....C.W. has few rivals as history teacher today....this rich offering of objects and information is not, however, sufficient by itself to make the past comprehensible. The interpretive mix needs, we believe, a new cohesive ingredient; the facts need a plot; the history a conceptual framework.'[8] The theme chosen? Becoming Americans. But what interpretation of history is reaching the visitors? The overwhelming message is the success of the WASP culture. Reality is mixed with fantasy and reproduction creating a sanitized, biased and bewildering experience. The 50% black and slave population in the eighteenth century is peculiarly absent. Beamish, the North of England Open Air Museum, has been criticised recently for its romantic and 'countrified' view of the past, that it represents 'the cultures of subordinate classes not in their real complexity but as a picturesque element'.[9] Ironbridge Gorge Museum has been said to produce a 'pedagogic-style history'. With a strongly masculine assessment of people and nation and inextricably involved with the history-making business, it legitimizes its own view of the past and its sense of self importance as educator and historian.[10]

As educators, these museums should be helping to question assumptions, not to reinforce them. There is obviously a great deal of mileage in working from historic sites; the context provided can be very successful at stimulating historical imagination. The rescue and rebuilding of whole buildings helps keep history out of glass cases. As educators, museums need to be aware of what they are teaching as well as what they would like to teach. The strengths of such museums must be the opportunity they provide for the study in depth of a particular period or place. Information can be supplemented with reading, other sources and with comparisons.

Living History, Drama, Demonstrators

Some of the historical pitfalls of this interpretation exist for living history. The greatest problem for living history is making clear to the learner what is fact and what is fantasy. If we are trying to assess the educational value of such exercises it is worth comparing historical 'empathy' exercises in schools. Asking pupils to imagine that they are villains visiting a medieval town, without studying the period in some depth, will produce little in the way of historical empathy; more information is needed for it to be history and not just imagination. A visitor to a nineteenth-century/early twentieth-century schoolroom 'experience' at Wigan Pier does not really have the framework necessary to get much 'history' out of the visit. It is quite enjoyable, but is it history?

The following models, based on a diagram by Robin Kripps, help illustrate just what *historically* we are asking our visitors to undertake.

Model I

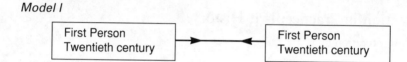

Examples are costumed interpreters, craft demonstrators, guides, etc. where demonstrators educate visitors about an aspect of the past. The demonstrators explain what they are doing and visitors are free to ask questions.

Model II

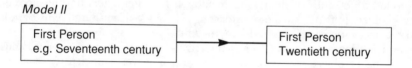

Examples include living history battles, or domestic working by interpreters in authentic period costume, also character actors, such as those found at Wigan Pier, Colonial Williamsburg, MOMI, etc. Here the interpreter, well-schooled in, say, seventeenth-century history to the point of using accurate language, tries to communicate to the modern visitor. In this instance, the visitor is not interested in moving away from the twentieth century. I have heard visitors ask whether the interpreter has a television and other such anachronisms. The interpreter is left saying, 'Well, I don't know what you mean by that' or, 'We don't have those around here...' It is better if there is no attempt to interfere. The History Re-Enactment workshop have acknowledged this problem and supply 'Red T-Shirts' (staff) to act as successful go-betweens.

Model III

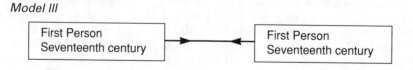

A typical example is the Victorian schoolroom, such as at Wigan Pier and the Welsh Folk Museum, where the visitor becomes part of the historical reconstruction. Alternative examples are the character actors at Wigan and Colonial Williamsburg, who try to take visitors back in time with them.

The only way that such 'experiences' can be educationally successful is for the participants to be properly prepared. This is less of a problem with visiting school groups, who will often base the visit around extensive project work. But we have to ask ourselves just what history does an ordinary one-visit person learn?

All living history events, whether professional or organised as educational activities, depend also for their (historical) success on authenticity, which demands a lot of hard work.

What living history events do bring to museums, however, is a sense of dynamism and of movement. Activity, when it involves you, can be exciting and very stimulating; to create genuine interest in the study of history is not contradictory to the aims of education. In addition, living history has enabled curators to put people back into the past, to explain processes and to tackle the complex problem of explaining social networks, rather than unrelated facts. Perhaps we must be content to stop the assessment here. The difference between Wonderland and the totally reconstructed 'experience' gets harder and harder to define.

Conventional Displays and Project Work

The majority of museum displays are housed inside buildings, both old and new, which offer marvellous opportunities for learning. It is also easier for the social history curator to 'control' the interpretative messages using text and labels than it is on an open-air site.

Museum displays are normally aimed at the general adult visitor rather than at children, but as a result their potential use as an educational resource is enormous. A well presented, clearly-expressed exhibition is the social history curator's best means of 'publication'. In addition to the 'educational' intent of the exhibit, i.e. that the visitor should learn something, any number of projects can be based upon an exhibition. The increasing emphasis in social history museums upon participation and involvement by the local community can ensure that these museums remain relevant and dynamic, challenging and 'living' places to visit, learn from and have fun in, such as is possible in 'The Story of Hull and its People', to name just one!

Outreach/Publications

The education process need not be confined to the parameters of the museum building. An increasing number of outreach and community projects are reaching an audience that the museum might not otherwise succeed in attracting. Self-guided town trails and site interpretation, guided trails, travelling exhibitions, reminiscence work, helping groups to create their own exhibitions outside the museum – all these activities present themselves as educational possibilities for the social history curator.

GCSE

GCSE provides perhaps some of the best opportunities for social history curators to be involved in the process of education. The strength of GCSE is that it involves learning history in the way that historians 'do it'. The emphasis in at least some areas of GCSE is upon the methods of studying history; the use of evidence, the study of the local area or buildings, for example, and the need to evaluate that evidence before reaching a conclusion. It may be some time before museums are brought fully into the educational arena, but new opportunities exist and much depends upon the response of social history curators. They can seize the opportunity to promote their collections and resources, with the help of education staff, to establish museums as essential motivators of ideas about social history, setting high standards of interpretation and closing the gap between the academic history still written in universities and the real life experiences of people.

Notes and References

1. E.J.Frostick, 'Museums in education: a neglected role?', *Museums Journal*, vol.85, no. 2, 1985, pp. 67-74.

2. R.Aldrich, *An Introduction to the History of Education*, Hodder & Stoughton, 1982.

3. G. Kavanagh, 'Melodrama, pantomime or portrayal? Representing ourselves and the British past through exhibitions in history museums', in a Symposium, 'Making Exhibitions of Ourselves: The Limits to Objectivity in the Representation of other Cultures', British Museum, 1986.

4. Museums Association definition of a museum.

5. W.H. Burston, 'The place of history in education', *Handbook for History Teachers*, Methuen, 1962.

6. J. Bruner, *The Process of Education*, Harvard University Press, 1982.

7. A term first described by Jean Piaget, Swiss psychologist, 1896-1980.

8. *Teaching History at Colonial Williamsburg*, Colonial Williamsburg Foundation, 1985.

9. Tony Bennett, 'Museums and "the people"', in Robert Lumley (ed.), *The Museum Time Machine*, Comedia/Routledge, 1988.

10. Bob West, 'The making of the English working past: a critical view of the Ironbridge Gorge Museum', in Robert Lumley, op cit.

Bibliography

Educational theory

Aldrich, R., *An Introduction to the History of Education*, Hodder & Stoughton, 1982.

Bruner, J., *The Process of Education*, Harvard University Press, rev. ed. 1982.

Frostick, E.J., *The Secondary School History Syllabus: What Have We Forgotten?*, unpublished, 1984.

Hargreaves, D.H., *The Challenge for the Comprehensive School: Culture, Curriculum and Community*, Routledge, 1982.

White, J., *The Aims of Education Restated*, Routledge, 1982.

History and history teaching

Ballard, M. (ed.), *New Movements in the Study and Teaching of History*, Morris, Temple, Smith, 1971.

Burston, W.H., *Handbook for History Teachers*, Methuen, 1972, 2nd ed.

Carr, E.H., *What is History?*, Penguin Books, 1987.

Dickinson, A., Lee, P.J., and Rogers, P.J., *Learning History*, Heinemann Educational 1984.

Lowenthal, D., *The Past is a Foreign Country*, Cambridge University Press, 1985.

Marwick, A., *The Nature of History*, Macmillan, 1970.

Education in museums

Ames, M., 'De-schooling the museum: a proposal to increase public access to museums and their resources', *Museum*, no. 145, 1985, pp. 15-31.

AMSSEE, *Museums and the Curriculum*, AMSSEE, 1988.

AMSSEE, *Museums and the New Exams*, AMSSEE, 1988.

Bassett, D.A., 'Museums and education: a brief bibliographic essay', in Thompson, J.M.A. (ed.), *Manual of Curatorship*, Butterworth, 1984.

Carter, P.G., 'Educational services', in Thompson, J.M.A. (ed.), *Manual of Curatorship*, Butterworth, 1984.

Colonial Williamsburg Foundation, *Teaching History at Colonial Williamsburg*, CWF, 1985.

Davies, M., 'Circular arguments', *Museums Journal*, vol. 89, no. 2, 1989.

Divall, P., 'Museum education – a new era?', *Museums Journal*, vol. 89, no. 2., 1989.

Durbin, G., 'Getting started; educational activities for children', *Journal of the Social History Curators Group*, vol. 16, 1988-9.

Fassnidge, J., 'GCSE for curators: history', *Museums Journal*, vol. 87, no. 1, June 1987.

Frostick, E.J., 'Museums in education: a neglected role?', *Museums Journal*, vol. 85, no. 2, September 1985.

GEM, GCSE Supplement, *Journal of Education in Museums*, vol. 8, 1987.

GEM, 'Role play and drama in the museum context', *Journal of Education in Museums*, vol. 9, 1988.

GEM, 'Multiculturalism and education', *Journal of Education in Museums*, vol. 7, 1988.

Lumley, R. (ed.), *The Museum Time Machine*, Comedia/Routledge, 1988.

Moffat, H., 'Museums and the Education Reform Act', *Museums Journal*, vol. 89, no. 2, 1989.

Rees, P., 'GCSE for curators: local history', *Museums Journal*, vol.89, no. 2, 1989.

Schlereth, T.J., 'Historic house museums: seven teaching strategies', in *Artefacts and The American Past*, American Association for State and Local History, Nashville, 1980.

Whincop, A., 'GCSE for curators', *Museums Journal*, vol. 87, no. 1, June 1987.

Winterbothom, N., 'Why bother with children?', *Journal of the Social History Curators Group*, vol. 16, 1988-9.

University of Leicester, Department of Museum Studies, *A Bibliography for Museum Studies Training*, University of Leicester, 1988.

Useful Addresses

Group for Education in Museums (GEM)
Secretary: Susan Morris
63 Navarino road
London E8 1AG
tel. 071-249 4296

For information about the National Curriculum and GCSE see useful addresses in :

Durbin, G., 'Getting started: educational activities for children', *Journal of the Social History Curators Group*, vol. 16, 1988-9.

Printed in the United Kingdom for HMSO
Dd294217 3/93 C13 G3397 10170